A CRITICAL HISTORY OF
CHILDREN'S LITERATURE

A CRITICAL HISTORY OF CHILDREN'S LITERATURE

*A SURVEY OF CHILDREN'S BOOKS IN ENGLISH,
PREPARED IN FOUR PARTS UNDER THE EDITORSHIP OF
CORNELIA MEIGS*

REVISED EDITION

by

CORNELIA MEIGS   ANNE THAXTER EATON

ELIZABETH NESBITT   RUTH HILL VIGUERS

Decorations by Vera Bock

MACMILLAN PUBLISHING CO., INC.
New York
COLLIER-MACMILLAN LTD.
London

1. Children's Literature — History and criticism

I. t

Macmillan Publishing Co., Inc.
866 Third Avenue, New York, New York 10022
Collier Macmillan Canada, Ltd.

Library of Congress catalog card number: AC67-10271
ISBN 0-02-583900-4
Printed in the United States of America

10   9   8   7   6   5   4

For

ANNE CARROLL MOORE
BERTHA MAHONY MILLER
FREDERIC G. MELCHER

*Three great leaders
in the knowledge and understanding
of children's literature*

Introduction
to the Revised Edition

By Frances Clarke Sayers

When *A Critical History of Children's Literature* made its initial appearance in 1953, it shot across the sky, a brilliant exploratory satellite. No such rocket had ever before been launched from an American base. Now, nearly two decades later, it reenters the earth's atmosphere in a revised and enlarged form.

Originally the brainchild of Doris Patee, then editor of children's books at Macmillan, it took form under her direction. The subtitle declared its purpose: to "survey children's books in England and America from earliest times to the present." Four authorities who knew children's books as writer, critic, teacher, and librarian were invited to accomplish the gigantic task, under the editorship of one of them, the distinguished Cornelia Meigs. Each of these experts could have changed roles with any other, as do experienced actors in repertory theater, each equipped by long rehearsal, interest, and knowledge to see her own part in relation to the whole. It seemed, therefore, an inspired as well as a practical plan to assign to each contributor a certain period of time in the history of children's literature as her portion of research and renewal.

Whenever a space vehicle returns to earth the initial and obvious reaction after splashdown is to ask questions. Has the atmosphere changed the character of the encapsulated matter? What of the world in which it claims reentry? Is it the same planet from which the launch was made? What possibilities for service and survival does this veteran of the skies offer the environment of the present and the future?

The basic plan remains, but the facts of history have played havoc with balance of parts as established in the first edition, the sheer proliferation of books for children in these well-nigh twenty years threatening to consume, like an insatiable Moloch, the whole of the historic past, putting the greatest burden of judgment and revision upon the last quarter of the book.

The revision of the first three sections consists of textual corrections of errors, most of them committed at the proofreader's level, and the addition of significant titles to the bibliographies. No body of rewriting has been undertaken with the exception of the recasting of an occasional paragraph. Time has not withered Cornelia Meigs' initial section "The Roots of the Past." She brings to her assignment the storyteller's narrative pace, the novelist's eye for endearing detail, and the scholar's control of historic perspective. Anne Thaxter Eaton, surveying the Victorian Age in both England and America, comes to grips with the social forces that echoed and reechoed throughout this era of great flowering of children's literature, the extent of her own reading and her pleasure therein enhancing paragraph after paragraph. The critic's endowment of analysis and appreciation lights up the pages of Elizabeth Nesbitt's section, which covers the period 1890 through 1920. Her pieces on Kipling, Howard Pyle, Walter de la Mare and Beatrix Potter remain timeless summations of their genius and reveal, in addition, the scaffolding and the scales by means of which the critic builds her premises and weighs judgment.

The last quarter of the book covers the time from 1920 to the present, a period which was, and continues to be "the best of times and the worst of times." The publication of books for children reached the proportions of an industry, "the obsession with children's books as gainful product" as Mrs. Viguers describes it, all but taking precedence over other values thought to be inherent in responsible publishing. Mrs. Viguers seems to have been tapped by Fate for her commitment to this period of time, for in the interim of the years since 1953 she has added to her accomplishments of writer, librarian, teacher and parent years of golden experience as editor of *The Horn Book*, the major fountainhead of knowledge, tradition and experience concerning children's books and the reading thereof. The actuality of her careful reading—one can hardly imagine the enormity of it—gives rare value to the pages she devotes to the present, and includes consideration of some of the forces brought to bear upon books for the present day child.

Lay hand on this book! The past is here, documented, its values assayed. The present is portrayed; tumultuous, many-faceted, with the reading of childhood now become the concern of psychiatrist and psychologist, educators and educational theorists, linguistic scholars with their schisms, social scientists, moralists, and reformers, artists, as well as men and women seeking among children an audience of listeners interested in stories told, songs sung, and facts revealed with that edge of eagerness which captivates the young. Small wonder that the trends, fashions, and pressures of the time compound the difficulty of sighting the most distinctive books of the period and those most likely to endure.

And what is to come? The sea of the future lies about this satellite, the black waters lapping at the threshold of the capsule. Who can dispute the terrors of disruption that froth the dark waves? When Dr. Henry Steele Commager wrote his erudite introduction to the first edition of this book, he spoke of the "awareness of evil so alien to the young." The young are no longer exempt. The exhilarated pace and immediacy of experience spread evil indiscriminately with good. Everyone knows simultaneously and sees upon the screen wars, crimes and the threat of atomic destruction. Everyone feels the impact of the slogans which deafen ear and dull sensibility through too much repetition: "Lack of Communication" at a time when a plethora of machines exist for the purpose of communicating: "Lack of privacy" yet the ill has been diagnosed as an alienation of person from person: "Lack of feeling" in a time when the rage of the young is disrupting campuses across the country. What idiotic paradoxes surround us.

Never doubt that children feel these anxieties and look to what they read for ways of effecting confrontations on their own terms. The psychiatrist is now a recognized character in books for children not yet in their teens. Divorce and the presence of parents in multiple numbers is a fact of life for many children. Too many children suffer not only because they are black or poverty-stricken or disadvantaged but because the certainties of dogma, belief, and behavior are shattered, for their parents as well as for themselves.

Children are never so brave as when they share a common danger with their elders. The hope of the world is to include them in fear and doubt as well as in courage and determination. Most children, like the young of the animal world, are predisposed to joy. They bring us a sense of wonder, an eagerness to know, their ability to make life bearable by the creation of explanatory myths of their own. Their sense of humor endures as does their brimming love of the earth and the mysteries that enfold it. These are among the elements to which the literature of childhood must always address itself. *A Critical History of Children's Literature* with its perceptive, wise summary of past and present, now assumes the role of the prophet, foretelling not what may happen but what *must* come to pass.

The Ojai

1 9 6 9.

Introduction
to the First Edition

By Henry Steele Commager

Here is something new and enchanting, a history of children's literature. But what, after all, do we mean by that term? Is it that literature written especially for the young—the fairy and wonder tales, the nursery rhymes and songs, the dull books of etiquette and admonition and moral persuasion, the stories of school or playing field or of far-flung adventure? It is all of this, to be sure, but it is far more. It is the whole vast body of literature that children have adopted, commonly to share with their elders, but sometimes to monopolize. It is, quite literally, *their* literature. For it is, in the end, not the parents, the teachers, the preachers, not even the authors, but the children themselves who determine what their literature is to be. Over the years they have followed their own rules or, better yet, their instincts; they have rejected most of what was deliberately concocted for them, and embraced what was not; and over the years their judgment has been vindicated. It is because the writers of this book have accepted, and even concurred in, this judgment, that they have given us our first critical and comprehensive history of children's literature.

They begin their chronicle with Celtic legends and tales, with the Arthurian legend so wonderfully re-created by Sir Thomas Malory, with Plutarch's *Lives*, with the stirring history of distant voyages retold by Hakluyt, and with *Pilgrim's Progress*. Now all of these stories and books have this in common, that they were not designed for the young at all. But very early the children took them over and made them their own, forced their elders, indeed, to revise and recast them in suitable form. This set the pattern for later generations, the pattern for almost the whole of English and American literature down to our own day. For, with important exceptions, that literature has not consciously recognized a dividing line between the young and the old, but has tended to see the world as a whole. It has not so much consciously, as instinctively, yielded to the claims of the young, recognized that they were entitled to enter into the world of the imagination, and made the pathway easy.

Had this not been the case, children would have been badly off (as they were in most Continental countries) for not until well into the nineteenth century was there a deliberate and successful effort to provide literature for children. Most of those books which we regard as classics of children's literature were written without children in mind and were taken over by them with cheerful disregard of what they could not understand. None of these were aiming at children: Hakluyt, whose stories have stirred the imagination of the young for three hundred years, nor poor John Bunyan, languishing in his gaol in Bedford, nor Daniel Defoe, old and cantankerous, nor the harsh and embittered Swift. Thackeray thought of his *Henry Esmond* as "a book of cut-throat melancholy"; but children did not find it so, and generations of boys and girls have admired Esmond and his gallant exploits.

And Sir Walter Scott, for whom was he writing, this Greatheart of the North? Who read *Ivanhoe* and *Quentin Durward* and *Rob Roy* year after year, who but boys and girls? Those who have not read Scott at fifteen will probably never read him. And so, too, with the incomparable Jane Austen, with the Brontë sisters—is not *Wuthering Heights* among the most popular of girls' books? Or we can turn to the greatest of them all, Charles Dickens who, except in his *Child's History of England*, did not consciously write for children but who, next to Hans Andersen and Mark Twain and Louisa Alcott, perhaps, is the most widely read and the most dearly beloved of children's authors. It is the children who weep over little Nell, who rejoice in David's good fortune when he finds a home with Betsy Trotwood, and who insist every year on the reading of *A Christmas Carol*.

This *History* makes clear how the Victorian era introduced new elements, and new departures, how it witnessed the beginning of literature written especially with children in view, and written not only to edify but to entertain. It rejoiced in the contributions of that wonderful galaxy of women, Mrs. Gatty, Mrs. Ewing, Mrs. Molesworth, and Charlotte Yonge. It saw Captain Marryat and others reviving the art of Hakluyt and Defoe, and Charles Kingsley, better remembered for *Westward Ho!* than for his novels of social reform. It saw too, in *Alice's Adventures in Wonderland* and the verses of Edward Lear, the triumph of nonsense, of a peculiar madness which no other people but the English have ever matched.

But at the same time, as if in reaction from this direct catering to the needs and desires of the young, came the beginnings of a change in the great tradition of literature. George Eliot and Anthony Trollope did not write for the young, nor were their books (perhaps *The Mill on the Floss* is an exception) welcomed by the young. Nor will children read those other giants of the late Victorian era, Meredith and Hardy and Henry James. Already we see in these that indifference to the needs of the young, that complexity of thought and manner so disconcerting to them, that awareness of evil so alien to children—all of those literary characteristics so prominent in the literature of our own day and so largely responsible for the growing divorce between the literature for adults and for children.

Yet the distinct tradition of writing the sort of literature which appealed to children as well as to adults continued to flourish through the Victorian age and into the twentieth century. It inspired Robert Louis Stevenson, the Stevenson not only of *Treasure Island* and *Kidnapped* but of *A Child's Garden of Verses*. It was maintained by Kipling, the Kipling of the *Jungle Books* and *Kim* and *Captains Courageous*. It presided over the writing of Conan Doyle, over his historical romances like *The White Company* and over the adventures of Sherlock Holmes. Every normal boy is a Baker Street Irregular.

In a different way, too, such a tradition inspired a number of authors who dedicated themselves almost exclusively to the service of children. Barrie is not quite of this company, though it is children who read him now, not adults. But Kenneth Grahame is, Grahame who was content to recall the Golden Age of childhood and whose every book was a classic. And so, too, is Andrew Lang, who made fairy tales live again and who is surely one of the greatest of all benefactors to the children of the world.

Even into the Georgian era, that era heavy with social problems, the pleasant tradition persisted, in the Wells of *Mr. Polly* and *Bealby*, in the Bennett of *Clayhanger*, in Conrad above all, that prince of story-tellers who has something for every age and for every stage of philosophy. It flourished even in the generation after the first war, though less assuredly now—with John Buchan who was the successor, and a not unworthy one, to Scott and Stevenson; with the neglected Quiller-Couch; with Hugh Walpole of the wonderful Jeremy stories, and perhaps even better, of *Fortitude*. Then the greater writers deserted it: what child can read James Joyce or Virginia Woolf, D. H. Lawrence or Aldous Huxley or Evelyn Waugh?

What an astonishing record it is when viewed as a whole, this record of children's literature stretching from the Arthurian legends to *Lord Jim*. It is a record that cannot be matched by any other country or by any other literature. France offers us the magic stories of Perrault and, much later, the fabulous world of Jules Verne; Italy submits Pinocchio; Switzerland the lovely tales of Spyri and Malot; Germany the folk tales collected by the brothers Grimm; Norway the fairy tales of Asbjörnsen and Moe; and Sweden the wonderfully imaginative stories of Selma Lagerlöf; and Denmark, of course, the greatest of all, the tales of Hans Christian Andersen. Yet nowhere is there anything to compare with the English achievement.

Nowhere, that is, but in America, which inherited and enlarged the tradition that served children. Call the roll of American writers from Franklin to Howells and from Bryant to Carl Sandburg; almost all of them wrote for children or wrote books which children have taken over. Franklin's *Autobiography* is a school-classic now, a book that children can understand and that they read and remember. Cooper was a novelist for adults, but up to our time he has been read by boys and girls in almost every country on the globe. With Poe it is children who work out the puzzles and the ciphers of his stories, or who learn by heart "The Raven" and "The Bells" and "Annabel Lee." Hawthorne was, of course, a children's author quite deliberately. Having started with *Grandfather's Chair* he went on to the retelling of classic myths in *A Wonder Book* and *Tanglewood Tales* where the myths were "purified from all moral stains."

Most of the poets of the American Golden Age wrote what served the needs of children or what children took as their own. Whittier, Longfellow, Lowell, and Holmes belong to both categories, those poets whose benign countenances stared out at us in the amiable game of authors once so popular. Much of Whitman was unsuitable to the young, but he was the poet of the young, nevertheless, the kind of poet they could understand. A bit later it was the gentle Sidney Lanier who somehow found energy for *The Boy's King Arthur* and *The Boy's Froissart* and even *The Boy's Percy.* Emily Dickinson wrote for children, as did Stephen Crane and, in a sense, William Vaughn Moody, while the best poems of those "minor" poets, Eugene Field and James Whitcomb Riley, are all of them about children and some of them, like "Little Boy Blue," destined to live long.

Neither of the two mid-century writers who have come to be most highly regarded in our own day, Thoreau and Melville, wrote consciously for children, but *Walden* is discovered anew by every youngster, who loves the idea of a hut on Walden Pond as much as the idea of a tree dwelling on Robinson Crusoe's island. *Moby Dick*, too, has made its way into the schools, where it is read as much as *Gulliver's Travels* was once read, parts of it, at least, understandable. Emerson addressed himself to the high-minded and the mature, but what boy or girl has failed to read him and take strength from him? It is a striking, and not a discouraging, consideration that our most famous philosophers, Franklin, Emerson, and William James are all read by the young.

Even the nineteenth century historians wrote for young readers as well as for their elders. It was true, of course, of the fantastic Parson Weems; it was true of Samuel Goodrich, the untiring Peter Parley. But with these it was deliberate. Children took over the more magisterial historians as well, not Bancroft, perhaps, for he was a bit heavy going, but Prescott who made the Inca and Aztec civilizations live again, and Motley who inspired an abiding interest in the history of the Dutch

Republic. And they took Parkman above all who could make of Pontiac's Rebellion a struggle worthy to put beside the struggle between the Persians and the Greeks, who wove an aura of romance about New France, the *coureurs de bois*, the Recollets, the great captains.

It was in this mid-nineteenth century that two women were writing books that were to be read and cherished for a century to come. Harriet Beecher Stowe did not design *Uncle Tom's Cabin* for children, far from it. But within a short time the children took over, the children of every land and every clime; it is they who have read it ever since and who have made little Eva and Topsy and poor Uncle Tom immortal. And along with Mrs. Stowe was young Louisa Alcott, the spinster who never really understood children, and who wrote perhaps the greatest child's book to come out of the New World. The children loved *Little Women* from the beginning, and have never ceased to love it. None of the sequels was quite as good, though nothing that came from that gifted pen could fail to be endearing. But *Little Women* belongs to itself, a classic as Andersen's *Fairy Tales* is a classic, or *Robinson Crusoe* or *Alice in Wonderland* or *Treasure Island*. Those little women of Concord have gone all over the world, they have gone into the hearts of children everywhere, giving them a feeling for America that nothing else gives in quite the same way.

But not alone; they have had noble company, notably in Tom Sawyer and Huckleberry Finn. It is an impressive thing that so many Americans should think that *Huckleberry Finn* is the great American novel. What other people, what non-English people would ever single out a child's book as their great national novel? The English might, to be sure, if they ever permitted themselves to speak in superlatives, but surely it would never occur to the Germans, the Spanish, the French. Mark Twain not only gave us the immortal Tom and Huck, he wrote half a dozen other books crowded with characters and episodes and morals too, books that have nourished the spirits and delighted the hearts of the young ever since.

William Dean Howells, who wrote an account of Mark Twain as tender as anything one writer ever wrote about another, had won the formidable title of Dean of American Letters. He was in a way a formidable figure—editor of *The Atlantic Monthly* and then of *Harper's Easy Chair*, author of thirty or forty novels, and a dozen books of criticism and another dozen of travel. Put him in France or Germany or Denmark and what would you have? A Hippolyte Taine, or a Jakob Burckhardt or a Georg Brandes; imagine any of these bothering himself about children. But Howells did; he wrote directly for the young and about them too. Is there a more charming picture of boyhood in American literature than *A Boy's Town*?

And so it goes, all through the nineteenth century and into the twentieth. No need to recall Bret Harte or the local colorists who were, most of them, children's writers as well. No need to celebrate those writers who are, perhaps, closer to Lewis Carroll and Beatrix Potter than to any of their American contemporaries—Frank Stockton whose stories were not quite fairy tales and not quite humor; Joel Chandler Harris whose *Uncle Remus* has gone everywhere.

We cannot speak of Lewis Carroll or Beatrix Potter, of Stockton or Harris, without thinking of the illustrators who made them live for us— of Tenniel who could never illustrate other books after he had done Alice; of Miss Potter herself whose drawings are as exquisite as her stories; of Frederick Church who made Uncle Remus and Brer Rabbit so real. For the children not only levied on writers; they levied on artists too, and the greatest of the nineteenth century illustrators delighted to serve them. It is one of the many virtues of this *History* that it has not neglected the artists; here are tributes to Kate Greenaway, to Randolph Caldecott, to Walter Crane and their many successors on both sides of the Atlantic, the wonderful Howard Pyle above all.

Not only did the English-speaking peoples produce a long succession of classics for children, they produced, too, the only really good juvenile magazines. America led the way with *The Youth's Companion*, a paper that served American youth for a generation and more. And America produced also the one indubitably great magazine for children, *St. Nicholas*. It was beautifully and lavishly illustrated; it contained departments—like the memorable League—that gave such pleasure as is difficult to imagine, now, in connection with a mere literary publication. Its reputation was such that everyone rejoiced to write for it. All this was the achievement of the great editor, Mary Mapes Dodge, whose true monument is not so much her book *Hans Brinker, or the Silver Skates* as *St. Nicholas* itself.

One thing that this book makes clear is that though our generation may not have any giants to compare with Mark Twain or Louisa Alcott or Stevenson or Kipling, the general quality of writing for children has by no means declined. Already some "classics" have emerged in this generation; who can doubt that children half a century from now will read about Winnie-the-Pooh or Mary Poppins or Dr. Dolittle; who can doubt that they will still delight in the story of *Understood Betsy* or the adventures of the doll *Hitty*, or find the Moffats and the Melendeys as interesting, perhaps, as the Marches; that they will be stirred by Will James's *Smoky* or by *The Yearling*?

"England could be reconstructed entirely from its children's books" writes Paul Hazard, and there is truth in the statement as well as exaggeration. Because the record is so long and so rich, because over the centuries almost all major writers have addressed themselves to children or written about children or been taken over by the children, we have in literature not only a continuous record of childhood, but a continuous record of society as a whole, and—what is more important—of the ideals and standards that society wishes to inculcate into each new generation. On the whole children's literature is literature on good behavior, literature consciously or unconsciously moralistic. English children's literature displays the sense of adventure; the feeling for Empire; the importance of the school and of the playing-field and the code of fair play developed on the playing-field; the fierce feeling for right and justice; individualism running into eccentricity; class consciousness; the importance of the nanny and the governess; the pervasive morality usually but not always allied with religion; the humor running so easily into nonsense and fantasy; the tenderness and gentleness and kindness and with it the courage and tenacity and loyalty; the deep feeling for nature—nature tame and neat—and for animals; all these traits that we recognize at once as part of the composite of the English character. From American literature emerges a different picture: equalitarianism rather than class consciousness; a stronger family feeling; adventure, but of a different kind—adventure in the American West rather than in distant lands, adventure that makes not for imperialism but as often as not for provincialism; courage and a hatred of the bully; self-reliance; work and the gospel of work; nature in the raw rather than tamed; democracy and humanitarianism, a feeling for fair play and for the underdog; ingenuity and mechanical skill; humor that ran to the boisterous and the tall story rather than to whimsy or nonsense; simplicity and morality.

What explains the English and American preoccupation with childhood, and the readiness of English and American literature to accept children as ends in themselves? The explanation is not easy nor is it simple; it is economic, it is social, it is philosophical and religious. First the English, then the Americans, have been in a position where they could afford to pamper their children. The English, to be sure, did not pamper all of them—certainly not the boys who worked in coal mines, the girls who worked in factories, well into the nineteenth century. But the English class society indulged those children to whom writers addressed themselves, and in the mid-nineteenth century the humanitarian revolution championed and even sentimentalized the victims of the industrial order. Americans on the other hand have always been in a position to indulge their children, to release them from much of the work which was taken for granted elsewhere, to provide schooling for as many years as was thought desirable, to pay for leisure and sports.

But more effective than this was the conviction that children were important in themselves, and that childhood was its own justification. The English sense of individualism, the English passion for liberty, has always made it easy and natural for them to regard children as individuals; the same qualities that make the English perhaps the best schoolmasters in the world, best able to combine intellectual with physical and moral training, make them able to provide the best literature. Americans have never believed that childhood was merely a preparation for life; they have insisted, rather, that it was life itself. This was the doctrine that Bronson Alcott taught at the Temple School, and if that school was not immediately successful, Alcott himself produced one pupil who compensated for all other failures. But it is the doctrine too of the most influential of American philosophers and educators, John Dewey.

There is, too, a philosophical principle here, one implicit rather than explicit, in much of the literature described in this book. From the beginning Americans have lived much in the future and for the future. This was true of individuals—after all the migration to America from the Old World was a vote of confidence in the future; it was true of society as a whole which was always making ambitious plans for the future, sometimes at the expense of the present. But this is simply another way of saying that Americans, more perhaps than other people, live in and for their children. And why not? Whatever may be the lot of the parents, who knows what may befall the children? The popularity of the Alger stories was rooted in experience and familiarity.

There is a further philosophical principle that operates in American literature. That is the principle of equality which Tocqueville saw as the most pervasive and persistent of all American characteristics. This principle has affected the position of children and the character of children's literature in America. Even English juvenile literature is class conscious —more class conscious than much of the Swiss and Scandinavian. But there is precious little class consciousness in American children's literature. Not only did the principle of equality create an immensely broad and uniform audience; it created a broad and uniform culture, and the two made possible a literature that would appeal equally to all classes and sections and faiths. Equality worked in another direction as well: it worked to blur if not to eliminate the differences between the sexes. Just as Americans early accorded a high position to women, and pioneered in education for girls and higher education for women, so they wiped out most of the differences between stories for boys and stories for girls. Where English juvenile literature addresses itself largely to boys, American knows no sex preferences.

Here then is a record not only of literature but of philosophy or, of what is perhaps better, sentiment. It is a record of a literature that makes peculiar demands upon imagination, upon the affections, upon sympathy and understanding and humility and humor. Almost anyone, one is tempted to say, can write a book for adults—and almost everyone does; but it requires a felicitous combination of qualities, intellectual and moral, to write a good book for children. That the English and the Americans should have written so many is a testimony not only to their imagination but to their virtue. "My ambition," wrote the great artist-author Howard Pyle, "in days gone by was to write a really notable adult book, but now I am glad that I have made literary friends of the children rather than the older folk. In one's mature years one forgets the books that one reads, but the stories of childhood leave an indelible impression, and their author always has a niche in the temple of memory from which the image is never cast out to be thrown into the rubbish-heap of things that are outgrown and outlived."

Here is a record of the books one does not forget, the books that leave an indelible impression, the authors who will ever occupy a grateful niche in the temple of memory.

Foreword

By Cornelia Meigs

This *Critical History* is written, first, in an attempt to capture the essence of that experience of delight which children have enjoyed in exploring their own literature from the beginnings of remembered history onward, the adventure of childhood itself in finding, pursuing, and even helping to shape the course of that reading which has grown up to be theirs in their own right. This book, moreover, sets out to refute the idea that children's literature has had only a brief and unimportant record. And finally, it undertakes to offer a critical analysis of what has endured and why, of how time and circumstance have affected the progress of children's literature as it has shaped that of adults, and to discuss what is best in that bewildering abundance of supply which is now available for young people's reading, and where are the contemporary books which, in their turn, may endure.

While much of the theme concerns the fact that children through the generations have had an instinct for finding and establishing what is to be their own in the world of literature, it is none the less true that children as individuals do need some guidance and advice in the choice of their reading among those books which are to establish standards and crystallize taste, and which will present much vicarious experience and will be long remembered. Much excellent work has been done in recent years by libraries and schools in making up book lists as guides to a discriminating selection. Constructive study in children's reading has properly become a part of the education of teachers. In regard to books of the past there have been bibliographical surveys of interest and importance. There have been, further, some extraordinary and beautiful collections made of early children's books. The gathering of them is one of the most elusive pursuits in the field of collecting, for the best loved and most precious are the rarest, having been bound to perish early under the hard usage of countless readings.

But with all this, the coordination of the whole sum of knowledge and understanding of children's literature—not merely that which was printed and bought and put before them, but the true literature which was sought out and cherished and carried in their hearts always—this was a piece of work long undone. In view of the scope and opportunity of children's literature of today, it seemed fully time that there should be a completed study of the basic elements and the developing factors which have brought it through a traceable history of more than three hundred years to be what it is now. To say that this book undertakes to accomplish all this is a pretentious claim; its excuse is that such a study needed so truly to be made.

The epithet, "a definitive work," is a large and formidable one, nor has there been an attempt to make it apply here. The very first exploration and discussion of the field showed at once the opportunity to march forward with the progress of a very great development, but along with it, the necessity of leaving to other hands an alluring number of detailed studies, and of focussed criticism of particular periods. Concerning an era when the printer's or publisher's name on the title page rather than the author's was the custom, there arose a myriad of beckoning possibilities for research. In dealing with our present age, where there is suddenly such immense wealth of material on all subjects, there are threads of influence and expected consequences that are yet to be picked up and followed to the end. No one knows better than the writers of this book how much there is still left to do in the study of children's literature. Yet they have, to the best of their ability, traced out a consecutive line of signposts along a road of extraordinary interest and variety.

Collaboration is often thought of as a mysterious process, yet here it has been simple, constructive and delightful. It was clear from the beginning that this was not an undertaking for a single hand, that though the whole continuity of the subject fell rather easily into definite periods, each of these needed a detailed approach, an individual judgment and a varied quality of criticism and interpretation. It is probably because the whole project was one for which this particular time was so truly ripe, that there appeared at once the proper persons, each suited to a particular portion of the work.

Collaboration has gone further than that, however, for the book was not begun without complete discussion and exchange of opinion concerning the whole field, without thorough settling of the general problems of trends and tastes, of historical causes and results, of promising advances and temporary retreats. Consultations were held also with generous advisers who were not only experts, but also conspicuous figures in the history being traced: Anne Carroll Moore, formerly of the New York Public Library; Bertha Mahony Miller of *The Horn Book*; Frederic Melcher of *Publishers' Weekly*, whose guiding and stimulating hand has been everywhere evident as the cause of children's reading went forward. Doris Patee, Juvenile Editor of Macmillan, has offered elsewhere information as to each of the writers who took part, but she has implied nothing of what her dynamic editorial ability contributed to the plan and how it was through her that it so successfully held together.

It has been, therefore, carefully compared opinion which determined what to include, how parts were to be divided, how authors and periods were to be compared, and what, alas, had to be left out. At first, it was so easy to think, happily, that this was an all-embracing project; so difficult to determine that, for practical purposes, so many cherished items must be omitted. A full study of the illustrators of children's books, which could so appropriately have gone along with the record of children's authors, had to be abandoned, although artists whose work has made books notable by the right of the pictures rather than the text have been given their rightful due. And in the final comparison of first drafts, it had to be admitted that not all the writers who were well worth knowing could possibly be included, that some must be passed by for the sake of doing justice to those who were greatest and most significant.

Footnotes have been kept to a minimum and are offered only for the practical purpose of identification. It has been taken for granted that the bibliographies appended to each chapter would be understood to stand as the authority for statements of fact in the text. The bibliographies themselves have been made brief; they contain the titles of the most suggestive and the most helpful works and they may well be used for more specialized study into any subject or period. To gather and check all necessary information has not been an easy task, for exploration in an unstudied field has its difficulties. Librarians everywhere have been interested and helpful. The writer of this Foreword, whose task gave patient librarians the most trouble of all, would like to acknowledge the untiring support and assistance of Miss Sara Geist of the Bryn Mawr College Library, the aid of Miss Rich of the Rare Book Room in the Philadelphia Free Library, of Miss Van Winkle and Miss Bubb of the District of Columbia Central Library, and of Mr. Ted Arnold of the Library of Congress.

The authors are especially grateful to Dr. Henry Steele Commager, distinguished critic and literary historian, whose keen insight into the literary content of children's books and whose knowledge and appreciation of their contribution to the whole wide field of literature is reflected in his excellent Introduction to this *History*.

One book cannot accomplish everything; even encyclopedias have their disappointments. It has been necessary again and again for the writers to remind themselves of what was their original purpose—to make a study, from the critical point of view, of the worth, the kind and the power of those contributions to children's literature which have given that literature its now acknowledged place in the civilization of today. Good books for children have always been within their reach, lamentably few of them in the far past, increasing in number as time went on, until now they are a veritable flood. Each condition has had its drawbacks and dangers. For those who feel it their responsibility to see that children find the best, for the writers, teachers, and librarians, for the editors and booksellers, for the parents—for all of those whose purpose is to embrace to the fullest extent the opportunities in their hands, this book is presented by these writers as the product of their joint labor.   [1953]

Acknowledgments for the revised edition should include the names of Mrs. Ellin Greene of Rutgers University, Miss Ruth Freitag of the Library of Congress, Miss Avima Ruder, formerly of Macmillan, and Miss Angeline Moscatt of the New York Public Library's Central Children's Room, who have all taken part in making the bibliographical checking. To these names are added those of Miss Deborah Listzwan and Miss Robin Wheeler, who assisted with the index.   [1969]

Contents

Part One BY CORNELIA MEIGS

ROOTS IN THE PAST UP TO 1840

Part Two BY ANNE THAXTER EATON

WIDENING HORIZONS 1840–1890

Part Three BY ELIZABETH NESBITT

A RIGHTFUL HERITAGE 1890–1920

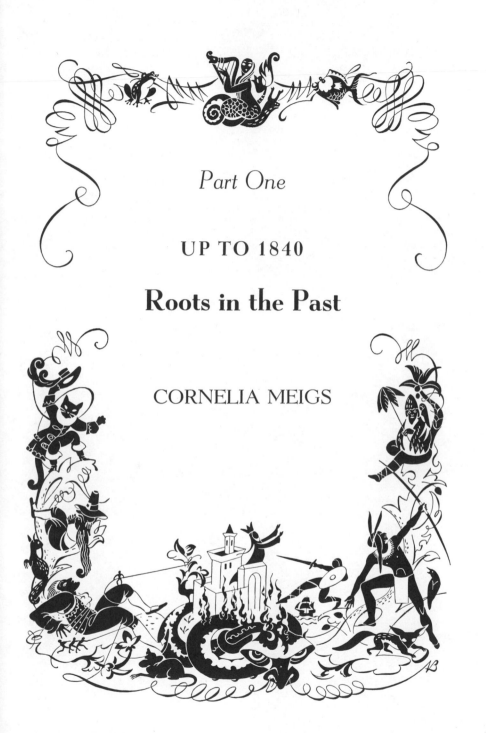

Part One

UP TO 1840

Roots in the Past

CORNELIA MEIGS

· 1 ·

The Deepest Roots

To be aware of the greatness of a literature is not always to understand it fully, since to have interest and regard for it does not imply entire knowledge of what it is and how it came to be. But if thinking people are to have any part in shaping the literature of the present and the future, they should have a fuller understanding of it as a whole and of its past. Literature for children not only has its greatness and an entity of its own in our present day, but has always had it. Just as children, in spite of having long been treated as no more than smaller and more helpless editions of their elders, have always been something apart in vigor of personality, in vision and enterprise of mind, so has the reading of their choice, even though unrecognized as something separate, had its own characteristics, its own individuality, and its own greatness. It is time now to take some measure and to have some comprehension of this greatness, to know why it has lived, survived, and grown in stature, to see what have been its shining monuments and its unnoticed contributions.

In attempting to study the real origins and the determining forces of the juvenile literature of the English-speaking races, one must look very deeply into the past. It is necessary to journey back beyond the earliest stories deliberately written for children, beyond the triumphant landmark of the first printed book, beyond the great medieval manuscripts, with their pages illuminated in scarlet and gold and their jeweled covers that are symbols of the unique treasures within. It is necessary to go beyond even these, although some of them are a thousand years old.

Among all of them, there was always found something that was of interest and delight to children. Even before the beginnings of the art of writing, our remote ancestors had a literature in the vast collection of dear, familiar stories told around the cottage fires in humble houses, or in the great poetic narratives recited or sung in the halls of palace and castle. These last were recounted to the harp music of those gifted wanderers, called variously scops or bards or gleemen or minstrels. Some of them composed their own lays; some repeated, word for word, what had been first sung by their remote masters.

Among those listening to the cottage tales there was always a goodly proportion of children, young persons who hearkened and remembered and told the same stories to their children in their own time. And if we try, for a moment, to picture those richly dressed audiences of court and castle, it is easy to see that those who listened with the deepest attention, the most thrilling response, were those of the company of boys present in every great house for the learning of the arts of war and the graces of chivalry. Such groups go all the way back to the "boy corps" at the court of King Conor of Ulster, which, history tells us, had its day in the first years of the Christian era. The great vellum *Book of Leinster* (circa 1150), recording the tales of Cuchulain,[1] tells us that it was the boy corps that came to the aid of the hero when he lay grievously wounded, and that they perished, every one, even to the king's son, in protecting him.

In that ancient world of primitive ideas and primitive impulses, there was little distinction between what entertained the elders and what entertained the young. In a somewhat more sophisticated time the elders had begun to outgrow their interest, but the young had not. It is the abiding memory of many children and the research of a few devoted scholars which have preserved for our time those humble tales which we call folklore, the slowly accumulated and especially rich treasure which is the heritage of English and, with it, American children's literature.

When one examines the quality of that inheritance, one sees, as when a tulip bulb is cut, both the root and the flower of that imaginative and varying taste which was to give distinctive character to all the literature that was to come. There are a power and life in those stories which have penetrated through every superimposed layer of time, through conquest and growth and Christian conversion. They are qualities which have survived the staggering changes of the reformations, both religious and political, even through periods of destructive and suspicious disregard for old things which occasionally has taken possession of a society which believes itself to be building an entirely new age. Besides the ineradicable root of living imagination, there was the blossoming of fancy and poetic genius, even in the days when men could not write, to preserve the creations of their minds from the dangers of oblivion.

We see, in these folk stories of immense age, above everything else man's effort to explain to himself the forces of which he was so vaguely and reverently aware in the material and spiritual world around him, to explain them without the help of science or the illumination of revealed religion. During that time, long before there were books for anyone to read, there was, none the less, forming among children's minds, as well as among their elders', that basic foundation of taste and imagination and recognition of truth wherever it was encountered which one genera-

---

[1] Pronounced Cu-hóol-in.

tion was to pass on to another. Children learned for their own part how to accept and reject, to perpetuate the good and forget the useless. Thus there began to be a world of literature for children of their own choosing, in spite of much that was thrust upon them in which they had no real part. The importance of this is not to be discounted, since it makes clear how, as Paul Hazard says, "children have defended themselves"[1] by taking for their own, masterpieces from their elders' literature, and determinedly forgetting that which was supposed to be for them.

In the case of the British child's heritage of folklore, there is a singular variety and richness. The Celtic inhabitants of the British Isles were telling their tales and listening to their bards before the Romans came, those fleeting conquerors who left behind them, along with the tessellated pavements and ghostly configurations of ancient camps, a scattering of Mediterranean gods and goddesses that got themselves curiously mixed with the stories of the countryside. The Danes, even more than the Romans, were conquerors who left legends behind them. Servants in their households would have heard and passed on to their native kinsfolk the ringing stories of Hading, who had a giantess for a nurse, of Swanwhite, his warrior daughter, of the giant friend of King Frode's fatherless children, and of the evil triplets who were all three called Grep. Most evidently they heard of Amleth, the prince who feigned madness in order to avenge the murder of his father. Yet the traces of the conquerors are as nothing to the vivid elements that lived in the Anglo-Saxon and the Celtic imaginings.

The Quality of Saxon Fancy

When we speak of the English fairy tales, we are apt to mean that group which has stoutly kept its Anglo-Saxon cast, even though adopting and adapting tales from other sources. In the study of races, of their wanderings and their far connections across Asia and Europe, the tracing of similar stories is often the clue to some hidden kinship. But for the study of this literature, it is the differences and the variety that are important, the quality of detail and the spirit of the narrative which show the racial impulses and ambitions and longings which have gone into the telling of the tales.

The English stories are direct, compact and forthright; they have to do with things of the imagination but, for the most part, in a comfortable and eminently practical way. It is the part of fairies to make the butter come, to do the housework at night if the family is in trouble. The head and front of English magic lore is Robin Goodfellow, who, though some legends declare he is a child of Oberon, is English to the core of his strange being. He is Puck whom Shakespeare makes much of; he is Lob-lie-by-the-fire from whose legend one of the most beautiful of Mrs.

[1] Paul Hazard, *Books, Children and Men,* translated by Marguerite Mitchell (Boston, The Horn Book, 1944), p. 47.

Ewing's stories is derived. He enters into Barrie's *Dear Brutus*; he is the Lubber Fiend of whom Milton speaks in *L'Allegro*. Kipling's portrait of him in *Puck of Pook's Hill* is as fine a likeness as any enthusiast could ask for; he is shown as the early folk tales show him—broad of face, big-eared, hairy, the soul of wit and resource. He is endowed with strange indefinite powers and an infinite knowledge of all the magic which has passed through England within his limitless memory. Kipling calls Puck the "oldest Old Thing in England," but one might differ from him. It is just as possible that the Cornish Piskeys and the Welsh Fair Family are older, or the Irish Leprechauns, who have stored away great riches in gold from unnumbered years of fairy shoemaking.

Sir Walter Scott has said that Tom Thumb and Tom Hickathrift came into England with Hengist and Horsa, so ancient are they. Tom Thumb exploited his smallness and his agility of wit to triumph over all obstacles that came in his enterprising way. Tom Hickathrift, on the other hand, seems not to have been a fellow of towering intellect, but with his monumental strength he became a great sportsman, a phenomenal carrier of heavy weights, and boldly made a way for travelers by slaying a giant with a cart for a club. The land thus freed was given to the poor for common grazing and his reward was that he "was called Mr. Hickathrift before he died."

Jack the Giant-Killer is so thoroughly adopted in the English tradition that his story cannot be called other than an English fairy tale, although Jack himself, as the rhyme records, was a Cornishman and became in time a knight of the Round Table, though Sir Thomas Malory has left the fact unnoticed. Jack got from a slain giant the coat of invisibility, the sword that cut all asunder and the shoes of swiftness, but his achievements do not turn on the possession of these magic properties; he conquers instead by character and invention.

The English fairy tales show a certain rude disregard for human life; heads are cut off, blood flows, miscreants suffer the most dire punishments. But in curious contrast there are a number of them that are carried by the compelling force of pure nonsense which comes by natural gift and is impossible to imitate. Even in the brief absurdity of "Sir Gammer Vans" it is a promise of what other Englishmen were to achieve later. "Last Sunday morning at six o'clock in the evening as I was sailing over the tops of the mountains in my little boat . . ." One sees in this ridiculous use of the impossible a glimpse of that beloved White Rabbit who hurries along looking at his big watch and murmuring, "I shall be too late."

Celtic Fairyland

When we come into the presence of the Celtic fairy story, as distinguished from the English, we enter another realm of fancy entirely, where the existence of the land of Faery is so well known and so recognized that nearly every narrative turns on the nearness of the one world to the other. Celtic stories have this one factor in common, but they vary greatly among themselves, Scotch being unlike Irish, and Welsh differing from both of them and from Cornish, which unhappily is almost lost to us, going the way of the old Cornish language which has perished from common memory.

Scotch stories, so the folklore scholars agree, have got more or less interwoven with the English, for both have long since crossed their own borders. But the Scotch tales still tend to show the character of much older narrative; they are less explicit, briefer, and cruder in their details. In "The Black Bull of Norroway," found in English collections, there is evidence of its Scottish origin, partly in its romance, partly in the formula at the beginning when each daughter says to her mother, "Bake me a bannock, and roast me a collop, for I'm going away to seek my fortune." A bannock seems, in more stories than one, to be a necessary thing to have with one when setting out into the world.

"Tamlane" is a typically Scottish tale also, where the young son of the Earl of Murray, plighted to Burd Janet, was so rash as to go widdershins—in a direction against the sun—around the hill and so was subject to being carried away by the fairies. Burd Janet, standing at Miles Cross at midnight on Halloween, cast a compass about her with holy water and saw the court and the train of the Queen of Elfland ride by. Among them was her lover on a white horse and with a star in his crown, this honor being his due as a "christened knight." Her love rescued him, even after he had been turned into a red-hot glaive. Many of the ancient tales, like this one, have survived in the Scottish ballads, along with those of later date and of recognizably historic times.

The Piskey Folk of Cornwall

The procession of the Queen of Elfland reflects the tendency of the Celtic stories to deal with fairies in flitting throngs and with the nature of the fairy world. The Cornish legends, collected by Enys Tregarthen, absolutely revel in the doings of the small people—the Little Invisibles, the Knockers, the Spriggans, and most of all the Piskeys. Benet Chegwidden, in the story of "The Piskey Revelers" saw the whole fairy host, in their little gold coaches no bigger than a large turnip, their footmen dressed in scarlet and green, their horses the size of kittens, the lords and ladies in their rich finery of laces and velvets and jewels. Young Merlin Legassick saw Bucca Boo's Little Merry Men, Bucca Boo being the Cornish Neptune, rowing in their little boat which was "curved like a moon on her back" and lay "a burning wonder on the quiet water."[1]

---

[1] Enys Tregarthen, *Piskey Folk* (New York, John Day, 1940), pp. 132, 148.

The Cornish tales have a grace and a grotesqueness all in one, a charm wholly their own, like the Piskeys, who are not quite matched by any other fairies anywhere. The Cornish Knockers have been translated to this country, for in the deep mines for gold and copper in the Rocky Mountains where many Cornishmen work, the tapping of their hammers, so it is said, can be heard beyond the shaft, a sound that bodes disaster.

Genius Concerns Itself with Fairies in Ireland

There is rich variety and resourcefulness of wit in the tales of Eire, which have been collected under particularly happy circumstances. As scholars have pointed out, storytelling in Ireland was still practiced as an art and a profession when wise minds began to be concerned with the oral literature which was rapidly dying out elsewhere. James Stephens with his greatness of poetic imagination has retold some of the hero narratives in *Irish Fairy Tales* (1920), while William Butler Yeats, with the able help of Lady Gregory, set about gathering the fireside stories for his collection *Fairy and Folk Tales of the Irish Peasantry* (1888). He has distinguished between "the Trooping Fairies" and "the Solitary Fairies," like the Pooka, and the Merrow, who is a mermaid, the Banshee and the Leprechauns. If you catch a Leprechaun and hold him until he promises to share his wealth with you, then you are made for life, since he has crocks of gold hidden everywhere.

The Fairy World and the Welsh

By the firesides of Wales, stories were told in which the world of the supernatural seemed to come closest of all to the world of men. Do we not hear of Morgan Rhyss, who was so tormented by the constant presence of fairies in his house that he decided, on advice, to pack up and pretend that he was preparing to move and live elsewhere? When he had just got all his possessions loaded on a cart, a neighbor stopped to ask him whither he was going, and a little voice spoke out of a churn, "We are going to live in Ystrad Towy."[1] This was so discouraging to Morgan that he took his effects back into his cottage, but at last got rid of his troublesome guests by the charm of cooking a sparrow in a nutshell.

The Welsh lore tells you things of great interest, that a white dog with silver eyes can see the wind, and that if you are to travel with fairies and are given your choice, you must choose mid-wind, since above the wind is terrifying and giddy, while below it you are carried bumping through bogs and briers. There is a recurrent tale in many versions of wanderers stumbling upon a cave where warriors of the most ancient days lie asleep. They are Arthur and his knights and a touch on an enchanted bell wakes them from their slumber.

[1] William Jenkyn Thomas, *The Welsh Fairy-Book* (New York, F. A. Stokes, 1908), p. 16.

The Cinderella Story

Students of folklore have traced the tale of Cinderella almost literally from China to Peru, with a vast number of variations. The one which has proved most acceptable to English-speaking children is the French version, brought into England in the translation of Perrault. He was far from inventing the tale, but the attributes of the French story—the pumpkin coach, the mice turned into horses, even the fairy godmother— are unlike the native British form, but have caught the fancy of British and American children. The English, Scottish, and Irish, however, all have their own variants.

The simplest, and probably the oldest, of them all is the tale of Tattercoats, the granddaughter of a lord who would have none of her because her mother died when she was born. She wandered in the fields with no comrade but the gooseherd, while the lord sat brooding over his sorrows. Then the king came to visit a nearby town and gave a ball at which the prince, his only son, would choose a wife. Tattercoats and the gooseherd went barefoot to the castle; there was no gold coach, no lizard footman, not even a glass slipper. She appeared dressed in her torn petticoat, with the gooseherd playing music on his pipe which cast a love spell upon the young prince. The prince carried Tattercoats away, the lord returned to his brooding and the gooseherd was never seen again.

A more elaborate version and one well loved until the Perrault story displaced it is that of Catskin, which we hear of as being told, in a later age, to the Vicar of Wakefield's children. Catskin, although she achieved a coat of silver cloth, one of beaten gold and one made of the feathers of all the birds of the air, is none the less an able and practical heroine who gains her end and a royal wedding by native wit and not by magic. It is a thoroughly English narrative, told and retold before Goldsmith mentioned it.

The Scottish Cinderella is Rushen Coatie, whose stepmother and jealous sisters made her toil in the kitchen and wear no garment save one made of rushes. Her mother had left her a little red calf who granted all her wishes and kept her from starving. The sisters were going, not to a ball, but to the three days of successive church services for Yuletide, and by aid of the calf Rushen Coatie went also, suitably attired on each of the festival days. A prince fell in love with her and in proper tradition identified her by the slipper which she lost on running away. This slipper had distinguished properties, for it leaped from the prince's pocket when that "dirty thing that sits in the kitchen nook and wears a rushen coatie" was brought before him, and fitted itself upon the lady's foot.

The most elaborate tale, full of the most magic and romance, is the

Irish one of Fair, Brown and Trembling, wherein the lady rides to church in "a dress as white as snow and green shoes for my feet," on a "white mare with a golden saddle and bridle" and with "A honey-bird to sit on your right shoulder, and a honey-finger to put on your left," these being the gifts of the henwife. It is a longer and more complex narrative than the others, not coming to an end with the slipper, but reaching a satisfactory conclusion at last, one which embraced fourteen children.

England Inherits All

Once established in their own character, the stories have held true to type to a curious degree. As divided Britain became one kingdom with a common speech, the tales overran their own local boundaries and went everywhere. It has been suggested that Shakespeare did something entirely new in *A Midsummer-Night's Dream* when he presented fairies as small, airy, intangible creatures like Moth and Peas-blossom, putting them with the classical supernaturals like Oberon and Robin Goodfellow. But Shakespeare may have been only turning to the Fair Family, the Little People, nor can we possibly know what person of Wales or Cornwall had got so far from home as Warwickshire or London and spread his tales abroad to reach in time those keenly listening ears of genius. Shakespeare knew enough of the matter to be aware that in the magic world the high and lordly humans see very little of what is really about them, and adventures with the Little People must be set among simple folk. Bottom is the most delightfully and profoundly silly of all Shakespeare's men of little wit, but he could do one thing that his superiors could not: he could see a fairy.

That accumulated wealth of legend and imagination, the touchstone of beauty and fancy that came to belong to every person in Britain, was a treasure that was carried abroad with the adventurers to a new country. Not even the stern self-denial of the Puritans could leave it at home. Like the little voice that spoke from the churn, English folklore was heard again by English firesides in a different land. In the development of literature that was to follow, the British folk stories and their kindred descendants of magic fantasy have had curious alternations of eclipse and appreciation and eclipse again. But as time goes on, as literature swings away from the artificial and returns to the natural, they always reappear, kept alive by the ever-renewing interest of children and scholars. They invariably come back when the time is once more ready for them. As one of the Celtic storytellers so sensibly observed—

"There is no end of treasure hidden in the mountains of Wales, but if you are not the person for whom it is intended, you will probably never find it."[1]

[1] Thomas, *op. cit.*, p. 184.

Bibliography

Jacobs, Joseph, ed. *Celtic Fairy Tales*. New York, G. P. Putnam's Sons, 1892.
———— *English Fairy Tales*. New York, G. P. Putnam's Sons, 1890.
———— *More English Fairy Tales*. New York, G. P. Putnam's Sons, 1894.
Saxo Grammaticus. *The Swords of the Vikings, Stories from the Works of Saxo Grammaticus*, retold by Julia Davis Adams. New York, E. P. Dutton, 1928.
Thomas, William Jenkyn. *The Welsh Fairy-Book*. New York, F. A. Stokes, 1908.
Tregarthen, Enys. *Piskey Folk; a Book of Cornish Legends*, collected by Elizabeth Yates. New York, John Day Co., 1940.
Yeats, William Butler, ed. *Fairy and Folk Tales of the Irish Peasantry*. London, W. Scott, 1888.

2

The Quickening Life

The shadows of the Romans and the Danes passed over Britain quickly as we measure time now. The Normans thought to take possession of England, but in the end were possessed by her. We must look elsewhere than among the armed legions and the dragon ships for the real conquerors of Britain; they were men of another stamp and a totally different aspect. For the real conquerors of the British Isles were the Christian missionaries. They had as great courage as the soldiers of Caesar, or "the heathen men" of the marauding Viking bands, or the plumed and armored knights of William. Without exercise of arms, these devoted men brought first to Ireland and then to England the forces and influences that changed the face of history. Pope Gregory, seeing the Anglian slaves in Rome, saw with his shrewdly appraising ecclesiastical eye not merely the beauty, but the spiritual possibilities of this distant people.

Even before his emissaries had reached England, Ireland had been converted through men who had traveled thus far under the protection of the Roman occupation. St. Patrick and St. Augustine could not join hands across the hundred and fifty years that parted them in time, but they were one in their purpose and results. With the Christian doctrine came confidence and new vision; there came also the arts of reading and writing, there came shared knowledge and extending scholarship. The soaring Celtic fancy, the sturdy Anglo-Saxon imagination, now no longer limited by ignorance, began to follow the path of enlightened thinking, going forward each in its own way. They mingled without losing character, absorbed new cultures or overflowed them and found voice in a new Christian literature. And it was now a written literature whose enduring existence did not depend on the chance recollection of one generation or another.

How much of the old oral tradition was lost cannot now be calculated, nor how much it was changed. The humble folk stories continued to be told, although the spirit of Christianity touched them with an altering hand, leaving only some of them openly and frankly pagan. Just as the old Druidic festivals, such as Yule and Midsummer Eve, became identified with Christian feasts and seasons of the Church, so did the stories take on Christian mysticism instead of superstitious magic. Imaginations fed on the beauty and fancy of fairy lore can rise easily to the higher and truer belief in the miracles of God. We hear very early, for instance, of the good Beuno, who used to preach on Sunday at Llanddwyn off the coast of Anglesey, walking thither on the sea with his book of sermons under his arm. It was, however, only little by little that the simple fireside tales were written down, casually and by chance. Christianity had brought the two great gifts—writing and, with it, the love of learning; yet these two did not affect greatly the lives of the humble.

A more assured existence and perhaps, therefore, a more definite influence on the writing that was to come was the literature of the castle as distinguished from that of the cottage. The great hero tales, sung to harp music in the hall of lord or king, varied little in form, since they had to keep to the musical accompaniment and were, moreover, of wording jealously guarded and handed on from one bard to another. It was these which made their way into the great medieval manuscripts, written down by the order of some nobleman to perpetuate the events of his own realm or the reputed deeds of his own ancestors. Or they were put down by the devoted labor of some quiet monk living far from the world's affairs but hearing, none the less, the echoes of its greatness, writing in the scriptorium, that one spot in the monastery where it was a little warmer than elsewhere, so that the ink would not freeze. Here have survived those narratives of saints and heroes which were listened to by children in their own time and, in ours, have passed through the hands of scholars to come back to children again. Even after the inevitable changes, we can still trace the varied character of their origin.

The cycle of tales having to do with the Irish hero Cuchulain is one whose quality is undimmed even by countless repetitions, by long passage of time, and by diversity of sources. The manuscripts from which the full sequence is drawn are of a considerable number, the oldest being the *Book of the Dun Cow*—the *Leabhar na h-uidri*—getting its odd title merely from the kind of parchment upon which it is written. It was compiled and inscribed in the monastery of Clonmacnoise on the River Shannon, about the year 1100. It differs somewhat in extent but not in essential detail from the *Book of Leinster*, drawn up for King Dermod MacMurrough, ruler of Leinster who later in the twelfth century invited the Normans to come over from Wales to help him against his enemy neighbors. The background scene of the stories is of extraordinary richness, with the great scythe-armed chariots, the plunging horses yoked with silver, the helmets set with carbuncles and crystals, and the mighty two-handed swords.

The character of Cuchulain is like no other in all the roster of heroes; he is the epitome of youth; there is in him a lightness, a flame of wild courage, a frantic elation, which comes upon him when mortal combat is joined. He is only four years old when he comes to King Conor's court to begin his training in arms and fighting; he is still a child when he slays the dreadful dog of Culain and takes upon himself the title of the Hound of Culain, later to have friends and enemies alike call him the Hound of Ulster. While still nothing but a boy he chooses the day for his dedication to a life of arms, and is warned by a wise Druid that it is an ill-omened selection, for it means, to the warrior dedicated on that day, a short life, though a glorious one.

"Though the span of my life were but a day," Cuchulain says— " 'Bec a brig liomsa sin' ar Cuchulaind"—"Little should I reck of that, if but my noble deeds might be remembered among men."[1]

The war between Ulster and Connaught begins in the cattle raid of Cooley, concerning which incident alone there exist almost a hundred tales. The climax of the struggle comes when Ferdia, Cuchulain's dearest friend and comrade in arms, is bribed by Queen Maeve of Connaught to take her side and to meet his loved Cuchulain in single combat. The two warriors sit by their campfire together at night recalling all the pleasant days of their training in arms; when morning comes they rise to try, one against the other, all the dreadful devices that were taught to them both. Ferdia falls at last, Maeve admits defeat, and there is peace for a long space of time. But in the end Maeve's bitter hatred leads her to join the powers of darkness against Cuchulain and she enlists magic to destroy him. Three spears, three swords, given surprisingly by Vulcan, bring him to his death. His surviving horse, the Grey of Macha, carries his chariot driver and the fateful message home.

The *Book of Leinster* gives us also the story of Deirdre, calling it "The Tragical Death of the Sons of Usnach." It has been made familiar to us all by each of three great Irish poets—Synge, Stephens, and Yeats. The Irish hero tales are prone to be tragic; the story of Deirdre is one of the *Three Sorrowful Tales of Erin*, the others being "The Tragical Fate of the Children of Lir" and "The Tragical Fate of the Children of Tuireann." The tale of Cuchulain is Cuchulain himself, with a concentration of interest and suspense in the narrow circle that lights his own heroic figure. In the story of Deirdre, the central theme is not her beauty or her childlike innocence and lovableness, but, as the old title in the manuscript indicates, the real action is in the single-minded devotion of all the brothers and their support of the passionate love for Deirdre which has taken possession of one of them. Time and repetition have rendered some of the hero stories more and more complicated as the

---

[1] Eleanor Hull, *The Boys' Cuchulain* (New York, T. Y. Crowell, 1910), p. 1.

generations go by, but the sense of single interest has never been lost from these Irish epic narratives.

Heroes of Wales

In the library of Jesus College, Oxford, is a Welsh manuscript dating from the fourteenth and fifteenth centuries. The *Red Book of Hergest*—the *Llyfr Coch o Hergest*—is a collection of tales that once were the songs of bards, varying in subject and also in quality, many of them dealing with King Arthur and his court, some of them reaching back into still more ancient legends. Extensive translations from this book were published, beginning in 1838, the work of Lady Charlotte Guest (1812–1895). This remarkable woman had thrown herself as a constructive partner into her husband's great iron business, the largest in the world, with a most enlightened interest and care for the welfare of his twenty thousand employees. She was the mother, also, of a very large family of children. But even these were not enough and she managed to gather sufficient scholarship to read and translate these ancient stories of Wales, her adopted and deeply loved home.

She called her published collection *The Mabinogion*, plural of Mabinogi, a bard's narrative in song, belonging to an age far older than the manuscript itself. The *Red Book of Hergest* is a compilation, rather than a single cycle, and shows a long sweep of legend, some of it frankly pagan, some touched with Christianity, but all of it shot through with mystery and magic. Lady Charlotte translated only a part of one group of narratives, which have been added to later, making complete for young people in our time a story of a less-known hero than Cuchulain, but one of equally striking character. The tale, of which parts appear in Lady Charlotte's *Mabinogion*, is offered entire in Kenneth Morris' *Book of the Three Dragons*, published in 1930.

The hero is Manawyddan, the center of a succession of adventures unified by his single character and full of delicate complexities of rare poetic beauty, abounding in color, strange landscapes, and incredible events. Behind the action is the fact that the gods have decided to raise a mortal to their own stature and have chosen Manawyddan, who must pass through ordeal after ordeal as a divine testing. His long trials and journeyings, covering the span of a lifetime, end in his coming face to face with a flame-bright dragon, the most glorious dragon in literature one might well say, with its sun-colored wings and sapphire sword, with its power and subtlety in fighting. Combat between these two lasts from one day to another and another. Manawyddan is more and more seriously wounded, he is exhausted to the point of death, but every hour his admiration and love of the dragon grow, until at last he bows down in worship, knowing that his adversary is a god, Gwron Giant himself, the Heartener of Heroes, clothed in his mantle of blue flame.

In these Welsh hero stories one gets, more than anywhere else, an idea of the Celtic gods, who otherwise loom only vague and wonderful behind the tales of mortal men. The gods of Greek and Roman mythology are far more definite in our minds, for they had pagan poets to celebrate them who have left their written works unchanged to posterity. But in the case of this equally complex Celtic hierarchy, of Lugh and Gwron and Ceridwen, the Mother of the World, the words of the pagan bards have only been preserved to us by the hands of Christian scribes, with the glory of the old deities waning as belief in them came to an end.

The first four stories in Lady Charlotte Guest's *Mabinogion* have to do with King Arthur and the companions of his court. It is a different Arthur and a very different company from that with which young readers have later become familiar. But the foundations of the whole Arthur literature of medieval romance and later modern poetry can be seen in these early Welsh narratives. Arthur here is a monarch of purely Welsh blood; he is possessed of magic powers which are shared by his attendant warriors. Kai, his seneschal, had "this peculiarity," that his breath lasted nine days and nine nights under water, and when it pleased him he could render himself as tall as the highest tree of the forest. The accounts are full of beauty and color; Kilhwch, riding to ask Arthur's help in winning his bride, is mounted on "a steed with head dappled gray, of four winters old, firm of limb, with shell-formed hoofs, having a bridle of linked gold on his head, and upon him a saddle of costly gold." The youth carries in his hand two silver spears "of an edge to wound the wind."

Related in the beginning by professional storytellers and singers, the narrative is often a tour de force of unbelievable memorizing, recounting the names and qualities of Arthur's companions and enumerating the details of the thirty-eight tasks which are laid upon Kilhwch by his bride's father. The most telling recital is Arthur's presentation of that list of things which are his dearest treasures—his ship Prydwen, his sword Caledvwlch, and his Queen, Gwenhwyvar.

The Golden World

All this, with its complexity and discursiveness, seems a far cry from the kind of story to absorb and please the young reader of the present day. There is no doubt that the accounts of Cuchulain, of Manawyddan, and of Arthur need much alteration for such a purpose, but it must not be forgotten that here we see already the excuse and reason for the constant retelling of the stories through the ages. It is easier to understand their greatness and how they have enriched and leavened the literature of all time if we look at their sources and recognize the beginning and the germ of the living power in them. A group of tales having a similar oral origin, but belonging to a somewhat later chapter of medieval times, have descended to us, not in the form of the epic cycle, but of the popular ballad. They belong to the great and the simple alike, and their subjects come from every walk of life. A certain collection of them attaching to one figure, as legendary yet as realistic as Arthur himself, are the ballads of Robin Hood.

Who that bold and lovable outlaw was or whether he really lived at all are questions that have never been settled. Some of the accounts of him are as early as the fourteenth century, while others have evident origin of a much later date. All of them not only follow the career of the same hero, but reflect a certain mood of lighthearted courage, of generosity, of a carefree approach to even the most bitter problems that men have to meet. And there is also, of which all readers become aware, a sense of delight in the free, the green, the leafy freshness of Sherwood forest.

> When shaws beene sheene, and shradds[1] full fayre,
>   And leaves both large and longe,
> Itt is merrye walkyng in the fayre forrèst
>   To heare the small birdes songe.[2]

This is the opening of one of the oldest, "Robin Hood and Guy of Gisborne," but a beginning of very similar wording belongs to "Robin Hood and the Widow's Three Sons," a tale wherein Robin Hood, in disguise, gets the sheriff of Nottingham to hire him as his hangman, and is thus able to free the three condemned brothers. Robin Hood is the people's hero, the figure of protest against the corruption and the avarice of that privileged class which was engendered by the feudal age. He is as English as Cuchulain and Manawyddan are Celtic; he has deep but unspoken devotion to a great principle of loyalty to the poor, but he never, outwardly, takes himself with great seriousness, and for him life is always direct and gay and good. Shakespeare knew this essence of his character, for Charles, in *As You Like It*, thus reports of the banished Duke,

> They say, he is already in the forest of Arden, and a many merry men with him; and there they live like the old Robin Hood of England . . . and fleet the time carelessly, as they did in the golden world. (I, i, 122)

A few attempts have been made at collecting the Robin Hood ballads, but what older scholars have accomplished less well, a modern prose writer has fully achieved. Howard Pyle's *The Merry Adventures of Robin Hood* captures to our deepest satisfaction the full quality of that gay-hearted hero, making us aware of that history which is the heritage

---

[1] twigs.
[2] *A Book of Old English Ballads* (New York, Macmillan, 1896), p. 106.

of both English and American readers, and lets us see it at its very springtime.

Scottish ballads, and those of the Border where there was never any lack of hotly contested frays, have a march and a swing to them that are inseparable from their stirring content. Sir Philip Sidney says in his *Defense of Poesy*, "I never heard the old song of Percy and Douglas that I found not my heart moved more than with a trumpet." So does any reader feel as the ballad of Chevy-Chase unfolds before him. Who can fail of an inward stirring on reading the tale of Johnie Armstrong and that bold fellow's upbraiding of the Scottish King:

> "To seek het water beneath cauld ice,
>   Surely it is a great follie—
> I have asked grace of a graceless face,
>   But there is nane for my men and me!"[1]

There is a roughness of style in the old ballad not to be imitated in the new, nor is it appropriate to modern themes. Through the Middle Ages and some time beyond, the ballads were everywhere, but they sank presently to the doggerel of the chapbooks, vended by strolling peddlers. They were revived in 1765 by the publication of Percy's *Reliques*, to be followed by another collection, Walter Scott's *The Minstrelsy of the Scottish Border* (1802–1803). Their impact on a languid and sterile phase of English poetry was startling. Wordsworth has testified how great a debt he and his contemporaries owed to the old ballads which ushered in another form of verse. One has only to reread *The Rime of the Ancient Mariner* to realize that in the hands of real genius true balladry can live again in English literature. Later attempts at the older form in new settings have been less fortunate. Critics have pointed out that the merit of the old ballads was that their authors believed the stories they were telling, a requisite hard to supply in more modern attempts in the same medium. But children's response to them should give present-day writers a key to what elements in poetry children most easily enjoy—swift narrative, rough-cut character, stark rhythm, and the repeated refrain which sings in the mind long after the page is turned.

So far we have looked at those manuscript treasures of the Middle Ages which preserved the spoken poetry and narrative of a much older time. It is plain, of course, that even before the invention of printing, books and the knowledge of reading increased together, and through the monastic schools there grew up a body of readers and a growing literature of contemporary event and contemporary taste. No one had as yet

---

[1] Robert MacIntyre, ed., *Ballads Ancient and Modern* (London, Thomas Nelson, 1935), p. 46.

written for children, but the sources of that awareness of good literature, the possession of which was to stand children in such good stead, begin to be more and more evident. One further influence there was, indirect, but potent none the less.

The Corpus Christi Festival

Children had heard stories, had listened to the lays of minstrels, and joined in the refrains of ballads; they had, moreover, stood absorbed and entranced before those vivid pictorial dramas of action and color which we call the Mystery, the Miracle, and the Morality plays. We owe their beginnings to the Church, as we owe the art and practice of writing itself. But very soon the Biblical and saintly dramas came down from the steps of the cathedrals and were presented for a wider and more secular audience in the public streets. Here in the open these early plays were free for all to see. They were, at the time of their highest glory, the work of guilds and companies drawn from the people themselves, and there can be no doubt that many in their audiences were children. We can picture them with their elders, streaming over the great stone bridge under the shadow of York Minster in the bright weather of late May or early June to see the town gay with banners for the plays to be given on Corpus Christi Day.

The big pageant wagons would draw up to the chosen spot, the brightly dressed figures would come forward on the stage—Noah in his long robe expostulating with his unconvinced wife, Isaac trudging along after his father, carrying the wood for the sacrifice and asking innocently where the creature was that was to be laid on the altar. There would be the shepherds with their rough jokes, playing tricks on each other, then reduced to silent awe as they came into the presence of Mary and the Holy Child. After them would come the gorgeous visitation of the Kings of the East, presented by the goldsmith's guild as having greater resources for the purpose than the other companies. All through the fourteenth and fifteenth centuries this lavish entertainment was offered once a year, spreading out from York and Coventry to other places, extending the scope of the drama to include St. George and the Dragon and other legends. The Morality plays developed wherein men, women, and children, too, listening and watching, learned the meaning of allegory and symbols. Could there, one wonders, have been *Pilgrim's Progress* without *Everyman* to show the way?

Romance and the Middle Ages

Besides the plays, creative writers and receptive readers of the Middle Ages began to throw themselves into romance. It was a type and manner of literature which came into England from the Continent, but the nucleus of its story was often some Celtic or English legend, so overlaid with new matter and ideas foreign to the original spirit that the real beginnings are scarcely recognizable. Two, in particular, were of immense popularity, both on the Continent and in England, and have, moreover, often been listed in later times as tales especially acceptable to children. These are *Sir Bevis of Southampton* and *Guy of Warwick*. *Bevis* is a story which, like many others of its time, took its material from the long struggle of Christian Europe against Islam for the possession of the Holy Land. It contains a Saracen princess, Josian, and the capture of a comic giant whom Josian takes as her page.

Guy of Warwick is distinctly the more important of the two and was offered in children's editions for a long time after the invention of printing made such publication possible. The name of its English hero was a byword for strength, boldness, and piety all over Europe as well as in England. It tells a story which was earnestly asserted to be true, citing the relics preserved at Warwick Castle as testimony. It was, besides, deeply consistent with the ideas and ideals of its time. The hero, son of the steward of Warwick Castle, falls in love with Felice, the daughter of the earl, and to win her he performs enormous feats in wars, in tournaments, against dragons and monsters. He wins her at last, but immediately after their marriage a change comes over his spirit.

"For Beauty I have shed a world of Blood," he declares, but now "I'll go thro' Hell itself to purchase Heaven." He sets off, with staff and scrip, to make a pilgrimage of penitence to the Holy Land. Years later he returns home, old, broken and unrecognizable, to settle down as a hermit in a hut near Warwick Castle. Only on his deathbed does he reveal himself to Felice, who has been living a life of devotion and alms-giving, always looking for the return of Guy. The place of his retreat, a high, bold hill with a stream below and a stretch of woods, was ever after known as Guy's Cliff. When King Henry V came in state to visit Warwick Castle, he urged the earl of that day to set up a shrine to Guy's memory, since all men in Europe and even Islam gave honor to his name.

Speculation as to the names of the authors of these romances has revealed no certain answer. They are Norman in quality, rather than the hearty Anglo-Saxon English on which the Robin Hood ballads were nurtured. Not only in spirit, but in form, are they typical of those stories which originated in England, were carried abroad, and returned overlaid by the conventions and elaborations of a very different taste. The same evolution occurred in the case of another group of legends to be considered in the next chapter, a set of stories as old as our knowledge of England itself, which traveled afar, took to themselves the very different aspect of continental romance, and came home to be remade into a glorious record by the hand of a very great English gentleman.

Bibliography

Baugh, Albert C., ed. *A Literary History of England*. New York, Appleton-Century-Crofts, 1948.

A Book of Old English Ballads. New York, Macmillan, 1896.

Child, Francis James, ed. *The English and Scottish Popular Ballads*. 5 Vols. Boston, Houghton Mifflin, 1883–98.

Clarke, Sidney W. *The Miracle Play in England*. London, W. Andrews, 1897.

Cuchulain. *The Boys' Cuchulain: Heroic Legends of Ireland*, by Eleanor Hull. New York, T. Y. Crowell, 1910.

—— *The Cuchullin Saga in Irish Literature*; compiled and edited with introd. and notes, by Eleanor Hull. London, D. Nutt, 1898.

Guy of Warwick (Romance). *The Noble and Renowned History of Guy, Earl of Warwick*. 5th ed. London, A. Bettesworth, 1711.

Lang, Andrew. *Custom and Myth*. 2d ed., rev. London, Longmans, Green, 1885.

Mabinogion. *The Mabinogion*. Translated with notes, by Lady Charlotte Guest. London, B. Quaritch, 1877.

McGurk, J. J. N. "Learning and Society in Ireland Before the Norman Conquest." *History Today*, Vol. 16 (Feb., 1966), pp. 85–93.

MacIntyre, Robert, ed. *Ballads Ancient and Modern*. London, Thomas Nelson, 1935.

Morris, Kenneth. *Book of the Three Dragons*. New York, Longmans, Green, 1930.

Percy, Thomas, Bp. of Dromore. *Reliques of Ancient English Poetry*. 3 Vols. Edinburgh, W. P. Nimmo, 1869.

Schreiber, Lady Charlotte Guest. *Lady Charlotte Guest; Extracts from Her Journal, 1833–1852*. Edited by the Earl of Bessborough. London, J. Murray, 1950.

—— *Lady Charlotte Schreiber; Extracts from Her Journal, 1853–1891*. Edited by the Earl of Bessborough. London, J. Murray, 1952.

3

The Multiplying Leaves

The "Knyght Presoner" and His Story of King Arthur

For five hundred years the name of Sir Thomas Malory (circa 1400–1471) was surrounded by mystery. Through centuries scholars have looked for information concerning his life; and even his work, a great epic in English prose, was available to readers only through the medium of another man's mind. When William Caxton (circa 1422–1491) published his version of Malory's King Arthur stories he altered and edited them according to his own notion, some of his ideas being good, some being far from that. Caxton or his successors suffered the manuscript from which he worked to be lost or destroyed, so that for these hundreds of years it has been thought that none existed. For long it has been accepted that we could know little more of Malory than his name and the work which Caxton gave us.

Scholarly research during the past sixty years, notably the discoveries of the late Professor George Lyman Kittredge, presented us with some startling new facts about Malory, but they have served, indeed, to make him more of a man of mystery than ever. Court records give evidence of his turbulent career, of his long imprisonment, and his almost unnoticed death. They seem to help very little in the involuntary attempts of any reader to see, behind his pageantry of knights and battles, something of the greatness of spirit and personality of the real Malory. But the comparatively recent finding in the library of Winchester College of an actual manuscript of his *Morte Darthur* has made clearer our understanding of what Malory had set about doing and what he had really intended when he was drawn little by little into rendering the Arthurian romance into English "oute of Freynshe."

We know now that he, like Shakespeare, was a native of Warwickshire, and we can recognize that green landscape of great ancient trees, stretches of woodland and of flowery meadow which both writers so evidently remember, and of which Falstaff was babbling when he died. The Malorys were Norman-English, modest gentlefolk who lived on the manor of Newbold Revel. It was natural that Thomas's father, M.P. for Warwickshire, should have the desire and the opportunity to place his son in the service of the great lord of the neighborhood, Richard de Beauchamp, Earl of Warwick. This Richard traced his ancestry back to Guy of Warwick of earlier romantic fame, with unforgetting reverence for that great warrior's story. When Richard Beauchamp, in his own turn, journeyed to the Holy Land, he was waited on by a messenger from the Sultan, who told him that even here they had heard of Guy of Warwick and circulated the story in "books of their own language."

The career of Beauchamp was the actual education of young Thomas Malory, the source of his knowledge and his deep impressions concerning knighthood and leadership, and the greatness and glory of a career of arms in those years of the waning Middle Ages. We do not know in what year Thomas joined his patron; we know that he was with him in Calais some time before Henry V's triumph at Agincourt. We know by record that Richard Beauchamp held command in Rouen on that fearful day when Joan of Arc was burned in the market place. Beauchamp's duty was to provide the guards surrounding the place of execution; it may have been that Malory was one of them; certainly there could be no one in Rouen that day who did not witness the terrible spectacle. Three times in Malory's stories are women bound to the stake, condemned to death by burning; but unlike the tragic Joan they are always saved at the last minute by the appearance of a champion.

Such were the activities of Malory's earlier years; such was the hero, the great earl whom he had always before his eyes. And if Beauchamp was not hero enough, there was also the striking figure of King Henry V leading his men to desperate victory, dying romantically at the height of his glory.

The records show that Malory returned to Warwickshire after the end of the fighting in France, that he was an M.P. as his father had been and then—astonishing denouement—there is the undeniable witness of the legal archives that he was accused of breaking and entering, of robbing Coombe Abbey of jewels and ornaments of the church and of two bags of money, finally of having lain in wait to assassinate Humphrey, Duke of Buckingham, kinsman of the royal family. Buckingham presided over his trial and, as is not surprising, the knight was condemned to imprisonment which lasted virtually all the rest of his life.

It was a lawless time, with the quarrels of the houses of Lancaster and York beginning to sweep over England. Malory's friend and patron, Richard Beauchamp, was dead, his place taken by Richard Neville, maker and unmaker of kings. It was a time also when tempting opportunity had brought about corruption in certain quarters of the heavily propertied Church, with Coombe Abbey as one of those accused of flagrant injustice and extortion practiced upon its tenants. Malory's act of breaking and entering at the head of a band of a hundred rioters may have been a matter of taking the law into his hands for forcible restitution. For the alleged threat to Duke Humphrey's life there seems to have been very little evidence. Was he a headstrong crusader? Was he a political victim? Or had long campaigning broken down his moral sense and was he in truth a thief, a housebreaker, and a riotous person as the indictment declares? Research has not yet found the answer; it is sufficient that we know that for the remaining twenty years of his life he was an imprisoned culprit, spending the longest period of that unhappy time in Newgate Prison in London.

We feel that Malory speaks of himself as "a knyght presoner," that he asks, at the conclusions of his different books, for prayers for his deliverance and that, as he writes of Tristram's captivity, he gives most moving witness of his own suffering and his own despair. "For all the while a prisoner may have his health of body he may endure under the mercy of God and in hope of good deliverance; but when sickness toucheth a prisoner's body, then may a prisoner say all wealth is him bereft, and then he hath cause to wail and to weep. Right so did Sir Tristram when sickness had undertaken him, for then he took such sorrow that he had almost slain himself."[1]

More than one great piece of literature has been written in prison; this study will presently have occasion to examine another. Here, more than under any other circumstances, do the character and the content of the writing depend upon what is latent in the author's own mind, what he can look back upon in the past when the present affords nothing but a dim procession of monotonous days. Malory could look back upon splendor and color and the crowded action of that great expedition undertaken when "fair stood the wind for France," upon English arms and English martial enterprise when they were at the height of their glory. Moreover, being a follower of Richard Beauchamp, who was a scholar and lover of letters as well as a warrior, Malory had become familiar with the French romances which celebrated the greatness of medieval chivalry. It was a system which was already slipping to its destruction, although few were aware of this.

Certain privileges were allowed him in prison on account of his rank, one of them being access to the books in the Greyfriars Library across the road, the first city library in London, which had been founded by one Sir Richard Whittington, four times Lord Mayor. Beginning on a project which might help to shorten the interminable days, Malory set about the translation of some of the French romances into English. Most particularly he was interested in the great cycle of stories of King Arthur. Recorded by the *Mabinogion*, paraphrased by Geoffrey of

---

[1] Sir Thomas Malory, *Le Morte Darthur* (London, Macmillan, 1900), Vol. I, p. 419.

Monmouth and other writers who followed the old Welsh hero tales, they had become so famous everywhere that they had gathered to themselves the elements and grace of the continental romance and had come back to England clothed not only in the language, but in the style and panoply of almost contemporary European chivalry.

With the first of them, "The Noble Tale of King Arthur and the Emperor Lucius," Malory concerned himself only with an account of military adventure wherein Arthur makes a conquering journey to Rome and is there crowned emperor by the Pope, but prefers to return to reign in England. But from the moment of his describing the birth of Arthur in the storm-beaten castle of Tintagel on the Cornish coast, the story laid its spell upon Sir Thomas. He could not stop with the return of Arthur and the founding of the Round Table, that circle of a hundred chosen knights who were dedicated to the very spirit and essence of romantic chivalry. He had introduced at the court a young knight errant, a real genius in the pursuit of military prowess who is loved by Queen Guenever, that strange woman combined of charm, shrewdness, restlessness, and passion. Loving her in return, Launcelot sets out to seek adventures which will prove him worthy of her, just as did Guy of Warwick for his lady love in the story with which Thomas Malory was so familiar.

The story of Tristram and La Beale Isoud followed, the tale of love induced by a magic potion, love that was purified by tragedy and adversity. It contains that unforgettable person, Sir Palomides, Isoud's cheerfully unsuccessful lover, the bold Saracen who had been converted from his Mohammedan faith but who would not accept baptism until he had proved himself a true Christian knight by winning victory in seven combats.

After leaving Tristram, Malory returned to Launcelot, completely absorbed now in his deepening theme and with no thought of bringing his task to an end. He moved from a narrative of earthly and military glory to one of spiritual triumph as the knights of the Round Table scattered to seek the Holy Grail; how Launcelot pursued his quest, how his worldliness and earthly love finally stood in his way so that he saw only a partial vision of it, one which almost destroyed him—in recounting all this Malory passed from a translator's inspired power to the greatness of creative genius. "For when I sought worldly adventures for worldly desires," Launcelot says, "I ever enchieved them and had the better in every place. . . . And now I take upon me the adventures of holy things, and now I see and understand that mine old sin hindereth me and shameth so that I had no power to stir nor speak when the holy blood appeared afore me. So thus he sorrowed till it was day, and heard the fowls sing; then somewhat he was comforted."[1] It was Launcelot's

---

[1] Malory, *op. cit.*, Vol. II, p. 254.

son, Galahad, who saw the Grail and died before the terrible beauty of the vision.

In "The Piteous History which is of the Morte or Death of King Arthur" Malory tells of the downfall of the Round Table and of Arthur's kingdom wrecked by the treachery of his nephew Mordred and by the ill-advised obstinacy of his other nephew Gawaine, the implacable enemy of Launcelot. Arthur is slain and the sword Excalibur is received by the hand uplifted from the water. But in spite of Malory's deep reverence for Arthur, Launcelot is his real hero. Conscious of his sinfulness and his share in the destruction of the Round Table, Launcelot retires to spend the rest of his life at "an hermitage and a chapel that stood betwixt two cliffs."[1] It was Guy's Cliff, which Malory had seen so often during those stripling days at Warwick castle when his career was just beginning. Here is the end and climax of the story.

Malory's prose, with its moving simplicity, its sincerity, and its unfailing beauty of tone, rises with his subject as he goes from the glory of battle to the glory of God and back to the unescapable truth that men are sinful and cannot be made perfect even by the glimpse of a heavenly vision. In it he has told the story of feudal chivalry itself, dedicated to brave deeds, seeking the inspiration of heavenly truth, but inadequate and doomed to that end which always overtakes a privilege-engendered system of society. Moreover, the progress of the work shows an evolution in the very heart of the writer, the change from a soldier and adventurer, lawless within justifiable or unjustifiable bounds, to a man grappling with his own spirit in the solitary contests of imprisonment, tentatively beginning a chronicle of military achievement, going on to realize more and more the height and the depth of his spiritual theme. We see him struggling through despair to higher aspiration, becoming a great writer where he had failed of the opportunity to be a great soldier.

"And here is the end of the death of Arthur. I pray you all, gentlemen and gentlewomen that readeth this book of Arthur and his knights from the beginning to the ending, pray for me while I am alive, that God send me good deliverance, and when I am dead, I pray you all pray for my soul. For this book was ended the ninth year of the reign of King Edward the Fourth, by Sir Thomas Maleore, knight, as Jesu help him for His great might, as he is the servant of Jesu both day and night."[2] So he ends his collection of stories, based on older English sources and coming through those French romances which he has made his own— and England's. The book itself has brought his memory that good deliverance for which he so earnestly prayed.

That ninth year of the reign of Edward IV was the year before

[1] Malory, *op. cit.*, Vol. II
[2] *Ibid.*, p. 505.

Malory's death in 1471. That his work was copied and recopied and read in manuscript is known by the fact that it was already, fifteen years later, one of those important books of English literature which William Caxton selected for printing. It appeared in 1485, but not in the form that had left Malory's hand in Newgate Prison. Instead of its being a collection of separate stories, it had been rendered by Caxton into one, called *Le Morte Darthur*. He believed that a single narrative would more generally interest his readers. As a result, for his editing was fairly superficial, there are repetitions, inconsistencies, and an outpouring of minor events and military detail that are no longer focused on one central hero or arranged to lead up to one final, decisive combat. The result can be somewhat bewildering to a casual reader, although nothing can diminish the effect of Malory's prose or the towering stature of his central figures.

The single manuscript now known to scholars, brought to light in 1934 by the Librarian of Winchester College, Mr. W. F. Oakeshott, and reported to the literary world by Eugène Vinaver, has at last made it plain that Caxton's seemingly discursive version was not what Malory intended. Here we see the separate romances, each complete in itself with its own continuity and unity, meant to be read alone, pondered over and digested before a reader should go on to another. It was a very different form from that into which Caxton metamorphosed it. But we must be grateful to Caxton, none the less, for offering to the public, thus early, one of the greatest works of English literature. His is a noble volume, of which only one perfect copy has survived, now to be seen in the Pierpont Morgan Library in New York. The place of the discovery of the unique manuscript is singularly appropriate, for Malory speaks of "the City of Camelot, that is in English Winchester."[1]

Composed in an age even franker than our own in its manner of speaking of sex, these stories of Malory's, as they came from his hand, cannot be called wholly suitable writing for children. But as they have been edited by Sidney Lanier or retold by Howard Pyle, as they may very well be edited again for younger readers in the light of the discovery of an older version, they are the basis of narratives many times repeated. They are, moreover, the prime source of our own idea of medieval chivalry, of that essence of romance and courage and high action which appeals to young readers of all ages. Even those who have never read any of the tales direct know who Arthur was and what was the quality of his greatness, who Launcelot was and how high-minded were his bravery and his ambition. Even with retelling at second or third hand, there is always a response to that thrilling sense of what great deeds were done in England once upon a time.

[1] Malory, *op. cit.*, Vol. I, p. 77.

"I, Wyllyam Caxton, Symple Persone, Present Thys Book . . ."[1]

It is scarcely a grateful or even a graceful gesture to criticize Caxton for his treatment of Malory, since without him we might not have had Malory at all, or might, by bare possibility, have had to wait until 1934 for him. That Caxton erred in his treatment of the Malory text is the judgment of our own day, but he may have had his own reasons, born of a closer knowledge of his own readers. His great venture, taken as a whole, was so courageous and so crowned with success significant for his time and for posterity, that we must treat his decisions with respect.

A shrewd and prosperous merchant, who took up printing as a hobby and literature as a dilettante student of the European romances, is what Caxton really was but not what he afterward became. Born "in kente in the weeld" in 1421 or 1422, he was apprenticed to a mercer—a dealer in textiles—a man who rose high in his calling and became Lord Mayor of London during the boy's apprenticeship. There was close and important intercourse between England and the Low Countries during that period, particularly in the cloth trade. A mercers' guild of Englishmen had been established at Bruges in Burgundy, which is now Belgium.

To Bruges Caxton took his way when he began to act for himself and here carried on his business with such competence that he became governor of the Merchant Adventurers, called for its importance in the Low Countries "The English Nation beyond the Sea." In Bruges the rulers of Burgundy held their court, the most splendid in Europe of that time. The Duchess, wife of Charles the Bold, was Margaret of York, sister of King Edward IV of England. Part of Caxton's duties as governor of his association was to negotiate with the court of Burgundy for mercantile concessions and privileges for English trade. He thus became acquainted with the ruling family and eventually entered the service of the Duchess Margaret. With her sharp good sense, she was deeply interested in the commercial intercourse between the two countries and highly valued this Englishman who had done so much to establish the prestige of his trade abroad. She was, moreover, a patron of letters and employed copyists to produce manuscripts for her libraries at Malines and Binche. Even so successful a man as Caxton would have had little access to the treasures of the European libraries had it not been for her influence and backing. He began to study the French and Flemish romances and to become more and more interested in the new art of printing so lately come into Flanders from Germany.

He spent various periods in Cologne to learn all the technicalities then known to the printer, while he had already begun to translate into English some of the French romances in the Duchess's library. His interest in this form of literature, entirely new to the middle-class Englishman,

---

[1] Caxton's prologue to *Le Morte Darthur*.

his vision of what the new mechanics of printing might accomplish for the world of writing, and his warm love for his own country all combined to bring him back from Burgundy to begin a new career in England. It is thought that there went with him that Alsatian boy, Jan van Wynkyn, who afterward became his successor, taking the name of Wynkyn de Worde from his native place of Worth.

King Edward of England, having fallen out with the king-maker, had spent a year in exile, taking refuge in Burgundy at his sister's court, as did also his brother-in-law, Lord Rivers. The king returned to England five years before Caxton but was ready with friendship and patronage when the merchant-turned-printer arrived in 1476 to settle down and set up his printing business at the sign of the Red Pale in Westminster, near the Abbey. The first book which Caxton printed in England was Lord Rivers' translation, *Dictes or Sayengis of the Philosophres* (1477).

Publishers have to be bold, but few have been so bold as Caxton. With him, English literature entered upon an entirely new history, books suddenly multiplying at a speed out of all proportion to the slow creation of manuscripts so painstakingly carried forward for hundreds of years. Caxton's avowed purpose was to introduce English readers to the high culture of European romance. Although he held to this program, it was not long before English prose and poetry began to possess him and he set about publishing, besides the romances, the work of Chaucer, Lydgate, Malory, and a long list of others. He was concerned not only with writers, but with adding to the number of readers, and he did not forget the young ones. Among the books he issued in his first year of printing in England was the *Booke of Curtesye*, brought out in 1477.

The *Booke of Curtesye or Lytyll John* has been ascribed to some unknown monk who wrote verses in the manner of John Lydgate; it puts its maxims and instructions into rough and homely rhyme for the better recollection by boys of how to mind their manners in the households of the great. Intricate directions are given as to saying of prayers on rising; on dressing, on behavior at table, on serving a superior, on walking in the street. All of them are to the intent that anyone who looks upon the young person will involuntarily say, "A goodly chyld ther passeth by the waye." *Stans Puer ad Mensam* appeared in the same year and is attributed to Lydgate himself. It is in couplets also, and offers in briefer form much the same sort of admonition, all reflecting the rigid etiquette which was taught to boys as their preparation for social and military life. Caxton followed them with *Reynard the Fox* (1481), Æsop (1484); *The Book of Good Maners* (1487), aiming to improve the "condicions & maners of the comyn people," and *The Book callid Caton* (1483) which is for the study of "yonge children in schole."

Caxton seems to have subscribed at once to that instinctive adult belief, showing itself as soon as books for children began, that the

young should read only what would instruct and improve them. Even
from that period of the middle and later fifteenth century we have a
list of similarly edifying and duly neglected works—John Russell's
Boke of Nurture (between 1460 and 1470), Peter Idley's *Instructions
to His Son* (mid-fifteenth century), and *The Babees Book*, this last a
translation from the Latin and meant for young gentlemen and not those
of such tender age as the title suggests. Its date is difficult to determine,
since it existed in so many versions, but it is of this same time. Thus
began the long succession of books of edification and admonition which
in different forms were to be thrust upon childhood year after year,
generation after generation. Nothing could be more immovable or more
dismaying than this settled conviction, this stubborn blindness to the
fact that children take what they like while admonition blows its windy
breath in vain. Never, so it seems, did it occur to Caxton that in Malory
he had a finer guide to courtesy and manners than any number of
rhymed instructions to youth could ever bring forth.

But besides *Le Morte Darthur*, published in 1485, he brought out
two other books which in lesser and greater degree have made themselves a place in children's reading. *The Historye of Reynart the Foxe*,
Caxton's own translation of a romance and satire by the Flemish poet
Willem, has been much chuckled over by grownups and children in all
later times. Satire, of course, means nothing to the very young, yet the
spectacle of beasts talking and behaving like human beings has always
fascinated them when it is well presented. In many ways it is not especially suitable for children's reading, but the fact that it is a beast fable,
elaborated into romance, must be its main recommendation. The bitterness of its wit cannot fail to permeate the action and the style of telling,
yet it is thoroughly amusing with its characterization of the clever
animal who outwits all the rest—the resourceful Reynard who keeps
getting the better of every creature who is sent against him.

What was far more important to a posterity of young readers was
Caxton's publishing of the *Fables of Esope*. About Æsop himself we
have only legend to inform us, with no guarantee that legend is correct.
That he was a Greek slave living in the sixth century B.C. is what we
are told. That he was small, misshapen, and of extraordinary nimbleness
of wit, by which he was always getting his master out of comic difficulties and so in time earned his freedom—this legend adds with even less
plausibility. Scholarship complicates the record by saying that he was
not one man but several.

The stories themselves can be seen to have origin in times older still,
some of them from ancient Egyptian and other Oriental sources. They
went through many hands before they were gathered up by Stainhöwel,
a fifteenth century German, and then were translated from his version
into French by Jules Machault, a monk of Lyons. It was from his

work that Caxton translated them into English. Even through all these changes of hands, they have not lost the touch of some original genius, their reflection of the instinctive friendship between man and the animal kingdom, their cheerful presentation of human weaknesses recognizable to anyone, even the very young reader. It is difficult to imagine what our English speech ever did without recourse to the early bird, to the fox and the sour grapes in whom the simplest person can see himself, to the tortoise who has brought encouragement to generations of plodders.

Caxton finished the last of his translations on the day he died in 1491. His volumes, the first printed books which Englishmen and English children were to have offered to them in their own country and their own language, were in outward form of a standard not easily equaled. The ample pages, the broad margins, the black-letter type which suggested manuscript, all contributed to their beauty and dignity, to their worthiness to be England's first widespread realization of her own literature. Caxton has been criticized because, living at the dawn of the great period of the Renaissance, he paid so little attention to the works of the Greek and Roman classical age just being rediscovered by Europe. But in spite of his own enthusiasm for translating French romance, he recognized the unerring hand of Malory for its superior style and forbore to meddle with anything but Malory's structure. Finally, he did give to the English world and its posterity perhaps the oldest and the most widely beloved of the ancient classics. People have long read *Æsop* who could not read the *Æneid*.

Bibliography

Æsop. *The Fables of Æsop, as first printed by William Caxton in 1484*, edited and induced by Joseph Jacobs. 2 Vols. London, D. Nutt, 1889.

Aurner, Nellie (Slayton). *Caxton, Mirrour of Fifteenth-Century Letters*. London. P. Allen, 1926.

Baugh, Albert C., ed. *A Literary History of England*. New York, Appleton-Century-Crofts, 1948.

Furnivall, Frederick J. *Early English Meals and Manners*. London, N. Trübner, 1868. Includes John Russell's *Boke of Nurture, The Boke of Curtasye, Stans Puer ad Mensam*, and *The Babees Book*.

Hicks, Edward. *Sir Thomas Malory, His Turbulent Career; a Biography*. Cambridge, Harvard University Press, 1928.

Malory, Sir Thomas. *Le Morte Darthur*, edited by A. W. Pollard. 2 Vols. London, Macmillan, 1900.

——— *The Works of Sir Thomas Malory*, edited by Eugène Vinaver. 3 Vols. Oxford, Clarendon Press, 1947.

Reynard the Fox. *English. The History of Reynard the Fox, from the Edition Printed by Caxton in 1481*. London, Reprinted for the Percy Society by T. Richards, 1844.

4

"The Compass of the World"

It is natural that the very period of untutored and unquestioning minds should hand on to children of later ages much that they would read and cherish. The Middle Ages, too, with their clash of arms and their tales of aspiring adventure were to offer their large contribution to young people's literature. Yet it is, at first glance, surprising that the era of the Renaissance, that time of broadening views and extending enterprise of spirit, should, in point of numbers at least, have produced so little for young readers. When we look more closely, however, we see once more the source and foundation of a great deal that was to come later; we see diligent hands preserving for future eyes those records and recollections of events whose real story and real worth might otherwise have been lost forever.

At the time when Caxton returned from Bruges, bringing his printing press with him, a young Genoese named Christopher Columbus was making a voyage to the coasts of England and, in 1485 when British readers were opening the first copies of Malory's *Le Morte Darthur*, just published, this same Columbus was offering his first proposals to the King and Queen of Spain, with his idea of looking for the Indies by the westward passage. The Middle Ages touched the modern world in that year, though none of those concerned were in the least aware of such a fact. But with the voyages of Columbus, following as they did the earlier discoveries of Portugal's adventures to the south, a new, fresh wind began suddenly to blow across European thought. With it came all at once a sense of the great size of the earthly globe and a realization of what infinite possibilities lay before the men who would dare to pass from the safe and narrow seas between England and the Continent, to the high seas of unknown boundary and practically mythical farther shores. From the East, along with the great classics of the ancient world, brought by scholars to Europe after the fall of Constantinople, there came also the Arabian knowledge of astronomy, of the measuring of latitudes, and the guiding power of the stars. There came also and always the tales of the riches of India and the scattered islands of the Indies. The reading world of Europe and, in the end, of England turned its attention to accounts of the new world and all its promises, and also to ancient history of a world of infinite age and to an ancient and noble literature. In matters of the mind it was a more subtle and sophisticated age than any which had gone before it; in the realm of material affairs it was a time for bold minds and hardy spirits. Many of its records are outside the reach of young minds, but the Renaissance affords at least two invaluable pieces of writing for future generations, reflecting the two great themes of interest of the time, Hakluyt's *Voyages* and Plutarch's *Lives*. There is another which deals with things of the spirit, but has a different office.

They That Go Downe to the Sea in Ships

Richard Hakluyt (circa 1552–1616) in his Epistle Dedicatorie to his first edition of 1589, tells us that when he was a boy at Westminster School he visited his cousin, also Richard Hakluyt, in his chambers at the Middle Temple and saw upon his table "certain bookes of Cosmographie with an universall Mappe." The older and kindly cousin gave him a brief lecture on "All the known Seas, Gulfs, Bayes, Straights and Capes" visible on the map and concluded his homily with a direction to read the 107th Psalm. There the younger boy read "They that go downe to the sea in ships, and occupy their business in great waters; These men see the works of the Lord, and his wonders in the deepe." All this, he says, were "things of high and rare delight to my young nature" and he became thenceforward an avid geographer. As a student and later as a lecturer at Christ Church College, Oxford, he threw himself into the study of languages that would serve his purpose and into examination of the changes and reforms that were taking place in the old maps where cosmographie was turning into real and accurate geography. He took holy orders, as most scholars did, and for five years served as chaplain to Sir Edward Stafford, Queen Elizabeth I's ambassador to the French court. This gave him priceless opportunity to study the records of voyages of French, Portuguese, and Spanish explorers. He came to the conclusion that the English voyages had never received proper public justice and, if recounted, would prove a greater glory in his country than any of those by the adventurers of Europe. The task of collecting the evidence for a complete account had been neglected so far, on account of "the huge toile and small profit to insue."

He apologizes for undertaking the work himself, but since there is evidently no other hand to do it, he sets himself to the task. He had already translated a journal of the French discoverer Laudonnière concerning voyages to Florida. Coming home, he was content to settle down as a country clergyman of the Church of England in a little parish in Suffolk, where he could pursue with unquenchable interest his investigations of his great countrymen's great voyages. In 1589 there appeared in print *The principall Navigations, Voiages and Discoueries of the English nation made by Sea or over Land, in the most remote and farthest distant Quarters of the earth at any time within the compasse of these 1500 yeeres.* This was a single folio volume to which Hakluyt added as time went on and his researches brought in further matter. This first edition of his work was printed in London by George Bishop and Ralph Newberie, the latter a name interesting to note, for we shall presently meet it again. Between 1589 and 1600 the successive volumes of the final form appeared, expanded now to include such accounts as that of the victory over the Spanish Armada and a record of "the English valiant attempts in searching almost all the corners of the vaste and new world of America."

That he was undertaking a thorough and conscientious account is shown by his beginning with "the voyage of Arthure, King of Britaine to Island (Iceland) and the most Northeastern parts of Europe, Anno 517." He is one of the few historians who undertake to attach a date to Arthur's reign, a date which throws the background of Malory into great confusion. He goes on to English voyages overland severally to Russia, to Judea, and the River Euphrates.

Hakluyt is not an author; he is an editor, a collector and recorder of data which grow more authentic and more and more interesting as he approaches his own time. The real value of the whole account is in the narratives of the great Elizabethan voyages, each in the words of an eyewitness, covering the adventures of Hawkins, Frobisher and "The Famous Voyage," that of Drake in the *Golden Hinde* around the world. He completes his task with the newest map then extant, a piece of work of great detail as to known territory, frankly ending in thin air where information is lacking. It is remarkable for the amount that it gets right as well as for what it gets wrong. His list of acknowledgments includes the names of Sir John Hawkins, Sir Walter Raleigh, and "my kinsman Master Richard Hakluyt of the Middle Temple."

Hakluyt, as an editor himself, has one view in mind—to show the prowess of English discovery. He needs re-editing for our own time and for young readers, but few narratives could be more valuable to go along with the study of geography, to show what are the real facts of those first great voyages, which made known the true shape of the world. Young minds would learn to know geography as Europe of that time learned to know it—through Hawkins, the trader in slaves who went from place to place along the coasts of Brazil, Mexico, and the West Indies trying to find the best prices for his human cargo; through Frobisher, looking hopefully for gold along the coasts of Greenland and only incidentally for the passage to India; through Drake, getting personal satisfaction out of plundering Spanish shipping and making the east coast of South America so hot behind him that he could not return and, once having passed the Straits of Magellan, having to go home by the Cape of Good Hope. There is a dash and boldness about Hawkins —part of the account of his three voyages is in his own hand—that make one feel like forgiving him even for the slave trade. He describes, as though they were matters of everyday, disease, mutiny, and the rousing fight in the port of San Juan de Ullua where his kinsman, Francis Drake, was with him. " 'Now' said I, 'I am in two dangers and forced to receive one of them.' "[1] One of the dangers is that the Spanish fleet with its treasure of close to two million pounds might be sunk; the other is "the Queen Majesty's indignation in so weighty a matter." He loses his flagship and escapes with only two small vessels but gets home at last to Mount's Bay in Cornwall "Praised be to God therefore."

Frobisher's three patiently courageous voyages to Greenland and Hudson's Bay make one deeply admire the intrepid determination of the English explorer. Cold, hunger, floating ice, danger of losing his way forever in those frozen fields of the northern sea, danger of mutiny—he faced them all. He insisted on pursuing his explorations in spite of the peremptory order to lade his ships with the black ore which contained iron pyrites and was vainly thought to be rich in gold. The narrative, written by one of his captains, commander of the *Anne Francis*, is full of picturesque detail and at every turn reminds one of the *Rime of the Ancient Mariner*. This is no coincidence, for Coleridge based much of his description on the account of this voyage, scarcely less terrible than the Ancient Mariner's own. The account sheds significant light on the attitude and the power of Queen Elizabeth. She commended them so greatly for their courage and good order, "every man so ready to his calling . . . that she gave so great encouragement to all the captains and gentlemen that they, to continue her Highness' good and honorable opinion of them, have since neither spared labour, limb nor life to bring this matter, so well begun, to a happy and prosperous end."[2] There is no mention of other reward than her Majesty's good opinion for their monumental labors.

The Famous Voyage, the journey of journeys, is Drake's circumnavigation of the world, bringing home to Englishmen, as by no other means, the knowledge that they lived upon a globe. It made clear also that to treat the Americas as a negligible barrier between Europe and the Indies was not to make for success. The account of the journey is written by one of Drake's men-at-arms. It has, therefore, more to do with battles and plunder than with geography and navigation, but nothing can hide the importance of the voyage nor the perils into which Drake

---

[1] Richard Hakluyt, *Principall Navigations* (New York, E. P. Dutton, 1926), Vol. VII, p. 57.
[2] Hakluyt, *op. cit.*, Vol. V, p. 229.

sailed so boldly. England and Spain were not then at war, but Drake suffered losses in the fight at San Juan de Ullua and felt himself quite justified in recouping them wherever he found opportunity.

In the port of St. Iago they found the great Spanish ship laden with treasure from Peru, "25,000 pesos of very pure and fine gold"; later they came on a Spaniard asleep on the shore beside thirteen bars of silver that weighed 4,000 ducats Spanish. "We took the silver and left the man."[1] Nothing, it seemed, was too large or too small for their acquisitions. "The Treasure of the World," Drake called this flow of riches which was pouring from South America toward Spain, but which he so thriftily diverted into his own pockets and into the coffers of his sovereign. Through all the voyages one gets continually the sense of their devoted service to Elizabeth, of her greatness, of her vivid enthusiasm not merely for the riches gained, but for the glory of the discoveries. Some of the glory would have perished if it had not been for Hakluyt, working away in his country parsonage for the greater renown of English seamen.

He was not, of course, writing consciously for children. Only those will read him direct who are of true historic impulse and who are anxious to grow expert, as children so often can, in some one important particular. Yet simplicity and honesty of treatment and magnificence of material and detail are not lightly to be passed by. He did, however, offer a Treasure of the World to writers and readers of a later age; Kingsley and Macaulay, Kipling and Charles Boardman Hawes, and a host of others let you see his spirit walking once more as their narratives unfold and a myriad of young readers wait breathlessly to see how the far-reaching adventure will end.

Lives of Great Men

Historically minded children will also get pleasure out of reading Plutarch, whose work entered English literature and became a part of it through Sir Thomas North's translation made in 1579. They will see the known world extend into another direction unexplored by Englishmen before the Renaissance, the distant world of the remote past. Plutarch could have gone even further back than he did, so he insists, although he began with Theseus and Romulus. "Even so, in this my history, I could speak of strange things, and more ancient and further from men's memory," he says when discussing the barrier between the two worlds known and unknown. He makes close-packed reading, but breaks, at proper intervals, the array of factual narrative. He lets you see the twin gods, Castor and Pollux, appear in the market place of Rome, their horses white with foam as they come in divine haste to announce vic-

---

[1] Hakluyt, *op. cit.*, Vol. VIII, p. 59.

tory. He makes you realize the boyish admiration that Theseus had for Hercules, a sense of emulation which molded one hero's life in the image of another's. He makes convincing that free, hardy life which made such lusty fellows of the Spartan youths, so that their games, their wrestling matches, and their sparse living seem of extraordinary attractiveness to youth of a later age. We have many small, undying by-words in the reference of our talk whose origins we have usually for-gotten. We do not generally remember that it was Plutarch who first gave us the tale of the Spartan boy with a fox hidden under his coat.

He has a curiously quick ability to give the reader a sense of charac-ter, to make clear that it was the stubborn pride of Coriolanus which was the undoing of a man who could have been an unforgettable hero in the history of his great city, or to show us what part the slyness and adroitness of Mark Antony played in the destiny of Rome. It is not to be wondered at that he appealed so greatly to Shakespeare, with his dramatic situations and his compelling personalities.

He has come to the young persons of our day, and to those who have written for them, through the medium of several hands. Plutarch him-self (living approximately from 46 to 120 A.D.) was a Greek phi-losopher, who lectured in Rome and made deep study of Roman history as compared with that of his own country. Comparison, he felt, was the soul of the real understanding of the past, so that he conceived the idea of his great series of biographies, not merely as the narratives of the lives of separate men, but as men set in pairs in the two countries, with outward circumstances and undertakings somewhat similar. Thus we have Theseus and Romulus, legendary founders of great states; Lycurgus and Numa, lawgivers to their society; Alexander and Julius Caesar, military geniuses.

His original version was in Greek, but far more widely read through the centuries since has been the Latin translation. The Latin was ren-dered into French by Jacques Amyot, Bishop of Auxerre, a scholar deeply respectful of history which, so he said, "was used among men before there was any use of letters at all." Sir Thomas North (circa 1535–circa 1601), the scholarly and unprosperous younger brother of a titled family, translated Amyot's French into the vigorous fine English of his time with an economy and compactness of prose that lost nothing of Plutarch's power. North had fought in the war with Spain whose cli-max was the battle with the Armada, he held a pension from the Queen "for good and faithful service done unto us." His book was published with the title *The Lives of the Noble Grecians and Romaines, Compared Together by that Grave Learned Philosopher and Historiographer, Plutarke of Chaeronea.* He dedicated it to "The Most High and Mighty Princess Elizabeth . . . for who is fitter to give countenance to so many great states than such an high and mighty Princess, who is fitter to revive the dead memory of their fame then she that beareth the lively image of their vertues?"[1] One can say of North's able and powerful prose that he himself bore the image of his master's virtues. "Some talk of Alexander and some of Hercules, of Hector and Lysander and such great names as these." Plutarch was one who talked of them and with sublime authority, with Sir Thomas North as a not unfitting second in command.

Man's Inhumanity to Man

Belonging to this period, but having its era of so-called usefulness to the reading public at a somewhat later date, is Foxe's (1516–1587) *Book of Martyrs*. To name it in the list of children's book is an anomaly, but there it stood for years, immovable and unassailable. Few children of the Puritan age escaped reading it under the stern behests of parents or pastors; no child has ever been recorded as having done so willingly. The book was written abroad by an Englishman, published there first in Latin and brought out in England in 1563.

It has been said that it came to be the greatest vehicle for Puritan intolerance and was so employed for generations. This use to which it was put, with the fact that it was inflicted upon Puritan children as a task which they could not escape, has given Foxe a bad name and has done his great work of historical research much less than justice.

He lived too early to be involved in the Puritan controversies, although it is quite clear that he was of a Puritan quality of mind. He was, instead, a devoted follower of the Reformation, of the teachings of Martin Luther, new in England during the time that John Foxe was growing up, the days when King Henry VIII was on the throne. He was expelled from Magdalen College because of his too zealous Protestantism, which outran even the king's decrees. He went into exile during the reign of Mary, Henry's Roman Catholic daughter; it was during his residence in Germany and Switzerland that he began his vast book which he called first *The Acts and Monuments*. It was not intended for propaganda for Puritanism, nor even, strictly speaking, for Protestants. It grew from his burning zeal to resist what he thought—and rightly—was a blot upon the history of his age, the practice of putting men and women to cruel death because of sincerely and bravely held religious beliefs.

Mary Tudor, half Spanish herself and married to the Spanish Philip, went far toward employing some of the methods of the Inquisition in England with the execution by burning of those who did not con-

---

[1] *The Lives of the Noble Grecians and Romaines*, Compared Together by that Grave Learned Philosopher and Historiographer, Plutarke of Chaeronea. Translated . . . into English, by Sir Thomas North Knight (London, Richard Field, 1603), title page.

form to the established state religion. After Mary's death and the end of the executions for heresy against the Roman Catholic Church, Foxe maintained his stand firmly against the practice as carried on by those of his own faith. It was no safe thing to champion the cause of people who had been condemned for nonconformity, but Foxe wrote letters to the ministers of government, even to the Queen herself, begging for mercy to men whose only sin was honesty of belief. "To burn up with fiery flame, blazing with pitch and sulphur, the living bodies of wretched men who err through blindness of judgment rather than deliberate will, is a hard thing."[1] This he dared to say to Elizabeth.

He labored with the prisoners themselves; he visited them in their condemned cells, trying to convert them and to save them. But his efforts were in vain. With all the enlightenment of the Renaissance age, the cruelties of an earlier and more savage time still persisted and Foxe's was a voice crying in the wilderness. He was, therefore, more determined than ever to show the whole history of martyrdom, its early beginning in Rome with the tossing of the first Christians to wild beasts, through the Inquisition and from thence onward to his own time and the executions under Mary and Elizabeth. He took immense pains to consult records and hear the stories of eyewitnesses—of how greatly Latimer and Ridley had died, and Rowland Taylor and that John Rogers of whom we hear more later. The separate biographies are all brief and eminently factual, always reaching the climax of a violent end. The whole story is one depicting inspired heroism; it is, further, a terrible indictment of the intolerance which men, even to a later age, disguised to themselves as righteousness.

As historical record the *Book of Martyrs* is of true importance, as reading for children it is extraordinarily unsuitable. Only a child's fascinated and shivering instinct to dabble in horrors could lead any one of them to open the book voluntarily. Children were required to read it to make them properly aware of what difficulties earlier Protestant believers had gone through and, by analogy, to emphasize the persecutions laid upon those Puritans who thought of themselves as the sum and summit of the Protestant movement. It was, indeed, used as a fire to keep unforgiving intolerance alive, a purpose for which Foxe never meant it. Since later generations of children have repudiated it so completely, we can hope that even the little Puritans were able to put it out of their minds and did not go to bed to dream of crackling faggots and choking smoke. And we can comfort ourselves with the knowledge that Puritanism gave children also such a book of beauty and truth that in their delight in it Foxe's fearful tale could be forgotten.

One thing more that the Renaissance offered to the world of chil-

[1] James F. Mozley, *John Foxe and His Book* (New York, Macmillan, 1940), p. 87.

dren's literature through its contribution to the world at large was its beautiful language. People sometimes confuse quotations from Shakespeare with those from the Bible; that is because they are both in the Renaissance English, which is almost as distinctive as personal style. The variety, the life, and the richness of that English have been caught and held in those two great works, Shakespeare's plays and the King James version of the Bible, perfected by a group of churchmen and scholars—certainly with some poets among them—in 1611. That Bible, which a little earlier men and women had been hanged and burned for reading in English, was now available to all. So deeply was it read by devout-minded persons and in family prayers in religiously trained families, so contagious is its dignity and simplicity, that it has affected the style of a myriad of writers. It inspired and influenced one above all, that same Puritan classic which is the gift of that age to children of all time. We may be certain that Bunyan, in his dark prison, read his Bible every day before he took up his pen to go forward with *Pilgrim's Progress.*

Bibliography

Foxe, John. *Fox's Book of Martyrs,* edited by William Byron Forbush. Philadelphia, J. C. Winston Co., 1926. Forbush has dropped the Elizabethan spelling of Foxe's name.

Hakluyt, Richard. *The Principall Navigations, Voyages, Traffiques & Discoveries of the English Nation.* 12 Vols. Glasgow, J. Maclehose, 1903–05.

——— ——— 8 Vols. New York, E. P. Dutton, 1926–31. (Everyman's Library).

Mozley, James F. *John Foxe and His Book.* New York, Macmillan, 1940.

Plutarch. *The Lives of the Noble Grecians and Romaines, Compared Together by that Grave Learned Philosopher and Historiographer, Plutarke of Chaeronea. Translated out of Greeke into French by Iames Amiot . . . and out of French into English, by Sir Thomas North Knight.* London, Imprinted by R. Field, 1603.

——— *Plutarch's Lives,* englished by Sir Thomas North. 10 Vols. London, J. M. Dent, 1898–99.

——— *Shakespeare's Plutarch,* edited by the Rev. Walter W. Skeat. London, Macmillan, 1875.

——— *The Children's Plutarch; Tales of the Greeks,* by F. J. Gould. New York, Harper, 1910.

——— *The Children's Plutarch; Tales of the Romans,* by F. J. Gould. New York, Harper, 1910.

5

Three Tales of Travel

"Some Said, 'John, Print It . . .' "

Inexperienced writers who listen in bewilderment to the conflicting comment of friends can always take heart when they read John Bunyan's Apology for *The Pilgrim's Progress*, when they hear rehearsed the argument over the possible merits of his new undertaking. He thus quotes his advisers—"Some said, 'John, print it,' others said 'Not so'" and others in their wisdom pursued "Well yet I am not fully satisfied, 'That this your book will stand when soundly tried.'" Nearly three hundred years have given it a fairly sound trial and there can be no question as to how it has stood.

As John Bunyan (1628–1688) saw his best years going by in one prison cell after another, his turbulent, self-searching mind, cut off from preaching, turned itself to writing to make life endurable. His immensely imaginative spirit went over and over again all of his own religious experiences and those of men he knew; he scourged himself with repentance for his misguided early life. It is very probable that those years were far less wicked than his self-condemnation in *Grace Abounding to the Chief of Sinners* (1666) would lead us to believe. One examination into spiritual life after another came pouring from his hand, until finally, within the four harsh walls of Bedford County Gaol, the fancy took possession of him to write in an allegorical, not a direct medium.

Though he pushed it aside, the impulse came back again and again, until, merely to get peace in which to go on with his more sober work, he let the idea have its way and put down the story. It was of that man Christian who is all men, and who takes his way from the City of Destruction to another city, built of pure gold, where men dwell in eternal life.

In his theology and his deepest thinking Bunyan was a Puritan. He was, as all men know, a tinker like his father. He was not the irresponsible wanderer up and down the lanes of England that we think of in that term, but a respectable artisan who had his own economic place in his own community of Elstow in Bedfordshire. There are few words which have been more widely applied than the word Puritanism, few whose meaning has been so loosely used and so often mistaken. Puritanism unseated a king and beheaded him; it held firm in the face of imprisonment and execution; it carried an intrepid race to a far and forbidding country; it upheld them through trials that were almost worse than the persecutions at home. It left so strong a stamp on the thinking of English and American people that the period of its influence cannot be measured. It fell into error at many turns of the way, just as all human institutions do, and it left us *Pilgrim's Progress*.

The Church in England, based on the deepest of religious beliefs, was by natural tendency Protestant in form. But after it was made definitely so by the decree of one English king, was returned to Roman Catholicism by his elder daughter and made Protestant again by the younger, it was not surprising that it could not escape confusion, opportunism, and worldly standards in high places. Puritans arose to cleanse the religious life of England of those corruptions. That was its primary motive; and all else came later, the sitting in judgment, the intolerance of other beliefs, the sternness in ordering how men should believe and act. Bunyan's Puritanism was of this first form; it stood for the cleansing of a man's own life, as well as of the Church; it stood for a return to simple good and for an understanding of man's relation to God and to eternal truths.

He was so convinced of his own duty in relation to what he believed that he felt that he must preach, even though preaching without a license and without the authority of the Church was accounted a crime. Preach he did, although he was arrested and released and arrested and imprisoned again and again. When his voice was silenced within four walls, his pen went busily on. His greatest sermon was not spoken but written.

Its simplicity appeals to children because it is a simplicity that has its foundation in the deepest truths of which human beings are conscious. *Pilgrim's Progress* finds its universal qualities through many reasons, not the least of them being the fact that one can never read it without ending by recognizing one's self among the myriad characters, even if it is only in Mr. By-Ends or Mr. Short-Wind. With all the host of figures which the story embraces, just as innumerable figures touch a real life and move away again, one never loses the vivid sense of individuality in the principal persons. The mind follows them in sympathy and suspense, and the thread of the story is never lost.

Christian is a character full of great purpose, full of fears and doubts, with inspired courage to press on through the confusion of his trembling human timidity. The first part of his journey he must take alone as a test of his intention; he must pass the Slough of Despond and the Valley of Humiliation, where occurs the tremendous battle with Apollyon, the monster who straddles the road, huge, with the wings of a dragon and with fire in his belly. Then Christian must go through the Valley of the Shadow of Death. Later he is allowed to have Faithful for a companion, and when Faithful is condemned and executed in the wicked town of Vanity Fair, he is joined by Hopeful. Thus he is not to go alone, even when he falls into the hands of the dreadful Giant Despair, and he has Hopeful's hand to lead and sustain him when, still trembling and hesitating, he goes down to the river and passes over to the other side.

The geography of their journey is as clear as are the main persons— the meadow beyond the town, the wicket gate, the long straight way. We see without effort the plains, the hills, the first glimpse of the Delectable Mountains from whose summit a pilgrim catches his first sight of the Eternal City. For young readers there is always action and more action, new dangers just when the way seemed safe, new help and encouragement just when the difficulties and terrors seem past bearing. Among this cloud of witnesses to men's failings and their virtues there is always a touch of humanity. There is Ignorance, setting out headlong for the Eternal City without thinking how to discover the way to get there. We have Mrs. Timorous, rushing off to report to her friends that Christiana is of a mind to follow her husband and take her children. We see Mercy's blushing shyness which cannot stand in the way of her unconquerable desire to go with Christiana. Even when she looks back on the way through the Valley of the Shadow of Death and sees "something most like a lion and it came a great padding pace after," even then she only goes closer to Mr. Greatheart and presses forward still.

One of the most beloved characters in the book is Mr. Greatheart with his resourcefulness, his hearty reassurances, his generous courage. There are few moments in all literature more memorable than that when Christiana and her family are lingering at the rest house, wondering how they shall dare go forward and "Now, about this time, one knocked at the door. So the Porter opened and behold, Mr. Greatheart was there." He has come to guide them, to walk before and meet all the terrors first, to answer all the little boys' questions and to give good counsel to Christiana. He and his friend, Mr. Valiant-for-Truth, go with her all the way and bid her be of good courage when the moment comes for her to enter the river and cross over to where the chariots and messengers are waiting. Mr. Greatheart does not go; he has other work to do, but Mr. Valiant-for-Truth follows her "and all the Trumpets sounded for him on the other side."

The long theological dialogues are not for children's reading; in modern editions for young readers they are omitted. When children, long ago, had no such edited copies, they doubtless skipped them. But beyond that, the story, that tale of humble-minded heroism, is so full of color and imagination that a child will follow it with untiring interest and be the richer and the better for it all his life thereafter. The first part of *Pilgrim's Progress* was published in 1678; the second, offered with more confidence and less discussion from friends, in 1684. The world of Christian thinking has been the better for it, also, for almost three centuries.

In one way Bunyan failed of his intention, yet wrote to far better effect than he could ever know. Every child who reads the story thinks of it in terms of an actual and vivid journey, moving from place to place, covering real miles of changing landscape and ever-renewed adventure. It is doubtful whether many grownup readers do otherwise. If you should tell young persons that Bunyan had in mind people of his own village, who lived all their lives in one place, saw the same neighbors and did the same things day after day, few would believe it. For all time readers will follow the story and not the allegory. The allegory is the deep thought of a devout man, but the story is the work of a great creative genius.

Bunyan's religious narratives, *The Life and Death of Mr. Badman* (1680) and *The Holy War* (1682), have none of the elements which endear them to children and without them seem to have had no power of survival. His one book that was really intended for young readers, *A Book for Boys and Girls* (1686), will be discussed elsewhere, although there is no great power in its verse. Yet we cannot say that Bunyan could not make good verses, for there is a single unforgettable lyric in *Pilgrim's Progress*:

> He that is down need fear no fall,
> He that is low no pride,
> He that is humble ever shall
> Have God to be his guide.[1]

It is sung by the shepherd boy upon the hillside, but there is more pure poetry in the prose passage which follows, when Mr. Greatheart says of him, "I will dare to say that this boy lives a merrier life and wears more of that herb called heartsease in his bosom than he that is clad in silk and velvet." That is what Bunyan was seeking, the crown and reward of his long work, the herb called heartsease.

"O, Solitude, Where Are the Charms . . . ?"

Toward the end of July 1703, Daniel Defoe (1659–1731) stood three times in the pillory before Temple Bar in London, a "middle-sized,

---

[1] John Bunyan, *Pilgrim's Progress* (Philadelphia, John Winston, 1933), p. 251.

spare man, about forty years old, of a brown complexion, . . . sharp chin, grey eyes, . . ." So runs the advertisement put out to offer reward for information that would lead to his arrest. The fault for which he was suffering was the authorship of a "libellous and seditious pamphlet" having to do with the religious-political controversies of the day and called, *The Shortest Way with the Dissenters*. Readers had misunderstood the irony of his censure of the High Church party; and, bewildered and surprised, he found himself condemned to public humiliation and a long term in Newgate Prison. The result was the complete ruin of his tile-making business and his own reduction to practical beggary. Yet he kept busily writing in every waking hour that he lay in jail, and the ruin of his business turned him even more completely to his chosen vocation.

Freed from prison by the intercession of his patron, the Earl of Oxford, he set out with spirits undampened to further adventures in political pamphleteering. Nor did he keep to that alone. His observation and his interest in people and politics were keen, his sense of timing was excellent. He had, indeed, composed in jail a satirical *Hymn to the Pillory*, which, hastily printed by a friendly publisher, was profitably circulated and sold in the crowd which came to see the execution of his sentence.

His party connections have little to do with the present matter. It is sufficient to say that he and Jonathan Swift, who hated each other cordially, had two things in common in their pursuit of political journalism—their hatred of the Duke of Nottingham and their unswerving devotion to Robert Harley, Earl of Oxford and one of Queen Anne's most important ministers. Defoe's was an amazing output—histories, biographies, accounts of apparitions, a record of a *Journey to the Land of the Moon*, and a series of tales for the reading and moral improvement of rogues and criminals. He had among his many gifts an extraordinary faculty for assuming different personalities. His biographies, some of them semifictional, some of them wholly so, were nearly all presented as journals or first-person accounts. In them he identified himself with his subject so completely that in many cases it has never been known how much, if any, was the contribution of the central figure and how much was pure Defoe. He was fifty-eight years old, expert in his craft, and full of worldly experience when he turned himself to his greatest impersonation of all, the writing of *The Life and Strange Surprising Adventures of Robinson Crusoe of York, Mariner* (1719). It made him immortal, a result as unexpected as had been his landing in the pillory from the publication of an ill-judged political pamphlet.

In 1712 had been published the account of the sojourn of a sailor, Alexander Selkirk, on the Island of Juan Fernandez. He had deserted his ship and had lived alone for four years, until a chance vessel came by and took him back to England. The narrative was meager in detail, given at secondhand by the captain of the rescuing ship, but the fact of the adventure and the man's problem of survival struck Defoe's fancy and he set out to become, in imagination, a simple-hearted British mariner cast suddenly into this solitary and dangerous situation.

As a book for adults, *Robinson Crusoe* was immensely popular in its own time and has been highly regarded ever since. The loosely jointed, episodic narrative has become a model to all later literature for that kind of biographical yarn. It is a form directly natural for children's liking, with no confusing complication of structure, with effortless unity of place and character, and, above all, with vividness of dealing with natural things and natural adventure. It was exactly that for which children had looked so long in vain. It is as a tacit declaration of independence of all that their elders would thrust upon them that young readers have so firmly and persistently supported the books which they have chosen for themselves.

A man thrown on his own resources on a desert island is an irresistible subject, but this man was peculiarly appealing in his ways and methods. He was no marvel of knowledge and inventiveness, as is the paterfamilias of *The Swiss Family Robinson*. What he did, though he accomplished wonders, was done as slowly, as laboriously and clumsily as any ordinary boy would do it, with the constant danger of utter failure. His most inefficient and long-drawn out method of building his bower, his constructing of a boat that, in the end, was too large for him to move, his making of pots which were "ugly things" are none of them the work of any superman. But the baking of the clay in the fire is one of the dramatic episodes in the book; in the end he had "three very good, I will not say handsome, pipkins" after which life goes on to more ingenuities.

The pioneer spirit still dwells in the human race in spite of crowded civilized surroundings, and in no portion of mankind does it dwell so lustily as in children. The instinct of survival is ever-living in human beings, and the why and how of achieving it is no matter of course to the young. Any boy reader (or any girl with a little stretch of wishful imagination) can, without a great leap of fancy, see himself as Robinson Crusoe, building his house, capturing his goats, teaching Friday to talk to him. Little by little the reader becomes so identified with Crusoe, just as Defoe was, that he can see himself at the end in command of the final dramatic situations of great hazard, called governor of the island, giving orders to captains of ships and always looked up to as the leading spirit, the rescuer.

It is doubtful which is the more fascinating figure, Crusoe dealing with cannibal savages or Crusoe in his solitary existence, a grotesque picture with his goatskin costume, his umbrella, his attendant goats and parrot. The real charm of the story is in knowing just how he did everything, and so convincing is Defoe in his explicit descriptions, that we quite overlook some of the things which he does not explain. We are not told how Crusoe got fire, even though we see him cooking goat's flesh and baking red pots. Only long after, he speaks of having a tinder box, but it was made with "wild-fire" which he must have got in the forest rather than from the ship. He says it was very necessary to have an umbrella that will open and shut but "However, at last, . . . I made one to answer," is as far as Defoe can go. He is vague, too, in the matter of baskets.

One does not expect this denizen of eighteenth century London to be omniscient in the matter of life on a desert island, even though he sets himself up to be. The real heart of the story is the fact that there is never a dull moment; when the exercise of ingenuity has lost its novelty there are the earthquake, the explorations in the little boat, finally the footprint in the sand. Almost anyone who looks back upon the book from maturity has the indefinite memory that the footprint was Friday's, but in real fact of narration it was five years later and in quite another part of the island that Friday first made his appearance. The story ends in a fine welter of battles, escapes, meetings, surprises, and final departure. Even the journey back to England has its hazards and adventures, but Crusoe arrives at last, very satisfactorily, for he has picked up, here and there, a fortune of almost thirty-three thousand pieces of eight. Pieces of eight are Spanish silver dollars, such as have been absorbed into our own currency, but which will always be a romantic measure of fortune and success.

So great was the prestige of the first *Robinson Crusoe* that it was followed by a host of others, so that a generic name has been applied to them, Robinsonades. The earliest, published in 1727, was *The English Hermit or Unparalleled Sufferings . . . of Mr. Philip Quarll* by Longueville. The story begins with a wealth of detail about the hermit's establishment as discovered by a traveler, before one gets any glimpse of the hermit himself as a center and focus of the description. Defoe on the other hand, makes us so interested in Crusoe and so sympathetic with his misfortunes that every small matter of what he does and how he does it becomes the object of our curiosity. *The Swiss Family Robinson* by Johann Wyss, published in English in 1814, is the most famous of these followers of Crusoe; it is typical of its age, full of moralizing and lecturing by Robinson Senior, with complete unreality as to natural facts. Not even a child reader will believe that every fruit and every animal of temperate and tropical climes could have come together on a single island. There is even an *American Family Robinson*, so poorly written that there is no need to mention more than its existence.

Writers in all later times have taken inspiration not only from the form, but from the content of *Robinson Crusoe. Treasure Island* unconsciously borrows even some of its phrases and some scenes, but none the less is most gloriously Stevenson's own. And what is even more important, small boys everywhere and in all places have played at being Crusoe themselves, even as Tom Sawyer did. It is a far cry, but Mark Twain could hardly have found a better romantic substitute for Juan Fernandez than an island in the Mississippi River.

Mr. Lemuel Gulliver

It seems incongruous to believe that Jonathan Swift (1667–1745) and *Gulliver's Travels*, a unique personality and a unique work, have anything in common with those two great tales and their authors which came immediately before them. But Swift's allegory, unlike as it is in spirit to Bunyan's, rose out of the same sort of deeply creative fancy. And *Gulliver's Travels* (1726), with its record of far journeys, of shipwreck and strange lands, of ingenious contrivances for survival and comfort, seems curiously, and one can hardly believe it is not deliberately, like *Robinson Crusoe*.

"I found the island to be all rocky, only a little intermingled with tufts of grass and sweetsmelling herbs. I took out my small provisions, and after having refreshed myself, I secured the remainder in a cave whereof there were great numbers; I gathered plenty of eggs upon the rocks and got a quantity of seawood and parched grass, which I designed to kindle the next day, and roast my eggs as well as I could, for I had about me my flint and steel, match and burning glass." This might be Robinson Crusoe, newly shipwrecked; but it is not—it is Gulliver's first coming to land in Balnibarbi, over which hovers the Island of Laputa. He says of an earlier voyage, "The ship lay very broad, so we thought it better spooning before the sea than trying or hulling." Swift copied his nautical expressions, word for word, out of a seaman's manual, but it seems rather as though he had opened the book at random.

Just as there can be unbelievable differences in nature between one man and another, even though they are both in the same image, so there can be equal distance between two books of allegory. Bunyan felt love and hope for his fellow men, Swift openly professed to feel nothing toward them but indignation and scorn. "I have ever hated all nations, professions and communities," says he, "and all my love is for individuals. But principally I hate and detest that animal called man." Yet his friends, so Carl Van Doren, one of his biographers, insists, "always spoke of his sweetness, his charm, his delightful temper, his hearty affection, his honest generosity."[1] Certainly he was a faithful friend to those whom he really loved.

[1] Carl Van Doren, *Swift* (New York, Viking, 1930), p. 185.

One of the most interesting studies in character that can be found is in his connection with the two great politicians of his age, Oxford and Bolingbroke, who worked together yet despised and distrusted each other, while both trusted and loved Swift. That brief period of worldly glory to which they raised him is of absorbing interest, too. In contrast with his lonely boyhood, his dependent youth and young manhood at Moor Park as a retainer of Sir William Temple, after his taking holy orders and holding an insignificant living in Ireland, he emerged suddenly into an honored place in the world of politics and of the court. These two great men had discovered the power of his bitter pen and spared nothing to enlist him on their side. He was surrounded by so-called friends, by the outward professions of admiration and respect, yet he was honest with himself and others. With Oxford and Bolingbroke he worked for the downfall of the great Duke of Marlborough, because he himself truly thought that long war was ruining England and that the Duke's towering ambitions were prolonging the conflict. Yet his own ambition for preferment in the Church was almost as great.

During his political life in London he belonged to various clubs—the Kit-Cat, the Beefsteak, and others. But what meant the most was his membership in a circle of five—himself, Dr. Arbuthnot, and the three young poets, Parnell, John Gay, and Alexander Pope. He had given them a name—he loved ridiculous names—the Scriblerus Club. These were his true friends, those with whom he had both mind and heart in common. They filled their evenings with talk of the foolishness of the world, and among them they evolved the plan of a satire of ridicule, based on the blundering character of a certain Dr. Martin Scriblerus and his errors and enormities. Arbuthnot had already written the early story of Martin's younger years and of his education. Pope, looking for material for his share of the work in examples of human failings, laid the foundation for his later poem about dunces. And Swift, being appointed to show Martin on fabulous journeys to far countries, was preparing to recount his travels "among pigmies, among giants, among fantastic scientists."

The death of Queen Anne scattered the ministry, scattered the Scriblerus Club, sent Swift to the only appointment within his reach, that of Dean of St. Patrick's in Dublin. It sent him to Ireland where he was born but which he considered a land of exile. The idea of Dr. Martin and his absurd adventures went with him, to lie in his restless and rebellious mind during the twelve years that passed before he saw England again. He had always fully carried out his clerical duties as he saw them; he bestirred himself now to defend Ireland, and the Church in Ireland, against certain injustices which England was putting upon her. In 1724 he gave utterance to the principle of which men were already beginning to talk, "All government without the consent of the governed is the very definition of slavery."[1] It was to be heard again, louder and louder, as the century passed.

Through all these years he had been thinking of Dr. Martin Scriblerus, then of a larger and more effective concept of his own, of plain Lemuel Gulliver, who was not a fool, only a very ordinary man, who was to see strange worlds and show, in contrast, what England and Europe were like in Jonathan Swift's eyes. He wrote to a friend in April of 1721, "I am now writing a History of my Travels, which will be a large volume and give account of countries hitherto unknown." The voyage to the land of horses was the part which had been least discussed among the friends. The Island of Laputa was to be number four of the countries visited. But all the force of his satire, all his judgment of the world around him, all his dislike and his despair concerning "that animal called man," had been poured into the study of the Houyhnhnms and he set it last as the climax of his attack on his fellow human beings.

By 1723 his friends were urging him to revisit England, but it was not until 1726 that he came, the manuscript ready for the printer in his hand, *Gulliver's Travels into Several Remote Nations of the World*. He and his friends thought that there would be much difficulty in finding a printer for this terrible indictment of England and the court, this blistering satire of society in high places. When one printer expressed himself willing, the manuscript was dropped outside his house in the dark from a hackney coach. But there need have been no such precautions, only laughter and delight followed the book and it was prophesied that it would have "as great a run as John Bunyan." The secret of authorship was not long kept.

The Princess of Wales was said to be greatly pleased over the rumor that she was portrayed in the person of the Queen of Brobdingnag, although there is little personal detail in the figure of her gigantic majesty. Flimnap, the chief courtier to the King of Lilliput who could caper higher in his master's presence than any other, was supposed to be Walpole, while the sourest and most hostile minister of Gulliver's acquaintance among the little people was said to resemble the Duke of Nottingham. The war between the Big-endians and the Little-endians was the differences between Roman Catholic and Protestant, while the Island of Blefuscu, whither the surviving Big-endians fled, was France.

One could say that the greatest irony in all of Swift is the fact that his famous work has survived in general reading only as a book for children. But there is far more than irony in such a truth. The deepest genius is in the workmanship, the true literary quality of ingenuity and imagination; those endure while the savage satire is something readers

---

[1] Van Doren, *op. cit.*, p. 175.

laugh over briefly and then forget. The man who was so deeply kind to little Hester Johnson that he won a lifetime of her devoted friendship was not blind to the things that please children. It can be said that he had a genius for perfection in an exasperatingly imperfect world. But it is the perfection that makes *Gulliver's Travels* so pleasing to children, the exactness and consistency of things being to scale, small or large, the exquisite details of littleness, the delicate proportions, the practical way in which Gulliver makes two stout stools of the highest trees in the king's park and thus is able to step over the walls of the palace courtyard without danger of knocking them down—such are the matters in which young readers revel. The manners of the court are only oddly curious to children, who do not bother their heads with possible resemblances. Here is a man writing, not as one who hates his fellow beings, but as one who loves, as children do, a fine exactness of fancy.

The land of Lilliput will always be the children's favorite. With the voyage to Brobdingnag the scene darkens, although not many young persons will worry much over the king's opinion that Europeans must be very vicious little creatures. Very few, old or young, will fail to be bored by the Island of Laputa, where little happens and the reflections on overscientific life are intricate and often repulsive. Swift said that he was moved to write of the Houyhnhnms and the Yahoos by the terrible poverty and degradation of the lower class in Ireland. But the picture shown in the final voyage is too depressing even for children to ignore, though it is the most interesting of ideas to think of horses as really fulfilling, somewhere, all the promise which their look of nobility and that instinctive friendship between children and animals would suggest as possible. And there is ingenuity of a pleasant kind in the details of the horses' housekeeping, and in the appropriateness of the countryside, waving with fields of oats.

Swift received a great ovation when he returned to Ireland; all the bells of Dublin City rang as his ship came up the bay. The officials of the town came out over the water to meet him and escort him in. He had served his Church, he had served Ireland, he had served mankind in ways that he had not intended. In spite of all, he had made himself beloved as well as famous. It must have been the highest day of his life.

Bibliography

Bunyan, John. *Bunyan's Grace Abounding to the Chief of Sinners; Heart's Ease in Heart Trouble; The World to Come, or, Visions of Heaven and Hell.* Albany, J. R. Abatt, 1833.

Case, Arthur E. *Four Essays on Gulliver's Travels.* Princeton, Princeton University Press, 1945.

Craik, Henry. *The Life of Jonathan Swift, Dean of St. Patrick's, Dublin.* London, J. Murray, 1882.

Ehrenpreis, Irvin. *The Personality of Jonathan Swift*. London, Methuen, 1958.
Lee, William. *Daniel Defoe, His Life and Recently Discovered Writings*. 3 Vols. London, J. C. Hotten, 1869.
Van Doren, Carl. *Swift*. New York, Viking Press, 1930.
White, William Hale. *John Bunyan*. New York, Scribner, 1904.

6

The Bible and Sun

The Candle of the Lord

There have been various children who, usually without their own knowledge, have played important parts in the forward progress of human thinking. Among those, quite unsung by fame, were a certain group remarkably privileged—the son and the grandson of the Earl of Shaftesbury; the son of Sir John Banks; the two children, son and stepdaughter of Lady Masham; and a small Quaker boy residing in Holland, Arent Furley. These were the children taught and loved by John Locke and, as they learned from him, he learned by their aspirations, their disappointments, their affections, and their stubbornness what children are really like. It is interesting to speculate on what it would be like to have one's early education taken charge of by a great philosopher, but it is probable that no party to the affair was aware that this was the case. Rousseau, in imagination and spirit, superintended the education of the fictitious Émile and rendered him, on paper, a delightful and spirited youth. Locke makes no mention of his actual pupils; his *Some Thoughts Concerning Education* (1693) concerns not one child, but all children; and this series of informal letters, written to his friend Mr. Edward Clarke and afterward developed into the printed essay, mark a great point in literary history for the young. For the first time a truly great mind speaks with authority on children as children and tells their parents how to behave toward them, instead of inevitably instructing children on their whole duty to their parents.

Locke, born in 1632 and dying in 1704, was during his life subject to the strifes and contentions of that same general and troubled age which saw the birth of *Pilgrim's Progress*, *Robinson Crusoe*, and *Gulliver's Travels*. His great *Essay Concerning Human Understanding* (1690) in which he brought the force of reason and experience to bear on established ideas was written in the exile which he shared with his patron, the Earl of Shaftesbury. It has been said that this new philosophy was an unintended encouragement to skepticism, but it must be remembered also that Locke was the stimulus and inspiration of the young Jonathan Edwards, who hearkened so earnestly to Locke's precept, "The light of reason is the candle of the Lord." Locke's own candle was held up to shed illumination on the dark ignorance of his time as to how children's minds should be cherished and spared, rather than roughly and peremptorily handled. It was the first real light to be cast upon the subject.

"Children should be treated as rational creatures,"[1] he declares. "They should be allowed their liberties and freedom suitable to their ages. . . . They must not be hindered from being children, nor from playing and doing as children; but from doing ill."[2] He adds further what has been the foundation of modern thought in education, "They love to be busy, change and variety are what deligt them"[3]; ". . . curiosity is but an appetite after knowledge, the instrument nature has provided to remove ignorance."[4] He undermines the foundation of a whole system when he says, "Do not charge children's memories upon all occasions with rules and precepts which they often do not understand and are constantly as soon forgot as given."[5]

Oh, shades of the *Bookes of Courtesie!* It is hard to realize what a direct contradiction this was to the established belief of elders that children were but smaller vessels of their own kind, ever open and into which they could pour the accumulated wisdom which they themselves often were not able to assimilate. Again and again Locke comes back to the idea, children must have their liberty.

They had taken it, without anyone's ever really granting it, they had made a choice of reading guided by that richness of taste which sprang from the very roots of English literature. He did not live to see them embrace *Robinson Crusoe* and *Gulliver's Travels* as their own, but he could have forseen that they would. He is quite definite but not very optimistic in regard to existing books for children. "When by these gentle ways he begins to be able to read," he directs, "some easy pleasant book should be put in his hands, wherein the entertainment that he finds might draw him on." *Æsop's Fables*, preferably illustrated, is best for the purpose, he thinks, dwelling on a child's natural interest in animals. "*Reynard the Fox* can be brought in for the same purpose. . . . What other books there are in English of the kind above mentioned, fit to engage the liking of children, I do not know."[6] It is to be noted that

---

[1] John Locke, *Some Thoughts Concerning Education.* In *Works*, Vol. IX (London, T. Davison, 1801), p. 40.
[2] *Ibid.*, p. 53.
[3] *Ibid.*, p. 62.
[4] *Ibid.*, p. 115.
[5] *Ibid.*, p. 45.
[6] *Ibid.*, pp. 147, 148.

both these books were of Caxton's printing and even as published works were over two hundred years old.

We could not ask that he would go the whole way into modern thought concerning the treatment and education of children. Some of his ideas sound unnecessarily grim and harsh, although he does say that "the rough discipline of the cudgel" is not to be used at all. "But we make no excuses for the obstinate," he insists; "blows are the proper remedies for those. . . ."[1] And further, "Children should submit their desires and go without their longings, even from the cradle,"[2] self-denial being a principle to be followed even for its own sake. "Be sure that he [the child] is capable of submission and understands in whose power he is"[3] sheds light on his conception of parental authority.

His thoughts spread slowly, so that it is long before we see real results. But a turning point was definitely reached with Locke, so that henceforth one mind after another was to regard children's real needs. Yet it was not until fifty years later that they were to find their real champion.

The Running Stationers

That long process by which children were selecting the material that pleased them and rejecting that which was thrust into their hands becomes vaguely apparent at this time in the business index of books sold and unsold. In the store of little volumes carried up and down England by the chapmen of the time, we begin to see indication of an attention to children's interests, rather than to the forming of manners. The chapmen liked to be called the "running stationers" and for the improvement of the young they cared very little. Shakespeare's Autolycus, the shrewd peddler of *The Winter's Tale*, carried broadsides and ballads in single sheets, but nothing of a more literary nature. *The Winter's Tale* has no more date than Bohemia has a seacoast, but it is very plain that this most thorough of knaves was of Shakespeare's own time. Successors of Autolycus a hundred years later, more established in their business and undoubtedly more honest, carried a more extensive kind of book, small and meager though the eighteenth century chapbooks were. Their character may be judged by the classifications into which they fell: Religious, Diabolical, Supernatural, Superstitious (interpretations of dreams and charms), Romantic, Humorous, Legendary, Historical, Biographical, and Criminal. Nothing there was composed actually for children, none the less children had their own favorites. We have from a rather unexpected quarter direct witness of what was available, in the record of James Boswell, an immensely grownup young man of twenty-

[1] Locke, *op. cit.*, p.74.
[2] *Ibid.*, p. 32.
[3] *Ibid.*, p. 33.

two, putting down in his *London Journal* on July 10, 1763, an account of meeting some of his old favorites.

". . . some days ago I went to the old printing-office in Bow Churchyard kept by Dicey, whose family have kept it fourscore years. There are ushered into the world of literature *Jack and the Giants*, *The Seven Wise Men of Gotham*, and other story-books which in my dawning years amused me as much as *Rasselas* does now. I saw the whole scheme with a kind of pleasing romantic feeling to find myself really where all my old darlings were printed. I bought two dozen of the story-books and had them bound up with this title, *Curious Productions*."[1] Dicey was the great printer of chapbooks for the running stationers' trade and put out those little tales which Boswell, a young reader at the mid-century, had consumed with avidity.

He would have seen the chapbooks in their heyday, and at twenty-two still cherished affection for what reminded him of his "dawning years." His collection of *Curious Productions* finally ran to three volumes, now in the Child Memorial Collection of Chapbooks owned by Harvard College. Although he has included some which were palpably not for children, the list gives some idea of what reading, slowly collected through the centuries, was now available to English children. There are *Jack and the Giants*, *The Seven Champions of Christendom*, *The Famous and Renowned History of Guy*, *Earl of Warwick*, *The History of the King and the Cobbler*, *The History of Sir Richard Whittington*, *Thrice Lord-Mayor of London*, *The Famous History of Johnny Armstrong of Westmoreland*, *The Babes in the Wood*, *The Friar and the Boy*.

Other collections than Boswell's contain—always including *Jack the Giant Killer*—*Reynard the Fox*, *Valentine and Orson*, *Fortunatus*, *Jack Horner*, *Robin Hood Ballads*, *Tom Thumb*, and *Robinson Crusoe*. Richard Steele writes in the *Tatler* of seeing his godson absorbed in reading *Don Belliamo of Greece*, *Guy of Warwick*, *John Hickathrift*, *Bevis of Southampton*, and *St. George*. An acquisitive young person might collect a fair library now, except that the books were greatly abridged from the original narratives, poorly printed, and with strange and distorted pictures. They filled a need in their time and they went their way to oblivion when something better offered. Some of them were a good deal like the present-day comics; the humorous ones seem inexpressibly vulgar to us now, yet they belonged to a time when language, even before children, was far more outspoken than it is today.

In one of the volumes Boswell has written on the flyleaf words which show that the ideas of Locke, once set rolling, have directly or indirectly gone very deep into thinking minds.

[1] James Boswell, *Boswell's London Journal, 1762–1763*, Frederick A. Pottle, ed. (New York, McGraw-Hill, 1950), p. 299.

"James Boswell. Inner Temple, 1763. Having when a boy, been much entertained with *Jack the Giant Killer* and such little Story Books, I have always retained a kind of affection for them, as they recall my early days. . . . I shall certainly some time or other write a little Story-Book in the stile of these. It will not be a very easy task for me; it will require much nature and simplicity and a great acquaintance with the humours and traditions of the English common people. I shall be happy to succeed, for He who pleases children will be remembered with pleasure by men."

Although Boswell, as far as anyone knows, never undertook that "not very easy task" but went on to pursue larger game in the person of Dr. Samuel Johnson, he spoke with an insight that would have been unknown no more than a few years earlier.

At Saint Paul's Churchyard

Those same ideas of Locke's had been turning in the mind of a man almost a generation older than the young Boswell, one who was now, in 1763, at the summit of his chosen enterprise. Boswell probably did not know him. Dr. Johnson, however, and Goldsmith and Newbery had already become well acquainted.

Young people who have had an orthodox education have already met John Newbery (1713–1767) without knowing it. In Goldsmith's *The Vicar of Wakefield*, when Dr. Primrose, returning from a heartbreaking journey, falls ill at an inn and find himself penniless, "It is possible the anxiety from this last circumstance alone might have brought on a relapse, had I not been supplied by a traveller, who stopped to take a cursory refreshment. This person was no other than the philanthropic bookseller in St. Paul's Churchyard, who has written so many little books for children; he called himself their friend, but he was the friend of all mankind. He was no sooner alighted, but he was in haste to be gone; for he was ever on business of the utmost importance, and was at that time actually compiling materials for the history of one Mr. Thomas Trip. . . . from him I borrowed a few pieces, to be paid at my return."[1]

Dr. Primrose was only one of many, for even the great Doctor borrowed small sums from John Newbery, whose delight was to place his large, practical, and sensible generosity at the service of his friends. Goldsmith has said of him directly that he was the patron of more distressed authors than any man of his time. Goldsmith explored to the full all of the potentialities of Newbery's unending good nature and even at times ventured a little further than Newbery's patience could reach.

Newbery is, indeed, a Goldsmith character—simple, jolly, resourceful, journeying up and down England in a great flurry of business,

[1] Oliver Goldsmith, *The Vicar of Wakefield*. Everyman's Library. (New York, E. P. Dutton, 1965), p. 101.

wearing a slightly shabby, mud-splashed coat, knee breeches, and buckled shoes. Books were his main interest, but he had many others, just to make certain that there was sufficient profit to go forward with the books. Patent medicines, especially Dr. James's fever powders, were part of his stock in trade and were famous for other reasons than that a lack of them destroyed the father of Goody Two-Shoes. Horace Walpole swore by their excellent qualities.

John Newbery was son of a poor farmer in Berkshire and was born in 1713. He came naturally to the book trade, for he was a descendant of Ralph Newberie, who was a famous publisher in his own day and brought out Hakluyt's *Voyages* (1589). John Newbery had a certain amount of formal education but at sixteen was already getting his experience in business, working for a merchant in Reading and reading intensively whenever he had the opportunity. Dr. Johnson said of him later that he did not know whether Newbery had "read or written" the most books. At Reading he became associated with the printer and newspaper owner William Carnan. When Carnan died, he took over the business and also married Carnan's widow. He traveled indefatigably to London, St. Albans, Hull, Lancaster, and sold haberdashery and cutlery as well as books of which he was already printing a good number.

Reading did not give sufficient scope for a man of such broad talents, and he moved to London in 1744, trying two locations before he settled in 1745 at St. Paul's Churchyard, "over against the north door of the Cathedral," in the shop which he called the "Bible and Sun." His bustling energy in business enterprise, his interest in literature and writers, his deep and sincere love for children, and his gift for friendship all began now to contribute to his truly astonishing success. He had chosen an utterly untried direction, that of publishing for children. He had read and pondered Locke, he had observed the chapbooks and children's taste as measured by the popularity of their favorites, he had taken keen note of the success of one most significant book which directly followed the educational ideas of Locke. *The Child's New Plaything* had been published elsewhere in 1743 and dedicated to the young Prince George, a more appropriate offering than Gay's *Fables* had been for an earlier prince. Being a spelling book, as the title page explains, it is intended "to make the Learning to Read a Diversion instead of a Task."

It contained the enduring classic, "A Apple-Pye, B bit it, C cut it," and it goes on to increasingly elaborate lessons which finally contain chapbooks of the time, *St. George and the Dragon, Fortunatus, Guy of Warwick, Reynard the Fox, The Wolf and the Kid.* It was, in fact, a book written directly and fully for children and published with their interest and entertainment in view, rather than only their instruction. It gave Newbery not only food for thought, but encouragement, so that in the next year, 1744, we see him bringing out *A Little Pretty Pocket-Book*, not in the drab cheapness of the chapbooks, but already in the gilt and embossed paper covers which were to be the mark of Newbery's taste, his understanding, and his astute business sense.

"The books are given away," he says in an alluring advertisement, "only the binding is to be paid for." And for this the thrifty price was sixpence. For the sake of the parents he quotes Locke's advice on the care of children; for the sake of the children themselves, he includes two letters from Jack the Giant Killer, whose sentiments are very lofty indeed and his advice to Master Tommy most uplifting.

John Newbery did not by any means desert the idea that books for children must teach them to be good, but his moral precepts, most of them included for the sake of the parents who were after all the purchasers, were all of the gentle and understanding kind which stressed the difficulty of avoiding naughtiness, rather than the more intricate philosophy of avoiding sin. In *The Wisdom of Crop the Conjuror*, Billy Learnwell is told, as the fortune which Crop tells for him, "You will be a great man, for you mind your book, you shall have horses and coaches a-plenty and everything you wish for, if you continue in the same good way you are now in." "Obstinate boys," Crop observes, "are like people who walk on their heads and of course, see everything the wrong way."[1] The fortune of Billy Learnwell is contrasted to that of Miss Lydia Indolent, who "thought it very vulgar to rise early in the morning, and with a foolish pride said it might answer for boys who followed the plough or maids who milked the cows, but for herself she chose rather to lie and dream of a coach than get up and possess one."[2] It need scarcely be added that she never was so rewarded. Coaches and horses, Newbery declares, are so much in the minds of children that they are always to be shown as the rewards of merit, there is nothing else which will answer so well. Even if fortunate youths become Lord Mayor of London, or fortunate and virtuous girls marry and become the Lady Mayoress, the real token of achievement is still stressed as riding in a coach, preferably a golden one.

The most significant passage among these books of improving fancy is contained in *Nurse Truelove's New Year's Gift*, published in 1760. The book itself is "designed for a present to every little Boy who would become a great Man and ride upon a fine Horse, and to every little Girl who would become a fine Woman and ride in a Governour's gilt Coach. But let us turn over the Leaf and see more of the matter." It

[1] *The Wisdom of Crop the Conjuror* (Worcester, reprint by Isaiah Thomas, 1786), p. 15.

[2] *Ibid.*, p. 18. Where no copy of a Newbery first edition can be found and the date is unrecoverable, the book can often be read in Isaiah Thomas's reprint, with A. S. W. Rosenbach's *Early American Children's Books* giving such information about the Newbery edition as is available. For Isaiah Thomas see Chapter 10 of this History.

contains various brief stories, even sketches so simple as to be less than stories, but entertaining in themselves with their gay descriptive scenes and occasional verses. "Innocent Pleasures of a Country Life, or The Haymakers" is enlivened by lines that fairly dance themselves to a jig tune.

> In came the jolly mowers,
> To cut the meadow down,
> With bottle and with budget
> And ale that's stout and brown.
>
> > [You see the picture of
> > the budget, a small bag
> > for bread and meat.]
>
> Sweet jug jug jug jug jug
> The nightingale doth sing,
> From morning until evening,
> While they are haymaking.[1]

Finally the collection reaches "The History of Mrs. Williams and Her Plumb Cake, with a word or Two concerning Precedency and Trade."

"Mrs. Williams, when I first became acquainted with her, was a widow gentlewoman and kept a little college in a country town for the Instruction of young Gentlemen and Ladies in the Science of A.B.C. The books she put into the hands of her young pupils were—"[2] there follows a list of Newbery publications. The story describes her making a plum cake and cutting it geometrically in wedges. She offered Master Hawes his choice before any of the other boys. Whereupon "Master Long, only son of the Lord of the Manor," objected, saying that he didn't want any cake because "Tom Hawes, who was a tradesman's son, had been served before him, though his father was Lord of the Manor and kept his Coach and Six."[3]

Mrs. Williams replies with a brief discourse first on pride and then on the importance of trade. In the cake, "that Plumb came from Turkey, and this from Spain, the sugar we had from Jamaica, the . . . candied sweetmeats from the Barbadoes, and the Spices from the East Indies. A Man of Fortune, my dear, that does no Good, does Harm, for he who lives an idle Life, lives like the Drone in the Bee-Hive by the Labour of others. . . ." "Here Mrs. Williams stopt. Master Long blushed and all the rest bowed respectfully and cried out 'Trade and Plumb Cake forever, Huzza.' "[4]

One might say this was the basis of Newbery's literary philosophy: good, solid English trade and the highest ideal of success and honor in

---

[1] *Nurse Truelove's New Year's Gift* (Worcester, Isaiah Thomas, 1786), p. 16.
[2] *Ibid.*, p. 48.
[3] *Ibid.*, p. 52.
[4] *Ibid.*, p. 57.

commercial life, all this held out to children well flavored with plum cake and the whole bound in gilt and flowered boards for sixpence. How comforting a contrast to the bare and drab homilies for the instruction of the young which had preceded this happy day when children found a real friend at last! Thanks to Locke and to Locke's theory and to John Newbery's practice, books for children finally stood on their own feet. Literature for the young was to have its vicissitudes later, but it was never really to go back into the no man's land where it had wandered for three hundred years.

Newbery offered books of stories as well as the generous collection in which he brought together games and puzzles, riddles, maxims and instruction: The *Circle of the Sciences* (1745), *The Land of Cakes* (1746), *The Nutcracker* (1750), *Be Merry and Wise* (1758, second edition), and *Giles Gingerbread* (1765) (who acquired learning by a peculiar process, for, his father being a baker, he ate a gingercake every day with the alphabet stamped upon it). A gilt coach, of course, was waiting in the offing for such an industrious scholar to reach great erudition.

The *Lilliputian Magazine* was a special kind of publication in itself, although it was hardly, in truth, a magazine at all, since it appeared all in one volume in 1751. Its full title is *The Lilliputian Magazine or the Young Gentleman's and Lady's Golden Library*, being an Attempt to mend the World, to render the society of Man more Amiable and to Establish the Plainness, Simplicity, Virtue and Wisdom of the Golden Age . . . Printed for the Society . . . at Mr. Newberry's, the Bible and Sun, in St. Paul's Churchyard." The contents make up a miscellany of all that the other individual volumes contain—stories, jokes, riddles, games, a bit of advertising—"Master Peter Primrose, when he was but seven years old . . . by reading the *Circle of the Sciences* had obtained some knowledge of men and things."[1]

In *Jack Dandy's History of Birds and Beasts* (attributed to Goldsmith) the knowledge is so deliberately entertaining that it is not always entirely accurate. "Goats are remarkable in the care of their young, which care, when the dam grows old, is returned with becoming gratitude by the young one, who brings her food and water."[2] The text is intermixed with verse and more than intermixed with useful precept.

> The bear in coldest climate lives,
> Screen'd by his shaggy hair,
> But boys may cold and hunger dread
> Who naught for learning care.[3]

[1] F. J. Harvey Darton, *Children's Books in England* (Cambridge, Eng., University Press, 1932), p. 127.
[2] *Jack Dandy's Delight or the History of Birds and Beasts* (Worcester, reprint by Isaiah Thomas, 1786), p. 15.
[3] *Ibid.*, p. 24.

Passages from the Bible are often quoted, longer ones are inserted for reading exercise, and the goodness of God is a theme which appears and reappears. Not wrath or punishment but the direct love of God for children and the love of children for God make the real philosophy which underlies the very gentle preaching—since of course some preaching there must be. The books, so it was advertised, were only for good little masters and misses, "those who are naughty shall have none." It is pleasant to realize that there is no trace of a record of any young customer's ever having been turned away.

The association of Newbery and Goldsmith is a delightful subject for both contemplation and speculation. Newbery loved to do good, to befriend the unfortunate, and who could have been a better subject than gifted, unthrifty, shabby Oliver Goldsmith, whom even his best friends pronounced a fool in all practical matters? Newbery had practical sense enough for both of them and many more. He measured Goldsmith's abilities at once and employed him, first, to write for his periodicals, and later, in the more difficult task of writing for his children's library. Only two books can be absolutely identified as Goldsmith's, a revision of *Plutarch's Lives* (1762) and *An History of England* (1764). One is tempted to attribute to Goldsmith one or another of the most clever and sprightly volumes on the Newbery list: the *Mother Goose* (1760), with commentary much in the style of Dr. Johnson, but always absurd; *Tom Thumb's Folio* (1768) and, most important of all, *The History of Little Goody Two-Shoes* (1766, third edition).[1]

Newbery published this little story with the unblushing statement that it was "from a manuscript found in the Vatican with illustrations by Michael Angelo." Various biographers say that Goldsmith avowed *Goody Two-Shoes*, but the scholarly record is not really clear. Goldsmith, brought up in the country, had sympathy enough with the tenant class of farmers and their sufferings under harsh landlords, but Newbery, whose father was a poor farmer, also had equal knowledge of such hardships as poor Meanwell suffered before he died. Moreover, in *Nurse Truelove's New Year's Gift*, the sketch of Mrs. Williams, with her speech on trade and plum cake, could hardly be from any other hand than Newbery's own. Trade was no deep concern of Goldsmith's. The same Mrs. Williams and her "college for instructing little gentlemen and ladies in the Science of A.B.C." appear in *Goody Two-Shoes*, for Margery Meanwell is her successor, teaching very much in the method suggested by Locke. Mr. Smith, the benevolent clergyman who is forced to turn Goody Two-Shoes and her brother out of doors because of pres-

---

[1] Darton gives this date as 1766, being that of the third edition, since no copy of an earlier one is obtainable. Rosenbach gives April, 1765, for the first edition. Washington Irving, citing convincing authority in his *Life of Oliver Goldsmith*, gives 1765.

sure from "that tyrant of the parish, Graspall," ejaculates with tears, "Lord have mercy on the poor," the same words used in the anecdote in Dick Whittington concerning the indentured servant.[1] When Dick, setting out from London because of the cruelties he had suffered, sits down on a stone near Halloway, he hears Bow bells "of which there were then only six" ringing the refrain "turn again. . . ." "What would one not endure to be Lord Mayor of London and ride in a fine coach?" Dick reflects, and rises up to go back. He did better even than marry his employer's daughter and ride in the mayor's coach. In the last year of his mayoralty he entertained King Henry V and his queen. These three sound a good deal more like Newbery than Goldsmith, but who is to judge until documentary evidence is really uncovered to show which of these two men, who had the same taste, the same flavor of humor, the same industry in production, wrote which books?

In a noticeably different style is *Tom Thumb's Folio* (Mr. Thomas Thumb was the son of Mr. Theophilus Thumb of Thumb Hall in Northumberland), which concludes with Tom Thumb's Song on the "Plays of Youth." It is of very different caliber than, for instance the clumsy doggerel verses of Crop the Conjuror. Thus the school boy sings—

> Now from the school I haste away,
> And joyful rush along to play.
> Eager I for my marbles call,
> The whirling top, the bouncing ball.
>
> The changing Marbles to me show,
> How mutable all things below,
> My fate and theirs may be the same,
> Dashed in one instant from the Game,
>
> Tops which in restless circle wind,
> Paint the wild image of my Mind
> Giddy, unfixed, I murmuring weep,
> Fancy still fluttering when I sleep.
>
> . . . Thus in my sports I read my State,
> Balls, Tops and Marbles warn my Fate.
> I see myself in every Toy,
> The Play's the Picture of the boy.[2]

Is this Goldsmith? Is it Giles or Griffith Jones, who also contributed to the Newbery Library? If *Goody Two-Shoes* is Newbery's, this is

---

[1] Reprinted by Isaiah Thomas, Worcester, 1787.
[2] *Tom Thumb's Folio for Little Giants* (Boston, Thomas and John Fleet, 1780), p. 30.

hardly his. The question remains open for future researchers and may they some day find the answer.

Newbery and his successors, his son, nephew, and stepson Carnan, did not neglect the old favorites of the chapbook list, whose popularity had given him the first encouragement. We find *Æsop*, *Robinson Crusoe*, and *Gulliver's Travels*. We find *The Children in the Wood*, that unaccountably immortal ballad which no generation could resist. Others of the older stories appear in further collections. Newbery's use of the title of "Mother Goose" was taken from Perrault's *Contes du Temps Passé* which had as a frontispiece *Ma Mère l'Oie*, telling her tales to children.[1] It was Newbery's idea to attach the name to the first important collection of ancient rhymes, some of them so long current in England that they are as old as literature itself. There can be much interesting study of their quaint and hidden symbolism, but their true charm, felt by every child almost from the moment that he is aware of words at all, is in their unfaltering rhythm and their compact and arresting variety of character and incident. Mother Goose is one of the indestructible treasures of the human race.

Something must be said, even if it can be only in passing, of the contribution of the illustrator Thomas Bewick (1753–1828) to the Newbery books. He did not come upon the scene until after John Newbery's death; it was Newbery's successors who introduced Bewick to the child's world. Anyone who has had the opportunity to see modern reproductions of his watercolors of birds and animals, such as those collected and published by David Croal Thomson, will realize at once what grace of line and rare delicacy of composition were within his grasp. Old woodcuts suffered fearfully from clumsiness in the cutting of the blocks and too generous a hand in the inking, so that it was only a comparative measure of the artist's abilities that resulted in the finished product. Bewick cut his own blocks, and there was greatness in his touch, but even in that case reproduction could be very inadequate and we have to look past it to realize what Bewick really achieved. He illustrated Gay's *Fables* and Æsop's and Berquin's *Looking Glass for the Mind* and many others of real note.

John Newbery's great day of publishing was from 1744 to 1767. He died in that latter year at the age of fifty-four, and for a time his kind of work was carried forward by his son and his nephew, both named Francis Newbery, and by his nephew's widow, Elizabeth, from 1769 to 1801. Never, however, was there again such a master hand for the direction of his chosen project. Though he wisely reprinted classics for children, he was, actually, not responsible for any new one. There is greatness in *Goody Two-Shoes*, simplicity and unconscious reflection

---

[1] Reprinted by Isaiah Thomas, Worcester, 1794.

of the conditions of English rural life. There is, for history, a glimpse recorded of what children did and thought and said in the first half of the eighteenth century. His real achievement was that, with his extraordinary gift for practical business, he demonstrated the high possibilities in publishing for children; he made the first large venture and showed all others afterward how well a man might prosper who took young persons for his chosen readers.

Yet it was not for the sake of business alone that he embarked on such an enterprise. No man who was the first in that sort of undertaking could ever have won success who did not have a deep and generous and understanding love for children. That God-given generosity which was the very core of his nature was responsible for something that was utterly new, a collection of books which were intentionally and entirely the children's own. They were cheap—deliberately so; they were gay and beautiful to look at; they were frail and they have, practically all of them, perished under the loving hands which received them. But when, either before or after, was there ever so much to be bought for sixpence?

Bibliography

Ashton, John. *Chap-books of the Eighteenth Century*. London, Chatto and Windus, 1882.

Boswell, James. *London Journal, 1762–1763*. Prepared for the press, with introd. and notes, by Frederick A. Pottle. New York, McGraw-Hill, 1950.

Cuff, Sister Mary Louise. "The Limitations of the Educational Theory of John Locke." Washington, 1920. Thesis (Ph.D.)—Catholic University of America.

Darton, Frederick Joseph Harvey. *Children's Books in England; Five Centuries of Social Life*. Cambridge, Eng., University Press, 1932.

Halsey, Rosalie V. *Forgotten Books of the American Nursery*. Boston, C. E. Goodspeed, 1911.

Irving, Washington. *Oliver Goldsmith, a Biography*. New York, G. P. Putnam, 1849.

Locke, John. *Works*, Vol. IX. *Some Thoughts Concerning Education*. London, T. Davison, 1801.

Rosenbach, Abraham Simon Wolf. *Early American Children's Books*. Portland, Me., Southworth Press, 1933.

Welsh, Charles. *A Bookseller of the Last Century. Being Some Account of the Life of John Newbery, and of the Books He Published, with a Notice of the Later Newberys*. London, For Griffith, Farran, Okeden & Welsh, 1885.

7

The Little Female Academy

The Age of Admonition

It is strange that in a time when the elders were reading with breathless interest the great novels of their day, *Clarissa Harlowe*, *Tom Jones*, *Evelina* and the others, they should still be so content that their children should have only the meager fare on which their minds had starved for so long. Newbery was too unusual and too bold to have any immediate followers who could do his work with the same measure of inspiration and success. The original genius had gone out of the enterprise. No one examined what had pleased children through the past generations; no one recognized, even from the success of John Newbery, that children's stories must have action and gaiety and sympathy with children's lives, or they were not stories for children at all. Newbery had always been shrewd enough to see that unless his little books carried a moral, parents would not buy them, so the contrast between good and bad, between the successful virtue that was rewarded by riding in a coach, or reprehensible idleness and folly that led to the jail or to beggary was made plain. Beyond that he would not push his young readers or interfere with their interest and enjoyment.

Up to this time it was only masculine hands which, intentionally or unintentionally, had produced work that was acceptable to children, or was destined for them without being acceptable. But at this point we observe the stage direction, *Enter the Ladies*. Women, interested in education and the necessity for it, feeling closer to children on account of more constant contact, came, by a natural right, to undertake their share of those experiments, all of them so well-meant and most of them so full of error, which were to follow Newbery's signal and unique success. It is easy to point out their conspicuous failings and their absurd blindness of judgment; it is far less easy to see how genuine was their motive for good in attempting to create literature in a new medium; it is easy to forget that they broke ground for better informed and more gifted writers who were to come.

Many of the shortcomings of this group of women writers can be laid to the time in which they lived and worked, the latter part of the eighteenth century when terrifying changes were going on all about them. Locke's theories on education had already reversed many of the comfortable old methods of bringing up children or, at least, of leaving them to servants to bring up. We will see later how Locke, once assimilated, was to be followed by the far more disturbing and startling Rousseau, but his power in England was still to come. There had been the dragging disillusionment of "the American war," followed by the crashing fall of the French monarchy and the thunder of Napoleon's cannon rolling across Europe. Sarah Fielding, the first to be discussed, lived in a less agitated world, but with the others we see an ever greater determination to retain or to establish a proper world for the young, unlike the rocking civilization in which they so dismayingly found themselves. The only method they could see was by strict and literal clinging to what they saw as truth, and by preaching laid upon preaching and edifying advice piled upon improving counsel. Under their hands the stern and often grim representations of what we may call the Age of Admonition settled down upon defenseless English youth and upon the new reading public growing up in America.

The Impeccable Governess

An almost forgotten writer, but one who is an important link in the chain of literary development is Sarah Fielding (1710–1768), sister of the novelist, who published one book for children, *The Governess; or, The Little Female Academy* (1749, second edition). Interest in education made her turn her mind and pen to offering, in rambling and eventless narrative, her idea of an exemplary establishment for the forming of the manners and characters of girls. Mrs. Teachum is the head of this institution; she is the widow of a clergyman, "who was a very sensible man and took great delight in improving his wife."

The most effective feature of her system is an excellent one, for she studies to efface herself and her authority, and leaves it to the girls themselves to talk things over in the summerhouse as to their problems and difficulties. Each one is shown as a distinct personality—Miss Jenny Peace, whose part in the story is manifest from her name, Miss Sukey Jennet, Miss Lucy Sly. Every girl "tells the story of her life," each one a brief account which does not aim at anything dramatic or startling, but which actually gives a cross section of the situations out of which children's characters are formed. The whole adds up, although Sarah Fielding does not directly emphasize it, to the fact that English children spent an appalling proportion of their time with hireling nurses or governesses, usually ignorant, often dishonest, and sometimes vicious.

The personal narratives are interspersed with stories told or read aloud, all dull, one interminable. Mrs. Teachum gives warning that "giants, magic, fairies and all sorts of supernatural assistances in a story are introduced only to amuse and divert, for a giant is called so only to express a man of great power." She adds that she cannot "recommend them to your reading, except, as I said before, that great care is taken to prevent you being carried away by these high-flown things."[1] Thus we hear pronounced that embargo on matters of the fancy which was to be so firmly supported by the literary effort which came thereafter. If the worthy ladies had really had their way, they would have brought into being a line of priggish, but otherwise perfect, little mortals who had suffered, however, a complete stultification of the imagination.

Mrs. Barbauld and Dr. Aikin "At Home"

Anna Letitia (Aikin) Barbauld (1743–1825), with her slim elegance and her classic profile, made a figure in London literary society which moves in and out of very many of the letters and journals of the last third of the eighteenth century. She was considered one of the significant authors of her day, although nothing that she wrote has thrust itself very forcibly upon the attention of a later age. Her publications for children were small in quantity, but, compared with Sarah Fielding's, Mrs. Barbauld's influence was immeasurably greater and more tenacious. She was a woman of deep thought and conviction, who lived so surrounded by new and conflicting ideas that she almost inevitably fell into some of the errors that went along with the enlightenment.

Her brother, John Aikin, some years younger than she (1747–1822), was instrumental in bringing out her first book of poems and, later, *Miscellaneous Pieces in Prose* by J. and A. L. Aikin. These were for adults and were sufficiently well spoken of to establish her as a literary personage. After her marriage to the Reverend Rochemont Barbauld, she took part with him in establishing a boarding school for boys at Palgrave, Suffolk, which became notably successful. Hers were the very young pupils, a class of teaching for which she had unusual gifts. Her own literary reputation brought prestige to the school. She made a point of teaching her students to write good English.

Having no children, she and her husband adopted the son of John Aikin, little Charles, for whom she wrote *Lessons for Children, from Two to Three Years Old* published in 1778. It is a small book of the Newbery style, with large print and pictures on every page. In four parts it adapts each one to a different age, Part II being for children three years old. "Good morrow, little boy," it begins, "Bring your little stool and sit down by me, for I have a great deal to tell you. I hope you have been a good boy . . ." We will see later that this understanding simplicity is only achieved by an adaptable and discerning person.

---

[1] Sarah Fielding, *The Governess* (London, T. Clarke, 1765), p. 52.

Hymns in Prose for Children followed in 1781, a paraphrasing of biblical passages reduced to greater simplicity for the reading of children. "Behold the shepherd of the flock, he taketh care for his sheep, he leadeth them among the clear brooks . . . Who is the shepherd's shepherd, who taketh care of him?"

So well known and so prosperous did the school become, that Mrs. Barbauld found it possible and often necessary to spend the vacation time in London, where a widening circle of literary acquaintances made her more and more welcome. Finally, with the decline of her husband's health, the school was given up, and the Barbaulds settled at Stoke Newington to be nearer to Dr. Aikin with whom his sister had already begun to collaborate on their series, *Evenings at Home* (1792).

Much the larger portion of the work was done by Dr. Aikin, but it is certain that the planning and arrangement were done in close consultation, though so much of the writing is his. The basic project, which evidently arose from the practice of the school, is a very sound one. A series of stories, short plays, instructive articles, are, supposedly, written by various people who, when possessed of some interesting idea or anecdote or bit of information, put it down for the benefit of others. All the manuscripts are deposited together in "the budget of instruction and entertainment." "Opening the budget" was an evening pastime, with one thing and another drawn out at random. Night First for instance offers "The Young Mouse, a Fable," with a moral on the advantages of filial obedience. "Traveller's Wonders," as related by Captain Compass, bring this remark from little Jack, "I have been vastly entertained while you were abroad, with *Gulliver's Travels*," and when asked if he would like to hear Captain Compass tell of his adventures he responds, "Pray do."

People of a generation old enough to have had *Evenings at Home* surviving on their shelves when they were children can come across the book in later life, look into its battered pages, and think suddenly, "Why here was where I first heard about King Canute's ordering back the sea, and about Alfred's burning the cakes." There is some very basic information of this kind scattered through the volumes, there is something for everybody's taste, there are admonitions against everyone's temptations. So widely were these publications read and so large was the dignity of Mrs. Barbauld as a literary figure, that she stamped the limitations of her ideas firmly on the whole character of stories for children of her time. They are literal, they are prosaic, they take account of the limitations of children's knowledge and experience, but they have no vision of the wider world which children's imaginations long to explore. Charles Lamb complained bitterly that "Mrs. Barbauld's stuff" had driven out the old favorites beloved by John Newbery. Nothing was on the bookshop shelves now but little narratives of puss and a crow and a squirrel, or useful explanations of how paper is made. How Mrs.

Barbauld and John Aikin would have rejoiced in the anecdote of Washington and the little hatchet, but it did not reach English shores in time.

The Fabulous Robins

A lady of stern stuff and direct intention, someone even of firmer though kinder character than Mrs. Teachum herself, is Mrs. Sarah (Kirby) Trimmer (1741–1810), resident of Brentford, near London, and mother of six sons and six daughters whose education she earnestly supervised. With her and her writing there entered a factor in literature for children which gave it a deeper purpose, but, unfortunately, which tended to emphasize even more conscientiously the importance of moral teaching.

Robert Raikes, of Gloucester, a newspaper owner and successful man of affairs, had become deeply concerned over the pitiful ignorance of the very poor and the utter lack of provision for instruction of their illiterate children. He devoted a lifetime of effort, money and a gift for publicity to the founding of Sunday schools for children and untutored adults. Sunday schools they had to be, for children and adults alike were at work for wages twelve hours a day through the other six days of the week. The movement spread widely and rapidly as does any effort which is bitterly needed. Sarah Trimmer was one of his early adherents and matched his burning zeal with her own to bring education into the barren wastes of English poverty. Her interest in writing for children went hand in hand with her belief that all children had a right to learn to read.

Mrs. Barbauld's *Lessons for Children* inspired her to undertake *An Easy Introduction to the Knowledge of Nature* (1782), a set of conversational lessons on the same plan, written with less skill and grace and more of that insidious sense of patronage which creeps into even the most wholehearted of these educational efforts. Henry is invited to partake of these lessons with his older sister Charlotte. "Though he is young he is a sensible little fellow and will be able, I dare say, to understand many things which we shall have occasion to talk of." The children are conducted across the meadow, the discourse ranges rapidly from grain to turnips, to flax, to cabbages, to the dire consequences of a boy's eating green fruit, to mining in the bowels of the earth, to dairying, to beans. The *Easy Introduction* was so successful that Berquin translated it for his young audience, after which it made its way back into English by retranslation. Madame de Genlis' *Adèle et Théodore* suggested to Mrs. Trimmer her *Series of Prints*, with copperplate scenes from biblical history and accompanying lessons.

Her *Fabulous Histories* (1786) may have been a larger project which did not get beyond *The History of the Robins*, though finally, in a later edition, there were added a few "Anecdotes of Animals." Since it is practically impossible to write anything for children without involving the use of some imagination, she finds herself in the embarrassing situation of having created a family of robins who must and will talk to carry out the intention of the story. For this she apologizes in her introduction and makes everything clear by saying, "Before Henry and Charlotte began to read these Histories, they were taught to consider them, not as containing the real conversations of Birds (for that is impossible as we shall ever understand) but as a series of Fables, intended to convey moral instruction." It may be that Locke's approval of Æsop rendered the fable seemingly innocuous, whereas the fairy story was fraught with corruption.

In the account of the robins she offers a reflection of family life and all the problems that arise in children's day to day experiences. We see the consequences of small selfishnesses, of intolerance of others' feelings, finally of the master fault disobedience, all set forth in the actions of Robin, Jr., Dicky, Flapsy, and Pecksy. Where the consequences of the errors of the young birds are not clear enough, we have Father Robin making everything quite plain in his brief lectures to Mother Robin and the children. His language is worthy of the queen's drawing room; he needs only an embroidered waistcoat and ruffles to make him complete. "Your present humility" he remarks to the erring Robin, Jr., "disarms my resentment . . . We will therefore say no more on a subject which gives so much pain to both of us."[1] Mrs. Benson, mother of the children for whom the lessons on robin life are spread out, wastes no opportunity either and, as is natural, she outdoes the cock robin in loftiness of language. "I am delighted, my dear children, with your humane behaviour towards the animal creation . . . but though it is a most commendable propensity, it requires regulation."[2] The hand of Dr. Samuel Johnson lies heavy on the whole literary convention of the time, and even writers for the young must be exceptional to escape it. Mrs. Trimmer's solid good sense and her honest desire to make children treat animals well show through the inappropriateness of her style, although it hardly recommends her to immature readers. She introduces, with great inaccuracy of detail, a bird which manifestly does not belong in this habitat, and conscientiously explains in a footnote, "The Mock-Bird is properly a native of America, but is introduced here for the sake of the moral."[3]

Her stern principle on the matter of the falsity of imaginative fancy was to grow on her, even as her interest in Sunday schools and in children's education increased. She founded the *Family Magazine*, which ran from 1788 to 1789 and was specially designed for the "instruction and amusement of cottagers and servants, calculated to improve the mind

[1] Mrs. Sarah Trimmer, *Fabulous Histories* (London, Longman, 1786), p. 102.
[2] *Ibid.*, p. 9.
[3] *Ibid.*, p. 105.

and lead to religion and virtue." Her purpose was eminently good, so, seemingly, was the journal's avowed policy "to counteract the pernicious influence of immoral books." Among these harmful books, however, she vehemently classed *Robinson Crusoe*, which would lead, she declared, "to an early taste for a rambling life and a desire for adventures." So little did she really know children that she did not realize that this last is an inevitable factor in every child's make-up. *Mother Goose* was only fit to "fill the minds of children with confused notions of wonderful and supernatural events." She denounced *Cinderella* as leading to undutiful notions about stepmothers, and even bore down upon *The Governess* for containing those fanciful fables which Mrs. Teachum had taken such pains to render harmless. But for all her care, her hand slipped once. In *The History of the Robins* she accidentally stumbled into mention of the office of Robin Redbreasts in the ballad of *The Children in the Wood*. The fantasy of the past had, after all, risen up to embrace her.

Cowslip Green

When Hannah More (1745–1833) went up to London from Bristol, aged twenty-eight and gloriously independent in the possession of a small annuity settled upon her by a friend, she was received at once in every group of the current literary society of that brilliant year of 1773. She found her path crossing, but not often coinciding with, that of Mrs. Barbauld. They both moved in the circle surrounding the great Dr. Johnson, although Hannah turned on a much closer orbit than that of the already distinguished Anna Letitia. She spoke with amusement of Boswell's idolatry of Johnson; she was too late to know Goldsmith or John Newbery. She would probably, on various counts, have disapproved of both of them.

One sees in her letters, even then, the deep sense of piety which later was to be the dominating theme of her life. Possessed of charm, wit, and a genuine capacity for friendship, she was also inflexibly established in certain principles of her own, which kept uncaptured, in the midst of that gay whirl of intellect and amusement, some inner core of her being. A friend of the Garricks, at whose house she was to spend many of the ensuing winters, deeply regarded by Sir Joshua Reynolds and his sister, petted by Johnson, developing acquaintance with Horace Walpole who was to be her friend and correspondent for twenty years—she could hardly have asked for anything further. Her writing during this period was mostly verse, graceful and adroit some of it, but not to be called poetry. Although inwardly she disapproved of the theater, she wrote a play, *Percy*, which Garrick himself directed, the production being a great success. Far more than any achievements of her own, she enjoyed the brilliance of the minds around her and the keen edge of intellectual give and take.

By the time she was forty-four the satisfaction in all this had gradually diminished and she realized that her tastes and impulses lay in a different direction. She acquired a little place near Bristol which she called Cowslip Green, and here she was joined by her older sisters who had retired from their very successful school for girls in Bristol. They built themselves a house outside Bath, where they spent the fashionable season, but more and more they began to be drawn into a very different and much larger occupation.

They had observed the ignorance and moral degradation of the working people about them and coupled the hard facts with the knowledge that there were no schools for children in their neighborhood and only the most distant and indirect ministrations of any church. Roused by the examples of Raikes, Sarah Trimmer, and others, they set about founding one school after another, straining their resources to hire buildings and employ teachers, accepting help from all walks of life and every kind of people. "One of the farmers seemed pleased and civil," Hannah More wrote to a friend, "he was rich and covetous, a hard drinker and his wife a woman of loose morals but natural sense; she became our friend sooner than some of the decent and formal and let us a house, the only one in the parish."

The able More sisters had capacity to do well anything to which they set their hands. The first school at Cheddar was followed by many others, while the sisters laid out sound plans of instruction, took over some of the teaching themselves, covered miles of difficult travel to hold endless interviews with parents, patrons, and possible teachers. Hannah, among them all, had something more to give. She could write.

It was in 1789 that the new enterprise was begun, the year that the French Revolution broke forth in furious upheaval, later in bloody horror. Hannah More had already been asked by friends if she could not write something which would counteract the influence of the Jacobin and the atheistic propaganda which was beginning to spread through England. She was aware, also, that children being taught to read should have suitable reading matter ready to be put before them. Her reply was the launching of the plan for *Cheap Repository Tracts*, containing a story, a brief set of verses, and a direct but short sermon, to be read, or read aloud in the schools. An advisory committee was formed to assist her in choosing and treating subjects. It has been said, with evident truth, that she consulted the committee more than the tastes of the children. Three tracts a month were issued for a period of three years from 1795 to 1798; they were sold in tens of thousands, finally in millions. There had been nothing like it before in output for children's reading.

The Shepherd of Salisbury Plain is one of the most famous, and perhaps is completely typical. The stories had inevitably fallen into an established pattern concerning how to live a good life, more emphatically how to be industrious, thrifty, and content "in that state of life into which it had pleased God to call us." The Shepherd, in numbers of long speeches, sets forth his situation to kindly Mr. Johnson, depicting his happy life with a wife crippled by rheumatism and five children in a house with leaky thatch and a broken chimney. When he is given a crown by the benevolent gentleman, he uses it to pay the doctor who tended his wife last winter when she was ill unto death. He fears that he can get no more medical aid until the debt is paid, nor will he buy meat for himself or the children until the doctor has had his due. By great good fortune the old clerk of the parish dies at this juncture and the shepherd gets his place and his weatherproof cottage, with "a large light kitchen" where he and his wife are to conduct a Sunday school. The author had no idea that she was transmitting to posterity an unconscious picture of privilege, patronage, criminal neglect, and unbelievable penury. *Black Giles the Poacher, Tawny Rachel the Fortune-Teller, The Happy Waterman, The Two Wealthy Farmers* followed, indicating as soon as their titles are read just what the reader is to expect. Since many were taken from actual events, they often open with a situation or a character of some reality, but the purposes of the story throughout prevent any natural unfolding of the plot. Virtue is always rewarded, usually by the accidental meeting with a charitably inclined person; vice gets its due in the gaol or, when the worst comes to the worst, by transportation or hanging.

Swift, many years earlier, had observed the similarly appalling poverty and degradation of the peasants in Ireland and wrote of his fellow men as brutes and Yahoos; Hannah More, far less of an artist, made it her business to work daily toward bettering the unfortunate lot of the poor and looked upon them and served them as suffering human beings. She faced criticism and abuse for her attempt to educate working people "until they were no longer fit for servants," as it was said against her. She made an honest and courageous attempt to reach their minds by teaching and writing; the attempt is what is important, far more so than the fact that she, like the rest of society, did not fully know how. And what is equally important, she drew her material from the vast record of everyday life, writing of the humble, the simple, and the unpretentious, out of whose human experience the solid truth of literature had long been wrought, whether for old or for young.

Her poetic impulse, her rich background of broad and brilliant acquaintance, and her familiarity with the beautiful and intellectual things of life could not fail to give something more of substance and humanity to her work than would otherwise have been possible. She never went back to her old interests, although she kept up her friendships until the end of her years. In her correspondence with Horace Walpole, which she continued until his death, the old sparkle still revives and she gives due answer to those witty and affectionate letters from him which show him at his best.

"Thou mightest be one of the cleverest of women if thou didst not prefer being one of the best," he said to her. "When I say one of the best I have not engaged my vote for the second."[1]

Mrs. Mason

To the list of these untiringly admonitory ladies there must be added one more, displaying most of the faults and few of the virtues of their form of literature. Mary Wollstonecraft's (1759–1797) *Original Stories* (1788) imitated the others, added nothing, and showed the whole method in its stark nakedness. So successful had been Mrs. Barbauld and Mrs. Trimmer that, so E. V. Lucas surmises, the publisher Johnson, of St. Paul's Churchyard, suggested to Mary Wollstonecraft, later to be Mary Godwin, that she turn her vigorous pen to the same kind of task. The resulting book, written to order by one who had small knowledge of children and, it might be added, not much skill in composing a juvenile story, was all that one could expect. It was published in 1788 and shows Mrs. Mason undertaking the training of two motherless little girls, and gives us ample view of her method. She knows everything and never fails to impart information and moral teaching with every breath. More than half of the pages of the little book, by actual count, are monologue by Mrs. Mason, who partakes of the natures of Mrs. Teachum of *The Governess* and Mrs. Benson, the human mother in *The Fabulous History of the Robins*. She leads the children to dark and eerie places and there recounts to them unwholesome stories of death and insanity as the result of wrongdoing. With the best of intentions for the welfare of her young charges, she and Mary Wollstonecraft could scarcely have done worse.

A curious detail is that William Blake, employed to make drawings for the story, seems to have been entirely on the side of the children. Although he has presented Mrs. Mason as slim, lissome, and goodlooking, one sees her always in a studied pose, the conscious teacher, while the children look wistfully out from the page as though glancing surreptitiously at that wider and more natural world which their conductress will not allow them to enter. The book has been thoroughly forgotten and for obvious reasons. But it remains an interesting object of study, written by an intelligent and well-meaning woman, the sum and unadorned pattern of the kind of story which the adult world had decided firmly was best suited for the younger one. It was high time for the Little Female Academy to develop something better, if it were only a

---

[1] Horace Walpole, *Letters*, Peter Cunningham, ed. (London, Henry Bohn, 1866), Vol. IX, p. 470.

broader background of thought and a style that was not overcast by the ponderous shadow of Dr. Johnson.

Bibliography

Barbauld, Anna Letitia. *The Works of Anna Lætitia Barbauld. With a Memoir by Lucy Aikin.* 2 Vols. London, Longman, Hurst, Rees, Orme, Brown, and Green, 1825.

Hopkins, Mary Alden. *Hannah More and Her Circle.* New York, Longmans, Green, 1947.

More, Hannah. *The Letters of Hannah More,* selected with an introd. by R. Brimley Johnson. London, J. Lane, 1925.

Roberts, William. *Memoirs of the Life and Correspondence of Mrs. Hannah More.* 4 Vols. London, R. B. Seeley, 1834.

Trimmer, Sarah (Kirby). *Some Account of the Life and Writings of Mrs. Trimmer.* 2 Vols. London, Printed for F. C. and J. Rivington, 1814.

Walpole, Horace, 4th Earl of Orford. *The Letters of Horace Walpole, Earl of Orford.* Edited by Peter Cunningham. Vols. IX and X. London, R. Bentley, 1857–59.

—— *The Yale Edition of Horace Walpole's Correspondence,* edited by W. S. Lewis. 34 Vols. New Haven, Yale University Press, 1937–65.

8

Launching a Century

Little Henry

There was interesting variety in Hannah More's life, but it was, after all, passed between narrow social limits, as was also that of Mrs. Barbauld and of Mrs. Trimmer. Yet all three women had for one object of their writing the careful preservation of those limits and that narrow society. Mary Butt Sherwood (1775–1851), however, looked out upon broader scenes. She, like the others, took up writing primarily for the sake of moral teaching and, like them, wrote for the sake of the charity schools in which she was also interested. But she carried her technique and her results far beyond anything that these other women had achieved.

Brought up in a country parsonage, she regarded life, even from her very early years, with a curiosity and interest that never flagged. As she grew older, although the literary circles of London did not know her, she had a taste of the wit and intellect of a smaller society, the group at Lichfield, which touched the greater world at a dozen points of contact. Center of the group was Miss Anna Seward, called "the Swan of Lichfield," who wrote verse and a good many rather unreliable memoirs and was arbiter of the literary standards of the place. Here Dr. Johnson—he crosses every horizon—was born and often came for visits with Boswell in attendance. Here was the house of the actor Garrick's brother, where the great David was often entertained. Through young Mary Butt's diary we get our first glimpse of "that dashing young widower" Richard Lovell Edgeworth, "one of the most fascinating men in conversation," and of his friend, Thomas Day. Edgeworth, Mary declares with regret, was an open infidel, on account of his pursuit of the French philosophers; she is kinder concerning "poor Mr. Day," although she admits that religiously he is "little better."

Part also of the scenes of her youth were the surroundings of the rectory at Stanford, with wide lawns and orchards going down to the borders of the River Teme, with hills rising to heights beyond and with everywhere bits of woods, farms, ancient manor-houses, and churches with their lifting spires or their square towers. The chief factors in a girl's education of that day had to do with posture, manners, and the wearing of the proper clothes in the proper way. Parental policy in regard to these matters was firm, one might even say tough. The little girl was made to wear an iron collar and a backboard to insure erectness and stood in wooden stocks as she studied her lessons. But once she was free of all this at the end of the day, she ran happily in the fields and let all the English beauty strike deep into her memory. She was to have need of it.

She read *Robinson Crusoe, The Little Female Academy*, and *Æsop's Fables*, and once acted Miriam in Hannah More's sacred drama, *Moses in the Bulrushes*. Mary heard much of Hannah More from a neighbor who had once worked with her and in time, under this friend's guidance, Mary Butt began to teach in the Sunday schools and to learn to understand children's minds. She was taken by this Mrs. King to Bath and there saw Hannah More, an old woman sitting in an invalid armchair, watching her with "magnificent dark eyes" and talking like an oracle. Young Mary wondered, "If I ever become a celebrated writer, should I be disposed to hold forth like this lady?" She decided later, "I need not have deranged myself by this fear."[1]

Although she had been writing little stories since she was six, it was not until 1802, when she was twenty-seven, that her first real book was published, *Susan Gray*. She frankly stated that it "has religion for its object" just as did those of her predecessors. The next year she was married to her cousin Henry Sherwood, an army captain, and in 1805 she set sail with him for India where he was to be stationed for so many years. She left a baby daughter behind her; she went through fantastic hardships on the way, with no privacy, with dirt, and with suffocating quarters, and in the end a battle with two ships of the French navy. She began teaching soldiers to read even on the voyage out.

She settled to her picturesque and difficult life first at Dinapore, then at Berhampore, later, after a long journey up the Ganges, at Cawnpore. Her son Henry was born at Berhampore, an ailing baby with all the cards stacked against him—hot climate, a nurse who gave him opium to keep him quiet, flies and disease all about him. Nothing that Mary Sherwood ever wrote elsewhere is so moving as the simple record in her diary of how she walked, in the golden sunset light, up and down the long verandah with her little boy in her arms and knew that he was dying.[2]

After small Henry's death, "an easy, careless, good-natured" chaplain

[1] F. J. Harvey Darton, ed., *The Life and Times of Mrs. Sherwood* (London, Wells Gardner, Darton, 1910), p. 128.
[2] *Ibid.*, p. 298.

could give her no comfort through her own and her father's Church of England doctrine. But she fell in with a young missionary, who put before her the Calvinistic belief in predestination and original sin. It was of extraordinary relief and support to her for, as she says, she had thought heretofore that she was the only complete sinner in the world. A daughter was born to her before little Henry died, but this child she lost also.

She founded schools for the soldiers' children, since the government had made no provision for their being taught. She wrote *Margery*, which was turned into a primer for the schools; she began the *Infant's Progress;* she went forward with her teaching and her writing, her unfailing industry. She said that a big Indian house is lonely, one can't go out in the heat, there is little to read, and nothing to do but listen to the click of the punkahs. She made the most of the lonely quiet.

Much of her work now was in preparing material for her schools, which were extended by this time to native children. She found it hard to reach their alien little minds and to answer their questions, "What is a barn? Can they walk out at noon without a *chatta*? Are they not afraid of serpents in the grass?" She began a collection of stories which she called the *Child's Manual*, which later grew into *The Fairchild Family*.[1]

When the agony of sorrow over the loss of her first son had worn down during the years, she wrote *Little Henry and His Bearer*, finishing it in 1809, a story of what that baby, in whom she saw such spiritual possibilities, would have done had he lived. She sent it to her sister at home, who arranged for its publication; it was printed in 1814 and was an immediate success. Even Kipling, two generations later, in his story *William the Conqueror*, speaks of it. "They came to an India . . . of palm-tree, palmyra-tree and rice, the India of the picture books, of 'Little Henry and His Bearer,' all dead and dry and baking heat." For years it was the picture of India which most English people had foremost in their minds.

Little Henry in the story is an orphan, his father has been killed attacking natives in a mud fort, his mother dies soon after, a rich and indifferent but kindly woman assumes charge of him, and leaves him entirely to the care of servants. His bearer, Boosy, loves him deeply, nurses him through illness, teaches him his own heathen religion, for the rich lady has instructed him in none. A young girl who has traveled out to India to marry a missionary comes to visit; she undertakes to teach little Henry, has some difficulty in making the subject of sin clear to him and all the fine-cut doctrines of eternal punishment. He learns to read and she leaves him with a Bible. From this he reads to

[1] Darton, *op. cit.*, p. 393.

Boosy, sitting on his heels in the cool passage, with the Bible on his knees. He is pale and evidently suffering, but he has no complaints. When the girl, now married, sees him again, she is shocked by his appearance but he reassures her that "death is very sweet." "You will live to be a judge yet, with seven silver sticks carried before your palanquin," she declares, but Henry fades into death, leaving a devout and broken-hearted Boosy who does not long survive him. The story has the errors of its time, the open sanctimoniousness and the narrowness of doctrine which limit its meaning, but it has the sense of human sorrow and the pathetic picture of a child in conditions under which he has so little chance of life.

With *The Fairchild Family*, begun in 1812, she turned her eyes back to England, to gay and happy English life and to the green landscape of Stanford. "From the top of this hill one might see Mr. Fairchild's house, standing in a pleasant garden, and also many beautiful cornfields and little coppices and meadows . . . the long green lane which led to the village too was visible from the hill and John Trueman's neat cottage. . . ." Mr. Fairchild had a school for poor boys in the village and Mrs. Fairchild one for girls. With their children, Lucy, Emily and Henry, they used to go there two or three times a week "to see the children and give rewards to those who had behaved well."[1] The separate stories extended to four series, brought out in 1818–1847. The incidents are the simple ones that make up children's lives; the problems are of obedience, patience, and good temper. While the moral issue is always the primary factor in every happening, the lesson is presented through the situation, not from the long-winded explanation and preaching of any one character. Mary Bush tells of how she was led into mischief by wicked children so that she distressed and neglected her dying mother. Mrs. Fairchild tells her own story—beginning with a funeral as so many of these narratives do—and recounts her being led astray by the ill-taught Nancy into breaking the Sabbath and eating forbidden cherries. Later in the book, when the young visitor, Bessie, behaves in so headstrong a manner that she gets herself caught in the rain and ruins her clothes—a frequent tragedy among the young of this time—when she has nothing to wear and the other children are going to "an evening party in Miss Pimlico's orchard," Mrs. Fairchild says nothing of an improving nature but stays at home with her, helps her put her ruined dress to rights, and makes her happy again. The manner of telling these life stories is direct and forcible and each partakes of the character of the teller. Mrs. Fairchild's great merit is that she rises to a real command of fine English.

In a famous passage in the book, not to be found in later editions,

[1] Mrs. Sherwood, *The Fairchild Family* (London and Edinburgh, T. C. and E. C. Jack, n.d.), p. 12.

Mr. Fairchild takes his children to see the body of a man hanging from a gibbet, a man of high position, hanged in his own garden in blue coat and silk scarf, but hanged none the less because he has murdered the brother with whom he had been in the habit of quarreling from childhood. It is a story told with no stress on horror, but merely on the facts; it has a moving power quite unknown to the sentimentalities of the preceding writers. The wisdom of this particular choice of incident is very doubtful, but generally speaking, there has been evolved in Mrs. Sherwood's hands a style really suitable for children, a point of view that reflects their own thinking and a power and purpose that reaches them.

After her return to England in 1816 she set up a little boarding school for girls, mostly for those whose parents were in India. She wrote indefatigably in the years that followed—*The History of Henry Milner* in four parts (1823–37), *The Lady of the Manor, Roxobel, The Hedge of Thorns, The Ayah and the Lady, Lucy and her Dhaye*. She did some editorial work and, rather surprisingly, turned her disapprobation upon *The Little Female Academy* for its imaginative fables about giants and pretty little dwarfs. She issued a new edition of the book shorn of those misleading tales. "Since fanciful productions of this sort can never be rendered generally useful it has been thought proper to suppress [them] . . . substituting in their place such appropriate relations as seemed more likely to conduce to juvenile edification."[1] The substitutes were of the allegorical type which could mislead (or interest) nobody. Even Mrs. Sherwood with her sharper observation and deeper understanding could not get away from the unhappy phrase, "juvenile edification."

Fables and More Fables

Even after so long a term of protest against the story of imagination, it had not been found possible to banish completely such an essential factor in literature for the young. The name fable was adopted to cover the sort of imaginative thing that was considered admissible, although its definition became more and more indefinite. As a truly fanciful story it was condemned; as an allegory presenting vague personifications of good and evil, the right way and the wrong way, it was hesitatingly approved.

Lady Eleanor Fenn (1743–1813), during those same busy 1780's, wrote *Cobwebs to Catch Flies, or Dialogues in Short Sentences*, closely allied, as were so many similar efforts, to Mrs. Barbauld's *Lessons*. Her *Fairy Spectator* (1789) was dominated by a firm Fairy Guardian. But her *Fables in Monosyllables* (between 1780–1790) is most revealing

---

[1] F. J. Harvey Darton, *Children's Books in England* (Cambridge, Eng., University Press, 1932), p. 97.

of the principles of the time and in it she makes an attempt at a distinction in the matter of what fables are. Fables are stories to teach children what they should do, "by showing them what may happen to them if they do not act as they ought to do." If a boy goes near a horse, she explains, after he has been forbidden to do so, and the horse kicks him, "that is not a fable but a tale." But the story of the good Kid (Lady Eleanor was innocent of modern slang) who obeyed his mother, and the other of the naughty Kid, who did not mind the orders which the Goat left, and so was devoured by the Wolf, "that is a fable." The distinction is still somewhat hazy and probably rather beyond the reach of Little William, to whom it is presented, but the dialogue ends, as all of them do, in the simple sentiment, "but it is certain that children, if they will not obey their parents, will come to harm for their disobedience."

That her *Fables* was written in monosyllables is merely a matter of printing and, while those for Little William, aged three and a half, are fairly simple, those for the mature George, of the age of five, call for some rather heavy intellectual effort. "*George.* The good young Crab, who was will-ing to sub-mit to the re-stric-t-ions which his mo-ther should please to lay on him, would find se-cu-ri-ty in his o-be-di-ence. Mamma, *did* the Fox get him?"[1] George seems to be speaking in his own person in the last sentence and in more congenial language. The matter of animals being able to speak, a gross falsity to nature which has troubled every author of this period, is met by Lady Eleanor thus: "*Boy.* Frogs . . . cannot speak, can they, Aunt? *Lady.* No, my dear, but this man [Æsop] says for the frog what we may think the poor thing would say if it could speak. *Boy.* Why, Aunt? *Lady.* To teach you, my dear."[2] Everyth.ng returns to this simple purpose, which scarcely any author of this period could lose from sight. One—a famous one—did stage a revolt, stubborn but ineffective, as we shall presently see.

William Godwin (1756–1836), who married Mary Wollstonecraft, turned aside from his political writings, which set conservative tongues wagging, and set up a small publishing company which brought out a number of children's books, calling his collective presentations *The City Juvenile Library.* He wrote for his own part and under the name of Edward Baldwin *Fables, Ancient and Modern* (1805) and *The Pantheon, Ancient History for Schools and Young People* (1806). His second wife took what was probably more than nominal charge of the company and, what was their most important venture, besides the early publication of the *Swiss Family Robinson,* brought out that small group of books written for children by Charles (1775–1834) and Mary Lamb (1764–1847).

[1] Lady Eleanor Fenn, *Fables in Monosyllables* (Philadelphia, Thomas Dobson, 1798), pp. 6, 7.
[2] *Ibid.*, pp. 18, 19.

These two had been cheerfully unaffected as to juvenile writing by the prevailing trend toward moralistic teaching. They had in mind something quite different. In that curious life which they led together, surrounded by devoted literary friends but cut off from so much by Mary's looming tragedy of recurrent mental illness, their great solace was reading and sharing with each other their keen enjoyment of great literature. It was their idea that children could be helped to appreciate those larger beauties which, so far, adult choice had made no effort to put before them. The Godwins printed their work, but evidently with no complete sympathy for this special kind of undertaking. Charles Lamb, who said briefly as a description of himself, "A small eater but not drinker," had an equally terse and apt phrase for William Godwin, "A middle sized man, both in stature and understanding." For the second Mrs. Godwin he had unconcealed dislike, since her taste and his ran in strong counter currents.

The Lambs' first important published work was, actually, in this phase of writing for children, and the *Tales from Shakespeare* was their primary venture, published in 1806.[1] Mary paraphrased the comedies and Charles the tragedies. The project itself was a difficult one and left little chance for much of their own character and style to be represented. But it is remarkable how well they have avoided pure summary of the immortal William's intricate and sometimes incredible plots. They capture the spirit and essence of each play, and they give one so strong a sense of the central character and his or her vital problem, that even a young mind can get an immediate unity of impression to carry away with him until the high moment when he reads and then sees the play in its own form. There is a discernment and economy in the retelling that only real creative power could have achieved. It was a unique effort in the direction of opening to children that world of pure literary delight which so far they had only been able to enter occasionally through their own determined exploration.

There followed in 1808 the *Adventures of Ulysses* by Charles Lamb alone. Practically speaking, it was the first time since the translation of Plutarch into English that anyone had introduced a great figure of classical literature in a form remotely within the reach of children. Charles used Chapman's translation of the *Odyssey* with a free hand, and in his own prose was able to convey a fine sense of the glory of the original story. Neither of the two books made very great headway against the general idea that what children read must be openly and avowedly for the purpose of instructing them. Mrs. Godwin was insistent as to what was the really proper kind of publication, though she realized the Lambs' gifts and would not relinquish them. *Poetry for*

---

[1] Darton in *Children's Books in England*, p. 198, speaks of the *Tales* as "2 vols., 1806 but dated 1807." On page 165 he observes, concerning children's books of this period, "The dates, where given, are apt to be confusing."

Children was published in 1809, of which Charles said defiantly that it was "written to order by an old bachelor and an old maid." It will be discussed elsewhere in considering the whole body of early verse for children. In the same year appeared *Mrs. Leicester's School*, mostly the work of Mary, although Charles's hand is in three of the sections. It succumbs to Mrs. Godwin, and moreover quite openly follows the pattern of *The Little Female Academy*, giving the life history of each pupil just as Sarah Fielding did. But there is great difference, for here is real imaginative power, here is the capacity to look back upon childhood and reclaim some of its fine memories. One can recognize the recollections of young Charles's and Mary's visits to their grandmother in a world of fields and sunshine, seen through children's eyes, with, alongside the pleasure in country freedom, a faint homesickness for London streets. The charm of that style which was to mark Charles Lamb's later work of real genius is apparent here, although nearly submerged in the essential pattern and purpose set up by the earlier *Governess*. Evidently the argument over this production was too bitter to be endured, for soon after this Charles escaped into the larger greatness of *Elia*, and exacting children's publishers had seen the last of him.

Charles Lamb, as has been noted earlier, lamented bitterly that Mrs. Barbauld and her like had driven away the simple stories of childlike fancy, the old wives' tales and even the early Newbery reprints of *Gulliver* and *Crusoe* and the once-beloved *Goody Two-Shoes*. In spite of his setting up the standard of revolt, the strong forces of the Age of Admonition were too much for him. But it is pleasant to note that *Tales from Shakespeare* is still a classic which children's libraries cannot do without and Mrs. Leicester has gone the way of Mrs. Teachum. Actually this children's book of the Lambs is the only one of all this period which has really survived, to be a part of the literature that is used and enjoyed today.

A Dog, a Mouse and a Pincushion

There are other writers of this time who leave a gently pleasant memory and whose merit is that they did not err too greatly because they did not undertake too much. Edward Augustus Kendall (1776?–1842), with *Keeper's Travels in Search of His Master* (1798), gives a chronicle of simple events illustrative of the sterling qualities of a faithful dog. Mary Jane Kilner (1753–?) and her sister Dorothy (1755–1836) wrote for children in the decade of 1780 to 1790. The publisher Marshall advertised their wares as offering, "a different style from the Generality of Works designed for young People, being divested of that prejudicial Nonsense (to young Minds) the Tales of Hobgoblins, Witches, Fairies, Love, Gallantry, etc. with which such little Performances heretofore abounded."[1] Dorothy Kilner became a friend of Mrs. Trimmer and evidently was inspired by the *History of the Robins* to undertake her *Life and Perambulations of a Mouse* (between 1780 and 1790). There is a gay note in the tone of the story, which is supposedly dictated by the Mouse himself. Nor, on introducing himself, does he apologize and explain away his being able to talk. She wrote further, *Little Stories for Little Folk* and *History of a great many Little Boys and Girls of four and five Years of Age*. She signed her books M.P.

Her sister, Mary Jane, whose signature was S.S., wrote *Jemima Placid, or The Advantages of Good-Nature, exemplified in a Variety of Familiar Incidents*, a title which gives one good indication of what to expect, although the familiar incidents do indeed have the merit of being those natural ones of child's day-by-day life. Her *Memoirs of a Peg-Top* was widely read and it followed faithfully the pattern of the good child contrasted with the bad one. "Charlotte was a very fair-complexioned and pretty girl, but you cannot imagine how ugly her ill-humor made her appear."[2] The advantages of Good-Nature are still being pointed out to the extent that her sister, "browner, and pitted with small pox," was a more agreeable child to look at. The *Adventures of a Pincushion* (also between 1780 and 1790) was even more popular and has an appealing simplicity and approach. Two little girls fall out over the breaking of a toy tea set but make up again in the manufacture of a pincushion, so exceptional a pincushion indeed, that it observes, on the printed page, "I will take the liberty to speak for myself and tell you what I saw and heard in the character of a Pincushion."[3]

This, of course, is too fanciful to pass without the usual apology, "it is to be understood as an imaginary tale in the same manner as when you are at play, you sometimes call yourselves gentlemen and ladies, though you know you are only little boys and girls."[4]

The Pincushion goes on a journey in Eliza's pocket as she sets off for boarding school, it is witness of her ill-judged behavior in eating Portuguese preserved plums, a crime which is confessed, although another girl, Betsey, tells a lie about going for a walk, whereupon, when she goes for the walk again a horse kicks her and she is crippled for life. "This instance may serve to convince you . . ."[5] The Pincushion is what drama scholars call a chorus character, who observes and comments but does not take much part in the action. Part I of the *Adventures* ends with the Pincushion's being rolled under a bookcase by a

[1] Darton, *Children's Books in England*, p. 164.
[2] *Ibid.*, p. 167.
[3] Mary Jane Kilner, *Adventures of a Pincushion* (Worcester, Isaiah Thomas, 1788), p. 13.
[4] *Ibid.*, p. 13.
[5] *Ibid.*, p. 49.

kitten; Part II goes on to slightly more subtle situations, all of which "serve to convince you . . ." as before.

Lady Eleanor Fenn's books, discussed earlier, were also published by Marshall and come well within the charmed circle which is guaranteed free from Hobgoblins and other prejudicial Nonsense. The Dialogues in her *Fables* always begin with the stage setting, *Parlour. Children employed.* It is a favorite scene with all the writers of this time; the children being so safe there and so open to the good counsel of their elders.

The Inescapable Rousseau

The years which we have been discussing saw the end of the eighteenth century with its wit, its lace ruffles and small-swords, its history-shaking revolutions. They pass into the beginning of the nineteenth, where all the results of these drastic political upheavals are still to be explored. Even in the first decade or two there is already to be observed a subtle change in writing for children. This is not always an alteration for the better, but it gives promise for a best that is still to come. The outward pattern remains the same; there is still the important lesson, either intellectual or spiritual, to be laid down in unsparing distinctness, the lesson which is taken as the invariable excuse for writing at all. Indeed, as we go forward, the pattern seems more inflexible than ever, although beneath it there is an advance of naturalness, of understanding of children, of good taste in what is to be offered them. The mind responsible for much of this, both for better and for worse, is without question that of Jean Jacques Rousseau.

Mrs. Barbauld, whose husband was of French connections, took note of Rousseau early and owed to him some of the excellence of her teaching. Mrs. Trimmer, guardian of morals, regarded him with aversion, Hannah More with shuddering horror. Mary Wollstonecraft quite evidently agreed with him. Lady Eleanor Fenn introduces her *Fables* with a quotation from him, to the effect that those impressions made upon a child's mind are written there for life "en caractères ineffaçables." In that no one could dispute him. The value and responsibility of that opportunity were becoming more and more clear and of a wider illumination.

The Reign of Terror in France went by and the wave of atheism diminished, after so greatly alarming God-fearing Britons as being more contagious even than radical democracy. England saw plainly that the French were still a great people and were rising from the ruins of the ancient and inequable society which they had overthrown. Not even the threatening person of Napoleon could dispel the knowledge of that greatness. A new and more liberal kind of thinking began insensibly to affect even those who thought they were standing fast in their original firmness. Besides these elders, there had grown up a fresh generation of English working people who had come into a new literacy which had been denied their parents. This was thanks, in great part, to the devoted labor of some of those writers of the time whose blind conservatism and conventionalism we are tempted to condemn. Moreover, a whole generation had passed since the publication of Rousseau's *Émile* in 1762. Rousseau's ideas, some of extraordinary vision, some of extreme impracticability, had begun to infiltrate the minds of almost all of those having interest in children's education and thus, inevitably, came to affect all those who had concern with children's literature. The results of his influence on individual persons, on their writing and on young people's literature as a whole were both curious and unexpected.

Bibliography

Lamb, Charles. *The Works of Charles Lamb*, edited by William Macdonald. 12 Vols. (*Mrs. Leicester's School*, Vol. 7, pp. 3–112). New York, E. P. Dutton, 1903–16.

Lucas, Edward V. *The Life of Charles Lamb*. 2 Vols. New York, G. P. Putnam's Sons, 1905.

Sherwood, Mary Martha (Butt), and Henry Sherwood. *The Life and Times of Mrs. Sherwood (1775–1851) from the Diaries of Captain and Mrs. Sherwood*. Edited by F. J. Harvey Darton. London, Wells Gardner, Darton, 1910.

9

Rousseau and His Companions

Rousseau (1712–1778) quarrels with Locke at almost every turn in his exposition of the ideal education of his French pupil, but in the end their ideas supplement each other. As has been said, Locke's *Some Thoughts Concerning Education* never made real those children whom he actually taught and who thus helped him to form his ideas; Rousseau, on the contrary, makes completely vivid with humanity those fictitious young persons, *Émile* (1762) and Sophie. He shows Émile as spirited, eager, unspoiled, and receptive, while Sophie, who is being brought up to make him a suitable wife, is docile without being vapid, gentle without diminution in strength of character. Strength is expected of the Gallic wife and Rousseau sees that Sophie has it. Best of all, the two children seem to be endowed with sufficient and natural common sense to resist some of the impossible experiments which Rousseau proposes to perform upon them. "Émile will not know what a telescope or a microscope is . . . before using these instruments, I intend that he shall invent them."[1]

Locke had said that children must not be forced but must be guided and invited into learning, with their natural curiosity of mind supplying sufficient motive force to carry them to full education. Rousseau went further and declared that they must not be led, but accompanied in that search for knowledge, with the wise preceptor and friend always at hand to supply information when they ask it, to make things clear at the critical moment when self-instruction tends to turn into confusion. The theory is the firm basis of even present educational theory, but it has had to be mitigated and compromised, for, as Rousseau proposed it, the plan had one great drawback—it called for a superman or woman to carry it out.

Not for a moment did Rousseau pretend that he was that superman. "The mildness of my disposition would have made me a very proper person to teach," he says of himself and his brief experience in actual

---

[1] Jean Jacques Rousseau, *Émile*, W. H. Payne, ed. (New York, D. Appleton, 1905), p. 188.

instruction of his patronesses' children, "had not fits of anger mingled their storms with my work. As long as all went well and I saw my plans and labors succeeding, I could not do too much. I was an angel, but when things went wrong I was a devil. When my pupils did not understand me, I raved, and when they showed signs of ugliness I could have killed them."[1] One wonders just what fortunate child it was that helped Jean Jacques discover these wholesome truths about himself; there can be no doubt that the young person or persons took full measure of him and made the most of their raving tutor as an interesting spectacle.

Like Locke, he did immense service by making a study of children's minds as different from those of their elders, and further he offered his ideas in a blaze of convincing enthusiasm which carried them much farther than could his predecessor. It is no part of this study to trace the effect of his theories upon education, great as they have been. We have enough with which to concern ourselves in examining their effect upon literature. Rousseau had pronounced only one book suitable for children—Locke, it may be remembered, had been able to find two. Rousseau's choice was *Robinson Crusoe*, which showed man reduced to a state of nature and gradually building up out of his own spirit and ingenuity a workable scheme of living and security. But *Robinson Crusoe* was a work of genius which could not be reproduced at will, no matter how many there were who had tried it.

As a result, those who fell, directly or indirectly, under the influence of the Jean Jacques method had to invent something different, since examples of genius were so few and far between. There began, perforce, to emerge a stock literary character, the parent or relative or friend or teacher who knew everything, who could answer all the questions—provided the right ones were asked—who was always at hand to make a profitable lesson out of everything, to render every experience educational and almost always dull. The blight which this established figure has laid upon the work of the early nineteenth century is immense and deplorable; his shadow falls over all the writing of the latter portion of the Age of Admonition. His discourses run to paragraph after paragraph where one chosen sentence would have been enough for both the children in the story and the children who read it to have done with him.

Complications of the Simple Life

One sees this literary convention beginning to invade the well-meant efforts of Mrs. Trimmer and even of Hannah More, little as she suspected the origin of it. But the everlastingly wise person, the inevitable expounder of all pertinent facts, comes highly into his own in a

---

[1] Rousseau, *op. cit.*, p. 18.

slightly later age, first in his perfection in the work of Thomas Day (1784–1789). The blight lies not only on *The History of Sandford and Merton* (1783, 1786, 1789), but reaches out to a far better writer and lays a withering hand upon the gaiety and the sympathetic imagination of Maria Edgeworth.

It was one of the essentials of Rousseau's belief, recognizable in the ideas of many others who followed him, that life must be simple and unadorned, free from the luxuries of elaborate costume or complicated food, from the sophisticated pleasures of a too highly organized social life. In this matter primarily, as well as in others, he had the loyal adherence of those two incongruous friends, Richard Edgeworth and Thomas Day. Edgeworth's dedication was later tempered with experience and he found himself unable to support the unquestioned whole of the Rousseau theory. But with Day, loyalty was complete, so that he went through the whole of his adult years in unswerving devotion to his friend, to Rousseau's beliefs and to his scheme of life, most particularly to the last. To live according to his beliefs was so important to Day that all things must be subordinated to it—household, place of living, and marriage. He was a man of sound fortune and presentable intellect, although ladies did not find prepossessing his deliberate indifference to dress, to manners, and to the cutting of his hair. He offered himself to Edgeworth's sister, with careful specifications as to the kind of life they were to lead together, and was courteously refused. He offered himself to Honora Sneyd, the much admired friend of the Swan of Lichfield (the specifications had by now become a thick written thesis, which Day sent to the lady by the hand of his friend Edgeworth) and was again refused. When he passed his affections on to her sister, Elizabeth Sneyd, he did consent to make some effort to civilize his manners and appearance, but even after his manful struggles under French dancing and fencing masters the lady unappreciatively declared that she had liked him better in his more natural state. Certainly she could not marry him. Richard Edgeworth had become a widower, his first wife, mother of Maria, having died. He, instead of Day, captured the affections of the beautiful Honora, and on her death history repeated itself and Edgeworth married Elizabeth. After Day's well-known and disappointing experiment of bringing up two foundling girls as candidates for the position of Mrs. Day, a friend discovered the right person for him in Miss Milnes of Yorkshire and the years of search were over.

During the interval of seeking French polish, Day had been accompanied by Edgeworth to France, where they visited Rousseau; Richard Edgeworth had brought his son, young Dick, who was being educated strictly by the Rousseau method. The boy was taken to see the philosopher, who invited him for a walk and looked into the results of the training. He reported to the anxiously waiting father that Dick had distinct and untrammeled abilities but that he was full of pride and national prejudice. It may be that it was at this moment that Edgeworth's hitherto unwavering faith in the Rousseau system began to falter.

Day's life in the country was happy. He deliberately set himself to copying the rural existence of Cincinnatus. He and his wife visited the Edgeworths in Ireland and there saw Richard and Honora Edgeworth beginning a collection of stories, *Harry and Lucy* (published 1801), something of the nature of Mrs. Barbauld's *Lessons* which had been a model for so many other authors. Day set out to write a story of his own to add to theirs and thus embarked on *Sandford and Merton.*

From a man who pursued with such undeviating devotion every idea which had enlisted his sympathy, *Sandford and Merton* is exactly the book which one would expect. Tommy Merton, son of a rich Jamaica planter now retired, is an overindulged, delicate, and ill-mannered little boy. He is saved from the bite of a snake by the rugged Henry Sandford, who so arouses the respect of Tommy's father that the two boys are placed together under the tutelage of the worthy Mr. Barlow, a clergyman of the neighborhood. This gentleman seems to have had few duties in connection with his church, so fully does he give himself over to the boys. He is, as is to be expected, a fountain of useful information, which gushes from him at the slightest touch of incident or question. He is a storyteller, also, but with so little sense of continuity that his narratives are difficult to follow. Tommy Merton's reclamation is not accomplished without a struggle, but of course all is thoroughly well before the end.

Harry Sandford is, of course, as close to being Émile as an English background and a somewhat clumsy English hand can compass. There is introduced a rather extraneous character in the person of a young lady visiting at the Mertons, Sukey Simmons, who is like Sophie even to the possibility of possessing some of her charm. But Day, as an author, has an unfortunate characteristic: any person in whom he is really interested he immediately renders odious by pompous dialogue and unnaturally aggressive virtue. "If little Harry, while eating his dinner, saw a poor wretch who wanted food, he was sure to give him half, sometimes the whole . . . He would often go supperless to bed, that he might feed the robin redbreasts."[1] When he, who is six years old, is asked to dine at Squire Merton's house, he observes to his host, after having remonstrated with him on the too-great delicacy of the dinner, "Therefore it is not fit that we mind what we live upon, but we should take what we can and be contented, just as the beasts and birds do, who lodge in the open air and live upon herbs and drink nothing but water and

[1] Thomas Day, *The History of Sandford and Merton* (Boston, Lee and Shepard, 1875), pp. 3, 4.

yet they are strong and active and healthy."[1] Rousseau, so Day surely thought, would be pleased with that speech.

Besides its pompous style, the structure of the book is appalling; direct narrative is interrupted for the telling of long stories, mostly derived from classical legends, which must be related in sections and sometimes are even interrupted by other stories, also in sections, which must be completed before the dismembered portions of the first ones can be brought together.

With all this it is difficult to account for the popularity and authority of the book, for the editor of a new edition a hundred years later feels justified in saying that it "has charmed, instructed and ennobled the young hearts and minds of more than half a century with a constantly increasing celebrity." One must remember that it appeared in its three sections at a time when it had few rivals. There had been short stories by Mrs. Barbauld and others, but a full-sized narrative for children, practically a juvenile novel in three volumes, was something they had never had before. It is full of action, in spite of being so weighted down with moralizing. And there is some invisible force that wholehearted and unfailing sincerity bestows that does not wholly go to waste, even in the midst of egregious blundering.

Day's only other writing for children is the very brief *History of Little Jack*, published in 1788. It tells of a foundling boy, adopted by a soldier, suckled by a goat, and thus growing to hardihood in the most natural manner. The Edgeworths pronounced the goat ridiculous, but Day would not give it up. Jack, on his benefactor's death, becomes a worker in a smelter, a servant, a marine, a Robinson Crusoe on one of the Comoro Islands, a traveler to India, and a friend of wild Tartars. This appeared as part of the *Children's Miscellany*, a series of stories whose publication was backed by "some gentlemen of fortune who deplored the lack of good reading matter for children." Day carried the plan forward alone for a time but abandoned it before the series grew to any length. But *Sandford and Merton* established itself as the model book for the young and was thus to have a stubborn influence on the richer and more promising work which came immediately after.

Philosopher and Friend

Richard Edgeworth had definitely modified his allegiance to Rousseau by the time his daughter Maria (1767–1849) reached her formative years, but the stamp of his early thinking and of Day's was not to be eradicated from her impressionable mind and her work. With all her literary gifts, combined with her great practical sense and administrative ability, Maria, through love, sense of duty, and early formation of

[1] Day, *op. cit.*, p. 8.

taste, was wholly receptive to that scheme of thinking which so commanded these two men's minds. Second child of Edgeworth's teeming twenty-two, of whom most lived to grow up, she was always a special figure in the remarkable Edgeworth household. Richard Edgeworth fell in love easily and often, and was most properly happy with each one of his four wives, except in the last years of the first one. But Maria was something apart, her father's other self. One gets the impression that in the midst of that thronging Irish household these two alone really understood each other.

Maria was born at her grandfather's house near Oxford and spent the first thirteen years of her life in England, only returning to Ireland for anything like permanent living after she had passed some time in a boarding school at Derby and in another in London. Her holidays were often spent with the Days, where Thomas, for her father's sake and her own, watched over her with the most affectionate care. He strongly disapproved of feminine authors, nor did the Edgeworths, father and daughter, publish any of their collaborations during his lifetime. She was twenty-two when he died, but there had been great opportunity to share what he thought, what he wanted, and what he hoped for concerning education and literature for children.

Richard Edgeworth took charge of his children's education himself; he and Maria collected endless data on their observations of what methods worked best on the pupils so ready to their hands. Maria's early stories were written out on a slate, corrected and read to the young family audience, and only copied and preserved if they seemed to meet approval. In 1796, when she was twenty-nine, the first book of her stories for children was published, *The Parent's Assistant*, a sort of companion piece for *Practical Education* (1798), a book of essays which she and her father had written together.

Although Richard Edgeworth took no part in composing Maria's actual stories, he had no hesitation in applying his criticism and corrections on any of them, whether for adult or young readers. While she was away on a series of visits in 1805, "Your critic, partner, father, friend has finished your *Leonora*,"[1] he writes her blithely. He specifies that he has "cut out a few pages, one or two letters are nearly untouched, the rest are cut, scrawled, and interlined without mercy." It seems clear that he felt he had a completely free hand on his own part. Maria makes no demur, and after her father's death, when she has got through the long task of finishing his memoirs—how one wishes that she had written her own instead—she continually laments the loss of his advice. She wrote very little through her remaining years. *The Parent's Assistant* was followed by her very successful novel *Castle Rackrent*

[1] Grace Oliver, *A Study of Maria Edgeworth* (Boston, A. Williams & Co., 1882), p. 211.

(1800) after which came *Moral Tales* (1801) and *Popular Tales* (1803). Short stories for children were produced from time to time as the years passed, and were generally embodied in new editions of *The Parent's Assistant* and *Popular Tales*. The specially famous story of "Rosamond and the Purple Jar" had appeared in the first *Parent's Assistant*, but a Rosamond Series finally took form in 1813, when a number of tales continuing the Barbauld and Edgeworth plans for *Early Lessons* appeared. In them we find *Frank* and a continuation of *Harry and Lucy*.

Although the big, crowded, rather dilapidated house and estate in Ireland, Edgeworthstown in the county of Longford, was surrounded at different periods with the famines, the unrest, and the political violence which marked Irish history during the end of the eighteenth and the beginning of the nineteenth century, such turbulence seemed only at separated moments to come very close to Maria's own life. She was the mainstay of the household, she was continuously happy with her successive stepmothers, the last one considerably younger than herself; she visited friends in the neighborhood, friends in England, made excursions to conventional resorts on the Continent. Her *Castle Rackrent* brought her immediate acclaim as a novelist, and as her novels progressed she rose steadily to stand higher and higher in the regard of English, Irish, and Scottish readers. Probably the very highest tribute that ever reached her was Walter Scott's. He said that it was the example of her Irish novels and her keen observation and interpretation of Irish life that prompted him to turn from romantic poetry and try to succeed with the Scottish countryside and character as she had done with the Irish. She died at Edgeworthstown at the age of eighty-three.

Harry and Lucy, the undertaking begun by Richard Edgeworth and Honora Sneyd Edgeworth in the manner of Mrs. Barbauld and later finished by Maria, bears perhaps the strongest evidence of her father's limiting influence. Frank and Robert in "Little Dog Trusty," part of the Harry and Lucy Series, are respectively truthful and lying boys with a whipping for Robert, and Trusty given as a reward to Frank. "The Orange Man, or the Honest Boy and the Thief" is another of the same series and pattern; Charles fights Ned to protect the man's oranges, which have been entrusted to him, while a moral-minded horse kicks Ned as retribution. Harry and Lucy themselves are taken for walks, not to take the air, but to take instruction; they learn about ships and hammocks and the skimming of milk, as Sandford and Merton take a survey of their own cabbages and kings under the lectureship of Mr. Barlow. Harry has been away, living with an uncle, and is newly come home to be introduced to the family educational method: He is shown a man making bricks by hand and piling them up in a wall to dry. He inadvertently knocks over the wall and the laborer in great indignation says that half his day's work is ruined and that Harry must pay for them. Harry, taking refuge in an appeal to his father, is told by that worthy gentleman, "I did not spoil them, therefore it is not necessary that I should pay for them." What a cheerful homecoming, what a sense of refuge and security his father's method offers! Harry is taken further to see a horse shod, but it is doubtful whether he gets much out of it. Lucy, more cautious and adroit, fares much better in the matter of discovering the secrets of horn spoons and tortoiseshell combs.

The Harry-and-Lucy paterfamilias—and he may be Mr. Edgeworth himself—has his counterpart in Rosamond's mother. Poor Rosamond, carried away by the color and form of the purple jar in the "chymist's" window, infinitely prefers it to a new pair of shoes—what child would not?—and is allowed to buy it. When she finds that the jar is full of bad-smelling liquid she asks for a bowl into which to pour it, to which request her mother replies, "That was more than I promised you, my dear, but I will lend you a bowl." It is then revealed that it was the liquid which was purple and the jar of clear glass was nothing. Not only is Rosamond's love of beauty the essence of a natural child, but so is her final conclusion, "I am sure—no, not quite sure, but I hope I will be wiser another time."

Far more developed as to form, material, and substance are some of Maria's later stories, although none of them escape the exposition of wisdom spoken by a character or by the author. Rousseau's idea of instruction by association had given rise to this convention of a person always ready to give forth important words. Rousseau's intention was that such a being was to be the vehicle of educational instruction, the English variant made use of him even more for moral edification, nor does he fail to play his part in the hands of Maria.

But her tales, unlike those by any earlier hand, are the work of a skilled novelist who was also adept at suiting her tone and narrative to the qualities of the young. The stories have suspense, dramatic sequence, and a fine unity of their own. There recur the themes of industry, thrift, stalwart honesty, and contentedness with small means; the contrast of good and bad persons is still the backbone of the composition. Yet there is a growing reality of character, so much so that in "Waste Not Want Not," for instance, the portraits are so true to life that Maria cannot keep us from liking the heedless Hal far better than the solid Ben, though such was not her intention and though Mr. Gresham is always at hand to make the issues clear. Lady Diana Sweepstakes alone would save the story from mediocrity. "Simple Susan" is touched with the picturesque charm of English cottage life, and the glimpse of children dancing on the green which has been assured them for a playground is not easily forgotten.

One does resent the abundance of patronage, which is always the way by which the unfortunate rise from their mean surroundings; one shivers at the question, "What is a fair good day's work for a [small] boy of his age, come at six and go at six?" and on hearing of a family of orphans as being evicted from their cottage and suffered to go to live in the open ruins of an abandoned castle, while the youngest girls, six and seven years old, are so fortunate as to have opportunity to cut and sort rags at twopence a day in a nearby paper mill. To these social outrages, Maria Edgeworth was blind, even as were all of her contemporaries with a few crusading exceptions.

She has, also, a custom of giving the moral maxims in her own person, rather than always putting them into the mouth of a character in the story. "Those who never attempt to appear what they are not," she observes, "those who do not in their manners pretend to anything unsuited to their habits and situation in life, never are in danger of being laughed at by sensible, well-bred people of any rank; but affectation is the constant and just object of ridicule";[1] etc. and again etc. None the less, we see in Maria Edgeworth the measure of a true artist, delighting to show scene and character, not setting out with the single purpose of teaching a truth and looking with secondary interest for the material with which to clothe it. In spite of Richard Edgeworth, in spite of Thomas Day, in spite even of Jean Jacques Rousseau, Maria was too great a writer to suffer herself to be led completely astray.

When Knights Were Bold

Walter Scott's (1771–1832) tribute to Maria Edgeworth, makes an interesting beginning to the entry on the juvenile scene of Sir Walter himself. As early as 1816, three years after the appearance of *Waverley* he was already at work on a history of Scotland, always thinking of it in terms of being for young readers, chiefly for his grandson, little Johnny Lockhart. *Tales of a Grandfather* (1828–1830) was long a cherished project with him; in 1816 he spoke of having been some time at work upon it and revising it with great care. The work was a delight to him.

"This morning was damp, dripping and unpleasant," he wrote in his diary of October 8th, 1827, "so I even made a work of necessity and set to the Tales like a dragon. I murdered Macllen of Bomby at the Thrieve Castle; stabbed the Black Douglas in the town of Stirling; astonished King James before Roxburgh; and stifled the Earl of Mar in his bath in the Cannongate. A wild world, my masters, this Scotland of ours must have been."[2] In spite of his enthusiasm, the book was not to see the light of day for some time to come.

---

[1] Maria Edgeworth, *The Parent's Assistant* (Philadelphia, Ashmead and Evans, 1865), p. 151.
[2] John Gibson Lockhart, *Memoirs of the Life of Sir Walter Scott* (Boston, Houghton Mifflin, 1902), Vol. V, p. 125.

In the end, Scott was one of those writers whom children sought out on their own initiative, even though it was his intention to go to meet them. In the long period between the beginning and the ending of the undertaking, Scott the historian got the better of Scott the storyteller and *Tales of a Grandfather* shows only a gleam, here and there, of the beauty and romance which it was his great gift to portray. Children with a deep interest in history—and there are many such—can enjoy it for its clarity and comprehensiveness. But the usual young reader will turn instead to the pure romance, which he gave in such abundance to a waiting world.

Out of the long list of the Waverly Novels, those which have the power of appealing to young readers and have been crowned with their commendation are *Rob Roy* (1817), *Ivanhoe* (1819), *The Talisman* (1825), and possibly *Quentin Durward* (1823). Barrie, in *Sentimental Tommy*, has given us a convincing picture, even though it is of fictitious children who are captured by the spell of *Rob Roy*. Mark Twain, in the person of Tom Sawyer, who, as no one can doubt, represents himself, has told how the reading of romance could fill the barrenness of a lonely and uneducated little boy's life. In Scott's great stories, the remote and the real have reached just the balance that young readers love, and in these special books there is no great complication of plot or subtlety of character too difficult for young minds to follow. In his novels, literature for the young has been endowed with the great gift of romance; not since the Middle Ages had it been thus made available to them. It was a beginning from which has stemmed so much, which has led to the gathering of such great treasure that its worth is hardly to be computed. The adult romanticist and the young one have much in common. With these books of Scott's they meet on middle ground. Young readers had waited long for such riches to be put into their hands; they would wait a little longer before romance could be completely their own.

A chance remark of Scott's led to another flare of revolt against the moralizing story. Catherine Sinclair (1800–1864), born with the century, a writer of minor novels, set out to champion the cause of the too restrained child. Scott, she declared in her preface to *Holiday House* (1839), said to her that "in the rising generation there would be no poets, wits or orators, because all the play of the imagination is now carefully discouraged." The author announces her intention of painting "That species of noisy, frolicsome children, which is now almost extinct." This she proceeds to do and presents us with Harry and Laura, who set themselves riotously free of conventional restraints, who triumph over the tyrannical nature of their nurse, Mrs. Crabtree, and, at least in the short span of this set of stories, live their own lives as they choose. The book has much life, very little unity, and—alas—very little real probability, although it contains very real children. Catherine Sinclair's attempt was but a flash in the pan, yet it was to be followed before too long by other and more sustained efforts.

Bibliography

Buchan, John. *Sir Walter Scott.* London, Cassell, 1932.

Edgeworth, Richard Lovell. *Memoirs of. Richard Lovell Edgeworth, Esq., Begun by Himself and Concluded by His Daughter, Maria Edgeworth.* 2 Vols. London, R. Hunter, 1820.

Gignilliat, George Warren. *The Author of* Sandford and Merton; *a Life of Thomas Day.* New York, Columbia University Press, 1932.

Grierson, Sir Herbert J. C. *Sir Walter Scott, Bart.* London, Constable & Co., 1938.

Hopkins, Mary Alden. *Dr. Johnson's Lichfield.* New York, Hastings House, 1952.

Lockhart, John Gibson. *Memoirs of the Life of Sir Walter Scott.* 5 Vols. Boston, Houghton Mifflin, 1902.

Oliver, Grace A. *A Study of Maria Edgeworth.* Boston, A. Williams, 1882.

Rousseau, Jean Jacques. *Rousseau's* Émile; *or, Treatise on Education*; abridged, translated and annotated by William H. Payne. New York, D. Appleton, 1893.

10

Distinguished Foreigners

While the progress of children's literature had gone forward in its own steady growth, there had been occasional and signal contributions from other countries. On the whole, literature for the young had made greater and freer early advance among the English-speaking people than among other nations, and had offered more contributions than it had received. But those books and stories which have presented themselves from afar and won their own place as an integral part of the body of present-day children's inheritance are not to be passed by. They begin very far in the past.

It might be said that in this class fall *Reynard the Fox* and *Æsop's Fables*, but since they were already present at the very founding of English literature, one accepts them as our own from the beginning. A group of stories which almost qualify for the same position, but which, none the less, have remained somewhat apart is the *Gesta Romanorum*, little known now, but surviving here and there on dusty shelves, where children still peep into them with inquisitive half-comprehension, just as their great-great-grandparents did.

Time's Grandmother

People who have been to Hollywood talk of seeing, in various waste and vacant spaces, a vast collection of old sets of scenes—palaces, streets, jungles, and luxurious interiors, all recognizable as the backgrounds of old and favorite movies. When one opens the *Gesta Romanorum*, it is something like straying into a similar lumber room of the literary past; one sees here so many beginnings and the basic situations of books and stories and dramas of a later world. Scholars say that there is no direct evidence that Shakespeare ever read the *Gesta* itself as he so obviously read Plutarch. But here we find the legend of the father and daughter on which the situation of *King Lear* is founded, here are the stories of the three caskets and of the bond which appear in the *Merchant of Venice*, here are the detailed plots of *Pericles* and the *Rape of Lucrece*.

Shakespeare was not the earliest to have even indirect access to its contents; Chaucer and Lydgate in England and Boccaccio in Italy had all partaken of the same source.

The book came from Europe into the monasteries of England written in Latin and was supposedly a collection of tales which monks could use "in their discourses from the pulpit," as its subtitle avers, although that is not the place where we generally think of monks as being. It existed in manuscript long before being printed; a version of 1326 shows signs of successions of copying. Once it had been supposed to be an account, in story form, of the important events in the history of the Roman Empire, but it had acquired so many additions that, in the end, it was simply a book of tales of entertainment still, however, keeping its original solemn title. A separate group of stories especially appealing to British taste was finally circulated by itself, translated into English and published some time between 1510 and 1515 by Wynkyn de Worde, Caxton's successor.

Practically all of the stories, even those which are plainly of Oriental or Mohammedan origin, call the central figure "the Emperor." All were provided with an "Application," an allegorical interpretation, sometimes very loosely attached indeed, but serving to preserve the character of the work as a book for holy men. In one tale, for instance, a poor Roman clerk descends into a subterranean palace full of treasures, with people who had been sitting and feasting at a table, but now are turned to stone. Light comes from a great carbuncle, at which a stone archer is pointing a stone arrow. The clerk takes up a cup from the table to carry it away, the archer looses his arrow, shatters the carbuncle and extinguishes the light and the clerk perishes. This is one of the few which contrive to dispense with an emperor. The Application declares that the statue which indicates the steps leading down to the palace is the devil, the steps themselves are the passions, the carbuncle is life, the archer death, the cup represents worldly possessions.

Due to their ancient origin, the frankly sexual nature of the stories makes them unfit reading for children in general. They are so directly told as to be almost without detail, the bare bones only of situation and event. Their real interest is in their being so quaint and so extensive a storage house of beginnings. The tale of *Guy of Warwick* is there, although here he is called Guido. What is most interesting to our present study is the fact that a very definite number of Howard Pyle's stories, particularly those in *Twilight Land*, come obviously from this repository. Pyle's acknowledgment in the Introduction to the *Wonder Clock* is quite adequate. He visited Time's House, he said and "found all manner of queer forgotten things laid away and nobody but Time and his grandmother knew where they were."

"The Mouse Chirpeth I . . I . . ."

Just as fully as the *Gesta Romanorum* represents that literature of the Middle Ages which was fostered "in the deep silence of the cloister," so does the *Orbis Pictus* stand for the widening curiosity of the Renaissance. It was the work of the Moravian Bishop, John Amos Comenius, (1592–1671) who, as an orphan boy in what is now Czechoslovakia, struggled for an education and, on growing up, set himself to studying and advancing better methods of teaching the young. "Boyhood is distracted for years with precepts of grammar, infinitely prolix, perplexed and obscure," he declared. "Boys are stuffed with vocabularies without associating words with things or indeed with one another."[1] He became a teacher and a writer; he was driven from place to place by the depredations of the Thirty Years' War and the persecutions of his time; he wrote in the Czech tongue his profound work on educational philosophy, *Didactica Magna*. Fortunately he did not stop at that. In 1657 he brought out the work whose all-embracing title is *Orbis Pictus, the world of Sensible Things drawn; that is the Nomenclature of all Fundamental Things in the World and Actions in Life reduced to Ocular Demonstration*.

It has been called the first picture book for children. So important did Comenius think was the office of illustrations that he carried the manuscript to Nuremberg himself to make sure of a proper artist. The original copper plates wore out with constant use in time, and the book reappeared with clumsier woodcuts. He made sure that children should have a graphic view of every one of the things in Heaven and Earth which he included in his *World Illustrated*. The translation of the non-Latin portion into English was done by Charles Hoole and followed soon after. It was steadily reprinted in England; it was, indeed, called the most popular schoolbook in Europe for the whole of a century.

In form it is a combination of picture book, Latin text, and natural history. There are two columns of reading matter, one in Latin, opening with a dialogue between Magister and Puer, with the corresponding English opposite. "Invitation: *Invitatio. Master.* Come, boy, learn to be wise: *Veni, Puer, disce sapere.* Boy. What doth this mean, to be wise? *Quid hoc est, sapere? Master.* To understand rightly. Boy. See, here I am, lead me in the name of God."[2]

As in most schoolbooks of its kind, we have an alphabet, a long list of essential members of the animal and vegetable kingdoms, with their appropriate pictures and their equally appropriate sounds. "*Cornix cornicatur*: The crow crieth, a . . a. *Ventus fiat*: The wind bloweth, fi . . fi . . .

[1] S. S. Laurie, *Comenius* (Syracuse, N.Y., J. W. Bardeen, 1892), p. 22.
[2] John Amos Comenius, *The Orbis Pictus* (Syracuse, N.Y., J. W. Bardeen, 1887), p. 1.

The Horsefly saith ds . . ds . . . The Mouse chirpeth, i . . i . . ."[1] "The Globe of the Heaven is turned about upon an Axle tree, about the globe of the Earth in the space of XXIV hours,"[2] he explains lucidly. He tells us of the Terrestrial Sphere and its Continents, including "America whose inhabitants are Antipodes to us, and the South Land yet unknown."[3] He leaves very little unmentioned and unexplained. "A wind underground causeth an Earthquake."[4]

He wrote other books, war and persecution still pursuing him. He died at seventy-nine; in his last writing he thanked God that "he had been a man of aspiration." Those aspirations of a very great man had been as broad as the Renaissance itself, voiced by Master to Boy, "I will show you everything, I will name all things to you. *Ostendam tibi omnis, Nominabo tibi omnia.*"

"*Histoires ou Contes du Temps Passé. Avec des Moralitez.*"

A foreign visitor of a very different nature who came to stay forever in English hearts was our good friend Cinderella with her companions, the Sleeping Beauty, Puss in Boots, and Little Red Riding Hood. The author of their stories was Monsieur Charles Perrault (1628–1703), scholar, member of the French Academy and assistant superintendent of public works under Louis XIV's great minister, Colbert. One of Perrault's last official acts was to make sure that the gardens of the Tuileries were kept open to the public and in particular for the children, although there had been a movement on foot to close them and reserve them for the use of royalty alone. "I am persuaded that the gardens of Kings are made so great and spacious that all their children may walk in them," he insisted.[5]

Children, by his means, have walked ever since his time in a far more beautiful garden of fancy, for the backdrop of his fairy tales is a combination of an old and beloved France, of courtly manners and costumes, and the sunshine of pure imagination. Some strange elements are joined in them, for they are based on folklore of a past, untutored age, yet their retelling reflects the odd fact that it had become the fashion at the court of Louis XIV to tell fairy tales, just as, at a slightly later date and with the kingdom itself falling about their ears, the ladies of court circles were playing at being milkmaids. In no way could the stories have achieved such extreme simplicity except by the streamlining of years of telling and retelling, which polishes all superfluities away. Perrault was

---

[1] Comenius, *op. cit.*, pp. 3, 4.
[2] *Ibid.*, p. 127.
[3] *Ibid.*, p. 134.
[4] *Ibid.*, p. 10.
[5] Andrew Lang, ed., *Perrault's Popular Tales* (Oxford, Clarendon Press, 1888), p. xii.

genius enough to preserve that simplicity and add to it those small, enchanting touches such as Cinderella's gold coach or the gleaming knives and forks set with rubies which graced the christening feast of that princess who was to be the Sleeping Beauty. The stories have, inherently, a Celtic sprightliness and a Gallic delicacy which have set them forever in a class of their own.

It has puzzled many commentators to see that the dedication and, by implication, the book itself are by P. Darmancour, who was Perrault's young son. There are certain turns of phrase and of thought that a young boy could not have compassed; the courtly flattery of the dedication itself is the voice of a mature and sophisticated person. One might think of the boy's share as something like that of Christopher Robin in *When We Were Very Young*, supplying the taste and impulse through which the father turned back to the fancies and interests of a child.[1]

One forgets how few the stories are, "The Sleeping Beauty," "Cinderella," "Red Riding Hood," "Blue Beard," "Diamonds and Toads," (called by Perrault "The Fairies"), "Ricket of the Tuft," "Puss-in-Boots," "Hop-o-My-Thumb." One forgets also how extremely brief and to the point they are, though lacking no essential detail. In "Cinderella" there is no mention of the magic gifts of the girl's dead mother as in so many other versions. The girl is weeping because she cannot go to the ball; her godmother, "who was a fairy," as the story tersely states, appears and sets immediately to work. Paul Hazard has pointed out that the French fancy is practical, that it does not accept a gold coach without a pumpkin upon which to build. In the same way the coachman is the rat with the longest whiskers, and the footmen, lizards with their glittering coats. All the rest is pure action. Cinderella's beauty is excuse enough for the Prince to love her, although we have already seen, in her patience and generosity in helping the sisters prepare for the ball, that she is of what Perrault calls, almost untranslatably, "la bonne grace." She sees to it that the sisters are married to two great persons of the court on the same day as her own wedding. We have most of us forgotten that "as good as she was beautiful," an expression long useful in our language, was Perrault's phrase for Cinderella.

"Little Red Riding Hood" is hardly more than a game, with a great pounce at the end and, probably, a squeak of delighted horror from the small listener. The German version, "Little Red Cap," from Grimm's later fairy tales, with its rescue by the huntsman, has come to be the accepted history, but this one did very well until Grimm arrived. "Blue

[1] *Ibid.*, p. xxvii. The title page of this first edition of 1697 is here reproduced as *Histoires ou Contes du Temps Passé Avec des Moralitéz*. No name of the author is given but on the ensuing page the *Dedication* is signed P. Darmancour. Lang says that this was "because it did not become an Academician to publish fairy tales." Public opinion, however, has never failed to attach Perrault's name to them in the English-speaking countries.

Beard" is a strange tale of blood, but it lives by that moment of immortal suspense, "Anne, Sister Anne, is no one coming?"

Perrault's *Histoires ou Contes du Temps Passé* was published in France in 1697; the date of its translation into English has not been determined, but it is certain that it came soon after. Perrault was enough of a man of his time to send the stories forth with "des moralitez," but very gentle and unaggressive morals they are, set in pleasant verse at the end of each tale, and not often included in the English versions. Mrs. Trimmer, who so harshly condemned "Cinderella," could scarcely have read them, nor Peter Parley, who was so shocked by Puss-in-Boots as being a monster of deceit. Cinderella's "bonne grace" is offered as her excuse for being. "Feminine beauty is a rare treasure," says Perrault's graceful verse at the end of the story, "but it is beauty of spirit which is without price." It is as though he had foreseen the literal-minded Mrs. Trimmer and her concern over step-filial behavior. With a little more of irony he adds to "Cinderella" "Autre Moralité" to the effect that no matter what gifts you have, you get nowhere without godparents.

Except for the garbled and often vulgar tales in the chapbooks, these tales of Perrault, published in England, were the first fairy stories written down and printed just for them that British children had for their very own. Here, for the first time, was assurance that the story would be given to them again and again with no change of word or syllable, a matter in which listening children are very particular. As has been said earlier, Perrault was the first to enlist the backing of that famous figure, Mother Goose. The title page of his *Histoires ou Contes du Temps Passé*, shows her, Ma Mère l'Oie, telling a story to children, symbol of the recounting of old nurses' tales to an attentive audience. John Newbery may have violated copyright when he transferred her to his collection of nursery rhymes, but there she seemed so infallibly to belong that there she has remained. We must thank Perrault for her, however, even though we have no clue to where, in his rare discernment, he, or little Darmancour, could have found her. She has lived on in her own right without aid from the Perraults.

A Cat and a Monster

Thackeray's daughter, Lady Anne Thackeray Ritchie, in an introduction to a translation of Madame d'Aulnoy's (circa 1650–1705) *Contes des Fées* says with great penetration that the ladies and gentlemen of the French court who added to the lists of fairy tales "did not, I imagine, pretend to create their fairies, but rather to conjure up the old ones with new dresses and decorations, just as our pantomimes do every Christmas." This is visibly true of Madame d'Aulnoy's stories, published in French as *Contes Nouvelles ou les Fées à la mode* (1698) and appearing in English as *D'Aulnoy's Fairy Tales*, about 1717.

"Finette Cendron" suggests "Red Riding Hood"; Cabriole, the little dog in "Fair Goldilocks," performs some of the offices of Puss-in-Boots. In all the stories we find a richness of costume and background which they could not have had through the ages of their folklore existence. In the most famous of them, *The White Cat*, there appears "a dressing gown of some material frosted with gold, embroidered with small emeralds to form monograms," while the Youngest Prince brings home a millet seed in which is a piece of linen four hundred ells long and so fine that it passed six times backward and forward through the eye of a small needle!

Madame Le Prince de Beaumont (1711–1780) founded the journal *Le Magasin des Enfans* in 1757, and in its numbers introduced "Beauty and the Beast," often translated in those early days, "The Beauty and the Monster." The fine tide of French fairy tales, to which England was so warmly open, reached its crest in the middle of the eighteenth century, but after that, gave way before the solid institution of the British Moral Story. But France, indirectly, was to make one more contribution to fantasy still.

The Wonderful Lamp

Not only out of the far past, but also out of the far distances, the *Thousand and One Nights Entertainments* came into England, arriving first through the translation into French from an Arabic manuscript of 1578 made by Antoine Galland, "antiquary to the King." He burdened it with the usual gigantic title which was the fashion of that day, *The Arabian Nights' Entertainments, Consisting of 1001 Stories told by the Sultaness of the Indies. . . .* The work was published in twelve successive volumes, from 1704 to 1717. The English version came soon after, with Volumes I to IV appearing in March 1706, Volumes V and VI in November of the same year. The other volumes followed in parallel to the appearance of the French ones. They were at once widely read, with certain stories easily sifted out which were particularly entertaining to children. "Aladdin" is perhaps the most famous with "Ali Baba," "Sindbad the Sailor," "The King of the Black Isles," and the tales of Haroun al Raschid—Aaron the Orthodox, as scholars tell us his name is to be translated—these with a few more make up what we ordinarily think of as a special collection, the *Arabian Nights' Entertainments*. The most romance lies in those concerning Haroun al Raschid, who ruled over the Mohammedan Empire when it was in its largest single state, with Bagdad its capital, "a city of delight" with her fabulous gardens, her fountains, her mysterious archways and green, hidden courts. Sindbad the Sailor's voyages were tales inspired by the adventures and new discoveries of the Arab mariners; Aladdin is firmly announced at the beginning to be a Chinese boy, but the whole scene and color of the story is Arabian. Scholars tell us that the ultimate origin of the tales is, for the most part, Persian, taken over by the Arabs and colored by devout Mohammedan belief. There are some additions that are Egyptian, some Turkish. The group cited above make a collection of their own; the rest—that enormous body of tales of travel, of mysticism, of magic, of sex, of violence—form a whole literature rather than a single set of stories. Æsop has been said to be not one man but several. Scheherazade was not one raconteuse, she was a multitude.

In many of the long-established families of England, in many castles ancient beyond the casual conception of Americans, there were still treasured souvenirs of the East which some remote ancestor had brought back from the Crusades, just as in the village church there was still to be seen the ancestor himself, an effigy with his legs crossed and a cross on his shield to signify that he, too, had sought the Holy Land. A taste for spices, for silks, for Damascus swords, for luxuries formerly unknown in austere England came back to Britain with those returning warriors and their servng men, and with them came also stories. Such legends had been told sparingly as something apart, as belonging to the remote and heathen East. But they were a note that rang again when the new theme sounded in English literature with the coming of the *Arabian Nights*.

Professional storytellers still ply their trade in the bazaars of the East, and still tell the same stories. A favorite theme, so Joseph Campbell points out, is the unheroic hero, the innocent, ordinary and sometimes stupid person, whom clever enchanters and great persons must employ to carry out their ends. Aladdin is one of them; he is, as the enchanter knows, the only person who can lay hands on the magic lamp. His princess, whom he wins by the virtue of the lamp, is as simple as he, for she trades away the magic talisman when the enchanter offers to exchange "New lamps for old." Ali Baba is of no great resource alone; his slave girl, Morgiana, supplies the wit in emergencies and makes an end of the Forty Thieves.

It may be that the wide popularity of these exotic tales, the mystic flavor of Mohammedanism, which strict English conformists termed flatly "infidel," contributed the last straw of provocation for the prejudice against things of fantasy and imagination which rose so ominously in the later eighteenth century. Certainly no further important contribution from France was accepted for the young reading public until, as the century advanced, the moral story was firmly entrenched on both sides of the Channel.

To "Invest Virtue with New Charms"

Two French contemporaries of Mrs. Trimmer and Mrs. Barbauld, sharing the strict views of those ladies and offering the same kind of stories, were Arnaud Berquin and Madame de Genlis. Their work, duly translated, was embraced by those who guided the reading of their young persons with conscientious attention. The little narratives, with their Gallic variation of greater emotion and more sophisticated scenes, offered variety even within the accepted pattern.

Arnaud Berquin (1747–1791) was a native of Bordeaux. His parents were worried over his early education, for he would write verses which, they thought, "would render him incapable of more serious and important studies."[1] He went early to Paris and there gave himself over to literature, and children's literature for the most part. His *Collection of Idylls* for very young readers was published in Paris in 1774. A critic said of it that it was natural and real and calculated to "invest virtue with new charms." To our modern taste that was rather too determined and obvious a purpose in all Berquin's writing. He did not denounce the magic content of Perrault, but he declared, in general, that tales of the imagination had "a tendency to instill Chimerical errors and dangerous infatuations."[2] To correct this evil he sets himself valiantly to work.

His *L'Ami des Enfans* consisted of stories that came out in 1782 and 1783 in separate numbers, finally making up twenty-four volumes. The English translation by M. A. Meilan was published in London in 1783. There is no doubt, also, that children learning French were set to reading Berquin's little volumes, thus giving him double entry into the British nursery. In 1787 there was published by Elizabeth Newbery, widow of John Newbery's nephew and successor, an English set of selections from Berquin, *The Looking-Glass for the Mind; or, Intellectual Mirror*, translated by the Reverend W. D. Cooper. The second edition, 1792, had illustrations by Bewick. This was highly recommended in English reading circles. Berquin liked children, although he did not fully understand them, and wrote for them in a pleasant and friendly style. He had high standards for them, however; they must be obedient and well mannered, they must also be charitable, must eschew frivolity and behave with sedateness and adult discretion. In one of his tales Little Annabella loses her mother in the crowd when they are on their way to market. She has very rashly "stopped to look at a little chaise drawn by six dogs," and the result is disastrous. Only a poor old woman with a basket of eggs pays attention to the little girl weeping by the roadside, but she gives her plum cake and restores her to her mother. The old woman is suitably rewarded, her mother buys all the eggs and "even made her a small present." But Annabella is her friend for life. "Thus you see, my young friends, what are the consequences of good nature

---

[1] Arnaud Berquin, *The Children's Friend*. Selections from Arnaud Berquin with a sketch of his life and writings (Boston, Marsh, Capen, Lyon and Webb, 1840), p. 8.

[2] *Ibid.*, p. 9.

and humanity," Berquin concludes with no false ideas about hiding his moral under a bushel.

Madame de Genlis (1746–1830) had a picturesque background for her own youth and went back to it for her tales for children. But for conscience's sake she reduced the possible riches to barren moralizing and curbed the powers of her own recollection. "I will give my children neither fairy tales nor the Arabian Nights" she declared in *Adèle et Théodore, Lettres sur L'Education* (1783). Even the tales that Madame d'Aulnoy wrote are not suitable. *Adèle et Théodore*[1] was followed in 1785 by *Les Veillées du Chateau*, antedating *Evenings at Home* by eight years. It begins with the greatest promise, describing what was actually Madame de Genlis' childhood home in Burgundy; one sees clearly the great drafty castle, with its shabby, echoing halls, to which the family of the Marquis de Clémire has retired for reason of economy. To make the long evenings pass, the Marquise begins a series of stories, told every evening, stories which have action and variety and even melodrama at times, but are so interminable, so confused, so pointless except for the evident moral, that any modern reader puts down the book in despair.

The misleading spell of Rousseau was upon Madame de Genlis, as it was upon Berquin, and by it the makings of a good storyteller were lost in her. None the less, she had a great vogue both in France and in England; her *Théâtre d'Education*, a group of instructive plays for children, was translated in 1781, *Adèle et Théodore* in 1783 and *Les Veillées du Chateau* in 1785. Her fame brought her appointments at the court and finally led to her being put in charge of the education of the Duc de Chartres' children. Gossip and scandal came to surround her in this position; her straitlaced literary admirers could give her their approval no longer. Maria Edgeworth speaks in her letters of going to see her in Paris, a poverty-stricken old woman in a dark and dirty apartment, but still accepting literary homage as undeniably her due. It is significant of the time that so great a reputation had been made by writing books for children.

---

[1] English translation 1783.

Bibliography

Arabian Nights. *The Portable Arabian Nights*, edited and with an introd. by Joseph Campbell. New York, Viking Press, 1952.
Aulnoy, Marie Catherine, Comtesse d'. *Fairy Tales and Novels, by the Countess d'Anois*. Translated from the French, with a biographical pref. 2 Vols. London, Printed for Walker and Edwards by S. Hamilton, Weybridge, 1817.
——— *The Fairy Tales of Madame d'Aulnoy, Newly Done into English*. With an introd. by Anne Thackeray Ritchie. London, Lawrence and Bullen, 1892.

Berquin, Arnaud. *The Children's Friend: Being Selections from the Various Works of Arnaud Berquin.* With a sketch of his life and writings. Boston, Marsh, Capen, Lyon & Webb, 1840.

—— *The Looking-Glass for the Mind; or, Intellectual Mirror. Being an elegant collection of the most delightful little stories, and interesting tales, chiefly translated from that much admired work,* L'ami des enfans. *A new ed.* America: Printed at Providence, R.I., by Carter and Wilkinson, 1794.

Comenius, Johann Amos. *The Orbis Pictus.* Syracuse, N.Y., C. W. Bardeen, 1887.

Gesta Romanorum. *Gesta romanorum; Entertaining Stories Invented by the Monks.* Translated by Charles Swan. New York, E. P. Dutton, 1924. (Broadway translations.)

Hazard, Paul. *Books, Children and Men.* Translated by Marguerite Mitchell. Boston, The Horn Book, 1944.

Laurie, Simon Somerville. *John Amos Comenius.* Syracuse, N.Y., C. W. Bardeen, 1892.

Perrault, Charles. *Mémoires de Ma Vie. Voyage à Bordeaux.* Publiés avec une introd., des notes et un index par Paul Bonnefon. Paris, Renouard, H. Laurens, 1909.

—— *Perrault's Popular Tales,* edited from the original editions, with an introd., &c., by Andrew Lang. Oxford, Clarendon Press, 1888.

11

The New England Primer

When the *Mayflower* weighed anchor and sailed out of Plymouth Harbor, to thrust her blunt nose into the north Atlantic's autumn gales, she bore in her cramped and ill-smelling hold a weight of potential history such as few vessels have ever carried before or since. And what was unique for a ship bound on such an undertaking, she carried children. The first adventurers to Virginia and Jamestown were practically all men, with the woman to follow when home had been won in the wilderness. But this voyage was an expedition of true emigration; families went as a unit, with all their homely goods and chattels and with a pathetic ignorance of what lay before them. One wonders how many of the women went willingly. It is fairly certain, however, that for the children it was a wonderful adventure.

On arrival, when the harshness of the climate, the loneliness and barrenness of the country made them see at once how precarious was life itself in the new world, it was plain to them that if their ideals and purposes were to be carried into the future, their hopes must rest mainly on their children. They had left Leyden and the friendly Netherlands because they wanted their descendants to grow up Englishmen and Englishwomen, and now further, if they were not to survive long themselves, they were determined that their children should first know how to die well, and, if it be granted that they should live, that they should live in the Puritan faith, in the Protestant persuasion and in the sight of God. Family worship, parents' admonitions and home instructions, the early organization of schools, all were turned to this task of perpetuating in their children that for which they themselves had sacrificed so much to preserve for their own.

"The Easiest Room in Hell"

They had, of course, brought books with them, to the extent that the meager cargo space would allow. But they were a people apart, and what they read themselves and gave their children to read must be something apart also. One might think that the earlier English literature

was easily transported to a new world and more closely clung to because
of the alien newness of everything around them, that English influence
would have gone easily forward, merely transplanted to a new environment. But Puritan thinking and Puritan culture was a seed sown, not a
tree transplanted, and it grew and spread and bore fruit of its own kind
such as only a new soil would produce.

They were an intense people, sifted out and winnowed by hardship
and persecution; only those of the firmest spirit took ship and came to
America, only those of the strongest will had the power to survive. It
is little wonder that where literature at home turned toward the admon-
ishment and improvement of children, in America it bent to the
task with a renewed intention of rendering young minds so strong and
inflexible that they could withstand all temptations and all hardships.

*Spiritual Milk for Boston Babes. In either England: Drawn out of the
breasts of both Testaments for their Souls nourishment. But may be of
like use to any Children*, was written by John Cotton (1584–1652),
grandfather of Cotton Mather, and published in England in 1646.[1] He
had occupied a pulpit in Boston, Lincolnshire—the birthplace of John
Foxe—and came later to Massachusetts, where his prestige as a preacher
was supported by the authority of this book.

Its real substance begins, as many of this type of publication do,
with a question and answer portion which is not, so far, the official
Westminster catechism. "What hath God done for you? God hath made
me, He keepeth me, and He can save me. . . . How did God make you?
I was conceived in sin and born in iniquity,"[2] with several questions and
answers following on the nature of sin. As the questions go forward,
the Boston Babes get into deeper theological waters when they reach
"What is the bond of the Covenant by which the Church is joyned
together?" coming to the deepest point when the child is told that the
"reward which shall be given is that the Righteous shall go into life
eternal, and the wicked shall be cast into everlasting fire with the Devil
and his Angels."

As successive waves of Puritan emigration followed the first ones,
Bunyan and Foxe made their way to New England, no matter how small
was the room anywhere for personal possessions, but *Pilgrim's Progress*
was for a time the only work of imagination available to conscientious
small readers. Foxe's *Book of Martyrs* was required reading here, as well
as at home.

Spiritual Milk for Babes was the model followed in later publications,
and there evolved, along with the long esses and grotesque woodcuts,

---

[1] A. S. W. Rosenbach, *Early American Children's Books* (Portland, Me., Southworth Press, 1933), p. 3.
[2] Paul Leicester Ford, ed., *The New England Primer* (New York, Dodd, Mead,
1897), p. 186.

the little volume which was partly prayer book and partly school text, whose plain purpose was to teach children to read the Bible. It undoubtedly was a most successful instrument of instruction, for it carried the rudiments of all that the Puritans desired to teach their children: Biblical knowledge, intense Protestantism, instruction—vague it must have been—in the doctrines of election and original sin, awareness of possible early death and the necessity of laying up treasure in Heaven. It is a great deal for one book to undertake, but concerning the *New England Primer*, the witness of history tells us that it accomplished its whole duty.

The book had its origin in an English publication, but very early took on its own characteristics. Its progenitor was *The Protestant Tutor for Youth*, published and probably written by Benjamin Harris, a London printer "at the Stationer's Arms under the Piazza at Cornhill." He was put in the pillory for a later publication, *A Protestant Petition*, and thereupon left England to pursue his trade in Massachusetts, where he arrived in 1686. He set up a Tea and Chocolate Shop in Boston, and later a London Coffee House, but his real pursuit was publishing and we see him presently with a shop, "The Sign of the Bible over against the Blew Anchor." He issued, some time before 1690, the American successor to *The Protestant Tutor*, the *New England Primer*.[1] The *Protestant Tutor* had contained alphabets, large and small, pages of syllables to be learned by rote, the Lord's Prayer, the Creed and the Ten Commandments. Its chief literary feature was the account, paralleling that of Foxe, of the burning of the Reverend John Rogers, with a frontispiece of Rogers at the stake attended by his wife and nine children, one a suckling. The record of the execution was followed by John Rogers' poem written for his children just before his death, "I leave to you a little book. For you to look upon, That you may see your father's face, When I am dead and gone." The *New England Primer* contained all the features of the earlier work with little alteration except for the change in name. John Rogers is an integral element in all the following editions.

The purpose of the inclusion of this story of John Rogers is, like the insistence on the reading of Foxe's *Martyrs*, to keep alive the memory of those persecutions which had attended the dawning of Protestantism. Some license, so it is claimed, has been taken with this featuring of Rogers, who was indeed the first executed in Mary's regime, but with the circumstances and the poem belonging to another man.

Had the Puritans but known it, they would have been confounded to realize that the very name of the new book was of Roman Catholic origin. A Catholic *Book of Hours*, printed in 1490, was called as a

---

[1] No exact date for the first edition has been identified, but a second edition was advertised in 1691. Ford, *The New England Primer*, p. 17.

subtitle, *The Prymer for Salisbury*, and was followed later by a publication authorized by Henry VIII, standardizing his new church forms and called *A Goodly Prymer of English*, which contained the alphabet, the Creed, the Lord's Prayer, and a Hail Mary. The Elizabethan *Book of Common Prayer* stemmed from this original, as in the end, and more remotely, did the *New England Primer*. Later to the *New England Primer* was added the *Milk for Babes*, since both were really shaped for the same end—the reading of the Bible and the expounding of the Puritan belief.

The rhyming alphabet, which is the great feature of the *New England Primer*, went through various metamorphoses, which are not only amusing but revealing of their time, thought, and society. "In Adam's fall, we sinned all," has been standard from the beginning, but the more secular sentiment—"The cat doth play and after Slay," "the Dog will bite, A thief at night," and "An Eagle's Flight Is out of sight"—gave way in a few years to more strictly scriptural comment on the letters. An edition of 1762 shows this scriptural influence at its height, "The *Deluge* drowned The Earth around" displaces the watchful dog, and "Elijah hid, By Raven's fed" succeeds the Eagle. "The Judgment made *Felix* afraid" stands instead of "The idle Fool Is whipt at School." "The Lion bold the Lamb doth hold" is replaced by the more elaborate "Lot fled to Zoar, Saw fiery Shower on Sodom pour."[1]

Difficulties, of course, arise as the alphabet gets into its later reaches and are met with greater or lesser facility or ingenuity. Plainly, "Uriah's beauteous wife made David seek his life" must have given rise to a good many questions which taxed parents to answer, and was got over finally by omitting U and stating that "Vashti for pride was set aside." "Xerxes did die, and so must I" is a simple but not very satisfactory truth, since so many between Xerxes and the young reader had bowed to the same necessity. But the earlier version, "Xerxes the Great did die, And so must you and I," gives it a more contemporary touch and is the form that was finally revived. With "Zaccheus he Did climb a Tree," the alphabet makes a successful end which has stood the test of time

There follows an alphabet of Biblical quotations: "A wise son maketh a glad father," "Better is a little with the fear of the Lord!" Likewise this alphabet is taxed with X, which is "eXhort one another daily." The Lord's Prayer and the Ten Commandments follow, then the account of the burning of John Rogers. The *New England Primer* of 1841 includes the comment that John Rogers' descendants finally came to Massachusetts, where his great-great-grandson, another John Rogers,

[1] Later editions were issued as *The New England Primer* "Improved" or "Enlarged." Even one of the earliest copies extant, that of 1749, is already *The New England Primer Further Improved with various Additions*. Rosenbach, *Early American Children's Books*, p. 21.

became president of Harvard in 1682. But it must be repeated for historical accuracy that the first John Rogers was a clergyman of the Church of England and his offense was not Puritanism but assisting Coverdale and Tyndal in the translation of the Bible into English.

Rogers' poem to his children is followed by the classic so often quoted, so deeply significant of the tenor of Puritan teaching for children:

> I in the burying place may see,
> Graves shorter there than I,
> From death's arrest no Age is free,
> Young children too must die.

But after this the spirit of the whole is retrieved by the inclusion of Watts's sincerely beautiful "Cradle Hymn":

> Hush, my dear, lie still and slumber,
> Holy angels guard thy bed.

The solid body of the Westminster Shorter Catechism filled most of the remainder of the eighteenth century *Primer*. In an edition so early that scholars think that this special feature may be by the original hand of Harris himself is the Dialogue—so written—between Christ, Youth, and the Devil in which Youth, alas, succumbs to the Devil's wiles and repents at the sight of death but is penitent too late.

> If thou some longer time should have,
> Thou would'st again to folly cleave,
> Therefore to thee I will not give,
> One day on earth longer to live.

The *New England Primer* was perhaps the first work of American literature to be current abroad, for Puritan children in England and Scotland were set to read it, and its power and influence lasted for well over a hundred years and through a hundred editions. Its character lay heavy on the Puritan mind and even more heavily on the Puritan writing and printing for children. While original sin and the doctrine of election were always stressed, not too great an effort was made to be very specific on a subject which must have been frankly alien to small minds, no matter how devout. But the idea of early death and the necessity of preparing for it was a theme that was never laid to rest. One can deplore the blindness of parents who put such weight upon it, but one must see their pathetic necessity. It was not the idea that the good die young, which they wished to keep always in mind, but the tragic fact that in that age the chance of life for young children was cruelly small and that parents must teach their children to be ready for death among the first things that they must know. Cotton Mather in *The Family Well-Ordered* (1699) published a sermon particularly addressed to children in which, with what one can only call devilish insight, he portrayed hell as a place of complete darkness, rather than of fire, as a warning that children who "make light of their parents" must face eternal punishment of the kind which children would most particularly dread. In this he was earnestly doing his duty as he saw it.

This same doctrine of necessary preparation for death gave rise to a whole group of terrifyingly unwholesome writings and publications of which *A Token for Children* is the most conspicuous and probably the most dreadful example. Its further title was *An Exact Account of the Conversion, Holy and Exemplary Lives and Joyous Deaths of several young children*. It was by James Janeway (1632?–1674), an English minister, and was published in two parts, in 1671 and 1672. Later it was published in America in 1700 with the addition of *A Token for the children of New England of some Examples of Children in whom the Fear of God was remarkably budding before they died in several parts of New England, Preserved and published for the Encouragement of Piety in other Children*. This further portion was written by Cotton Mather.

It records the career of Mrs. (Mistress) Sarah Hawley, aged nine years at the opening of the account, and dead at fourteen; of John Clapp of Scituate, who was "abounding in gracious admonitions to other young people"; and Priscilla Thornton, who "left this world having first given demonstrations of an exemplary Piety"; and "Daniel Williams, whose dying speeches have been conscientiously collected." The book and its wide popularity gave rise to many of similar tenor; *A Legacy for Children* is an instance, "Being some of the Last Expressions and Dying Sayings of Hannah Hill, of the City of Philadelphia, aged 11 years and near 3 months, published at the ardent desire of the deceased."

Hannah is quoted as saying, "Oh that I could launch away like a boat with sails. Who am I but poor dust and ashes." *A Devout Contemplation on the Meaning of Divine Providence in the early Death of Pious and Lovely Children* (1714) is a sermon by Benjamin Colman and is published as a definite contribution to children's reading, stating in plain terms its recognition of the fact that "The abundance of the Children of Men and of our most hopeful, pious and promising children do Die young, Untimely Births, those who number only a few breaths, what multitudes die in infancy!" *The Rule of the New Creature*, published in New England in 1668, which even antedates the *New England Primer*, gives directions how to lead the exemplary life which alone can promote salvation. "Be sensitive of thy Original Corruption daily . . . groan under it and bewail it as Paul did" is the first admonition, nor is it necessary to go further.

One can see actually that the *New England Primer* and those attendant *mementos mori* form a pathetic documentary witness of the constant nearness of human tragedy. It bears evidence of more matters than this single one, however, for a book which passes through changing editions for a hundred and fifty years reflects in itself the growth of men's ideas. It is to be remembered that those first Pilgrims were but a generation removed from the Elizabethans, and that the life and spaciousness of the Renaissance was still a tradition and an instinctive taste with them. Thus, the first *New England Primer* is more liberal, comparatively speaking, nearer to the English *Protestant Tutor*, less demanding on the endurance of the child reader. As the Puritan population in New England grew, felt more secure and better established, the attitude of intolerance stiffened with the years of its isolation from the more mellowing forces of a larger and earlier society. The *Primer* of 1749 perhaps shows the highest point of that intolerance and strict Calvinism. But for nearly a hundred years, it had reflected those hard beliefs which are epitomized in that lengthy poem, *The Day of Doom*, written for adults in 1662 by Michael Wigglesworth (1632–1705). In describing the Calvinistic conception of Heaven and Hell, he permits the infants to speak, those numberless ones who died at birth and must languish in the abode of punishment since they had not been baptized nor had opportunity to be saved. Why should we suffer who have not sinned? they ask, but the Creator—in the image of Michael Wigglesworth—answers:

> "You sinners are, and such a share as sinners may expect,
> Such you shall have, for I do save none but mine own Elect.
> Yet to compare your sin with their, who lived a longer time,
> I do confess yours is much less, though every sin's a crime.
> A crime it is, therefore in bliss, you may not hope to dwell;
> But unto you I shall allow the easiest room in Hell."[1]

No one can doubt that the witch panic of 1692, set in motion by the accusing outburst of hysterical children, was a result of young minds being fed too long on terror and repression. The greater errors of the Puritan educational system carried the seeds of their own end, the lesser ones were more tenacious, and the *New England Primer* continued to be their spokesman for a curiously long time. But the world began to break in upon New England by the middle of the eighteenth century, and even the *Primer* began to retreat from some of its super-orthodoxy. The alphabetical rhymes began to grow secular again, and their content reflected more and more political change. "King Charles the Good, no man of Blood" went through several metamorphoses, but not so many or such sudden ones as did King George. Even "Kings should be good, no men of blood" had to yield to "The British King, Lost states thirteen." The same portrait of His Majesty himself came out labeled John

---

[1] Quinn, Baugh and Howe, *The Literature of America*, Vol. I. "The Day of Doom" by Michael Wigglesworth, p. 30.

Hancock, then Samuel Adams, at last George Washington with the legend, "By Washington, Great deeds were done."

The *Royal Primer* of John Newbery's printing reached America in time to offer wholesome competition to the stiff-necked New England edition of 1749 and earlier. It has much the same general format—alphabets, lists of syllables to be learned by rote, "chaw, draw, flaw, knaw," chanted in unison; it has biblical quotations and homilies, but hell fire is singularly absent and animals of everyday life creep into the illustrations. There is more verse, and it has less reference to the grave. "A divine poem by the most excellent Addison consisting of words not exceeding four syllables" is included. In spite of the restriction, Addison's verse is effortless:

> "My God, Thou mak'st the Sun to know
> His proper Hour to rise,
> And to give Light to all below,
> Doth send him round the Skies."

The Quaker, John Woolman (1720–1772), raising his voice to give young minds a better chance, brought out about 1766 *A First Book for Children*, full of their own spirit. There are some alphabets and syllables, but no admonitory rhymes, since Friends, eschewing music, were apt to have a limited ear for verse. But there is biblical rhythm in the lines, "The Lark will fly in the Field, The Cat doth run after the Mouse, The Chub swims in the Brook; And the Good boy will do good in his place." The assurance that "The eye of the Lord is on them that fear him; He will love them and do them good" is a welcome doctrine after all the threatened destruction for a world of young sinners.

A few books on courtesy mingled with those on moral behavior, some of them partaking of the nature of both. The *Rule of the New Creature* is religious and theological in its tone. *The School of Good Manners* deals with more secular things. How Locke with his disbelief in rules and precepts would have held up his hands—and possibly did so—at the "Twenty Mixt Precepts, the One Hundred and Sixty-Three Rules for Children's Behaviour, the Eight Wholesome Cautions and the Eleven Short Exhortations" with finally, by way of relief, "Cyprian's Twelve Absurdities." Among the rules of conduct in the Meeting House and on the Sabbath, there is also a good column of instructions on how to behave to parents, "never to sit in their presence without bidding . . . never to approach near them without a Bow." Sometimes the very language parallels that of the Books of Courtesy which Caxton brought out, although his selections have less to do with the Old Testament and its patriarchal conceptions of family life and parental authority.

Yet nobody can believe that this was all, that Jack the Giant Killer and Catskin and Robin Goodfellow and Guy of Warwick did not come to New England with all the other possessions, tangible and intangible, that Englishmen and women could not leave behind. As has been said, Walter Scott believed that Tom Thumb came into England with Hengist and Horsa; he undoubtedly traveled with the first settlers to America, and we find a copy of his story being sold in Boston in 1686. We feel ourselves justified in imagining that there were evenings when the *Book of Martyrs* and *The School of Good Manners* were put neatly on the shelf and the family had a fine round of Robin Goodfellow before going to bed. Robin could scarcely be called a good Puritan, although he was an acquaintance of Milton's. He was not even a good Protestant, but he was too old a friend of English mankind to be put off by any such consideration as that.

> Thus told the tale, to bed they creep,
> By whispering winds soon lulled to sleep.

If country people after a pleasant but exhausting day, could do so in Milton's England, can there be doubt that they did the same in the Puritans' America? Other highly recommended reading for the young was Chesterfield's *Letters to His Son*, first published in England in 1774 and brought out many times in America for the improvement of youthful manners.

Much discussion has just been given to the reading of Puritan children, because it was in New England where such thought and effort were given to the choosing of their reading, even though so much of that effort was ill-directed. But the parents of New England, in their deep concern for spiritual welfare, in their early and methodical establishment of schools, in their interest always in things of the mind, implanted something in their children which even bitter mistakes could not counteract.

In other portions of the country, children went more or less upon their own way. Certainly in the Southern colonies the link with England, both economical and cultural, was so close and maritime intercourse so direct that one can conceive of the children of Virginia and the Carolinas as reading much what the children "at home" were accustomed to do. America was an alert new country, its inhabitants eager in mind as well as energetic in body, both young and old. There was no dearth of readers; there was soon to be a sufficiency of reading—even for the young.

Bibliography

Halsey, Rosalie V. *Forgotten Books of the American Nursery*. Boston, C. E. Goodspeed, 1911.

Johnson, Clifton. *Old-time Schools and School-Books*. New York, Macmillan, 1904.

The New-England Primer; a History of Its Origin, with a reprint of the unique copy of the earliest known edition and many fac-simile illustrations and repro-

ductions, edited by Paul Leicester Ford. New York, Printed for Dodd, Mead, 1897.

The New-England Primer Improved. Boston, Printed and sold by S. Kneeland, 1762.

Rosenbach, Abraham Simon Wolf. *Early American Children's Books*. Portland, Me., Southworth Press, 1933.

The Royal Primer Improved: Being an Easy and Pleasant Guide to the Art of Reading. Philadelphia, J. Chattin, 1753.

Woolman, John. *A First Book for Children. Much useful reading being sullied and torn by children in schools before they can read, this book is intended to save unnecessary expence.* 3d ed., enl. Philadelphia, Printed, and sold by Joseph Crukshank, 1769?

12

Printer's Ink

The Gilt Coach in America

Oliver Goldsmith has given us a fortunate glimpse of the stout, red-faced, gay, and infinitely kind John Newbery of Reading and London. A contemporary has given us almost as accurate a portrait sketch of Isaiah Thomas (1749–1831), printer and publisher and bookseller of Boston and Worcester, the man who went about his own way of doing for American children what John Newbery had done across the water. "In his person he was tall and slender, stooping somewhat in his gait. His address was courteous . . . but something conventional, and his attention to appearance and dress was singularly precise and studied."[1] Just the same, the lean, stooping Yankee, whose life was full of quarrels and of shrewd philanthropy, and the bustling Englishman had this in common—they understood what children wanted and must have.

Isaiah Thomas wrote no children's books with his own hand, as contrasted with Newbery's busy output of "as many as he had read." Thomas made cuts for pictures, and extremely awkward ones at that, and some verses for popular broadsides. That was as far as actual creation went. By the custom of the time, he felt perfectly justified in the appropriation of Newbery's publications and in his printing his own editions of them. Young readers benefited, if Newbery did not, and the compliment was returned when British publishers printed Peter Parley's works in a multiplicity of versions which he could not even recognize as his own.

Thomas was an interested and enthusiastic printer, an organizer, and launcher of new journals and a man with a keen eye for the direction in which profit lay. It is said that he was a printer's apprentice when he was still a small boy of no more than six years old and set up a broadside, *The Lawyer's Pedigree*, before he could read. It was, perhaps, as well that he could not. Many of the broadsides of that time were of

---

[1] Clifford Shipton, *Isaiah Thomas* (Rochester, N.Y., Leo Hart, 1948), p. 73.

uncommon coarseness, like *The Friar and the Boy or The Piper's Pleasant Pastime* and *The American Sailor's Letters to his Sweetheart*.

It was in 1779, while the war of the Revolution was going on, that Thomas acquired a stout bundle of Newbery's little books—it has not been recorded by just what process of expert smuggling they came into his hands: *Goody Two-Shoes*, *Mother Goose* and *Robinson Crusoe* had thus arrived in New England. He imported and sold English children's books, but not until the war was over did he begin publishing them on his own account. John Newbery, now dead, was none the less his chief mainstay. It is notable that he selected the very best of Newbery's books: the *Mother Goose* of the pleasantly jocose edition which has been ascribed to Goldsmith, *Be Merry and Wise*, *A Little Pretty Pocket-Book*, *Nurse Truelove's New Year's Gift*, *The Lilliputian Masquerade*, and many others. He lived long enough to publish the work of Newbery's successors and to bring out books of other writers of the years following Newbery, such as Mary Jane Kilner's *Adventures of a Pincushion* and *Memoirs of a Peg Top*.

One observes that he printed only two of the innumerable editions through which the *New England Primer* went in the hands of many publishers. He had set up one of them during his very young apprenticeship, and seems to have had no further taste for the book. His choice of a school text was Webster's *Spelling Book*, of which he printed a great number. His first real publication for children was in 1785, Madame de Genlis' play, *The Beauty and the Monster*. The years 1787 and 1788 were his great period of publications for children, after that other enterprises rose up to engulf him. He was in business long enough to have had ample opportunity to present to America the *Little Female Academy* or some of Hannah More's *Tracts*, but for this he seemed to have had no desire. He stuck close to Newbery. The volumes were small, toy books like those which emanated from St. Paul's Churchyard. He used marbled or embossed paper for the bindings; the Dutch flowered covers, which had been so famous and which he had loved as a boy, were not to be had now.

He used Newbery's own method of advertising. In his version of *Nurse Truelove's New Year's Gift* (1786) Mrs. Williams of the Plumb Cake gives the pupils in her "college" a list of reading books which are "sold by I. Thomas" and a child who has dutifully studied the New Testament is given a prize of "one of the little Spelling Books and some of the other pretty Books which are to be sold by I. Thomas, in Worcester, near the Court House. . . ." He made some attempt to alter the content to suit the new country, but the gesture was a very sketchy one. Miss Polly Friendly, in *Nurse Truelove*, when she achieves the rewards of good conduct, marries in high places and rides in the "Governour's gilt coach." He neglected to go thoroughly through the story, however, and left it at the very end that thus Miss Polly became "a great Lady Mayoress and rode in a grand gilt coach." Whether it was from conviction or from mere inadvertence, he rewarded all his good children, as Newbery did, with riding away out of the story in a coach. We see that in his *Mother Goose* rhymes, first published in 1785, he altered "see-saw, sacaradown, which is the way to London town" into sending his young subjects to Boston instead. But children who played the game in later generations never gave up their quest of London.

He does not seem to have made any effort to increase his list by attempting to employ authors of his own country or time. After 1788 he apparently felt that he had exhausted the supply of good material and seemed to have turned his attention elsewhere. Early in his career as a printer, in 1761, when he was obliged to show a Prentice's Token as a specimen of his work, he had set up *Tom Thumb's Play Book to Teach Children their Letters as soon as they can Speak*. It too contained "A Apple-Pye, B bit it, C cut it, D divided it," etc. The alphabet is from a much older collection, White's *Little Book for Little Children*, for which the date can only be identified as between 1702 and 1712. It contained the more expansive rhyming alphabet, "A was an Archer and shot at a Frog, B was a Butcher and had a great Dog." Its one mild gesture at admonition is at the end, perhaps the best use of those late and difficult letters that we see anywhere. "W was a watchman and guarded the Door; X was expensive and so became poor." Tom Thumb's little book ends with the very small and simple prayer for children to say morning and evening, "I desire to lie down under Thy care and To abide forever under Thy blessing." It was a choice that casts vivid illumination upon Thomas's real taste and his understanding of children.

The Bible and Crown

Even as the eighteenth century comes to an end it is still necessary in America to look to printers and publishers of the period to discover what books were available for children of the age and in various parts of the country, since names of authors seem even more elusive among early American books than English. Isaiah Thomas was undoubtedly the most influential and enterprising of early American publishers who gave children their due measure, and thanks to his wide acquaintance and his extended partnerships up and down the country, his wares went far. In New York, Hugh Gaine (1726 or 1727–1807) began slightly earlier than Thomas to offer to a more limited public some of the same sort of reading, also largely drawn for his young customers from the Newbery treasure house. He called his shop the Bible and Crown, and he echoed Newbery's methods in the various directions of his flourishing business. He sold proprietary remedies, although none of them reached the eminence of Dr. James's powders. But he mentioned the good properties of his medications in the text of his publications, and on advertising title pages he made such announcements as that the book is "Printed by Hugh Gaine at his shop in Hanover Square where may be had a great variety of Books for little Masters and Misses."[1]

Gaine's record shows no such militant patriotism as did Thomas's, nor is it of much moment after so many years to look too deeply into where, during the Revolution, his allegiance really lay. Within Royalist and occupied New York his customers were British-born or British in sympathy, so direct reproduction of the Newbery items was entirely satisfactory to them. Gaine, however, printed the first *Journals of the American Congress* in 1775, and in the same year, the very anti-English poems of Philip Freneau. He was already interested in children's books and introduced *Robinson Crusoe* to new friends, importing it in 1753 and printing it in 1775, thus antedating Thomas in bringing that great man to America. Another prominent figure, also through him, made her first bow to the American public in 1775, Mrs. Margery Two-Shoes. Æsop's *Fables in Verse* with the *Conversations of Beasts and Birds by Woglog the Great Giant* had appeared or been imported as early as 1762, and *Watts' Divine Songs for Children* about ten years earlier (1753). His choice was wider than Thomas's nor did he confine himself so closely to Newbery. He, too, would have little to do with the *New England Primer*; his choice was Dilworth's *New Guide to the English Tongue*, "designed for the use of Schools in Great Britain, Ireland and America" and reported as the most popular spelling book of the eighteenth century. His importations and sales of English books covered a very wide field, but his big Bibles and his small books for children were his principal stock in trade. In those which he printed on his own part, including Bibles, there is a grace and proportion in the print and design of the page that is rare for that time. Among the very first of his books imported and advertised is Locke's *Thoughts on Education*.[2]

Other publishers of note did their share to promote children's reading, especially Mahlon Day in New York, Thomas and John Fleet in Boston, William Charles in Philadelphia, and, most prolific, the Johnsons, Benjamin and Jacob, of Philadelphia, the last two in partnership with Benjamin Warner. The list of these publishers is tremendous for its time. It covers chapbooks of the better kind for children, a few of Newbery's, *Watts' Divine Songs*, Mrs. Barbauld, Maria Edgeworth, and a generous quantity of Hannah More. *Sandford and Merton* seems to have had little patronage from American publishers, yet as an imported edition it is said that it sold as freely as did *Robinson Crusoe*. The test

[1] After 1775 he gave up the word "Crown" and thereafter called his place "The Bible in Hanover Square." Ford, ed., *The Journals of Hugh Gaine* (New York, Dodd, Mead, 1902), p. 64.
[2] *Ibid.*, p. 189.

of time has, however, righted any such temporary injustice and book-sellers' records tell a different tale now.

To Thomas Fleet of Boston we owe the odd confusion in people's minds of the real origin of Mother Goose. It is said that Fleet's mother-in-law was a Mistress Goose (or Vergoose as the accounts all take pains to add) who was much given to singing the old nursery rhymes to his children, a pursuit with which Fleet had small sympathy until it occurred to him to collect and print the little songs. It has thus been said that his publication in 1719 of a *Mother Goose's Melody* attached itself to this Mrs. Goose. As has been mentioned earlier, however, Perrault first introduced the world of young readers, both in France and England, to Ma Mère l'Oie. Newbery used her name for the collection of nursery rhymes which was published by him in 1760 and by Isaiah Thomas about 1785. Since that time, any other Mrs. Goose has shone only by reflected glory.[1]

The Sunday School Tracts

The organization which scattered far and near the *Cheap Repository Tracts* of Hannah More came into being to serve the first Sunday schools, and lived and had its branches and descendants for beyond the expectations of its founders. The Religious Tract Society, organized in London in 1799, had, at the beginning, the purpose of furthering general education, as well as providing religious teaching for the different denominations. This double responsibility was unlike what we think of as Sunday school instruction now. Early in United States history, when the smallness of industry and a less competitive way of living made child labor less of a menace to society, and when, also, schools for the whole population had been part of the original plans in many of the colonies, Sunday schools could concentrate on religious and sectarian instruction. Thus there was need for a different kind of publication. The New York Religious Tract Society and the New England Tract Society, after years of activity in their own territories, merged in 1825 to become the American Tract Society, with very definite ideas of what they would and would not offer for young people's reading. They printed toy books of something the same fashion as Newbery's, whose object, the society stated was "to do what they can to counteract the prevailing thirst in the rising generation for the mere entertainment of high-wrought fiction." The committee in charge of publications did recognize, however, "that the young demand something more than didactic discussion." They made the attempt, therefore, to enlist "authors of some reputation and experience," but it was only where some real enthusiasm for the cause of religious instruction already existed, that the invitation

[1] Darton, *Children's Books in England* (Cambridge, Eng., University Press, 1932), p. 103.

was accepted. Jacob Abbott responded and offered *The Young Christian*, *The Child at Home*, and *The Mother at Home*, with 100,000 sold of these three books. Thomas Hopkins Gallaudet, founder of the first Asylum for the Deaf and Dumb, had also given the committee, for general distribution, his *History of Joseph*, *History of Jonah*, and others, making a series of scriptural biography running to seven volumes.

With this society, the series became a favored device, one book running on into the next, until children's libraries were filled shelf by shelf with rows of little red and blue books. Usually one volume had the good fortune to strike, more or less by accident, the fancy of its intended readers and was worn out where the rest retained pristine newness. Youth's Biography Series, Youth's Narrative Series, etc., made up Youth's Christian Library, but the whole project set its face firmly against fiction. The Reverend Robert Hall deplored publicly the fact that Maria Edgeworth made light of religious truth, for, he said, "by exhibiting a perfect virtue without it" she had not set forth its real worth. Another critic of Scott said sadly, "I am well persuaded (alas by personal experience) that the evil effects arising from the perusal of one novel counteract the good effects of twenty sermons." Stories, however, thinly disguised under the mask of fables, because they carried more meaning, did begin to creep in, until finally Sunday schools admitted to the shelves of their libraries such fiction as they could thoroughly approve. There was a flood of it, all devoted so singly and so short-sightedly, and often so unskillfully, to the teaching of proper morals, that the stamp of Sunday school fiction as goody-goody books, fell like a blight upon a whole class of writing at a very critical moment in the development of juvenile books.

The well-meaning committees failed because they attempted to set up a literature of a certain kind, without any attention to what literature must have: freedom, reality, movement, and deep, rather than obvious, truth. Acquired by parents and families and Sunday schools for conscientious reasons, the books have survived in fact but not in spirit, and the scores of drab and dusty little volumes are piled in corners of storerooms and shops. They seem harmless enough as we look through them for some kernel of good and living matter, but they did do harm for they represent a blind alley in the exploration of the field. Their weight of platitudes and sentimentality was a dead load on the forward progress of a new literature of such infinite possibilities. Later, however, intelligent understanding of children's books has finally guided the policy of present-day publishing houses for Sunday school material. With a heavy handicap set up by previous lack of judgment in these early Tract Societies, they have risen to a high place in the selection and publication of the best sort of material for children and are rightfully distinguished for the worth of their product.

A Somnolent Dutchman and a Headless Hessian

From John Newbery to the early nineteenth century Sunday School Tracts seems a long and retrogressive step. But it was inevitable in a barren time that young people would find and select some favorites of their own, regardless of what their over-zealous elders were doing for them. There was opportunity for this in America as well as in England.

A young man, born in New York, possessed of an enterprising and enthusiastic mind, was to be the first to offer to elders what, in the end, was to become the prized possession of children. Washington Irving (1783–1859) had so young a mind that all his life he was to have particular pleasure in the company of young people, though firsthand knowledge of children he had none. He enjoyed his early and very carefree life among his friends in what had now become the nation's largest and most populous city. He enjoyed travel, seeing new places and new peoples and, with far more of the creative writer's instinct than that of the deliberate historian, he enjoyed looking into the past of those new peoples. Since his severe and conscientious Scottish father had been rather hard on this youngest son of a big family, his elder brothers later tried to make up to him what his father's lack of understanding had denied him. They gave him security and the opportunity to travel, and young Irving made the most of his chances.

When he went abroad, his warmth of personality and his ingenuous pleasure over all the new experiences that rolled out before him enlisted the interest and finally the friendship of his new literary acquaintances in England. And when, with his brothers' bankruptcy, he came suddenly into contact with hard reality, his new friends appreciated him more than ever, for he met a difficult situation with proof of real strength of character. A world war, with Napoleon as its personal storm center, had been followed by general depression, so that the task of taking care of himself and of an ill brother in Liverpool was not easy. Washington Irving had already done a certain amount of writing and publishing, mostly of light and pleasant satire and never with the object of self-support. Now he set to work in earnest.

There occurred to him the most fortunate idea, that at a time when British and Americans understood each other little and appreciated each other less, his was the opportunity of making each one better known to the other. The result was *The Sketch Book*, written in 1819 by "Geoffrey Crayon," a group of essays which were sent home and published in periodicals and later collected into a pair of volumes. They were gay but incisive familiar essays, a little like Addison and Steele, and perhaps a little like Charles Lamb. They gave Americans a view of English life and English manners just as they had appeared to this young traveler from America. They pleased Americans greatly, they pleased the British just as much. At a time of heavy-hearted effort to meet the inevitable aftermath of war—part of which had been even a war with the United States—the British public had tended to lose sight of the serene, established, pleasantly moving life which had once been possible to so many of them and which suddenly was made so vivid that it seemed it might be possible again. Glimpses of an earlier England, surviving in old customs, had so fascinated young Irving that his presentation of it was enthusiastic and convincing.

It was the good fortune of Irving to have been taken into the vivid and generous friendship of Walter Scott, to whom he owed very little in literary influence but a very great deal in practical help and advice. Scott introduced him to publishers who would otherwise have taken small interest in an unknown American writer, who reversed earlier refusals of his work and lived to be most thankful that they had. *The Sketch Book* was read everywhere with extraordinary pleasure on both sides of the Atlantic.

Irving's all-devouring interest in the new and the old had not stopped at the very old indeed. He always had an appetite for folklore, was intensely interested in what Scott and others told him of ancient Scottish legends, and began to wonder whether America had nothing of the sort to contribute to literature. English folk tales had not anchored themselves to any region of the strictly Puritan New England country, but it had been otherwise in the Dutch-settled region of the colony of New York. Stories that he had heard and only partly heeded in his youth began to come back to him, so that two of the first substantial items in *The Sketch Book* were the tale of "Rip Van Winkle" and "The Legend of Sleepy Hollow." They have the force of a vital human situation, such as all ancient stories have, otherwise they would not survive.

Usually a folk story is integrally connected with its own countryside, a fact which teller and hearer take for granted. But these tales were recounted for a far audience and one of very different connection, so that Irving had to supply the sense of place and kind of people, which he does with the care and precision of one who knows his own ground, both from a geographic and a literary angle. There is genial charm and warm-hearted humor whenever Irving sets out to tell a story. It would have been pleasant to hear him at the dinner table in Bracebridge Hall (1822).

Other uses that Irving made of his studies of folklore are well known. "The Spectre Bridegroom" grew out of a German tale which he transmuted into human possibility. While he was a secretary of legation at Madrid, a wise superior encouraged him to take time for research and writing, realizing that he could do both countries better service in that occupation than sitting at a desk and filling out government reports. His *Legends of the Alhambra* (1832) makes a deeper and more extended study of folklore than did anything else to which he set his hand. He could not resist supplying some details from imagination, but he kept to the spirit and fundamental facts of the old stories and was able to capture the oriental magic of the old and picturesque culture of the Spanish Moors.

Children who know them are apt to love them, and all of those who read them in early years not only retain a sense of rich and beautiful imagination, but scarcely ever fail to acquire certain unconscious standards of taste which Irving's unobtrusively brilliant and graceful style inevitably imparts. He is one of those writers whom Boswell wistfully described as pleasing children and being remembered with pleasure by men.

War Paint and the Glimmerglass

With the rise of the Romantic movement abroad, so spiritedly brought into the realm of the novel by Walter Scott, it would be remarkable if romantic influence did not soon invade the literature of America. Here we once more have Scott to thank, for James Fenimore Cooper (1789–1851) in New York set out to do for America what Scott had done for his own country. Cooper, like Irving, had no intention of writing for the young, but it is even less remarkable in his case, that with his taste for action and adventure and directness of plot, he produced books that, in the end, were adopted by young readers instead of their elders. His life experience gave him ample material for the kind of work he set out to do. His boyhood was passed at Cooperstown, a frontier village founded by his father. Thence he went to Yale, then to sea in the merchant marine, where he had the experience of having his ship chased by pirates. He then moved on to the navy and saw service on inland waters as well as the Atlantic. He had married and resigned from the service by the time the War of 1812 had begun. Having inherited a comfortable fortune from his father, he settled down to country life and the small but absorbing occupations of that sort of living. He had time now to mature the memory of his varied earlier adventures and his happy recollections of beloved scenes, all of them stuff out of which, in the right hands, novels eventually come.

History dominated his first books as it had Scott's, nor do these, *The Spy* and *The Pilot*, have much interest for the young. His first volume, in what became afterward the Leatherstocking Series, came late in the personal history of its hero—only afterward did Cooper go back and relate the stories that had to do with Natty Bumppo's earlier life. In that first book, *The Pioneers* (1823), he embarked on the subject which, without his being aware of it, was closest to his heart and to his literary ability. Indians will never fail to be an alluring theme for books for young readers and with Cooper the subject was a fresh one. Romanticist though he was, he did not regard the American red man as something impossibly noble and majestic. His Indians did not represent the "natural man" of Rousseau; his Indian was a human being with savage faults and savage courage, with loyalty and faithfulness and a moving affection for his own country and his own way of living.

Of the succession of books into which this first novel led him, *The Last of the Mohicans* (1826) was second and has come to be the one most highly regarded by young readers. The hero, Natty Bumppo, variously called Deerslayer, Pathfinder, Hawkeye, La Longue Carabine, and other titles, is Hawkeye here. There is no attempt to show him as a man of heroic stature; he is tough, uncomely, skilled in woodcraft, resourceful, but sometimes mistaken. Most important of all, he is a man who understands Indians and is loyal to those true friends he has among them.

Concerning the Indians, Cooper has said himself that in their differences from our culture, we see their most conspicuous faults: dirt, treachery where enemies are concerned, irresponsibility. But they have their heroic attributes also, and these attributes, he insists, deserve to be remembered and celebrated. In the other favorite in the series, *The Deerslayer* (1841), Cooper has gone back to Otsego Lake, the scene of his own small boy adventures in ranging the woods and the tributary waters. He is bound, in this story, that we shall see the Glimmerglass as it is here named, know the shape of its shores and the slopes and contours of the surrounding hills. "It may assist the reader in understanding the events we are about to record if he has a rapidly sketched picture of the scene placed before his eyes in a single view" he observes, and gives it with skill and power, so we not only know the topography of the place, but we are there in imagination. The very character of the happenings at Hutter's water-built castle and on his floating scow— the ark, the captures, the escapes, the drifting canoes—all depend on the character of the lake itself, actually one of the main figures in the story.

Cooper, like Scott, is extravagant with words and details, in pleasant confidence that his reader has plenty of time and will go all the way with him. Occasionally he builds suspense by the naive means of leaving the story at a critical juncture and taking us far away, with slow progress back again to rescue the hero just in time. It is not a method to be recommended, especially for the perusal of young readers, who are all too apt to skip. The books are full of bloody incident. *The Last of the Mohicans* particularly ends in tragedy, but it does so inevitably. The more one becomes attached to the Indian characters, Uncas and Chingachgook, the more one realizes that such is their situation that tragedy is the only possible end.

Cooper's novels, especially the Indian ones, were justly admired in America and were almost as widely read in England. English boys and girls were deeply interested in Red Indians, so-called to distinguish them from the brown inhabitants of India proper. The German editions were widely popular and read by the young of Europe who are more versed in languages than Americans. "At least I know your Lederstrumpf," a Greek gentleman will say who read him in his youth in German. The books are so essentially American that one can see little imitation of Scott in them, far more are they a response to Scott's inspiration and the challenging spirit of the time. Romance in America, for both old and young, was closer and more convincing than in the older countries. With Cooper, the young people of America came into their own heritage of adventures of changing scene and vital action. His was not the attenuated romance, mixed with sentimentalism, which came to be the reproach of the last stages of American romanticism. With Cooper, it was fresh, vigorous and robust, of the quality that young readers have always demanded.

Bibliography

Gaine, Hugh. *The Journals of Hugh Gaine, Printer*; edited by Paul Leicester Ford. 2 Vols. New York, Dodd, Mead, 1902.

Hellman, George Sidney. *Washington Irving, Esquire*. New York, A. A. Knopf, 1925.

Irving, Washington. *The Sketch Book of Geoffrey Crayon, Gent*. Reprinted from the original edition. Chicago, Belford, Clarke, 1884.

Rosenbach, Abraham Simon Wolf. *Early American Children's Books*. Portland, Me., Southworth Press, 1933.

Shipton, Clifford K. *Isaiah Thomas, Printer, Patriot and Philanthropist, 1749–1831*. Rochester, N.Y., Print. House of Leo Hart, 1948.

Thompson, Lawrance R. *The Printing and Publishing Activities of the American Tract Society from 1825 to 1850*. In Bibliographical Society of America, Papers, Vol. 35, 2d quarter (1941), pp. 81–114.

Van Doren, Carl. *The American Novel, 1789–1939*. Rev. and enl. ed. New York, Macmillan, 1940.

13

Two Indefatigable Americans

"A Sort of Intellectual Plum Pudding"

If Samuel Goodrich (1793–1860), who called himself before the world Peter Parley, had written only one book for children and that one about his boyhood, there is every chance that he might have presented us with a classic. As it is, he does little more than exist in literary records with scarcely any person's being more than vaguely aware that he wrote very busily for children over a long stretch of years. Goodrich's *Recollections of a Lifetime, or Men and Things I have Seen* (1856) reflects, even in his old age, such a richness of youthful happiness and appreciation of the delights of childhood that it is hard to believe that any such ardent, genuine, and highly receptive spirit could have, in later life, fallen so deeply into mediocrity. His affectionate account of his Connecticut home of Ridgefield, with its view of Long Island Sound, with a white wooden meetinghouse on a grassy square, and a tavern with a cannonball in the wall left over from 1777, with its "stone bees" where neighbors gathered to help clear a patch of land of that rocky outcrop of which Connecticut has so rich a supply—his picture of all this preserves the quality of small boy observation and happiness.

He had a deep and sincere love of nature, both of men and things. He knew birds and flowers without any necessity of instruction; he drank in knowledge, as a child who loves the green world about him will always do. Above his head, political society was being rent by the differences between Federalists and Democrats; they even dressed their parts, the small Samuel noted, with the Federalists still in perukes, broad-skirted coats, and low-crowned hats, while the Democrats brought in the fashion of short hair, pantaloons, and round hats with narrow brims. He records one of the greatest accusations of all those hurled against Jefferson, the arch-Democrat, that he wore leather shoestrings instead of the honest buckles such as had been good enough for his fathers.

It is when he discusses his reading that we begin to understand the source of that blight which fell upon his creative fancy in later life. We can see that as a boy he was of unusual sensitivity, living happily on dreams, as he said of himself. But the prolific and literal-minded 1780's and the literature which they had put forward colored the whole of what was available to him and stifled any impulse to bring the powers of fancy to bear on what he read. When he first encountered "Little Red Riding Hood" he was harrowed by the tragedy of the tale, which he took to be solemn truth, and then was outraged when his mother told him that it was not. The clever cat in "Puss-in-Boots" he condemned as a liar and a cheat, and he was revolted by the bloodiness of "Jack the Giant Killer." He later declared himself convinced that "much of the vice and crime in the world are to be imputed to those atrocious books put into the hands of children."[1] They belonged to a barbarous age, he thought, and should not be offered to children by Christian parents. He was ten years old when he read Hannah More's *The Shepherd of Salisbury Plain* and found it the single book which wholly pleased and satisfied him. "Twenty years after, I enjoyed the pleasure, I might almost say ecstacy, of passing over the scene of this inimitable story and of telling my experience to the author at Barley-wood."[2]

He was a homesick youth behind a clerk's desk, dreaming of running away to sea, as Irving had dreamed, then equally homesick behind the counter of a dry goods establishment, yearning for the education which was beyond his reach. At last, however, he was able to make a move in the direction of his real destiny, and in 1814 set up, with a friend, a small publishing business. For this he wrote a little arithmetic and half a dozen toy books, "though I never confessed their authorship." He began to plan with no great encouragement a series of school histories, manuals of chemistry and natural philosophy by different authors. He had great trouble with his eyes; a fall from a horse put him on crutches for a year and lamed him permanently; his wife and daughter died; his affairs "became embarrassed." Yet the idea of the need and opportunity for making better books for children did not fail him. One can realize that he genuinely loved children and wanted to understand them; that he was supremely happy in the recollections of his own childhood. As Samuel Goodrich, full of eagerness, curiosity, and sympathy, he was a lovable person and could have been a memorable author. Instead, as a result of the deeply rooted convention of his time, as a consequence of unfortunate choice in his immediate inspiration, he became Peter Parley, instructor-in-chief to the young, never forgetting himself in that self-chosen part.

In 1823, at the age of thirty, he went abroad; Americans were just

---

[1] Samuel Goodrich, *Recollections of a Lifetime* (New York, Miller and Orton Co., 1857), Vol. I, p. 169.

[2] *Ibid.*, p. 172.

discovering the "grand tour" and the advantages of education to be found in contact with older countries. Samuel Goodrich gazed open-mouthed at the wonders of Europe; he thought that England was "the most beautiful country in the world," with its greenness, its neatness, its ancientness. He visited Lichfield, which seems to enter so often into the annals of writers of this time; he saw Kenilworth and Edinburgh and London. But the peak of his experience was the visit to Barley Wood and Hannah More.

He describes her—and he describes people extraordinarily well—as small, greatly wrinkled, her hair "lightly powdered and frizzled, her eyes dark and penetrating, her dress dark red bombazine." She told him of the reasons for her beginning the *Repository Tracts* and of their immense sale; she explained that the Shepherd of Salisbury Plain was a real person, "although the events of the story were fictitious." The two were in complete agreement about the necessary factors in books for the young. "Do not children love truth? If so, was it necessary to feed them fiction? Could not history, natural history, geography, and biography become the elements of juvenile works in place of 'fairies and giants and mere monsters of the imagination?' " His vague ideas about publishing for children took fire, came into focus; he would take *The Shepherd of Salisbury Plain* and the other tracts for his general model, and he would produce, in kind and quantity, his own sort of thing in American version.

People were kind to this thin, limping, immeasurably enthusiastic visitor from America. He was introduced to Jeffrey, of the sharp critical tongue, to Blackwood, genial founder of *Blackwood's Magazine*; he gave his heart completely and wholly to Scott. He describes his "farmer-like aspect, his rough, freckled, weather-beaten face," his small gray eyes— "one of the pleasantest countenances I have ever seen . . . I leave you to guess my emotions, for I cannot describe them."[1]

He returned to America, moved his residence from Hartford to Boston to further his publishing business and also with the great plan in mind of juvenile authorship, although this last was not to be told abroad. Irving and Cooper were coming to the forefront of American writers, but, for the most part, American booksellers and publishers were doing little for children but reissuing or importing books of English authors. It must be remembered about Goodrich, a publisher and writer, that he was the first to offer young people American work—and works.

In 1827 appeared *Tales of Peter Parley about America* with the real authorship of the book a profound secret. "Nursery literature had not acquired the respect in the eyes of the world it now enjoys,"[2] he commented later. In 1828 there followed *Tales of Peter Parley about Europe*, in 1829 *Peter Parley's Evening Tales*, in 1830 *Juvenile Tales*, and so on

[1] Goodrich, *op. cit.*, Vol. II, p. 177.
[2] *Ibid.*, p. 279.

and so on, almost ad infinitum. By 1850 he had become the author of a hundred and seventy volumes (small ones) of which five million had been sold. He believed that one should write for children as though one were talking to them, and talk to them he did, fluently, garrulously, sometimes as a teacher, sometimes as a moral mentor. In 1830 alone his product included *Peter Parley's Tales of Africa, of Asia, of the Sun, Moon and Stars*. One of his late publications was a volume of selections, *Peter Parley's Thousand and One Stories of Fact and Fancy, Wit and Humor, Rhyme and Reason and Romance* (1858), edited by Samuel Goodrich. The secret of his connection with Peter Parley had long since been revealed. It was his intention, he said, to make it "a book of books, for the grave and gay, a sort of intellectual plum pudding."[1] Such was his whole work, although the plums were a lttle dry and the quality of the pudding underbaked. Newbery's "Trade and Plumb Cake forever" was a far richer confection.

He is best in his discourses on natural history, since that was where his real interest lay. *Peter Parley's Farewell* (1839)—but far from a final one—took the form of an account of a walk through a wheat field with Jane and James, who respond pleasingly to leading questions and are the recipients of much detailed and some interesting information. The frog —"the finest of all four-footed swimmers"—and the crocodile "with square scales disposed like parallel girdles" show close knowledge and enthusiastic study, although "the elephant's trunk terminated with an appendage resembling a finger" might seem to violate scientific truth. The intricacies of nature's wide organization are used to lead up to a summary of the nature of God.

He was fumbling for the right way of meeting children's curiosity, but he was far from discovering the true answer. That one person, with no specialized knowledge, could possibly give so much and such widely scattered information, could give it interestingly and convincingly, was an impossibility. His determined pursuit of the series idea led to deadening results. There have been many excellent series offered, especially for the young, but it is, at best, a dangerous device, which tends to dilute and extend the matter appropriate for a single book, rather than concentrate variety and richness in one piece of work. Goodrich ran the series plan thoroughly into the ground, but was never aware that he was so doing. It may have been that he was determined to equal his idol, Hannah More, in volume of sales and that this was his undoing. The public welcome of what he offered was his reason for going on and on with "more of the same" and still more in unvarying sameness of quality and content.

Peter Parley's Magazine was composed of shorter sketches of the

[1] Goodrich, *op. cit.*, Vol. II, p. 334.

same order. As his own work, it ran through 1833, after that it was sold and went on with no contribution from him. *Merry's Museum*, his longer-lived juvenile journal, of which Louisa Alcott was editor for a time, continued under his management until 1850. The extensive pirating of his work in England and elsewhere was a thorn in his flesh but it was proof of how truly popular his name had become. Certainly the act was not without justice, after the unlimited use that American publishers had been making of English work. The fact, however, tended to extend still further the flood of Parley literature, flowing evenly and smoothly outward from the apparently inexhaustible Parley source.

Yet he knew what he was doing, he knew what he intended to do, and he knew, even, the exact nature of his accomplishment. When he declared, at the end of a long and busy life, "I know better than anyone can tell me that there is nothing in this long catalogue that will give me a permanent place in literature,"[1] he disarms our condemnation. The goal of literary eminence was not, after all, the one which he was trying to achieve. He wanted to reach children everywhere, to reach their desire for knowledge in a world that was so new to them. In that we cannot say that he was wrong.

Beechnut and Phonny, Rather Than Rollo

It might seem at first glance that Jacob Abbott (1803–1879) had followed the same course as Samuel Goodrich, for we have again large output, extensive sales, and, in certain fields, a wide spread of material. Thanks to Harper and Brothers, his publishers, thanks to the distributing agencies of the Sunday School and Tract Societies, thanks perhaps to Peter Parley himself, who had plotted the commercial way, Abbott in his own turn ran into series, multiplied books of instruction, and reached a wide audience. But the fact remains that he was not imitative because he had something distinctive of his own, and he ended by offering one set of stories which went far beyond anything that Goodrich had ever conceived. He had a very vital sense of history and biography so that there was always a core of meaning and intention in his very colorful and often dramatic biographical narrative. And, what is more valuable still, he had a profound knowledge of children's minds, rising from his intense and thoughtful interest in them. Even in his books of instruction he seems to be showing, not what children ought to know, but what it would interest children to hear about. He was a minister, a teacher, and a writer, member of three professions which all tend to a deep and thorough examination of minds and hearts.

Like Parley, he was a New Englander, as rock-ribbed a denizen of Maine as Goodrich was of Connecticut. Rock-ribbed he was, at least in

[1] Goodrich, *op. cit.*, Vol. II, p. 334.

principle, but as to practice, he was possessed of a curious gentleness and tolerance that eminently belonged to a strong, rather than a yielding spirit. One of his sons spoke of his "patient and gentle inflexibility," a quality with which the Puritan spirit is occasionally, though rarely, endowed. His boyhood was of small-town life in Hallowell, on the Kennebec River, where there were long seasons for the enjoyment of winter sports—although it occurred to no one to call them that—for evenings by the roaring fire, of reading or hilarious games. It offered a little school and good teaching, which led in time to college at Bowdoin and theological training at Andover. He was deeply religious in impulse, having therewith a wide and lively interest in education, in the sciences of chemistry and geology, and in mathematics. At twenty-two he became a professor of mathematics at Amherst, at twenty-four he was licensed to preach. Three years later he left Amherst to become head of a newly founded school in Boston.

It is interesting to note that Boston's new Masonic Temple was being constructed soon after, and Abbott's establishment, the Mount Vernon School, growing with unexpected rapidity, arranged to move into the building as soon as it was finished. Jacob Abbott was consulted as to the planning of the great schoolroom on the third floor, with its long windows and unencumbered space. It was the same place which Bronson Alcott used afterward for his historic educational experiment, the Temple School.

Abbott concluded finally that both writing and preaching appealed to him more than school administration and he left, first to undertake a church, afterward, in 1836, to build a house in the country near Farmington and settle down to an intensive program of writing. Here at "Little Blue" he began adding to his series of Rollo books already begun in 1834. They are not the books of travel for which Abbott is frequently remembered, but they concern the development of a very small boy, *Rollo Learning to Talk*, *Rollo Learning to Read*, *Rollo at Work*, *Rollo at Play*, etc. Fourteen volumes are dominated by Rollo even before he and his widely informed uncle set forth on their European travels.

The theme in *Rollo Learning to Read*, voiced by Rollo's father, is that to learn to read is a very hard task and a little boy must summon all his courage and perseverance to meet it. Rollo rises to the occasion accordingly and surmounts all the difficulties. The actual mechanics of learning Abbott does not seem to consider as important as the challenge to a young pupil on which the emphasis is to be laid, his response and his pride in achieving something "very hard." Many religious books follow Rollo, then one series after another, the Jonas Books (1839–1842), the Lucy Books (1842), *Marco Paul's Travels and Adventures in Pursuit of Knowledge* (1843).

It was in 1843 that Jacob Abbott first traveled abroad. He covered

England and Europe with the same thoroughness and method with which he did everything, and came home with a richer and deeper mind, with his best work to follow immediately. He was fully impressed with the necessity for children of knowledge of the past and of their rather general lack of it. *Abbott's Illustrated Histories* were the first result of this larger stimulus, *Cyrus the Great, Darius the Great, Xerxes the Great, Alexander* (1848–1854); he seems to have had an eye especially for greatness and what it gave to the world. The series extends from Romulus through Peter the Great. He shows us that he had something of the larger, as well as the smaller, sense of the passage and drama of history. As Plutarch believed and as Abbott earnestly agreed, the lives of great men make the most convincing and memorable history; this fact being especially true of history for children. It was with this conviction that Abbott set himself to the task of this lengthy succession of volumes, just as little Rollo set himself to the great undertaking of learning to read. The books have unity, clarity and liveliness of interest. They suffer from the conventions of their time. Personal detail in biography was considered an intrusion on privacy and was largely omitted. Partisanship was apt to be heavily marked. The hero must be shown as a compelling and striking figure to justify the restoration of his past.

Foreign travel can often open people's eyes to a new and clearer perspective of their own country, a truer vision of home and earlier surroundings. This was eminently true of Abbott and brought him unwittingly to the work which he thought was of no great significance but which actually realized his own highest level and that of all writing for American children up to that time. The Franconia Stories (1850–1853) were "written in intervals of more important work" as he says in an introduction and with a tone of apology. Evidently they were the respite from his researches into the historical past. His mind went searching instead into the memories of his boyhood, into the experience of bringing up his own children. He thus created that delightful set of simple narratives of young people as living the uncomplicated and unrestricted life of little town and broad country, with all the small adventures and larger crises of a child's life. Mrs. Henry is the most unobtrusive aunt in literature, bar none; Ellen Linn is wise and sensible without being obnoxious; Mary Bell, even though she is such a mountain of industry, is appealingly natural just the same. Even Caroline, with her small vanities, is pleasantly human.

Earlier in life Jacob Abbott confided to a college friend that "in his youth an impetuous temper was his besetting temptation." The statement makes us believe that Phonny might have been himself, the boy who was always unthinkingly getting himself into trouble and so cheerily getting out again. He could easily have been the boy who sets out with a wheelbarrow load of implements to work in his garden, who leaves that, with everything scattered, to go fishing, who tires of fishing and then draws the wagon up to the woodpile, ties the reins to the shafts, and takes Malville for a long imaginary ride, talking rapidly of the scenery through which they are passing, "the streams and lakes and waterfalls, or the lofty precipices and the dark mountains which came successively into view."[1] He draws up at an imaginary inn and tells the landlord what entertainment they will require. He is brought down to earth at last. The "hired man" Beechnut (short for Antonio Bianchinette) wants to use the wagon and declares a penalty.

No one ever questions Beechnut's decrees and the penalties are always so ingenious that the culprit is filled with the liveliest curiosity as to what his fate is to be. We leave Phonny turning the grindstone for forty minutes since, as Beechnut sensibly declares, "your time is worth only half as much as mine" so that the penalty must be doubled. Beechnut's punishments are alluring because they are always so reasonable. Even now we can hardly find a more natural boy in any story for children than Phonny, who takes so little thought of consequences and is so surprised at his own frequent discomfiture.

The only thing that we deplore in the books is the rating of Beechnut as twelve years old, since no boy of his age, even a resourceful French orphan, could possibly have been so sagacious. But if this fact is overlooked, one takes Beechnut into the warmest of literary regard, for he is, truly, a matchless fellow. Jacob Abbott could not quite get away from the one utilitarian character who knows more than all the rest, but Beechnut's superiority is in nimbleness of idea, in breadth of experience, in fine common sense and unfailing humor. The horse steps on Phonny's foot and, amid his lamentations, he is warmly congratulated by Beechnut, since, so he says, every boy must get his foot stepped on at some time, and it is excellent to get the object lesson safely over. Would that education concerning automobiles could be as inexpensively bought!

The hard things of life, unescapable in that region of rigorous climate and narrow economy, are not ignored. Ellen Linn loses her aunt, with whom she lives, and her father in the same night of fearful storm; Mary Erskine goes through quiet but heroic struggle to make living possible for herself and her children in her cabin on the edge of the mountain wilderness. Even very young readers are conscious of what a comfort to her little Mary Bell was in her loneliness and sorrow. It gives a sense of the worth of children that no one had offered before. But these hard experiences are shown, not for sentimental or tragic effect, but just as things to be expected where human beings are coping with formidable surroundings. No one would take the whole impression as anything but interesting, stimulating, and representative of a free and happy life for children.

[1] Jacob Abbott, *Beechnut* (New York, Harper, 1850), p. 16. Beechnut was the Henry children's version of the boy's real name, Antonio Bianchinette.

Abbott has been reported by a friend as being a great admirer of Maria Edgeworth and to have read her tales assiduously. But he has far surpassed her in cheerfulness of tone, in the entire absence of sentimentality, and the naturalness of events in his stories. Gone completely is the violent contrast of good and bad boy. Phonny is foolishly irresponsible and very young; Stuyvesant is sober and methodically industrious; Rodolphus has been spoiled by an inept mother and falls first into bad company and then into serious trouble. But one knows that the child characters will all grow up into such men and women as make the solid citizens of the community. Situations and difficulties are worked out by the person's own efforts, be he old or young: there is none of the patronizing benevolence which, with such painful frequency, is the deus ex machina in the stories of Hannah More, and even Maria Edgeworth. The Franconia Stories are perhaps a small beginning, but they uncovered a vein in which writers for children could mine true gold.

Jacob Abbott failed to appreciate the Franconia Stories himself. He went conscientiously on with Rollo and took him to Paris, to Geneva, up the Rhine. Rollo's uncle is not so good a relative as Mrs. Henry, although he does have the wisdom to allow Rollo to make the choice of routes and places, and sends him out, with no knowledge of the language, to get tickets and make reservations, which Rollo does. Travel in Europe, even by diligence and uncertain river steamer, was simpler ideologically than it is today, and Rollo was to have little real difficulty over frontiers.

Sheer weight of numbers may have eclipsed the Franconia Stories in their own day, for Abbott's work ran to a hundred and eighty titles, outdoing even Goodrich's. More than a third of what Abbott wrote is for pure religious instruction or for use as school textbooks. The other two-thirds does not attempt to cover the field of earth, sun, moon, and stars, but remains within the believable limits of one man's effort. One book, although written for parents, must be noticed as of permanent importance, *Gentle Measures in the Management and Training of the Young* (1871). Wise, penetrating, sensible and progressive, it gives real revelation of children and what can be done with and for them by those who can stay their hands from the more obvious, but less successful "rough discipline of the cudgel." Abbott wrote perhaps too much, but with it he buried the *New England Primer*.

A man who was born a few years after him and died a few years later than he did was a person who could not write well, either for adults or children, but who has left his mark of deep influence on young people's literature just the same. Amos Bronson Alcott must have known Abbott by reputation, since his school so soon followed Abbott's at the Temple in Boston, although there is no record of any meeting between them. But Alcott with his ideas born of the Romantic movement and of Transcendentalism was a wise teacher to the same degree as Abbott.

Their beliefs partook of those of Locke and Rousseau, but they were ideas which had been sifted through more than a generation of experimenters, sifted and combined with wider practical knowledge. Both men were religious, Abbott fully orthodox, Alcott rigorously unorthodox in his scheme of thinking. To both the fullest justification for their conclusions about children was a deeply authoritative statement, "Of such is the kingdom of Heaven."

Abbott saw, what no man apparently had seen as clearly before him, that children's minds were not to be forced, their instinctive tastes were not to be violated or ignored. Never were they to be written down to. Moreover, to create literature for the young, children themselves must be the source and the inspiration; it was truly from love and understanding and knowledge of them that the whole vision must come. Jacob Abbott achieved it only when he went back to his own childhood and that of his children. Alcott never achieved such writing himself, since his pen was heavy-moving and too ponderous for easy reading, even by his philosopher friends. But he had, by the fortune that watches over men's advancement, that daughter Louisa on whom the gift of writing for the young had been generously bestowed. She never fully understood him, though she loved him dearly. But it was he who taught her —and us—the fullness of this real truth about children.

Bibliography

Abbott, Jacob. *Gentle Measures for the Management and Training of the Young.* New York, Harper, 1872.
——— *The Young Christian. With a Memoir of Jacob Abbott by his Son.* Very greatly improved and enl. New York, Harper, 1851.
Goodrich, Samuel Griswold. *Recollections of a Lifetime.* 2 Vols. New York, Miller, Orton and Mulligan, 1857.
Shepard, Odell. *Pedlar's Progress; the Life of Bronson Alcott.* Boston, Little, Brown, 1937.
Weber, Carl J. *A Bibliography of Jacob Abbott.* Waterville, Me., Colby College Press, 1948.

· 14 ·

"Some Excellent Verses for the
Education of Youth"

Early verse for children was, for the most part, little more than that
which the above title indicates, although it was only the name of a small
book by a Friend,[1] published and sold in Boston in 1708. On the list of
authors reaching into the beginning of the nineteenth century, authors
mostly admonitory, there are some exceptions, one shining one whose
"Little Lamb, who made thee?" has brought more real knowledge of
higher things than any of the preaching in all the others' work. There
arc also some who did well indeed for children, even within the rigidly
prescribed limit laid down by convention, the idea that a book, especially
in verse, must be improving. The small work mentioned above does its
whole duty as one brief quotation will show:

> Though I am young, yet I may die
> And hasten to Eternity.

And there are some, fortunately, who finally put admonition behind
them.

Country Rhymes for Country Children

As has been said before, Bunyan was a more liberal-minded Puritan
than those who came after him and had a gentler heart. In his writings,
in spite of his genius for poetic prose, his use of rhyme and meter
seemed, except on rare occasions, to bring him tumbling down to earth,
with only his pure honesty and sincerity to rescue him from oblivion as
a poet. He claims little for himself in the field of poetry, and in his single
book for the very young, he offers it only as *A Book for Boys and Girls:
or, Country Rhimes for Children* (1686). His knowledge of the countryside and its varied denizens is complete, and any one of its major or
minor objects is taken as appropriate for verse. There is a sharp and

---

[1] The Friend is Nathaniel Crouch (1632?–1725?), who wrote also under the
name of Richard Burton. A. S. W. Rosenbach, *Early American Children's Books*
(Portland, Me., Southworth Press, 1933), p. 6.

humorous observation, too, which would well catch a child's fancy. Of
the "Fatted Swine" he says:

> But, Hog, why look'st so big? Why dost so flounce,
> So snort and fling away? Dost thou renounce
> Subjection to thy lord 'cause he has fed thee? . . .[1]

However, what life and liveliness the verses might have are weighted
down by the allegorical "Comparison," sometimes as farfetched and
intricate as the "Application" of the *Gesta Romanorum*, although far
less sophisticated.

> The Bee goes out, and Honey home doth bring;
> And some who seek that Honey find a Sting . . .
> Comparison. This bee an Emblem truly is of Sin,
> Whose Sweet unto a many, Death hath been.[2]

After Bunyan's death his unassuming title was dropped, and the
collection of verses edited by a sterner Puritan hand than his. It was
reissued under the name of *Divine Emblems for Youth: or, Temporal
Things Spiritualized*, a designation that conveys more to parents than
to an inquiring child. Any of the verses which show even a quick flash
of Bunyan's humor are carefully omitted. But there is in them a spirit of
country freedom and vigor which not even the Comparison nor the
ponderous hand of the later editor can really quench.

"Soft, My Child, I Did Not Chide Thee . . ."

One who gave his gifts in kindly measure and his deep interest to
childhood was Isaac Watts (1674–1748). He was a Nonconformist
minister who spent most of his pastoral life in London, before he retired
from active preaching to devote himself to his chosen calling, the writing
of hymns. Like Locke, he learned about the nature of children's minds
by teaching them, being a tutor in a private family when he was a very
young man. The children were those of Sir John Hartop at Stoke
Newington. Science interested this young divine, as well as religious
philosophy, and his two important works in prose were *Logick or the
Right Use of Reason in the Enquiry after Truth* (1725) and *The
Knowledge of the Heavens and the Earth Made Easy, or the first Principles of Geography and Astronomy Explained* (1726). Like Locke, he
was led by teaching into thinking deeply about children's minds, their
capacities as well as their limitations. He believed that a child's understanding could join and contribute to religious worship, saying in what
is perhaps one of his greatest hymns:

---

[1] John Bunyan, *A Book for Boys and Girls* (New York, American Tract Society,
1928), p. 63.
[2] *Ibid.*, p. 36.

> Jesus shall reign where'er the sun
> Does his successive journeys run; . . .
> And enfant voices shall proclaim
> Their early blessings on His Name.[1]

Like Bunyan, he was one of the gentler Puritans, without that armor of defensive self-righteousness which some of them assumed in the face of persecution and the battle for existence in a harsh land. Watts loved to dwell on the beauty and majesty of religious thought, rather than upon the sinful nature of man and his descending punishment.

> Not to the terrors of the Lord,
> The tempest, fire and smoke
> Not to the thunder of that word
> Which God on Sinai spoke.[2]

When one reads the autobiographical line, "Oft have I laid the awful Calvin by,"[3] one catches a glimpse of the real nature of his thought. He is speaking of Calvin in the highest terms of honor and respect, but he is aware that man cannot live in the intense continuing light of that great man's unwavering rectitude. Of another great spirit he says, "Locke hath a soul wide as the sea, calm as the night, bright as the day."[4]

At the time that Watts lived, persecution of Puritans had died away, although there was still a deep gulf fixed between Anglican and Nonconformist. None the less, the Episcopal Hymnal contains a goodly treasure of his hymns: "Joy to the world," "When I survey the wondrous cross," "Come, Holy Spirit, heavenly Dove," and finest of all, "O God, our Help in ages past." All these are sung Sunday after Sunday with little recollection or acknowledgment of the power of that early eighteenth century religious poet.

His *Divine and Moral Songs for Children* was published in 1715, in the same general age and surroundings that produced *Robinson Crusoe* and *Gulliver's Travels*. In the *Divine Songs* he introduces children to a happier life in religious belief than Janeway or Mather would have allowed them. Tribute has already been given to his "Cradle Hymn," which sings itself in the mind of every mother and child, and which was one of the few redeeming features of the *New England Primer*, "Hush thee! my dear, lie still and slumber . . ." The holy angels which were to guard the child's bed were a vision bright enough to dispel those terrors by which a less convincing literature sought to surround young, impressionable minds. There is an unusually appealing touch in the last verse:

[1] (Episcopal) *Hymnal* (New York, James Pott, 1880), No. 261.
[2] *Ibid.*, No. 392.
[3] Isaac Watts, *Divine and Moral Songs*, Preface.
[4] Isaac Watts, *Poetical Works*. In *Selected British Poets*, Vol. IX, p. 331.

Soft, my child, I did not chide thee,
Though my song might sound too hard,
'Tis thy mother sits beside thee,
And her arms shall be thy guard.[1]

As printed in the *Divine Songs*, alternative words are offered in the place of mother—brother, sister, neighbor, friend—so that the sleepy child will know most particularly that the song is his very own.

The *Moral Songs* is a division entirely by itself in his book for children and contains many familiar lines and characters, usually recollected without acknowledgment to the author. Here we behold "How doth the little busy bee," a thoroughly reputable character this time and not the emblem of sin as Bunyan would have her. Here sounds "the voice of the sluggard," and here we are bidden to "let dogs delight to bark and bite." There is sympathetic acquaintance with children's failings and the gentlest of advice as to how to meet their temptations. Once in a while the intolerance of his age betrays Watts, but it is very seldom, so truly was he devoted to the task of showing children the wonderful works of God.

For a Very Little Prince

When Dean Swift paid his last visit to London, his advent was celebrated by a meeting of his favorite Scriblerus Club, where the germ of the idea for Gulliver had been fostered. The membership was still intact, except for the death of the poet Parnell. John Gay (1685–1732), one of its brightest spirits, was working on his *Fables* (published 1727), written ostensibly for the Duke of Cumberland, the son of the Prince of Wales, the little boy being six years old. The verses were to offer instruction that would assist and advise one who was in line to bear royal responsibilities. This is the dedication:

Accept, young Prince, the moral lay,
And in these tales mankind survey,
With early virtues plant your breast,
The specious arts of vice detest;
Princes, like beauties, from their youth
Are strangers to the voice of truth.

It is satire rather than moral teaching, which is the burden of the *Fables*, their language aimed far more at the elders than at children. They ran through many editions in their century, but no child and few grownups regard them now. They are keener and more ungentle than

---

[1] Isaac Watts, *Divine and Moral Songs* (London, James Nisbet & Co., 1866), p. 74. The first English edition was 1715. Rosenbach, *Early American Children's Books*, p. 37.

the kindly tales of Æsop, while the vehicle of long-drawn-out rhyme is much less effective than the old homely prose. In "Fable V, The Wild Boar and the Ram," a boar reproaches a flock of sheep for submitting to the butcher without resistance or attempted retaliation. An ancient Ram replies astutely:

> Know those who violence pursue
> Give to themselves the vengeance due,
> For in these massacres they find
> The two chief plagues that waste mankind:
> Our skin supplies the wrangling bar,
> It wakes their slumbering sons to war,
> And well revenge may rest contented
> Since drums and parchment were invented.[1]

One doubts whether the young Prince was any the better for having them read to him, or was any other child. Gay was at the same time germinating another and more congenial project, which had arisen from a suggestion of Swift's—that he base a comedy on the rogues and rascals of Newgate Prison with whom he was so well acquainted. It was to come into being later as *The Beggar's Opera* (1728) with Gay completely returned from his brief excursion into literature for the young.

Watts, of these three, made perhaps the most deeply concentrated effort to reach children in verse, and for this he was inspired by his sense of the necessity of religious teaching. Without that incentive few seemed to be moved to make the effort to appeal to children's minds which, as Boswell recognized, was less easy than writing for contemporaries.

Robert Southey's (1774–1843) poem beginning "You are old, Father William" may have been written for adults, nor has it, in its original form, survived to be remembered by older or younger readers; it needed Lewis Carroll's hilarious parody to make an immortal appeal to the young imagination. Southey's prose masterpiece, "The Three Bears," has fared better. Authorities declare that it was really his invention, not an earlier tale heard in childhood. It was published in his *The Doctor* (1834–1837) and has deservedly achieved the position of folklore in its own right.

The appearance of Wordsworth's and Coleridge's *Lyrical Ballads* in 1798, which did so much to change the face of all literature, was, in the end, to have great influence on the character and quality of children's literature also and to bring a full awakening of that understanding of children which is an utter necessity to a true literature for them. But the direct result was less than the indirect; Wordsworth (1770–1850) rather

[1] John Gay, *Fables by the late Mr. Gay* (London, J. and F. C. Revington, 1772), p. 24.

went over their heads with "Lucy Gray" and did not have them in mind with "The Daffodils" any more than Samuel Taylor Coleridge (1772–1834) did when he plunged into the fine terrors of "The Rime of the Ancient Mariner." There is still a generation which knew that poem in the huge folio edition with Doré illustrations, which had to be spread flat on the floor with the youthful reader on his stomach—preferably in an undisturbed position under the grand piano—to explore with something of the same bewilderment as the Wedding Guest, the kaleidoscopic and strikingly pictured journeyings of the Mariner.

"Little Lamb, Who Made Thee?"

It was the least heralded of the group of Romantic poets who left behind one of the deepest and most lasting of those few pieces of truly great poetry that have power to appeal to children of all time. This was William Blake (1757–1827) with his *Songs of Innocence* (1789). There are scholars who have spent half a lifetime trying to fathom the depths of Blake's message to mankind, nor, perhaps, will the full riddle of his strange mind ever be fully solved. He was barely noticed in his own time but has come slowly into high regard in the twentieth century. *Songs of Innocence* was composed, illustrated, lettered, engraved on copper plates, and printed, all by his own hand. They were the essence of the man himself.

Born in a shabby quarter of London, but close enough to its edge for a boy to walk out into bright fields and open country, he lived from his birth to his death in hard, unchanging poverty. His only real education was his apprenticeship to an engraver, but it taught him the mastery of line and design which was the fulfillment of his own artistic genius. He added much, by reading and the study of languages, to broaden his intellectual world, and his strangely inspired imagination explored a world far beyond that. To one who was preoccupied with angels, the details of poverty were unimportant; he worked to the fullest of his ability on drawing and poetry all his life and asked for nothing more.

Songs of Innocence was one of his earliest works. It cannot be said that it was actually written for children. It makes an attempt to picture the mind of man before maturity has set up what Wordsworth called the enclosing shadows of the prison house. The *Songs* represents, in contrast to his *Songs of Experience* (1794), the fullness of youthful glory before it has crossed that knife edge of difference between the thinking of the wholly young and the beginning of adult responsibility and knowledge. Thus Blake achieved, scarcely knowing it, that task which is the real goal of writers for children, the production of something out of the knowledge and recollection of childhood that is the very spirit of childhood itself. It was not to be achieved in poetry or prose for a long time after; it was something that had fallen unnoticed to the ground until both readers and writers of a later century understood literature and literature for children more fully and gratefully. He says in his "Introduction":

> Piping down the valleys wild,
> Piping songs of pleasant glee,
> On a cloud I saw a child,
> And he laughing said to me:
> "Pipe a song about a Lamb!" . . .[1]

The child is here the true spirit and import of the writing. There is nothing of preaching or searching for a point of attack to deliver a moral. Yet here, in a much fuller sense, is an awareness of heavenly beauty and a child's instinctive response to it. A very young mind's fumbling penetration and its divine curiosity are all embodied in the utter simplicity of that "song about a Lamb," piped to order as the "Introduction" declares:

> Little Lamb, who made thee?
> Dost thou know who made thee? . . .
> Little Lamb, I'll tell thee:
> He is calléd by thy name,
> For He calls Himself a Lamb.
> He is meek and He is mild;
> He became a little child,
> I a child, and thou a lamb,
> We are calléd by His name.
> Little Lamb, God bless thee![2]

To such unassuming teaching any child will respond where a hundred *Tokens for Children* and *Milk for Babes* fall to the barren ground of unheeding indifference. In Blake's more mature poems, there is something to which children will answer, even without asking for a meaning, which so often and so humbly they refrain from doing. "Tiger, Tiger burning bright in the forests of the night" is a picture that remains long in any child's inward eye. There are few, also, who will not thrill in answer to those resplendent lines:

> Bring me my bow of burning gold!
> Bring me my arrows of desire!
> Bring me my spear! O clouds, unfold!
> Bring me my chariot of fire![3]

Time and temporary oblivion shut swiftly down upon Blake, but it is good to know that there were to be great poets such as he to write of and for children again.

[1] William Blake, *Works* (London, Oxford University Press, 1925), p. 65.
[2] *Ibid.*, p. 67.
[3] *Ibid.*, "Milton," p. 370.

Meddlesome Matty and Her Brothers and Sisters

Like Blake, the Taylor family were engravers—the two daughters Ann and Jane, their brother Isaac, their father who had taught them their craft, their grandfather, Isaac Taylor, also, who had taught him. The Taylors of Ongay they came to be called, a household where father, mother, brother, and sisters all published books and needed to be distinguished from another literary family, the Taylors of Norwich. Isaac Taylor Second gave his daughters all their education and kept them for long hours at their lessons and for equally long hours when they came to take part in his business of engraving copper plates for the printers. Ann was the elder sister (1782–1866); she won a prize for solving puzzles in a magazine carried on by the publishers Harvey and Darton, after which she continued to contribute to the magazine and was presently followed by her sister Jane (1783–1824). It was the interest and encouragement of these publishers which led to the bringing out of their first book.

They were a gay and spirited family, of quick wit and vigorous minds. It is not often that those so young could understand children so fully, without an interval of growing perspective on their own early years. Verse came easily to them; Jane, when only eight or nine, wanted a garden and stated her desire for it in a set of stanzas after the style of John Gilpin. The Taylors' verses teach a lesson, of course; verses did not appear through the ordinary channels of publication without that excuse. They are, however, the unaggressive lessons of decorous and polite behavior which are presented, along with the larger virtues of good nature, obedience and tolerance. The ideas are as clear and simple as running spring water and the character of the verse is the same. But the meter has life, so have the children portrayed by it; there is freshness and naturalness of interest in the subjects and a varied sympathy with what befalls them in the very mild hazards and problems of English living.

> Little Anne and her mother were walking one day,
> Through London's wide city so fair,
> And business obliged them to go by the way
> That led them through Cavendish Square.[1]

Little Anne weeps at seeing fine ladies roll away in a coach "while we have to walk in the cold." Her mother, after the traditional manner of making children content, points out a beggar who is so much worse off than they that Anne speedily becomes happy again.

"The Churchyard" moves in singularly close parallel to Gray's "Elegy," but it is followed quickly by the more cheerful:

[1] The Taylor Family, *Original Poems for Infant Minds* (New York, F. A. Stokes, 1904), p. 5.

> Awake, little girl, it is time to arise,
> Come shake drowsy sleep from thy eye;
> The lark is now warbling his notes in the skies
> And the sun is far mounted on high.[1]

Meddlesome Matty is a heroine so well known that she needs no quotation. "Twinkle, twinkle, little star" has established itself firmly in every child's memory, this being Jane's, while "My Mother" and "Welcome, welcome little stranger, to this busy world of care" are Ann's.

Original Poems for Infant Minds by Several Young Persons (1804) was the title of their first book, coming from the hands of very young persons indeed, since Ann was twenty-two, Jane twenty-one, and their brother Isaac, who wrote one or two of the contributions, was seventeen. Since the publishers did not think the number of verses quite sufficient, they included in the volume some further poems for children by Adelaide O'Keefe (1776–1855), who was not known to the Taylors or associated with them in any other way. She was the daughter of an Irish playwright, lived with him at Chichester and Southampton, and wrote some books on her own account—*Original Poems Calculated to Improve the Mind of Youth and Allure It to Virtue* (circa 1808) and *Poems for Young Children* (circa 1849). She did not achieve much standing in her own right, while the Taylors, who had the charm and sparkle in their work which she had not, came immediately into immense public regard. Their pleasant picture of simple English life was true of countless households all over the British Isles. Everywhere people were reading delightedly about themselves. The *Original Poems for Infant Minds* was translated into French, German, and even Russian for people liked to read about England and about the young people who were so natural they were at home anywhere. They were as well beloved across the Atlantic as at home.

A second volume of *Original Poems* appeared in 1805, this time by the Taylors alone; it was followed by *Rhymes for the Nursery* in 1806 and by *Hymns for Infant Minds* in 1810 and 1811. In the next year Ann was married and the break in association brought the young poets' real career to an end. While each wrote her own poems, with a recognizable quality in the work of each sister, none the less the advantage of being together, of mutual stimulation and discussion, seemed to have been a large factor in the excellence of their work. Jane published a few further poems which never reached the reputation of those earlier ones. But the life of their first books went steadily on. In 1877 there was published a collected edition of all the poems of the Taylors, and an even later collection came out with Kate Greenaway's illustrations, *Little Ann and Other Poems* (circa 1883).

---

[1] The Taylor Family, *op. cit.*, p. 25.

Charles and Mary Lamb, evidently urged thereto by their publishers, who were impressed by the success of the Taylors, brought out in 1809 *Poetry for Children, Entirely Original*, by the Author of *Mrs. Leicester's School*. Charles joined in the enterprise with a very bad grace and said sourly of the subjects "picked out by an old bachelor and an old maid" . . . "Many parents would not have found so many." The brother and sister went back to their own childhood visits to the country for scenes and incidents. They depict "The Reaper's Child," "The Ride," "The Butterfly," all in mild and easy verse, now and then even achieving an energetic swing of rhythm. Charles, on his own account, brought out a longer set of verses, *Prince Dorus, or Flattery Put out of Countenance* (1811), which is ingenious and deliberately absurd and not much else.

The Butterfly and the Peacock

If it ever fails to be plain that children have an excellent ear for rhyme and rhythm and a distinct enjoyment of it, the fine popularity of *The Butterfly's Ball, and the Grasshopper's Feast* (1807) would be sufficient proof of it all over again.

> Come take up your hats and away let us haste
> To the Butterfly's Ball and the Grasshopper's feast . . .

The verses following these opening lines run at just the satisfactory pace to make the young imagination gallop away with it. Most of the poem is an enumeration of the guests—the Hornet "with jacket of yellow and brown," the Gnat, the Dragonfly and all their relations "green, orange and blue," and all the rest. The scene is one of color and movement and enticing variety. It was written by William Roscoe (1753–1831), a professional historian with side interests in science, but parent of a responsive son for whom he wrote the verses.

So completely was the poem taken to the heart of youth that its publisher, John Harris, who had in certain ways assumed the mantle of John Newbery, proceeded to follow it with a long string of others, *The Peacock "at Home"* (1807) by a Mrs. Dorset being the best of them. Here the invitation list is heavily weighted with the names of birds, with the poem having a sprightliness of its own. There were many others, *The Lion's Parliament* (1807), *The Rose's Breakfast*, *The Tyger's Theatre*. None of them approached the original, not even Ann Taylor Gilbert's *Wedding among the Flowers*.

English verse was read so contentedly by American children all through the seventeenth and early eighteenth centuries that they did not seem to miss the presence of poets of their own. "Mary Had a Little Lamb" was published in 1830 in the *Juvenile Miscellany* so successfully conducted for a few years by Lydia Maria Child. Mary's immortal story is by Sarah Josepha Hale, editor of Godey's *Lady's Book*, and was later published in her own volume of *Poems for Children*. It has been so universally adopted into children's literature that one almost forgets that it does not belong to Mother Goose, instead of ultimately to *McGuffey's Second Reader*.

"Down the Chimney St. Nicholas Came with a Bound"

In 1823 Clement Clarke Moore (1779–1863) came to the rescue of American letters and produced a real classic, for American children first, and later for children everywhere, *The Night Before Christmas*. So great and wide has been its beloved and, many times, oral career that time has streamlined it and made some alterations which the writer never contemplated. The title Moore gave it, *A Visit from St. Nicholas*, has given way to a more acceptable one; its conclusion "Happy Christmas to all and to all a Good Night" has become "Merry Christmas" by common consent—except perhaps Clement Moore's. Its rhythm is a perfect choice, echoing the prancing and pawing of each little reindeer hoof, giving scope for the sudden soaring to the roof and the bouncing entry of St. Nicholas into the room where the stockings hang.

Clement Moore was a professor of biblical learning at the General Theological Seminary in New York. Not even the study of minor saints would seem to come into the subject of his courses, but fortunately he had other fields of research. The poem was written for his own children; it slipped into the *Troy Sentinel* without his knowledge and without his name. Newspapers copied it everywhere although it continued to be anonymous until Mrs. Hale discovered the secret and gave it away. In an edition of Moore's verse published in 1844 it is included as his own.

In spite of the wide familiarity of all the world with his poem, Moore as a person tended to remain in undeserved obscurity. Anne Carroll Moore, as one item in her great and varied service to children's reading, has brought him back to our knowledge and friendship. Her *Nicholas, A Manhattan Christmas Story* is a boldly fanciful tale of that city upon which few people have remembered to look with imagination. Its delightful map guides us to "the Night Before Christmas Country," and its story gives us an unforgettable glimpse of Clement Moore himself and the district of New York where he lived—of the fields and orchards about his house "which he was already beginning to give away." We hear of his friend the Dutch farmer who gave him information about the saint and we feel that we know kindly, studious Clement Moore himself with the magic of Christmas in his heart. Children's literature has completely adopted his poem. Children's taste, too, with that power which has been the underlying force of the whole development of children's reading has exerted its authority and named it *The Night Before Christmas* for all time.

Bibliography

Blake, William. *The Complete Writings of William Blake*; with variant readings, edited by Geoffrey Keynes. New ed. London, Oxford University Press, 1966.

Gilchrist, Alexander. *Life of William Blake*. A new and enl. ed. London, Macmillan, 1880. Vol. I.

Irving, William Henry. *John Gay, Favorite of the Wits*. Durham, N.C., Duke University Press, 1940.

Moore, Anne Carroll. *Nicholas; A Manhattan Christmas Story*. New York, G. P. Putnam's Sons, 1924.

Taylor, Jane, Ann Taylor Gilbert, and Adelaide O'Keefe. *The "Original Poems" and Others*, edited by E. V. Lucas. New York, F. A. Stokes Co., 1905.

Watts, Isaac. *Divine and Moral Songs for Children*. London, J. Nisbet, 1866.

Part Two

1840 - 1890

Widening Horizons

ANNE THAXTER
EATON

1

The Victorian Family

When Charlotte Yonge as a little girl (she was born in 1823) went with her parents from Otterbourne to visit her grandmother, the journey was always made in a chariot with post horses. "I was always giddy, often sick, in a close carriage," she tells us in her autobiography, but, she adds, "there were delights. Papa read me the *Perambulations of a Mouse* on one of those journeys."[1] In adult life Charlotte Yonge paid tribute to *The Life and Perambulations of a Mouse* by Dorothy Kilner, *Jemima Placid* by Mary Jane Kilner, and to a number of other stories which had appeared toward the end of the eighteenth century. She edited them, with an appreciative introduction, in *A Storehouse of Stories*, published by Macmillan in 1870. Thus a writer, who has justly been called "a Victorian best-seller" and whose life and work coincided almost exactly with the reign of Queen Victoria, links the children's books before her time with the books for children which she and others were to produce so plentifully during the second half of the nineteenth century. Between 1844, when her first book, *Abbeychurch*, was published, and her death in 1901 Charlotte Yonge wrote over one hundred and twenty books. She is best remembered for her stories—family stories—and her historical tales.

There was never, perhaps, a writer more typical of her own age. Charlotte Yonge wrote of life as lived by the large families who were growing up in Victorian nurseries and schoolrooms. Her readers could find themselves and their own households in *Heartsease* (1854), *The Daisy Chain* (1856), *The Pillars of the House* (1873), *Magnum Bonum* (1880) and the rest. Though Charlotte had only one brother, who was considerably younger than herself, she grew up in close association with her cousins, the children of "Uncle and Aunt Yonge," who lived at Puslinch, five boys and five girls, just such a family of brothers and sisters as she was afterward to describe in her books. From an early age she had a sharp eye for character, an ear for conversation, and a retentive

---

[1] Charlotte Yonge, "Autobiography," in Christabel Coleridge, *Charlotte Mary Yonge, Her Life and Letters* (London, Macmillan, 1903), p. 63.

memory. Moreover, it was a habit of hers to write down actual conversations, which explains why the reader sometimes feels himself to be eavesdropping.

The age in which Charlotte Yonge lived was the age of the Family, a family far more self-contained and self-sufficient in its interests, its amusements, its aspirations, than families today. The Victorian Age was also a religious age and religion was deeply a part of the family's life. During Charlotte's young womanhood and early days of authorship, the state of the Church was a matter of vital interest. The Oxford Movement, sometimes called the Tractarian Movement, had begun in 1833 with a sermon preached by John Keble. Keble, John Henry Newman, James Froude, Edward Pusey, and others were trying to bring back the spirituality which they believed the Church had lost. *Tracts of the Times* began to appear in 1834. In 1841, Newman's famous *Tract 90*, in which he demonstrated that the Thirty-nine Articles were not inconsistent with Catholicism, brought consternation to churchmen and to some of the laity. Newman resigned his living and in 1845 joined the Church of Rome, a blow from which John Keble never recovered. All these matters were discussed with pained and eager interest around the evening lamp in many households. In the close-knit families of the day, young people listened to these discussions and shared the concern of their elders. It was natural, therefore, that the Church should play a large part in the lives of the boys and girls in Miss Yonge's books. She knew of what she wrote. John Keble was vicar of Hursley Parish, which adjoined Otterbourne. There was close intercourse between the two families, and Mr. Keble prepared Charlotte for confirmation when she was fifteen; she called it "one especial blessing of my life."

What had happened within the Oxford Movement, Newman's ordination as a Roman Catholic priest, the opposition which the Tractarians aroused among some members of the Church of England, deepened the loyalty of others. It was not only the religious belief that concerned them, but the ritual, the services, the music, the building itself, eager as they were to have the church which they upheld as perfect as their dedicated efforts could make it. Thus the discussion of church affairs by Miss Yonge's characters, their regular church going, their interest in parish work, seemed entirely natural to Miss Yonge's readers.

Charlotte Yonge, however, unlike the writers of the preceding century, did not write her stories for the sake of religious or moral teaching. She put into her books her own sincere belief in the Christian way of life, in the help the Church can give, in the importance of self-discipline; to her they were all a part of normal living. However, she sounded a new note, for in her stories she combined goodness and romance. She showed that a high standard of Christian life was not incompatible with fun and merriment, with common humanity and its failures, as well as with its aspirations fulfilled. Guy Morville of *The Heir of Redclyffe* (1853) may seem priggish to the modern reader, Amy's decision not to send one word of comfort to her suitor to show her belief in him, when she knows his banishment to be undeserved, may appear ridiculously scrupulous; and in *Heartsease* Helen Martindale's refusal to marry after eight years of waiting because of her old, decrepit, and imbecile grandfather may seem absurd. But Miss Yonge's contemporaries accepted it all and, no doubt, for the most part approved. The theme of filial obedience, which appeared again and again in Charlotte Yonge's books, was familiar and respected. Readers of the day—undergraduates at Oxford, bishops, statesmen, and soldiers—received *The Heir of Redclyffe* warmly and were moved by it. Rossetti shed tears over it; William Morris determined to model himself on its hero.

In *The Daisy Chain* there is much enthusiasm and lively discussion in the May family over the building of the church at Cocksmoor, for in this and in other books Miss Yonge shows us a dominant interest of her times, the building of churches, the outward sign of that core of Tractarian doctrine, belief in the Church. Many churches were built all over the country. A new church was built at Otterbourne, for which Charlotte's father helped prepare the plans. A church was built at Hursley, Keble's parish, and a church at Amphill, near Otterbourne, was rebuilt —three undertakings which Charlotte was able to watch from day to day.

Two other predominant interests of the period, interests very close to Charlotte's heart, are shown in her books, receiving special emphasis in *The Daisy Chain*. These are foreign missions and the Sunday schools. In 1854 (two years before *The Daisy Chain* was finished) a distant cousin of the Yonges, John Coleridge Patteson, decided to go out to New Zealand with Bishop Selwyn. Norman in *The Daisy Chain* seems to have been patterned after this "Coley" Patteson. Charlotte, feeling that the earlier voyages of the future Bishop Patteson in his mission ship had provided so many suggestions for imaginary incidents in this book, wished to turn over the proceeds of the book to the Mission. In 1859 this was done, and the money dedicated to the proposed college at Kolumarama. Already, in 1854, a substantial part of the profits from *The Heir of Redclyffe* had been handed over to Bishop Selwyn "toward the vessel for the Island Mission."

In *The Daisy Chain* the decision of Norman May and his wife Meta to go as missionaries to the Loyalty Islands, and Harry May's adventures there, are made romantic and thrilling for youthful readers and doubtless turned the thoughts of many Tractarians toward the mission field. Running through the book is Ethel May's dream of starting and teaching in a school for the untaught, neglected children of Cocksmoor, a dream which comes true. *Langley School*, an earlier book which appeared first in *The Magazine for the Young*, contained stories of the children taught at a similar school in Otterbourne and of those Charlotte Yonge's friend, Marian Dyson, taught at Dogmers Field. These tales were published in book form in 1850 and not only pleased the younger children for whom they were intended, but as one of Miss Yonge's biographers has said, "fired the imagination of girls in their teens and set a whole generation to school-teaching."[1]

These parish schools were important, for although the idea of compulsory education was in the air and Parliament had voted in 1833 twenty thousand pounds per annum in aid of schools for the people, it was 1870 before a bill was introduced to provide for general public education in England and Wales. The parish schools and the Sunday schools helped bridge the gap.

The coming general interest in education is foreshadowed in Charlotte Yonge's books, but there is in them no hint of that other phenomenon of the latter half of the nineteenth century, the rise in status of the middle-class woman. In fact, we find Charlotte expressing the characteristically Victorian belief in the inferiority of women, which it took so many years to wear down, as for example when Ethel May in *The Daisy Chain* is advised to sacrifice her desire to keep up with her brother Norman in his university studies, not only because of her home duties, but because a woman cannot hope to equal a man in scholarship. *Henrietta's Wish* (1850) is concerned with this same theme, and in her *Womankind* (1877) Charlotte came out frankly with, "I have no hesitation in declaring my full belief in the inferiority of woman, nor that she brought it upon herself . . ." (here she was referring to the apple and the Garden of Eden). "That there is this inequality there is no reasonable doubt. A woman of the highest faculties is of course superior to a man of the lowest: but she never attains to anything like the powers of a man of the highest ability."[2] Even as she so wrote, Florence Nightingale, a woman and her contemporary, had, in her organization of a hospital unit in the Crimean War and in her founding of the Florence Nightingale School and Home for Nurses at St. Thomas's Hospital in 1860, not only worked a revolution in the care of the wounded but set women well along toward the goal of independence and training for professional life. But of all this Charlotte was quite unconscious.

In 1865 in *The Clever Woman of the Family* Charlotte devotes nearly the whole book to making Rachel, the heroine, realize how much better and deeper were her husband's ideas than her own. Women

[1] Georgina Battiscombe, *Charlotte Mary Yonge* (London, Constable, 1943), p. 67.
[2] C. M. Yonge, *Womankind* (London, Macmillan, 1877), pp. 1–2.

were to think for themselves, to be sure, that Miss Yonge makes clear; but in the case of a disagreement, it is evident that she expected the woman or the girl in the case to come around to her husband's, brother's, or father's opinion.

There were also the beginnings of another movement during the 1840's, 1850's, and 1860's of which we find no hint in Charlotte Yonge's stories. The founders of the Sunday schools of the late eighteenth and early nineteenth centuries took into account that the children working in factories and coal mines had no opportunity for schooling but completely failed to realize the enormity of the fact that children of six and even younger were drawing coal trucks in mines and laboring in factories ten hours a day for a six-day week. In 1861 the Report of the Children's Employment Commission was published, a troubling document. The next year a poet spoke out when Elizabeth Barrett Browning wrote "The Cry of the Children" and stirred the reading classes when she asked:

> Do you hear the children weeping, O my brothers,
> . . . .
> They are weeping bitterly!
> They are weeping in the playtime of the others,
> In the country of the free.[1]

Dickens, along with the fun and fascination that his novels provided, pointed out to his readers the sad lot of orphans and charity-school children. Charles Kingsley roused public opinion in the matter of chimney sweeps. Yet reforms came slowly. The Victorians were not heartless, but the results of the Industrial Revolution, the growth of factories, the economic theory of non-interference with the laws of supply and demand, combined to keep things as they were, partly because people were bewildered and uncertain as to what should be done to improve conditions that had gone unquestioned for so long. Then, too, there was a sturdy optimism abroad; the hard-working, self-confident Victorians felt with Tennyson:

> Oh yet we trust that somehow good
> Will be the final goal of ill.[2]

Charlotte Yonge's charity was practical and personal; she thought in terms of individuals like Lovedy Kelland, the little girl in *The Clever Woman of the Family* who worked at lace-making for ten hours a day. Help in her mind was given from person to person or it was provided

[1] Elizabeth Barrett Browning, "The Cry of the Children," *Complete Poetical Works* (Cambridge edition), p. 156.
[2] Alfred, Lord Tennyson, "In Memoriam," stanza LIV, *Poetic and Dramatic Works* (Cambridge edition), p. 175.

under the direction of the Church and the Sunday schools which were so dear to her. In 1861 Charles Kingsley expressed himself as disturbed beyond measure by the Report of the Commission on Child Employment, but Charlotte Yonge in that same year was unaware of the beginnings of a movement, which aimed not to ameliorate destitution but to abolish it, in short that social reform was on the way.[1]

Because Charlotte Yonge transcribed into her books so much from the life around her, they naturally mirror in smaller matters the attitudes characteristic of her own day, so different from those of our own time that they tend to disturb the modern reader. Invalids are legion in her stories, sometimes brought to their sickbeds or to couches in the living room by an astonishing array of symptoms, their couches becoming the centers of the family's life. Very naturally no more attention is paid to the matter of infection or hygiene than was paid in real life at that time. In *The Pillars of the House* the family live in the closest contact with the father, who is dying of "galloping consumption." Babies appear unheralded, as in the famous incident in *The Dove in the Eagle's Nest* (1866), with a disconcerting suddenness. Only in *The Heir of Redclyffe* is the coming event openly discussed.

Though Charlotte's predecessor, Jane Austen, decried sensibility, hers was a lone voice; sensibility was not only characteristic of Victoria's reign, it was an admired characteristic. Not only women but men were easily moved to tears. The men were not ashamed of it and confessed, many of them without hesitation, to breaking down over the deathbed scene in *The Heir of Redclyffe*. Charles Kingsley found himself "wiping his eyes a dozen times before he got through *Heartsease*." After that he wrote to the publisher that the book was "wise and human and noble as well as Christian." It would have brought no shock to a contemporary to find Tom, the erring schoolboy, and his father, Dr. May, weeping together when Tom confesses his wrongdoing. Deathbed scenes are frequent in Miss Yonge's books, though no more so than in those of other writers of the day.

As we look at books of the time in general we see that there was less distinction between those for the young and those for older readers when Miss Yonge was writing. Books were written to appeal to a wider age range, perhaps because of the very general family habit of reading aloud. William Morris, Edward Burne-Jones, Dante Rossetti and others of the Pre-Raphaelite group read *The Heir of Redclyffe* and took it seriously. Henry Sidgwick of Trinity College, Cambridge, was impressed by *The Trial*, the sequel to *The Daisy Chain*. *Heartsease* got out to Crimea during the War and brought comfort to Lord Raglan before his death. Tennyson and Lewis Carroll were among Miss Yonge's admirers.

---

[1] Charles Kingsley, *His Letters and Memories of His Life* (London, Kegan Paul, 1877), Vol. 2, p. 124.

Sir Walter Scott's books, like Charlotte's own, were enjoyed by young and old. Scott was a deep influence in Charlotte's life. She described Lockhart's *Life of Sir Walter Scott* as "A book that was absolute delight to me, and is still, showing forth that most attractive character in its fulness. I may respect, admire, rely on other authors more, but my prime literary affection must ever be for Sir Walter!"[1] Nor was Charlotte Yonge unique in this feeling. Scott, with his reverence for tradition and chivalry, his joy in the high courage and gallant deeds of the past, his sympathy for the romantic and aristocratic Jacobite cause, was thoroughly congenial to the Tractarians. Whole families read him, Newman read Scott all his life, the Moberly children delighted in his stories. Maurice Baring in his autobiography says that Scott's novels were held before him and his sisters as an alluring bait. "When you are nine years old," he was told, "you shall read *The Talisman*," and he adds, "the reading of the Waverley Novels was a divine, far-off event, to which all one's life seemed to be slowly moving."[2] Charlotte herself made the acquaintance of Scott with *The Talisman* when she was ten. She was then allowed a chapter of Scott a day, provided she first read a chapter of Goldsmith's *The Roman History* or some other equally solid book.

Another writer who meant much to the Victorians, though without Scott's genius, was La Mott-Fouqué. Dürer's "The Knight and His Companions" hung over Charlotte's writing table, the influence of *Sintram* can be clearly seen in *The Heir of Redclyffe*, and there are allusions throughout Miss Yonge's books to this tale, so religious and so romantic. On this side of the Atlantic, Jo, in Louisa Alcott's *Little Women*, planned to spend her hard-earned pocket money for a copy of *Undine and Sintram*.

Yet if we look below the manners and customs and influences of that age, so different from our own, we can see that the excellence of Miss Yonge's character drawing is what really stands out. No more delightful portrait of a father has ever been painted than that of Dr. May in *The Daisy Chain*; generous, kind, impulsive, humorous, and understanding, sometimes impatient but quick to acknowledge when he is wrong. (The Moberlys, with their many children, were near neighbors and devoted friends of the Yonges. *The Daisy Chain*, indeed, seemed to derive from the large Moberly family.) Dr. George Moberly, Headmaster of Winchester and later Bishop of Salisbury, made Charlotte promise when she began writing sequels to her stories never to allow Dr. May to die, a promise she managed to keep, though with some difficulty because of the many years her books covered.

[1] Charlotte Yonge, "Autobiography," in Christabel Coleridge, *Charlotte Mary Yonge, Her Life and Letters*, p. 113.
[2] Maurice Baring, *The Puppet Show of Memory* (London, Heinemann, 1922), p. 49.

Ethel May, harum-scarum, impulsive, quick-tempered, but thoroughly lovable (Jo in Louisa Alcott's *Little Women* might be a lineal descendant), was perhaps the first really human heroine in a book for young people. She is more convincing than Norman, her favorite brother, though Norman too is real and the friendship between brother and sister one of the charms of the story. Equally close in affection were the younger pair, Harry and Mary. Felix and Geraldine in *The Pillars of the House* exhibit the same sympathy and understanding.

Thus her observation of families living, working, and playing together, her memories of happy childhood days spent with her cousins at Puslinch, all went into Charlotte Yonge's stories, so that while she may use a character to illustrate a principle, that character remains a real person and never becomes a type. Her characterization of younger children is excellent. Her description in *Countess Kate* (1862) of a sensitive, high-strung child has seldom been equaled.

So far nothing has been said of Miss Yonge's historical stories, although they comprise a large part of her writing. As a mirror of her time the family stories are enjoyed because of the fascinating glimpse they give us of Victorian life, yet they are out of print today. Interest in the historical tales has lasted longer. The best known are *The Chaplet of Pearls* (1868), *The Little Duke* (1854), *The Lances of Lynwood* (1855), *The Prince and the Page* (1865), *Two Penniless Princesses* (1891), *The Dove in the Eagle's Nest* (1866), *The Caged Lion* (1870) and *A Book of Golden Deeds* (1864). All of these except *The Chaplet of Pearls* are still in print and found in libraries today. Maurice Baring tells of reading *The Lances of Lynwood*, *The Little Duke*, and *The Chaplet of Pearls* when he was a boy.[1] He found the last named thrilling, but *The Little Duke*, a vividly told story for young children of Richard, Duke of Normandy, is the most generally popular. It is written with full understanding of children, for Charlotte did understand them, and with a pleasant simplicity of style. Miss Yonge had the happy faculty of seeing events and people from a child's point of view. In some respects she never left her own childhood entirely behind and she never wrote down to boys and girls. Her storytelling is better than her history, for her period sense was slight and she was inclined to look at all centuries through the eyes of the nineteenth. Her interest was in the characters whom she painted according to her own conception, which, it must be said, made them appear citizens of Charlotte's own world rather than their own. Some of her historical figures might electrify a modern historian, but her contemporaries were not too historically minded. The story was the thing for which children and grown-ups who read her books were looking and the story, as Charlotte told it, had drama and vividness.

[1] Maurice Baring, *op. cit.*, p. 49.

No account of Charlotte Yonge would be complete without mention of *The Magazine for the Young* and *The Monthly Packet*. The first number of *The Magazine for the Young* appeared in 1842. Almost at once Charlotte became a contributor and *Langley School* first appeared in its pages. By 1850, when *Langley School* was reprinted in book form, Charlotte had had four books published. *Langley School* in particular had made her name familiar to the reading public. Encouraged, perhaps, by this, Charlotte undertook a new literary venture, a magazine to be called *The Monthly Packet*. *The Magazine for the Young* was intended for the children of the working classes, *The Churchman's Companion*, in which Charlotte's *Two Guardians* was appearing at this time, was the High Church magazine and was controversial in tone. Miss Yonge's friends, Miss Marian Dyson and her brother, the Reverend Charles Dyson, felt that there was a place for a magazine for girls and young women planned for the home schoolroom rather than the village school. It was to be a Church of England magazine, it was to avoid personal controversy, and Charlotte was asked to edit it. She undertook the work with enthusiasm; modestly she gave all credit to the Dysons but in fact *The Monthly Packet*, the name finally decided upon (*The Maiden's Manual* was one of the titles suggested), was her creation; its tone and character, which she worked hard to maintain during her forty-eight years of editorship, expressed her own individuality and ideals. In the introduction to the first number, the editor wrote: "It has been said that every one forms their own character between the ages of fifteen and five-and-twenty, and this Magazine is meant to be in some degree a help to those who are thus forming it; not as a guide, since that is the part of deeper and graver books, but as a companion in times of recreation, which may help you to perceive how to bring your religious principles to bear upon your daily life, may show you the examples, both good and evil, of historical persons, and may tell you of the workings of God's providence both here and in other lands."[1]

No doubt it did, for it was very popular. Girls waited eagerly for the monthly issues, looking forward to the next instalment of the serial story by their favorite writer, Miss Yonge. *The Daisy Chain, The Trial, The Pillars of the House, The Little Duke, The Lances of Lynwood*, and others all appeared in *The Monthly Packet* as well as *Musings Over The Christian Year*, for Keble's *Christian Year* was a book cherished by Charlotte all her life. To these were added *Conversations on the Catechism*, the long series of *Cameos from English History* and in 1877, *Womankind*.

Among other contributors two outstanding names, in the early years, were those of Mrs. Alfred Gatty and Juliana Horatia Ewing. In 1858 Miss Yonge and Mrs. Gatty began to correspond; in 1861 they met for

---

[1] Georgina Battiscombe, *op. cit.*, p. 67.

the first time when Charlotte and her mother were persuaded to spend a night with the Gattys at Ecclesfield, on their way from York to Gloucestershire.

Beginning in 1852 Miss Yonge wrote a number of books for use in schools. Besides the *Cameos from English History*, which were reprinted in book form in 1868, there were also *Landmarks of History* (1852–1857), *Aunt Charlotte's Stories of English History for the Little Ones* (1873), and many others. *Little Lucy's Wonderful Globe* (1871) has a certain quiet charm and was still read by children in the 1920's.

On the whole these schoolbooks are seldom recalled today, but though her family stories are out of print and her historical tales less read than in the past, it is unlikely that Charlotte Yonge will ever be forgotten. She was not a great writer but she was an honest one. Her books are a true picture of another age, an age that seems to us today to hold the charm of a certainty and security that have passed away.

Bibliography

Baring, Maurice. *The Puppet Show of Memory*. London, Heinemann, 1922.

Battiscombe, Georgina. *Charlotte Mary Yonge; the Story of an Uneventful Life,* with an introduction by E. M. Delafield. London, Constable, 1943.

Coleridge, Christabel Rose. *Charlotte Mary Yonge, Her Life and Letters*. London, Macmillan, 1903.

Cruse, Amy. *The Victorians and Their Books*. London, Allen and Unwin, 1935.

Darton, F. J. Harvey. *Children's Books in England, Five Centuries of Social Life*. Cambridge, Eng., University Press, 1932.

Jackson, Mrs. Annabel Huth. *A Victorian Childhood*. London, Methuen, 1932.

Marr, Margaret and Alice C. Percival. *Victorian Best-Seller; the World of Charlotte Yonge*. London, Harrap, 1947.

Moberly, C. A. E. *Dulce Domum*; George Moberly (D.C.L. Headmaster of Winchester College 1835–1866, Bishop of Salisbury 1869–1885), His Family and His Friends by His Daughter, London, Murray, 1911.

Sewell, Elizabeth M. *Autobiography*; edited by her niece Eleanor L. Sewell. London, Longmans, 1907.

2

A Scientist, a Realist and a
Purveyor of Magic

Science and Margaret Gatty

Margaret Scott Gatty was very much of her own time, yet with her varied interests (her husband said that to live with her was a liberal education), with her ability to meet new situations and new people, it is much easier to transplant her in imagination to the twentieth century than so to transplant her contemporary, Charlotte Yonge.

It is natural to compare these two women, since they lived at the same time (Mrs. Gatty from 1809–1873, Miss Yonge from 1823–1901), and since they were both extremely popular authors and both prolific writers. Mrs. Gatty, however, by no means attained the number of books written by Miss Yonge. Each wrote chiefly, though not entirely, for children, and each edited a magazine for young readers.

Their work, however, differed widely. Miss Yonge's stories consciously emphasized Christian living, the church as the center of family life and the dominant note in the life of the individual. Mrs. Gatty and her daughter, Mrs. Ewing, were staunch churchwomen, too, but they were "Broad" rather than "High." In regard to the Oxford Movement their sympathies lay in another direction from Miss Yonge's. Mrs. Gatty resented what she called the attempted innovations in the Church and felt that Puseyism bordered on Popery. Religion was important in the lives of Mrs. Gatty and Juliana Ewing, but interests other than the Church play a larger part in their books than was the case with Charlotte Yonge's stories.

Mrs. Gatty in her writing crossed the boundary between fiction and science. As late as 1946 her two-volume *British Seaweeds* was still used as a reference book by the Scottish Marine Biological Association, and two scientist friends of hers were so pleased with the work she had done that they named their separate discoveries in algology after her. Sundials had always interested her and she wrote a book on them, published in 1872. She was interested in chloroform, which had recently become known to the medical profession, had fought prejudice against it, and persuaded the local doctor to make use of it. She was interested in lichens, fungi, and the stars. In short, had she lived today, she would have become, in all probability, an outstanding scientist. She also read German and Italian well; in her young days she invented a secret writing which she called an "ogham" and which she and her sister used in their correspondence. She experimented in etching on copper and some of her work is in the print room of the British Museum. She met Tennyson, who declared he admired "The Unknown Land," one of the *Parables from Nature*, as much as anything he ever read, and she stayed with the Tennysons five times, discussing with the poet such details in his poems as "daffodil skies" and "the sea-blue bird of March."

Margaret Scott was the daughter of a clergyman and married a clergyman. Dr. Scott, after a brief period in which he seemed to favor the young curate, Alfred Gatty, as a suitor for his daughter's hand, decided like a true Victorian father that Alfred's prospects were too uncertain and forbade all thought of an engagement. Fate brought Margaret and Alfred together again, however, and Dr. Scott proved less obdurate; Alfred obtained a better curacy in Southminster and the two young people were married. But Southminster, after all, was not to be their home, for while they were still on their wedding trip word came that Uncle Thomas Ryder had died, and the living of Ecclesfield, Yorkshire, which was in the gift of Margaret's uncle, Edward Ryder, was offered to Alfred Gatty. Originally for fourteen years, it turned out to be for life, for in Ecclesfield they remained and here their ten children were born.

How Margaret Scott Gatty accomplished all she did as the wife of a hard-working clergyman whose income was never sufficient to make both ends meet (Mrs. Gatty's checks for her books promptly went into the family budget), as the mother of ten children, eight of whom lived to grow up, as the author of more than a score of books and the editor of a flourishing magazine for children from 1866 until her death in 1873, is one of those Victorian miracles that we wonder at today. In addition she was plagued from 1849 till her death by the litigation over her grandfather's estate, of which, unfortunately for her, she had been put in charge.

The Fairy Godmothers (modern fairy tales with a moral), published in 1851, was Mrs. Gatty's first book for children. In 1855 appeared the first series of *Parables from Nature*. 'Worlds Not Realized' followed in 1856. "It is not a parable," Mrs. Gatty wrote, "but still it is all about beasts." *Aunt Judy's Tales* was published in 1859, many of the stories having first appeared in the magazine edited by Miss Yonge, *The Monthly Packet; Aunt Judy's Letters* came out in 1862. By 1871 the fifth series of *Parables from Nature* had been published. *Parables from Nature* is the book on which Mrs. Gatty's fame rests. The Parables were written to teach a lesson, but told with clarity and grace as they are, they have a quiet charm. Children, who are not frightened off by a moral as easily as we think (and when has a child not been aware of the possibility of skipping?), must have enjoyed these talking beasts, birds, and insects whose life experiences as recounted by Mrs. Gatty were not only completely accurate but often had a touch of drama.

More important than her own books, however, in the development of writing for children, was Mrs. Gatty's work as an editor. During the seven years she edited *Aunt Judy's Magazine* (1866–1873), her critical judgment and flair for discovering new writers are shown by the contributors she secured for the magazine and the favorable reviews it contained of such new works as *What the Moon Saw* by Hans Christian Andersen and *Alice in Wonderland* by Lewis Carroll. So much did Mrs. Gatty admire Lewis Carroll that she persuaded him to write a story for *Aunt Judy's Magazine*, and "Bruno's Revenge" appeared in its pages in 1867. When Carroll's *Sylvie and Bruno* was published in 1889, he said in his preface that the book grew out of the little fairy tale he had written at the request of the late Mrs. Gatty.

She delighted in Charles Kingsley's *The Water-Babies* when it appeared in 1863, though the scientist in her protested that the fashion in which the dragonfly shed his skin was not entirely correct. She included in the magazine a poem called "Shelter" by C. S. Calverley, the well-known writer of light verse, and thus she showed how the scope of children's reading was broadening.

Real Life and Mrs. Ewing

The most frequent contributor to *Aunt Judy's Magazine* was the editor's daughter, Juliana Horatia (the name of the magazine was taken from Juliana's family nickname, given her because of her popularity as a nursery storyteller). Both Mrs. Gatty and her daughter drew on the life and daily doings in their own home. In this home of eight brothers and sisters, the second daughter, Julie, as she was called, was the inspiration of most of the family fun. Dame Ethel Smyth in her *Impressions That Remain* says that "Aunt Judy had a positive genius for young people." There seems never to have been a dull moment. Julie was an excellent actress, a clever mimic, a ready writer and versifier. Private theatricals, home magazines, games and jokes, flourished. From her early years Julie had been an excellent storyteller, taking her inspiration from Grimm, Andersen, and Bechstein, and her brothers and sisters kept her busy. It was this happy family life that made Mrs. Gatty's two books, *Aunt Judy's Tales* and *Aunt Judy's Letters*, so popular, for the children were engagingly real and the description of a large group of boys and girls, with an older sister always ready to help them carry out their plans and provide new sources of entertainment, was very appealing to other children.

Juliana Horatia Ewing was born in 1841. Her first three published stories—"A Bit of Green," "The Blackbird's Nest," and "Melchior's Dream"—appeared in Miss Yonge's *Monthly Packet* in 1861. "The Brownies" was also published in *The Monthly Packet* and was a child-like story which became popular at once and, though the author never knew it, provided, years later, the name for the junior branch of the Girl Guides and Girl Scouts. In 1870 "The Brownies" with "Timothy's Shoes," "Amelia and the Dwarfs," "Three Christmas-trees," "The Land of Lost Toys," "Old Father Christmas," "Benjy in Beastland," "The Peace-egg," and "An Idyll of the Wood" were published by Bell as *The Brownies and Other Tales*, illustrated by George Cruikshank. All these stories combined reality and fantasy, a type of tale for which Mrs. Gatty felt that her daughter had special aptitude. It pleased Juliana when Cruikshank remarked that when he read her things "the fairies came and danced for him."

In the first number of *Aunt Judy's Magazine* (May 1866) there appeared Julie's first serialized story, *Mrs. Overtheway*. The next year Julie married Major Alexander Ewing. This marriage, like most Victorian marriages, had not come about suddenly. Alexander Ewing first met the Gatty family in 1856. He was a musician and a churchman (the fact that he composed the tune to which "Jerusalem the Golden" is sung naturally recommended him to the Gattys), and he was also a member of the Commissariat Department of the Army. During the Crimean War he was sent to Turkey, later to Australia and China, but in 1866 he returned to England and again saw his friends the Gattys. With his musical talents, his ability to write verse, and his enjoyment of theatricals, he fitted admirably into the Gatty family circle, but it was soon evident that his chief interest was in the clever, lively, generous-spirited Julie. The courtship was not without opposition. Major Ewing's prospects also were uncertain, Julie was not strong and besides she seemed almost indispensable for the magazine so recently started, as well as in the home. But parental reluctance was conquered; in 1867 the marriage took place and "Rex," as his wife always called him, and Julie sailed away immediately to Canada, where until 1869 they made their home in Fredericton, New Brunswick. There they studied Hebrew together, gardened, and collected dogs. The last two interests were always very dear to Mrs. Ewing as shown in her stories, where gardens and flowers are numerous and the dogs are so evidently drawn from life.

In Canada Mrs. Ewing wrote the last two stories in *Mrs. Overtheway's Remembrances*, "Reka Dom" and "Kerguelen's Land." "Three Christmas Trees" was also written in Canada. This story and "Christmas Crackers," a charming fantasy which she wrote after her return to England, and "Dandelion Clocks" (1876) show very strongly the influence of Andersen, a life-long favorite with Mrs. Ewing. "The Land of Lost Toys" was also sent to the magazine from Canada, and in 1868, the year before her return to England, she began her series of fairy tales which were published in the magazine in 1870–1876, and in book form by S.P.C.K. in 1882, with the title *Old Fashioned Fairy Tales*. Of these tales Mrs. Ewing said, "My aim is to imitate the old 'originals' and I mean to stick close to orthodox traditions. . . One of my theories is that all fairy tales should be written down as if they were oral tradition."

In 1869 the Ewings came home, where Major Ewing was stationed at Aldershot. There they lived till 1877 and this was Mrs. Ewing's most productive period. She enjoyed army life and keeping house in an army hut, and the climate agreed with her. Twenty tales were written and published during these years. Best known among them are *A Flat Iron for a Farthing* (1872) in which Mrs. Ewing went back to her own childhood to tell about the two little girls who, like her sister and herself, went to the sea for a holiday, rode donkeys, and found a shop where tiny flat irons were sold for a farthing and where they met the little boy who was the hero of the tale. Then there was *Lob Lie-by-the-Fire* (1874), telling how an adopted child brings luck to the ladies of Lingborough Farm; *Six to Sixteen* (1875) about the daughter of an English officer in the Indian Army, told in the form of a diary; *Jan of the Windmill* (1876), published in *Aunt Judy's Magazine* with the title "The Miller's Thumb," about a boy brought up by a miller who became a distinguished painter; "Our Field," about a family of flower-loving children, a delightful dog, and the meadow they found which became for them a little Earthly Paradise.

In 1876 the happy days at Aldershot ended, for Major Ewing was transferred to Manchester, and while he went on ahead to find a place for them to live, Julie remained behind to pack up their belongings, something which, for economy's sake, she always did herself. This was a proceeding that had to be repeated the following year when they moved to York, a proceeding that was always complicated by the fact that wherever the Ewings went, their piano had to go with them.

In "Madam Liberality," which first appeared in *Aunt Judy's Magazine* and was then published in *A Great Emergency* (1877), Mrs. Ewing drew her own portrait, we are told by her sister, Horatia Gatty, in a way that cannot be surpassed, though her sister adds, it was done quite unintentionally.[1]

Mrs. Ewing had an excellent dramatic sense, heightened, no doubt, by the theatricals which were so much a part of life in the Gatty home

---

[1] Horatia K. F. Gatty, *Juliana Horatia Ewing and Her Books* (London, S.P.C.K., 1885), p. 5. S.P.C.K. stands for the Society for Promoting Christian Knowledge, an organization established in England in 1698 which was intimately connected with the development of elementary education. In 1831 the Society began the publication of books.

in Ecclesfield. She also had a strong sense of time and place which she was able to transmit to the reader. The flowers in *Mary's Meadow* —the story of children who loved gardening and discovered Parkinson's *Paradisi*—and those in "Our Field" (which Ruskin said was not a story but a poem) are still blooming. In *Lob Lie-by-the-Fire*, we find a true picture of a nineteenth century village. Here live the little ladies, Miss Betty and Miss Kitty, practising their little economies and carrying out their little charities unknown to each other, and here lives John Broom, the gypsy child they adopt who becomes the hero of the tale. Here, too, we meet the parson, the Scottish farm-bailiff, Thomasina the maid-servant, for one of Mrs. Ewing's gifts was her interest in people and her ability to put into her books characters in all walks in life whom she met, talked with, and enjoyed. She got on with them all, whether she was helping an old woman iron her caps, "tidying up" an invalid or giving advice about economy in bonnets. "I do like Mrs. Ewing," said a villager, "she's such good company. No need for two to kill time when she's near."[1]

Fertile as she was in ideas for plots, Mrs. Ewing was far from feeling that plot was all that was needed to make a story. To her manner was as important as matter. She was a capable artist; many are the references to sketching in her letters and diaries, and in her mind the work of the artist with brush and pencil was closely related to the work of the writer. When asked for advice about the art of writing she always recommended Ruskin's *Elements of Drawing;* to his nine laws of the guidance of artists she added a tenth to the effect that "if a writer could express himself clearly in one word he was not to use two."[2] We have her own testimony that writing was not easy and that she spent long hours seeking for the right words and the best arrangements of sentences.

Dame Ethel Smyth, who took music lessons from Major Ewing and knew Mrs. Ewing well, speaks of her devotion to the British Army. This feeling comes out over and over again in Mrs. Ewing's books but is most clearly expressed in *Jackanapes* (1884) and in *The Story of a Short Life* (published as "Laetus Sorte Mea" in *Aunt Judy's Magazine*, 1882; in book form by S.P.C.K. 1885). In *Jackanapes* a soldier's son grows up, follows his father's career, and is killed saving a fellow soldier's life. This is Mrs. Ewing's best-known story, and if to the modern reader the moral may seem to be over-labored, it thoroughly appealed to the taste of the times. Part of its fame is due to the fact that it was illustrated by Randolph Caldecott. Mrs. Ewing fell in love with Caldecott's picture books, *John Gilpin* and *The House that Jack*

[1] Christabel Maxwell, *Mrs. Gatty and Mrs. Ewing* (London, Constable, 1949), p. 159.
[2] Horatia K. F. Gatty, *op. cit.*, p. 67.

Built. "I was daft about them," she writes, "the draughtmanship so nervous and fine, the whole artistic satisfactoriness so completely free of trick and so thoroughly the outcome of labour."[1] She went so far as to propose to George Routledge, the publisher, that Caldecott should illustrate a set of verses she wrote in 1879 called "A Soldier's Children" (published in *Aunt Judy's Magazine* during 1880–1883) offering to give up any payment for herself. Caldecott could not undertake the work at the time but promised they should work together later. The idea for *Jackanapes* was already in her mind; inspiration came to a head when news reached England of the Prince Imperial's death in battle when many people felt that the English soldier who accompanied him should have saved him or else perished with him. *Jackanapes* (1879 in *Aunt Judy's Magazine*, in book form, 1884) was Mrs. Ewing's contribution toward upholding the ideal of heroic obligation and example, and since there were scenes of horsemanship in the tale, Caldecott was the perfect illustrator. Mrs. Ewing knew what she wanted in an illustration and was exacting, but each admired and truly respected the other and they got along smoothly. After Mrs. Ewing's death in 1885 Caldecott contributed a sketch in her memory to *Aunt Judy's Magazine.*

The Story of a Short Life uses the camp at Aldershot as background and tells how a small boy, crippled in saving his dog from being run over, finds comfort during the rest of his short life by thinking of himself as a wounded soldier and trying to live up to the highest military ideals. In this book Mrs. Ewing shows her appreciation of the British soldier, who had not yet found a champion in Kipling. It was probably Kipling's intuitive feeling that here was a kindred spirit which caused him to say of *Six to Sixteen* in his *Something of Myself*, "I owe more in a circuitous way to that tale than I can tell. I knew it, as I know it still, almost by heart. Here was a history of real people and real things."[2]

One quality in Mrs. Ewing which appealed to Caldecott was her interest in different types of people, for it was like his own. Thus they worked together with great satisfaction on *Daddy Darwin's Dovecot* (1884). Caldecott wrote to Mrs. Ewing that he was very glad to hear she "liked the old gaffers, that they suited the story and the locality." The tale was founded on fact, using an actual incident when one hundred and twenty pigeons were stolen from Ecclesfield Hall in 1875.

When Caldecott was given the opportunity to choose between illustrating *The Story of a Short Life* and *Lob Lie-by-the-Fire* he chose the latter. *Lob Lie-by-the-Fire* had the distinction of being illustrated by both Cruikshank and Caldecott, for Cruikshank made drawings for the first edition, which was published in 1874 together with reprints of

---

[1] Christabel Maxwell, *op. cit.*, p. 208.
[2] Rudyard Kipling, *Something of Myself* (New York, Doubleday, 1937), p. 9.

"Timothy's Shoes," "Benjy in Beastland," "Old Father Christmas," and "The Peace Egg." Gordon Browne, who had illustrated Mrs. Ewing's first book, *Melchior's Dream* (1862), now illustrated almost her last one, *The Story of a Short Life*, with sensitive appreciation of the child hero.

The Story of a Short Life has had many admirers and has drawn many a tear. According to modern standards it is sentimental, for Mrs. Ewing did not escape the fondness for deathbed scenes which prevailed in the eighteeneth and nineteenth centuries. Sensibility is not now fashionable, but before being too harshly critical, it is well to note that in Mrs. Ewing's books the incidents and endings always follow naturally and that the pathos is genuine.

Mrs. Ewing is not read today as she was in her own time. The average child, brought up on more highly seasoned fare, tends to find her books slow and uneventful (though the British Broadcasting Corporation did broadcast two of her stories, *Jackanapes* and *Jan of the Windmill*, on their Children's Programme). But she is not likely to be forgotten. Back of superficial differences in custom and behavior, her books, which pass the supreme test of pleasing both children and adults, deal with things that do not change—children, flowers, and animals. They give us the satisfaction of a well-contrived plot, the outdoor atmosphere of wood and field and garden, characters that remain in the memory, all building up a true and gracious picture of an earlier day against a lovely background of the English countryside.

The Charming Cuckoo

Another well-known author of books for children, writing at the same time as Mrs. Ewing, was Mrs. Molesworth, as her name always appeared on the title page of her books, and like Mrs. Ewing she wrote more than a hundred books.

The journals kept by so many Victorian women and the voluminous correspondence they carried on were usually carefully preserved and served as fertile sources of information about their lives and the times in which they lived. Mrs. Molesworth may have been an exception to the rule, though it would seem certain that she must have carried on a large correspondence. But for some reason, perhaps because her place of residence was changed so often, perhaps because, unlike Mrs. Ewing, she had no sister or niece to care for her personal papers, we do not have accounts of her life in her own writing. What records exist tell us that she was born Mary Louisa Stewart in 1839, the daughter of Charles Augustus Stewart; her childhood was spent in High Legh, Cheshire, she became engaged to Major Molesworth before he went to the Crimea and married him on his return. There were five children, two boys and three girls, but it was not a happy marriage and Mrs. Molesworth, taking a step most unusual for the times, obtained a legal separation from the major. She then took her children abroad. They lived in France for many years, later they lived in Germany and finally came back to England. In a house in Lower Sloane Street, London, Mrs. Molesworth entertained authors and artists and seems to have known most of the literary and intellectual figures of her day. She lived until 1921. Her stories show an acquaintance with life on the Continent and an especial love and understanding of France.

Mrs. Molesworth's first books were written for adult readers, four three-volume novels were published between 1870 and 1874 under the pen name of Ennis Graham. But after her first book for children appeared, *Tell Me a Story* (1875), illustrated by Walter Crane and containing "Adventures of Herr Baby," "Little Miss Peggy," and "Nurse Heatherdale's Story," her books, with two or three exceptions, were all for children.

She was extremely popular, but is less well remembered than Mrs. Ewing and George Macdonald with whom contemporary criticism ranked her, probably because she lacked a certain universal quality found in Mrs. Ewing's books and George Macdonald's fairy tales. But she had distinctive gifts of her own which deserve recognition. From her own five children she learned what boys and girls are like and what they like and her storytelling never falters. Her books had a fascination for children which they still retain. They are of two kinds, those which combine magic and reality and those which are purely realistic. In the realistic tales her boys and girls are natural and lifelike. In her fanciful tales she never lost the single-hearted quality of true make-believe, and she wrote always with warmth and a gentle humor. *Carrots, Just a Little Boy* (1876), one of her most famous, belongs to the latter group. It is a story adapted to reading aloud to young children, for the hero is only five and the tale is told in a series of separate incidents. *Carrots* was followed by *Two Little Waifs* (1883) and *Us, an Old-Fashioned Story* (1885), about a little twin brother and sister who run away from home, both meant, like *Carrots*, for young children. For readers from ten on were *The Rectory Children* (1889), *The Oriel Window* (1896), *Miss Mouse and Her Boys* (1897), this last a pleasing story of a quaint and independent little girl and the five boys who were her playmates, and *The Carved Lions* (1895), a well-written account of school life, realistic except for one magical episode. This is to mention only four titles. Mrs. Molesworth also wrote several books for older girls, but these were not very successful and are not remembered today. She dealt very successfully with family life, but her great gift lay in establishing real characters and then taking them across the borders of the everyday world into a thoroughly convincing fairyland. Best known of these tales are *The Cuckoo Clock* (1877), *The Tapestry Room*

(1879), *Four Winds Farm* (1887), and *Christmas Tree Land* (1884), the most successful and best loved being *The Cuckoo Clock* and *The Tapestry Room*. The latter is built around the house in Arranches in Normandy, where Mrs. Molesworth lived for many years and where, in the story, two little cousins, a boy and a girl, are able on moonlight nights to find themselves adventuring into the castle and surrounding country represented by the tapestry on the walls of the little boy's room. In *The Cuckoo Clock*, the most charming of Mrs. Molesworth's stories, when nine-year-old Griselda, whose parents have left her for a time in the care of two elderly aunts, is bored and lonely, the Cuckoo she has watched so often comes out of the clock to be her guide to magical adventures. With him she visits the Country of the Nodding Mandarins, the room where the cuckoo clock was made for her beautiful mother, Butterfly-land, and the Other Side of the Moon. The Cuckoo is Griselda's mentor as well as her guide, for Mrs. Molesworth was unable entirely to resist the temptation to teach a lesson, but her moralizing was neither dull nor perfunctory and indeed the cuckoo delivers his admonitions with a brisk and enjoyable sprightliness.

Mrs. Molesworth was a skillful writer. She handled her tales, which combined fantasy and reality, with a fine balance; not only her real world but her wonderland is consistent and believable. It is visible to the mind's eye and almost tangible, for this author had a rare power to bring out the enchanting quality of *things*, something which a child feels and to which he readily responds. Surely some of the charm which cuckoo clocks have for many adults, as well as for children, and their popularity for generations in English nurseries may be laid to Mrs. Molesworth's story. The "faded yellow hangings in the great saloon," the Chinese cabinet all black and gold and carving, the potpourri jar, the carved ivory palanquin borne by four Chinese-looking figures with pigtails and bright jackets, the mandarin with his nodding head, create a gracious atmosphere that becomes a part of the child's own experience.

Bibliography

Gatty, Horatia K. F. *Juliana Horatia Ewing and Her Books*. London, S.P.C.K., 1885.

Laski, Marghanita. *Mrs. Ewing, Mrs. Molesworth, Mrs. Hodgson Burnett*. London, Arthur Barker, 1950.

Maxwell, Christabel. *Mrs. Gatty and Mrs. Ewing*. London, Constable, 1949.

Molesworth, Mary. "One Generation Passeth." *Blackwood's Magazine*, London, Vol. 262 (July, 1947), pp. 22–36.

Smyth, Ethel. *Impressions That Remain; Memoirs*. London, Longmans, 1919.

3

A Broader Field

An Irish Castle

It would almost seem as though Miss Yonge, with her enormous output, and the industrious Mrs. Ewing and Mrs. Molesworth must have provided most of the books read by English boys and girls in the 1870's and 80's. There were, however, stories by other authors who with only one or two books to their credit had a well-deserved popularity. One of these books was Flora Shaw's *Castle Blair*. This spirited account is of a houseful of children living very much according to their own sweet will in their uncle's home in Ireland while their parents are in India. It reads as well today as when it was published in 1878. Here, in a fresh and lovely setting of Irish woods and glens, are very natural and human children, for the author has characterized them with sympathy and understanding. The older and gentler French girl who comes to visit in Ireland is so different from the others that the vivid personalities of the Irish children stand out in striking contrast, possessed as they are of such vigor of enterprise, such burning enthusiasm, and such romantic and unreasoning attachment to their ideal of Ireland. Their headlong collision with equally unreasoning authority, which attempts to oppose them, is natural and inevitable. The story, progressing through natural and steadily rising action, reaches a climax of feeling and excitement that few books of this period have been able to achieve. The strength of this climax lies in its complete freedom from sentimentality.

Flora Shaw, afterward Lady Lugard (1852–1929), was a contemporary of Mrs. Molesworth, but her *Castle Blair* seems more modern than any of Mrs. Molesworth's tales because of its broader background. The fact that the Irish revolutionary movement plays a part in the story puts it on a larger stage than that of the nursery, schoolroom, or village tales that formed most of the reading matter for boys and girls of the 70's. Flora Shaw's other two books, *Phyllis Brown* and *Hector*, fell far below *Castle Blair* in force and interest.

Flora Shaw crossed the Irish Sea for the setting for *Castle Blair*. Two other writers had already gone farther afield, with the definite purpose of acquainting young readers with a country other than their own. As long ago as 1841 Harriet Martineau (1802–1876) had written *The Playfellow*, a four-story series, each later published separately. Of these four stories for children (three are *The Settlers at Home*, *The Peasant and the Prince*, and *The Crofton Boys*) *Feats on the Fiord* is the one best remembered. To a few children of today it has seemed dull, but the picture of life in the North with its smugglers, its peasant superstitions, and its adventures by water and by land gave interest and a wider scope to the tale than was usual in children's books of that time. The picturesque setting is so clearly presented that no young reader can fail to be aware of the threatening cold, the dangers of the stormy fiord, and the high airy slope of the summer pasture where someone must always "keep an eye on the cattle" because it is the firm belief of the watchers that the moment the protecting glance is withdrawn the fairies will turn them into creatures the size of mice and spirit them away underground.

Jane Andrews in her *The Seven Little Sisters Who Live on the Round Ball that Floats in the Air* (1861) told in successive chapters of seven little girls—Agoonack, the Esquimaux Sister; Gemila, the Child of the Desert; Jeanette, the Little Mountain Maiden; Pen-se, the Chinese Girl; Manenko, the Little Dark Girl; Louise, the Child of the Beautiful River Rhine—in a way that has pleased children from seven to nine through several generations of readers. A new edition was published as late as 1924. To balance matters evenly she wrote also *Ten Boys Who Lived on the Road from Long Ago Till Now* (1885).

Jane Andrews was an American writer. In 1865 another American published in the United States a book which still ranks high among stories of foreign countries. This was *Hans Brinker, or the Silver Skates* by Mary Mapes Dodge (1831–1905). Every detail of life and custom was so carefully verified by the author that the book was immediately accepted by the Dutch as the most faithful story of Dutch life known in Holland. Since the narrative contains, as the climax of the action, a race for a skating championship it is thus, in a way, a pioneer sports story. But the real interest lies in the sturdy character of Hans, a boy not too good or too wise, and with his sister, both gay and undefeated by their poverty. One sees them at the beginning, skimming over the ice on homemade wooden skates, which stick when they become wet, tripping the owners amid gales of contagious laughter. The unfolding of the plot is direct and natural, with the father's illness and loss of memory rendering deep hardship to the little family until he is restored by the skill of a great doctor who has become interested in Hans, while the savings which he has hidden and forgotten are found in time to help in his recovery. The two children stand by their mother with steadfast and unconscious courage. The whole is kept wisely and skillfully to the level of a young person's point of view, so that the race for the silver skates is the great moment of the book. Mrs. Dodge's *Donald and Dorothy* was a pleasant tale of a twin brother and sister. A slight mystery added to its interest and the book was a favorite for many years. Mary Mapes Dodge herself, with her signal achievements as editor of *St. Nicholas Magazine*, will be studied more fully in a later chapter.

A Swiss Alp

It is probable, however, that no other book of this time, showing a background foreign to English and American young readers, had such a success or has implanted itself so firmly in youthful memories as did *Heidi*. Written by the Swiss author Johanna Spyri (1827–1901), it was translated from the German in 1880 and with its snow-capped mountains, its free outdoor atmosphere, its happy children, simple pleasures, and warm affection between the characters, it is still delighted in by boys and girls. The reason for this is that Heidi herself is so honest, so genuine in her enjoyment of the life in her grandfather's cottage, that every detail of that life is glowing and memorable. One feels forever after that there can be no bed like a mattress stuffed with hay and laid opposite the open wooden shutter of a window facing a whole world of mountains and stars. Was there ever anything that seemed more delicious to the imagination than the hot, creamy goat's cheese with which her grandfather spread her thick-crusted bread? Heidi's adventures are small but spirited. The real accomplishment of the book is that it renders a hitherto alien scene not only familiar but beloved; it makes clear, not the hardships, but the deep and satisfying pleasures of peasant life. The book remains steadily in print with new illustrated editions appearing frequently. Other of Johanna Spyri's books were translated into English, but none of them reached the stature of *Heidi*.

An English School

In 1857 appeared the first great school story, *Tom Brown's School Days* by Thomas Hughes (1822–1896). It is real because the boys were human beings and the school an actual one. Up to this time there were few descriptions of school life other than a story or two of Maria Edgeworth's, Charles Lamb's account of the Blue Coat School in the *Essays of Elia*, and Dickens' "Dotheboys Hall" in *Nicholas Nickleby*. It is difficult to think of *Tom Brown's School Days* in the same class with the ephemeral school story of today, but it is not hard to understand why, over a hundred years after it was written, Hughes's book still has value and importance. The story lives by its own right, by our interest in the hero and his friend East, who become more and more characters whom we like and respect although we are never told to do so. We follow the intricacies, some of the absurdities and the intense feeling that are all part of school life and of a boy's developing consciousness of the world about him, and know that we are reading substantial truth. There is genuine boyhood in the story with the author's happy memories of the school upon which to found reality. But the sense of substance which the book gives us lies in the deep principles that underlay the writing. Beneath the boyish escapades and school customs the story has its roots in significant ideas of the time.

The author, like his friend Charles Kingsley (1819–1875), was a Christian Socialist. That term is never mentioned in the book but, through the behavior of Tom, the author expresses the Christian Socialist's personal ideal—bodily strength, manliness, readiness, indeed eagerness, to fight in a just cause, resistance to bullying, sympathy and help for the weak, warmth and loyalty of friendship, and a religious belief that meant turning to God for help in solving the problems of everyday life. These were the qualities which Hughes, one of the leaders of the Christian Socialist movement, showed as champion of the poor and the laboring classes, as a promoter of cooperational societies, and as one of the founders and then as principal of the Working Men's College.

Hughes's principles were far from being merely theoretical and it is no surprise to find that when, as a young man, he discovered that solitary policemen in lonely parts of the city were often attacked by crowds of laborers and thieves, he made up his mind to help the next victim he saw. This he did, saying in "Fragments of Autobiography," which was published in 1925 in the *Cornhill Magazine,* "I went hurling into the press and in a second was in the middle of it." It was thoroughly in keeping with Hughes's character that when he learned the policeman had been at fault in this particular instance rather than the man Hughes had helped to jail, he went to court the next morning to speak for the prisoner. Also characteristic was the fact that, noticing the poor physical state of the students at the Working Men's College, he, the principal, chose to teach a class in boxing, which was attended by the students with enthusiasm and excellent results.

Tom Brown's School Days is a landmark in another connection, for it is allied with a further movement of the day, that of educational reform. "The Doctor" of the book is Thomas Arnold, the great schoolmaster of the nineteenth century, whose reforms at Rugby spread to all the public schools in England. Thomas Hughes's unmistakable portrait of a great man helped contemporary Englishmen to grasp Arnold's educational ideals and to understand his "unwearied zeal in creating moral thoughtfulness in every boy with whom he came in personal contact." We leave Tom Brown standing by Arnold's tomb in Rugby Chapel, while the tribute paid by Hughes at the end of the book to Thomas Arnold is sincere and noble and moving today.

Hughes preaches in *Tom Brown*, it is true. In his preface to the sixth edition he states that his object in writing was to get the chance to preach. But even today when books for youngsters are geared so that he who runs may read, if a boy is directed to the account of the glorious fight between Tom Brown and "the Slogger," the school tyrant and bully, he will continue reading for the sake of the vitality of the tale, the naturalness of the boys and the descriptions of sports and games. He may, and probably will, skip the formal preaching but he will feel the book's depth and power since the high standards of the author, the best lessons, are found in the story itself. Within nine months after its appearance three editions of *Tom Brown's School Days* were published. The book is still famous as a picture of nineteenth century English life and is still rewarding reading for young people who have the background to appreciate it. *Tom Brown at Oxford* followed in 1861; it has less vitality than its predecessor and is interesting chiefly as showing the awakening of a group of young men to the ideas for social betterment which were in the air.

Two other stories of the mid-nineteenth century are known by name and fame, but, most understandably, are not read today. Harriet Martineau's *The Croften Boys* (1841) describes the experiences of Hugh, aged eight and a half, at a school where he is the youngest boy. This tale, which is concerned largely with the hero's struggles with his conscience, seems today too heavily moral to interest children. Still, it was read in its own time. Maurice Baring writes in his autobiography, "It is very difficult for me to understand now how a child could have enjoyed the intensely sermonising tone of this book, but I certainly did enjoy it."[1]

Eric, or Little by Little; A Tale of Roslyn School (1858) by Frederic Farrar (1831–1903), Fellow of Trinity College, Cambridge, in its own time rivaled *Tom Brown* in popularity. Today it is hard to believe that such a combination of moral teaching bordering on priggishness and sentimentality, so much dividing of the sheep and the goats, so many tears and more than one deathbed scene, could have been read by boys. But thirty-six editions were published. Sensibility, however, still prevailed in the mid-nineteenth century, along with a tendency still to look upon books as a means of encouraging moral behavior. Thus Victorian parents hastened to supply their sons with copies of *Eric* and its sequel, *St. Winifred's*. The author wrote in all sincerity (and quite without humor), describing what he called "the darker shades of school life" from a sense of duty but with honest sorrow. It would doubtless have grieved him very much to know that in the 90's the three irrepressible heroes of Kipling's *Stalky & Co.* were guying Eric and his school fellows without mercy.

[1] Maurice Baring, *The Puppet Show of Memory* (London, Heinemann, 1922), p. 19.

In America was published in 1883 a school story as typical of the New World as *Tom Brown* was typical of the older world across the sea, *Hoosier School Boy* by Edward Eggleston (1837–1902). It is a comfortable, pleasant, and cheerful book with a flavor of the soil in setting and character. The figures of the story are distinctive pioneer types and the reader is made well aware of the difficulties to be surmounted in those days by a boy ambitious for an education.

The Rector of Eversley

Though Charles Kingsley never wrote a school story and Thomas Hughes never strayed into the world of fantasy, it is natural to think of the two men together. They were friends and both were Christian Socialists; both helped to found the Working Men's College; both were vigorous men of action who delighted in sports, nature, and outdoor life.

Kingsley, a man of deep sympathies, found himself living through a period of social revolution. He had a passionate desire to see set right the wrongs which were troubling the consciences of many people of his time. He sympathized with the Chartist revolution, though both he and Hughes felt that the Chartists were going the wrong way to obtain the reforms they wanted. Kingsley's novel *Yeast* was written in protest against the Corn Laws; in *Alton Locke* he spoke for the poor who, like the woman in Thomas Hood's "Song of the Shirt," were victims of the sweating system. He wrote many pamphlets designed to help the overworked and underfed, but found that, like other Christian Socialists, he was not always understood or listened to by those he was trying to help. He was happiest in his parish at Eversley in Hampshire, where he knew every man, woman, and child, talked with them about all sorts of things and told stories to the children. Even the rough and lawless population of poachers and squatters who made up a part of his parish looked upon him as a friend because of his outspoken hatred of the tyrannical game laws. Kingsley was a country parson in every sense, for besides his interest in his parishioners, he loved every aspect of nature and delighted in sharing what he observed with his own children and his child friends.

In Eversley he wrote his best novels, *Hereward the Wake* and *Westward Ho!*, both read by boys and girls. *Westward Ho!* (1855), while it belonged to the general class of historical romance which people were coming more and more to read, was a book of such body and substance that it has stood firm in a place all of its own. For many readers with a taste for historical novels it is a firm cornerstone in the fabric of that affection. Kingsley could, when he wished, turn aside from his direct crusade for social reform and look at the glories and errors of a time long past. He was a good follower of Hakluyt, one of those who realized the greatness of that record which the sixteenth century scholar, also a country parson, had toiled so long to collect. The full title of the book is *Westward Ho! or the Voyages and Adventures of Sir Amyas Leigh Knight, of Burrough, in the County of Devon in the Reign of her most Glorious Majesty Queen Elizabeth*. It shows all the glory and boldness of English sea adventure, especially of those courageous men of Devon about whom romance inevitably gathers from the remembrance of their great exploits. The book was not written for children, its end is tragic, and in its bitter details of the Spanish Inquisition as carried to America it reflects Kingsley's hatred of all cruel and tyrannical acts. But a young person's impulse for hero worship, a growing mind's instinctive sympathy and understanding of that great time when the limits of the known world were being pushed back, are fully enlisted here. A new edition in 1933 with illustrations in color by N. C. Wyeth that do justice to the heroic scenes through which it passes, has given it back to young readers of a later day.

The Classical Legends Revived

In the year after *Westward Ho!* Kingsley, who could retell tales of wonder as well as create new fantasy, wrote *The Heroes, or Greek Fairy Tales for my Children*, dedicated to Rose, Maurice, and Mary, to whom he wrote in the Preface, "There are no fairy tales like these old Greek ones for beauty, wisdom, and truth." To a friend he explained that he had adopted a simple ballad form and tried to make his prose as rhythmical as possible. Writing as both scholar and poet Kingsley told the stories of Perseus, Theseus, and Jason in a smoothly flowing narrative that succeeds perfectly in accomplishing the author's aim, to "translate the children back into a new old world, and make them, as long as they are reading, forget the present."[1]

Kingsley, however, was not the first to put the Greek myths within the reach of child readers. In 1852 in America, Nathaniel Hawthorne (1804–1864), who enjoyed and understood children, published *A Wonder-Book for Boys and Girls*, to be followed in 1853 by *Tanglewood Tales for Boys and Girls; A Second Wonder-Book*. Older readers often prefer Kingsley as more Greek in spirit, and it is true, as Hawthorne himself states in his preface to *A Wonder-Book*, that his retellings have the Gothic and romantic touch which was the spirit of his age. They are, however, little masterpieces of prose and introduce children to the satisfactions of good style as well as to mythology. Moreover *A Wonder-Book* and *Tanglewood Tales* together contain twelve legends while *The Heroes* comprises only three. The little interludes between the tales in the two books by Hawthorne, with their real children and the young

[1] Charles Kingsley, *His Letters and Memories of His Life* (London, Kegan Paul, 1877), Vol. 1, p. 354.

college student who told the stories beside the brook, in the woods or on a hilltop, bring a breath of outdoors and suggest a fresh and lovely American scene.

Many enterprising children, their appetite whetted by Kingsley and Hawthorne, found still more myths to delight them in Thomas Bulfinch's *The Age of Fable; or Stories of Gods and Heroes* (1855), although this attempt to popularize mythology was planned not for children but for the general reader. Many editions have been published and in revised and enlarged form this is a book usually found in libraries today.

Mother Carey and Little Tom

Kingsley's most famous book for children was not *The Heroes* but *The Water-Babies; A Fairy Tale for a Land-Baby*, published in 1863. One day in the preceding year his wife had said to him, "Rose, Maurice and Mary have got their book, and baby must have his." Kingsley promptly went into his study, locked the door, and came out half an hour later with the story of little Tom. It was the first chapter of *The Water-Babies*.[1] Here Kingsley gave free rein to his love of children and nature alike. Also, by using as his hero a little chimney sweep, he expressed his indignation over one of the abuses of the age, the forcing of children to clean out soot-filled chimneys, and he thus helped to abolish this unjustifiable form of child labor.

One senses, too, in the book that the new scientific ideas of the day were in the back of the author's mind. Darwin's *Origin of Species* had been published in 1859; rationalism and doubt were in the air; it was not as easy to believe in organized religion as it had been in the past. Kingsley, to be sure, was one of those who found it possible to reconcile the new science with religious faith. He, of course, made no attempt to introduce any idea of conflict between religion and science in his book for children, but he skirts the problem of infidelity in *The Water-Babies* in the History of the Doasyoulikes, recounted by the Fairy Bedonebyasyoudid, and he never misses an opportunity to say a word for the Church.

The many children, however, who read *The Water-Babies* in the past were not troubled by the fact that the author now and again mounts to the pulpit, nor is the smaller number of child readers today. The story of Tom, the water-baby, his adventures with lobsters, sea anemones, and other sea creatures, with caddis flies, and dragonflies, the stately salmon and his wife, the otter family on their way to the sea, are sheer delight. Mrs. Doasyouwouldbedoneby, Mrs. Bedonebyasyoudid, Mother Carey, and the rest make a fascinating cast of characters.

[1] Charles Kingsley, *His Letters and Memories of His Life*, Vol. 2, pp. 126–127.

Kingsley moralizes, of course; it would have been out of character if he had not tried to make his readers, old and young, understand, as he wrote to F. D. Maurice, "that there is a quite miraculous and divine element underlying all physical nature," but he added that Maurice was to remember that "the physical science of the book was not nonsense but accurate and earnest." Mrs. Gatty, who knew natural history, praised *The Water-Babies* in the highest terms. Bruce Frederick Cummings who, under the pen name of W. N. P. Barbellion, published extracts from his diaries as *The Journal of a Disappointed Man*, in 1919, was said by his wife to have been started on his career as a biologist by having *The Water-Babies* read to him as a child. Later he puzzled through *Madam How and Lady Why* (1870), a book about earthquakes, volcanoes, and glaciers in which Kingsley was more teacher than storyteller. Even in *The Water-Babies* Kingsley allowed himself to indulge in long lists of names; they are blemishes from the artistic point of view but not so discouraging to a child as the modern adult supposes. There is much more in the book to delight children than to repel them. Kingsley, who was a poet as well as a writer of novels and tales, included in *The Water-Babies* three of his most charming poems, which are known in anthologies to many who have never read the book, "The Song of the River," "When All The World Was Young, Lad," and "The Lost Doll."

With *The Water-Babies* may be said to begin the succession of modern fairy tales which is one of the glories of English writing and which was to be continued in America. Before writing of Lewis Carroll's masterpieces, *Alice's Adventures in Wonderland* and *Through the Looking-Glass*, and their successors, it will be well to turn for a moment to the entry of the fairy tale into the reading of English-speaking children.

Bibliography

Hughes, Thomas. "Fragments of Autobiography;" edited by Henry Shelley. *Cornhill Magazine*, London, Vol. 58 (1925), pp. 280–289; 472–478; 563–572.

Kingsley, Charles. *Charles Kingsley; His Letters and Memories of His Life*, edited by his wife. London, Paul Trench & Co., 1888.

Williams, Stanley T. "The Parent of School Boy Novels." *English Journal*, Chicago, Vol. 10 (May, 1921), pp. 241–246.

4

The Return of the Fairy Tale

After the tranquillity and restraint of the eighteenth century, a restraint called classical because orderly beauty was also characteristic of the literatures of Greece and Rome, there was, as always, a swing of the pendulum. During the late eighteenth and early nineteenth centuries a new spirit was abroad. Reality was not scorned, but it was to be a reality of deeper feeling and wider vision. A desire not only for beauty, but for strangeness and mystery, turned people's thoughts to the Middle Ages. This was the atmosphere Sir Walter Scott sought in his novels; it played its part in the Tractarian Movement and the ideas of the Pre-Raphaelites; it stirred enthusiasm for Gothic architecture. The German poets and philosophers—Tieck, Schlegel, Herder, and others—explored folk literature and folk thought; in England the lyrical ballads by Coleridge and Wordsworth were published; Rousseau's philosophy inspired a return to nature and the simplicities of life. All of this together made up the Romantic Movement and during its flowering a group of sturdy woodland blossoms took root and flourished.

The German Brothers

Among these there were the *Kinder- und Hausmärchen*, the folk tales collected by the Brothers Grimm. Jacob (1785–1863) and Wilhelm (1789–1859) were both philologists. The *History of the German Language*, the *German Grammar*, the great Dictionary planned on so large a scale that it was impossible for the two brothers to bring it to completion, are works of magnificent learning known to the world of scholars. But the folk tales are known to thousands of men, women, and children who have no interest in philology. The poet and philosopher Herder, whose love for early literature paved the way for the work of the Grimms, declared prophetically that such a collection of tales would be a Christmas gift for young people of the future.

We are reminded of the universality of folklore and that, as Paul Hazard has said in his *Books, Children, and Men*, "The folk tale knows no frontiers," when we consider how these stories, collected in a European country more than a century ago, come to life everywhere for each new generation of boys and girls. Hansel and Gretel, the witch and her gingerbread house, the gallant little tailor with his seven at one blow and many others are an integral part of the childhood experience of English-speaking people and are handed down to the oncoming boys and girls because of the happy recollections of their elders.

The *Hausmärchen* were definitely a product of the Romantic Movement. Jacob Grimm, in compliance with his father's wishes, studied law. His professor at Marburg, Friedrich Karl von Savigny, and Savigny's library awakened Jacob Grimm's interest in early German literature. Through Savigny he made the acquaintance of *Des Knaben Wunderhorn* (The Boy's Wonderhorn), a collection of folk songs edited by Ludwig Achim von Arnim and Clemens Brentano, which gave him the keenest delight. Anything in the nature of a ballad, it is said, appealed to Jacob Grimm. When Savigny took him to Rome with him to help in collecting material on the history of Roman law, Jacob found time for some research of his own in another field. His brother Wilhelm had written him, "I have been thinking that you might look for some old German poems among the manuscripts. Perhaps you might find something unknown and important." However, it was a collection not of folk songs but of folk tales that Jacob determined on his return to undertake with his brother's help.

The two worked together in complete harmony. They spent all their lives under one roof, sharing books and other property, a happy partnership that Wilhelm's marriage did not alter.

In Hesse, where they lived, stories were to be had on all sides for the mere listening, and the Grimm brothers set out to do for the folk tale what Arnim and Brentano had done for the folk song, but with a difference. The brothers did not approve of the liberties taken by the compilers of the *Wunderhorn*, for to them the language and form of the old folklore were the things to be preserved as well as the story. Jacob wrote to Wilhelm in 1809, "They [Arnim and Brentano] are not content to leave the old as it is but insist on transplanting it to our time where it does not belong," a sentiment which shows the Grimms to have been far in advance of contemporary ideas on the subject. There was something of happy childhood in the delight these two serious scholars felt in folk literature that fitted them to interpret the old fairy tale to the modern world. The *Hausmärchen*, which appeared in Germany in 1812–1824, became a part of the life of the German people, and soon, crossing the Channel, was adopted by English nurseries.

The tales were translated by Edgar Taylor and published in England in 1823–1826 with the title *German Popular Stories*, illustrated by one of the finest artists of the time, George Cruikshank. From that day on, English-speaking children have been on terms of familiarity with a host of thrilling, entertaining, and lovable characters in Faithful John, the Elves and the Shoemaker, Rumpelstiltskin, Snow-White and the Dwarfs, and all the others. Everything that was satisfying in the old English folklore and legends was here again—brave deeds, familiar animals, glimpses of splendor, and of the sparse and adventurous peasant living. Child readers who were just beginning to have some mastery over letters and words could go through them without help from their elders, with little of their concentrated effort to be spent on side issues or passages of description. The story was the thing they were pursuing and to the story the authors kept faithfully. It is hard to remember how very laborious are the first efforts of the very young reader. Witness of the fact is that on the child bookshelf the volume of Grimm is usually the most tattered of all. Called sometimes *Grimm's Household Stories*, sometimes *Grimm's Fairy Tales*, they have appeared in many editions, and in addition to Cruikshank's, have had illustrations by such well-known artists as Walter Crane, Arthur Rackham, and Wanda Gág.

The Danish Ugly Duckling

Meanwhile another interpreter of the world of imagination was living a life that in itself seemed a kind of fairy tale. In 1805 Hans Christian Andersen was born in Denmark in the town of Odense. His family belonged to the respectable poor: his father was a cobbler, his mother took in washing, but the cobbler was self-educated—he read history and the Bible and he read the plays of Holberg, the Danish Molière, aloud to his son. Hans Christian's mother could not understand their laughter; she was never able to follow her son's flights of fancy but she surrounded him with warm affection and security. The imagination of one parent, the practicality of the other, blended together, made Hans Christian what he was.

Andersen's was a happy and sheltered childhood, and though the family lived in a house full of poor people, home was always a place of golden memories to him. He wrote in his autobiography, "The one and only little room, almost filled by the cobbler's bench and the bedstead and the folding bench in which I slept, this was my childhood home, but the walls were covered with pictures, there were pretty cups, glasses and knick-knacks on the chest of drawers, and over the cobbler's bench by the window was a shelf with books and songs. In the little kitchen a row of pewter plates hung over the larder, and the tiny space seemed vast and rich to me. The door itself, with a landscape painted on the panel, meant as much to me then as a whole picture gallery now!"[1] Once a year in May, when the golden-green beech leaves were out, the mother would join her husband and son in a trip to the woods. Always she

[1] Signe Toksvig, *The Life of Hans Christian Andersen* (New York, Harcourt, 1934), p. 3.

brought back an armful of fresh-leaved birch branches to put behind the brightly polished stove, and St. John's wort was stuck into the cracks in the rafters, to see how long the family would live.

Hans Christian's father made a toy theater for him, and the boy wrote plays for the doll actors. When he was about eleven he made a list of plays he intended to write, twenty-five of them; two of the titles were "The Evening Promenade, or The Cook and the Count," and "The Two Murderers." His father's mother, a gentle, blue-eyed old lady, was proud of her grandson; she told him tales of ghosts and goblins which he loved, although they terrified him. She tended the garden of the hospital for the insane poor and sometimes brought flowers to the Andersen house. Hans Christian was thrilled to hold them and arrange them in a glass of water. Perhaps he recalled these nosegays when he wrote "Little Ida's Flowers."

Many memories of Andersen's childhood are to be found in his stories. "The Red Shoes" may point back to the very special pair of dancing slippers that his father made but which failed to win the post for which he applied. Of the boxes which little Kay and Gerda in "The Snow Queen" called their garden, because herbs and two tiny rose trees were planted there, Andersen wrote in *The Story of My Life*, "In the rain-gutter next to the neighbour's house stood a huge box full of earth, in which grew garden herbs, and which was the only garden my mother had. In my story, 'The Snow Queen,' this garden is blooming still."[1]

The boy was a dreamer. He would sit under a tent made by his mother's apron and the gooseberry bush, gazing into the green leaves, lost in his imaginings. Then he went to school and learned to read. After that there was less time for dreaming, for he read with passionate eagerness anything he could lay hands on. If he heard that anyone had books, he went and asked that person to lend him some and he was not refused. In this way he made the acquaintance of Shakespeare and learned scenes from the plays by heart. He had a high, clear voice and when he sang by the river people came to hear him. His songs and recitations brought him a local reputation as an entertainer and this encouraged his secret determination to become an actor, but no one seems to have told him that for a stage career an education is necessary. His father died when Hans Christian was eleven, and three years later his mother married again. The husband, who was fifteen years younger than his wife, was not unkind but he had no interest in his stepson. His mother could not give him the same attention as in the past and it was her desire to apprentice him to a tailor, for since Hans Christian made costumes for his doll actors, tailoring seemed the obvious trade. Hans Christian, however, had other ideas and announced his intention of

[1] Esther Meynell, *The Story of Hans Andersen* (New York, Schuman, 1950), p. 4.

going to Copenhagen to become an actor. His mother, shocked at first, allowed herself to be persuaded by his arguments and Hans Christian set out like the heroes in the fairy tales to seek his fortune, armed only with a letter to a certain Mrs. Schall of the Ballet.

Years of struggle and hardship followed; singing, dancing, he tried them all, and all failed to impress those who might have smoothed his path to the stage. Yet his honesty, his eagerness, his enthusiasm, appealed to people; he made good friends and managed to exist. At length King Frederick VI sent him to school at public expense. In 1829, when he was twenty-four years old, Andersen's first book appeared. It was a fantasy called *A Walking Trip From Holmens Kanal to the East Point of Amager*, and a slight thread of plot enabled Andersen to put into the book all the ideas that had been simmering in the back of his mind while he was studying for his matriculation at the University of Copenhagen. Daydreams, what he observed, what he imagined, what he felt, all went into the book in a lively style that showed his gift for personification. The critics were kind. Copenhagen was charmed, and for Andersen it was a glorious springtime.

In 1830 a volume of his *Collected Poems* was published, and soon after, an unhappy love affair made Andersen's friends feel that he needed the distraction of travel. A traveling pension from the king made the journey possible, and Andersen set out for Germany. On his return he put the story of his trip into a little book called *Travel Silhouettes*, which was not praised by the critics. Two more years of travel followed —Germany, France, Italy—and then in 1835 came the turning point of his career with the publication of his novel, *The Improvisatore*, which met with deserved success.

In that same year Andersen began the work which, though he did not know it, was to bring him his greatest fame. He wrote four fairy tales for children which were published in a pamphlet—"trifles" he called them. Still he wrote another little book of tales because wherever he went children seemed to have read the first one. He wrote these stories in vigorous, homely, everyday speech, as they had been told to him and as he told them to children. "The Tinder Box," "Little Claus and Big Claus," "The Princess and the Pea," and "Little Ida's Flowers" were the first four stories, followed in the second booklet by "Thumbelina," "The Naughty Boy," and "The Traveling Companion."

In 1838 the king granted him a pension; now he was independent. Absorbed in playwriting, he nevertheless found time to write two more stories for children, "The Daisy" and "The Steadfast Tin Soldier." Travel again followed to Italy, Greece, Turkey; a journey was always refreshment to Andersen, who spoke of returning to Denmark with his "heart filled with the flowers of travel." The fairy tales were appearing, a small volume each year, and they carried Andersen's fame far beyond the borders of Denmark. Though Andersen called his tales "Wonder Stories for Children," he meant them to appeal to both young and old; this double appeal existed in Andersen's time, when he was in constant demand as a storyteller for adults, as well as children, and still exists today. Boys and girls who are enthralled by "The Steadfast Tin Soldier," "The Ugly Duckling," "The Nightingale," "The Wild Swans," and "The Snow Queen" turn to them again in later years and find a wisdom beyond a child's comprehension. At first, as Andersen explains in his autobiography, he told the old stories in his own way as he remembered hearing them as a child. But as he continued to write and publish he relied more and more on his own invention.

On one of Andersen's trips to Germany he decided to call on the brothers Grimm. The maid showed him in to Jacob, but Jacob did not recognize Andersen's name. Andersen felt shy and awkward and the interview was not a success. When he again met the brothers in Berlin, matters went better, Wilhelm Grimm saying, "I should have known you very well if you had come to me the last time you were here." And Andersen as he recorded this in his autobiography added, "I saw these two highly gifted and amiable brothers almost daily. The circles into which I was invited seemed also to be theirs; and it was my desire and pleasure that they should listen to my little stories, that they should participate in them,—they whose names will always be spoken of as long as the German volksmärchen are read."

Andersen, the son of poor parents, a youth who had almost starved in his early years in Copenhagen, was now on easy terms with the nobility. They not only liked his books, they appreciated his social gifts, his talk, his amusing stories. In their country houses, with their beech forests and the lakes, where the swans sailed by with slow dignity, he was at home and happy. In the summer of 1842, during one of those pleasant visits, he wrote "The Ugly Duckling," thinking of his own life, the wretched early years of misunderstanding, the secure and gracious present. Told in simple, everyday style it is a story for children; it is also a story, like so many of Andersen's, with a deeper meaning for the adult to ponder.

Andersen's fairy tales had a new and unique quality. Jacob and Wilhelm Grimm presented the dwarfs and elves and talking animals of the forest; the French storytellers, Charles Perrault, Countess Marie d'Aulnoy, and others, chose for their characters kings and queens and courtiers riding in splendid coaches; Andersen uses the furniture of the household, setting in motion a whole world of inanimate things, as well as birds and animals who are members of the household or barnyard characters. His pages are crowded with peg-tops, green peas, tin soldiers, darning needles, shirt collars, swallows, slugs, cats and hens and apple trees, all of which express themselves with the greatest clarity and individuality. They think and talk as the child thinks and talks, they see the world as he sees it and thus are completely understood by him.

In 1846 Andersen's tales were first translated into English by Mary Howitt, who called the book *Wonderful Stories for Children.* She also translated Andersen's *The Story of My Life*, giving it the title *The True Story of My Life; A Sketch* by Hans Christian Andersen, translated by Mary Howitt (1847). The dedication read:

> To Jenny Lind the English translation of her friend's life is inscribed in admiration of her beautiful talents and still more beautiful life, by Mary Howitt.

thus marking the faithful friendship between Andersen and Jenny Lind, the singer, which lasted until Andersen's death in 1875.

As is the case with *Grimm's Household Tales*, Andersen's *Stories* have been for more than a hundred years an indispensable part of the library of the English-speaking child.

Other Writers of Fairy Tales

Resistance to fantasy, so firm in the 1780's and 1790's, was gone at last. With the way paved by the success of the Grimm brothers' *Tales* and Andersen's *Stories*, with the persistence of Perrault's *Contes de Ma Mère l'Oie* (*Tales of Mother Goose*) and Countess d'Aulnoy's *Fairy Tales*, which had come to England in the eighteenth century and were reprinted in many editions, fairy tales became in the 1840's and 50's a recognized part of children's reading. Many fairy tales, some traditional, some original inventions, were either translated for the first time or assembled from earlier collections. Sir Henry Cole, under the pen name of Felix Summerly, frankly ranged himself on the side of imaginative reading for children by including many traditional fairy tales in his *The Home Treasury* (1841–1849); he also spoke out firmly for them in the prospectus, much to the annoyance of Samuel Goodrich who, as Peter Parley, was eagerly advocating the factual in children's books.

Anthony Montalba also defended the fairy story, for in the preface of his *Fairy Tales of All Nations* (1849) he declared that we had "cast off that pedantic folly of thinking fairy tales immoral." Richard Doyle had a way with fairies and fairyland and his fine drawings gave an added distinction to this book.

Among the fairy tales from Europe which were popular in translation were *Fairy Tales* (1802–1827) by Wilhelm Hauff, particularly "Dwarf Long-nose" and "Caliph Stork"; also Ludwig Bechstein's (1801–1860) *The Old Story-Teller* (1854), popular tales translated into English mostly from *Das Deutsches Märchenbuch*. This and a second volume, *As Pretty as Seven* (1872), were illustrated with many drawings by the German artist Ludwig Richter. In 1857 Annie and Eliza Keary retold the Norse myths in *Heroes of Asgard*; James Robinson Planché (1796–1880), poet and dramatist, but best known for his *History of British Costume*, translated *Four and Twenty Fairy Tales, Selected from Those of Perrault and Other Popular Writers* (1858). Many of these tales were adapted by Planché as extravaganzas for the stage.

The most important translation and one which has been the basis for all subsequent collections of Scandinavian folktales was Sir George Webbe Dasent's *Popular Tales from the Norse* (1859), from the *Norshe Folkeeventyr* of Asbjörnsen and Moe. Edouard de Laboulaye (1811–1883), a famous French lawyer, wrote for his little granddaughter a large number of fairy tales based on the folklore of many countries. These were published in England as *Fairy Tales* (1887) and in America as *Fairy Tales of All Nations* (circa 1866) and *Last Fairy Tales* (1884). *Abdallah; or, The Four-Leaved Shamrock*, translated by Mary L. Booth, was published in England in 1868; a later edition, published in the United States, was called *The Quest of the Four-Leaved Clover* and was translated by Walter Taylor Field.

Many of the fairy tales of Clemens Brentano were translated by Kate Freiligrath Kroeker, as *Fairy Tales from Brentano* (1885) and *More Fairy Tales from Brentano* (1888). These were published in England and the United States and included besides the famous and popular "Gockel, Hinkel and Gackeleia," the "Story of Brokerina," who was an excellent cook and who was also so hard to please that her father bade her bake a husband to suit her, which she did. There were also "The Story of Frisky Wisky," who befooled the Giant Stretch-Yourself and his wife, Burst-Your-Seams, and the story of "Old Father Rhine and the Miller."

The famous tale of *The Three Bears*, usually known as *Goldilocks and the Three Bears*, had appeared in 1834, an advance guard of the fairy tale in English. Now Richard Henry Horne (1803–1884), poet, dramatist and traveler, wrote *The Good-Natured Bear* (1846), an entertaining little story in which an educated bear tells of his amusing adventures with his German friends, Mr. and Mrs. Littlepump and their children. Horne's *King Penguin, A Legend of the South Sea Isles* (1848) tells of the hero's adventures on an island inhabited by these pompous, bowing birds, where he is befriended by their king. Horne's most famous book, which he wrote under the pen name of Mrs. Fairstar, was *Memoirs of a London Doll* (1846), which in its descriptions of the Christmas Pantomime, Twelfth Night Festivities, The Lord Mayor's Show, Punch and Judy, gives us an unforgettable glimpse of Victorian England's entertainments.

In America Christopher Pearse Cranch (1813–1892), best known for his witty but amiable caricatures of his fellow Transcendentalists, wrote

The Last of the Huggermuggers (1855) and its sequel *Kobboltozo* (1856). *The Last of the Huggermuggers* tells how a ship's company were wrecked on an island inhabited by a kindly giant and his wife, the Huggermuggers. When a ship arrives to rescue them, the sailors plan to take the giant home in order to exhibit him, but the giant, who has lost his dearly loved wife, goes into a decline and dies before the ship reaches port. The sequel, *Kobboltozo*, which appeared first in *The Atlantic Monthly*, tells of the downfall of a malicious dwarf who had been the cause of the giant's misfortunes. These stories enjoyed considerable popularity but they lack gaiety, and the death of the two giants seems needlessly sad. Cranch, indeed, admitted that his little son always cried over *The Last of the Huggermuggers*, and Cranch's friend, William Wetmore Story, called the tale lachrymose, bade Cranch read Andersen, and urged him to put into his book some of the humor which his friends knew he had.

Granny's Wonderful Chair (1857) by Frances Browne (1816–1879) consists of eight fairy stories connected by the pleasant device of a chair which responded to a little girl's request, "Chair of My Grandmother, tell me a story." The tales have a moral but it is unobtrusive; the style is charming and, strange to say, since the author was born blind, the stories have a vivid and lovely pictorial quality. They are kept in print and are still read and loved by children.

John Ruskin wrote *The King of the Golden River* in 1841, but it was not published until ten years later. This dramatic tale of the Black Brothers, Little Gluck, the South-West Wind, and the Treasure Valley, restored by Gluck's compassion, is still a favorite. It has a clearly indicated moral but a moral eminently satisfactory to children, and Richard Doyle's fine drawings, so completely in the spirit of the tale, added to its appeal.

A charming and amusing fairy tale was provided by Charles Dickens in *The Magic Fishbone*. This appeared as Part II of "A Holiday Romance," which was published serially in 1868 in *All the Year Round*. It dealt with the Princess Alicia, her eighteen brothers and sisters, her royal father, King Watkins the First, and the Queen, his wife, the Fairy Grandmarina and the talisman she so wisely bestowed and Alicia so wisely refrained from using until the right moment came.

Thackeray's *The Rose and The Ring; or the History of Prince Giglio and Prince Bulbo. A Fire-Side Pantomime for Great and Small Children, By Mr. M. A. Titmarsh* (1855) is a gay bit of nonsense which borrows the trappings of the traditional fairy tale and handles them with a delightful humor and sense of fun that is greatly aided by Thackeray's own cleverly absurd drawings. That a great critic and two of the great novelists of their time turned their attention to the fairy tale goes far to show how firmly it had now become established in its own place.

Bibliography

Andersen, Hans Christian. *The Story of My Life;* Now First Translated Into English and Containing Chapters Additional to Those Published in the Danish Edition, Bringing the Narrative Down to the Odense Festival of 1867. Cambridge (Mass.), Riverside Press, 1871.

Gooch, G. P. "Jakob Grimm." In *History and Historians in the Nineteenth Century.* London, Longmans, 1913.

Ker, W. P. "Jacob Grimm." In *Collected Essays.* London, Macmillan, 1925. Vol. 2, pp. 222–233.

Meynell, Esther, *The Story of Hans Andersen.* New York, Schuman, 1950.

Miller, Frederick DeWolfe. *Christopher Pearse Cranch.* Boston, Harvard University Press, 1951.

Toksvig, Signe. *The Life of Hans Christian Andersen.* New York, Harcourt, 1934.

· 5 ·

The Gift of Pure Nonsense
and Pure Imagination

An Old Tradition Goes Down the Rabbit Hole

As we have seen in the mid-nineteenth century, fairies and elves, giants and magicians, became once more the familiars of English-speaking children. In 1862 there quietly occurred something that was the real beginning of modern literature for children. On a July afternoon, "a golden afternoon," a young Oxford professor took the three little daughters of Dean Liddell of Christ Church on a picnic and, while rowing and drifting on the Isis, he told to the three, in response to their eager demand for a story, the tale of Alice, who followed the White Rabbit down the rabbit hole and found herself taking part in remarkable adventures.

Though written for children, perhaps no book has ever had an audience so evenly divided between children and adults. Scarcely a week passes that there is not an allusion to *Alice's Adventures in Wonderland* (1865)[1] or *Through the Looking-Glass* (1871) in editorial, newspaper column, courtroom, or novel. Quotations from these books are a part of everyday speech—"The *best* butter," "jam tomorrow and jam yesterday—but never jam *today*," "I didn't say there was nothing *better*, I said there was nothing *like* it," have passed into the language, and when someone remarks "I doubt it," how hard it is not to add "said the Carpenter, and shed a bitter tear." Some say, indeed, that the Alice books are for adults rather than for children, but the adults who say this fail to remember the hundreds, the thousands, of children who have read and are reading Alice not only in English, but translated into many other languages.

The revolutionary quality of Lewis Carroll's two books lies in the fact that they were written purely to give pleasure to children; moreover they were written purely for pleasure on the part of the author, too, for thus is a masterpiece made. Here, then, for the first time we find a story designed for children without a trace of a lesson or moral.

---

[1] Published 1865, withdrawn and published again in 1866.

In a sense the Alice story is childhood itself, with its wonder and its wisdom; with the grave little heroine, curious but never prying, anxious to please but never afraid, moving with the gentle grace of unspoiled childhood through all the extraordinary events and among the extraordinary characters of Wonderland and the Looking-Glass World.

When Lewis Carroll left his little guests at the deanery door that summer evening, ten-year-old Alice said, "Oh, Mr. Dodgson, I wish you would write out Alice's adventures for me." This was done and some months later Alice received it as "Christmas Greetings to a Dear Child," written out by hand and illustrated by her friend in a little green book. It was read not only by the Liddells, but by their friends. Mrs. George Macdonald read it aloud to her children and Greville, aged six, declared "there ought to be sixty thousand volumes of it." George Macdonald and others urged its publication, Tenniel was suggested as an illustrator, and on April 5, 1864, Mr. Dodgson, Tenniel, and Macmillan made final arrangements. *Through the Looking-Glass and What Alice Found There* followed in 1871.

Charles Dodgson, the young Liddells' gifted friend, was a professor of mathematics, an alternate field which seems, at first glance, to be far removed from that of the extraordinary imagination of the Alice books. But on further thought one realizes that part of the substance of the fantasy is the entirely graphic quality of the persons and places. Nothing is vague in the story except perhaps the Cheshire cat's slowly fading smile. One does not often stop to think how difficult it is to create impossible personalities, but so clear and convincing are Lewis Carroll's that it is nothing for us to learn "to believe three impossible things before breakfast." The White Knight, while he certainly suggests to everyone somebody or other whom he has known, is so real in his own right, not only in person but in spirit, that he is a notable addition to our cherished circle of friends. The Duchess was a conception of such positive attributes that Tenniel, in trying to envisage an appropriate presentation of her, finally had to have recourse to the ugliest portrait in the National Galley to find his inspiration.

The verse in the two books is of such ingenious and memorable quality that it is a basic part of our delight in *Alice*. As has been said earlier, Southey's poem "The Old Man's Comforts" has lived far more vividly in Carroll's version, "You are old, father William," than by its original reputation. Wordsworth himself comes in for what is never unkind, but only penetrating and adroit imitation, when "Resolution and Independence" becomes "A-Sitting on a Gate." Jane Taylor's gentle poem, "The Star," takes on surprising energy and bounce when it turns into "Twinkle, twinkle, little bat! How I wonder what you're at!"

Lewis Carroll and Tenniel made an author-artist combination rarely if ever equaled. They worked closely together, Carroll being very sure of what he wanted and Tenniel going along with him until it came to the thirteenth chapter of *Through the Looking-Glass*, when Tenniel declared that "a wasp in a wig was beyond the appliances of art." He also felt that the chapter was not equal in value to the rest of the book and Carroll, though he would hold out for what he wanted, in this case bowed to Tenniel's judgment. Tenniel never illustrated another book for children, saying that after *Through the Looking-Glass* was finished, his gift had forsaken him. The two Alices provide the perfect example of author and artist expressing the same thing in their respective mediums and, as Austin Dobson wrote, addressing himself to Alice:

> Naught but chaos and old Night
> Can part you now from Tenniel.

The Hunting of the Snark; An Agony in Eight Fits was published in 1876 with extraordinarily apt and amusing drawings by Henry Holiday and pleased both children and adults. Some readers have tried to prove that the poem was an allegory; Carroll himself, however, insisted it didn't mean anything but nonsense. *Phantasmagoria*, consisting of amusing verses, was published in 1869, and in 1883 the comic portions of *Phantasmagoria* and *The Hunting of the Snark* were published together with sixty-five illustrations by Arthur B. Frost and nine (the original Snark pictures) by Henry Holiday, with the title, *Rhyme? and Reason?*

Carroll's only other book for children was *Sylvie and Bruno* (1889) and in 1893 *Sylvie and Bruno* and *Sylvie and Bruno Concluded* were published in one volume. This book grew out of the short story "Bruno's Revenge," which Carroll wrote for Mrs. Gatty's *Aunt Judy's Magazine*. *Sylvie and Bruno* has had and still has its lovers among children and adults, but it is not well known nor often read today, and as a literary achievement it stands far below *Alice*. The fairy chapters are very pleasing, but Carroll unwisely tried to combine them with a human love story, the characters weaving back and forth from fairyland to reality in a way confusing to many readers. In addition he used the book as an opportunity to express his ideas about life and death, religion, art, love, and science, with a resulting lack of artistic unity. Still, the story holds delight for the persevering reader in the "Songs of the Mad Gardener" and in the Other Professor, who is one of the book's most amusing characters and whose inventions—his Outlandish watch with the reversal peg, his megaloscope and minifying glass, his umbrella boots for horizontal weather—remind us of the White Knight. Through the pages of *Punch*, Lewis Carroll became acquainted with the work of Harry Furniss and in 1885 wrote to ask him if he would illustrate *Sylvie and Bruno*. As was the case with the *Alice* books,

Carroll was exacting but the two men worked together with satisfaction, for if Carroll caused his illustrator an immense amount of work and trouble, Furniss declared that he was quite repaid by Carroll's generous appreciation and put it on record that Carroll was the only one of the many authors he had illustrated who cared about understanding the illustrations to his own book. The drawings for *Sylvie and Bruno* are both charming and amusing and admirably illustrate the story.

About Charles Dodgson himself (1832–1898) and the circumstances of his outward life, people in general know surprisingly little. It might be said that there was little to know, since there was so much that was beyond our reckoning. He was the Reverend Charles Dodgson, having taken holy orders, although he never pursued any other occupation than that of teacher of mathematics. He was the son and grandson of clergymen, was born in the rectory in Cheshire and then was moved to Crofts in Yorkshire—but not before he was old enough to become acquainted with Cheshire cats. He had a singularly happy boyhood, loving to wander about in the open country and scramble in the marle pits, shy and tending to solitary play, always seeming to find sufficient happiness in his own busy imaginings. He edited—and wrote—two small family papers, *Mischmasch* and, later, *The Rectory Umbrella*. His father, apparently deciding that his tendency to shyness should not be encouraged, sent him to Rugby for three years which, so Charles declared afterward, "no power on earth could induce him to go through again." Otherwise he made little direct comment on the school except to say that he "spent an incalculable time writing out impositions," the penalties of that educational period being calculated daily in so many lines of Greek and Latin. Charles's Rugby was not that of Arnold's day, but of Tait's, a less able successor.

At nineteen, Charles entered Christ Church College, Oxford, and there remained the rest of his life, first as an undergraduate, going on to scholarships and fellowships, an obscure, kindly, still shy Oxford bachelor, writing abstruse books on mathematics. The largest event in this scholastic life was his moving in 1868 from one set of rooms on Tom Quad to another, still overshadowed by the presence of the great clock tower and Big Tom, who chimed the curfew at nine o'clock every night, always, by ancient tradition, five minutes late.

So likeable was he that he became the friend of many distinguished people—Ruskin, Sir John Millais, the Rossettis, and Ellen Terry—but he moved little in formal society. His hobby, amateur photography, he pursued diligently and with great success. He was always truly happiest in the presence of children. He made friends with them wherever he went, always able to pull puzzles out of his pocket to amuse them on railway trains, or producing safety pins when a child on the beach wished to go in wading.

His friend Liddell was Dean of the magnificent Christ Church, which is really the cathedral of Oxfordshire. He spent thirty-six years at Oxford, Dodgson forty-seven. In 1932, at Charles Dodgson's centenary, his university, which had once been so unaware of him, made beautiful acknowledgment of the fame he had brought to her. She bestowed an honorary degree upon Alice Liddell Hargreaves, then aged eighty, with the citation "awakening with her girlhood's charm the ingenious fancy of a mathematician . . . the moving cause . . . of this truly noteworthy contribution to English literature; I gladly admit you to the degree of Doctor of Letters in this University." Alice's reply was brief. "I feel that Mr. Dodgson knows and rejoices with me in the honor you are doing him."[1]

There Was an Old Man of . . .

Though Edward Lear's *A Book of Nonsense* appeared in 1846, one thinks of Lear and Carroll together, for Lear's verses were as free from any attempt to sugar coat a moral as was Lewis Carroll's prose. There is nothing derivative about the Jabberwock, the Mock Turtle, and the Gryphon, but they were drawn in the same vein as Lear's "The Pobble Who Has No Toes," "The Dong With The Luminous Nose," and the elderly Quangle Wangle, and they would all undoubtedly have felt quite at home with one another. Lear's books, like Carroll's, belong to both children and their elders and Lear, like Carroll, is quoted frequently. Another likeness is that in the case of each one, his nonsense created a world of its own, different from the real world but a logical and consistent world according to the laws of nonsense. Lear's most famous book, like Carroll's, was written for child friends and was quite apart from that branch of art by which he hoped to earn his living, for Lear (1812–1888) was by profession a landscape painter and illustrator.

In his introduction to *More Nonsense* (1872) he says that "in days when much of my time was spent in a country house where children and mirth abounded, the lines beginning 'There was an Old Man of Tobago' was suggested to me by a valued friend as a form of verse lending itself to limitless variety for rhymes and pictures; and thenceforth the greater part of the original drawings and verses for the first Book of Nonsense were struck off with a pen, no assistance ever having been given me in any way but that of uproarious delight and welcome at the appearance of every new absurdity." Lear is best known for his *A Book of Nonsense* (1846) and *More Nonsense* (1872), but equally important are his Nonsense Alphabets, his Nonsense Geography, Natural History and Botany, and his Nonsense Stories which were published together as *Nonsense Songs, Stories, Botany and Alphabets* (1871).

---

[1] Florence Becker Lennon, *Victoria Through the Looking-Glass, The Life of Lewis Carroll* (New York, Simon and Schuster, 1945), Introduction, pp. ix–x.

All of them were illustrated by Lear's enormously original, imaginative, and hilarious drawings, with their apparent naiveté produced by the skillful hand of a master. *Laughable Lyrics*, containing "The Dong With The Luminous Nose," "The Pelican Chorus," "The Yonghy-Bonghy-Bo," "The Quangle Wangle's Hat," and others, appeared in 1877.

George Macdonald Takes His Readers to the Back of the North Wind

There were contemporaries of Carroll who also wrote tales of fantasy for children. The greatest of these was George Macdonald (1824–1905). He and Carroll were friends; Carroll told stories to the Macdonald children, to their great delight, and Macdonald urged the publication of *Alice in Wonderland*. Macdonald's own fairy tales deal with a world of the imagination, but a far different world from that of Carroll. In *At the Back of the North Wind* (1871), *The Princess and the Goblin* (1872), *The Princess and Curdie* (1883), and the fairy tales there is a serious atmosphere, a kind of other-worldliness characteristic of the author, indeed so much a part of him that it would have been impossible to keep it out. Macdonald was a visionary, and his children's stories, while not allegories, were filled with spiritual meaning. This by no means keeps them from being good stories, full of lively incident and appealing characters.

Who can forget the North Wind, in *At the Back of the North Wind*, beautiful with her flowing hair, blowing in through the knot-hole in the loft where Diamond slept, to carry the little boy away on wonderful journeys over land and sea? The glimpses which Macdonald gives us of the country from which she comes make perceptible that indefinite region of the imagination which differs deeply with different fancies but has eternal qualities just the same. Ancient and simple people of the British Isles called it simply Fairyland and had endless tales of those who went or were carried there and how the world looked to them when they returned. With another race of men it was called the land which lay "east of the sun and west of the moon," whither only gallant souls were privileged to penetrate. In a later and more sophisticated age it has been less easy to conceive; Barrie's Never-Never Land is one picture of it, Howard Pyle's Garden behind the Moon is another. At the Back of the North Wind is perhaps the most indefinable place of all, but its quality is clear to us, it has the magic of the spirit as well as of pure imagination.

One long remembers also, in *The Princess and the Goblin*, little Princess Irene climbing flight after flight of moonlit stairs in the palace to find a good great-great-grandmother to offer her counsel and comfort when she needs them. For George Macdonald's stories give children what they need—wonder, adventure, and a sense of security. The stories themselves in the two Princess books quietly suggest in every incident ideas of courage and honor. In two more of his books Macdonald drove home the moral he had in mind in passages that are definitely didactic, yet in *At the Back of the North Wind* certainly this does not keep children from enjoying the story. Five fanciful tales were published in 1867 with the title *Dealings with the Fairies*, illustrated by Arthur Hughes. These were "The Light Princess," "The Giant's Heart," "The Golden Key," "The Shadows," and "Cross Purposes."

Arthur Hughes (1832–1915) is always associated with Macdonald in the minds of those who have seen the illustrations Hughes made for *Dealings with the Fairies*, *The Princess and the Goblin*, *At the Back of the North Wind*, and *Phantastes*. The two men were alike in their insight into something beyond the actual and in their response to the things of the spirit.

Phantastes first appeared in 1858, a book not written for children but one which many young readers have found for themselves and enjoyed. The first edition had no pictures; later, an illustrated edition was published without Macdonald's sanction; the illustrations so distressed Macdonald's son, Dr. Greville Macdonald, that he persuaded Hughes to make pictures for a new edition in 1905.

Macdonald was a novelist, poet, and clergyman, as well as a writer of children's books. Born in Aberdeenshire, Scotland, he studied for the ministry and for three years held a pastorate in Arundel. At the end of that time he resigned because his congregation, while they respected and liked him, did not think his sermons sufficiently dogmatic. But formalism and rigid doctrinal interpretation were always in entire opposition to Macdonald's true religious fervor and the spirituality of his outlook. He preached occasionally in later life but never held another pastorate; and though his health was always delicate he supported his large family by writing, teaching, and lecturing. His novels of Scottish life were popular during his lifetime, his verse, which had a strong spiritual quality, was admired, and his poems are still found in anthologies; but he is best and most justly remembered for his children's stories. *At the Back of the North Wind* and the *Fairy Tales* are still read and *The Princess and the Goblin*, which has been a favorite with boys and girls since it was first published, shows no signs of losing favor.

Mopsa, the Brownie and the Little Lame Prince

Jean Ingelow (1820–1897), poet, novelist, and writer of children's stories, was a contemporary of Carroll's. Her novels and poems are largely forgotten, though the poem "Seven Times One" from her *Songs of Seven*, has been loved by many children and is still found in anthologies. In her own day she was much admired on both sides of the Atlantic and she was the friend of Tennyson, Browning, Oliver Wendell Holmes, Lowell, and Longfellow. C. S. Calverley parodied her cleverly in his *Verses and Fly Leaves*, though he was actually an admirer of her poetry. Her best-known book today is a story for children, *Mopsa the Fairy* (1869), a well-constructed tale of a little boy who finds a nest of fairies, puts them in his pocket, and flies into fairyland on the back of an albatross. Told with charm and a kind of logical make-believe, the book has enjoyed a long popularity. It has been published in Everyman's Library. An American edition (1927) was illustrated by Dorothy Lathrop. The beginning of *Mopsa the Fairy* has been compared to the beginning of *Alice's Adventures in Wonderland*, and the suggestion made that Jean Ingelow owed the idea of her story to Lewis Carroll. The resemblance between the hollow tree and the rabbit hole is hardly marked enough to indicate that Jean Ingelow was consciously or unconsciously imitating Carroll, but undoubtedly the author of *Alice* did much to create an atmosphere sympathetic to the fairy tale and thus set other writers free to use their imagination in children's books.

Dinah Maria Mulock (1826–1887), who became Mrs. Craik, wrote many books but is best remembered by one, *John Halifax, Gentleman*. Next best remembered are two of her books for children, *The Adventures of a Brownie* (1872) and *The Little Lame Prince* (1875). In the first the mischievous pranks of the brownie who lived in the coal cellar and the everyday life of the children whose playmate he became make a combination that has delighted several generations of young readers. *The Little Lame Prince* tells of Prince Dolor, who is imprisoned in a tower and whose Fairy Godmother sends him a magic traveling cloak that carried him on wonderful journeys. The story has a touch of sadness in it, but it is beautifully written and has a charm to which children still respond.

Mary De Morgan (d. 1907), whose brother William (1839–1917) became famous in the early years of the twentieth century for *Joseph Vance* and other novels, wrote some spirited, original fairy tales which were published in England (1876) and in America (1891) with the title *On a Pin-cushion, and Other Fairy Tales*.

Oscar Wilde (1854–1900) wrote two volumes of fairy tales, *The Happy Prince and Other Tales* (1888) and *A House of Pomegranates* (1891). Wilde used words full of color and music and there is beauty in the writing. Some of these stories, notably "The Selfish Giant," are enjoyed by children at the fairy-tale age, but because of the poetic quality of the style and the suggestion of allegory, these tales appeal especially to older boys and girls and to adults.

Bibliography

Ayres, Harry Morgan. *Carroll's Alice*. New York, Columbia University Press, 1936.

Collingwood, Stuart Dodgson. *Life and Letters of Lewis Carroll*. New York, Century, 1899.

Davidson, Angus. *Edward Lear*. London, Pelican Books, 1951.

Dean, F. R. "George Macdonald." In *Manchester Literary Club Papers*, 1948–49. Manchester, 1950, pp. 61–78.

Hall, W. C. J. "Jean Ingelow." In *Manchester Literary Club Papers*. Manchester, 1931. Vol. 57, pp. 145–165.

Holbeach, Henry. "George Macdonald." *Contemporary Review*, London, Vol. 19 (Jan., 1872), pp. 37–54.

Lennon, Florence Becker. *Victoria Through the Looking Glass, The Life of Lewis Carroll*. New York, Simon & Schuster, 1945.

Macdonald, Greville. *George Macdonald and His Wife*. New York, Dial Press, 1924.

6

The American Family

The Vale of Tears

In 1850 there appeared in America *The Wide, Wide World*, by Elizabeth Wetherell, the pen name used by Susan Bogert Warner (1819–1885), to be followed two years later by *Queechy* (1852). In both books the heroines are orphans and both are beset by many trials and tribulations which they surmount with Christian fortitude. Floods of tears are shed and the young heroines, gentle as they are, are much given to pointing out the better way and the joys of a religious faith to those dear to them. The author's sincerity, however, and the zest and freshness with which she describes everyday things—food and clothes, cooking, nut gathering—kept her books wholesome and made them popular. The daughter of a well-to-do farmer, Susan Warner was able to paint a picture of society in New York and the surrounding country that is still of interest.

Elsie Dinsmore, by Martha Farquharson Finley (1828–1909), who sometimes wrote under the name of Martha Farquharson, was published in 1867, the first of a long series which began with Elsie as a child, carried this heroine through childhood, girlhood, wifehood, motherhood, and widowhood, ending with a volume called *Grandmother Elsie*. There were still other volumes dealing with descendants and relatives and, in 1878, Miss Finley embarked on another series in which a new character named Mildred was the central figure. This series was less popular than the Elsie books, which were read for many years. They are remembered today when many better books are forgotten, for Elsie, with her firm religious principles, her insistence on obeying her conscience to the displeasure of her worldly father, and her final conversion of that gentleman to a practicing Christian, has come down through the years as the archetype of a little prig. Nevertheless, Miss Finley's books are full of incidents pleasing to children, described with the detail in which children delight. Her readers, too, enjoyed finding in book after book the same characters that made up Elsie's large circle of friends and relations. The Elsie books were read for forty years and up to the 1940's could be still found in print.

Life Grows More Lively

Many realistic stories for girls were written in America during the 1860's and 1870's. They dealt with home life and were for the most part intended for readers from ten years on. However, Sophie May, a pseudonym for Rebecca Clarke (1833–1906), began in 1863 a series for younger children with a book called *Little Prudy*, followed by *Little Prudy's Sister Susy, Little Prudy's Captain Horace*, and others. This series (1863–1865) was followed by three others, dealing with sisters or cousins of Little Prudy—the Dotty Dimple Series, Little Prudy's Flyaway Series, and Flaxie Frizzle Series (1867–1884). It has been the fashion to make fun of Sophie May and it is true that her family chronicles were prolonged to thinness, but her characters are very human and if a moral is sometimes too obviously insisted on, a sense of humor pervades her accounts of children, who are natural and engaging. Sophie May also wrote books for older girls, The Quinne-basset [or Maidenhood] Series (1871–1892), which took its name from the New England town that served as their setting. They are forgotten now, but *The Doctor's Daughter, Our Helen, Janet, The Asbury Twins, Quinnebasset Girls*, and *In Old Quinnebasset* are interesting, lifelike, unsentimental tales which were popular in their own time and read well today. Sophie May is a witness that books in a series are no modern idea.

Adeline Dutton Train Whitney (1824–1906), who was always Mrs. A. D. T. Whitney on the title pages of her books, was a writer of considerable substance. Beginning with *The Boys of Chequasset* in 1862, she published novels and poems as well as children's stories into the 1890's, but her best remembered books are those she wrote for girls. *Faith Gartney's Girlhood* (1863), *A Summer in Leslie Gold-thwaite's Life* (1866), *We Girls, A Home Story* (1870), *Real Folks* (1872), and *The Other Girls* (1873). Mrs. Whitney knew how to tell a story and could make her characters real. She wrote of the New England she knew so well in simple, easy fashion, and her homely details and a suggestion of dry humor gave her style strength and individuality. Her books maintained a high moral standard and she could not always resist the impulse to preach, but this habit lessened with time and *We Girls*, one of the most attractive of her stories, is almost free from sermonizing.

Elizabeth Stuart Phelps (1844–1911), who became Mrs. Herbert Ward, wrote novels with a strong religious tone. Her *The Gates Ajar* (1868) was very popular in England as well as America; she also wrote stories for young readers. Best remembered among her books for the young are the four volumes of the Gypsy Breynton series, *Gypsy Breynton* (1866), followed by *Gypsy's Cousin Joy*, *Gypsy's Sowing and Reaping*, and *Gypsy's Year at the Golden Crescent*. The last named tells of Gypsy's experiences at boarding school. These are pleasant tales of everyday life, told with a sense of humor. Gypsy is a lively, adventurous young heroine, showing that even before the advent of *Little Women* the type of girl heroine was changing. Gone are the blinding headaches, the tendency to fainting spells of Susan Warner's heroines and of Elsie Dinsmore. Gypsy was an outdoor girl who could row and skate and swim, play ball, make kites, coast and race and chop wood, and, greatest change of all, her brother Tom could say, "I don't believe Gypsy cries four times a year . . . with all her faults there's none of your girl's nonsense about her."

Sarah Chauncey Woolsey (1835–1905) used the pseudonym of Susan Coolidge. Her first book, *The New-Year's Bargain* (1871), is an imaginative and pleasing story in which two children are able to bargain with the Months for a story and a gift from each one; *Mischief's Thanksgiving* (1874) is another collection of tales. But the author's best books and those by which she is remembered are the Katy Did series, *What Katy Did* (1872), *What Katy Did At School* (1873), *What Katy Did Next* (1886), *Clover* (1888), and *In the High Valley* (1891). In this series, which was very popular and is still enjoyed, a group of young people grow up from childhood to marriage. The Carrs are a real and appealing family—from impulsive Katy, the oldest, to solemn six-year-old Dorry. In Dr. Carr, the father of these motherless children, the author drew a fine portrait of a lovable character. Susan Coolidge wrote well and her stories have much of the genuineness of Louisa Alcott's. The stories and poems of the young Carrs and the plays they wrote and acted remind us of the "Comic Tragedies," as Louisa Alcott called them, which were written and performed by the March girls in *Little Women*.

Harriet Beecher Stowe (1811–1896), whose *Uncle Tom's Cabin* was read by many boys and girls though written for their elders, wrote a story for girls which was very popular. It was called *Little Pussy Willow*, published in 1867–1868 in *Our Young Folks* and coming out in book form in 1870. In it the author used the device of contrasting a wholesome, happy country girl (Pussy Willow) with a city girl (Miss Emily Proudfit), a device always popular with young readers, and Pussy Willow and Emily Proudfit have their descendants in books of today.

In the same years, *Our Young Folks* published *William Henry's Letters to His Grandmother* by Mrs. Abby Morton Diaz (1821–1904), which came out in book form in 1870. Natural and unforced, these letters were written with the unconscious humor of a real boy, and the spontaneous little drawings with which William Henry is supposed to have illustrated them ring true. If Susan Coolidge's *What Katy Did At School* was the first thoroughly convincing school story for girls in this country, the William Henry *Letters* provides the first genuine picture of a small boy and his fellows in boarding school. Mrs. Diaz also wrote one of the earliest stories about dolls in her *Polly Cologne* (1881) and a book of cat stories, *The Cats' Arabian Nights* (1881), much loved by the younger children.

Helen Hunt Jackson (1830–1885) was the daughter of an Amherst professor. After her first husband's death and her marriage to William Jackson of Colorado Springs, she made her home in Colorado. There she wrote *Nelly's Silver Mine* (1878), an excellent story of a brother and sister whose family moves to sparsely settled mining country in Colorado. Two years later she edited *Letters from a Cat*, written by her mother, which had many years of popularity. Because she was so deeply concerned over the disgraceful treatment the Indians were receiving from the white people, Mrs. Jackson wrote *Ramona* (1884), a novel for adults but read by many young people in the 1880's and 1890's.

In 1880 *The Peterkin Papers* by Lucretia P. Hale (1820–1900), sister of Edward Everett Hale, was published. (A few of the Peterkin Papers had appeared in *Our Young Folks* and in *St. Nicholas*.) Ever since the book was available to children they have been entranced by Mrs. Peterkin's elaborate efforts to counteract the effect of the salt accidentally substituted for sugar in her coffee; chuckled over Elizabeth Eliza's playing the piano through the porch window because the instrument was turned the wrong way; followed Agamemnon as he prepared to write his book only to discover when he was ready to begin that he had nothing to say; and delighted in the Christmas chapter when Mr. Peterkin and the little boys in their India-rubber boots brought home a tree so tall that to make room for it the ceiling in Elizabeth Eliza's room had to be raised. The helpful "Lady from Philadelphia" has become a household word for common sense. In 1960 *The Complete Peterkin Papers* was published with the original illustrations and an introduction by Nancy Hale.

The Five Peppers Arrive

Margaret Sidney was the pseudonym of Harriet Mulford Stone Lothrop (1844–1924). In 1878 the magazine *Wide Awake* began the publication of her *The Five Little Peppers and How They Grew*. In 1881 it was published in book form, to be followed by *The Five Little Peppers Midway* (1893), *The Five Little Peppers Grown-Up* (1892), *Phronsie Pepper* (1897) and several other books on the Pepper family. Mrs. Lothrop wrote other stories for children, but her fame rests on the first four "Little Pepper" books. These stories deal in simple, homely fashion with the everyday life of a large family of limited means and have appealed for many years to a wide audience of readers.

The Man Without a Country

Edward Everett Hale (1822–1909), born in New England and a great-nephew of Nathan Hale, the American Revolutionary hero, was a clergyman and a writer. Best known of his stories is "The Man Without a Country" (published in *The Atlantic Monthly* in December, 1863), which was read by young and old. It is the sad tale of a young officer implicated in Aaron Burr's treachery, who impatiently expressed the wish at the court martial that he might never hear of the United States again. That was his punishment, for, transferred from one ship to another at sea, he was sent on voyage after voyage, all mention of the United States in his presence being forbidden and all references to his country being carefully removed from his reading matter. Told with remarkably realistic detail, this story, which is strictly fiction, has an air of truth so convincing and impressive that it undoubtedly fulfilled the purpose for which Hale wrote it, to deepen a feeling of loyalty in the North during the Civil War and to encourage enlistment.

These books make it clear that the realistic story for young people was establishing itself and a comparison of Katy Carr and Polly Pepper with Susan Warner's Ellen and Fleda shows that the nineteenth century girl heroine was steadily growing more human and natural. The stories mentioned in this chapter were written for children and eagerly read by them. In 1868 a book for young people appeared which was read not only by them but by their elders and was received with an enthusiasm that indicated the arrival of a great writer, as indeed this author was. The book was *Little Women* by Louisa May Alcott.

The March Family

Louisa May Alcott (1832–1888) cannot be considered apart from her family. She was the daughter of parents of marked individuality; her father, Bronson Alcott, a philosopher, a born teacher, so forward-looking for his time that his educational theories were in many ways those of the twentieth century; her mother, Abba May Alcott, brilliant, practical, versatile, with strong affections, immense loyalty and an irrepressible sense of humor. All of these characteristics helped to make their daughter into the person that we know. The rich, warm family life of the Alcotts, too, the never failing interest and pleasure which each member took in the doings of all the others, the never failing flow of ideas which left no chance for dullness or idleness, the friends attracted by a family so alive, so broad in interests—all these went into the books which came from Louisa Alcott's pen in the years between 1864 and 1888.

Amos Bronson Alcott (he soon dropped the Amos) came of old New

England country stock. As a boy he helped on the farm, but books were his delight and he wished to enter Yale. Since the family income forbade, he set out instead for the South, where he hoped to find a teaching position. Disappointed in this he began peddling small articles, almanacs, and tinware about the city of Norfolk, Virginia, and the surrounding country. This, of course, could not hold him for long, so he presently came north again, his mind once more on the thought of teaching. After four years in a position in Connecticut, where his ideas on education proved too advanced for the community, he went to Boston and there founded a small infant school where he could put his theories into practice. It was while he was teaching in Connecticut that he met Abigail May, daughter of Colonel May of Brooklyn, Connecticut, and in 1830 he and Abba May were married. Abba May's ancestors were Sewells, Quincys, and Hancocks. The Dorothy Q of Oliver Wendell Holmes's poem was a great-aunt, Madame Dorothy Quincy Scott, but always called by the name of her famous first husband, "Aunt Hancock." Abba May grew up in a home where life was simple, for Colonel May lost all his money during Abba's childhood. But it was a home rich in interests and in sympathy for those in need. That even when means are limited there is always a way to help others was a lesson Abba May learned from her father and one that she taught in turn to her daughters.

Anna Alcott, the oldest daughter of Bronson and Abba, was born in Germantown, Pennsylvania, where Alcott had gone to open a school under the patronage of the Quaker Reuben Haines. The next year the second daughter arrived and was named Louisa May, but the children were not to grow up in Philadelphia. To the Alcotts' great sorrow, their good friend Reuben Haines died, and without his help it was impossible for the school to continue. In 1834 the Alcotts were in Boston where, with Elizabeth Peabody as assistant, Bronson Alcott for the second time started an infant school, called the Temple School because its quarters were in the Masonic Temple. Thoughtful people were sympathetic with Alcott's ideas; Ralph Waldo Emerson all his life was Alcott's loyal friend and backer; the children in Alcott's school were happy and made progress but once again his ideas were too advanced for the parents. Moreover, Alcott was an abolitionist. The admission of a little Negro girl to the school proved the last straw. The school had lasted five years; now the last pupil had been removed, it had to close its doors. Alcott was in debt and sold his books and other possessions to pay his creditors.

Alcott discovered that children are active beings and that they learn better when they are happy, that working and playing together can be fun, that words are most easily learned when meanings go with them, that counting beans is for little children a practical way of learning arithmetic. All of this does not seem very startling today, whatever it may have seemed in 1834. It was, however, the publication by Alcott of his *Conversations with Children on the Gospels* that shocked orthodox parents into taking pupils out of the school. It was thought to be eminently improper to talk so familiarly of God to young children.

The world was not ready for Alcott's educational ideas, but he could and did use them in teaching his own little girls; his theories, combined with his wife's wisdom and common sense, certainly seem in the case of the four Alcott sisters to have produced admirable results. Though Bronson Alcott was never successful from a worldly point of view, though the Alcotts were poor, sometimes desperately so, though Louisa realized early in life that she must earn money to help her family, the father's courage and patience and his determination in standing by the principles in which he believed were dearly cherished by his family. After the Temple School was closed, they went to Concord, where so much of their life was to be spent. The Hosmer Cottage where they lived had a large garden; behind it were fields and a river. After Boston the children were delighted with the freedom of the country, especially Louisa, who was the tomboy of the family. Bronson Alcott worked hard at odd jobs—farm labor, wood cutting, gardening, anything that would help take care of the family. There was another little girl now, younger than Elizabeth, who was born in 1835. May needed her mother's care, and the older children spent much time with their father, though they learned to cook and to keep house.

When spring came, Emerson and other friends made it possible for Bronson Alcott to go to England to see the school which had been named for him and to talk with people who understood his ideas. The family waited eagerly for his return; what had been accomplished by his trip they did not know, but hopes were high. The immediate result of the journey, however, was something they could never have guessed. Bronson brought back with him two Englishmen and a boy, who were to live with the Alcotts for the winter. In the spring of 1843 they, with Alcott and others, were to start an experiment in communal living. This was the Fruitlands vividly described by Louisa in her story "Transcendental Wild Oats."

Life at Fruitlands was hard for Mrs. Alcott, who bore the brunt of trying to feed and clothe her family while doing most of the housework for the community. It was too hard, and when Charles Lane, one of the Englishmen, felt that Alcott should leave his family to devote himself to the communal idea, she stood firm. A family council was called, including the girls. They talked the matter over, Alcott and his wife in great distress; the girls went to bed in tears. No one, not even Bronson knew what the end would be. The next day, however, when Charles Lane returned from a trip, the matter was settled; after an interview between the two men, Bronson knew that his place was with his family. Lane and his son left. Then on a "bleak December day," so

Louisa Alcott tells it, "with their few possessions piled on an ox-sled, the rosy children perched atop and the parents trudging arm in arm behind, the exiles left their Eden and faced the world again. 'Poor Fruitlands! The name was as great a failure as the rest,' said [Bronson], with a sigh, as a frostbitten apple fell from a leafless bough at his feet. But the sigh changed to a smile as his wife added, in a half-tender, half-satirical tone,—'Don't you think Apple Slump would be a better name for it, dear?' "[1]

Abba Alcott's brother found them a house in Still River, a nearby town, and here for a time it seemed as though Alcott would never be his old self again. He had worked too hard, he was exhausted in body and spirit, but Abba Alcott's courage did not fail even now. Her loving care, the rest and freedom from perplexities, slowly brought back her husband's health and he bravely put behind him his grief for the great experiment that had failed. They moved to Concord, then to Boston, then back to Concord again, this time to a house that belonged to them, which they named "Hillside."

In spite of the many times they moved ("We have lived in twenty-four houses in twenty-two years," Mrs. Alcott once remarked), no young people ever grew up in a happier home than the Alcott girls, whether that home was for the time being in Boston or Still River or Concord. In spite of hard work and plain living there was no lack of plans and projects to keep the girls entertained and busy. Private theatricals were a perennial delight. The girls wrote the plays, made the costumes and properties, and acted the parts with gusto. In *Comic Tragedies Written by "Jo" and "Meg" and Acted by the "Little Women"* (1893) some of these plays are preserved.

The Alcotts delighted in traditional celebrations and old English customs. Bronson's *Journals* relates how he "brought a load of trees from the woods—spruce, larch and pines. Conveyed the children, consisting of several from the neighbourhood, with May-pole . . . to the Emerson's. The waggon was neatly trimmed with running pines, and a wreath of the same on our bonnets and hat, and as we passed along the road we sang, 'Merrily We Go.' At Emerson's several joined us, with the mothers and other company, and then the children danced around the May-pole."[2]

From the time she was thirteen until the autumn of the year she was sixteen, Louisa lived at Hillside and when she was fourteen she went for the first time to the district school. Though it was Bronson Alcott's joy to educate his children, he and their mother felt the girls needed companionship of their own age. Louisa was shy at first, but

[1] Louisa May Alcott, "Transcendental Wild Oats," *Silver Pitchers*, 1876, pp. 100–101.

[2] Bronson Alcott, *The Journals of Bronson Alcott* (Boston, Little, Brown, 1938), p. 178.

her liveliness and high spirits made her popular. The next year the girls returned to lessons with their father, and when Louisa reached sixteen she decided to make her first venture as a breadwinner. She started a little school in the barn at Hillside, Mr. Emerson's children providing most of the pupils. Her father had taught her to be a good teacher, though she never really liked teaching, but her energy and friendliness and resourcefulness made the children like her. It was during this time that Louisa wrote her first book. She had not thought of the little stories she wrote for Emerson's daughter Ellen about birds and fields and flowers as a book, but her father showed one of the stories to a publisher, who liked it. The stories were made into a small volume called *Flower Fables* (1855), and Louisa at twenty-three was an author, though she laughed at the idea and refused to take herself seriously.

The school had brought in little money, and the following year Louisa made a difficult decision. She decided to go to Boston where she hoped to find work of some sort. At least by earning her own living she would relieve the family of her support. She found an opportunity to teach, she did sewing, she was lonely and very homesick, but there were compensations. An occasional play and concert delighted her, and the Theodore Parker home was always open to her, where she met the most interesting people in Boston and heard good talk.

For Louisa, the prospective author, these lonely months in Boston were important, for she wrote constantly—melodramatic tales, lurid she herself called them, like nothing she knew or indeed like anything in real life, but she was gaining experience and when the stories found a market for modest sums in the second-rate magazines they helped the family finances. Louisa's first long story, a novel, was *Moods*, written in 1861 but not published till 1864. It did not have much success though a certain young book reviewer named Henry James, after criticizing the story as unnatural, praised the book's beauty and vigor.

In 1858 Elizabeth died. Louisa had gone home to help nurse her through her last illness, an experience that she was afterward to describe so movingly in *Little Women* that thousands of readers have sorrowed with her over gentle Beth's passing. Soon after, Anna announced her engagement to John Pratt. Louisa liked John but to lose Anna from the household made her feel doubly bereaved.

When the war came, Louisa made up her mind to go as a nurse. She knew the work would be difficult and dangerous, but she only said, when anyone tried to dissuade her, "The blood of the Mays is up, I must go." Out of this experience came her first successful book, *Hospital Sketches*, based on the letters written to her family from the Union Hospital in Georgetown. This was a far better book than *Moods*, for it was written out of her own experience and her deep sympathy with the wounded men.

She was not physically strong enough to stand the strain of nursing and, after six weeks of struggle to care for the wounded in spite of inadequate quarters, unsanitary conditions, and complete lack of equipment, a serious illness made it necessary for her to return home. In 1867 the firm of Roberts Brothers in Boston asked her to write a book for girls, and after some hesitation she agreed to try. The result was *Little Women* (1868). She herself was not impressed with the book, thinking the first part dull, but she admitted it read better than she expected, saying "We really lived most of it, and if it succeeds, that will be the reason of it."

It is remarkable that in an age when reticence was the fashion in life and in books, Louisa Alcott had the insight to realize that what girls wanted was truth and warmth and that she had the courage to let them share the intimacy of life in her own home, for the Marches in *Little Women* are clearly and unmistakably the Alcotts. Girl readers and older readers, too, lived with and loved the four March sisters, loving Jo best of all, for this irresistible Jo, everybody's favorite character, was Louisa herself. Among those amazingly real portraits, she is the most real, the most convincing of all. Impulsive, quick-tempered, awkward, she is all of these in the book, for the author did not spare herself, but since it is a true portrait, Jo's courage, honesty, and unselfishness were bound to come out, too, to complete the picture of a splendid character.

So popular was *Little Women* that a sequel was called for and *Little Women, Part II* was published in 1869. *An Old-Fashioned Girl* (1870), which reflects some of Louisa's experiences in earning her own living, and *Little Men* (1871), which dealt with the later years of the March family, followed. *Eight Cousins* (1875) and its sequel *Rose in Bloom* (1876) give an account of a larger family, with the aunts and uncles and the various young people all settled in one neighborhood. Like Father Bhaer's handling of the boys in the Plumfield School, Uncle Alec's plans in *Eight Cousins* for Rose's education illustrate many of the theories which Louisa had learned from her father. There is a happy boy-and-girl companionship in the book, as shy Rose learns to know and enjoy her seven lively boy cousins who remembered a Scottish grandfather, called themselves the Clan, and took pleasure in Scottish songs, dances, and bagpipe music. *Under the Lilacs* (1878) and *Jack and Jill* (1880) came out serially in *St. Nicholas*. The latter begins with a coasting accident but the year's invalidism for the little heroine that results, in contrast to the stories of an earlier day, is handled with common sense and liveliness, Jill's room becoming the center of amateur theatricals, tableaux, and all the ingenious good times of a group of boys and girls.

Young people having good times together, understanding elders, enjoying warmth and security—both *Little Men* and *Under the Lilacs*

begin by describing how a forlorn, small boy finds a home and affection
—all these things appeal to young readers and have kept Louisa Alcott's
books alive for generations of children.

Jo's Boys, the last of the full-length stories, appeared in 1886 when,
in Louisa's words, "The curtain falls forever on the March family."
Work, which represented her own personal experiences, was published
in 1873, though written much earlier. *A Modern Mephistopheles* was
brought out in 1877 among the earlier volumes of the No Name Series.
Miss Alcott says, in the preface to a later edition published under her
name, "it was very successful in preserving its incognito," and many
people still insist it could not have been written by the author of
Little Women. With it, when published in 1889, was "A Whisper in
the Dark," which Miss Alcott called "a sample of Jo March's necessity
stories, which many girls have asked for."

Many volumes of short stories were brought out from 1868 on—
*Aunt Jo's Scrap-Bag, Silver Pitchers, Proverb Stories, A Garland for
Girls, Spinning-wheel Stories*, and *Lulu's Library*, this last consisting
of stories which Louisa wrote for her little niece, the daughter of May
Alcott Nieriker, whom Louisa brought up after May's death. All these
were cordially received by children, but it is on her long stories that
Louisa Alcott's fame rests, most of all on *Little Women*. Because it is a
true and very human account of real people, their aspirations and mistakes, their failures and their triumphs, *Little Women* has something of
universal human nature in it. If this were not so, the story would not
appeal as it does to readers a hundred years after it was written and
also to readers in other countries. It has been translated into fourteen different languages, among them Finnish, French, Hungarian,
Chinese and Japanese. In spite of differences in customs and conventions,
the human quality in Miss Alcott's stories, her knowledge of young
people, and her sympathy with youth have kept her books alive.

It is one of the miracles worked by books that a quiet New England
woman, a century ago, should have opened a door through which
thousands of readers all over the world are still passing to share
the life of an ideal home with its moral earnestness, innate refinement,
and its liberality of thought.

Bibliography

Brown, Janet E. *The Saga of Elsie Dinsmore*. University of Buffalo Studies, Vol.
17, July, 1945. Vol. 3, No. 4 of Monographs in English.
James, Henry. *Notes and Reviews*. Cambridge, Mass., Dunster House, 1921.
McCuskey, Dorothy. *Bronson Alcott, Teacher*. New York, Macmillan, 1940.
Meigs, Cornelia. *Invincible Louisa*. Boston, Little, Brown, 1933.
Salyer, Sandford. *Marmee: the Mother of Little Women*. Norman, University of
Oklahoma Press, 1949.
Sanborn, F. B. and W. T. A. Harris. *Bronson Alcott; His Life and Philosophy*.
2 Vols. Boston, Ticknor Brothers, 1893.

7

The Field of Adventure in England
and America

Two important changes in writing for children took place in the latter half of the nineteenth century. For some time the belief that instruction was the primary object in books for the young was weakening. Then Carroll's *Alice's Adventures in Wonderland* pointed the way to entire freedom of the imagination in children's books and to complete banishment of the obvious moral. It followed naturally, when entertainment was recognized as a legitimate aim for the writer of books for children, that the reading tastes of different ages should be taken into consideration. It occurred to publishers and authors that there are vast differences between the seven- and nine-year-olds and their older brothers and sisters. The home story by Louisa Alcott, Susan Coolidge, and others took care of the girls; there now sprang up a crop of adventure stories for boys, though their sisters read them as well.

Walter Scott, for many years an author read by whole families, had perhaps helped to show what was the sort of story that appealed to the growing boy or girl, at the age when the most reading is done. Scott was ably seconded by Cooper, who, as has been said earlier, set children everywhere to playing that they were scouts and Redskins. Sir Sidney Colvin, the friend of Robert Louis Stevenson, remembered playing Indian "according to Cooper."

At Sea with Marryat and Others

Scott was a landsman and thus left the whole range of romantic possibilities that lie in the sea story for other writers to cultivate, both in the adult novel and in the story for boys. Cooper, with *The Pilot* (1823), wrote the first sea story of the period, but Captain Frederick Marryat (1792–1848), who was to take the sea as his special province, was hard on his heels with his *The Naval Officer; or, Scenes and Adventures in the Life of Frank Mildmay* (1829), to be followed by other novels and at last by *Peter Simple* (1834) and *Mr. Midshipman Easy* (1836). These two, although they were, like the rest, written for adults, were read at once by boys and greatly enjoyed by them. The fact that midshipmen began naval life at the ages of fourteen or even twelve made the account of their first years in the service congenial and absorbing reading to boys of the same age. So many of them were fired with enthusiasm for a naval career that Marryat has been called the best recruiting officer the British Navy possessed. Yet he had not romanticized the hard life where boys, shy and awkward and utterly inexperienced, must learn their way by hard knocks and under unsparing taskmasters or by the chance assistance of a loyal friend.

Marryat himself entered the service at the age of fourteen. He had made several attempts to run away from school and go to sea before his father consented to his becoming a midshipman on the frigate *Imperieuse*. At twenty-three he was a commander and the hero of numerous cutting-out expeditions and privateer chases; when he left the navy at thirty-eight he had witnessed some fifty naval engagements. When he was in command of the sloop *Beaver* he was given the guard duty of the island of St. Helena, where Napoleon's presence, even in captivity, had so long been a latent threat to the peace of Europe. "An English man-of-war was always kept cruising to windward of the island," so the record has said, for there was ever the possibility that some desperate effort at rescue might set him free to harry the world again. But Napoleon was dying now and it was Marryat who brought the despatches back to Europe announcing the fallen emperor's death.

In 1830 on returning from India, he gave up his command and was never appointed to another ship. But he had published *Frank Mildmay* and had a new profession to which to turn. His many novels were successful and justly so. His style is clear and lively, his tales are seasoned with humor and include scenes of pure comedy based on real incidents and actual characters, for he came to know many types of men and was a shrewd observer of human nature. Yet when he attempted elaborate plots he was weak and even absurd; his heroines are what might be called negligible. The qualities of his writing belong essentially to the kind of book that boys like and this, presently, he himself came to see. Boys were already reading his novels, but he set out to write for boys themselves with *Masterman Ready* (1841), *The Children of the New Forest* (1847), and *The Little Savage* (1848). *Masterman Ready* shows steadfast character, humble courage, and devotion to duty which win our deepest respect. The story has to do with shipwreck and a desert island, but it is no mere imitation of *Robinson Crusoe*, for it has strong individuality of its own. *The Little Savage* has a somewhat similar, but cruder, theme.

Of *The Children of the New Forest* more special note must be taken. In spite of its age and of a certain leisureliness of style which belongs to a period when spare hours for reading were more abundant, it has still so many of the requisites of a good child's book that teachers and critics of children's literature and writers in that field can well come back to it to study its many excellencies. It has more of the elements of romance in it than any other piece of Marryat's writing, the romance of picturesque history and striking background. The story is simple, that of four royalist children who are orphans who have lost their home following the defeat of King Charles, and are carried by an old servant to the safety of his cottage in the New Forest. Upon the old man's death not long afterward, they are thrown on their own resources, a well-known situation and always interesting to the young, so well carried out here that there is nothing stereotyped in the able treatment. The material elements of the story—the capture of the wild ponies, the taming of the wild cattle, the forest cottage itself—are all alluring. The treatment of character is wise and plausible; we learn to like and admire Edward's bold and not always wise courage, Humphrey's patient and cheerful ingenuity, the elder sister's responsible care of the youngest. Marryat's narrative style is here at its best in its clarity, its steady forward progress, its unpretentious vigor. He had learned much in his years of novel writing; it was children's literature that was to reap the benefit.

A goodly number of writers followed Marryat and Cooper into this field of telling tales of adventure, some with little more to offer than a facility for stringing incidents together, some with very much larger powers and experience which resulted in books of much more permanent value. Of the better ones there can be mentioned first Thomas Mayne Reid (1818–1883), who was born in Ireland and at twenty sailed for America and betook himself into the wilderness as a trader. Then, having received a commission in the United States Army, he fought as a second lieutenant in the Mexican War. He was wounded and during his convalescence began to write. His first book was *The Rifle Rangers* (1850). After his return to England he went on to a long succession of stories. His novels were inclined to be lurid and were forgotten, but his stories for boys were in great demand for many years. They included *The Scalp Hunters, or Romantic Adventures in Northern Mexico* (1851), *The Boy Hunters* (1852), and *The Young Voyageurs* (1853). His style was spirited; he could handle a plot; he was not above giving instruction, chiefly on the subject of natural history, but not to the extent of greatly impeding his story. It has long been said that his information was detailed and accurate, but the accuracy which we demand of authors in a specialized field today was somewhat beyond him. He slips in some small matters as does a man whose life has not been spent amid the background which he is using. It was once a current legend in the West that big-horn sheep could leap from tremendous declivities and land safely on their hoofs. This is an idea long since exploded, but in *The Desert Home* (1852) Reid describes them as doing so, bouncing high, turning over in the air and landing on their feet. Boys read him eagerly and unquestioningly, however, and longed for adventure in the West.

Reid's contemporary, Robert Michael Ballantyne (1825–1894), was a native of Edinburgh and a nephew of James Ballantyne, Sir Walter Scott's publisher. At sixteen he became a clerk with the Hudson Bay Company in Canada, where he gathered a store of experience to be used to great advantage in his books. On his return to Edinburgh and after working seven years in the publishing business of Thomas Constable, he settled down at the age of thirty as a writer. Later he journeyed to Norway and Africa to collect material and managed to produce eighty books. His first, *Snowflakes and Sunbeams, or The Young Fur Traders* (1855), was very successful. It dealt with the Hudson Bay Company, as did *Ungava, A Tale of Eskimaux-Land* (1857). In the next year appeared *The Coral Island*, perhaps his best-known and best-loved story. Stevenson praised it and mentioned Ballantyne, Kingston, and Cooper in the poem which precedes the title page of *Treasure Island*.[1]

The ship's company that was wrecked on *Coral Island* appear again in a sequel, *The Gorilla Hunters*. The boy readers of Ballantyne's high-spirited tales were carried along from one astonishing adventure to another, to their entire satisfaction. Ballantyne was remembered with affection by many of these readers in middle age.

The other popular writer for boys mentioned by Stevenson was William Henry Giles Kingston (1814–1880). His father was in business in Portugal where Kingston therefore spent much of his youth. He wrote novels and books of travel, but it is for his books for boys, over one hundred of them, that he was best known. The first, *Peter the Whaler*, appeared in 1851. While Kingston and Ballantyne had much in common, Ballantyne was the better writer. The books of both authors were full of incredible adventure. Both were concerned with keeping a healthy moral tone, Ballantyne's efforts, however, being less obvious.

George Alfred Henty (1832–1902) was for several reasons the most important figure among this special group of the nineteenth century writers of adventure stories for boys. Like the other writers of the day, he drew on his own experiences, but those were experiences of a different sort, for Henty was a war correspondent and one who ranked with the best. He left Cambridge University to volunteer for service in the Crimean War and stayed in the army until 1865, when he joined the London *Standard* and remained with that paper until his death. The *Standard* first sent him to Italy, where the war with Austria was going on. Later he followed Garibaldi in the Tirolean Campaign; he went to Ethiopia with Lord Napier and attended the opening of the Suez Canal in 1869. The next year he was sent to Germany to report the Franco-Prussian War, then to Turkestan with the Russian Army,

---

[1] Robert Louis Stevenson, "To the Hesitating Purchaser," *Treasure Island* (London, Cassell, 1883), Prologue.

to Africa with Lord Wolseley for the war with the Ashanti, and to Spain for the Carlist War. His last campaign was the Turkish-Serbian War in 1876. At its close his health forced him to go home, and it was then that he began to write.

His first stories were told to his own children. At the suggestion of a publisher he wrote one out and it was accepted. From that time on, he had a definite purpose in his writing. He would not only make a living by it, he would put military history into books for boys, and he would give English boys a sense of the British empire. This was, in a sense, a labor of love, for Henty liked nothing better than to tell the tale of great campaigns and battles. It was a period, since censorship was not strictly enforced, when a war correspondent could go wherever the soldiers went, and Henty chose to be always at the front. With war much less mechanized than it is today, there was a greater chance for picturesque personalities and stirring deeds to emerge. Henty's life coincided with Victoria's reign. He wrote with pride of England and the expanding empire, but he was fair, for though he wept in public over Britain's disaster at Majuba Hill, he considered the Boer War a disgraceful and humiliating chapter in British history.

He never drew a moral in so many words, but his books convey the lesson that determination and courage win in the end, and when he magnified brave exploits, he showed that gentleness and magnanimity go with true courage. His style is clear and interesting and his military history accurate. Of *The Young Buglers* (1880) he wrote, "The military facts, with the names of generals and regiments, the dates and places, are all strictly accurate, and any one who has read with care the story of 'The Young Buglers' could pass an examination as to the leading events of the Peninsular war."

Though he liked best the wars of the nineteenth century, those of the eighteenth century coming next and then those of the seventeenth, his books cover a wide range of time and place. *The Cat of Bubastes* (1889) gives a picture of Egypt in the reign of Thotmes III; *The Dragon and the Raven* (1885) deals with Alfred's struggle with the Danes; *Under Drake's Flag* (1883) ends with the defeat of the Spanish Armada; *By Pike and Dyke* (1889) tells of William of Orange and the sieges of Haarlem, Leyden, and Antwerp. In *St. George for England* (1885) the young hero takes part in the battles of Crécy and Poitiers; *With Wolfe in Canada* describes the massacre of Fort William Henry, Louisbourg, Ticonderoga, and the battle of Quebec; *With Kitchener to the Soudan* (1903) was published after Henty's death. Hardly a period or an important military operation is missing from the list. Henty's belief in his country, his staunch and genuine patriotism, fitted well with the expanding empire. Romance for the most part he avoided although in the last chapter of *With Clive in India* there are a well-written love scene and four weddings. Henty had little gift for characterization; his heroes have a genuine quality but also a sameness which caused Miss Muffet, the heroine of Samuel Crothers' *Miss Muffet's Christmas Party*, to say of Mr. Henty's boys, "There seem to be a great many of them, but I've sometimes thought there may be only two, only they live in different centuries and go to different wars." Nevertheless Henty's books, of which there were more than ninety, made history for many young readers. His reading public in his own lifetime was enormous, and his popularity continued well into the twentieth century.

The Riches of Treasure Island

During the years from 1840 onward, boys were exploring remote regions, sailing the high seas, escaping from cannibals or Redskins in the company of heroes who, even when created by different authors, bore a marked resemblance to one another and who were, on the whole, pegs on which to hang adventures rather than individual characters. Early in the 80's, however, something of an entirely different class appeared, and another milestone in writing for children was passed, when Robert Louis Stevenson's (1850–1894) *Treasure Island* came out in *Young Folks* in 1881–1882 and in book form in 1883.

Written for boys, it was seized upon by adult readers as well. Augustine Birrell said "we could almost have raised a statue in the market place to Stevenson for having written *Treasure Island*" and advised Lord Arthur Balfour to get a copy without delay, which Lord Balfour did. William Ernest Henley called it the best boy's book since *Robinson Crusoe*. Lord Randolph Churchill told Balfour that everyone was reading the new novel, *Treasure Island*. Andrew Lang wrote, "except for *Tom Sawyer* and the *Odyssey*, I never liked a romance so much."

Here were adventure, suspense, drama, all set down by the hand of recognizable genius. At the same time, in Jim Hawkins, the young hero, in Squire Trelawney and Dr. Livesey, who set off with Jim to outwit the buccaneers, and in Long John Silver, were characters so real, so consistently drawn, that the reader half expected to meet them on the street. The thrilling force of the dramatic moments arises from the actor's feeling and emotional response to them, rather than from the material events themselves. No one will ever forget Jim Hawkins hidden in the apple barrel.

Stevenson wrote *Treasure Island* with delight. "It's awful fun, boys' stories" he told Henley. "You just indulge the pleasure of your heart." And so his readers can indulge the pleasure of their hearts too.

The Black Arrow, his other book for boys, also appeared first in *Young Folks*. This was a tale of the Wars of the Roses and had a heroine as well as a hero. Stevenson called it "a tale of tushery," the name which he and Henley had used for stories of the Ivanhoe type. He did not think highly of it himself, but many young people and their elders have been thrilled by its disguises, outlaw bands, and fighting men. It appeared in book form in 1888. *Kidnapped*, published in 1886, has always been popular with boys and girls though it was written for adults. *Catriona*, its sequel, passes a little beyond their reach.

American Adventurers

The British writers for boys—Mayne Reid, Ballantyne, Kingston, and, above all, Henty—were read with enthusiasm in America, where Marryat, too, has always had considerable standing. The American adventure tales also made their way to England. The best known were those of "Oliver Optic," Harry Castlemon, Elijah Kellogg, and J. T. Trowbridge. To these names, that of Horatio Alger (1834–1899) must be added. Alger's first story for boys was *Frank's Campaign*. He had already published a rather poor novel but after *Ragged Dick*, which appeared in 1867, found an enthusiastic audience of boys he wrote for them only, producing over a hundred books in series of six each—the Ragged Dick series, Luck and Pluck series, Tattered Tom series, and others.

Alger wrote the same story over and over. His heroes, whether newsboy, bootblack, or street musician, all climbed the ladder of success. He did not write well, but his books, with their theme of the poor boy's triumphal rise over obstacles through perseverance and hard work, suited the times. He was read by thousands, and the way the Horatio Alger hero has become a symbol of the proverbial "rags to riches" is proof of his wide popularity in his own times and for a generation afterward.

Artificial as his plots are, Alger had a genuineness of sympathy with his heroes, a naive confidence in the unfailing power of thrift, cheerfulness, and industry, which enlist a reader's willingness to see one more working out of the same old formula. Alger himself was so deeply interested in the condition of boys who were making their own way in New York that he went to live at a newsboys' home, so that he could better know and assist them. And assist them he did in a multitude of kindly ways. Only one story, *Phil the Fiddler*, directly attacks a social abuse, the begging racket in the New York of his day. Alger's heroes are not only universally successful, but they are always so cheery as they go whistling through their adverse circumstances and misadventures that it is a pleasure to see them arrive at the deserved reward.

William Taylor Adams (1822–1897), who wrote as Oliver Optic, was a New England school teacher. For approximately twenty years, while continuing to hold his principalship, he wrote under his pseudonym, rivaling Peter Parley with over one hundred full-length books. Finally in 1865 he resigned his position to devote all his time to authorship. He also edited magazines for children—*Oliver Optic's Magazine for Boys and Girls* which ran from 1867 to 1875, *Our Little Ones and the Nursery*, and *Student and Schoolmate*. Optic's books were written in series, according to the fashion of the day, but they are not a mere string of incidents, for he had a sense of dramatic climax and could make the trial of a boy falsely accused, or the outcome of a boat race, scenes of excitement and suspense. His heroes were travelers and in the Yacht Club series (1854), Woodville series (1861–67), Army and Navy series (1865–94), Starry Flag series (1867–69), and many more, the reader accompanied the hero on exciting adventures in distant places, learning geography and science as he went. Optic's boys were courageous and upright, but though he was consciously a moral writer, he did not allow the moral to interfere with his lively well-told stories, and he was read with enthusiasm by more than one generation of boys and girls.

Harry Castlemon's real name was Charles Austin Fosdick (1842–1915). He was the uncle of Harry Emerson Fosdick, the clergyman, and Raymond Fosdick, the lawyer and publicist. Of all the writers for boys in this country in the last half of the nineteenth century, he was perhaps the most read, successfully rivaling Henty and Optic. Franklin P. Adams called him "the boys' own author." He wrote some fifty-eight volumes in the Gunboat, Rocky Mountain, Sportsman's Club, Boy Trapper, Rod and Gun, Afloat and Ashore, and Pony Express series. Fosdick served in the navy in the Civil War and drew on his own experience for the Gunboat series, of which *Frank on a Gunboat* was the second. *Frank the Young Naturalist* was in his Frank and Archie series. His style was brisk and lively. He himself said, "Boys don't like fine writing. What they want is adventure, and the more of it you can get into 250 pages of manuscript, the better fellow you are." "If I have any message for the boy of today," he said on another occasion, "it is this: Success lies in application, and in doing what you can well, and with tenacity of purpose."[1]

Elijah Kellogg (1813–1901) was a Maine boy. Before going to Bowdoin College and Andover Theological Seminary, he spent three years on a farm and three at sea, so he knew the life he later described in his books, a life which with its fishing and shipbuilding and logging had a strong flavor of pioneer days. Kellogg's first and best book, *Good Old Times* (1867), tells of his grandfather's life as a Maine backwoodsman a hundred years earlier. Kellogg did not formally draw a moral, but his tales emphasize the importance of courage, endurance, upright living, and the dignity of work. He himself is said to have exemplified these qualities. He was eagerly read; he liked and understood boys and knew many of them. Tradition has it that he was the first man to climb

---

[1] Jacob Blanck, comp., *Harry Castlemon, Boy's Own Author* (New York, R. R. Bowker, 1941), pp. 5–6, 13–14.

the college tower at Bowdoin to place the president's hat there, and his books show that he never lost a boy's love of fun. Kellogg's stories have specific local color, for his characters speak in the Down East vernacular, and his setting is recognizably Maine.

John Townsend Trowbridge (1827–1916) wrote novels, narrative poems, and stories for boys and girls. It is the last named which made his reputation. With Lucy Larcom and Gail Hamilton he edited *Our Young Folks*, and many of his stories first appeared in the pages of this magazine. He was born in Genesee County, in western New York State, but lived most of his life in New England. His *Cudjo's Cave* (1864), the adventures of an abolitionist Quaker schoolmaster in Tennessee in the days before the Civil War and his escape from his persecutors, was adopted by young people although it was meant to be antislavery propaganda for adults. For his popular Jack Hazard stories, Trowbridge drew on his recollections of his early life on the banks of the Erie Canal. *Jack Hazard and His Fortunes* appeared first as a serial in *Our Young Folks*, and with four other titles was published in book form as the Jack Hazard series (1871–1875). Trowbridge raised the level of writing for young people. He was interested not only in boys but in human nature in general. His characters are well differentiated and hold the attention of the reader not merely for the adventures which come to them, but as individuals. One of Trowbridge's poems, "Darius Green and His Flying Machine," is an early example of verse in lighter vein; the young inventor who attempted to fly from the roof of the barn has amused many boys and girls, and the poem is still found in anthologies.

Richard Dana Goes to Sea

The severe attack of measles that forced Richard Henry Dana, Jr. (1815–1882), to leave Harvard was responsible for one of the best sea narratives ever written. *Two Years Before the Mast* is a thrilling tale, which also served to present a vigorous, unbiased account of a sailor's life from the forecastle's viewpoint. In 1834, for the sake of his health, Dana shipped as an ordinary sailor in the brig *Pilgrim* around Cape Horn to California. He kept a journal which was lost. *Two Years Before the Mast* (1840) was reconstructed from letters sent home and a rudimentary log. The young Harvard student was observant and sensitive. No details of a sailor's life escaped him. He was shocked by the brutal treatment the sailors received, and the indignant sympathy which he put into his book aroused public interest in the sailor's lot. Written more than a hundred years ago, Dana's book still reads well. Appropriately enough, after he entered law practice, maritime cases appealed to him especially. His next book was *The Seaman's Friend* (1841), a standard manual of the sea.

Noah Brooks (1830–1903), born in Castine, Maine, was a journalist and editor who served on many papers and magazines in both the East and the West. He wrote essays, history, and biography but is best remembered for his books for boys. *The Boy Emigrants* (1876), his most well-known book, recounted the adventures with Indians and wild animals of boys who crossed the continent in '49. *The Boy Settlers, or, Early Times in Kansas* (1891) tells of emigrants, Indians, border ruffians, and buffalo hunts. *First Across the Continent* (1901) is an account of the Lewis and Clarke expedition and *The Fairport Nine* (1881) is the first baseball story. Brooks's books were lively and very readable.

Jules Verne Conducts Excursions to a Hidden World

To the many nineteenth century milestones along the road of children's literature must be added one more, the rise of the scientific adventure story. Jules Verne (1828–1905), its progenitor, was a Frenchman, but it is doubtful if the boys and girls who so quickly took his tales to their hearts ever realized that these tales had not been originally written in English. Men as well as boys read them, for they were a type of fantasy that had a special appeal for the nineteenth century.

Strange and marvelous were the feats of Verne's heroes, but to those who had seen the steam train supersede the stage coach, the steamship the clipper, Verne's tales seemed to hold the germ of possibility. These stories served, too, as escape literature for those late Victorians who found themselves confronted with the fact that the Industrial Revolution and all the scientific and technical achievements of the century had not brought the millennium, that slums and poverty and ignorance still flourished. The hero most acceptable to these Victorians was the man of action, the man successful in the field of practical endeavor, and admirably Jules Verne's heroes filled the bill. Another craving, too, was satisfied by Jules Verne. Defoe's *Robinson Crusoe* had set men to thinking of desert islands and resourceful heroes who mastered circumstances. Jules Verne said himself that it was his passion for the Robinson-Crusoe-inspired adventures that put him on the road he was to follow, and his *The Mysterious Island* (1875) is one of the best desert island stories ever written.

Far distant lands, the unknown depths of the ocean, the limitless airways attracted Verne as fields of activity in which his courageous and resourceful heroes might display their powers. He did not deal deeply with character, though Captain Nemo of *Twenty Thousand Leagues Under the Sea* (English edition, 1869) who, like Sherlock Holmes, had to be resuscitated because of popular demand, and the laconic Phileas Fogg of *Around the World in Eighty Days* (1870), caught the fancy of boys and girls. Romance was practically excluded, but accuracy was high. Verne took infinite pains with the description of a storm, of a geological period (*The Child of the Cavern* deals with the carboniferous epoch), with the development of the telescope, with many more scientific and technical matters, and his mistakes are few.

Five Weeks in a Balloon was Verne's first scientific adventure story. It was published by Hetzel in France in 1863. After Hetzel's *Magazin d'Education* began publication in 1864, each year one of Verne's stories appeared, to be published later in book form.

A Voyage to the Center of the Earth came out in 1864. *Twenty Thousand Leagues Under the Sea* (1869) and *Around the World in Eighty Days* (1872), which won the French Academy prize, are rivals in popularity; the latter was adapted for the stage in 1874 and again in 1948 and a motion picture based on it appeared in 1956. *From the Earth to the Moon* (1866) was the most famous moon story until H. G. Wells's *The First Men in the Moon* appeared in 1901. *Michael Strogoff* (1876) was and is a favorite. Verne's books are still read. The author's evident faith in his characters, and their doings, his way of quoting from actual newspapers and advertisements give a zest to his writing which is contagious. For many readers today there is a thrill in seeing how inventions that are now taken for granted were dreamed of by Jules Verne long before. During the 1870's and 1880's Verne's books, resplendent in red and gold, were welcome gifts to French children; and they were deeply cherished, too, by English and American boys and girls.

Bibliography

Allott, Kenneth. *Jules Verne.* London, Cresset Press, 1940.

Blanck, Jacob. *Harry Castlemon, Boys' Own Author,* Appreciation and Bibliography. New York, R. R. Bowker, 1941.

Castlemon, Harry. "Inventor of the Boy Thriller." *Literary Digest,* New York, Vol. 50 (Sept. 11, 1915).

Chambers' *Cyclopedia of English Literature.* London, W. R. Chambers, 1901–1938. Vol. 3.

Ford, H. S. "Henty." *Saturday Review of Literature.* March 2, 1940.

Jordan, Alice M. *From Rollo to Tom Sawyer.* Boston, The Horn Book, 1948.

McGrath, M. "Centenary of Marryat." *Nineteenth Century,* London, Vol. 106, pp. 545–555.

8

Illustrators Who Were More
Than Illustrators

Art for Children in England

All in all it can safely be said that the most brilliant accomplishment in illustrated books for children occurred in the nineteenth century. At its beginning, Thomas Bewick had done much of his work with children in mind. Blake, that great poet and artist, who had no successors in a direct line, had written poems about children with love and understanding and had drawn pictures for these poems in the same spirit. William Mulready made pictures for William Roscoe's *The Butterfly's Ball* (1806), a poem so popular that it was followed by a large number of similar poems by other authors, *The Elephant's Ball*, *The Lion's Masquerade*, and others, all illustrated by Mulready. But successful as was Mulready's work, it was only a faint foreshadowing of what was to come. Thomas Stothard (1755–1834), in addition to illustrating *The Arabian Nights*, *Gulliver's Travels*, *Robinson Crusoe*, *Pilgrim's Progress*, and other classics, drew a set of six charming groups of children at play and made a graceful frontispiece for Thomas Day's *The History of Sandford and Merton*. John Flaxman had made pictures for the *Iliad* and the *Odyssey* which, though intended for adults, have pleased children for more than a hundred and fifty years.

These artists owed much to the art of the steel engraver, which reached a high point in the last quarter of the eighteenth and the first quarter of the nineteenth century. Bewick, however, using a new graving tool and developing the use of the "white line," and of the end-grain block, revived interest in the woodcut. By the middle of the century, engraving on metal had practically ceased and the woodcut had become the favorite method of reproduction. The magazines helped to make it popular; *Penny Magazine* began in 1832, *Punch* in 1841, *The Illustrated London News* in 1842, and the artists began at once to draw on woodblocks for them. *Once a Week*, starting in 1859, and the *Graphic* (1869) offered further opportunity to artists, while three children's magazines—*Good Words for the Young* (1869–1877), *Aunt Judy's Magazine* (1866–1885), and *Little Folks* (1871–1933)—encouraged a high level of illustration.

In 1841–1849 appeared Felix Summerly's *Home Treasury of Books, Toys, Pictures, etc. purposed to cultivate the Affections, Fancy, Imagination and Taste of Children.* Summerly (Sir Henry Cole, 1808–1882) was a public-spirited art critic and government official who organized the Great Exhibition of 1851 and was one of the founders of the South Kensington Museum. He admitted that the *Home Treasury* was undertaken partly because of personal need, his own family of young children being numerous, and partly, so it is said, to combat that literalmindedness which Peter Parley was inflicting on the young public.[1] The *Home Treasury* contained folk tales, fairy tales, and ballads, and "Sir Hornbook," a verse exercise by Thomas Love Peacock to teach the parts of speech. "All," wrote Sir Henry in the prospectus, "will be illustrated, but not after the usual fashion of children's books, in which it seems to be assumed that the lowest kind of art is good enough to give the first impressions to a child. In the present series, though the statement may perhaps excite a smile, the illustrations will be selected from the works of Rafaelle, Titian, Holbein, and other old masters. Some of the best modern artists have kindly promised their aid in creating a taste for beauty in little children." It is clear that young people's book illustration owes a considerable debt to this wise and kindly gentleman who was genuinely interested in children.

Cruikshank's Bent for Fairy Art

George Cruikshank (1792–1878), an artist of imagination, originality, and daring, made pictures for *Grimm's Fairy Tales* when they were translated into English in 1823 that have never been surpassed in their humor, their exuberant fancy and the way in which they are at one with the spirit of these sturdy folk tales. Beginning as a boy of twelve, Cruikshank had worked with his artist-father making designs for nursery tales, valentines, and Twelfth Night Characters. He lived in London all his life and knew it thoroughly, as is seen in his illustrations for Dickens, his *Mornings at Bow Street*, and the *Comic Almanacs*, which appeared in 1835–1853. His pictures for Grimm had the honor of being republished in Germany with the original text. He had a feeling for the magic of the folk tale, and besides his drawings for Grimm he made frontispieces for *Popular Romances of the West of England or the Drolls, Traditions and Superstitions of Old Cornwall*, collected and edited by Robert Hunt. In the first series, the Giant Bolster is shown in the act of making a six-mile stride from Beacon to Carn Bred; the second series shows a fine flight of witches on broomsticks over the sea. In the frontispiece for Thomas Keightly's *Fairy Mythology*, elves, dragons, dwarfs, witches, gnomes, fairies, and pixies whirl about a weathercock with amazing animation and individuality for such tiny

[1] F. J. H. Darton, *Children's Books in England* (Cambridge, Eng., University Press, 1932), p. 240.

figures. *George Cruikshank's Fairy Library* was published in four volumes in 1853 and 1854, and contained the stories of "Puss in Boots," "Hop-o'-my-Thumb," "Jack and the Beanstalk," and "Cinderella." The illustrations are in Cruikshank's most enchanting vein, but unfortunately Cruikshank had now acquired the reformer's spirit and attempted to improve the morals of the old tales. Thus in "Cinderella," the Fairy Godmother, just before the wedding, delivers a sermon on temperance, and the King, convinced of the error of his ways, orders a bonfire to be made of all the wine, beer, and spirits in the country. When Mrs. Ewing's stories began in 1866 to appear in *Aunt Judy's Magazine*, they were illustrated by Cruikshank, to the great satisfaction of the author.

It is perhaps significant that as fairy tales were establishing themselves in English nurseries, the artists who made pictures for children's books should find themselves very much at home with the fairies. Richard Doyle (1824–1883) joined the staff of *Punch* in the third year of that paper's existence. Though only nineteen, he held his own in the distinguished company of John Leech, Douglas Jerrold, and the others who composed the *Punch* staff. His "Manners and Customs Sketches," his "Brown, Jones and Robinson," delighted the readers of *Punch*, and he illustrated Dickens, Frederick Locker-Lampson, and other authors, but all through his life he seems to have taken pleasure in depicting the fairy world. His fancy was as lively as Cruikshank's, but his fairy beings were drawn with a gentler touch and he preferred elves to giants. His first fairy pictures were drawn for stories from Grimm called *The Fairy Ring* (1846). He illustrated Montalba's *Fairy Tales of All Nations* in 1849, Mark Lemon's *The Enchanted Doll* in the same year and in 1851 drew some of his most famous pictures for children in Ruskin's *The King of the Golden River*. Those who first knew that story with Doyle's drawings can never think of Gluck and the Black Brothers or South-West Wind, Esq. or the King himself in any other way than as Doyle drew them. For Thomas Hughes's *Scouring of the White Horse*, he drew, in 1858, pictures full of lively action. *In Fairyland* (1870) was a series of fairy fantasies, designed with delicacy and great charm. They were accompanied by a poem of William Allingham's, but in 1886 the pictures were reissued with a story written around them by Andrew Lang and called by him *The Princess Nobody*. With one piece of Doyle's work every reader of *Punch* is familiar—the famous cover design for the magazine which Doyle made in 1849. Other artists made cover designs—Hablôt Knight Browne (Phiz), Kenny Meadows, Sir John Gilbert, and others—but Doyle's was chosen as best representing the spirit of Mr. Punch, and Doyle's circle of dancing, climbing, swinging elves surrounding Mr. Punch and his dog Toby, all depicted in this artist's droll, spirited, and altogether inimitable way, has served as *Punch's* cover to this day.

Lesser artists were Harrison Weir (1824–1906), an artist who drew animals with great accuracy (he was expert in the matter of cats and dogs and founded the London Cat Show), and Alfred Crowquill, a pen name for Alfred Henry Forrester (1804–1872). He and his brother Charles Robert (1803–1850) used the pseudonym jointly, one drawing, one writing, until Charles died and Alfred continued alone. His best-known work was the spirited, amusing drawings he made for *Comic Nursery Tales* (1845) by Frederic William Naufor Bayley, including "Blue Beard," "Robinson Crusoe," "The Little Red Riding Hood" and "Jack the Giant Killer."

John Tenniel (1820–1914), who also worked for *Punch* and contributed masterly cartoons, illustrated only two books for children, Lewis Carroll's *Alice's Adventures in Wonderland* and *Through the Looking-Glass*. Superb in their ingenuity, their humor, their imagination, so utterly satisfying to child readers, these pictures are famous as well for their perfect harmony with the story. In fact, they so became a part of the story that *Alice* without Tenniel is to many no longer *Alice*. When after the *Alice* books Tenniel declared his invention for children's illustration was exhausted, Carroll looked for an illustrator for *The Story of Sylvie and Bruno* in 1889. He was fortunate in discovering Harry Furniss, whose wit and imagination caught to perfection the half-fanciful, half-real, sometimes nonsensical, and sometimes poetic atmosphere of the book.

The Sober Grace of Arthur Hughes

Arthur Hughes has always been associated with George Macdonald. He also illustrated Thomas Hughes's *Tom Brown's School Days*, made an exquisite set of drawings for Christina Rossetti's *Sing-Song*, and drew fairy pictures for William Allingham's *The Music Master*. But most of his work appeared in Macdonald's stories for children. Hughes drew no droll dancing elves; his beings from beyond the borders of the real world and the children who meet them have a grave and serious beauty; even the goblins of *The Princess and the Goblin* and *The Princess and Curdie* are not figures of fun but suggest the spiritual quality of the tales. In Hughes's work we see black and white at its best.

Thackeray, in 1855, had made his own irresistibly jolly drawings for *The Rose and the Ring*, which along with the rollicking fun which pleases children has a touch of gentle satire to amuse the grownups.

Gordon Browne (1858–1932), who made the pictures for Mrs. Ewing's last book, *The Story of a Short Life*, in 1885, illustrated a long and varied list of books from Henty, George Manville Fenn, *Gulliver's Travels*, and *Robinson Crusoe* to such fantasies as Alice Corknan's *Down the Snow-Stairs* and Harry Jones's *Prince Boohoo and Little Smuts*. He worked in black and white with an admirable feeling for design, a fine free line, and a delightful humor. He seems to have been equally happy depicting real life or pure fantasy.

An earlier artist for children was "E.V.B.," initials which stood for Eleanor Vere Boyle (1825–1916). Her *Child's Play* was first published in 1852 and reprinted in the 1860's. *A Second Child's Play* appeared in 1879. In 1882 she illustrated a dozen of Andersen's fairy tales with twelve large drawings in color. Forgotten today, she won high praise in the 1870's and 1880's. Her draftsmanship was not beyond reproach, but her pictures had a unique charm. There is a naive simplicity about them and a quality that might almost be called tangible, as if one could pick up her charming round babies or walk into the delightful kitchen pictured in "The Ugly Duckling."

Linley Sambourne (1844–1910), another *Punch* artist, did not illustrate many children's books, but his pictures for Charles Kingsley's *The Water-Babies* are well known and highly satisfying, and the *New Sandford and Merton* (1872), a burlesque of Thomas Day's instructive work which Sambourne wrote and illustrated, while hardly to be classed as a child's book, is clever and amusing.

The Decorative Grace of Walter Crane

We come now to the three great names of the century: Walter Crane, Randolph Caldecott, and Kate Greenaway. With them we find, for the first time, color used with skill and imagination to make children's books truly a thing of beauty. To Edmund Evans, the printer, our gratitude is due for this new development. An artist in his own right, a lover of beautiful things, he was also a determined and highly skilled craftsman, and, had it not been for his pioneer work in the field of color printing, none of these three artists would have been able to make the picture books for which they are so justly famous. For while these artists were illustrators, and good ones, they were primarily picture-book makers, at their best when they were creating characters out of their own imaginations. In the old fairy tales and the nursery rhymes used by Crane and Caldecott for their picture books they were free to draw the characters as they saw them in their mind's eye. In Kate Greenaway's case the children, though true to the spirit of childhood, came straight out of that lovely world of flowers and meadows that her own fancy created.

Walter Crane (1845–1915), the son of a portrait painter, was apprenticed to W. J. Linton, the wood engraver. During his lunch hours he would wander over to Fleet Street and the *Punch* office to look at the cartoons in the window. His first independent work was making designs for the paper covers of cheap railway novels; these were printed by Edmund Evans, who was at that same time protesting against the cheap, crudely colored illustrations in children's books. He felt sure that paper picture books could be made beautiful in color and design and still sell for sixpence if printed in sufficiently large quantities. Crane liked the idea and was ready to take part in the experiment. The publishers, however, were hesitant; the public, they felt, was satisfied with the current illustrations, crude though they might be. Would the public buy this new type of picture book? Warne, however, had the courage to be a pioneer, and Crane's first nursery picture books—*Sing A Song of Sixpence, The House that Jack Built, Dame Trot and Her Comical Cat,* and *The History of Cock Robin and Jenny Wren*—were published in 1865–1866 by this firm. Then Routledge became interested, and in the two series issued between 1867 and 1876 under the Routledge imprint thirty-five picture books appeared. There is great variety in them; *The Fairy Ship* and *King Luckieboy's Party* are perhaps the best. Besides the *Absurd ABC* and *Baby's Own Alphabet,* there are nursery rhymes, *One, Two Buckle My Shoe,* and *This Little Pig Went to Market,* and there are fairy tales, *Bluebeard, Beauty and the Beast, Puss in Boots,* and others.

Crane had a strong interest in design. Like William Blake who, more than fifty years before, had produced in his *Songs of Innocence* and *Songs of Experience* pages where poem and picture form a perfect design, Crane was convinced that text and illustration should be planned to make a harmonious whole. He was the first of the modern illustrators to put this belief into effect. Flat colors and a firm black outline were characteristic of his picture-book work; those books published by Routledge show the influence of the Japanese prints which so delighted him. He was interested in William Morris's Arts and Crafts Movement, and one can detect the influence of the Pre-Raphaelite School in his drawings. Crane made many designs for wallpapers, hangings, and friezes and he said himself that he was in the habit of putting into his picture books "all sorts of subsidiary detail that interested me and often made them the vehicle for my ideas in furniture and decoration." For this reason Crane is found difficult by some children; on the other hand, his own interest in the scenes he was creating makes him, as Gleeson White says, "the true artist of Fairyland, because he recognizes its practical possibilities and yet does not lose the glamour that never was on sea or land."[1]

One of Crane's loveliest series of pictures and one of the least known is the series he made for *The First of May, a Fairy Masque* by J. R. Wise. When Crane was seventeen he had gone with Wise to make illustrations for the book Wise was writing on the New Forest. They became friends in spite of the difference in age and when Wise went to Sherwood in 1878 to write his fairy masque he sent for Crane

[1] Gleeson White, "Children's Books and Their Illustrators," *The International Studio,* Winter Number, 1898, p. 32.

to join him. For two springs they worked in Sherwood Forest. Crane's drawings were so in harmony with Wise's text that the book seemed the work of one person, and Crane's love for the forest was so strong that he brought his family to spend the summer there while he worked on the pictures. Cruikshank and Doyle had brought the elves from fairyland to dance among mortals; Crane, in *The First of May*, entered the fairy realm itself, where he found the Fairy Queen of the May, woodland elves and fairies, and birds and beasts and insects who dance and frolic around their own Maypole. The drawings were made in pencil and reproduced in photogravure by Goupil and Co. in Paris. They give the silvery, delicate effect of pencil drawings and since no type was sufficiently delicate to harmonize with the drawings, Crane lettered the text by hand. The cost of reproduction was great, it could only be published in a limited edition, hence its rarity today.

Crane and Evans produced two books of old rhymes, with the music on one side of the page and the illustration on the other. These were *The Baby's Opera* (1877) and its successor, *The Baby's Bouquet* (1879). The tunes were arranged by Crane's sister, Lucy. These were followed by *The Baby's Own Aesop* (1886). The rhymed text for this was done by Crane's old master, W. J. Linton. These little books have great charm and still hold their own as favorite picture books. *Pan Pipes*, another book of songs arranged from old traditional English tunes, each song enclosed by Crane in a decorative border, appeared in 1888, printed by Evans and published by Routledge. That same year was marked by the appearance of Grimm's *Household Stories* with Walter Crane's illustrations, the text translated by Lucy Crane. This contains some of Crane's best work in the pictures themselves and in the decorative head and tail pieces. Among the children's story books illustrated by Crane are *Carrots*, *The Cuckoo Clock*, *The Tapestry Room*, and others by Mrs. Molesworth, Hawthorne's *A Wonder Book*, which Crane was asked to illustrate when spending a year in America in 1891–1892, Judge Parry's retelling of *Don Quixote*, Mary De Morgan's *Necklace of Princess Fiorimonde*, Mrs. Harrison's *Bric-a-Brac Stories*, and Oscar Wilde's *The Happy Prince*.

John Gilpin Rides Again

Randolph Caldecott (1846–1886) drew almost from his cradle. At six he was making pictures of animals, modeling them in clay, or cutting them out of wood. At fifteen, however, as his father did not encourage his artistic tendencies, he was working in a bank at Whitchurch in Shropshire. He lived out of town, however, and his spare time was spent in getting acquainted with the country around him and with country life. The sights and the sounds of the markets and cattle fairs, of the meets of the hounds, the hunting and fishing of those Shropshire days, which he stored away in his memory, were to be used later in his picture books. He was transferred to a bank in Manchester and worked five years there, and then, having decided on art as a career, he began sending contributions to the magazine *London Society*. Henry Blackburn was the editor, and he and Caldecott became lifelong friends. In 1872 Caldecott went to London, where publishers and editors recognized his skill and gave him plenty of opportunities for the character delineation at which he was so successful. When he was twenty-six, Sampson Low sent him abroad to illustrate a book of travel in the Harz Mountains. His sketches were published by *Harper's Magazine* in the United States, and for years he sent to the London *Graphic* contributions in which he was both artist and author. In 1872, 1873, and 1874, he made sketches for *Old Christmas*, a selection of chapters from the *Sketch Book* by Washington Irving, an author with whom Caldecott had much in common. But the work by which Caldecott is best remembered began in 1877 or 1878, when he made the first of a series of picture books, a series that continued until a year before his death. *The Diverting History of John Gilpin* was the first, to be followed by sixteen others, including *The Babes in the Wood*, *Come Lasses and Lads*, *Elegy on the Death of a Mad Dog*, *The Farmer's Boy*, *The Fox Jumps Over the Parson's Gate*, *The Frog He Would A-Wooing Go*, *The Great Panjandrum Himself*, *Hey Diddle Diddle and Baby Bunting*, *The House that Jack Built*, *The Queen of Hearts*, *Ride a Cock Horse to Banbury Cross*, *A Farmer Went Trotting Upon His Grey Mare*, *Sing a Song for Sixpence*, and *Three Jovial Huntsmen*.

These were published singly in paper for a shilling. Later several were issued together, as bound books, and after Caldecott's death a large and beautiful edition engraved by Edmund Evans was published by Routledge, called *The Complete Collection of Pictures and Songs, With a Preface by Austin Dobson*. Never perhaps was there a maker of pictures for children who felt so instinctively what children want. Caldecott's animals come to life on the page, one feels the rush of wind that removed Gilpin's hat and wig as he galloped through Islington, one enters the cozy room with the Frog who would a-wooing go, watches him gallantly kiss Miss Mouse's tail, while his friend, Mr. Rat, serenely sits in a chair against the wall and drinks a glass of beer. *The Farmer's Boy*, *The Three Jovial Huntsmen*, *The Fox Jumps Over the Parson's Gate*, bring the English countryside before the reader's eyes. There are sly touches of character, the severe face glimpsed at the window tells us that the pretty maid late in returning from the Maypole dance in *Come Lasses and Lads* will receive a grim welcome. To look at Caldecott's pictures is excellent training for children; never was so much told with such an economy of line. The fun in them is so genuine, the spirit so gay, and at the same time so gentle, that they are fine examples of true humor.

Caldecott illustrated three of Mrs. Ewing's books. They worked together happily, for they had much in common; each admired the other's work and when Mrs. Ewing was planning her famous *Jackanapes* she asked Caldecott to make her a picture to "write to," saying that she knew he had profound sympathy with horses and he "must not be afraid to trust her with the ghost of an old Posting House, horses, highwaymen and an old Postillion," though "if a coloured sketch would be easily concocted out of a laddie with an aureole of yellow hair on a red-haired pony full tilt among the geese over a village green," he was to give her "the decayed Postillion in pen-and-ink." The frontispiece which Caldecott made to this specification is one of the best known and best loved of Caldecott's drawings.

The Quaint and Beautiful Art of Kate Greenaway

The third of the great three is Kate Greenaway, a unique figure in the history of books for children. At first thought it seems absurd to couple her name with William Blake, yet the two had something in common for, unlike as their work was, both artists discovered and understood the spirit of innocent childhood and transferred it to their pages.

Kate Greenaway (1846–1901), daughter of John Greenaway, a well-known wood engraver and draftsman, was born in London the same year as Randolph Caldecott, but her childhood included country life, for she and her brother and two sisters spent much time on the farm of a great-aunt in Nottinghamshire. Here Kate made the acquaintance of the flowers, the gardens, fields and hedgerows with which she was to fill her books later on. "You can go into a beautiful new country," she wrote when she was fifty, "if you stand under a large apple tree and look up to the blue sky through the white flowers. I suppose I went to it very young before I could really remember and that is why I have such a wild delight in cowslips and apple-blossom—they always give me the strange feeling of trying to *remember*, as if I had known them in a former world."[1] The flowers that she loved from earliest childhood are everywhere in her pictures, tucked into a corner of the border design if there is no other place. Her children in *Under the Window*, her first picture book, published by Routledge in 1878, and in her *Marigold Garden*, which followed in 1885, gather daisies, troop out of school, play at battledore and shuttlecock, drink tea sedately, gaze at London Town from the top of a hill, or walk out with Grandmamma past houses of warm red brick.

[1] M. H. Spielmann and G. S. Layard, *Kate Greenaway* (London, Black, 1905), p. 189.

Kate Greenaway would never have called herself a poet, but her simple verses are a perfect accompaniment to her drawings. They appeal to children as do the pictures themselves, for so true to real childhood are Miss Greenaway's children that modern boys and girls recognize them as children like themselves, in spite of the quaint costumes of an earlier day in which the artist dressed them, and which are one of the charms of her books. "I like making cowslip fields grow and apple trees bloom at a moment's notice," she wrote in a letter to Ruskin, "that is what it is, you see, to have gone through life with an enchanted land ever beside you." This enchantment and childlike wonder she kept alive in her own heart and filled her pictures with them for others.

Kate Greenaway illustrated a number of books by other authors, including two by Charlotte Yonge, but this was not her happiest field of endeavor. Her finest work is in her picture books, in the two already mentioned, in her *A Day in a Child's Life* (1881), with music by Myles Foster, which contains some of her most delightful flowers, in her charming *Mother Goose* published in the same year, and in her *Pied Piper of Hamlin* (1888). The freshness and originality of *Under the Window* made it a success at once. Twenty thousand copies of the first edition were published and were soon sold out, and reprinting up to seventy thousand was necessary. It carried her fame across the Channel, for the book was received with enthusiasm in Germany, France, and Belgium, her costumes were adopted, and for a time, it is said, she dressed the children of two continents. Of Kate Greenaway's *Birthday Book for Children* (1880) not only were 123,000 English copies sold, but 13,500 French and 8,500 German copies were placed on the market. For this charming duodecimo volume, with verses by Mrs. Sale Barker, Miss Greenaway made 382 drawings; 370 were minute uncolored figures, with a full page in color for each month.

It is said that *The Birthday Book* inspired Robert Louis Stevenson to try his hand at the verses which became *A Child's Garden of Verses*.

One of Kate Greenaway's best known and most successful undertakings was her series of *Almanacs*. These exquisite little volumes were issued from 1883–1897 (only 1896 being omitted). In 1883 she made pictures for the verses of Jane and Ann Taylor in a volume called *Little Ann and Other Poems*. For these poems, which she had loved as a child, Kate made some of her most springlike drawings. The *Language of Flowers* contained some of the artist's most exquisite figures and flowers, and though Ruskin did not care for it, it sold well in both England and America. *Mavor's Spelling Book*, which Kate Greenaway illustrated with beautifully engraved cuts printed in sepia, was without doubt one of the loveliest schoolbooks ever printed. It was not, however, successful, but when the publisher decided to issue the capital letters alone in a 48mo volume, nearly 25,000 copies were sold. *A Apple Pie*, which contains some of her liveliest pictures, was popular in America and France as well as England. *Kate Greenaway's Book of Games* appeared in 1889, the title indicating that her name had a selling value.

The friendship between Kate Greenaway and John Ruskin, which lasted from their first meeting in 1882 until Ruskin's death in 1900, was important to them both. Letters were exchanged almost daily. Ruskin criticized, praised, instructed; Kate listened and received adverse comment gracefully, but though humble in her attitude toward her own work she had strong opinions and continued to draw in her own way. Her friendship with Ruskin brought forth an interesting new edition of *Dame Wiggins of Lee and Her Seven Wonderful Cats*, an old rhyme first published in 1823. In 1885 Ruskin asked Miss Greenaway to draw some cats for the extra verses he had made. They were printed as she drew them, rough pencil sketches, since as Ruskin put it, "My rhymes do not ring like the real ones and I would not allow Miss Greenaway to subdue the grace of her first sketches to the formality of the earlier work." In 1887 Kate Greenaway illustrated *The Queen of the Pirate Isle* by Bret Harte. These drawings were more realistic than any of her others and as Ruskin had often demanded more realism, this volume called forth his warm approval. To most people, however, it hardly seems to deserve his estimate of the best thing she had ever done. As to that, he must have changed his mind for in May, 1889, he wrote, "*The Piper* [published 1888] is the best book you ever did and the Piper himself unsurpassable."

Frederick Locker-Lampson was another lifelong friend of Kate Greenaway. *Little Ann and Other Poems* is dedicated to his children; through him she became acquainted with Browning and the Tennyson family. Quietly as she pursued her life, which was almost entirely given over to her work, she was a well-known and respected figure in the London of the 1870's and 1880's. Her circle of friends was large, yet it would have undoubtedly surprised that modest artist to know that a hundred years later the circle is still large and added to each year as a fresh generation of children makes the acquaintance of her books.

Illustrators in America

The picture books of Walter Crane, Randolph Caldecott, and Kate Greenaway were as familiar to American children as they were to boys and girls in England. When Crane and his family made a trip to America in 1891–1892, Winthrop Scudder of the Riverside Press commissioned Crane to illustrate Hawthorne's *A Wonder-Book*, which was completed in 1892 and became one of the most popular editions of this American classic.

The first edition of Hawthorne's *A Wonder-Book for Boys and Girls* was published in Boston in 1852 and illustrated by Hammatt Billings. In 1884 another edition appeared with spirited, imaginative drawings by Frederick Stuart Church (1842–1924), an artist who, in 1881, had illustrated with J. H. Moser, Joel Chandler Harris' *Uncle Remus; His Songs and His Sayings;* in 1884, with W. H. Beard, he illustrated *Nights With Uncle Remus.* In both books Church's drawings have a fine spontaneity and humor. In 1895 and the early 1900's A. B. Frost (1851–1928) made drawings for various collections of the Uncle Remus stories. Again Harris was fortunate in his illustrator. Frost had an active sense of humor, great sincerity, ability to catch the local flavor of whatever he illustrated, and a thorough sympathy with Harris' tellings of the Uncle Remus stories; his pictures have the same zest and gaiety as the tales.

The magazines for children which flourished in America in the second half of the nineteenth century and the magazines for older readers, as well, were largely responsible for the fine work done by American illustrators. It was a drawing in the old *Life*, of a small boy stung by a bee, that made Mark Twain decide to have Edward Windsor Kemble (1861–1933) illustrate *Huckleberry Finn* (1884). *St. Nicholas*, under the editorship of Mary Mapes Dodge, with Frank R. Stockton as associate editor, published in the years from 1880–1887 many of Stockton's stories with illustrations by E. B. Bensell and Reginald Birch (1856–1943). Bensell made the amusing and quite unforgettable pictures for Charles Carryl's *Davy and the Goblin*, published in book form in 1886. Birch illustrated Carryl's *The Admiral's Caravan*, which appeared in *St. Nicholas* in 1891–1892, and in book form in 1892. Birch's best-known illustrations are those he made for Frances Hodgson Burnett's *Little Lord Fauntleroy*, drawings at which readers of a later generation were inclined to smile. This was not due to the drawings themselves, for Birch was an excellent draftsman, his work always individual and charming, but to the temper of the times. After the 1890's velvet suits, lace collars, and long curls for boys were out of fashion, and indeed the very memory became anathema to adults who in middle life felt they had been victimized in childhood when their mothers dressed them like Mrs. Burnett's hero.

Rather unexpectedly we find Thomas Nast (1840–1902,), the cartoonist whose satiric pencil was largely responsible for breaking up the Tweed Ring, making pictures for children's books. In 1867 he made the pictures for a new edition of Mary Mapes Dodge's *Hans Brinker*. He also illustrated *Robinson Crusoe* and *A Visit from St. Nicholas*, and, surprisingly enough, several of Sophie May's *Little Prudy* books. His own work appeared in a separate volume, Thomas Nast's *Christmas Drawings for the Human Race* (Harper, 1890), a book which must have delighted boys and girls with its many jolly pictures.

Joseph Greene Francis (1849–?) added to the gaiety of *St. Nicholas* with his original, humorous drawings and the nonsense rhymes that went with them. Pictures and rhymes were published by The Century Company in 1892 with the title, *A Book of Cheerful Cats and Other Animated Animals*. Animated they certainly are, these little cats demure or mischievous, or the assorted group of animals riding happily on a giraffe until "they came to grief when their charger bit a leaf;" or the Owl Schoolmaster, or Duck's barber shop where the Lion insists on a haircut. These cleverly drawn pictures reflect the innocent fun of the unsophisticated child and the little oblong volume has been cherished by many generations.

Mrs. Laura E. Richards (1850–1943), whose nonsense verse will bear comparison with Lear, published in 1881 a volume called *Sketches and Scraps* for which her husband, Henry Richards, made the pictures. They were drawn with a firm outline in bright colors and were supremely satisfying to children. "The Seven Little Tigers and the Aged Cook," "Skinny Mrs. Simpkin and Fat Mrs. Wobblechin," and "The Frog of Lake Okifinokee" were ineradicable memories to those who were children in the 1880's.

Palmer Cox (1840–1924) is seldom mentioned today but his brownies were a dearly loved feature of *St. Nicholas*. They ran through many years, the verb is appropriate for they were always in a state of great activity. Beginning with *The Brownies: Their Book*, in 1887, eleven Brownie books were published, the last being *The Brownies and Prince Florimel* (1918). Large as was the Brownie band, the artist managed to give individuality to each member. The Dude, the Dutchman, the Policeman, and others were easily recognizable, their behavior was consistent, and children could follow the adventures of their favorites through book after book.

Bibliography

Blackburn, Henry. *Randolph Caldecott*. London, Sampson Low, 1886.

Crane, Walter. *An Artist's Reminiscences*. New York, Macmillan, 1907.

James, Phillip. "Children's Books of Yesterday." London, *The Studio*. Autumn number, 1933.

Lang, Andrew. *Illustrated Books*. In *The Library*. London, Macmillan, 1881, pp. 122–179.

Mahony, Bertha E., Louise Payson Latimer, and Beulah Folmsbee, comps. *Illustrators of Children's Books: 1744–1945*. Boston, The Horn Book, 1947.

Pearson, Edmund Lester. "Wizards and Enchanters." In *Books in Black or Red*. New York, Macmillan, 1923.

Smith, Janet Adam. *Children's Illustrated Books*. London, Collins, 1948.

Spielmann, M. H. and G. S. Layard. *Kate Greenaway*. London, Adam & Charles Black, 1905.

White, Gleeson. "Children's Books and Their Illustrators." London, *The International Studio*. Winter number, 1898.

9

New Horizons

The Bodleys Lead the Way Through Europe

In the last three decades of the nineteenth century there appeared a new kind of book for children—the travel story book as distinct from those books of instructive travel which Peter Parley and Jacob Abbott first introduced. Horace Scudder's Bodley family were the first of these book travelers; other writers followed suit and sent groups of young people journeying far and near. As always, children's books were reflecting what was happening in the world. A railway had been built across the United States from ocean to ocean; steam navigation, taking the place of sail, made it a simpler matter to go from continent to continent. Polar exploration was bringing the Far North into people's consciousness; Stanley and Livingstone had focused attention on Africa. Armchair travel had become popular with adults, and writers for children felt that here was a kind of book that could be made both entertaining and profitable to young readers. It was natural that Horace Scudder (1838–1902), with his interest in children and in education, should start the ball rolling with his Bodley books.

In his first series—*Doings of the Bodley Family in Town and Country, The Bodleys Telling Stories, The Bodleys on Wheels, The Bodleys Afoot, Mr. Bodley Abroad* (1875–1880)—Mr. Scudder tells how an amiable New England family explored New England on foot and on wheels, learning New England history as they did so. In the second series—*The Bodley Grandchildren and their Journey in Holland, The English Bodley Family, The Viking Bodleys* (1882–1885)—the Bodley grandchildren journey to Holland, not only for sightseeing, but to trace the footprints of their ancestors and to connect Dutch and American history. In the second book in the series they meet a descendant of the English branch of the family, in the third they try to find records of their Viking ancestors and also visit the home and haunts of Hans Christian Andersen. The Bodley books are not read today, though perhaps they would be if children's travel books, good, bad, and indifferent, were not supplied in such abundance, for the Bodleys have well-defined personalities and there is a natural and pleasant family relationship. Mr. Bodley is informative, it is true, but he is not dull and his talks about what they see are interspersed with much lively conversation.

Hezekiah Butterworth (1839–1905), for many years assistant editor of the *Youth's Companion*, wrote a travel series which appeared in the 1880's and 1890's. Butterworth took his idea from a book, *Voyages en ZigZag*, by a Swiss teacher named Rodolphe Toepffer (1749–1846), who led a class of boys on a "zigzag" journey through Switzerland. So Mr. Butterworth, with a group of imaginary boys in mind, set out (first stop the Public Library) on *Zigzag Journeys in Europe; Vacation Rambles in Historic Lands* (1880), to be followed by sixteen other volumes. In the first eight the travelers are members of the Zigzag Club of the Academy of Yule, in Massachusetts. The aim of the club was to visit historic places without regard to routes of travel, which explains why the books became history and folklore rather than descriptive travel books. At their meetings the club told historic stories and legends of these places. In *Zigzag Journeys in India* the club is left out altogether and the book is a collection of folklore, wild animal stories, and tales from history, put together with many pictures. The author was interested in folk literature, ballads and legends, and his inclusion of this material pointed out the cultural contribution of different countries and gave his books their chief value. The Zigzag travels were bought in large numbers by approving elders and were read by many boys and girls, some of whom bear testimony today to the enjoyment these books afforded.

Charles Asbury Stephens (1845–1931) was engaged by the editor of the *Youth's Companion* in 1870 to write exclusively for that magazine at an annual salary and, during the sixty years that this arrangement continued, turned out thousands of stories. His travel stories appeared in two series. The Young Yachters series (1872) comprised *Left on Labrador; Off to the Geysers, or The Young Yachters in Iceland*; and *On the Amazon*. The Knockabout Club series consisted of the *Knockabout Club in the Woods, Alongshore, In the Tropics*. Stephens had the gift of writing for young people, as his tremendous following in the *Youth's Companion* showed; he had also taken journeys to Florida, the West Indies, Mexico, Spain, and North Africa, which were reflected in his books.

Thomas Wallace Knox (1835–1896) grew up on a farm, taught school later on, but was drawn by the Gold Rush to Colorado and there became a newspaper editor. After the Civil War, in which he held a commission as lieutenant-colonel on the staff of the governor of California, he joined the staff of the *New York Herald* and as correspondent began his world travels by crossing Siberia in sledge and wagon with the American Telephone Company. Colonel Knox, as he was always called, did the most traveling of any of the writers of travel books for young people. He made two voyages around the world and explored unfrequented paths in the Orient. His personal recollections gave liveliness to his books. When he visited Siam, some fifteen years after Anna Leonowens had undertaken the education of the king's children, he was responsible for the adoption of a system of education modeled upon American public education. After this visit he wrote *Boy Travellers in the Far East* in five volumes and for *Part II, Adventures of Two Youths in Siam and Java*, which the king declared the best description of Siam ever written, he received the decoration of the Order of the White Elephant. *Part III* took the two boys, Frank Bassett and Fred Bronson, with their uncle, Dr. Bronson, to India and Ceylon, *Part IV* to Egypt and the Holy Land and *Part V* to Africa. In ten more volumes Knox practically covered the globe. Altogether he produced nearly forty travel books for boys; all of them conscientious and accurate. Dr. Bronson taught Frank and Fred the art of travel and encouraged self-reliance by leaving the arrangements of the trips to them. Classics of travel and history are suggested, and Knox quotes liberally. The boys write diaries and letters home, including in them history and something about social conditions which they are encouraged to observe. Knox, however, was not merely factual in his approach, he tried in his books to show that human nature is the same all the world over. The boys are concerned over the condition of the people in Mexico, they contrast the attitude of Japanese children toward their parents with that of American children, not to the advantage of the latter. In the later volumes Frank's sister Mary and their mother join the party. Mary shows the same eagerness to learn as the boys and is soon talking intelligently on history and on contemporary subjects of which the boys are ignorant. She has been called by a critic of the day "perhaps the most intelligent of the party." Knox used a large number of illustrations, Harper's store of pictorial material was available to him, engravings were sometimes borrowed from foreign countries and the author ingeniously fitted pictures to text. Knox really provided useful information for the traveler and for those to whom thoroughness and substance appealed. On the whole, however, the Bodley books and the Zigzag travels were more popular.

Meanwhile Mrs. Elizabeth Williams Champney (1850–1922) wrote in the 1880's a series of travel stories for girls, beginning with *Three Vassar Girls Abroad. Rambles of Three College Girls on a Vacation Trip Through France and Spain for Amusement and Instruction. With Their Haps and Mishaps* (1883). Mrs. Champney and her husband, J. Wells Champney, a well-known New York artist (he made the drawings for his wife's books), lived abroad. *Harper's* and *The Century* published Mrs. Champney's articles about her experiences while traveling in England, France, and Spain, but it was when she began to write for girls that her name became known. From 1883 till 1892, her Vassar Girls traveled, in eleven volumes, through Europe, South America, and the Holy Land. The girls provide a nice variety of character and personality. Some are daughters of wealthy parents and travel for pleasure; others have a high moral purpose and plan to be missionaries or to study medicine in the hope of doing good. Some of the girls have artistic gifts, and Mrs. Champney contrived in many ways to make art and architecture play important parts in her stories. She also laid a refreshing stress on international understanding and the overcoming of prejudice. One of the girls suggests, early in the series, that prejudice comes from imperfect knowledge, and if prejudice exists among the girls a few months of meetings and excursions with their hosts and hostesses and the latter's friends are quite sufficient to break it down. An international marriage is frequently introduced, either as a cause, or as a result, of international understanding. Mrs. Champney is at her best when writing of the countries in which she had lived and traveled herself; Switzerland, France, and Germany fare better than the Amazon or Russia. She preferred to write of what she knew at first hand, but her publishers demanded books about more and more countries whether she had visited them or not.

The Witch Winnie series (1889–1898) was about young women artists at home and abroad. There was a story in each volume, often a slight mystery, and usually a touch of romance. Beginning in New York at a boarding school, where Winnie and her friends were pupils, the stories range from Paris to Holland, Italy and Spain. Winnie and her fellow travelers are forgotten today, but they had significance for the period when the books were written. The series maintained a high standard of behavior and was very popular.

Romance—Fauntleroy and Lady Jane

The last quarter of the nineteenth century not only offered a new type of book in these travel stories, it set a new style in the story about home life and real people. For some time stories had dealt with characters like those in Miss Alcott's books or in Susan Coolidge's stories, characters such as the reader, if he were lucky, might know in everyday life. In the 1880's and the 1890's stories began to appear in which the characters had reality but in which the events, while not fantasy, were more highly colored and more dramatic than the usual happenings of everyday. In other words, stories for girls grew more romantic, with a stronger emphasis on plot. *Little Lord Fauntleroy* (1886) by Mrs. Frances Hodgson Burnett (1849–1924) was the first of these. This account of a little boy born and brought up in America, who turns out to be heir to an English dukedom, has come in for a deal of harsh criticism in the present century. Cedric's velvet suit, lace collar, and long curls appealed to many mothers at the time, but not to the boys who were sometimes forced to wear them. However, it should not be overlooked that in Cedric, Mrs. Burnett drew a natural, courageous, and honest child. The readers who delighted in the book and those who saw the highly successful play made from it, undoubtedly enjoyed the flavor of English nobility. They may have done so with an unconscious snobbery, but the hero himself was as free from class consciousness as the most ardent democrat could wish.

Mrs. Burnett's next important story for children was *Sara Crewe; or, What happened at Miss Minchin's* (1888). Like *Little Lord Fauntleroy*, this appeared first as a serial in *St. Nicholas*. In 1903 Mrs. Burnett dramatized the book under the title *The Little Princess* and the play was so successful that she was persuaded to rewrite the story, basing the new version on the play and including characters which were not in the original story. *Sara Crewe* has the elements to enchant a child reader. When Sara, whose father's death in India had changed her from a favored pupil in Miss Minchin's boarding school into a little drudge, climbs to her attic room, tired, cold, and hungry to find it transformed, with a fire in the grate, a kettle hissing and boiling, a rug, a little table spread with covered dishes, warm bed coverings, a wadded silk robe, and some books, it is the Cinderella story brought into real life. While to have the magic continue and to discover at last that the invalid next door is her father's friend, who has been searching for her to tell her that she is no longer a friendless, penniless orphan, is for a child the perfect happy ending. *Sara Crewe* has more substance than *Little Lord Fauntleroy* though it was never so well known. The happy ending was not due to mere chance. Sara is a consistently drawn character, she was no weakling and the ending was the result of a moral victory as well as good fortune. *Editha's Burglar* (in *St. Nicholas*, 1881, later in book form), the story of a little girl who persuaded a burglar to carry out his job quietly without waking her mother, was admired in its own time and laughed at later. The tale, while much less convincing than the two already mentioned, was not unreasonable since nineteenth century burglars did not carry arms. Also this particular burglar departed with his spoil. Fifty years earlier, Editha would have persuaded him to leave it behind and sent him away a reformed character. Mrs. Burnett's best story for children was not written until 1910. In *The Secret Garden* she successfully combined plot, a charming setting consisting of an old house and a lovely garden, and three well-drawn children, who prove a knowledge of child psychology on the part of the author. *Little Saint Elizabeth and Other Stories* (1891) contained "Behind the White Brick" and other tales which had appeared in *St. Nicholas* and were popular with children. Over many years Mrs. Burnett, who was born in England but spent most of her life in America, wrote novels for adults. Many of them had great success at the time, but her reputation today grows from her three books for children, *Little Lord Fauntleroy*, *Sara Crewe*, and *The Secret Garden*.

Mrs. Cecelia Viets Jamison (1837–1909), artist and author of many novels, is best known for two of her children's books, *Lady Jane* and *Toinette's Philip*. Both appeared in *St. Nicholas*, illustrated by Reginald Birch, before the Century Company published them in book form in 1891 and 1893 respectively. The scene of both books is the French quarter of New Orleans. When Lady Jane's widowed mother dies, the child is left in the hands of an unscrupulous woman who ill-treats her. In desperation little Jane runs away and is rescued by the head of an orphans' home, where she is taken care of until discovered by relatives. In *Toinette's Philip* the boy hero also loses his parents and is brought up by Toinette, the kindly Negro servant who lived with his mother. Philip is adopted and taken to New York. Unhappy with his adopted parents he runs away, manages to get back to New Orleans. There, through the papers Toinette had left with Père Josef, who finds them waiting for him when he gets back from a long journey, Philip's parentage is discovered and a home and happiness is secured for him. Lady Jane had golden hair and eyes of violet blue. Dea, Philip's little friend, had a face as delicate as a Roman cameo. Current fashion has its influence on the criticism of children's books, elegance in looks has gone out of style; today the child heroine is likely to be freckled, rough-haired and dressed in blue jeans. But if superficial matters of dress and appearance are disregarded, these stories read well today. Mrs. Jamison could handle a plot in a way that few writers for children have equaled. If the plot is accepted, the events of the tale proceed inevitably. Mrs. Jamison's and Mrs. Burnett's tales are often dismissed as too highly colored; actually they have a greater reality than stories of a later period which are made up of events too palpably invented for children's consumption.

Books for Boys Show Tougher Fiber

As if to balance the swing toward romance in books for girls, books for boys turned to greater realism. Two of the most famous books for children, or at any rate read by children, for the second book was actually written for an adult audience, distinguished the last quarter of the nineteenth century—Mark Twain's (1835–1910) *The Adventures of Tom Sawyer* (1876) and *The Adventures of Huckleberry Finn* (1884). Based on the author's recollections of his boyhood in Missouri, they combine adventure, imagination, realism, humor, and human nature to a degree which makes them—especially *Huckleberry Finn*—great books and books that are essentially American. *Huckleberry Finn*, in fact, has been called "the great American novel." The background for the exploits of Tom and Huck and their friends, the midwestern town where they live, the life along the Mississippi, is a true picture of the American scene a hundred years ago.

Tom and Huck were preceded by another very real boy, though he is perhaps a less striking character and is described in a quieter way in Thomas Bailey Aldrich's *The Story of a Bad Boy* (1870). This book, too, is reminiscent of the author's youth; the Rivermouth of the book is Portsmouth, New Hampshire, and the tale of young Tom's mischief, his good times, his adventures and misadventures is told with charm, humor, and verve. Charles Dudley Warner's *Being a Boy* (1878) is more of an autobiographical essay than a story and better known to adults than to children, but the author's reminiscences of life on a New England farm in the mid-nineteenth century are full of humor and human nature.

J. T. Trowbridge (1827–1916) wrote realistically in his many stories (see page 222). James Otis Kaler (1848–1912), who used James Otis as a pen name, wrote in *Toby Tyler; or, Ten Weeks with a Circus* a story that is still a favorite because of its genuine portrait of a boy and its true picture of circus life and what the young hero thought of it. The story of the monkey, who is very important in the book, is continued in the sequel, *Mr. Stubbs's Brother*.

In 1872 *A Dog of Flanders* by Marie Louise de la Ramée (1839–1908), the first modern dog story, was published. Under the pen name of Ouida, this eccentric author wrote *Under Two Flags, Held in Bondage* and many other flamboyant, melodramatic novels which were widely read in the 1870's and 1880's. She was the daughter of an English mother and a French father. After leaving England in 1871 she made a brief stay in Belgium and then lived for twenty-three years in Italy. Ouida loved dogs, she kept a large number of them as pets in Florence where it is said they ruled her villa, and she was always ready to add an abused or starving dog to her household. The affection and admiration she felt for her dog friends she put into her story of Patrasche, the Belgian work dog, and his young master, Nello, the boy who might have become a great artist had he lived. The devoted dog and his master, dying together from hunger and exposure before the great Rubens painting in the cathedral, have drawn tears from several generations of readers. Burne-Jones is quoted by Sir Shane Leslie as saying, "I remember Ruskin and Cardinal Manning routing on their knees amongst some books to find *A Dog of Flanders* which they loved," adding, "but the style is bad I will confess."[1] The story bears the earmarks of the romantic period, but, its sentimentality notwithstanding, it has a convincing quality that has kept it alive for years. More cheerful are her

[1] Eileen Bigland, *Ouida, the Passionate Victorian* (London, Jarrolds, 1950), p. 76.

The Nürnberg Stove, and *Bimbi*, published in a collection called *Stories for Children* in 1882.

Discovering History

The writing of history for children had not developed in the nineteenth century to the same extent as the writing of fiction. Following Jacob Abbott's large number of biographies for young people, which ranged from Alexander the Great and Hannibal to Genghis Khan and Mary Queen of Scots, Thomas Wentworth Higginson (1823–1911) wrote *Young Folks' History of the United States* (1875), a book which marks the beginning of modern history writing for children. Such a book was needed and Higginson was asked by George B. Emerson, a Boston educator, to write it. Somewhat to the author's surprise it became popular at once; a few weeks after its publication 6,000 copies had been sold. It was translated into French, German, and Italian, and was adopted in 1879 by Boston Public Schools. An endorsement which especially pleased the author was that of an eight-year-old boy who told Higginson, "I like your History of the United States about as well as the Odyssey."[1] Higginson also wrote *A Book of American Explorers* (1897), a selection of extracts from the narratives of explorers, ranging from the legends of the Vikings to the establishment of the Virginia and Massachusetts colonies.

George Makepeace Towle (1841–1893) wrote history in the form of biographies, a series called Young Folks' Heroes of History, which included *Magellan* (1880), *Marco Polo* (1880), *Pizarro* (1878), *Ralegh* (1882), *Vasco da Gama* (1878), and *Drake* (1883). These were prosaic but useful since such material was scarce.

Charles Carleton Coffin (1823–1906) was correspondent during the Civil War for the *Boston Journal*. Boys of several generations have delighted not only in those books he wrote for young people, *Boys of '76* (1876), *Boys of '61* (1884), *Building the Nation* (1883), and *Old Times in the Colonies* (1880), but have enjoyed those written for adults, *My Days and Nights on the Battle-field* (1887), the Drum-beat of the Nation series (1888–1891), and others. Battles are described with the vividness of an eyewitness account and *Boys of '76*, in particular, has enjoyed long popularity.

Grace Greenwood, pseudonym of Sara Lippincott (1823–1904), wrote several volumes of historical tales and legends, *Merrie England* (1855), *Bonnie Scotland* (1861), *Stories and Sights of France and Italy* (1867), *Stories from Famous Ballads* (1860). Her interest was chiefly in legend, and she emphasized the romantic quality of history. Her graceful poetic style gave charm and atmosphere to her tales and

[1] M. T. Higginson, *Thomas W. Higginson, The Story of his Life* (Boston, Houghton Mifflin, 1914), p. 288.

made them attractive to nineteenth century readers. Much of Grace Greenwood's writing appeared in the magazine *Little Pilgrim*.

Two books of tales from history for children stand out because of the importance of their authors. Following Sir Walter Scott's *Tales of a Grandfather* (1831) was Nathaniel Hawthorne's *Grandfather's Chair, or True Stories from New England History 1620–1803*, written by Hawthorne while he was employed at the Salem Custom House. They were published in three parts by his friend and sister-in-law, Elizabeth Peabody, who had set up a kind of transcendental bookshop and homeopathic drugstore in Boston. The series consisted of *Grandfather's Chair, a History for Youth; Famous Old People, Being the Second Epoch of Grandfather's Chair*; and *The Liberty Tree, with the Last Words of Grandfather's Chair*, all published in 1841. The books were successful and were republished the following year by Tappan and Dennet. They attracted little critical attention, though Evert Duyckinck in the second issue of his journal *Arcturus* gave the first of the series a kindly word. "The best test of a sentimental author," he wrote, "is the production of a good book for children. If he can write so as to engage the hearts of both young and old he must have a portion of the poet's youthful soul, which grows no older though the furrows on the brow deepen or the world without presses with its cares." He said that those who remembered *Little Annie's Ramble* would need no introduction to *Grandfather's Chair*.[1]

The Chair of the tales was made from an oak that grew in the park of the English Earl of Lincoln and was given to his daughter, the Lady Arbella, when she went with her husband to the New World. It then passed into the hands of Roger Williams, Anne Hutchinson, Cotton Mather, and many others, it was used by Washington in Cambridge at the time the British were leaving Boston at the end of the Revolutionary War, it came at length into the possession of Samuel Adams, Governor of Massachusetts and at his death the Grandfather who tells the stories purchased it. The Chair thus serves as a link between the important events which are described. The narrative is discursive as was the fashion of the time, but characters and happenings are clearly and even dramatically described, with a genuine feeling for New England history.

It is surely an excellent way, perhaps the best way, for children to absorb history through the historical story if that story is sufficiently well done. The beginning of the well-written story with authentic historical background can be seen in the 1880's, though its full development came later. In 1883, however, a most significant book was published in this country. This was *The Merry Adventures of Robin Hood*

---

[1] Bertha Faust, *Hawthorne's Contemporaneous Reputation* (Philadelphia, Univ. of Penn., 1939), pp. 37–38.

of Great Renown, in Nottinghamshire, written and illustrated by Howard Pyle. The stories had first appeared in *Harper's Young People*. This truly great children's book has been read by children and their elders for over eighty years and there are no signs of its losing its popularity. To make his book, Pyle used the old English ballads that told of the life and exploits of Robin Hood, blending them into a perfect whole which has a magical power of re-creating medieval England. Child reader or adult reader finds himself in the green glades of Sherwood, or watching the life of the day as it passes on the high road, sharing the springtime adventures that could only have taken place in a younger, more innocent world. For Howard Pyle the book was a labor of love and this, with his care for accuracy, his artist's eye for detail, did what no book for children had done up to this time— it not only gave them information about a past age, but created for them in authentic and thoroughly convincing fashion the atmosphere of that day so long ago.

Bibliography

Cantwell, R. *Nathaniel Hawthorne, the American Years*. New York, Rinehart, 1948.

Haviland, Virginia. *The Travelogue Story Book*. Boston, The Horn Book, 1950.

Higginson, Thomas Wentworth. *Letters and Journals of Thomas Wentworth Higginson; 1846–1906*. Edited by Mary Thacher Higginson. Boston, Houghton Mifflin, 1921.

10

Magazines for Children in the
Nineteenth Century

Children's Magazines in England

Attempts were made in the early years of the nineteenth century to establish more reasonable and more permanent magazines for children. *The Child's Companion; or, Sunday Scholars' Reward* began publication in 1824 and continued into the twentieth century. *The Children's Friend*, beginning in 1826, lasted into the 1860's. The Rev. Carus Wilson, its editor and publisher, wrote in the spirit of the early 1800's and provided countless examples of pious infants whose conviction of sin was profound and whose deaths were edifying. A certain interest is attached to Mr. Wilson because he was known to Charlotte Brontë. Memories of him when, at nine years of age, she was a pupil at Cowan Bridge, the Clergy Daughters' School which Mr. Wilson founded, remained, and they were not pleasant ones. In *Jane Eyre* she drew a highly unattractive portrait of him as Mr. Brocklehurst, founder and inspector of the school at Lowood and incumbent of Brocklebridge Church. This portrait was challenged, for Mr. Wilson had many admirers. He was a respected leader in the Evangelical Movement and a friend of Wilberforce and Shaftesbury. *The Children's Friend*, however, confirms Miss Brontë's characterization of the man. It is dull, lacking in real sympathy for children, and devoid of humor.

The Youth's Monthly Visitor, solemnly announcing that it proposed to "attend to the solid improvement of the Youth of both sexes," was established in 1822; when it was reprinted the name was changed to *The Youth's Miscellany of Knowledge and Entertainment*. These magazines and many others with similar titles obviously bore little resemblance to the later ones. Their purpose, like that of the moral tale, was to inform and instruct.

The first real magazine for children did not appear until the fifties. This was *The Charm*, which began publication in 1852, edited by Addey, the partner of Cundall, who had published Felix Summerly's *The Home Treasury*, and his successor. No doubt his association with *The Home Treasury* and Sir Henry Cole (who used the pseudonym

Felix Summerly) had its influence on the new magazine. The prospectus stated that "space would always be given to legends of those gentle creatures who dwell in the realms of fairy." Unfortunately *The Charm* only lasted two years; the time was not ripe for the tales of the imagination offered by *The Charm*. Moral and instructive tales which were still considered by many adults to be the proper food for boys and girls were supplied by *The Boys' and Girls' Companion for Leisure Hours* (1857–58) edited by John and Mary Bennett, which continued three years longer as *The Companion for Youth*, and by *The Youth's Instructor* (1858). This last, however, after nine months was merged with *The Boy's Own Magazine* (1855–74), a much livelier publication and one of the many enterprises of the active Beetons. The magazines edited by this husband and wife were enormously successful. The price was low. *The Boy's Own Magazine* was sold at first for twopence, the price rising to sixpence in 1863 when it had a circulation of 40,000 copies a month. The popularity of the Beeton magazines was not due, however, to their cheapness but to the fact that the editors took into account children's tastes and printed what children wanted rather than what their elders thought they should have. *The Boy's Own Magazine* contained adventure stories. W. H. G. Kingston and J. C. Edgar were among those who wrote for it. There were stories from history dealing with kings and knights that appealed to the young reader's love of chivalry and romance. There were school stories and tales with a pseudo-Gothic atmosphere to satisfy a taste established in the early years of the century. There were also articles by specialists in their fields. J. C. Wood wrote on the Zoological Gardens, and Pyecroft wrote on cricket. There were articles on chemistry, with experiments; articles on the Army and Navy, and an excellent puzzle page. In addition, *The Boy's Own Magazine* offered attractive prizes to readers, such as watches and pencil cases, and among the winners was a future bishop of the Church of England. The magazine was octavo in size, with double columns of what today would be called impossibly small print. Woodcuts were used to illustrate the most exciting incidents in the stories. In 1863, when the price of *The Boy's Own Magazine* had risen to sixpence, the Beetons brought out *The Boy's Penny Magazine* also. *The Boy's Yearly Book* appeared in 1863. *Beeton's Annual; a Book for the Young* (1866) included contributions by Mayne Reid, Clement Scott, W. H. Davenport Adams, and Austin Dobson.

In the 1860's children's magazines came into their own. Their importance as a source of entertainment as well as of instruction was recognized, and editorial policies grew broader. Most of the best stories for children of the day appeared first in magazines. Charlotte Yonge's own stories were published in the magazine which she edited, *The Monthly Packet*, to which Mrs. Gatty and her daughter, Mrs. Ewing, were contributors; but after *Aunt Judy's Magazine* was started in 1866 under the editorship of Mrs. Gatty, Mrs. Ewing reached a wider public in its pages. The Gatty family, first and last, accounted for a good part of the content of *Aunt Judy's Magazine*. Mrs. Ewing's stories appeared one after another as serials for many years. Mrs. Gatty, as editor, conducted the department called "Aunt Judy's Correspondence," her son Alfred Scott Gatty set poems to music, Dr. Gatty wrote articles from time to time. There were distinguished names other than those of the family on the list of contributors. Many of Hans Christian Andersen's stories were published by Mrs. Gatty. Lewis Carroll wrote "Bruno's Revenge" at her request, and in the first number she included C. S. Calverley's "Shelter," an amusing poem, about a water rat, with a surprise ending. In Number Eleven the magazine began to publish book reviews, the first ones were enthusiastic notices of *Alice's Adventures in Wonderland* and Andersen's *Fairy Stories*.

Aunt Judy's Magazine emphasized home and family. *Boys of England; A Magazine of Sport, Sensation, Fun and Instruction* (first number November 29, 1866) was of quite another stamp. "Our aim," said the prospectus, "is to enthral you by wild and wonderful but healthy fiction." Wild and wonderful fiction it seems to have been; the villains were bloodthirsty, the epithets highly colored. At the end of six months the circulation was 150,000 a week but it reached the height of its popularity in 1871 when E. J. Brett, the editor, introduced his readers to Jack Harkaway, a character who might be compared to the American Nick Carter. *Boys of England* lasted until 1899 when it was incorporated into a magazine called *Up-To-Date Boys* which ceased publication two years after. *Boys of England* was well printed, with many illustrations, and its popularity was increased by a scheme for distributing 1400 prizes, including a Shetland pony, rabbits, and watches. Many other magazines for boys were published in the 1860's. *Boys of England*, poorly written and sensational, may be taken as a typical example.

It was concern for the low state of children's reading matter, as indicated by these "blood and thunder" magazines, that prompted the Rev. J. Erskine Clarke, Vicar of Derby, to found a new magazine on a higher level, which, he hoped, would inculcate ideals of piety and virtue. This magazine was *Chatterbox* (founded 1866). Two years before, Mr. Clarke had founded *The Children's Prize*, later called *The Prize for Girls and Boys*. He not only edited the work of his contributors (and usually with an unsparing hand) but wrote much of the contents of both magazines himself and his writing was clearly inspired by the Sunday school movement. There were stories in *Chatterbox*, biographical and scientific articles, and many pictures, but the whole effect was not one of gaiety and charm. Ruskin disliked Mr. Clarke's taste in illustrations and in his *Fors Clavigera* severely criticized *The Prize* for its complete lack of beauty,[1] a criticism indicating that the time had come when children's magazines were being taken seriously. The first editor's aim to "instill Christian principles" was all too evident; nevertheless, *Chatterbox* went on for many years and there was an American edition as well as the English one. It was, however, read far more in America as an annual, than as a current magazine.

With *Good Words for the Young*, published from 1869–1877, we come to a magazine of real distinction. Edited first by Dr. Norman Macleod and then by George Macdonald, it had a distinguished list of contributors. Charles Kingsley's "Madam How and Lady Why" was published in its pages. There were stories by William Brighty Rands, Dinah Mulock Craik, and William Gilbert, the father of W. S. Gilbert the dramatist; the latter, signing himself "Bab," illustrated his father's two stories, "The Magic Mirror" and "King George's Middy." Thomas Hood the younger provided a humor and a puzzle section. It is noteworthy that the names of the illustrators are listed in the table of contents. Arthur Hughes's name appears frequently. He illustrated not only George Macdonald's stories but "Innocents' Island" by William Brighty Rands. *Good Words for the Young* with its illustrations, its poetry, its excellent stories, its interesting informational articles, its editors who understood children's tastes and interests, was the first modern magazine for children.

In 1871 appeared *Young Folks*, interesting because Stevenson's *Treasure Island* first appeared serially in its pages, from October 1881 to January 1882. This was a landmark in magazine serials for here was adventure handled as literature rather than sensationalism. *Little Folks*, which aimed at a younger group of readers, recognized the importance of illustrations by announcing on the title page of the first volume that it contained about five hundred pictures. It had simplicity, variety and in a friendly, natural way, set out to amuse children. It was successful and, with some changes in scope, lasted until 1933. There was an American edition, *Little Wide-Awake; An Illustrated Magazine for Good Children* (1875), edited by Mrs. Sale Barker, who wrote the verses for Kate Greenaway's *Birthday Book*, which was truly Victorian in appearance and content. On the cover of the 1880 volume a Kate Greenaway picture showed a little girl in a long red coat, a fur muff and plumed bonnet, paying a morning call, the personification of Victorian childhood. This magazine published Mrs. Molesworth's "The Boys and I." *Little Wide-Awake* was planned for the middle-aged children with special pages for the little ones. It emphasized both fairy tales and the family pages and lasted till 1892. It was distinct from the American *Wide Awake* (see page 255).

[1] John Ruskin, *Fors Clavigera* (London, George Allen, 1875–1887), Letter L.

These magazines, interesting as they are in themselves, did not affect the main current of magazines for children. One, however, appeared in 1879 which was to outlive all the other children's magazines in England and which, from its beginning, marked out fresh paths and established a high standard of excellence. This was *The Boy's Own Paper*, not to be confused with *The Boy's Own Magazine* mentioned earlier. It was published by the Religious Tract Society, which has never confined itself to bringing out tracts alone. *The Boy's Own Paper* had its ideal of conduct, and goodness and honesty were treated as a matter of course. It recognized and rejected vice, but quietly, without moral fanfare. The firm's general editor was at first in charge, but at the very outset he called in George Andrew Hutchinson, who edited the magazine till 1912. An ideal editor, he quietly and unobtrusively saw to it that the magazine kept its character, its quality, and its ideals. Its policy was to emphasize both naturalness and manliness. The manly boy inevitably becomes a type, something which does not, as a matter of fact, disturb the average boy reader but there were well-known names among the contributors that kept the writing at a uniformly high level. Kingston's *From Powder-Monkey to Admiral* appeared in the first volume. Frank Buckland, zoologist, and Talbot Baines Reed, who enlarged the range of the school story, were also contributors. In Volume II were included Ballantyne, Jules Verne, and Ascott Hope (A. R. Hope Moncrieff), who besides his guidebooks to different parts of England wrote many stories for boys. Captain Webb wrote on swimming, W. G. Grace on cricket; Whymper, J. G. Wood, Maskelyne, and other specialists wrote on their fields. Far-flung, romantic adventure was as popular as ever, but Jules Verne (all of whose stories made their first English appearance in this magazine) proved that scientific adventure could be as thrilling as any other kind. Harvey Darton in his *Children's Books in England* declared that when *The Boy's Own Paper* celebrated its fiftieth anniversary and a Prime Minister of Great Britain was the principal guest, his presence as a speaker and the tribute he paid to the beloved magazine were unmistakable social history.[1]

Children's Magazines in America

The first children's magazine in America that was (in spite of its name) really childlike, appeared in Boston in 1826. It was called *The Juvenile Miscellany*, with Lydia Maria Child as its editor. The famous poem beginning "Mary Had a Little Lamb," by Sarah Josepha Hale, first appeared in its pages. However, Lydia Maria Child was an abolitionist; her views were unpopular at that time and the magazine had to cease publication.

[1] F. J. Harvey Darton, *Children's Books in England* (Cambridge, Eng., University Press, 1932), p. 306.

The other early children's magazines were born of the enthusiasm for the Sunday school movement. *The Children's Magazine* (1829) was Episcopal; *The Encourager*, Methodist. There was a *Catholic Youth Magazine* about 1850. *The Juvenile Instructor* was Mormon, and there was a *Youth's Temperance Advocate*. *Parley's Magazine* which, as one would expect, was instructive in tone, began publication in 1832 but after a few years Samuel Goodrich, its founder and editor, was obliged to give it up on account of ill health. The magazine called *Merry's Museum* for which Peter Parley was also responsible lasted longer. *The Child's Friend*, published in Boston 1843–1853, was attractive in form but dull in material. In the 1840's and 1850's Charles Fithian of Philadelphia edited *The Boy's and Girl's Penny Journal* and *Fithian's Miniature Magazine*, which contained stories, biographies, and foreign and local news. Grace Greenwood and Leander Lippincott edited a magazine called *The Little Pilgrim*. Caroline Hewins in her *A Mid-Century Child and Her Books* tells with what pleasure she looked forward each month to the arrival by mail of *The Little Pilgrim*, and to the reading of Grace Greenwood's "stories of history and travel, which made Shakespeare, Scott and Byron, the royal prisoner, James I of Scotland, Jane Beaufort and Catherine Douglas, Guy of Warwick and Sir Philip Sydney real living persons. . . ."[1] Whittier's "Barefoot Boy" appeared in *The Little Pilgrim*. It lasted three months of 1854, suspended, and then began again in 1855. Oliver Optic (the pen name for W. T. Adams) started several children's magazines; the one called *Oliver Optic's* lasted longest. It was another of his magazines, *Student and Schoolmate*, that started Horatio Alger on his career as a writer for boys by publishing his *Ragged Dick*.

In the second half of the century children's magazines grew to their full stature. They became of consequence for themselves and exercised influence on the whole field of children's reading. One of the most important was *The Riverside Magazine*. Though its life was short, only three years, from 1867 to 1870, its editor, Horace E. Scudder, was to be a moving force in the field of children's books for years to come. He felt strongly that only the best was good enough for children, and significantly, that true criticism should be applied to children's books. He believed, too, that the line dividing books for the young and books for the old should not be too strictly drawn. Scudder and Hans Christian Andersen became friends, a friendship that meant much to both, and a number of Andersen's stories first appeared in *The Riverside Magazine*. Frank R. Stockton, Alice and Phoebe Cary, Mary Mapes Dodge, Edward Everett Hale were other contributors. H. L. Stephens, Thomas Nast, E. B. Bensell, John LaFarge and Winslow Homer pro-

[1] Caroline Hewins, *A Mid-Century Child and Her Books* (New York, Macmillan, 1926), p. 69.

vided illustrations, for Mr. Scudder wanted "pictures of child life from painters who were not mere professional book illustrators." A new feature in the magazine, of great importance for the future of children's literature, was the articles which Scudder introduced on the subject of children's reading and the choice of books.

Though *The Riverside Magazine* ceased publication, Mr. Scudder continued to exercise his fine critical powers on behalf of children. Associated for many years with Houghton Mifflin Company, he was responsible for The Riverside Literature Series for Young People, for he was convinced that whole works were superior to the fragments in the old-fashioned school readers. Many important books for children were published during his years with Houghton Mifflin—Sarah Orne Jewett's *Betty Leicester*; Eliza Orne White's fine stories for little girls, *When Molly Was Six*, *An Only Child*, and others; Whittier's distinguished anthologies, *Child Life*, *A Collection of Poems*, and *Child Life in Prose*; Hans Christian Andersen's *Wonder Stories for Children* in an edition that still ranks high. Scudder, indeed, studied Danish in order that he might be sure that Andersen was properly translated. Mr. Scudder himself made some excellent selections of fables, folk tales, and legends and wrote a life of Washington. In 1881 his *The Children's Book* was published. Though unfortunately out of print this is the ideal volume to acquaint children with the best that has been written. In twelve sections it contains fables; favorite nursery tales; poetry (including lyrics, storytelling poems, and ballads); a representative selection of Andersen's tales; selections from *The Arabian Nights*; parts of "A Voyage to Lilliput" from Swift's *Gulliver's Travels;* and *The Travels of Baron Munchausen;* a few older stories with a moral, such as Maria Edgeworth's "Waste Not Want Not," ending with four great tales from Greek mythology.

Our Young Folks, published in Boston from 1865 to 1873, was edited by Lucy Larcom, Gail Hamilton, and J. T. Trowbridge. Gail Hamilton, however, dropped out after a short time. Lucy Larcom and Trowbridge were blessed with critical judgment and had a keen interest in children's reading. Trowbridge's *Jack Hazard and His Fortunes* appeared in *Our Young Folks* as a leading serial.

Lucy Larcom had literary taste and genuine sympathy with children, her moral sense was also strong though gentle in its expression. Her own poems appeared frequently; Whittier, whom she helped with his anthologies, Longfellow, and James Russell Lowell contributed poems. Thomas Bailey Aldrich's *The Story of a Bad Boy* appeared in *Our Young Folks* in 1869, and Charles Dickens's "The Magic Fishbone," which was published in England in *All the Year Round* as the second part of *A Holiday Romance*, appeared in *Our Young Folks* in 1868, just after the author's visit to America. *The William Henry Letters* by Mrs.

Diaz and Lucretia P. Hale's Peterkin family, which was to continue its perpetually baffled existence in *St. Nicholas*, made their first appearance in *Our Young Folks*.

The illustrations preserved a high standard, for they were the work of such artists as Winslow Homer, John Gilbert, and H. L. Stephens. There were departments for letters from correspondents and for puzzles. In 1874, however, not because of any falling off in popularity, but for business reasons, *Our Young Folks* was sold to Scribner's in New York to become part of a still more famous magazine, *St. Nicholas*. Another magazine was to be combined eventually with *St. Nicholas*. This was the American *Wide Awake*, founded in 1875 by Daniel Lothrop, and published in Boston. In size and general appearance it resembled *St. Nicholas* and was designed for the same public. It had many pictures, and pages in large type for the youngest readers. Louise Chandler Moulton, Elizabeth Stuart Phelps, Mary H. Catherwood, Edward Everett Hale, Mrs. A. D. T. Whitney, and Sarah Orne Jewett were among the contributors, as well as Hezekiah Butterworth, Sophie May, J. T. Trowbridge, and Margaret Sidney, who became Mrs. Lothrop. Her stories about the Five Little Peppers, which were published in *Wide Awake* before they came out in book form, had a strong appeal for child readers and did much to make the magazine a success. The early volumes of *Wide Awake* sometimes used material from England and in its first year it published George Macdonald's *A Double Story*. Semi-annual volumes of *Wide Awake*, bound up with the title *Wide Awake Pleasure Book*, were popular birthday and Christmas gifts.

St. Nicholas and Mary Mapes Dodge

St. Nicholas, the most famous of all magazines for children, began publication in 1873 under the guidance of a gifted children's editor, Mary Mapes Dodge. As Mary Elizabeth Mapes she was born in New York in 1831. Her father, who was a scientist, undertook to build up a broken-down farm in New Jersey, making experiments that were to prove of immense benefit to the farmer; indeed Horace Greeley, editor of the *New York Tribune*, declared that American agriculture owed as much to him as to any man who lived or who ever had lived. Lizzie, as she was called, kept the books, helped plan the rotation of crops, and shared with her father the editing of a magazine called *The Working Farmer*. In 1847 the Mapes family moved to the farm and it was there that one of their many visitors, a lawyer named William Dodge, persuaded Lizzie to become his wife. She was only twenty when she married, and so when her two little boys came she was young in years as well as in spirit. After a short seven years, however, this happy marriage was ended by the death of William Dodge, and Mary Mapes Dodge and her two boys were back in her childhood home. Determined to be independent, she proposed to write. Her father liked her first story, "Captain George the Drummer-Boy," which had had its beginning as a tale told to her sons. Horace Greeley and George Ripley, who reviewed books for the *Tribune*, read the manuscript and approved. A publisher accepted it and in 1865 her first book, *Irvington Stories*, appeared. The plots of the eight stories were taken largely from United States history; "Captain George the Drummer-Boy" was included. That same year another publisher asked Mrs. Dodge for a story for boys, suggesting that she again use the Civil War as a background. Mrs. Dodge's thought, however, turned in a different direction. Holland had interested her from the time she had read Motley's *Rise of the Dutch Republic* years before, and she now began to write *Hans Brinker; or, The Silver Skates*. She wrote all day in her work room and read the day's work in the evening to her family. In 1865 *Hans Brinker* was published. It was successful from the start and still retains its popularity. The 1867 edition was illustrated by Thomas Nast and F. O. C. Darley. At the end of thirty years it had been printed in more than one hundred editions and in half a dozen languages, and Mrs. Dodge had been awarded the Montyon Literary Prize by the French Academy, an honor achieved by few Americans.

After her father's death in 1866, Mary Mapes Dodge continued to write stories, articles, and poems; *A Few Friends and How They Amused Themselves* was published in 1869, *Theophilus and Others* in 1876, *Rhymes and Jingles* in 1874 and *Along the Way* in 1879. Meanwhile, in 1868, a new magazine called *Hearth and Home* was started in New York City, devoted to farm, garden, and fireside. This enterprise was to give Mrs. Dodge further editorial experience. Donald G. Mitchell, who wrote his books under the name of Ik Marvel, was the editor-in-chief; Harriet Beecher Stowe was a member of the editorial staff and after two years Mrs. Dodge was asked to edit the home-making department. She entered on the work with her usual energy and enthusiasm. Leaving the boys with her mother, she moved to New York, going to the farm for weekends.

Dr. Josiah Gilbert Holland (1819–1881), author of *Arthur Bonnicastle* (1873) and *Sevenoaks, A Story of To-day* (1875) was at this time one of the directors of Scribner & Co., which was loosely allied to the book publishing firm, and had persuaded his well-to-do friend, Roswell Smith, to join the board of directors. To him Dr. Holland unfolded an idea which had come to him, an idea that was to have far-reaching consequences. This idea was nothing less than a magazine for children, a magazine of lively, well-written stories, poetry, and articles, a magazine with the same high standards as the monthly which they published for adults. The other directors agreed, the venture was decided upon and Mrs. Dodge was asked to take the editorship.

It was perhaps the thought of how much her own boys would enjoy such a magazine as this promised to be that helped her make up her mind. At any rate, she did decide to accept the position and almost at once a name occurred to her, *St. Nicholas; A Magazine for Boys and Girls.*

Dr. Holland had chosen wisely and well. The new editor was suited by temperament, ability, and by her interest in young people to make *St. Nicholas* the outstanding magazine for children for all time. At the beginning of her work she wrote out the following editorial policy, which she never changed:

To give clean, genuine fun to children of all ages.
To give them examples of the finest types of boyhood and girlhood.
To inspire them with an appreciation of fine pictorial art.
To cultivate the imagination in profitable directions.
To foster a love of country, home, nature, truth, beauty, and sincerity.
To prepare boys and girls for life as it is.
To stimulate their ambitions—but along normally progressive lines.
To keep pace with a fast-moving world in all its activities.
To give reading matter which every parent may pass to his children unhesitatingly.

In the first issue she wrote, "Let there be no sermonizing . . . no spinning out of facts, no rattling of dry bones. . . . The ideal child's magazine is a pleasure ground." With the advent of *St. Nicholas* didacticism as the chief element in reading for children fled away forever. There were, of course, in its pages interesting, highly readable articles on science, history, and biography, but the chief function of *St. Nicholas* was to provide imaginative reading in the form of stories, poetry, and nonsense that had genuine appeal to boys and girls.

St. Nicholas not only delighted the fortunate children who were given subscriptions, but attracted the attention of the reading world. Established authors were glad to write for it, and Mrs. Dodge, with a flair for discovering genius and a gracious tact in approaching the authors she wished to enlist as contributors, secured many distinguished names. Horace Scudder and Mrs. Dodge were like-minded in their insistence on nothing but the best for children. When Mrs. Dodge went to Boston to talk over her plans with Mr. Scudder, she met and enjoyed a lively young writer named Frank R. Stockton. His stories had been published in *The Riverside Magazine;* when it ended they came out in *St. Nicholas* and within the year Stockton became Mrs. Dodge's assistant editor. His "The Floating Prince," "The Griffin and the Minor Canon," "The Queen's Museum," were among the glories of the magazine's early years.

In 1873 the new magazine was in the mails, and boys and girls for the first time read on the cover, *St. Nicholas; A Magazine for Boys and Girls*. In a country more unified than it is at the present time, *St. Nicholas* was more widely known than it could be today. It is proof of the editor's understanding of young people that boys and girls in India, in China, in London, read *St. Nicholas* and wrote to the editor, telling her how much they liked it.

Louisa Alcott's *Jo's Boys* appeared as a serial in *St. Nicholas*, as did her *An Old-Fashioned Girl* and *Eight Cousins*. Howard Pyle, when he was twenty-three, sent in a verse with black-and-white sketches called "The Magic Pill." Roswell Smith, recognizing the promise of the work, passed it on to Mrs. Dodge, to whom Pyle sent directly some animal fables, illustrated by woodcuts. Richard Watson Gilder, editor of the *Century Magazine*, heard Kipling say he would like someday to write for children and passed the word on to Mrs. Dodge. When they met, Kipling agreed to Mrs. Dodge's suggestion that he should write an animal story for her, or one about India. He did both, for after "The Potted Princess" and "Polly Cla" came "Toomai of the Elephants," the first of the Indian stories which appeared in *St. Nicholas*, to be published later as *The Jungle Book* and *The Second Jungle Book*.

Kipling spoke to Mrs. Dodge of Oliver Herford, a young Englishman who could both draw and write. Julia Ward Howe had also sent a word of recommendation of this artist to the editor; his verses and pictures were soon appearing in *St. Nicholas* and adding to the popularity of the magazine. The association between Kipling and Mrs. Dodge was a happy one, though Kipling did not care for Reginald Birch as an illustrator for his Indian tales. "*St. Nicholas* has come in," Kipling wrote to Mrs. Dodge, "and—Birch does not know too much about monkies. He's gone and put a man coming back from a dinner in a pith hat—the sort of thing you go and stalk tigers in! His old buffalo is an Italian beast and the yoke is a patent I don't know. He's an upsnorter at the Fauntleroy act but menageries isn't his stronghold. All the same, people who haven't been in India won't know."[1]

Reginald Birch may not have been at home in India but he charmed the readers of *St. Nicholas* with the children he drew for Mrs. Hodgson Burnett's *Little Lord Fauntleroy* and *Sara Crewe*, with his pictures of Dorothy and her unusual companions in *The Admiral's Caravan* by Charles Carryl and with those he made for Mrs. Jamison's *Toinette's Philip* and *Lady Jane*.

For the first issue Lucretia P. Hale (1820–1900) had written a story called "Anna's Doll." Soon *The Peterkin Papers* were brightening the pages of the magazine. *St. Nicholas* introduced Joel Chandler Harris'

[1] Alice B. Howard, *Mary Mapes Dodge of St. Nicholas* (New York, Messner, 1943), p. 177.

Uncle Remus, Brer Rabbit, Brer Fox, and the rest to the children. Laura E. Richards' nonsense verses brought them fun and gaiety. J. G. Francis' humorous contributions have been noted in Chapter 8.

Master Skylark by John Bennett (1865–1956), a story of Shakespeare's time that has never been bettered, appeared as a serial in 1896; Howard Pyle's stirring tale of pirates, *Jack Ballister's Fortunes*, in 1894. Sarah Orne Jewett, Mark Twain, Edward Everett Hale, and Thomas Bailey Aldrich all wrote for *St. Nicholas*, whose list of contributors reads like a list of the most distinguished names among American writers. Jack London, when he was a lawless boy on the San Francisco waterfront, read in the bound volume of *St. Nicholas* for 1884, which he picked up in the Oakland Public Library, a story by E. M. White which so impressed him that he decided to give up his wild life, offer his services to the state fish patrol, and learn to be a writer. He made good in that service and his stories were published. In 1902 his "Cruise of the Dazzler" appeared in *St. Nicholas* and marked the fulfillment of his ambition.

In addition to her own charming, childlike jingles, the nonsense rhymes of Tudor Jenks, Oliver Herford, Laura Richards, and others, Mrs. Dodge published poems by Longfellow and Whittier and selections from Emerson and Thoreau. William Cullen Bryant, when he sent her a poem, enclosed a note addressed "To the Young Lady whose directness and honesty pleased this old Quaker poet long ago."

St. Nicholas was not all stories and verse, however. Mrs. Dodge never forgot that an item in her original plan was "to keep pace with a fast-moving world in all its activities." Articles were needed on science, on technical progress, and these she obtained from people who knew how to write them. Biography she wanted, too, and E. S. Brooks (1846–1902) supplied biographies of Washington, Lincoln, Franklin, and other famous Americans.

There was a How To Do and Make Department and a department that not only reviewed but discussed books, under the direction of Donald G. Mitchell. One of his topics was the background of *The Arabian Nights*. Later this department was in charge of Hildegarde Hawthorne. In "Jack-in-the-Pulpit," as the editor's column was called, Mrs. Dodge discussed all manner of things—a cookery book printed by some children, the making of such modern articles as buttons and door knobs. Letters came in from children asking questions or suggesting topics for future discussions. The best of these letters were published in the "Letter Box."

In 1898, the year that the Century Company bought *St. Nicholas*, a famous feature was added to the magazine, the St. Nicholas League. Albert Bigelow Paine, who had been conducting a children's page for the *New York Herald Tribune*, was working on a special feature for that page. When the page was done away with, William Fayal Clarke, who had been an assistant editor of *St. Nicholas* from its beginning, thought there was a place for such a department in *St. Nicholas*. So Paine moved over to Union Square, where the Century offices were, and in the summer of 1898 Mrs. Dodge and Mr. Paine worked out the details of the St. Nicholas League. The motto was "Learn to live, and live to learn," the membership badge was a large button with the name of the organization and the stars and stripes of the American flag. The aims were, as printed in the magazine, "creative adventure for young people from five to eighteen which will stimulate them to strive toward higher ideals both in thought and in living, to protect the oppressed, to grow in understanding of all forms of nature."

The St. Nicholas League offered gold and silver badges for good writing in prose and verse and published it in the St. Nicholas League Department. Among those who won their spurs in the League were Ring Lardner, Richard Bentley, Deems Taylor, Corey Ford, all the Benéts, Alan Seeger, Cornelia Otis Skinner, Babette Deutsch, Peggy Bacon, Elinor Wylie, Norman Bel Geddes, Bennett Cerf, Sigmund Spaeth, and Edmund Wilson. Thus *St. Nicholas* trained writers for the future and also exercised a tremendous influence on the writers of the day. In the editors' realization of the desire that young people have to create something, in the opportunity the League gave them to carry out this creative urge, there was a foreshadowing of the richer, freer education that was to come in the twentieth century.

Withdrawing more and more from the active management of the magazine, Mrs. Dodge spent the last seventeen years of her life in Onteora in the Catskill Mountains. Her cottage, which she named "Yarrow," was a gathering place for friends and neighbors—Maude Adams, Brander Matthews, John Burroughs, Frank R. Stockton, and others. During these years Mrs. Dodge collected from back volumes of *St. Nicholas* the verses for younger children which were published by the Century Company as *Baby World* and *New Baby World*. Her own verses were published in a volume called *When Life is Young. The Land of Pluck*, by Mrs. Dodge, which contained a history of Holland and stories, was published in 1894. In 1883 *Donald and Dorothy*, which had appeared as a serial, came out in book form.

In 1905 Mrs. Dodge died, and few tributes have been more sincere and universal than those paid at her death. The procession at her funeral was made up spontaneously by the children of the community who loved her and thought of her as one of themselves. *St. Nicholas* came to an end in 1940, but there are no signs of its being forgotten. It is still the standard by which magazines for children are measured. The set of bound volumes is a rare and desirable possession. Professor Henry Steele Commager, in his two *St. Nicholas* anthologies, has made it possible for those who never knew *St. Nicholas* in its lifetime at least to taste of the joys that were once a monthly treat.

Probably no one has ever had more influence than Mrs. Dodge in establishing a high level of children's reading. *St. Nicholas* brought to them not written-down material, but writing that was genuinely good, and, more often than not, good reading for any age. There is an often told story of Kipling's asking Mrs. Dodge if she was not going to suggest that he contribute to *St. Nicholas* and her quick reply, "Do you think you are equal to it?" She formed young people's reading taste, not only for the immediate present, but for the future, for the names the children became familiar with in *St. Nicholas*, they found waiting for them in the adult book world. As Professor Commager has said, that was the time "when majors wrote for minors."

Five years after *St. Nicholas* began, another publishing house, Harper and Brothers, decided to add a magazine for young people to those it was already publishing for adults. In 1879 a prospectus announced "An illustrated journal of amusement and instruction" to be called *Harper's Young People;* later, the name was changed to *Harper's Round Table*. Kirk Munroe (1850–1930) was its first editor; often his own stories—"The Flamingo Feather," a tale of the Seminole Indians, "Derrick Sterling," "Dorymates," and others—appeared in *Harper's Young People*. Munroe had traveled over the United States and had been a surveyor in the West, had met Buffalo Bill and Custer, and drew on his own experience for his books. He was much read in the 1880's and 1890's, but his books have not survived.

Many of the *St. Nicholas* authors and illustrators also worked for *Harper's Young People*. Howard Pyle's *The Merry Adventures of Robin Hood* was published there, though Pyle made new pictures for the stories when they appeared in book form.

The Youth's Companion

Of all the magazines for young people in this country, *The Youth's Companion* had the longest life. Starting in 1827 under the editorship of Nathaniel Willis, father of the poet N. P. Willis, it continued till 1929 when it merged with *The American Boy;* the latter ceased publication in 1941. Like *St. Nicholas*, *The Youth's Companion*, which was a weekly, meant much in family life; many households subscribed to both magazines. *The Youth's Companion* started out with certain self-imposed restrictions. It proposed to "exile death from its pages," tobacco and alcohol were not to be mentioned, nor, indeed, were they through all the magazine's long life. Love was not allowed to figure until late in the 1890's and then only in circumspect fashion. Daniel Sharp Ford followed Willis as an editor, Hezekiah Butterworth was assistant editor during the 1880's and 1890's. The editor's name was never permitted to appear and an imaginary company, "The Perry Mason Company," was invented as a publisher. So excellent were the contributions, so normal and happy the characters in the stories, that readers were unconscious of any restrictions in the editorial policy. The list of those who wrote for *The Youth's Companion* is imposing—Tennyson, Gladstone, Frederic Farrar, Henry M. Stanley, Barrie, Kipling, H. G. Wells, Sarah Orne Jewett, Longfellow, Phillips Brooks, Mark Twain, Oliver Wendell Holmes, Jack London, and Theodore Roosevelt. Part of *The Youth's Companion*'s popularity was due to the inviting premiums which it offered. They were often of real value, providing excitement and gratification to young readers and helping to make the magazine a welcome weekly visitor.

Bibliography

Altstetter, M. F. "Early American Magazines for Children." *Peabody Journal of Education*, Nashville, Vol. 19 (Nov., 1941), pp. 131–136.

Eakin, Mary K. and Alice Brooks McGuire. "Children's Magazines Yesterday and Today." *Elementary School Journal*, Chicago, Vol. 49 (Jan., 1949), pp. 257–260.

Egoff, Sheila A. *Children's Periodicals of the Nineteenth Century*. London, The Library Assoc., 1951.

Mott, Frank Luther. *A History of American Magazines*. Cambridge, Harvard University Press, 1938. Vol. 3, p. 508.

Howard, Alice B. *Mary Mapes Dodge of St. Nicholas*. New York, Messner, 1943.

11

Poetry for Children in the
Nineteenth Century

Poetry provided for children changes less through the years than other kinds of reading. Much of the poetry read by children in the Victorian Age had come down from an earlier time, and today, though much excellent verse for children has been written since the beginning of the present century, the book of poems that is still the best known to parents and teachers is Stevenson's *A Child's Garden of Verses*, published in 1885.

Persistence of Early Verse

Original Poems for Infant Minds by Jane and Ann Taylor, published in 1804, and its immediate successors, *Rhymes for the Nursery* and *Hymns for Infant Minds*, had long life in the original volumes, a life that was prolonged in anthologies. In the 1840's the Taylors' poems were still much read, as were the verses by Mrs. Turner in her *The Daisy* and *The Cowslip*.

Though hardly poetry perhaps Heinrich Hoffmann's (1809–1894) *Struwwelpeter* should be mentioned. It reached England probably in 1844 in translation under the title *The English Struwwelpeter; or, Pretty Stories and Funny Pictures*. These rhymes about Casper who wouldn't eat his soup and grew thinner like a little bit of thread till on the fifth day he was dead, about Pauline who played with matches and set herself on fire, and other wilful and unfortunate children, shown in brightly colored drawings, were intended as awful warnings in their native Germany but in England and the United States have never been considered as anything but wildly hilarious. William Roscoe's (1753–1831) charming and childlike *The Butterfly's Ball* was published in 1807. Laura E. Richards' heroine used it to soothe a frightened little boy in *Hildegarde's Holiday*, which was published in 1891, so it is evident that Mrs. Richards said or sang it to her own children.

However, the growing respect for children as individuals was extending the field. It brought it about that a considerable amount of real poetry written for adults was included in anthologies prepared for children and, perhaps what was even more important, because of the greater accessibility, in readers. No child was starved for poetry when *The Gradual Reader* and Swan's *Grammar School Reader*, to cite those mentioned by Caroline Hewins in her *A Mid-Century Child and Her Books*, brought him Gray's "Elegy Written in a Country Churchyard," "The Deserted Village," "The Shepherd and the Philosopher," and Wordsworth's "Fidelity." McGuffey's famous readers are noted for the poems of real value they contained.

As for the anthologies, it is somewhat startling to find in *The Home Book of Poetry*, a tiny volume published in the 1860's, no compiler nor authors' names being given, Herrick's "Daffodils" and Scott's "Lament for a Highland Chief," side by side with "I love little pussy, Her coat is so warm" and:

> Where do you come from
> Little drops of rain,
> Pitter patter, pitter patter
> On the window pane?

Yet these nineteenth century compilers were wise, for the value of a collection for children is to suit all tastes and a wide age range.

The nineteenth century had its poets who wrote expressly for children. Two popular authors who composed for the nursery group, though their efforts, to be sure, resulted in verse rather than poetry, were Lady Hawkshaw (1812–1885) in England and Mrs. Eliza Follen (1787–1860) in America. Lady Hawkshaw's *Aunt Effie's Rhymes for Little Children* (1852) and Mrs. Follen's *Little Songs* (1833) were loved by several generations of children and many poems from both volumes appeared in collections. Mrs. Follen showed understanding of little children's tastes and a proper appreciation of the importance of nursery rhymes when she wrote in her preface, "It has been my object . . . to endeavour to catch something of the good-humoured pleasantry, the musical nonsense which make Mother Goose so attractive to all ages." Many of Mrs. Follen's poems—"Little Annie's Garden," "Oh, look at the Moon, She is shining up there, O mother she looks like a lamp in the air," and, "Where is my little basket gone, Said Charley boy one day"— are recalled by the middle-aged and elderly as familiar to them in childhood.

William Howitt (1792–1879) and his wife, Mary Howitt (1799–1888), who translated Andersen (see page 190), wrote verses for somewhat older children that here and there had an authentic note of poetry. "The Fairies of the Caldon-Low" has a charm that not only suited the Victorian child's taste, but has pleased children ever since.

> "And where have you been, my Mary,
> And where have you been from me?"

"I've been to the top of the Caldon-Low,
The midsummer night to see!"

. . . .

"Then take me on your knee, mother,
And listen, mother of mine:
A hundred fairies danced last night,
And the harpers they were nine,"[1]

This ballad form lends itself well to the story, for Mary has seen the fairies not only dancing but going about their chosen work. They have rolled water down the hill to turn the wheel of the anxious miller whose mill race was almost dry. They have wafted clean winds over the field of the blind widow's corn, so that the mildew is blown away and the grain stands strong and green again. They have scattered seed in the weaver's croft, springing up in blue flax blossoms which promise him an abundant crop. Finally a brownie declares:

"I've spun a piece of hempen cloth,
And I want to spin another—
A little sheet for Mary's bed
And an apron for her mother!"

"And with that I could not help but laugh,
And I laughed out loud and free;
And then on top of the Caldon-Low,
There was no one left but me."[2]

As Mary went down the hill she saw the results of the fairies' kindness.

"Mabel on Midsummer Day," included in *Fireside Verses*, though not so good a poem, tells a story fascinating to children. Although the authorship is usually forgotten, Mary Howitt's are the lines known everywhere, " 'Will you walk into my parlor?' said the Spider to the Fly." That William Howitt's "The Wind in a Frolic" was a favorite we can guess by the way its movement and gaiety catch the ear of the modern child when it is read to him.

Fairies and Little Things

William Allingham's (1824–1889) *Rhymes for the Young Folk* was published in 1887 with pictures by Helen Allingham, Kate Greenaway, Caroline Peterson, and Harry Furniss. Allingham is remembered by "Wishing"—

---

[1] J. G. Whittier, editor, *Child Life* (Boston, Houghton Mifflin, 1871), pp. 111–112.
[2] *Ibid.*, p. 114.

> Ring-Ting! I wish I were a Primrose,
> A bright yellow Primrose, blowing in the Spring!
> The stooping bough above me,
> The wandering bee to love me,
> The fern and moss to creep across,
> And the Elm-tree for our King!
> Nay,—stay! I wish I were an Elm-tree . . .[1]

What the mention of Allingham's name immediately suggests, however, is "The Fairies," a poem whose rhythm alone stands for the tempo of dancing feet, "Up the airy mountain, Down the rushy glen," a delightful poem which has been included in many collections of verse for children. In 1870, *In Fairyland* was published, combined with a series of fairy pictures by Richard Doyle. (See page 227.) The book is usually listed under Doyle's name, and the drawings are better known and, justly so, are more admired than the text. Still *In Fairyland* is a charming and ingenious play in verse with fairies and elves for characters, which makes an appeal to the imaginative child.

A children's poet of more substance was William Brighty Rands (1823–1882), who wrote also under the pseudonyms of Henry Holbeach and Matthew Browne. In 1864 his *Lilliput Levee*, illustrated by Millais and others, was published. The title poem tells how matters are reversed so that children and not parents are in authority, an idea that would certainly have startled the Victorian child. It has been reprinted in many anthologies. *Lilliput Levee* also contained "Polly," which Whittier thought worthy to be included in his *Child Life*, and a number of story poems, among them a nonsense tale of "Giant Frodgedobbulum's Fancy." Nonsense verses were becoming a recognized part of children's reading since Lear and Carroll had pointed the way. In 1871 Rands published *Lilliput Lectures*, mostly prose, and *Lilliput Legends* in 1872. All three appeared anonymously, but in 1899 the John Lane Company published an attractive volume called *Lilliput Lyrics* edited by R. Brimley Johnson and illustrated by Charles Robinson. This had W. B. Rands on the title page and contained verses from the three original volumes and also selections from Rands's contributions to magazines. Charles Robinson's highly original and imaginative illustrations are in the true nonsense vein. The freedom and smoothness of Rands's verse is perhaps best shown in his "Wonderful World:"

> Great, wide, beautiful, wonderful World,
> With the wonderful water round you curled,
> And the wonderful grass upon your breast,
> World, you are beautifully dressed.
> . . . . .

[1] Burton Stevenson, editor, *The Home Book of Verse* (New York, Henry Holt, 1915), Vol. I, p. 130.

You friendly Earth, hcw far do you go,
With the wheat-fields that nod and the rivers that flow,
With cities and gardens, and cliffs and isles,
And people upon you for thousands of miles?[1]

The best of George Macdonald's verse for children, with the same unusual qualities of imagination that adorn his prose, appears in various anthologies. An arresting example is "The Wind and the Moon."

Said the Wind to the Moon, "I will blow you out;
    You stare
    In the air
    Like a ghost in a chair,
Always looking what I am about—
I hate to be watched, I'll blow you out."[2]

In America, Lucy Larcom (1824–1893) and Lydia Maria Child (1802–1880) wrote simple, childlike verses which appeared in the magazines for children, and in 1875, Lucy Larcom's *Childhood Songs* was published with illustrations by Winslow Homer, Harry Fenn, and Arthur Lumley. Celia Thaxter (1835–1894) published *Poems for Children* (1884) and *Stories and Poems for Children* in 1895. She wrote chiefly on nature; her best-known poem, "The Sandpiper," is found in many collections.

Goblin Market

In the midst of what was, for the most part, merely pleasant verse for children, Christina Rossetti (1830–1894) provided them with one real, one can even say, one great poem, in *Goblin Market* (1864). Magical in word and thought, this is a poem which brings a truly imaginative experience to the child who reads it. There is an abundance of color and image, of action and feeling, all matched by the subtle variety of the ever-changing verse.

Morning and evening
Maids heard the goblins cry—
"Come buy our orchard fruits,
Come buy, come buy:
Lemons and oranges . . .
Swart-headed mulberries,
Wild, free-born cranberries . . .
Bright fire-like barberries, . . .
Sweet to tongue and sound to eye,
Come buy, come buy."[3]

[1] Stevenson, *Home Book of Verse*, Vol. I, pp. 118–119.
[2] *Ibid.*, p. 125.
[3] Christina Rossetti, *Goblin Market*, illustrated by Arthur Rackham (Philadelphia, J. B. Lippincott, 1933), pp. 9, 34.

The poem strikes not only the fantastic note but the human one in the devotion between the two little girls, Laura and Lizzie. Laura cannot resist the importunate "Come buy, come buy," although the very aspect of the goblins is enough to tell her there is ill fortune in yielding to them. She tastes their wares, she longs for more and more of them, she goes home to pine away because she can get no more of the magic fruit. Lizzie, seeing her sister about to perish, dares to go back to the haunted glen, where the goblins try in vain to get her also to taste of what they bring to market. She stands resistant.

> Though the goblins cuffed and caught her,
> Coaxed and fought her,
> Bullied and besought her,
> Kicked and knocked her,
> Mauled and mocked her . . .

She still remains determined not to give in.

> White and golden Lizzie stood
> Like a lily in a flood,
> Like a rock of blue-veined stone
> Lashed by tides obstreperously,
> Like a beacon left alone
> In a hoary, roaring sea,
> Sending up a golden fire . . .

By resistance to the goblins she wins the power to lift the spell from her sister. The most charming scene of all is that of the sisters, grown to woman's estate, telling their own children of their terrific adventure.

Christina Rossetti wrote also one of the most charming books of poetry for little children, *Sing-Song* (1872). It is in the nursery rhyme form and while some of these little verses are adult in outlook, in most of them the poet has caught the very feeling of young childhood and of the adult who loves and understands it. There is also that appreciation of very small things which some poets and almost all children have in common.

> The city mouse eats bread and cheese;—
> The garden mouse eats what he can;
> We will not grudge him seeds and stalks
> Poor little timid furry man.[1]

Many who are dealing with children today at home or in the school room find that "Who Has Seen the Wind" and "Currants on a Bush" are among the happiest poetry experiences they can give them. *Sing-Song*

---

[1] Rossetti, *Sing-Song* (New York, Macmillan, 1924), p. 29.

was illustrated by Arthur Hughes with drawings of rare charm and tenderness. (See page 228.)

We may be sure that Victorian boys and girls who, according to Amy Cruse, all over England were declaiming, "How Horatius kept the bridge, in the brave days of old," loved not only Macaulay's *Lays of Ancient Rome* but the old ballads as well. William Allingham's *Ballad Book* was published in 1865 with "Fourscore of the best old ballads," as he said in his preface, including "Thomas the Rhymer," "Hynd Horn," "The Wife of Usher's Well," "The Lytell Gest of Robin Hood," and "Tamlane."

Some Collections

When we come to Coventry Patmore's *The Children's Garland from the Best Poets* (1863) and J. G. Whittier's *Child Life* (1871) we find how the new attitude toward children and their reading had progressed. In his preface to the *Garland* Patmore wrote "This volume will, I hope, be found to contain nearly all the genuine poetry in our language fitted to please children . . . Children will not like this volume the less because, though it may contain little or nothing that will not at once give them pleasure and amuse them, it also contains much the full excellence of which it will be long before most of them are able to understand." Blake, Shakespeare, Tennyson, Marlowe, Keats, Matthew Arnold, Coleridge, Browning, Shelley, Byron, Poe, Ben Jonson, Milton, and Wordsworth are among the poets represented in the anthology.

In the preface to his thoughtfully made *Child Life, A Collection of Poems*, John Greenleaf Whittier said that in looking over several volumes of selected verses for children he noticed in nearly all of them much that seemed lacking in literary merit and that it occurred to him that a selection might be made "combining simplicity with a certain degree of literary excellence, without on the one hand descending to silliness, or, on the other rising above the average comprehension of childhood."[1] It is gratifying to find how high Whittier rated the comprehension of childhood and that he did not hesitate to include James Russell Lowell's "The Changeling" and his "The First Snow-fall," Bryant's "Robert of Lincoln," Tennyson's "The Brook," Elizabeth Barrett Browning's "Romance of the Swan's Nest," Hood's "I remember, I remember," and Southey's "Battle of Blenheim," along with such favorites for the youngest as Olive Wadsworth's "Over in the Meadow" and "Dame Duck's First Lecture on Education" from *Aunt Effie's Rhymes*. Here are such much-loved poems as "Lady Moon, Lady Moon, Where are you roving?" and George Macdonald's "Little White Lily." The opening poem is Macdonald's "The Baby," which begins: "Where

---

[1] Whittier, ed., *Child Life*, p. vii.

did you come from, baby dear?" Here we find Jean Ingelow's "Seven Times One." Nonsense is here too, represented by Lear's "The Owl and the Pussy-Cat," illustrated with a truly magnificent woodcut for which the artist's name is not given. All in all, the child who possessed Whittier's *Child Life, A Collection of Poems* and in addition his *Child Life in Prose*, started on his way with a foundation of real literature.

The Child in His Own Garden

A golden gift which the 1880's brought to children was from the hand of Robert Louis Stevenson (1850–1894). Graham Balfour says that Stevenson was first prompted to try his hand at verse for small readers and listeners by Kate Greenaway's *Birthday Book for Children*, saying, "These are rather nice rhymes, and I don't think they would be very difficult to do." The result was *A Child's Garden of Verses* which, in somewhat abbreviated form, was privately printed and published originally as *Penny Whistles* (1883). Here was poetry that children read or heard or repeated for pleasure, because it told of the things that were nearest them, it appealed to their instinctive taste, the poet realizing that the unspoiled child was himself poetic. That children at once and for all time took this book to their hearts is a proof of the understanding of this great children's poet.

If we look into the matter more deeply, if we ask why adults also get so much from it, we see that the power of this collection of simple verses lies in the fact that it offers, not a glimpse, but the whole contour of the child's hidden world. It shows the life that a child lives within himself and takes so completely for granted that he seldom speaks of it, usually because he cannot. In later days he recollects brief moments of sharp impression, he responds gratefully to anything which reminds him of that which he had forgotten. Stevenson has here recaptured not only a part, but the whole of that hidden life, and has set those recollections forth in just the terms that children would use, could they put them into words at all. Here are the quaint conceits and errors, the imaginative interpretation of that region which is beyond their experience, all the unquestioning philosophy that has to do with home and parents and "being good." Not only the interesting and, when one is once reminded of them, the entirely familiar recollections are here: "In winter I get up at night," "My bed is like a little boat," "I have a little shadow that goes in and out with me." There is also that deeper experience which reaches into the invented world of adventure which every child must have.

> At evening, when the lamp is lit,
> Around the fire my parents sit;
> · · · ·

Now, with my little gun, I crawl
All in the dark along the wall,
And follow round the forest track
Away behind the sofa back.

. . . .

These are the hills, these are the woods,
These are my starry solitudes;
And there the river by whose brink
The roaring lions come to drink.[1]

Or we have the world of wonder about him:

The lights from the parlour and kitchen shone out
Through the blinds and the windows and bars;
And high overhead and all moving about,
There were thousands of millions of stars.

. . . .

The Dog, and the Plough, and the Hunter, and all,
And the star of the sailor, and Mars,
These shone in the sky, and the pail by the wall,
Would be half full of water and stars.[2]

A child's imaginings not only explore the whole of his experience and beyond, they are creative also; wherever there is a need, imagination can fill it.

When children are playing alone on the green,
In comes the playmate that never was seen.
When children are happy and lonely and good
The Friend of the Children comes out of the wood.

. . . .

Nobody heard him and nobody saw,
His is a picture you never could draw,
But he's sure to be present, abroad or at home,
When children are happy and playing alone.[3]

Last of all, to make the round complete, there is the child's simplified version of the knowledge that there is full partnership between duty and happiness.

I woke before the morning, I was happy all the day,
I never said an ugly word, but smiled and stuck to play.

[1] Robert Louis Stevenson, *A Child's Garden of Verses* (New York, Scribner, 1898), p. 93.
[2] *Ibid.*, p. 38.
[3] *Ibid.*, p. 81.

And now at last the sun is going down behind the wood,
And I am very happy, for I know that I've been good.[1]

That which so many other children's poets have tried to reach and rediscover, Stevenson has brought together in its entirety and has presented us with his small but perfect nosegay gathered in the child's own garden.

[1] Stevenson, *A Child's Garden of Verses*, p. 36.

Part Three

1890 - 1920

A Rightful Heritage

ELIZABETH NESBITT

A New Era

"But everything must have a beginning," wrote Howard Pyle (1853–1911), and added, "I often think that my beginning must have begun in a very bright and happy childhood."[1] His biography and his own reminiscences clearly indicate the truth of his statement. For one of his temperament, abilities, and innate interests, the environment and conditions under which he grew up were enviable, not to say ideal.

It is notable that the word used most often in comment upon him is American. It is used not so much as a designation of race; rather it is a descriptive word used to define the unique and diversified quality of his art, whether in literature or in illustration. There may be significance in the fact that Pyle, born on March 5, 1853, grew to manhood in the quarter century preceding the centennial celebrating America's first hundred years of independence. Emerging from its early struggles to establish itself as a nation, from the internal strife of the Civil War, this country was developing into an entity during these years, proud of its history, confident of its future, with faith in its ability to create its own institutions and its own culture. His childhood was spent in Wilmington, Delaware, a city with a sense of history, rich in traditions, advanced in intellectual and cultural movements in which his father and his mother took leading parts.

To read of his childhood is to wish that every child, especially every gifted child, might have so serene, secure, and rich an environment. His relationship with his mother was a particularly happy and sympathetic one. She was a woman of wide interests, with a quick responsiveness to the true and the beautiful, and a deep spiritual sense. Constantly she introduced to her children that which appealed to her in literature and in art. Always quick to sense and participate in mood and emotion, always sensitive to beauty and drama, always alert to the inner meaning and significance of a thing read or seen, Pyle absorbed, under his mother's guidance, all the best that was available in literature and in

[1] Howard Pyle, "When I Was a Little Boy," *Woman's Home Companion*, Vol. 39 (April, 1912), p. 5.

art. In particular, she gave to him not only a knowledge of the material of great folk literature, but also a keen perception of the spirit of folklore.

Throughout his childhood, he showed an intense desire to create through writing and drawing. In this, too, his mother stimulated and encouraged him.

It was almost inevitable that Pyle should decide upon a career in the arts and reject the idea of college. For three years he studied under Mr. Van der Weilen, who conducted a small art school in Philadelphia. From this excellent and demanding teacher, Pyle received a foundation of technique which constituted the only formal instruction he ever had.

During the early seventies, William Pyle's leather business was in financial difficulties, and much of Howard Pyle's time was spent in working with his father. His earlier ambitions toward a career in the arts were to some extent forgotten. Nevertheless, the urge toward writing and drawing showed itself in numerous ballads and short stories which he illustrated.

Then, in the spring of 1876, came a fortunate occurrence. Pyle visited Chincoteague, an island lying off the coast of Virginia. His quick interest was caught by the atmosphere of the island, by the catching and branding of the wild ponies, and by the men who did this work. When he returned to Wilmington he wrote an essay about the island, and drew sketches to accompany it. Margaret Pyle, his mother, perceiving the quality of the writing and drawing, prevailed upon him to send the essay to *Scribner's Monthly*. Not only was it accepted, but *Scribner's* wrote, urging that Pyle come to New York, to develop his talents by drawing and writing for magazines.

So began his three years in New York, where he formed friendships with other artists, among them Chase, Abbey, Homer, Shirlaw, Beckwith, and Frost. His plans, thought, and work during this period are most vividly portrayed in letters to his mother. These reveal a confidence in his ability to write in spite of the fact that his mother and others urged him to pursue illustrating as his special field, and in spite of occasional frustration which he himself felt. Like many who struggle with words, the feet of his ideas seemed clogged with the difficulties of expression.

> I can't open the flood gates of my mind and pour out my thoughts onto the paper. The sentences will not "round up" so as to contain the thought in the shell of a few distinctly expressed words. I have to strike again and again with simile and hyperbole before I can crack that invisible, intangible wall that separates my internal thought from the perception of others.[1]

[1] Charles D. Abbott, *Howard Pyle; A Chronicle* (New York, Harper, 1925), p. 32.

Nevertheless, he persisted in his writing, and came to feel more and more that his chief forte lay in writing for children. His memories of his own childhood seem to have been extraordinarily vivid, memories not so much of incidents and events as of impressions, the effect upon him of scenes and moods, of books and pictures. At first, his writing and drawing for children consisted chiefly of short illustrated fables, published largely in *St. Nicholas Magazine*. The fable was undoubtedly for him a natural form of literature by means of which to express his ideas. He retained in his adult life the instinctive, unaffected, childlike but not childish, response to the symbolism of folk literature, to folkways of thought and expression, to the habit of personification, to the humor and wisdom of folklore in any form.

Much of his reading, while in New York, was in old sources of folk-tales. In a letter written November 26, 1876, he speaks of reading Thorp's *Northern Mythology*:

> . . . a dry and prosy collection of medieval legends, many of which I have selected to make note of, and I shall try whether I can infuse a little fairy-tale juiciness into them. It is a rich mine to select from, though a dull book to read.[1]

He outlines the plots of three of the stories, pointing with discernment to incidents and qualities which could be elaborated. And "*what* illustrations they would make!" he says. "I think I see myself turned loose in a boundless wilderness of quaint dwarfs, ugly trolls, ridiculous kaboutermannekens, and lively elves, with here and there a spicy smack of the awful in the shape of a hobgoblin or two."[2] In April 1877, *St. Nicholas* published a story called "Hans Gottenlieb, the Fiddler," clearly based on one of the legends from Thorp's book, one which Pyle had outlined in his letter written to his mother. It may well be that, in his omnivorous reading, he came across the *Gesta Romanorum*, since four stories in *Twilight Land*—"The Fruit of Happiness," "The Talisman of Solomon," "Much Shall Have More and Little Shall Have Less," and "The Salt of Life"—resemble stories in the *Gesta* either in incident or basic idea. "The Salt of Life" uses the well-known motif of Catskin, an English Cinderella variant, and of other folk tales the world over, and borrowed by Shakespeare in *King Lear*.

For many years he continued to write fairy tales, all of them animated by the richness of his knowledge and appreciation of the spirit of the genuine folk tale. His development in this field of writing is curiously like that of Andersen. At first, his stories were retellings, elaborated and enhanced, of old tales. Gradually he put more and more

[1] *Ibid.*, p. 93.
[2] *Ibid.*, p. 96.

of himself into the stories, adding original details and ideas, until only the skeleton of the source remained. Finally, he created his own stories, so like the folk tale in characters, expression, and spirit, that only Pyle's unique touches of style distinguish his work from a genuine folk tale.

In 1883 he proposed to *Harper's Young People* that he write several humorous verses, printing them by hand and decorating them with pen and ink sketches. These were to be published in *Young People* and later collected in a children's gift book. Before these were so collected, it was decided that an equal number of fairy tales should be combined with the verses and that the book should be called *Pepper and Salt; or, Seasoning for Young Folk*. The book was published in 1886, the first of Pyle's collections of fairy tales, to be followed by *The Wonder Clock* in 1888 and *Twilight Land* and *The Garden Behind the Moon* in 1895.

The prefaces and introductions to these books clearly reveal the zest and joy Pyle found in the writing of them. In *Pepper and Salt* he writes, "If I can only make you laugh and be merry for a little while, then my work will be well done, and I will be glad in the doing of it." In the preface to *The Wonder Clock*, he speaks of the "queer forgotten things" laid away in Time's attic. In the introduction to *Twilight Land* he reveals his deep knowledge of the sources of the folk literature of many countries. It is not surprising that he should know the *Arabian Nights* and Grimm, and English and Scandinavian folk tales, for these he mentions in his reminiscences of his childhood reading. But it is interesting that he should mention the *Bidpai*, and intriguing to find here also a mention of *The Blacksmith Who Made Death Sit in His Apple-Tree*, which must be a parallel of one of the more beautiful of the Russian skazki, *The Soldier and the Demons*, the general theme of which is also used in the play *Death Takes a Holiday*.

The stories in *Pepper and Salt* and *The Wonder Clock* show how complete was Pyle's mastery of the form and structure of the folk tale, which has often been called the most perfect short story form. From his beginnings, with their succinct setting forth of setting, situation, and character, through the closely motivated incidents which form the plot, to the complete and satisfactory conclusion, he re-creates a form of literature which, through years of oral telling, reduced and refined a story to a compact and close-knit entity. The fact that his stories are so extraordinarily tellable bears witness to this point. Structure and form, however, may be cold qualities unless enlivened with power of imagination and of style. Pyle's feeling for the folk tale went far beyond his grasp of its structural pattern. He had instinctive appreciation of the fundamental and significant meaning of folk literature and of the flavor of expression of a folk people, and these things he could re-express in his own way, an inimitable way. The words that come immediately to mind when thinking of his style are sincerity, enthusiasm, vigor, joy-ousness, picturesqueness of phrase and metaphor. Since it is just these qualities that make the greatest appeal to children, it is not surprising that six times as many copies of *The Wonder Clock* were sold in 1919 as in the first year of its publication.

The appeal of the stories in these two books is inexpressibly enhanced by the appeal of the illustrations, which form a perfect complement to the stories. It is almost impossible to do justice to them. They exhibit the same superb sense of form, the same fitting selection of detail, the same power of imagination, the same simplicity and strength and convincingness, the same humor and action, as do the stories. They are storied pictures, defying analysis, so completely do they fulfill Pyle's own theories that illustration should first of all tell a story and tell some phase of it better than written words do and that illustration is not merely decoration, but objectification of thought and feeling.

The general consensus of opinion seems to be that *Twilight Land* compares unfavorably with the first two collections of fairy tales. Such a comparison seems invalid, to some degree. The stories are of a different order than those in the first two books, several of them seeming to derive from Eastern sources. They are more mature, possibly less child-like in their appeal, and more subtle in their points and meaning. They may seem to be less compact in their structure, lacking in the zestful spirit and the rich quality of incident and phrase which distinguish the earlier stories. Pyle's biographer, Charles Abbott, says that Laurence Hutton claimed that one of the stories, "The Talisman of Solomon," was one of the best Pyle ever wrote but "this could hardly be said for the rest of book," which Abbott thinks lacks the inspiration of the two preceding volumes. This may well be, and yet, if *Twilight Land* were to stand alone as Pyle's sole contribution to fairy tale literature, it would still mark him as a master of the form.

The Garden Behind the Moon is distinguished from the other three books in that it is a long allegorical fairy tale in the tradition of George Macdonald and others of the great writers of fantasy in England in the latter half of the nineteenth century. It is an interesting example of Pyle's work, since it is the product of his own creative imagination, less derivative than his short stories. Its writing makes Howard Pyle the peer of the classic writers in the field of fantasy. Here he exhibits to the fullest extent his power to convince, his ability to select and stress telling detail, and above all, his gift for word pictures, a gift already demonstrated in *The Merry Adventures of Robin Hood* and which was to prove a most beautiful quality in the King Arthur stories. The vivid-ness of the following passages is due to the fine combination of appeal to sight and hearing, and to Pyle's clean-cut power of visualization.

On one side was the ocean, on the other side rose beetling cliffs that towered high, high into the air, the summit swimming dizzily against the blue sky and the floating clouds. High aloft against the face of the cliffs flicked and fluttered the white wings of the sea-gulls, and their clamor sounded incessantly through the ceaseless thunder and crash of the breakers.[1]

It was a queer, quaint little village in which little David lived . . . It had steep roofs, one climbing up over the other as though to peep over one another's shoulders at the water below. Nearly at the top of the cliff was a church with a white steeple, and beyond that was an open common, where there was grass, and where the geese and the cows fed, and where the boys and the girls played of an evening.[2]

During the years when he was writing his fairy tales, he had become interested in the possibilities in the retelling of medieval legend and tradition. As a boy, he had been thoroughly acquainted with the Robin Hood ballads in the collections of Bishop Percy and Ritson, and with the Arthurian legend in Malory's *Morte d'Arthur*. His response to the pageantry and drama of history, his sympathy with traditional literature, his strong spiritual and mystical temperament, caused him to be completely at home in the tradition of the Middle Ages.

In 1883, *The Merry Adventures of Robin Hood*, discussed in an earlier chapter, had been published. Here it is necessary only to re-emphasize that, in the opinion of many, this is Pyle's best and finest work. In design and illustration, in story quality and style, in spirit and interpretation, Pyle's is the most perfect re-creation of the ever appealing Robin Hood material.

After the success of *Robin Hood*, it was almost inevitable that the idea should come, to Pyle and others, of retelling the King Arthur stories. On March 3, 1902, he wrote to Scribner's:

It has been suggested to me that I write a book somewhat matching the *Robin Hood* but giving the adventures of King Arthur and his Knights. The suggestion has been lying in my mind for some time and the more I think over it the more feasible the project seems to me to be. It should, I think, be written in the same direct and homely English of the *Robin Hood* but with a more mature and poetic finish. As the *Robin Hood* was my first work I should, probably, make this the last of its kind . . .[3]

---

[1] Howard Pyle, *The Garden Behind the Moon* (New York, Scribner, 1895), pp. 112–113.

[2] *Ibid.*, p. 11.

[3] Abbott, *op. cit.*, p. 127.

Although Scribner's had other Arthur books on their list, they approved the idea, saying rightly that they could "easily imagine that Howard Pyle might give a distinction both of form and of substance to the Arthur legend which would detach it decidedly from all other books dealing with the same subject."[1]

The original plan was to have three volumes, but the material was so tremendous that it was decided that there should be four volumes. The task was colossal. It is almost incredible that the man who did so much else in writing, illustrating, and teaching could have mastered the entirety of Arthurian literature as Pyle did. When one considers the length of time over which Arthurian legend grew, the contributions to it of various periods, races, and individuals, it is hard to believe that Pyle performed his task of research, writing, and illustrating in seven years. *The Story of King Arthur and His Knights* appeared in 1903, *The Story of the Champions of the Round Table* in 1905, *The Story of Sir Launcelot and His Companions* in 1907, and *The Story of the Grail and the Passing of Arthur* in 1910. In these four volumes the many cycles of Arthurian romance are brought together and individual romances interwoven with them.

A few contemporary reviews of these books are somewhat critical, deploring the loss of Malory's spirit and ruggedness and accusing Pyle of diffuseness. In judging the validity of these comments, it is to be remembered that only a few writers had preceded Pyle in the retelling of classics for children and that the general public was not accustomed to the reshaping of such material to the immaturity, the interests, and the viewpoint of children, without loss of the essential significance and spirit of the original. What Pyle saw and enhanced in the literature of chivalry are the qualities which attract children to that literature— its high idealism, its consecration to a cause, its devotion to duty, its adherence to honor and loyalty, its adventure of spirit and body. As Nathaniel Hawthorne presented his point of view and his defense in his Preface to *A Wonder-Book and Tanglewood Tales*, so Pyle describes his purpose and method in a letter written to Edith Dean Weir:

> I have had great trouble in treating the character of Sir Gawaine to fit it to the purposes which I have in view. I wish to represent in my book all that is noble and high and great, and to omit, if it is possible, all that is cruel and mean and treacherous. Unfortunately the stories of chivalry seem to be very full not only of meanness and of treachery, but of murder and many other and nameless wickednesses that discolor the very noblest of the characters—such, even, as the character of King Arthur himself. In the more generally accepted histories, the characters of Sir Gawaine

[1] Abbott, *op. cit.*, p. 127.

and his brothers do not seem, unfortunately, to be worthy of the high tribute which you pay to the chief hero of the group. I must follow the thread of the better-known legends, for it is not advisable for me to draw upon the less well-known narratives. So I try to represent those which are known in the best possible light. Accordingly, I try to represent Gawaine as proud and passionate, quick to anger, but with a broad basis of generosity and nobility as an underlying stratum of his nature.[1]

How well he succeeded in fulfilling his ideas of the character of Sir Gawaine is manifested in the charming and whimsical story of the "Marriage of Sir Gawaine," which comprises the last two chapters of *The Story of King Arthur and His Knights*.

Pyle's comprehension of the spirit of magic and enchantment, of the haunting sense of the mystery of life and of the inevitability of fate, of the romance and spiritual and physical adventure of the medieval legend was as complete as his grasp of the spirit of the folk tale. The supernaturalism of the Middle Ages was quite a different thing from that of the folk and fairy tale, a more subtle and complex thing. The conception of good as beautiful and evil as ugly changed to a realization that evil may masquerade under the guise of extraordinary loveliness. So Pyle writes of Vivien:

> Now, there was at the Court of Queen Morgana le Fay, a certain damsel of such marvellous and bewitching beauty that her like was hardly to be seen in all the world. This damsel was fifteen years old and of royal blood, being the daughter of the King of Northumberland; and her name was Vivien. This damsel, Vivien, was both wise and cunning beyond all measure for one so young. Moreover, she was without any heart, being cold and cruel to all who were contrary-minded to her wishes.[2]

There is something almost Celtic in his inherent response to the mystery of human destiny, to the significance of nature in the life of man, to the spiritual quality of these stories; and at the same time he is akin to the youthfulness, the delight in living, the exuberance of spring, the love of adventure for its own sake, the joy in a story for the sake of story—qualities that are equally innate in the material with which he was dealing.

It is academic criticism to complain of his diffuseness of style, and to say that the spirit of Malory has been lost. It is true that a comparison of Pyle with Malory is apt to leave an immediate impression that

---

[1] Abbott, *op. cit.*, p. 128.
[2] Howard Pyle, *The Story of King Arthur and His Knights* (New York, Scribner, 1903), p. 164.

Pyle is verbose and lacking in the strength frequently imparted by succinct statement and understatement. The stateliness and lovely formality of his prose, the rhythmical cadence of the long, flowing sentence structure, the music of the word sounds, have an interpretative power achieved by no other reteller of the Arthurian stories for children. All the pageantry of the Middle Ages—the ritual and color, the symbolism and imagery—are carried over to the reader. Pyle has the gift of creating mood through description of place and the Celtic habit of "magicalizing nature," as Matthew Arnold phrases it. His descriptions are integrated with the mood and action of the story, setting the keynote for what is to come, never extraneous.

And this was a very wonderful land, for, lo! all the air appeared as it were to be as of gold—so bright was it and so singularly radiant. And here and there upon that plain were sundry trees all in blossom; and the fragrance of the blossoms was so sweet that the King had never smelt any fragrance like to it. And in the branches of those trees were a multitude of birds of many colors, and the melody of their singing ravished the heart of the hearer. And midway in the plain was a lake of water as bright as silver, and all around the borders of the lake were incredible numbers of lilies and of daffodils. Yet, although this place was so exceedingly fair, there was, nevertheless, nowhere about it a single sign of life of any sort, but it appeared altogether as lonely as the hollow sky upon a day of summer. So, because of all the marvellous beauty of this place, and because of its strangeness and its entire solitude, King Arthur perceived that he must have come into a land of powerful enchantment where, happily, dwelt a fairy of very exalted quality. . . .[1]

So often in Pyle's word pictures, the scene created by his keen artist's eye for detail and color and contrast has a vividness and reality which is almost startling, and yet the component parts of the picture are so exquisitely simple and so fundamentally familiar.

Now toward the slanting of the day he drew nigh to that place, and lo! he beheld before him a large and considerable town of many comely houses with red walls and shining windows. And the houses of the town sat all upon a high, steep hill, the one overlooking the other, and the town itself was encompassed around about by a great wall, high and strong . . . Now, at that time of day the sky behind the tower was all, as it were, an entire flame of fire, so that the towers and the battlements of the castle and the roofs and the chimneys thereof stood altogether black against the brightness

---

[1] Pyle, *op. cit.*, pp. 67–68.

of the light. And, behold! great flocks of pigeons encircled the towers of the castle in a continual flight against that fiery sky.[1]

It is no wonder then, that over the years the four volumes of Arthurian legend should have made their appeal to children in the idealistic, romantic, chivalry-loving stage of reading interest. And this appeal is immeasurably heightened by Pyle's illustrations. These carry to a high degree the simplicity, strength, vigor, and beauty characteristic of all his illustrative work. Done in pen and ink, they are magnificent in their representation of the outward semblance and inner spirit of the Middle Ages and its institution of chivalry. Particularly notable is his power of portraiture. The pictures of Merlin and Vivien are superb in the deep meaning of their character portrayal.

No period of history has produced better books of the realistic historic type of fiction than have the Middle Ages. Among these, Howard Pyle's *Otto of the Silver Hand* (1888) and *Men of Iron* (1892) have always taken high place. The first of these, a story of medieval Germany and the robber barons, is a study in contrasts, as were the Middle Ages themselves—contrasts in gentleness and savagery, in ways of war and ways of peace, in love and in hate, in action and in meditation, in the lust for material gain and the search for spiritual truth, in the pathos of helplessness and the self-assertion of brute strength. As always, Pyle's foreword sets the keynote for the essence of the story, one which is replete with the eternal drama of human life, sin and atonement, and the ultimate power of good to conquer evil. Hjalmar Boyesen wrote of it to Pyle, "There is a note in your book—strong, wholesome and sympathetic—far removed from sentimentality—but vibrating with true sentiment—in short it is a lovely book."[2] So poignant and so permanently true are the meaning and spirit of the book that even an age that is overly afraid of sentiment and has lost the distinction between sentiment and sentimentality cannot call it sentimental. It is too actual and too convincing, thoroughly authenticated by Pyle's tremendous and infinitely detailed knowledge of the period, never weighty or obtrusive, but always present, a firm foundation for incident and character. Nowhere is Pyle's wealth of background demonstrated more clearly than in the illustrations which all critics have compared with Dürer's work. Joseph Pennell, in his *Pen Drawing and Pen Draughtsmen*, writes:

> In his *Otto of the Silver Hand* . . . there are compositions which are almost entirely suggested by Dürer. But who has not made use of the suggestions of other men? . . . There is probably no draughtsman as successful as Howard Pyle in working in the manner of the

[1] Pyle, *op. cit.*, p. 83.
[2] Abbott, *op. cit.*, p. 117.

sixteenth-century artists, always, however, adding something of his own.[1]

To the child, however, and to most readers, the charm of the illustrations lies in the completely satisfactory rightness of the detail, in the story quality, and in the exact harmony between picture and text.

Men of Iron is laid in England in the fifteenth century during the reign of Henry IV. This is a story of vigorous adventure, unified by the central character of Myles Falworth and motivated by Myles's steady intention to redeem the loss of position and estate suffered by his father as a supporter of Richard II. It is a book to make glad the heart of any active boy, full of action, of tournaments, and of feats of skill and strength. It demonstrates to the fullest Pyle's ability to draw character, to center a plot on the viewpoint of a central figure, and to maintain continuing interest in the destiny of that character. Less delicate and subtle in its handling than much of Pyle's other work, it demonstrates his versatility and adaptability, possessing qualities in tune with plot, situation, and character, physical qualities of virility, vigor, and swift action, and moral qualities of honor and integrity. The illustrations are in keeping, done in black-and-white oil reproduced by photographic process.

Always appealed to by the romantic, Pyle had a deep interest in the history of buccaneers and pirates. It is said of him that he was never happier than when he found some forgotten account of a notorious pirate and could spend time poring over it. The summers spent after his marriage in the seaside town of Rehoboth, Delaware, did much to strengthen this interest. Legend says that the sand dunes to the north of the town were the hiding places of the illegal loot of many a rover of the seas. Pyle began to collect books on the subject of piracy and became, apparently, as much of an authority on this subject as on folk literature and medievalism. His enthusiasm and interest led to the writing of several articles and stories illustrated with remarkable pictures, and to the illustration of articles by others. One of these Frederic Remington coveted. "Too good—too good," he wrote Pyle, "the pirate captain dead on the sand. If I get that I will worship you, it, and once more take stock in humanity. As for what you will get—anything I have." And later, after receiving the picture, "I have the defunct pirate and it goes right up in my collection. It is simply all-fired satisfying. . . ."[2]

When he turned to colonial life in America for material for a boys' book, *The Story of Jack Ballister's Fortunes* (1895), Blackbeard was one of the central characters. The subtitle reveals how completely in the tradition of romantic adventure this book is—"Being the narrative

---

[1] Abbott, *op. cit.*, p. 118.
[2] *Ibid.*, p. 145.

of the adventures of a young gentleman of good family, who was kidnapped in the year 1719 and carried to the plantations of the continent of Virginia, where he fell in with that famous pirate Captain Edward Teach, or Blackbeard; of his escape from the pirates and the rescue of a young lady from out of their hands." Published first in *St. Nicholas*, and in 1895 in book form, it is, as one of the editors of *St. Nicholas* said, "a noble story and an admirable picture of the time with which it deals." Certainly he shows here that amazing command of the most minute details of American history which caused his students to reminisce enthusiastically and nostalgically about his informal talks that brought vividly alive scenes of the past.

An attempt has been made to stress the quality of Pyle's illustrations; surely they are "excellent in beauty." Much more could be said as to his influence on illustration through the example of his own work and through the fineness of his teaching. If he had written nothing, he would still be famed for the impetus he gave to book and magazine illustration. For years he exemplified in his incredible amount of work such sincerity, authenticity, technical skill, creative imagination, and dramatic power that many later illustrators echo Robert Lawson:

> His spirit shines in much of the best illustration of to-day . . . No illustrator worthy of the name can look on the work of Howard Pyle and then do careless or insincere work himself without feeling a sense of personal reproach, a sense of shame that he has failed this good and honest master. His presence is in every decent studio; inspiring, encouraging, helpful, corrective or justly wrathful.
>
> And in the minds and hearts of innumerable others there are still dreams and visions of color and romance, glimpses of another world of beauty and chivalry, planted there long ago by the incomparable work of this simple, sincere craftsman.[1]

The many similar tributes paid to him by those he taught at the Drexel School of Arts and Sciences, in his summer classes at Chadds Ford, Pennsylvania, and in his own school in Wilmington, are moving in their admiration of him as artist, teacher, and man.

Whether Pyle's first distinction lay in the field of writing or in the field of illustration may always be an arguable question, but there can be no doubt as to the rightness of the title so often given him, the first great American illustrator. There were others of his own period whose work was notable—Remington, Abbey, and certainly A. B. Frost; but among them all, Pyle is supreme. More than any other, through example and precept, he raised the art of American illustration to a high peak

[1] Robert Lawson, "Howard Pyle and His Times." In Mahony, Latimer, and Folmsbee, *Illustrators of Children's Books: 1744–1945* (Boston, The Horn Book, 1947), pp. 105–106.

from which it was never again to sink into the stagnation of inanity, mediocrity, and imitativeness which had made it lifeless before his time.

The period in which Howard Pyle did his work frequently has been spoken of as that Golden Age in children's literature that was to last for the decade to follow. It is difficult to do justice to his contribution to the shining quality of that era. The magnitude and diversity of his work eludes definition. Creative artist and born story-teller, each aspect of his two-fold genius enriched and interpreted the other. Lover of romance, he was able to discipline himself to the demands of realism and to infuse his realism with significance. Reteller unexcelled of classic traditional material, he could create wonder stories of his own, unique in their originality of conception and execution. Student and man of integrity, he established standards of workmanship which constitute a permanent measuring stick.

It was well said of him after his death in Florence in 1911, "We shall not see his like again." Still, he himself wrote his own best epitaph.

My ambition in days gone by was to write a really notable adult book, but now I am glad that I have made literary friends of the children rather than the older folk. In one's mature years, one forgets the books that one reads, but the stories of childhood leave an indelible impression, and their author always has a niche in the temple of memory from which the image is never cast out to be thrown into the rubbish-heap of things that are outgrown and outlived.[1]

[1] Abbott, *op. cit.*, p. 131.

Bibliography

Abbott, Charles D. *Howard Pyle; A Chronicle.* New York, Harper, 1925.
Lawson, Robert. "Howard Pyle and His Times." In Mahony, Bertha E., Louise P. Latimer, and Beulah Folmsbee, comps. *Illustrators of Children's Books: 1744–1945.* Boston, The Horn Book, 1947. Pp. 105–122.
Mahony, Bertha E., Louise P. Latimer, and Beulah Folmsbee, comps. *Illustrators of Children's Books: 1744–1945.* Boston, The Horn Book, 1947.
Moore, Anne Carroll. *Cross-Roads to Childhood.* New York, Doran, 1926.
——— *New Roads to Childhood.* New York, Doran, 1923.
——— *Roads to Childhood.* New York, Doran, 1920.
——— *The Three Owls; a Book About Children's Books.* New York, Macmillan, 1925.
——— *The Three Owls, Second Book; Contemporary Criticism of Children's Books.* New York, Coward-McCann, 1928.
——— *The Three Owls, Third Book; Contemporary Criticism of Children's Books, 1927–1930.* New York, Coward-McCann, 1931.
Pyle, Howard. "When I Was a Little Boy." *Woman's Home Companion*, Vol. 39 (April, 1912), p. 5.

· 2 ·

A Rightful Heritage

Surely no type of literature has suffered such persecution as have the folk and fairy tale, nor has any other shown such indomitable and irrepressible vitality. Considered worldly and immoral in the Puritan period, impractical and frivolous in the didactic age, it has lived from generation to generation in the memories of the common people. The chapbooks had given it the security of print. Charles Perrault had introduced it to its true realm, the field of children's literature. The early collectors, the Grimms in Germany and Asbjörnsen and Moe in the Scandinavian countries, had established its respectability as a literature worthy of an adult's time and study, and had been followed by others who preserved the wealth of folk literature existent in many different countries. At times of its greatest disrepute, there were rebels against prevailing doctrine who had spoken on its behalf. William Godwin had expressed himself as to the value of imaginative literature for children. Charles Lamb expended some of his choicest invective in defense of the fairy tale. He wrote to Coleridge after trying in vain to buy some fairy tales for the Coleridge children:

> Mrs. Barbauld's stuff has banished all the old classics of the nursery. . . . Mrs. Barbauld's and Mrs. Trimmer's nonsense lay in piles about. Knowledge, insignificant and vapid as Mrs. Barbauld's books convey, it seems must come to a child in the shape of knowledge; and his empty noddle must be turned with conceit of his own powers when he has learnt that a horse is an animal, and Billy is better than a horse, and such like instead of *that beautiful interest in wild tales*, which made the child a man, while all the time he suspected himself to be no bigger than a child.[1]

And again in a more wistful vein:

> We crush the faculty of delight and wonder in children, by explaining every thing. We take them to the source of the Nile,

[1] Florence V. Barry, *A Century of Children's Books* (New York, Doran, n.d.), p. 152.

and shew them the scanty runnings, instead of letting the beginnings of that seven fold stream remain in impenetrable darkness, a mysterious question of wonderment and delight to ages.[1]

But for the most part, these were voices crying in vain against the "creeping paralysis of seriousness." It was not until the latter half of the nineteenth century that children received romance in the form of folk literature expressly selected and adapted for them. Though there had been earlier collections of folk literature, these were not compiled with children in mind. Even in the nineties, the uneasy distrust of fairy tales was not completely gone. For that matter, it was never to vanish completely. Agnes Repplier in an essay called "Battle of the Babies" records a "warfare the echoes of which have hardly yet died sullenly away upon either side of the Atlantic." An American periodical devoted to the training of parents attacked the ancient nursery classics on the score of cruelty, helpless suffering, and implausibility. On the other side of the Atlantic, Andrew Lang rushed to the defense. Miss Repplier's essay is worth a reference, since its author makes therein a statement so incontrovertible as to be a final answer to all those, in many periods, who have inveighed against the use of fairy tales with children.

> That which is vital in literature or tradition, which has survived the obscurity and wreckage of the past, whether as legend, or ballad, or mere nursery rhyme, has survived in right of some intrinsic merit of its own, and will not be snuffed out of existence by and of our precautionary or hygienic measures.[2]

A changing conception of the child and of children's literature lay back of the recognition of the "intrinsic merit" of the literature of folk peoples the world over. Possibly the change was in part an aftermath of the literary revolution with its spirit of freedom from restriction. Writers of the romantic school had turned to folk tale, mythology, legend, and saga for material, thus bringing the beauty and quality of this literature to the attention of the English-speaking world. Simultaneously there was a lessening of the puritanical and didactic attitude in literature for children, attended, or possibly produced, by a more intelligent understanding of the child as a child rather than a miniature adult, as an individual, and as an individual who changed from year to year. Creative literary criticism was beginning to assert that literature could exist for the purpose of giving pleasure and delight, and there was a consequent lessening of insistence on "useful" knowledge at the expense of imagination and joy. Many of these ideas had come into being

[1] Charles Lamb, "Play-house Memoranda." In A. C. Ward, ed., *Everybody's Lamb* (New York, Harcourt, 1933), p. 302.
[2] Agnes Repplier, "Battle of the Babies," *Essays in Miniature* (Boston, Houghton Mifflin, 1895), p. 204.

in the first fifty years of the nineteenth century. In the last fifty years they became more firmly established, giving impetus to new ideas and forms in children's literature, and producing, among other types, the folk tale, epic, and saga, compiled or retold for the reading pleasure of children.

The selection and retelling of folk tales introduce a peculiar problem as regards criticism and evaluation. The thing to be dealt with is not an original work in the usual sense, but an adaptation of an original literature which, by its very nature, has strong qualities of interest and value for children. The high imagination of the folk tale, its wealth of symbolism, its interpretation of the fundamental experiences of life, its concentration on great moral ideals, rather than moral precepts or admonitions, its sense of wonder, make an immediate appeal to the child's mind. These qualities are put forth in a literary form polished by generations of oral storytelling, which makes stringent demands as to structure and expression. The narrative method is direct and artistically objective, the plot strongly constructed and closely motivated, the themes are vital and universal in their significance.

Plot and theme are of supreme importance. Character portrayal is nonexistent as such, the characters being types of human beings or of animal life or of supernatural creatures. The stories have an inevitability about them which arises from a high selectivity of incident, a stressing of essentials, an avoidance of unnecessary or superfluous explanation. The style meets the final test of literary quality, fitness of form to thought. Whether the story be romantic or realistic, humorous or serious, supernatural or matter of fact, the expression is in tune with the dominant quality of the tale. Always there is varied charm in the telling of these tales, the charm of humor, of poetic yet simple imagery, of rare and exquisite objects, of strange and wonderful events. All these qualities are characteristic of folk tales from every land. In addition, each country creates its own folk characters and reflects in its folk literature its own image, its customs and beliefs, its hopes and ideals, its ways of thought and expression. Even the physical, yet somehow spiritual, aspect of the country itself underlies and individualizes the literature of a single people. It is just these qualities of folk tales in general, of a country's folk literature in particular, which constitute their chief value as literature and their chief appeal to children. It follows that these are the qualities which a selector should represent in his selection, and a reteller retain or re-create in his adaptation. While certain liberties of omission and change are permissible in order to make the story understandable to children or to rid it of possible surface indications of a primitive civilization, its unique qualities of imaginative power, of dramatic structure, of symbolic truth, of fitting expression, should not be blurred or destroyed.

The pioneer compilers and retellers of the folk and fairy tale brought to their work a two-fold respect and knowledge—respect for their material and for children and knowledge of their material and of children's interests. They rightly refused to oversimplify and rightly believed that children should be provided challenge and stimulus to thought and imagination.

There are many adults who respond with vivid and delighted recollection to the mention of the "color" fairy books. Because of their perennial appeal, the children of today are fortunate that these books have been reissued by David McKay in modern editions. The compiler and editor was that same Andrew Lang (1844–1912) who so vigorously defended the fairy tale in that international controversy described by Agnes Repplier. Born in 1844 at Selkirk, Scotland, he was descended from Scottish gypsies, which may account for the elfish quality in the man himself, a quality which fascinated and frustrated his friends and contemporaries. A brilliant and incredibly versatile man, he was poet, critic, essayist, anthropologist, folklorist, and "King's-craftsman of fairy tales." To the confusion and dismay of his colleagues, he preferred fantasy to realism; literature, to him, should bring forgetfulness of trouble and provide the anodyne of dreams. That he should become "the historian of all the elves in all the colours of the spectrum," was quite in accord with his particular genius. As a boy in the "ghost-ridden" country of Scotland, he had been interested in observing the occurrence of tales with similar motifs in widely separated countries. As a man, he read voraciously in the literature of magic and folk peoples. As a folklorist, he successfully promulgated the theory that folklore is not the remains of a higher mythology, but rather the foundation on which mythology rests; that many folk tales have their bases in the events and experiences of human life—in birth and death, in warfare and conquest, and bondage, and in the beliefs, the rituals, and observances accompanying these universal experiences. From this profound background of knowledge, out of his constant search for stories, and for the oldest and best versions, came the "color" fairy books, of which the *Blue Fairy Book*, published in 1889, was the first and possibly always the most popular. It was followed by the *Red*, the *Green*, and the *Yellow*, and for many years, a new color appeared each year. Mr. Lang wisely interpreted "fairy" as the child interprets it, for the books contain not only folk fairy tales, but modern fairy tales as well, such as those of Madame d'Aulnoy and of Andersen. And if this mingling of folk and modern brought down upon the editor the wrath of the learned Folk-Lore Society, as Lang indicates it did in his preface to *The Yellow Fairy Book* (1894), the editor is well able to defend himself, and generations of children have approved his defense. These books represent a harvesting of stories from practically every country in the world, for all ages of children, selected with keen awareness of children's response to the romance and adventure of fairy lore. Some of the stories are taken directly from source collections, others have been translated or adapted by various people, whose help and work are acknowledged in the prefaces to the books. The purist may claim that the sources used are not always the best, that the adaptations vary in quality, and that, as is true, the selection of stories in the later volumes is not always wise. The fact remains that to hundreds of children of the past, present, and future, the "color" fairy books, *The Red Fairy Book* (1890), *The Green Fairy Book* (1892), etc., represent fairyland, and the first and most vivid acquaintance with Aladdin and Dick Whittington, with Cinderella and the Sleeping Beauty, with that roving spirit, the Half-Chick, with the castle that lay east o' the sun and west o' the moon, and with many another character and tale without a knowledge of which no education is complete.

In his preface to *The Yellow Fairy Book*, Andrew Lang gives to one of his colleagues a delightful "commercial." Sharing with Lang the disapproval of the Folk-Lore Society was Joseph Jacobs (1854–1916), who, says Lang, "has published many delightful fairy tales," and in a footnote, "You may buy them from Mr. Nutt, in the Strand." Jacobs and Lang may well have been kindred spirits. They were astonishingly alike in their extraordinary breadth of interests, in the versatility of their written work, and in their absorption with folk literature. Joseph Jacobs, however, introduced a new note in collections of folk tales intended for children. There had been those, like the Grimms, who collected folk tales from the folklorist's point of view. There were those, like Lang, who selected and adapted from source collections stories for children. Jacobs combined both processes. He collected from printed and oral sources, but he intended his collection to be for children, and so he adapted and retold as he transcribed. His theory and method of retelling, which set standards, is best described in his own words taken from the prefaces to the *English Fairy Tales* (1890) and the *Celtic Fairy Tales* (1893).[1]

> In the majority of instances I have had largely to re-write these Fairy Tales, especially those in dialect. . . . Children, and sometimes those of larger growth, will not read dialect. I have also had to reduce the flatulent phraseology of the eighteenth-century chapbooks, and to re-write in simpler style the stories only extant in "Literary" English. I have, however, left a few vulgarisms in the mouths of vulgar people. Children appreciate the dramatic pro-

[1] There are variations in first dates of publication for some of Jacobs' retellings. In every case the dates given in the British Museum Catalog have been used. These books are now published under the titles *English Folk and Fairy Tales* and *Celtic Folk and Fairy Tales*.

priety of this as much as their elders. Generally speaking, it has been my ambition to write as a good old nurse will speak when she tells Fairy Tales. . . . This book is meant to be read aloud, and not merely taken in by the eye. In a few instances I have introduced or changed an incident. I have never done so, however, without mentioning the fact in the Notes. . . . They indicate my sources and give a few references to parallels and variants. . . .

While I have endeavored to render the language of the tales (i.e. the Celtic tales) simple and free from bookish artifice, I have not felt at liberty to re-tell the tales in the English way. I have not scrupled to retain a Celtic turn of speech, and here and there a Celtic word, which I have *not* explained within brackets—a practice to be abhorred of all good men. A few words unknown to the reader only add effectiveness and local colour to a narrative, as Mr. Kipling well knows.

English Fairy Tales and *More English Fairy Tales*[1] (1894) constitute outstanding collections in their representation of the typical quality of the folk tales native to England and in their retelling which retains the peculiar flavor of the English tale. As Jacobs himself pointed out, these stories are essentially colloquial and rarely rise into romance; rather, humor is the outstanding trait. Indeed, they are frequently almost matter-of-fact and are told in an easy, unpretentious and idiomatic manner which is highly suitable. And yet there are stories, like *The Buried Moon*, which approach the romantic in imaginative quality and which have a strange, vivid, almost inarticulate beauty which Jacobs captures extraordinarily well; while Childe Rowland has a vein of mystery and magic which is close to the Gaelic.

In *Celtic Fairy Tales* and its companion volume, *More Celtic Fairy Tales* (1894), Jacobs shows his versatility as a reteller by his ability to adapt himself to quite a different type of retelling, necessitated by a different type of story. For while there are in these volumes humorous stories "perhaps more comic" than the English ones, there are many long romantic tales, characterized by the mystery and wonder, the color and magic and charm, the sense of beauty and of sorrow, characteristic of the Celtic folk imagination. His handling of such exquisite stories as "Deirdre" and "The Fate of the Children of Lir" is exceptional in the retention of the beauty and spirit of the originals. As one is impressed by the number of stories for little children in the English volumes, in the Celtic one is struck by the fact that these collections, as a whole, offer the greatest appeal to the older children in the romantic stage of fairy tale interest. The *Indian Fairy Tales* (1892), drawn from the Jatakas, the Bidpai and other Sanskrit sources, re-emphasizes

---

[1] Now published under the title *More English Folk and Fairy Tales*.

Jacobs' appreciation of children's tastes and his knowledge of the qualities in storytelling to which they respond. In all these books, the Notes and References, from which the children are amusingly warned away in the English and Celtic collections, comprise a wealth of intriguing information to any one fascinated by the phenomena of folk literature, particularly the matters of variants and parallels.

So the fairy tale came into its own realm, given the sanction of respectability by the work of serious scholars and men of letters. Although it might, in the future, be again the innocent cause of argument and debate it was never to vanish entirely from its right place in the field of children's literature. Equally significant is the fact that editors and retellers, like Lang and Jacobs, having knowledge of and respect for their material and children, established standards and methods of selection and retelling; they used original printed or oral sources, they selected with a child audience in mind, they made adaptations designed to make the stories suitable and understandable to children, at the same time keeping the integrity of the original.

America, which had already made great contributions to imaginative literature, notably in the work of Frank Stockton, Joel Chandler Harris, and Howard Pyle, contributed during the first twenty years of the twentieth century its share of folk tale collections. Storytelling, as it was practiced in the kindergartens and children's rooms of public libraries in the early years of this century, undoubtedly gave impetus to the interest in folk literature and intensified the need for stories. It may be worth noting that some of the collections published in the early 1900's were done by teachers and storytellers. Among these are the five volumes that make up the Library of Fairy Literature, edited by Kate Douglas Wiggin (1856–1923) and her sister, Nora Archibald Smith (1859?–1934). The excellence of the selection of the folk and fairy tales and the fables in *The Fairy Ring* (1906), *Magic Casements* (1907), *Tales of Laughter* (1908), *Tales of Wonder* (1909), and *Talking Beasts* (1911) is in large part due to the collaborators' enthusiasm for their work. In her autobiography Kate Douglas Wiggin writes:

> The younger sister read . . . uncounted tomes of fairy tales, culled from the literatures of all languages, and decided on the choicest three hundred for the purpose of selecting the best one hundred and fifty. These were the subjects of long discussions and frequently of spirited argument, until we agreed on one hundred, the situation becoming so acute that now and then we were obliged to 'trade off' our individual favorites. . . .[1]

East o' the Sun and West o' the Moon with Other Norwegian Folk Tales (1912), by Mrs. Gudrun Thorne-Thomsen (1873–1956), gives

[1] Kate Douglas Wiggin, *My Garden of Memory; An Autobiography* (Boston, Houghton Mifflin, 1923), p. 340.

evidence of the fineness of folk and story quality obtained when a gifted storyteller retells for children tales of her native land with which she is temperamentally and psychologically in sympathy.

From 1900 to 1920 collection after collection appeared in England and America, prophetic of the plentitude to be offered children in the future; *The Arabian Nights: Their Best Known Tales*, edited by Kate Douglas Wiggin and her sister, and *The Arabian Nights' Entertainments*, edited by Frances Jenkins Olcott, a pioneer children's librarian, who also made several other compilations; miscellaneous collections drawn from all the world, like F. J. H. Darton's *A Wonder Book of Beasts* (1909) and Eva Tappan's *The Golden Goose* (1905); stories from specific countries, showing an ever widening horizon—from India, in the *Jataka Tales* (1912) by Ellen Babbitt and *Tales of the Punjab* (1894) by Flora Steel—from Russia, in *Russian Wonder Tales* (1912) by Post Wheeler, and *The Russian Grandmother's Wonder Tales* (1906) by Louise Houghton—from Ireland in the earlier work of Seumas MacManus—from Wales, in William Thomas' *The Welsh Fairy-Book* (1908)—from England in Ernest Rhys's *Fairy-Gold* (1906) and from Scotland in Elizabeth Grierson's *The Scottish Fairy Book* (1910)—from the various tribes of the American Indian in collections by Eastman, Grinnell, Linderman, Lummis, and Kennedy. Possibly the interest in romantic literature and Howard Pyle's work with the Robin Hood material stimulated the prose retelling of ballads, since in the early 1900's were published three fine collections of retold ballads—Tappan's *Old Ballads in Prose* (1901), Mary MacLeod's *The Book of Ballad Stories* (1906), and Grierson's *Children's Tales from Scottish Ballads* (1906).

The search for literature with which to enrich the background and reading life of children went beyond the folk tale into the magnificent richness of heroic myth, epic, saga, and romance. Again, in previous periods there had been indications of what was to come. There had been *The Adventures of Ulysses* by Charles Lamb, the romantic telling of the Greek myths by Nathaniel Hawthorne, and the more classic telling by Charles Kingsley. There had been the work of James Baldwin with the Nibelungenlied and the Roland epic and Lanier's *Knightly Legends of Wales* (1881).

Like others of his time, Alfred J. Church (1829–1912), an English scholar, clergyman, and teacher, believed in the value of a thorough knowledge of the classics and in their power to form standards of taste and to give pleasure and delight. It is well for children's literature that, at this time in its growth and expansion, there were those who recognized the place that could be filled by retellings of the great world epics, with their vast horizons and cosmic implications, by the fundamental truths of human life which they portray, by the vital quality of their adventure and action, by their incomparable literary quality, and possibly, most of all, by the beauty of the "epic sorrow." Few have contributed more to children's literature in this respect than Church. His *Heroes of Chivalry and Romance* (1898), containing stories of Beowulf, King Arthur, and the Nibelungenlied, remains excellent in spite of later competition, following faithfully, as it does, the original sources in incident and style. His *Stories of Charlemagne* (1902) is still excellent reading. His greatest contribution, however, is in his retelling of the Greek and Latin classics and particularly of the *Iliad* and *Odyssey*. In 1892 he published *The Story of the Odyssey* in which he followed the order of events as they occurred in the original and in which the Homeric style was clearly reflected. *The Story of the Iliad* was also published in 1892. In 1906, *The Odyssey for Boys and Girls* appeared and in 1907 *The Iliad for Boys and Girls*. These are for younger children than the first two, simpler in adaptation and in style. Together, they constitute high examples of originals reduced to their essentials, yet retaining in event and phrasing the true spirit of the original. Matthew Arnold has said that there are four main Homeric characteristics: rapidity of movement, plainness of style, simplicity of ideas, and nobility of manner. No greater tribute can be paid to Church than to say that in simple, dignified, and admirable English he impressively retains the essence of Homeric style. From their first publication to their reissue in Macmillan's *New Children's Classics*, the fine illustrations of John Flaxman have been associated with them. Many of Church's books, most of them concerned with Greek and Latin classics, are unobtainable. It is a matter for gratitude that *The Odyssey for Boys and Girls* and *The Iliad for Boys and Girls*, still the best versions for the introduction to younger children of the grandeur of the Greek epics, are extant under the title of *The Iliad and the Odyssey of Homer* (Macmillan, 1964).

A fortunate accident led to the introduction of the Icelandic sagas to children. In a bookstore, on a second-hand counter, Allen French (1870–1946) picked up a copy of *The Story of Burnt Njal*. "The first two pages were enough to fascinate me with a glimpse of life in Iceland a thousand years ago." This was Dasent's translation of the great Icelandic saga, which French retold as the *Heroes of Iceland* (1905). Like all the Icelandic sagas, it reflects clearly and with detail the lives of the early Icelanders, forming a sharp contrast with the epics from the southern and eastern countries. The literature from Iceland is realistic, stark in its quality of understatement, terse in its treatment of human drama and emotion, grim in its reflection of man's combat against the forces of nature, greatly courageous in its acceptance of tragedy, strong in its simplicity. It reflects a people who were just and law-abiding, honorable men who respected truth and bravery, who were daring and adventurous, and who lived vigorously. With full appreciation of these distinguishing characteristics, Allen French has retold the story with remarkable fidelity to the spirit of the original, at the same time ridding it of much unnecessary or irrelevant detail, and concentrating on the main line of narrative.

His interest once aroused, French read other sagas from the Icelandic, among them the translation of the *Grettir's Saga* by Eiriker Magnusson and William Morris, which he retold in the *Story of Grettir the Strong* (1908). His straightforward and direct narrative style heightens the remarkable quality of the supernatural elements in this story. The combat with the spirit of Glam, the thrall, is one of the most gripping incidents of this kind in all literature.

In 1904 French published what he considered, with some justice, to be his best Icelandic book, the *Story of Rolf and the Viking's Bow* (1904), an original story the inspiration for which came from his knowledge of the Icelandic sagas. It is a fine and dramatic story, well and vigorously told, with excellent use of action and suspense. Aside from the inherent worth of the story itself, it has a peculiar value in that it provides as good an introduction as could be desired to the heroic literature of epic and saga.

The interest in Icelandic literature and the desire to broaden the horizons of children, to bring to them the thought and beliefs and aspirations of various early peoples probably account in part for the retellings of Norse myths that appeared during this period. These had been preserved in the Eddas of Iceland. Thomas Carlyle had drawn attention to the qualities of these myths, qualities of thoughtfulness, sincerity, strength, homely truthfulness, quite different, as he asserted, from the graceful lightness of Greek paganism. In 1882 Hamilton Wright Mabie (1845–1916) had rewritten these in his *Norse Stories Retold from the Eddas* (1894),[1] a version following the original closely and characterized by fine feeling for the special character of the Norse myths. Abbie Farwell Brown (d. 1927), many years later, retold them in her *In the Days of Giants* (1902) for children younger than those to whom Mabie's book appeals, emphasizing their strong storytelling element, their adventure and action. Still later, Ethel Wilmot-Buxton's *Stories of Norse Heroes* (1909) offered another retelling, which is marked by a simplicity and economy of words and style that aptly reflects the manner of telling of the original. In addition to the fact that these books brought the Norse myths to stand beside the Greek myths as retold by Hawthorne and Kingsley, they illustrate the desirability of different methods of retelling. Both by reason of age and temperament, children are sharply individual. That which makes an

[1] Several different dates were found for Mabie's *Norse Stories Retold from the Eddas*. The date found in the early printed *Catalog of Books in the Children's Department of the Carnegie Library of Pittsburgh*, is used here.

immediate rapport with one child will not always appeal to the inherent taste of another. The universality of appeal and significance of mythological and heroic traditional literature is such as to render it subject legitimately to various interpretations and emphases.

In 1883 Helen Zimmern (1846–1934) had published her *Epics of Kings; Hero Tales from Ancient Persia; retold from Firdusi's Shah nameh.* While this was a book more interesting to students of folklore than to many children, it had found its way into some collections for children in public libraries. Reminiscent of Greek hero tales in places, this epic is, however, strongly differentiated by the imaginative quality of Eastern lands and by the folk characters and beliefs that imagination evolved. Two versions for children were published in the early 1900's. Ethel Wilmot-Buxton's *Stories of Persian Heroes* (1908) lays emphasis on the historic aspect of the epic and uses for the tragic story of the slaying of Sohrab Matthew Arnold's poetic version. Search for additional storytelling material for a library club of boys interested in hero tales produced the *Story of Rustem and other Persian hero tales from Firdusi* (1909) by Elizabeth Renninger, based upon English translations of the Shah nameh. Although the telling at times shows a strain and effort which gives a semblance of affectation, this is, in the main, an acceptable version, reflecting the author's experience in telling the stories before they were written down.

In his preface to *Celtic Fairy Tales*, Joseph Jacobs pointed out that nowhere else than in Celtic folk literature is there so large and consistent a body of oral tradition about the national and mythical heroes. "I could have more than filled this volume with similar oral traditions about Finn. But the story of Finn, as told by the Gaelic peasantry of today, deserves a volume by itself, while the adventures of the Ultonian hero, Cuchulain, could easily fill another." Others have commented on the amazing bulk of Irish heroic literature extant. It has been estimated that the stories belonging to the Ulster or Cuchulain cycle alone would fill two thousand pages, and this and the Finn cycle are only two of the three great cycles of Irish mythological, heroic, and romantic storytelling.

The Irish literary renaissance, beginning about 1890, undoubtedly aroused interest in this great and extraordinary mass of material, an interest which, in the late nineties and early years of the twentieth century, amounted apparently to a fascination with all things Celtic, particularly with the mystery and beauty of Celtic literature. Lady Gregory (1852–1932), a leading figure in the revival and translation of the ancient Celtic heroic and romantic tales and legends, translated and retold, in a lovely English permeated with Irish idiom, the story of Cuchulain in her *Cuchulain of Muirthemne: The Story of the Men of the Red Branch of Ulster* (1902) and the story of Finn in her *Gods and*

Fighting Men (1904), which included also some stories from the earliest cycle of storytelling, the cycle of the Tuatha De Danaan. In his preface to Lady Gregory's *Cuchulain*, Yeats writes: "I think this book is the best that has come out of Ireland in my time. Perhaps I should say that it is the best book that has ever come out of Ireland; for the stories which it tells are a chief part of Ireland's gift to the imagination of the world—and it tells them perfectly for the first time."

To attempt to retell for young people stories from any of the bardic literature of Ireland is a task requiring courage, thorough knowledge of the originals, and temperamental sympathy with the stories. These cycles are complex in structure, profuse and fantastic in their detail, passionate in their emotions, prodigal in style, with a supernatural quality that is at times grotesque and at times possesses an unearthly beauty. Matthew Arnold, who so aptly established the fundamentals of Homeric style, is no less keenly aware of the elements that distinguish anything touched by the Celtic genius. The Celt, as described in Arnold's essay *On the Study of Celtic Literature*, is one who is very quick to feel impressions, and to feel them strongly. He is always ready to rebel against the despotism of fact. He constantly strives to express the inexpressible, and this, together with his feeling for all that is noble and distinguished, lends to his work an "intoxication of style." One of his chief gifts is his power to magicalize nature, to render vivid not only the beauty, but also the weird power and the fairy charm of nature.

This long approach to the retellings of the Celtic heroic and romantic material is more pertinent than it may seem to be. If it is an accepted premise that the recasting of a literary work of art is justifiable only when the qualities which make it unique are retained or re-created, then those qualities must be defined and understood. The intrinsic merit of the Greek epics, their balanced and polished beauty, is a matter of longstanding knowledge. The distinctive qualities of the Northern epics are those which have characterized much of the literature, traditional and sophisticated, of these countries, though it may be of interest to note Arnold sees a Celtic strain in Icelandic literature. The Celtic spirit, which transformed everything it touched, is less familiar and less akin to most temperaments. It is, consequently, a piece of good fortune that the two retellers of Celtic bardic literature were enthusiastic students of the literature with which they worked.

Eleanor Hull (1860–1935) had written a history of the Cuchulain Saga before she retold it as *The Boys' Cuchulain* (1910). This is heroic material, complex in its structure, and diverse in its quality. It is rich in color, in imagination, in drama, and in description. The characters are many and each an individual. As Dr. Douglas Hyde has said, no quotations can do full justice to the style. There is in it poetry of a supreme order, as in the laments of Deirdre over the bodies of the Sons

of Usnach, and of Emer over the body of Cuchulain. The story of the
death of Cuchulain is one of the most powerful pieces of objective storytelling to be found in all literature. Primitive and barbaric in places,
the saga offers also gentleness and tenderness, chivalry and romance,
humor and pathos. In her retelling, Eleanor Hull has rightly refused
to sacrifice this diversity in the interest of simplification. Using a
variety of sources, in manuscript and printed form (one of the difficulties
being the variety of versions), she has woven into the main Cuchulain
Saga related stories and small cycles of stories, rearranging and con-
densing, at times expanding, but always, with fine integrity, keeping
the quality of the original in matter and spirit. The result is one of the
finest retellings in children's literature.

In *The High Deeds of Finn* (1910), Thomas W. Rolleston (1857–
1920), whose *Myths and Legends of the Celtic Race* (1911) is rewarding reading, brings together from many sources stories from the three
cycles of storytelling, excluding those told by Eleanor Hull. Where reshaping seemed desirable, it has been done, but "nothing has been done
in the framing of this collection of Gaelic romances without the consideration and care which the value of the material demands and which
the writer's love of it has inspired" (Preface). Whereas *The Boys'
Cuchulain* excels in the unity of the whole, the excellence of *The High
Deeds of Finn* lies in the beauty and poetry and imagination of the individual stories. The inclusion alone of such unusual and exquisite stories
as "The Story of Etain and Midir," "King Iubdan and King Fergus,"
and "The Quest of the Sons of Turenn" would justify the book.

The partisanship of these retellers for their own material is interesting and ingratiating. Church was a scholar in the classic tradition,
steeped in the literature of ancient Greece and Rome. French believed
in the superiority of the Northern epics over the Southern. Eleanor Hull
in her introduction to *The Boys' Cuchulain* claims that "these tales have
a sprightliness and buoyancy not possessed by the Arthurian tales, they
are fresher, more humorous, more diversified; and the characters, more
especially those of the women, are more firmly and variously drawn."
Whether or not these opinions are biased, the results for children's
literature were all to the good. These writers brought to children great
literature of the past, and they wrote it with infectious enthusiasm, an
always telling quality in children's books.

They gave to children's literature an even greater gift in the spirit
of their retelling. They refused to ruin a thing of beauty in order to
bring it within the understanding of the immature or mediocre mind.
They had faith that a child might be raised to the level of greatness,
and they had too great a respect for greatness to compromise with their
faith. They enabled critics of children's books to establish criteria for
right evaluation of retellings of classic literature, and they set high

standards for those who were to follow them when the great modern period of children's book production began in the 1920's.

Bibliography

Arnold, Matthew. *On the Study of Celtic Literature and Other Essays*. New York, E. P. Dutton, 1932. Pp. 13–136.

Barry, Florence V. *A Century of Children's Books*. New York, Doran, n.d.

Darton, Frederick Joseph Harvey. *Children's Books in England; Five Centuries of Social Life*. Cambridge, Eng., University Press, 1932.

Gordon, George. *Andrew Lang; Being the Andrew Lang Lecture Delivered before the University of St. Andrews, December, 1927*. Oxford University Press, 1928.

Green, Roger Lancelyn. *Andrew Lang. A Critical Biography with a Short Title Bibliography of the Works of Andrew Lang*. Leicester, Eng., Edmund Ward, 1946.

Lamb, Charles. "Play-House Memoranda." In Ward, Alfred Charles, editor, *Everybody's Lamb*. New York, Harcourt, 1933. Pp. 290–305.

Repplier, Agnes. "Andrew Lang." *The Catholic World*, Vol. 96 (Dec., 1912), pp. 289–297.

————— "Battle of the Babies." In *Essays in Miniature*. Boston, Houghton Mifflin, 1895. Pp. 195–206.

Wiggin, Kate Douglas. *My Garden of Memory; An Autobiography*. Boston, Houghton Mifflin, 1925.

· 3 ·

A New Impulse in Romance

It has been noted of more than one man that he was born out of his time. Chronologically the work of Robert Louis Stevenson (1850–1894) belongs to the preceding section. *Treasure Island*, first issued as a serial in *Young Folks*, was published as a book in 1883, the year in which Howard Pyle's *Robin Hood* appeared. Symptomatically and influentially, *Treasure Island* belongs to the last decade of the nineteenth century. Written for the amusement of Stevenson's stepson, Lloyd Osbourne, this book, like so many others similarly initiated, grew into something which, in significance, far transcends its origin.

As a boy, Stevenson loved Scott, Ballantyne, and Marryat and the pasteboard toy-theater plays of Skelt, with their stories of treasure, of pirates and highwaymen. The romance of adventure was thus a natural field for Stevenson, as it is a favorite category of reading among children. Rarely, however, has so conscious and analytical a skilled craftsman written this type of story for young people. One of his critical essays, "A Gossip on Romance" (1882), should be known by all those who have anything to do with children's books and children's reading. In this essay he not only defines the nature of romance, he also touches upon the difference between the immoral and the amoral, a problem which has plagued and distorted the criticism of children's literature from the Puritan Age to the present; and he is possibly the first to state at least two invariable factors which largely determine the reading tastes and interests of children—the attraction of incident and the necessity for selectivity.

His thesis in this essay is that the charm of romance is largely dependent upon incident; character, eloquence, and thought are secondary, as are moral and intellectual interests. It is incident for which children read, and it is incident that woos the grown reader out of his reserve, that alike delights "the schoolboy and the sage." While drama is the "poetry of conduct" and exists solely on moral grounds, romance is the "poetry of circumstance" and may be concerned with that which is not immoral, but simply a-moral; which either does not regard the human will at all, or deals with it in obvious and healthy relations; where the interest turns, not on what a man shall choose to do, but on how he manages to do it; not on the passionate slips and hesitations of the conscience, but on the problems of the body and of the practical intelligence, in clean, open-air adventure, the shock of "arms or the diplomacy of life."[1]

To maintain its full effect, however, incident must be "fit and striking," that is to say, selective.

The right kind of thing should fall out in the right kind of place; the right kind of thing should follow. . . . The threads of a story come from time to time together and make a picture in the web; the characters fall from time to time into some attitude to each other or to nature, which stamps the story home like an illustration.[2]

In another essay, "A Humble Remonstrance," he answers Henry James, who in his *Art of Fiction*, claimed that there is little or no difference between the novel of character and the novel of incident. Stevenson reiterates that character to the boy is a sealed book. In the novel of incident the author may admit character within certain limits, but only within certain limits. Danger is the matter with which the story of adventure or incident deals, and characters should be portrayed only so far as they realize the sense of danger and provoke the sympathy of fear. "To add more traits, to be too clever, to start the hare of moral or intellectual interest while we are running the fox of material interest, is not to enrich but to stultify your tale."[3]

Because *Treasure Island* so thoroughly exemplifies Stevenson's principles, it is an event in the development not only of romance but of children's literature as a whole. There had been adventure tales before, but in them the element of adventure had been watered down by ulterior motives of piety or morality, or crudity of style had rendered unacceptable the quality of "brute incident—not mere bloodshed or wonder,"[4] which Stevenson so stressed. *Treasure Island* is that increasingly rare thing, an excellent story written for story's sake and written with a craftsmanship that raises it to the level of art. In its beginning and its climax, in its incidents and its characters, in its settings and situations, the book demonstrates the rightness of Stevenson's conception of the true nature of romance.

[1] Robert Louis Stevenson, "A Gossip on Romance," *Memories and Portraits* (New York, Scribner, 1904), p. 251.
[2] *Ibid.*, pp. 255–256.
[3] Stevenson, "A Humble Remonstrance," *Memories and Portraits*, pp. 289–290.
[4] Stevenson, "A Gossip on Romance," *Memories and Portraits*, p. 249.

In considering *Treasure Island* the emphasis must be on narrative method and style, since the interest is held, not by conduct, not by effect of character upon circumstance, but by sheer adventure appropriate to situation and setting and therefore, in Stevenson's estimation, romantic. Certain situations demand certain events, certain settings call aloud for a certain sort of story, he writes in "A Gossip on Romance." From the beginning to the end the story marches with rapid inevitability from incident to incident, with action so predetermined by quick-moving events that morality in the sense of hesitations and doubts of the human conscience is irrelevant.

No story of its kind has ever had better opening chapters, as one by one, vividly, and with a gripping quality of mystery, the characters who are to precipitate the action are introduced. One by one they arrive at the "Admiral Benbow" inn—Billy Bones, with the dirty livid saber cut across his cheek, and his constant watch for the "seafaring man with one leg;" Black Dog, whose appearance had so awful an effect upon Billy Bones; and finally the blind beggar, tapping his way down the road to the inn. Not least among the merits of the book are the word drawings of these villains. Stevenson holds true to his theory that sufficient character portrayal can be admitted to make real the sense of danger and to arouse the sense of fear. As each arrival increasingly threatens the sheltered, uneventful life of the inn and countryside, filling the bitter cold winter days with a terrible atmosphere of dark deeds and emotions, past and present, the sense of fear and unavoidable involvement mounts. Unforgettable as these early characters are, the figure of Long John Silver overshadows them, with his slyness and cunning, his seeming geniality and innate cruelty. The most effective scenes of the book, and those which constitute the true climax of the tale are those in which Silver saves Jim Hawkins from the vengeance of the crew and at the same time insures that he himself will be saved. Here again, Stevenson fulfills his own requirement—that the "characters should fall from time to time into some attitude to each other or to nature, which stamps the story home like an illustration."[1] This is, however, not so much a result of character analysis or portrayal as of narrative technique. Essentially, the characters are type characters, types necessary to the nature of the story—on the one hand, Jim and the doctor and the squire, simple, average, uncomplicated, undistinguished; on the other hand, Long John Silver and his companions, animated by lust and greed, true and typical ruffians and villains. In both cases it is situation that reveals character, rather than character controlling and creating situation.

The reminiscent point of view and the use of the first person play a large part in inducing in the reader the right mood of suspense and

---

[1] Stevenson, "A Gossip on Romance," *Memories and Portraits*, p. 256.

anticipation. It is a well-known fact that children dislike the use of the first person, realizing instinctively that often the "I" introduces too much of the subjective and introspective. In *Treasure Island*, as in *Robinson Crusoe* and *Gulliver's Travels*, they accept it, since in these books the emphasis is on action, not on thought and feeling. Emotion may be and is present, but it is made apparent by being inherent in situation, rather than by analytical dissection of a character's response to situation. Consequently, there is no hindrance to the reader's identification of himself with the "I"; in this case, Jim Hawkins. The sense of ineradicable memories, strongly felt in the opening phrase of the true story, "I remember him as if it were yesterday," is sustained to the last paragraph, where it is again forcibly expressed. Throughout, it does much to deepen the convincingness of the story and to heighten its reality. This effect is strengthened by the character of Jim and the place he occupies. Standing between Dr. Livesey, an ordinary able and calm adult, and the devious and cunning Long John Silver, he is a boy with a normal boy's courage and resourcefulness. Again, it is circumstance and situation and the accident of being in a certain place at a certain time which call forth these qualities in Jim and which make him the central moving figure in many of the episodes. He is the victim of circumstance, not the instigator of it.

A prime requisite of adventure fiction is obviously continuity and rapidity of action. To create a story which mounts steadily in intensity, to invent successive incidents which shall be varied and plausible, to draw background and scene as inherent parts of the action, is in itself an art, an art compounded of storytelling ability and power of style, an art produced by a creative imagination, disciplining itself by reality. Stevenson may not have created the tale of adventure as a type, but he is one of the few to tell it as it should be told, as a story which must stand or fall on its merits, as a story untrammeled by other motives. He was, above all things, a storyteller and a lover of good tales, one who believed that the act of reading should be "voluptuous," that one should "gloat over a book." To have a good tale to tell is, however, not enough. It must be told with a power of style which makes it credible, which sustains the initial interest aroused by the type of story, which enables the reader to immerse himself in the setting and to participate in the action.

Stevenson was not only a lover of tales, but equally a lover of words and phrases. He was a meticulous searcher for the right word for the right thing, a builder of phrases precise and exact. He had two of the greatest gifts a writer may possess, the gift of selectivity and the gift of stressing of essentials. The tight economy of detail and word, the strict adherence to the relevant, the fine precision of phrase, combine with a faculty for observation, a sense of the relationship between scene and mood, and a facility in harnessing imagination to reality to make a story that wholly absorbs the reader. Characters and scenes are etched upon the memory forever because of the fine clarity of description, the emphasis upon distinguishing and distinctive characteristics. Background is drawn sparingly, with a keen awareness of the part it plays in enhancing mood. The romantic, the dramatic, and the picturesque are so tempered by realism as to enable the reader to be convinced of any event, no matter how remarkable. The story progresses unimpeded, each sentence carrying the action forward, each chapter offering a faultlessly motivated episode, each bit of the amazingly actual dialogue contributing its share. The very matter-of-factness and objectivity with which the passions of greed and lust are treated make the story wholesome and rid it of any tinge of morbidity; for here the interest is concentrated, not on the problem of good and evil in man, but on the pitting of strength against strength, of wits against wits, in healthy combat.

It is no wonder this book made Stevenson a popular author. It appealed to boys and to the eternal boy in men; to the story-loving spirit which had treasured the chapbooks and perpetuated folk literature by word of mouth for generation after generation. In Stevenson's own day, the combination of robust, vigorous adventure and artistry of execution must have been a shock. Consequently Stevenson, like Howard Pyle, fostered the recognition that writing for children is a field of writing which should call for the best in technical excellence. To us, in retrospect, *Treasure Island* anticipates the escape from previous limitations of Puritanism and didacticism into complete freedom of form, idea, and substance.

In "A Gossip on Romance," Stevenson spoke of the hold which the Hawes Inn at the Queen's Ferry exerted upon his imagination. The physical details of the setting, the spirit which seemed to brood over the place, called for a tale. The real opening action of *Kidnapped* (1886) takes place at this same Hawes Inn.

In many ways *Kidnapped* is an interesting contrast to *Treasure Island*. It is altogether a more subtle, complicated story, involving a far deeper analysis of human character, mood, emotion, and motivation. The response to *Treasure Island* is a physical one, compounded of the love of adventure, the longing for vicarious experience, the desire for escape from everyday monotonous living. The response to *Kidnapped* is an emotional one, compounded of the tragedy of lost causes, the pathos of almost forgotten heroisms and loyalties, the sorrow felt for the hopeless gallantry of men doomed to defeat, the dramatic and picturesque quality that surrounds the Jacobite Rebellion and its aftermath.

This is not to say that the factors of action and incident are lacking. The combat in the roundhouse on board the *Covenant* is the equal, for sheer excitement, of any scene in *Treasure Island*. In *Kidnapped*, Stevenson, the romancer, again delights in a profusion of varied incident, in suspense and climax, in narrow escapes from threatening danger; in a manner almost reminiscent of the Gothic novel, he draws upon the romantic implications of the wild beauty of the highlands to underline the mood and tone of the story. However, a new note enters *Kidnapped*; Stevenson, the moralist, joins Stevenson, the romancer. The moral issues are treated with the artistry so characteristic of the writer—not by sermons, not by pointing to the moral to be drawn from this or that situation, not even by a description of the issues involved, but rather by juxtaposition of character and point of view, seen most notably, of course, in the constant contrast between David Balfour and Alan Breck. The latter is Catholic, Jacobite, and highlander, recklessly brave, indomitably gallant in the face of odds, immensely vain, inordinately proud, aggressively self-confident, a man to whom loyalties rate above moral scruples or personal safety. The former is Presbyterian, Whig, and lowlander, cautious, reserved, given to consideration rather than action, ruled and governed by his conscience, slow to take offence, but slower to forgive.

The friendship between these two, based on attraction of extreme opposites, is one of the chief merits of the book, and the means whereby the moral aspect of the tale transcends the merely moral, and comes to represent two opposing and irreconcilable ways of life and attitudes toward life. The relationship, the joining of fortunes of Alan Breck and David Balfour, serve more purposes than one. As a technical device, it is most excellent. It brings together the two threads of the plot, the effort of David to gain his inheritance, and the historical narrative of the plight of the highlanders stemming from the murder of Colin Campbell. It imbues a story of greed and treachery with the romanticism of the fugitive and outlawed highland chieftains, hiding from the king's troops, their safety dependent on the unwavering loyalty of ragged, hungry men. So what might have been a tale of mere adventure becomes a historical, romantic, and psychological novel, but with all these aspects so serving to provide appropriate background for plot and story, that boy and man may read with equal pleasure, though possibly with different interests.

As in *Treasure Island*, the style makes no small contribution to the vividness and vitality of the story. Fluent and graceful without affectation, lucid and pure without loss of graphic detail, rich in word use without ostentation, it demonstrates again the rightness of the comment so often made, that Stevenson's is the art that conceals art.

It has been said that Stevenson was not an original genius. This may be true in the sense that he originated no new type. His gifts to the onward progress of children's literature are none the less great and even unique. He was one of those who retain, with sincerity, the optimism and buoyancy, the love of life and living, the play spirit, the faculty for dramatization, the power of transforming imagination, which make the daily life and play of children so absorbing and exuberant. His books, so impregnated with these qualities, fulfill without strain or effort the child's fundamental conception of what a book should be—a thing to be gloated over, a thing which will sweep the reader away from the here and now. Stevenson was eternally right when he said it is for this pleasure, above all others, that children read. He may not have created the adventure tale as a type, but he raised it, and with it, the child reader, to the level of greatness. The eternal boy and the serious craftsman in Stevenson combined to create works which make child and adult equals.

Historically, these are the qualities that constitute the importance of Stevenson. For the immediate present there is added significance in the kind of book he wrote and in the way he wrote it. This is a period, like many past periods, of uncertainty, of fears and tensions. In such a time, concern for children deepens. Such concern is in itself admirable; but its very intensity frequently results in distortion and lack of perspective. It is inevitable and even right that the literature of an age should reflect the problems of that age, and this is no less true of children's literature than of adult. If there is anything proved by a survey of the development of children's books, it is that the prevailing tone of the period is a determining factor in the purpose, content, and quality of the contemporary writing for children. Historical perspective enables us to see the unwholesomeness and morbidity of the books of the Puritan era, the stultifying quality of the utilitarian pedanticism of the didactic age, the barriers to freedom and liberality of thought, idea, and form erected by any age that rates ulterior motive higher than literary excellence. We are not so clearsighted about the shortcomings of our own time. We are losing hold of the fundamentals of literary criticism—that distinctive literary types call for distinctive content and treatment; that mere propaganda and didacticism are rarely movingly and lastingly persuasive and convincing; that conviction is a matter of the heart as well as of the head and comes only from true literature, which reconstructs, imaginatively and interpretatively, universal and significant aspects of human life; that literalness is often mistaken for genuine realism; that even in such an age as this, there will be, and should be, books that escape the immediate problems and confusions and are therefore, in a certain sense, amoral; and that such an escape is the rightful heritage of children. A study of Stevenson's critical essays and stories might have a clarifying effect.

Bibliography

Balfour, Graham. *The Life of Robert Louis Stevenson*. New York, Scribner, 1915.

Darton, Frederick Joseph Harvey. *Children's Books in England; Five Centuries of Social Life*. Cambridge, Eng., University Press, 1932.

Stevenson, Robert Louis. "A Gossip on Romance." *In Memories and Portraits*. New York, Scribner, 1904. Pp. 247–274.

—— "A Humble Remonstrance." In *Memories and Portraits*. New York, Scribner, 1904. Pp. 275–299.

· 4 ·

The Great Originator

In the eighties and nineties, while Howard Pyle was writing and illustrating his fairy tales, retold romances and historic fiction in America, and Stevenson was giving new impetus to the tale of romantic adventure in England, the writings of a new and original genius startled the "precious" era, which was an aftermath of Pre-Raphaelitism and the aesthetic movement.

In 1889, at the age of twenty-four, Rudyard Kipling (1865–1936) came to London from India, already an object of wonder, an exciting and controversial figure because of the fame of his short stories. It is little wonder that he had so spectacular an effect upon that period. Even now it is hardly possible to analyze his genius, compounded of so many things—of inheritance and environment, of natural endowment and temperament, of training and experience.

His mother was Alice Macdonald, one of whose sisters married Sir Edward Burne-Jones. It was in their home that Kipling, as a small boy, found escape and relief from the bitter, unhappy experience of the years when he was committed to the care of a woman incredibly unsuited to assume responsibility for a child. His father was John Lockwood Kipling, a man of culture, architectural sculptor in the Bombay School of Art.

Rudyard Kipling was born in Bombay on December 30, 1865. As a child, he learned to speak Hindustani; indeed it must have seemed to him his natural language, since it is recorded that he had to be urged to speak English to his parents. From babyhood he was steeped in the legends and folk tales of a country which is a cradle of folk literature. All his life he was to keep the love of imagery and metaphor gained in his early years. At the age of six, after five years of normal, happy child life, he was sent home to England to live in the house of a woman who, together with her son, reminds one inevitably of some of Dickens' more fantastic character creations. The terrible unhappiness of his life at this time, so vividly remembered in *Something of Myself*, was relieved only by the holidays spent in the normal, happy and gracious home of his uncle, Sir Edward Burne-Jones. That he returned from these vacations with a tragic submissiveness to the indignities suffered at the hands of the woman to whose care his parents had unwittingly given him, and that he maintained silence about his ill-treatment, are facts not so unnatural as they may seem. His behavior in this respect is indicative of the pitiful helplessness a child may feel, in greater or lesser degree, under the domination of an adult world. It is possible also that this experience deepened the innate tenderness and sympathy he felt for children all his life. Fortunately his school life in the United Services College at Westward Ho! North Devon, where he was sent at the age of thirteen, was more normal.

On leaving this school at seventeen, Kipling returned to India and took a position on the staff of the Lahore *Civil and Military Gazette.* The next several years were the most important and influential of his life. Inherently, he was a great literary journalist, and his experience, first on the *Gazette* and later on the *Pioneer* at Allahabad, sharpened and developed his natural talents—his power of observation, his insatiable curiosity, his acute sensitivity to the romantic, the dramatic, and the actual, his quick response to humor and to pathos, his great sense of fact and at the same time of the truth and significance underlying fact, his human interest in all classes of society and in all kinds of people. The discipline of his daily work, which had to be carried on in spite of tropical heat and consequent illness, taught him compression and the art of vigorous re-creation of experience, situation, and character made colorful and vital by highly selective wording and phrasing. His experiences as a reporter convinced him of the truth of Edmund Gosse's principle that there is nothing in life itself that is not fit material for literature.

His experience and his genius bore fruit in the shape of short stories, some of them written while he was still in his teens, collected in *Plain Tales From the Hills* (1888). It is little wonder that these stories, reaching England before Kipling did, made people aware of a new note in literature. They combined a new kind of realism and a new kind of romanticism. On the one hand, they dealt with the color, the mystery, the exotic quality of the East; and on the other hand, they did not scruple to introduce sordid realities. Through the power of imagination and of style, they rendered the commonplace significant. They were disconcerting, but they could not be ignored.

It is inevitable that so original and experimental a writer should cause controversy. Contemporary criticism accused him of vulgarity, later criticism of imperialism. In the opinion of many, these accusations reflect upon the validity of the criticism, rather than upon Kipling. To him, to paraphrase a line of his own, there was nothing common in all God's earth. The blemish of imperialism, if it exists at all, is unimportant in relation to the profound and universal morality which underlies his writing. Fortunately, unless exaggeration and distortion enter, such arguments have little relevance to the present discussion concerned with Kipling's books for children. Here, the point of supreme importance is that, with the possible exception of Lewis Carroll, Kipling is the most original, the least derivative of writers for children up to his time and, in these respects, unexcelled since.

In 1892 Kipling married an American, Caroline Balestier. From 1892 to 1896 they lived in Brattleboro, Vermont, where *The Jungle Books* were written (1894, 1895). Not without significance is the fact that critiques of Kipling's work by those not personally nor professionally concerned with children's literature include discussion of his books for children. Still more important is the fact that these books are described frequently as something more than new childhood classics, since such comment indicates growing realization that literature for children may be, and often is, valuable in the study of an author's work and in the study of literature as a whole.

As has been pointed out by Darton among others, in *Children's Books in England*, the initial idea of *The Jungle Books* has precedent in legend and history. Nowhere, however, in traditional or sophisticated literature, has the theme of a human boy reared and nurtured by animals had so unique or meaningful a treatment. No doubt the beast-tale was known to Kipling, acquainted as he was in childhood with the folk literature of India. *Stalky & Co.* (1899) gives evidence of the impression made upon him and his boyhood friends by Joel Chandler Harris' classic Uncle Remus stories. But Kipling's treatment of animals in *The Jungle Books* is, as always with him, an innovation. His literary work stems not from other literature, but from life itself, and from the experience of life, whether animal or human.

Of the fifteen stories in the two books, eight are concerned with Mowgli and the jungle. The world Kipling has created in these stories has an impelling reality. Once known it exists in our minds forever, vivid and familiar as an actual experience. It is an elemental world, and it deals with elemental and eternal things—love and hate, fear and courage, loyalty and treachery, honor and dishonor, honesty and deceit, struggle for existence and the survival of the fittest. Its deepest compulsion is toward obedience to the law, a law which is not an arbitrary thing imposed by authority, but rather a code evolving inevitably from fundamentals of living. It follows that the chief quality of these stories is that of a high ethic, a morality transmuted by imagination into something both functional and inspirational. The basic idea is that of responsibility; from a sense of responsibility comes willing obedience to the law, which is made for the good of all. It is the old, old idea of the obligation owed by the one to the many and by the many to the one.

It is the concept of true freedom, for only those who are truly free can discipline themselves so that liberty does not become license.

Vitalized by Kipling's great power as a writer, this moral code transcends didacticism and becomes something immensely convincing and unquestionably acceptable. The stories have a gripping quality, drawing one into themselves, necessitating no effort at acclimatization on the part of the reader. The mingled humor and pathos, so frequently made up of little things—it is in little touches that Kipling most excels—make the strange setting of the jungle, the weirdness of the Cold Lairs, the primitive quality of some of the incidents, familiar and even intimate. In contrast are the majesty and grandeur of the moments of drama, many of which have epic quality—for a supreme instance, the moment when Akela, his leadership challenged, faces the Pack with dignity and reserve, holding to the Law of the Jungle. Indeed, it is Akela and his kind who dominate the stories, and rightly so, since it is they who have hewn out the Law of the Jungle. True to their types, they are yet individuals—Baloo the bear, Bagheera the panther, and Kaa the serpent. The monkeys are the essence of monkeyishness and still the prototypes of all who are outside the law, because they have no ability to persist, to progress, no sense of responsibility. In the center of it all is Mowgli, nurtured, loved, and educated in the law by the leaders of the jungle, but innately and irrevocably man, so that even those who love him cannot look into his eyes for long. Story, emotion, drama, and character are interpreted for the reader by Kipling's style, by its simple dignity and formality, its lovely cadence and haunting phrase.

The incidental stories are the equals of Kipling's best short stories, especially "Rikki-Tikki-Tavi," "The White Seal," and "Toomai of the Elephants." Many of the poems, which, in accordance with his frequent custom, open and close the stories, may be numbered among his finest poetry. "Seal Lullaby" is a perfect exemplification of its kind, with its slow, swinging rhythm, and the recurring, drowsy "s" and "l" sounds. "Mowgli's Song," recited over the body of Shere Khan, is reminiscent of the ancient epics in its repetitive quality, its defiance and triumph, its measured chant.

One more of Kipling's books for children was conceived during his stay in New England. Dr. James Conland, the family physician, had been a sailor in his youth, and Kipling listened to his tales of life aboard coasters and fishing vessels. Characteristically, his interest was caught by the hardy figures of the New England fishermen, by the way their lives molded their characters, by the drama and adventure of their life at sea. As the idea for *Captains Courageous* took form, he made a trip to Gloucester and spent some weeks among the Gloucester men.

In *Captains Courageous* (1897), as in *The Jungle Books*, Kipling the effective moralist is present. It is a story of the redemption of a spoiled, brash, and objectionable boy, who, through an accident, finds himself on board a fishing vessel. Indulged, pampered, selfish, he is now surrounded by men whose natural straightforwardness and realism have been heightened by their lifetime struggle with the elements, men whose seeming hardness is belied by their capacity for generous sympathy when the right occasion calls. They have neither the time nor the inclination to indulge the whims of anyone, much less a boy whose life they have saved, whose potentialities as a liability they do not intend to see realized. So by dint of unescapable work and discipline, the boy who had been well on the way to becoming a useless member of society becomes an honest and a responsible person. Essentially this is the theory of Rousseau and of his followers in England who formed the didactic school of writers. Kipling even uses, but with greater artistry, the technique of contrast which they employed. There is another and fundamental difference in Kipling's handling of the theme. The didactic writers were in love with their theory; it must be proven at all cost, even at the expense of reality of event and of human nature. Kipling is not only a moralist, he is a great reporter in both the professional and literal sense of the word. His reverence for accuracy, his intense curiosity about all kinds of men, his superior power of observation, his sense of reality, could never permit him to distort essential truth to fit preconceived theory.

In 1896 Kipling returned to England, and eventually established his home in Burwash, Sussex. One of the most penetrating analyses of the spirit of Kipling's writing has been made by a Frenchman, André Chevrillon, who, in his essay, "Rudyard Kipling As a Frenchman Sees Him," gives an equally penetrating description of the spirit of the Sussex country.

> This county of Sussex by the sea is a land of memories . . . The country folk lead the same rustic, Christian life as their forbears . . . The old men have a wisdom . . . that comes from the long years of a life given to the things of woods and fields, and beyond that from the experience of past generations . . . There is the same ancient marriage of a certain race and a certain soil as in our Brittany . . . But some of the songs [in Puck] date from farther back . . . from the bygone times of all those dead whose ashes, mingled with this soil, give it its healing virtue. They have left their traces everywhere: in the old lines barred by gates that have always been there, in the manor house with its smoke curling up behind the wood, in the trees on the village green, in the low Norman church watching over the tombstones on which Eighteenth Century dates are still visible.
>
> Looking round his familiar landscape, Kipling marvels to think

that the men and things of to-day are the same as those of distant
ages . . . that old man Hobden, who clips the Squire's hedge, comes
from a Hobden who in those far-away days clipped the hedge of a
knight.[1]

As *The Jungle Books* and *Kim* are implicit with an understanding and
love of India, so are *Puck of Pook's Hill* (1906) and *Rewards and
Fairies* (1910) inspired with a love of the spirit of the English land
akin, in its intensity, to that felt by the Elizabethans. Indeed, in these
books, Kipling is in the great and beautiful tradition of English writing
from the Anglo-Saxon and Celtic epics through the medieval romance
to generation after generation of writers; the tradition which envisions
the physical and spiritual aspects of the country as one, and the spirit
of England as a changeless and timeless entity. The view of history as a
continuing stream has never received a more telling demonstration than
in these stories, told to Dan and Una by personages from history and
legend, brought back by Puck, the "oldest Old Thing in England."
These books are historic fiction of a kind never written before and never
duplicated since. Told in the manner of fairy tales, and revealing
Kipling's knowledge and love of ancient English folk tradition, still
they have authenticity of truth to place and incident, and the greater
authenticity of imaginative truth which points, with stimulus and inspiration, to the significance underlying fact. Tying the stories together
is the ancient spirit of England, persistent and triumphant, enduring
through invasions, wars and changing civilizations.

Viewed as stories, they are a high exemplification of Kipling's mastery
of short-story technique, which encompassed the realistic and the fanciful. They are so spontaneous as to seem to have a life of their own, an
existence independent of print and paper. And yet, this spontaneity is a
consciously artistic achievement, a product of Kipling's grasp of essential detail, his vivid sense of the pictorial, and his command of a classi-
cally simple prose style. Enhancing the spirit and the moods of the
stories are the songs which precede each chapter, with "Puck's Song"
sounding the key-note for the whole book.

> She is not any common Earth,
> Water or wood or air,
> But Merlin's Isle of Gramarye,
> Where you and I will fare.

It may be that of all his books for children, the *Just So Stories* (1902)
is the book written chiefly for the purpose of entertainment. As such,
it is as great an innovation as his others. These stories, written in the

---

[1] André Chevrillon, "Rudyard Kipling As a Frenchman Sees Him," *Around the
World with Kipling* (Garden City, N.Y., Doubleday, Page, 1926), pp. 73-75.

sophisticated twentieth century, constitute an incredibly apt re-creation of the primitive impulse which gave rise to the many how and why tales which form a part of all folk literature. As might the early peoples, so does Kipling seize upon the distinguishing physical characteristic or native trait of elephant or camel, leopard or cat or butterfly, and weave a story which is an utterly satisfying explanation. Beginning with a distinctive variation on the time-honored folk tale opening, "In the High and Far-Off times, O Best Beloved," and ending on a note of finality, the *Just So Stories* preserve throughout the atmosphere of inescapable logic, of statement without protest, which is so innate a quality of ancient myth. Even more astonishing is their inner semblance of stories of the beginning of all things told in the beginning of the world; a kind of naiveté pervades them, a sense of wonder and curiosity uncontaminated. Yet again it is Kipling who gives them their inimitable form and flavor —Kipling's wit and wisdom, his feeling for the right word and capacity for picturesque phrase and, above all, his dominating sense of story make the *Just So Stories* incomparable.

Kim (1901), though it was not written for children, defies any limitation by age, upward or downward. Not so much a book as a spiritual adventure, it is something to be apprehended rather than comprehended. It is many things to many people, as a true work of art always must be. It is the story of a street urchin, shrewd, clever, indomitable, presented first in a startlingly vivid, unforgettable picture—a boy wearing a turban, perched on a gun "in defiance of municipal orders." It is the story of the quest of the old Lama, unworldly, saintly, with the unassailable dignity of pure innocence. It is the story of the great love between these two, between a precocious child and a childlike old man. It is the story of India, with all its contradictions—mysticism and realism, beauty and ugliness, gentleness and brutality, chivalry and cruelty, loyalty and treachery, truth and deceit. It is a vast panorama of the country— villages and towns, mountains, fields, and rivers—and of its people. It teems with multitudinous life and is permeated with a spiritual quietness. It has plentiful humor of situation and character and is poignant in its great spirit of compassion. It is realism, stark and naked, and romance with a sense of enchantment. It offers the easy appeal of mystery—excitement and suspense—and the subtle appeal of the eternal search for the secret of human destiny. It is a tremendous texture, inextricably woven of the elements of life itself, and to dissect it into its component parts is presumptuous and destructive.

To deal with Kipling's gift to children's literature is to deal inevitably in superlatives. He was one of the greatest of storytellers, one of those who narrate with authority, as one who has seen or heard these things. His intense interest in all sorts and conditions of men, his acute sensitivity to the drama implicit in human and animal life, his universality of interpretation, his imaginative power, endow his stories with a vitality that makes them living entities in their own right. The strength of his belief in the imperishable decencies lends them lasting significance. His masterly command of the English language, his ear for cadence and rhythm, his gift for creating mood, emotion, and atmosphere through sheer use of words, give his style an almost magic quality. His originality of mind, his utter lack of dependence upon past or existent patterns, make him the great innovator of form and type. The vigor of his mind, the keenness of his insight, the breadth of his knowledge, enrich his stories with freedom and profundity of thought.

By the end of the first decade of the twentieth century, Howard Pyle, Robert Louis Stevenson, and Rudyard Kipling had established literature for children as literature in every right sense of the word. What is more important, they had established it as a force to be considered by literary men as an integral part of the development of literature as a whole.

Bibliography

Canby, Henry Seidel. "Estimates of the Dead. 1. Rudyard Kipling." In *Seven Years' Harvest; Notes on Contemporary Literature*. New York, Farrar and Rinehart, 1936. Pp. 20–29.

Chevrillon, André. "Rudyard Kipling As a Frenchman Sees Him." In *Around the World with Kipling*. New York, Doubleday, Page, 1926. Pp. 61–76.

Darton, Frederick Joseph Harvey. *Children's Books in England; Five Centuries of Social Life*. Cambridge, Eng., University Press, 1932.

Gerould, Katherine Fullerton. "The Remarkable Rightness of Rudyard Kipling." *The Atlantic Monthly*, Vol. 123 (Jan., 1919), pp. 12–21.

———— The Man Who Made Mulvaney. *Harper's*, Vol. 172 (April, 1936), pp. 531–538.

Hart, Walter Morris. *Kipling the Story-Writer*. Berkeley, The University of California Press, 1928.

Hooker, Brian. "The Later Work of Mr. Kipling." *The North American Review*, Vol. 193 (May, 1911), pp. 721–732.

Kipling, Rudyard. *Something of Myself; For My Friends Known and Unknown*. Garden City, N.Y., Doubleday, 1937.

Le Gallienne, Richard. "Rudyard Kipling's Place in Literature." In *Around the World with Kipling*. Garden City, N.Y., Doubleday, Page, 1926. Pp. 45–51.

5

Classics in Miniature

It is not an easy task to write for children of any age. The child audience is a demanding and a critical one, with positive likes and dislikes, intolerant of condescension, insincerity, or artificiality. Children live largely in a world created by themselves, resentful of the intrusion of the ordinary adult, but welcoming with wholehearted enthusiasm the adult who can, without affectation, enter that world and accept it with imaginative sympathy.

To write for very little children is even more difficult. To create a world in which little children are at home, to scale down adventure and action and life and joy and sorrow to the confined limits of a small child's experience, to make a book understandable and at the same time interesting and significant, to clothe a story in language which is intelligible to a four- and five- and six-year-old and at the same time imbue it with literary quality, require a mind and temperament which can recapture the sensitivity to impressions, the ever new excitement roused by small incidents, the fresh sense of wonder characteristic of little children. There must also be the ability to tell a story as a small child wants it told, with a beginning that gives character, setting, and situation, with a comfortable basis of the familiar, but with the familiar transformed by the unfamiliar, with emphasis on action and incident, yet with the right amount of selective detail and with a satisfactory and definite culmination.

It is worthy of note that those authors who have made their way into the hearts and minds of generations of children are often those who have not so much written a book as created a world, peopled with unforgettable characters and filled with incidents which are right and inevitable—the world of *Alice in Wonderland* and *Doctor Dolittle*, the world of Wanda Gág and Kenneth Grahame, of Rudyard Kipling and George Macdonald, and the miniature world of Beatrix Potter (1866–1943), who in the early 1900's wrote a number of genuine classics for small children.

Whereas some of the most successful writers for children have had their creative ability brought to fruition by the vivid memory of a happy and contented childhood, others have created to escape harsh and unpleasant realities, past or present. To the latter group, Beatrix Potter belongs. Through childhood, adolescence, and young womanhood, she was a virtual prisoner of convention and class distinction. She and her brother had interests in common, but as a boy he was sent away to school, and as a man he took the first opportunity to create a life of his own. Beatrix, being girl and woman, was less fortunate. Having neither the companionship of her parents nor of those of her own age, she led an abnormally lonely existence, driven in upon herself, creating a life for herself quite divorced from that of her parents, developing in extreme privacy interests and talents peculiarly her own. Even this solace might have been denied her had it not been for the holidays spent in Scotland and the Lake Country. These vacations gave to her and her brother their only opportunities to lead a free and untrammeled life.

It is possibly true that, as Beatrix Potter herself wrote in later life, "It sometimes happens that the town child is more alive to the fresh beauty of the country than a child who is country born." But the fascination which human and animal life in the country held for her was something far more extensive than a surface appreciation of beauty or the welcome relief of a novelty. In the London house, she was like an island; about her, the affairs of daily living flowed on with a dreary monotony, regularized and artificialized until they became remote, vague and shadowy. In the country, all living was reduced to the elemental, the fundamental, the essential. It was vital and exciting. There must have been in her, too, that curious inner feeling of oneness with nature that many children have, and a child's natural love of small things. There was charm for her, also, in the unselfconscious dignity of labor, in the quality of necessity of the work done in fields and farmhouses and cottages. These impressions never left her; until she was able to make such a life for herself they sustained her and gave to her imaginative power that combination of realism and fantasy which is one of the marks of her genius.

The joy and magic of these summer holidays lasted to some degree through the winter season in London. The children brought home with them flowers, plants, and leaves, insects and even dead animals. Little handmade notebooks were filled with drawings, painstakingly and accurately done. Beatrix even managed to acquire pets, a pair of mice, a rabbit, a hedgehog called Tiggy.

The years passed by with a persistent sameness. As Beatrix grew up, she was still isolated from normal companionship, growing more and more shy and reserved. With only a few adults did she feel at home. But with children she made friends easily. With the children of her cousins and of a former governess, she could establish an immediate companionship. To her, as to Kenneth Grahame, children were the only real people, and she had perfect sympathy with their sense of wonder, their love of small things like themselves. To them she wrote letters and in these letters are the indications of the little books that were to be an unexcelled contribution of the early twentieth century.

One of the letters, written to Noel Moore, the oldest child of her former governess, when he was ill, opens with the now almost world-familiar, rhythmic beginning of *The Tale of Peter Rabbit* (1902). "Once upon a time there were four little Rabbits, and their names were Flopsy, Mopsy, Cotton-tail, and Peter." There follow the adventures of Peter in Mr. McGregor's garden, and each incident of the story is illustrated with small, completely satisfying sketches. It is little wonder that Noel kept the letter and had it ready to lend to the author when the idea came to her that she might make a book out of it. It is a thought-provoking fact and a proof of the universality of childhood that so many favorite books have been written for one child and have later pleased hundreds of children, from one generation to another, as initially they pleased the one child for whom they were created.

Beatrix Potter enlarged the original story, added a few illustrations, and submitted *The Tale of Peter Rabbit* to Frederick Warne and Company. They rejected it, as did other publishers to whom she sent it. At last she had it privately printed, a small book, with an illustration on every other page, and only a few lines of text on each page, the perfect book in format and size for the small child. The book sold so well that she was thinking of a second edition when Warne's notified her that they would like to publish it if she would do colored illustrations for it, rather than black and white.

She worked on the new drawings at her brother's farm in Roxburghshire, having no difficulty with the rabbits, but finding Mr. and Mrs. McGregor a problem. "I never learnt to draw figures," she wrote. She was, if anything, overanxious that the illustrations should be satisfactory to the publisher. In spite of her concern, the drawings went well, and she took great joy in the work, which gave her the novel and pleasant feeling of an individual and independent existence.

In the meantime, she had visited Gloucester where she had heard a strange story of a tailor who had left a coat unfinished, and the next morning found it finished but for one buttonhole. To it had been fastened a piece of paper on which was written "no more twist." The charming mystery of this tale tantalized her and stimulated her imagination. She sketched the house and the street in which the tailor was supposed to have lived, made drawings of the interiors and furnishings of old cottages in the district. Out of this grew *The Tailor of Gloucester* (1903), written first in a notebook for Freda Moore, Noel's sister—"Because you are fond of fairy tales, and have been ill, I have made you a story all for yourself—a new one that nobody has read before. And the queerest thing about it is—that I heard it in Gloucestershire, and that it is true—at least, about the tailor, the waistcoat, and the 'No more twist.' "[1]

She felt that it was a better book than *The Tale of Peter Rabbit*, and, indeed in the opinion of many it is her masterpiece which Masefield has called "a gem of English prose." She hesitated to show it to Warne's, believing that they would not be interested in another book so soon after the publication of *The Tale of Peter Rabbit*. So once more she paid to have it privately printed. A copy of this edition was sent to Norman Warne, who evidently, judging from a letter written him by Beatrix Potter, liked it, but suggested abridgment and the omission of some of the rhymes. Publication by Warne was delayed, in order to see how the private edition sold. Apparently it went well, for the next year, 1903, she began work on a new edition, with new illustrations, for publication by Warne. The exquisitely detailed pictures of eighteenth century costumes were copied from historic costumes in the South Kensington Museum.

In that same year, 1903, *The Tale of Squirrel Nutkin* appeared, an unquestionable success, since it brought the author her first letters of appreciation from her child audience. As is the case with so many of her books, the germ of the story is in a letter, written several years before to a child of her acquaintance, where she mentions an American legend about squirrels that voyaged on a river on little rafts, using their tails for sails. The owl, in *The Tale of Squirrel Nutkin*, was a former pet of her brother's who had the unpleasant habit of sitting with a mouse's tail hanging out of his mouth.

The Tale of Benjamin Bunny, a cousin of Peter Rabbit, was published in 1904, and for the next ten years, the little books appeared, sometimes one, sometimes two or three a year. They took shape from her memories of her childhood pets, like the hedgehog in *The Tale of Mrs. Tiggy-winkle* (1905), who was "just like a very fat, rather stupid little dog," but a very clean and neat little animal; from her letters to Noel Moore, his brothers and sisters, and to other children.

> My dear Eric, Once upon a time there was a frog called Mr. Jeremy Fisher, and he lived in a little house on the bank of a river.[2]

> Once upon a time there was an old cat called Mrs. Tabitha Twitchit, who was an anxious parent.[3]

[1] Margaret Lane, *The Tale of Beatrix Potter* (London, Warne, 1946), pp. 64–65.
[2] *Ibid.*, p. 55.
[3] *Ibid.*, p. 56.

Many of them were subjected to the searching criticism of children before they were put in their final form. "The words of the squirrel book [*Squirrel Nutkin*] will need cutting down, to judge by the children here; I have got several good hints about the words."

Others of her stories grew out of the life and surroundings of Hill Top Farm in the Lake Country, which she had purchased in 1905. This would seem to have been an unprecedentedly independent step for a daughter of the Potters. However, it took place in the same year that saw her engagement to Norman Warne, which had brought down upon her the heavy disapproval of her parents, who would not sanction the engagement since the Warnes were in the "trade" of publishing. Under these circumstances, the purchase of a farm was a very minor matter. But to Beatrix herself, it was the beginning of life as she had always wanted it, and it is good to know that she had this solace when, in December of 1905, Norman Warne died.

The years that followed her acquisition of Hill Top Farm saw much of her finest writing done. Her satisfaction in a place of her own, the love of the way of life it represented, the fascination which all the small details of daily living and of the surroundings had for her—all of this found expression in the books she wrote and illustrated during the years that preceded her marriage. Those lovers of her books who have visited the vicinity which inspired so much of her writing have commented with delight on the fact that over and over again, in text and pictures, are exact re-creations of the house, its attic and cupboards and furnishings, of the garden and the farmyard, of the fields and woods and hills.

With her marriage to William Heelis in 1913, and her complete removal to life on the farm, came the end of her best writing. Having achieved in reality the life she had for so long lived in imagination, it was as though she wanted to divorce herself completely from everything connected with the past years, even from the writing and painting which had given her her only escape. Having attained independence, she worked hard at it, developing, almost self-consciously, eccentricities of habit, thought, speech, which would mark her more intensely as an individual. She was no longer Beatrix Potter, the author and illustrator, but Mrs. William Heelis, wife, housewife, and country woman, descendant of "generations of Lancashire yeomen and weavers, obstinate, hardheaded, matter-of-fact folk," as she once wrote. She resented deeply any intrusion on the seclusion of her life. So rigidly did she and her publishers maintain her privacy that few people in England realized that Beatrix Potter was still living. Americans had greater access to her than did her own countrymen, possibly because those Americans who sought her out were personally and professionally interested in children's books. At least, her biographer, Margaret Lane, attributes her reception of American visitors, first, to the "serious and intelligent attitude toward children's literature, and the flattering American appraisement of her own work" and, secondly, to the "comforting sense of personal security conferred by the Atlantic."

In 1929, *The Fairy Caravan* was published in America by McKay. This story of a circus troupe of animals who travel in a caravan about the country surrounding the farm where Beatrix Potter lived suffers in comparison with her earlier books. In great part, this is due to the structure, since the book is a medley of tales told by the animals, strung on the connecting thread of the incidents and adventures connected with their travels. The beautiful irreducible minimum of incident and expression, so characteristic of her earlier work, is lacking, and in its place there is a rambling and profuse quality, together with occasional irrelevancy. However, there are plentiful remnants of the former charm and humor and style; the inevitable casting of the guinea pig as a Sultan of Zanzibar, the details of the making of his costume, the flavor of some of the stories woven into the main plot, the beauty of the descriptions of the countryside; all these are dim reflections of the unique character of the earlier books.

The Tale of Little Pig Robinson, a second book published in America by David McKay Company in 1930, and simultaneously by Warne in England, is the longest of her single-plot stories, and a disappointment to those accustomed to the artistry of the compactness and plausibility of plot in previous books.

Wag-by-Wall is the last of her books, and was published in book form by The Horn Book in 1944 after the death of Beatrix Potter in December 1943. She had once thought of it as a companion piece to *The Tailor of Gloucester*. Later it had been included in *The Fairy Caravan* but was omitted before that book was published. It is a gentle little story of an old woman who finds a treasure in a stocking. One could almost guess that this had been written in her latter life. Lacking in vitality, still it has a dreamlike semblance to the work of the younger Beatrix Potter.

It is difficult to capture the excellence and unique charm of Beatrix Potter's writing. The greatness of her books lies chiefly in a complete harmony of story expression and illustration. To analyze is to run the risk of shattering the totality of impression and of making commonplace the little world she created. If the plots of her stories were summarized, they might seem to be similar to many other shallow and footless stories written for little children. It is the delicate and discerning quality of imagination, the exquisite, disciplined economy of incident, detail, and words, the unusual perception of what pleases little children, which give them distinction and which mark her as an author of authentic genius.

Possibly the best way to attempt a critical evaluation is from the viewpoint of her contribution to literature for little children. The little books are perfect picture-story books, with complete harmony between picture and story, perfect placement of pictures, and detail in illustration which literally illustrates. It is difficult to contemplate what might have been had Beatrix Potter not had the twin talents of writing and drawing. There is, in her illustrations, an enhancement of the spirit of the story, its characters, its action, its humor, its pathos, set always against a background of unobtrusive beauty. From the beginning, any child can sense the mood of Peter Rabbit, as he stands with his back toward his mother and sisters, a stubborn, withdrawn look on his face. Many a child has wept over the pathos of the frightened little rabbit, with one foot over the other, one paw pressed against his mouth, the other against the locked door, under which "there was no room for a fat little rabbit to squeeze." And any child can chuckle sympathetically and with relief, over the Peter Rabbit, safe at home, but hiding under the bedcovers, only his ears showing, as his mother stands over him with a dose of camomile tea.

The manner in which she manages to humanize her animals, and still keep them animals, is mysterious and intriguing, and is the secret of that rare combination of reality and fantasy which gives her work so deeply genuine a quality and sets it apart from inferior works. With her, there is no caricature, no silly exaggeration, no vulgarity. Instead there is humor and pathos and a simple naturalness, which causes one to accept without question. Though they may be dressed in clothes, and performing human functions, her animals remain true to themselves and therefore convincing. Mrs. Tittlemouse, asleep in her chair, is the absolute exemplification of the exhausted and frustrated housewife, and still she remains mouse. The fidelity to detail of animal appearance and of scenes lends the pictures extraordinary authenticity and beauty—the woodland glade in *The Tale of Squirrel Nutkin*, with Nutkin, running just as squirrels do, the vista to be seen from the chimney of Tom Kitten's house, the lovely snowy street scenes in *The Tailor of Gloucester* are the finest art. Yet this background of beauty is never allowed to intrude upon the story quality of the pictures. Remaining background, it heightens the reality of the story, as do the lifelike interiors of cottages and farmhouses and shops—the fireplace in *The Roly-Poly Pudding* (1908), a replica of Beatrix Potter's own fireplace at Hill Top Farm, the cupboards and dressers, the old china. A child may sense, without conscious realization, the emotional quality such pictures contain, the pride, the serenity, and security imparted by loved, accustomed, prized possessions.

The stories themselves are swift-paced, action-full, chary of description. Always there is the comfortingly familiar, completely informing beginning, and the ear-appealing sounds of the proper names.

> Once upon a time there was a little fat comfortable grey squirrel, called Timmy Tiptoes.

> Once upon a time there were three little kittens, and their names were Mittens, Tom Kitten and Moppet.

> Once upon a time there was a wood-mouse and her name was Mrs. Tittlemouse.

Equally satisfying are the endings of the stories, with their finality and security, for while a small child wants suspense, he will not tolerate tragedy at the end.

The animals are little, appealing, familiar animals, living in a world of their own. Each animal lives in just the right kind of home for him. Mrs. Tittlemouse in a "mossy bank under a hedge"; the four little rabbits in a sandbank under the root of a very big fir tree; Mrs. Tiggywinkle in a hill with a door that opened on a "nice clean kitchen with a flagged floor and wooden beams, just like any other farm kitchen"; Tom Kitten and his family in a real house, as befits a household pet. To the little child, whose instinct for personification is strong and who must necessarily interpret everything in terms of his own experience, it is entirely credible that animals should live so, and entirely acceptable that familiar surroundings and incidents of everyday life should be shared by animals. While Beatrix Potter does not hesitate to introduce hazard and danger and near tragedy, her books are permeated with a feeling of intimacy and coziness and of the pleasant life.

Her characters are uninvolved, one-type characters, consistently true in speech and deed to themselves. Mrs. Tittlemouse is a "most terribly tidy particular little mouse, always sweeping and dusting the soft sandy floors." Mrs. Tabitha Twitchit is an "anxious parent"; a wealth of characterization is in those two words. Peter Rabbit and Benjamin Bunny and Squirrel Nutkin are small rebels—set in contrast to their more docile and amenable companions. The events of the story develop naturally from the nature of the primary character.

Brief and toned-down for the little child as the books are, still there is no inanity, that frequent curse of writing for the very young. Common sense and shrewd humor give them strength; action and genuine adventure—even danger—give them suspense; sentiment without mawkishness gives them sincerity of emotional quality; the manner of their telling puts upon them the seal of imaginative truth. Beatrix Potter knew well that realism may be sound without being literal, and that truth goes beyond mere truth to fact.

In spite of the brevity of the stories, there is a plentitude of the right kind of detail, the kind of detail which is so eminently satisfying because it tells all and no more than one wants to know. It is concrete, specific, selective, and often imbued with an imaginative quality which gives vividness and a sudden sense of actuality. In Mrs. Tiggy-winkle's kitchen there is a "nice, hot singey smell," a phrase which produces an immediate sense impression so clear, so reminiscent as to transport the reader, or the hearer, immediately to the scene. Mrs. Tittlemouse has a fitting dinner for a mouse, cherry-stones and thistle-down seed. When she got rid of her unwelcome and untidy visitor, she "began a spring house-cleaning that lasted a fortnight. She swept and scrubbed and dusted; and she rubbed up her furniture with beeswax, and polished her little tin spoons." And then, like any proud housekeeper, she gave a party before her house should get dirty again. Mrs. Tiggy-winkle's "print gown was tucked up, and she was wearing a large apron over her striped petticoat. Her little black nose went sniffle, sniffle, snuffle, and her eyes went twinkle, twinkle."

If a squirrel should play marbles and ninepins, he would, of course, play marbles with "oak-apples—yellow and scarlet" and ninepins with a "crab apple and green fir cones for ball and pins." Old Mrs. Rabbit earned her living by selling "herbs, and rosemary tea and rabbit-tobacco (which is what we call lavender)." Much of the beauty of *The Tailor of Gloucester* lies in its descriptive detail. "One bitter cold day near Christmas-time, the tailor began to make a coat (a coat of cherry-coloured corded silk embroidered with pansies and roses) and a cream-coloured satin waistcoat (trimmed with gauze and green worsted chenille). . . . There were twelve pieces for the coat and four pieces for the waistcoat; and there were pocket-flaps and cuffs and buttons, all in order. For the lining of the coat there was fine yellow taffeta, and for the buttonholes of the waistcoat there was cherry-coloured twist. . . . There were roses and pansies upon the facings of the coat; and the waistcoat was worked with poppies and corn-flowers."

Beatrix Potter's style is permanent and vital proof of the fact that literature for little children need not lack the stimulation of good, sound, and beautiful English prose. She herself has implied that she wrote and rewrote, tried out her writing with children, and then wrote again. But nowhere is there evidence of selfconsciousness or of writing down. There is the dignity of simplicity, the music of well-chosen words, the lilt of rhythm.

> In the time of swords and periwigs and full-skirted coats with flowered lappets—when gentlemen wore ruffles, and gold-laced waistcoats of paduasoy and taffeta—there lived a tailor in Gloucester.[1]

[1] Beatrix Potter, *The Tailor of Gloucester* (London, Warne, 1903), p. 9.

The moon climbed up over the roofs and chimneys, and looked down over the gateway into College Court. There were no lights in the windows, nor any sound in the houses; all the city of Gloucester was fast asleep under the snow.[1]

Pervading style and story is the feeling of deep love for the English countryside, not only for its physical beauty, but also for its spirit and tradition. So much is this aspect a part of the whole, so integrated is it with plot and style, that one may search almost in vain for descriptions of garden and hill and meadow. Only in *The Fairy Caravan* do such descriptions appear. Yet it is this quality of identification of story with a specific and real country which, as much as any other quality, places Beatrix Potter as a writer in the finest tradition of English prose.

The imaginative power that never degenerates into trivial fancy, the creativeness that never deteriorates into mere inventiveness, the ability to create plot and to infuse characters with life, the mastery of a simple and pure style, the knowledge of a small child's world—all these are hers. But there is something more elusive, less easy to define, which gives to her permanent distinction, and which, for more than fifty years, has called forth the warm response which small children lavish in such great measure upon books which are truly theirs. In all her writing, there is a convincingness, an effect of belief in her own story. In part, this is due to her almost matter-of-fact presentation, refreshing as a drink of cool water when contrasted with the preciousness, the over-elaboration and straining for effect characteristic of less able writers of fantasy. But there is something deeper and more significant here; underlining her stories are the eternal verities of life—love of home and countryside, the dignity of work, the decency of simple, average beings, the mingled humor and pathos of existence. It is the reflection of these imperishable truths which makes the tales of Beatrix Potter classics in miniature.

---

[1] Potter, *op. cit.*, p. 37.

Bibliography

Lane, Margaret. *The Tale of Beatrix Potter; a Biography.* London and New York, Warne, 1946.

Mahony, Bertha E. "Beatrix Potter and Her Nursery Classics." *The Horn Book*, Vol. 17 (May–June, 1941), pp. 230–238.

——— "Beatrix Potter in Letters." *The Horn Book*, Vol. 20 (May–June, 1944), pp. 214–224.

6

A Landmark in Fantasy

Beatrix Potter was not the only creator of beauty in children's books in the opening years of the twentieth century, although her pre-eminence as a writer for the nursery age is unquestionable, then as now. In letters she wrote to some of her American friends, there is an implication that she did not know of the work of some of her contemporaries who enriched children's literature for all time with beauty of idea, of execution, and with an understanding of children comparable to her own. "In the main, children's literature has not been taken seriously over here—too much left to the appeal of gaudy covers and binding and the choice of the toy sellers." Her biographer, quoting this, comments that "she seems, mysteriously, to have been quite unaware of her wonderful contemporary E. Nesbit." Not so mysterious perhaps, but equally regrettable, is the probability that she may have been unaware of Kenneth Grahame (1859–1932). There is deep spiritual kinship between Peter Rabbit and Grahame's *The Wind in the Willows* (1908); and the children who, in their nursery days, become acquainted with the literature of Peter Rabbit, at an older age are readily at home in the imaginative world of *The Wind in the Willows*.

There is, indeed, spiritual kinship between Beatrix Potter and Kenneth Grahame, different as were aspects of their backgrounds and personalities. Both had a liberality of idea which prevented them from ever descending to the commonplace and which enabled them to treat the seemingly trivial and ordinary in the light of its larger significance. In this respect, they were outstanding, even in a period when writing for children was distinguished by freedom from narrow restrictions of form and content. Both were endowed naturally with a genuine, instinctive understanding of the child's attitude toward life, and of the things a child holds important. Both retained, all their lives, what Kenneth Grahame called the "wonder of the world." To an American admirer, he said:

> Children are not merely people: they are the only really living people that have been left to us in an over-weary world. Any

normal child will instinctively agree with your own American poet, Walt Whitman, when he said: "To me every hour of the day and night is an unspeakably perfect miracle." In my tales about children, I have tried to show that their simple acceptance of the mood of wonderment, their readiness to welcome a perfect miracle at any hour of the day or night, is a thing more precious than any of the laboured acquisitions of adult mankind. . . . As for animals, I wrote about the most familiar and domestic in *The Wind in the Willows* because I felt a duty to them as a friend. Every animal, by instinct, lives according to his nature. Thereby he lives wisely, and betters the tradition of mankind. No animal is ever tempted to belie his nature. No animal, in other words, knows how to tell a lie. Every animal is honest. Every animal is straightforward. Every animal is true—and is, therefore, according to his nature, both beautiful and good.[1]

Beatrix Potter would have thoroughly appreciated the last few sentences.

Kenneth Grahame was born in Edinburgh on March 8, 1859, in a house facing the one in which Sir Walter Scott had lived. Although the Grahames moved away while Kenneth was still a baby, he retained, all his life, a memory of his father's pride in living so close to the home of Scott.

In 1860 James Cunninghame Grahame, Kenneth's father, became Sheriff Substitute for Argyllshire. The family moved to Ardrishaig to await the building of their permanent home at Inverary. It is quite probable, as Grahame's biographer believes, that at Ardrishaig the small boy first felt that fascination for water, boats, and small water animals which was to be the moving spirit of his great fantasy.

When the boy was five, his mother died, and the children were sent to live with their grandmother, first on the Thames, and later in Cranborne, Windsor.

In 1868 he was sent to St. Edward's School, Oxford, where he became head of the school and captain of the rugby. It was his great desire to go on to the university but the family decided against this on the ground of expense. So in 1879 Grahame received an appointment to a clerkship in the Bank of England, in which institution he rose to be Secretary. After his death, it was written of him that he "conferred a distinction on the institution of which he was a member comparable to that with which Charles Lamb honored the East India House."[2]

Kenneth Grahame first came to the attention of the literary world

[1] Clayton Hamilton, "Frater Ave Atque Vale," *The Bookman*, Vol. 76 (Jan., 1933), p. 72.
[2] Patrick Chalmers, *Kenneth Grahame; Life, Letters and Unpublished Work* (London, Methuen, 1933), p. 119.

in the 1890's as one of the young writers of promise whom William Ernest Henley gathered about him and who were contributing to the *Scots Observer* and to its successor, the *National Observer*. Henley, sensing Grahame's potential quality as a writer, urged and in fact almost demanded that he become a professional man of letters. But Grahame steadfastly refused, preferring, it is said, the orderliness and security of the life which his business provided for him. This may be so, but it is also probable that he knew well the peculiar and intimately personal nature of the thoughts and ideas which occasionally he was impelled to put into written words, that he was aware that the well of his inspiration would run dry if drawn upon too often. He protested once that he was a spring, not a pump, and again, that to "toil at making sentences" meant sitting indoors for many hours, cramped over a desk; yet out-of-doors, "the wind may be singing." The singing of the wind gave the world one book, unsurpassed of its kind, and it may be well that Grahame did not yield to the demand for more.

In the midst of a group of writers of unusual and varied talent and personality, he seems to have stood out as a rare spirit. The impression he made, even on casual acquaintances, was extraordinary. He was a shy, extremely reserved man. Yet his presence in any group was a deeply felt thing. Over and over, spoken and written comment dwells upon his physical beauty, and the comparable beauty of his spirit and personality. Apparently the inner quality that distinguished him was something difficult to capture in words, a fact which led to seemingly extravagant efforts to describe his nobility, his charm, his strange unworldliness.

His writing also seemed to individualize him and to set him apart from the others. Among the literary set who wrote for the *National Observer* and later for the famous *Yellow Book*, an article of his was an event. With the publication of "The Olympians," his reputation as a writer of originality on a new subject became fixed.

"The Olympians," later to become the Prologue to *The Golden Age*, was included in the first edition of *Pagan Papers* (1893), a collection of essays which had been published previously in the *National Observer*. The book was received enthusiastically for its style and for that quality which was to be a supreme characteristic of all Grahame's writing, his joy in life and living. This unassumed and unassuming pleasure in a way of life indifferent to the artificial rules of society seems to have made a great impression on the critics of the conventionalized nineties. This impression was heightened and a new element added by "The Olympians" and its companion articles, which firmly established Grahame among those rare writers who can write knowledgeably about childhood and children.

When, in 1895, the collection of story sketches about children called

The Golden Age was published; its effect was astonishing. The praise poured forth in reviews may seem exaggerated to an age more skeptical and more inclined to destructive criticism. As Swinburne, Anatole France, and others have pointed out, it is an art to be able to write adequately and acceptably about children. *The Golden Age* and its companion, *Dream Days*, which appeared in 1898, are more than adequate and acceptable writing about children. They are books instinct with the imagination of a time of life when a day of wind and sun initiates one into the secret life of the earth; when a clump of rhododendrons by a pond can be transformed into a tropical forest, or a hay wagon into the deck of the *Revenge;* when the visit of the mummers on Twelfth Night can bring hopes that on some quiet winter night Merlin might come, or "Ogier the Dane, recalled from Faëry, asking his way to the land that once had need of him! Or even, on some white night the Snow-Queen herself, with a chime of sleigh-bells and the patter of reindeer's feet, halting of a sudden at the door flung wide, while aloft the Northern Lights went shaking attendant spears among the quiet stars!"[1]

These books about children were not intended to be for children but for adults, those Olympians whose existence

> seemed to be entirely devoid of interests, even as . . . their habits [were] stereotyped and senseless. To anything but appearances they were blind. For them the orchard (a place elf-haunted, wonderful!) simply produced so many apples and cherries . . . They never set foot within fir-wood or hazelcopse, nor dreamt of the marvels hid therein. The mysterious sources, sources as of old Nile, that fed the duck-pond had no magic for them. They were unaware of Indians, nor recked they anything of bisons or of pirates (with pistols!), though the whole place swarmed with such portents. They cared not to explore for robbers' caves, nor dig for hidden treasure. Perhaps, indeed, it was one of their best qualities that they spent the greater part of their time stuffily indoors.[2]

In fairness to the Olympians of Grahame's time, it must be said that they recognized, perhaps nostalgically, the truth and value of his depiction of the realities of child existence and of the gulf of incomprehensibility that divides the child world from the adult world. If this led them to type him as a specialist and to disappoinment when his fourth, last, and greatest book appeared, they were not the first nor the last to fall into the fallacy of expecting an author constantly to repeat himself.

The origin of *The Wind in the Willows* is well known. Kenneth Grahame had been in the habit of telling his small son at bedtime

[1] Kenneth Grahame, *The Golden Age* (London, John Lane, 1899), p. 122.
[2] *Ibid.*, p. 5.

stories of a water-rat, a mole, and a toad. When the boy was sent to the seaside for a vacation, he exacted a promise that written installments should be sent him. So they were, in the form of letters which his governess kept and returned to Mrs. Grahame for safekeeping. How these stories, many of which had been told orally, finally were put into a connected written form, seems uncertain. Patrick Chalmers, in his biography, says they were finally "committed to foolscap in the author's own distinct write-of-hand." Mrs. Grahame, in *First Whisper of "The Wind in the Willows,"* says they were "more or less in manuscript form," when a representative of *Everybody's*, the American magazine, begged Grahame, in 1907, to write something for the magazine. Kenneth Grahame claimed that he had nothing written and would not promise to write anything. But Mrs. Grahame remembered the stories about Rat, Toad, and Mole and suggested that they be submitted for publication. Consequently, *Everybody's* was sent a manuscript called *The Wind in the Reeds*. And *Everybody's* rejected the manuscript, keenly disappointed that it was not another *Golden Age*. Mrs. Grahame tells with understandable glee of the aftermath of this error.

> Therefore Kenneth asked for the MS. to be sent back, and it was forthwith published in England, and when the head of that American firm saw how the book made its way into the hearts of its English readers he was a sad man, and lived to call his beautiful American country-home by the name of "Toad Hall."[1]

In 1908 the book was published under the title of *The Wind in the Willows* by Methuen and Company in London and by Scribner in New York. Graham Robertson had suggested the change in title, since a collection of Yeats's poems was called *The Wind Among the Reeds*. The reviews show clearly that the editor of *Everybody's* was not the only one to feel disappointment. However, one reviewer, Richard Middleton, writing in *Vanity Fair*, did not allow his love for the older books to blind him to the beauty of the new one.

Gradually the book made its way, not only into the hearts of English readers, as Mrs. Grahame said, but into the hearts of Americans and of people the world over. Kenneth Grahame sent a copy to Theodore Roosevelt, who had once written that he and his wife could pass an examination in *The Golden Age* and *Dream Days*, especially in the psychology of Harold. Roosevelt, at first indisposed to be impressed by any book which omitted the irresistible Harold, succumbed gracefully and graciously to the delight of *The Wind in the Willows*. From all over the world came moving letters of appreciation, including one

---

[1] Mrs. Elspeth Grahame, ed., *First Whisper of "The Wind in the Willows" by Kenneth Grahame* (New York, Lippincott, 1945), p. 4.

from the Prime Minister of Australia, expressing his gratitude and admiration.

From America, again, comes a tribute from a lesser person than the President of the United States and the Prime Minister of Australia. Clayton Hamilton tells of it in the previously mentioned article in *The Bookman*. On a visit to the Grand Canyon, he found at the beginning of Bright Angel Trail, a little bookshop, the chief stock of which consisted of the kind of books tourists read in Pullman cars. In the place of honor, on the center table, was a copy of *The Wind in the Willows*. The woman proprietor told him that she had been a clerk in a bookstore in Chicago when *The Wind in the Willows* was published, and she had promised herself that if she ever owned a bookstore, there would always be a copy of the book in the place of honor.

It is rather lonely here—most of the people who drift into my bookshop are merely tourists—But I can always tell a real person by the look that comes into his eyes when he sees *The Wind in the Willows* . . . you, for instance, are the first real person who has come here in three months and seventeen days.[1]

And in England, A. A. Milne, who himself has written for children in the fine English tradition which has contributed so many permanent treasures to children's literature, also thinks of the book as a touchstone.

A Household Book—[one] which everybody in the household loves and quotes continuously ever afterwards. . . . When you sit down to it, don't be so ridiculous as to suppose that you are sitting in judgment on my taste, still less on the genius of Kenneth Grahame. You are merely sitting in judgment on yourself. . . . You may be worthy; I do not know. But it is you who are on trial.[2]

So a President of the United States, a Prime Minister of Australia, an English writer and a lonely bookseller express the feeling of those who "are worthy," for *The Wind in the Willows* holds many things for many people, yet basically the same thing. The chapter which dwelt with Theodore Roosevelt was "Wayfarers All," which expresses so vividly the spirit of him who must wander; others, when they think of the book, think first of "Dulce Domum," the Christmas chapter, with its mood of poignant, nostalgic longing for home. Others, and many others, feel that the whole book culminates in the magic, mystery, and poetry of "The Piper at the Gates of Dawn." It is a book which has one motif, but plays upon that motif in many different keys. The motif is the "spirit of divine discontent and longing." It is played upon with warmth

[1] Hamilton, *op. cit.*, pp. 69–70.
[2] A. A. Milne, "A Household Book," *Not That It Matters* (New York, E. P. Dutton, 1920), p. 88.

and sympathy in the first chapter when Mole finds enchantment and contentment by the river. In contrast, the nonsensical treatment of the disconcerting adventures of Toad heightens the spirit of restlessness characteristic of those who are in constant pursuit of new sensations. There is gentle understanding of the eternal longing for the security of one's own place in the homesickness of Mole as he scents, on the cold winds of Christmas Eve, the home that he had forgotten. Again, in contrast, there is the colorful romanticism of the Sea Rat's description of the call which drives those who are wayfarers at heart. Finally there is the sense of awe, of mystery and of mysticism in the music of the Piper, as Mole and Water Rat heard that music in the strange and unearthly dawn.

All of this is expressed in a prose style which changes color as the mood of the book changes. From the publication of *Pagan Papers* in 1893 on, Kenneth Grahame was acclaimed unanimously as a master of English prose. He had an ear for the nobility and majesty of English style and once claimed that there were not more than six men in the United Kingdom who inherited an ear for prose, of whom one was Rudyard Kipling. Amid all the praise lavished upon him as a writer, two tributes stand out, the first by Clayton Hamilton, the second by F. J. Harvey Darton.

> It is a truth that, on that day [July 6, 1932, the day of Grahame's death], the translators of the King James version of the Bible, seated at an eternal council-table, admitted to their fellowship the last great master of English prose. . . .[1]

> In *The Wind in the Willows* he simply enjoyed himself, though he indulged the poet in him in two passages of the finest modern English prose.[2]

It is a fascinating, if tantalizing, pastime to attempt to identify the two passages referred to by Darton, passages which Darton, irritatingly, does not identify. Worthy of notice, surely, is the description of the river as Mole first discovers it; or the description of the "Terror of the Wild Wood," with the masterly, breathtaking ending to one paragraph. "And he—he was alone . . . and far from any help; and the night was closing in." Surely there is more than one part of "The Piper at the Gates of Dawn" which might be selected—this, for example:

> The line of the horizon was clear and hard against the sky, and in one particular quarter it showed black against a silvery climbing phosphorescence that grew and grew. At last, over the

---

[1] Hamilton, *op. cit.*, p. 74.

[2] F. J. Harvey Darton, *Children's Books in England* (Cambridge, Eng., University Press, 1932), p. 322.

rim of the waiting earth the moon lifted with slow majesty till it swung clear of the horizon and rode off, free of moorings; and once more they began to see surfaces—meadows wide-spread, and quiet gardens, and the river itself from bank to bank, all softly disclosed, all washed clean of mystery and terror, all radiant again as by day. . . .[1]

or this:

Breathless and transfixed the Mole stopped rowing as the liquid run of that glad piping broke on him like a wave, caught him up, and possessed him utterly. He saw the tears on his comrade's cheeks, and bowed his head and understood. For a space they hung there, brushed by the purple loosestrife that fringed the bank; then the clear imperious summons that marched hand-in-hand with the intoxicating melody imposed its will on Mole, and mechanically he bent to his oars again. And the light grew steadily stronger, but no birds sang as they are wont to do at the approach of dawn; and but for the heavenly music all was marvellously still.[2]

There are echoes of Pyle in that passage, which is not really surprising, since both Pyle and Grahame were steeped in appreciation of the beauty of English style as it is revealed in the Bible, in Milton, in Shakespeare. One of Darton's passages must certainly be in "Wayfarers All," which is full of word pictures as brilliant as those of Joseph Conrad. As the first chapter is the expression of the spirit of spring, so "Wayfarers All" is the epitome of autumn, when there is a "feeling in the air of change and departure," a call that the Sea Rat and those like him cannot resist.

And the talk, the wonderful talk flowed on—or was it speech entirely, did it pass at times into song—chanty of the sailors weighing the dripping anchor, sonorous hum of the shrouds in a tearing North-Easter, ballad of the fisherman hauling his nets at sundown against an apricot sky, chords of guitar and mandoline from gondola or caique? Did it change into the cry of the wind, plaintive at first, angrily shrill as it freshened, rising to a tearing whistle, sinking to a musical trickle of air from the leech of the bellying sail? . . . Back into speech again it passed, and with beating heart he was following the adventures of a dozen seaports, the fights, the escapes, the rallies, the comradeships, the gallant undertakings; or he searched islands for treasure, fished in still lagoons and dozed day-long on warm white sand. Of deep-sea fishings he heard tell, and mighty silver gatherings of the mile-

[1] Kenneth Grahame, *The Wind in the Willows* (New York, Scribner, 1961 ed.), p. 130.
[2] *Ibid.*, p. 133.

long net; of sudden perils, noise of breakers on a moonless night, or the tall bows of the great liner taking shape overhead through the fog; of the merry home-coming, the headland rounded, the harbour lights opened out; the groups seen dimly on the quay, the cheery hail, the splash of the hawser; the trudge up the steep little street towards the comforting glow of red-curtained windows.[1]

As Richard Middleton has said, it is hard to be critical of a book which offers such wealth of beauty and fun, of sense and nonsense, of joy and seriousness expressed in words whose music is a joy in itself. The very inconsistency with which the characters, who bear the names of small animals, are treated is in itself endearing, and somehow, an inevitable trait of the book as a whole. Sometimes they are animals, sometimes animals endowed with human traits, sometimes neither animal nor human. If this places the book on a lower plane than *Alice in Wonderland*, with its logical inevitability, the lovers of *The Wind in the Willows* believe that in this case certainly inconsistency is the bugbear of little minds. As has been said, it must have been fun to write it because it is fun to read it. And yet that is not all—into it Kenneth Grahame put the whole of himself and his love of life and of living things.

That it is, and that it will remain, his best-loved book is attested by the number of printings and editions issued. It was published first (1908) without illustrations except for a frontispiece by Graham Robertson. Five years later, in 1913, it was issued in an illustrated edition for the first time with pictures by Paul Bransom, pictures which emphasized realistically the animal aspects of the characters. In contrast is the edition (1922) illustrated in color and in black and white by Nancy Barnhart, whose illustrations point up the qualities of humor, imagination, and beauty inherent in the story. In the view of many, the unpretentious black-and-white sketches of Ernest H. Shepard, first published in 1931, give fullest expression to the spirit of the book, blending with the text so that story and pictures become a whole. In 1936 George Macy, director of the Limited Editions Club, suggested to Arthur Rackham that he illustrate *The Wind in the Willows*. Rackham received the suggestion with pleasure tinged with emotion. When the book was first published, he had been asked by Kenneth Grahame to make illustrations for it, and had refused, due to press of other work. Like the editor of *Everybody's*, he had lived to regret his refusal. It is satisfying to know that Rackham's last work was done for a book which he had longed to illustrate. Much of the work was done in his last illness, part of it when he could work only a half hour a day. In spite of this handicap, the illustrations are typical Rackham, with their soft, misty colors, their imaginative detail, and their technical excellence. A limited edition, designed

[1] Grahame, *op. cit.*, pp. 182–183.

by Bruce Rogers, was published in 1940. In 1944 the Heritage Press reprint appeared, containing twelve colored illustrations and numerous charming black-and-white drawings at the heads of chapters.

In 1900 *The Golden Age* and in 1902 *Dream Days* were reissued with illustrations by Maxfield Parrish. These new editions procured a new audience for these two books. In *Dream Days* there was a chapter which many considered the high point of the book. This was the story of the Reluctant Dragon. In 1938 Holiday House brought out this story in a beautiful format with illustrations by Ernest Shepard. It is a story Stockton-like in its gentle satire and gay humor, told in a style which is Grahame at his best.

Patrick Chalmers says that Grahame gave of his best when he gave to a child, and Graham Robertson writes that Grahame's best is "about as near perfection as may be compassed by our poor mortality." His gift to children's literature is small, but classic in its quality. The names of Howard Pyle, Robert Louis Stevenson, Rudyard Kipling, Beatrix Potter, and Kenneth Grahame make it clear that the passing of the nineteenth century and opening of the twentieth saw the creation of books for children unexcelled in originality, in beauty and breadth of conception and execution, in universality of appeal.

Bibliography

Chalmers, Patrick. *Kenneth Grahame; Life, Letters, and Unpublished Work.* London, Methuen, 1933.

Clayton, Walter. "An Interrupted Pan Resumes His Piping." *Forum*, Vol. 41 (Jan., 1909), pp. 83–85.

Darton, Frederick Joseph Harvey. *Children's Books in England; Five Centuries of Social Life.* Cambridge, Eng., University Press, 1932.

Grahame, Elspeth, ed. *First Whisper of "The Wind in the Willows" by Kenneth Grahame.* Philadelphia, Lippincott, 1945.

Grahame, Kenneth. *The Golden Age.* London, John Lane, 1899.

Hamilton, Clayton. "Frater Ave Atque Vale." *The Bookman*, Vol. 76 (Jan., 1933), pp. 69–74.

Macy, George. "Arthur Rackham and 'The Wind in the Willows.' " *The Horn Book*, Vol. 16 (May–June, 1940), pp. 153–158.

Milne, Alan Alexander. "A Household Book." In *Not That It Matters.* New York, E. P. Dutton, 1920. Pp. 85–89.

7

Extensions of Reality

From the year 1865, made famous by the publication of *Alice's Adventures in Wonderland*, to the present, one of the manifestations of the free and romantic spirit in literature has been the form known as fantasy. The first two decades of the twentieth century gave to children a rich endowment of classics in this type of literature. There is no doubt that these, together with the exceptional work of Rudyard Kipling, Beatrix Potter, and Kenneth Grahame, gave prestige to children's literature and made it a force to be reckoned with in the literary world. They were written by great writers and great thinkers who were gifted with creative imagination and who had something to say and could say it with power of style.

Too little attention has been given to the universality of fantasy. Whether it be nonsensical or philosophical or spiritual, its appeal is to the non-literal mind, in whatever country or time that mind exists. This is true because fantasy has to do with elements common to all mankind, with ultimate desirabilities not limited by race, creed, or color, with the weakness and greatness of men, with their hopes and fears and aspirations, with the everlasting conflict between good and evil. Realism, in the usual sense of the word, is compounded of elements which change from period to period, from country to country. The reality of fantasy is an unchanging and universal reality, extended into a dimension of its own.

It follows that the first requirement of fantasy must be convincingness; that the reader, having achieved Coleridge's "willing suspension of disbelief," must be enabled to maintain that suspension. Within implausibility, there must be plausibility; within irrationality, rationality; within the dream, actuality. Consequently, to be acceptable at all, fantasy must be the creation of a high order of imagination, free and yet controlled by the nature of the world created by itself. Its values are those of the imagination, values of compassion and understanding, of vision and faith, of stimulation and inspiration.

A second inherent characteristic of fantasy is originality. One of the most striking qualities of this kind of romance is the strong individuality of the various books. There is only one *Alice's Adventures in Wonderland*, only one *The Wind in the Willows*, only one *The Three Mulla-Mulgars*, only one *The Tale of Peter Rabbit*. Attempts at imitation are pallid and shallow in comparison with the color and depth of the original. This is inevitable, because to be successful, fantasy must be emotionally persuasive; to be persuasive, it must be sincere; to be sincere, it must be the expression of an individual mind and temperament. Certain basic devices may be, and are, used over and over again—the passage from one world to another by an actual means, the intermingling of two worlds, the dream technique. Certain themes occur and recur— nonsense for the sake of nonsense, the quest for spiritual treasure, the struggle between forces of good and forces of evil, the symbolic expression of a good way of life. But the spirit, the tone, the flavor, of each book are different.

Inevitably, creativity of imagination and originality of conception must be accompanied by unique power of style. Here inarticulate longings must be made articulate, the elusive must be captured, the intangible must be expressed, the unattainable must be made apprehendable. Therefore, power of style is the thing to be insisted upon; the power which bends words to its will, the power of so selecting and combining words as to underline them with limitless and illuminating significance. Not the least of the great values of fantasy is its literary excellence.

All literature began as story, the expression of man's imaginings in the form of fable and folk tale, myth and legend, heroic epic and romance. Deriving as it does from this honorable ancestry, fantasy, too, in the last analysis must be a story compounded of all the elements which make a good tale—of plot and theme, of character and incident, of adventure and suspense and climax. As story, it is again unique in its imaginative reconstruction of truth, in its breadth and wealth of idea, in its power to evoke stimulation and response to the liberating qualities of good humor and tender satire, in its capacity to instill compassionate appreciation of the essential and universal decency of mankind.

The fantasy of the first twenty years of the twentieth century is representative of the universality, the wide and rich variety, and the high quality of the type. The books of a Scottish mother, an English dramatist, an English poet, a Swedish novelist, and an American essayist bring honor to the countries of origin, but belong to the world. All moods are here, the sheerly nonsensical, the shrewdly humorous, the whimsical, and the spiritual. In setting and situation, they range from the basically realistic, somehow touched by the implausible and the unrealistic, to a complete other-worldliness. In conception and execution, in story and appeal, each is distinctive, so distinctive that it is difficult to devise a neat pattern of discussion. These books will not be pigeon-holed or reduced to formulae.

It is possible to bring together those whose appeal is to the younger children, those children who respond spontaneously and without inhibition to the humor of absurdity, the fun of nonsense, and who delight in personification of small animals. Even these few books illustrate the diversity so characteristic of fantasy for children.

The Story of Little Black Sambo (1899) by Helen Bannerman (1862?–1946) was written by a mother in a moment of homesickness for her two children left at home while she returned to India. It is plainly the work of one who had intimate knowledge of little children and certain knowledge of what they want in a story. One absurd incident succeeds another, and all are told with precise and specific detail, and with an air of solemn reasonableness which heightens the fun. The tale culminates, as it should, in a final chuckle-rousing exaggeration.

A certain amount of disapproval pertains to the term "bed-time stories." In point of fact, any story suitable for a small child is a bed-time story. Unfortunately the phrase has frequently been used to specify a type of story, footless, inane, and without character, usually concerned with animals treated fancifully, but not imaginatively. In recent years, some of this disapprobation may have rubbed off on the seven volumes of the *Old Mother West Wind* (1910) series. These books afford a good illustration of the frequently ill-defined line between an idea well handled and an imitation weakly handled. Thornton Burgess' (1874–1965) *Old Mother West Wind* stories are told simply and with charm. The personification of animals and the tales of their lives in the meadows are successful because they are convincing and interesting. The imitations are maudlin, artificial, and monotonous.

In contrast to these books is Stewart Edward White's (1873–1946) *The Magic Forest* (1903). To Jimmy, a small boy, conversant with Grimm and Andersen, the months spent with the Ojibway Indians in the forest were enchanted months. Here, a real experience, plausible in all its aspects, is transmuted into a thing of magic. The mystery of the forest, the excitement and adventure of the life there, the gentleness of the strange, dark people who befriended him, are the right ingredients of a fairy tale to Jimmy, endowed with the small child's sense of wonder and power of imagination. But when he tried to tell to adults the story of those months, they did not believe; "so he locked up the story of the Magic Forest in his heart, along with his firm belief in genii and water-babies and brownies and such folk."

Like Jimmy, David Blaize, of Edward Frederic Benson's (1867–1940) *David Blaize and the Blue Door* (1918), knew the stupidity of adults in regard to the really important things in life. He also knew, as did Wendy in *Peter and Wendy*, that children must grow up and become stupid; or, as David conceives it, soon after they are ten, they go "sound asleep," and lose all chance of ever seeing the real world. At the age of six, he naturally felt a pressing necessity to find the door into the real world of which so far he had caught only glimpses. When he finally discovered the shining blue door with a gold handle, he lost no time in opening it and locking it behind him. What follows is a story of sustained nonsense, than which there is nothing rarer. The slightly mad, consistently irrational world in which David finds himself is peopled with strange manifestations of things familiar to him—nursery rhyme characters, his Noah's ark family, his Happy Families Game.

Once the topsy-turviness of the world is accepted, there is, in regard to events and characters, that inevitable logic which is an inherent part of good nonsense. Indeed, Quiller-Couch's delightful phrase, "insane logicalities," which he applied to *Alice's Adventures in Wonderland*, applies equally to *David Blaize and the Blue Door*. The conceptions of the giraffe whose head went upstairs to brush its hair and of the animals who are so short that they have to go down to the cellar to tie their bootlaces are worthy of Lewis Carroll. In America it is a pity that so often nonsense like this is withheld from children until they reach that literal age which prevents them from accepting, with spontaneous joy, the delightful idiocy of this form of humor. It should be given to children who have an immediate background of the "divine nonsensia" of the nursery rhyme and of Edward Lear's verses; or to the child, or adult, who, all his life, knows the relaxing pleasure that good nonsense can give.

Another book with nonsense quality and tinged also with the flavor of the tall tale is Albert Bigelow Paine's (1861–1937) *The Arkansaw Bear* (1898). It is a delightfully irresponsible tale of a boy and a bear who travel through the South, the boy singing and the bear playing a fiddle. The songs have a swinging rhythm and the story has a carefree, humorous quality which is irresistible.

Fantasy, in the form of the short story, has provided children's literature with modern parallels of the folk tale, and with romantic literature, filled with zest of adventure, gaiety of humor, and beauty of enchantment. Those which parallel folk tales borrow folklore devices and characters, ways of thought and speech; the best of them re-create the flavor of the folk tale, at the same time that they imbue it with the grace of the conscious literary artist. Supreme in this group is the work of Howard Pyle in *The Wonder Clock* and *Pepper and Salt*. Others of these short stories are entirely original, influenced, however, by a rich background of folk literature and a far-reaching appreciation of the beauty and significance of folk and fairy tale, myth and legend. Of this order of fantasy is Henry Beston's (1888–1968) *Firelight Fairy Book* (1919) to which, in 1923, there was added a companion volume,

Starlight Wonder Book. These are stories filled with the laughter of nonsensical conceptions, with the golden charm of happy, far-off, simpler days, with the lasting values of courage and kindness, and with childlike wonder. They are told with a simplicity that is in tune with their nature, and in a style made lovely by the naturalist-author's sensitivity to the beauty of sun and wind, of sea and mountain.

Between 1894 and 1905 Laurence Housman (1865–1959), brother of A. E. Housman, wrote many short fairy tales characterized by highly individualized charm, rare imaginative power, and exquisite poetic prose. These stories are impregnated with a sense of romance, enchantment, and idealism difficult to convey. Such stories as "The Blue Moon" with its lovely musical prose and spell-binding beauty, its delicate play on the phrase "once in a blue moon," or "A Capful of Moonshine," with its expert recovery of the spirit of the traditional tale, or "A Chinese Fairy Tale," with its integrity of meaning, are unequalled among their kind. In 1923, when the original collections were out of print, Harcourt Brace republished a selection of Housman's stories in two volumes, *A Doorway in Fairyland* and *Moonshine and Clover*. *A Doorway in Fairyland* and *Moonshine and Clover* include stories originally published in *A Farm in Fairyland* (1894), *The House of Joy* (1895), *The Field of Clover* (1898), and *The Blue Moon* (1904).

The books written under the name of E. Nesbit (1858–1924) have never been surpassed in their blending of realism and magic, in their fresh, original invention, in their contagious humor, in their creation of delightful child characters and equally delightful magic characters. The juxtaposition of the real and the unreal, the association of natural humans and extraordinary supernatural creatures, inject into such stories as *Five Children and It* (1902), *The Phoenix and the Carpet* (1904), *The Story of the Amulet* (1906), and other fantasies by this author, a note as novel as when they were written in the early years of the 1900's.

This note is one of inexorable logic as regards the laws of magic in conflict with the laws of the natural world. In a sense, magic is shown wrong side out. A wishing ring is a thing to be longed for until a child wishes himself invisible and then loses the ring. Magic being what it is, he must stay invisible until the ring is found. The results consequent to an invisible child living in the midst of a family produce situations with which only E. Nesbit can deal. A magic carpet has endless and desirable possibilities, but it is literal and single-minded. If it is a Persian carpet, and is commanded to bring the most beautiful products of its native land, it naturally brings Persian cats, in the plural, one hundred and ninety-nine of them. Commanded to bring milk to feed the cats, it inevitably brings a cow. And if the resultant noise and confusion bring a policeman, to whom the children find it impossible to explain the inscrutable workings of magic, that is no concern of the carpet, faithful to its own nature and indifferent to the idiosyncrasies of the twentieth century. To find a Psammead, or sand-fairy, which can grant your wishes is the height of bliss until one discovers that the average person says "I wish—" several times a day, and that the sand-fairy reacts to the word "wish" like fireworks to a match, and with sublime disregard to the after effects.

It is almost ludicrous to use the weighty word "significant" in relation to the joyous and rollicking humor of such stories. Yet no lesser word will do full justice to E. Nesbit's contribution to fairy lore for children. No such fairy beings as the Psammead, the Phoenix, and the Mouldiwarp had ever existed. Indeed, the term "fairy being," partly through misuse, has a wrong connotation. Each of E. Nesbit's creations has a highly individualized personality. The Psammead, extraordinary in appearance and contrary by nature; the Phoenix, beautiful and vain; the Mouldiwarp, whom all white things obey, daisies and white feathers from pigeons' wings, snow, and white swans—these are alike only in their power of magic. In all other respects, they are differentiated as human beings are differentiated, and therein lies their convincingness. They were, and are, unique, although Mary Poppins is a sister under the skin.

Curious things happen in fantasy. A book may start out as fantasy and end by being something else as well as fantasy. A miracle may happen, and a book intended to be a textbook may become a classic in fantasy. Many adults have been charmed with the leisurely, witty, and wise essays of Samuel McChord Crothers (1857–1927), clergyman, essayist, lover of books and of children. Only such a man could have written *Miss Muffet's Christmas Party* (1902), to which were invited the best-loved book characters of many times. A fantasy in conception, actually it is an exceptional book on children's books, written with the tenderness and wisdom of one who knows what books may mean to a child. The adult reads it with nostalgia for the days when books were living things to him. The child reads it with quick response to the living reality of the book characters.

Selma Lagerlöf (1858–1940) was one of Sweden's greatest novelists, a member of the Swedish Academy, and winner of the Nobel Prize for literature. In view of these facts, it is noteworthy that many consider *The Wonderful Adventures of Nils* (1907) to be one of her finest works. The commission to write a geographical reader on Sweden given her by the National Teachers' Association seems to have held singular appeal for her. Born in the rural province of Värmland, on her father's country estate, Marbåcka, she was early steeped in the history and legends of Sweden. She had great love for the spiritual and physical aspects of the country. Before writing the story of Nils she spent three years gathering and assimilating the folklore of the various provinces of Sweden and pursuing nature study. All this time she pondered the form which the book would finally take. Finally, on a visit to her old home, the idea came to her of changing a boy into a tiny creature, who would fly on a gander's back with the wild geese over Sweden. For this visit, and the idea which came of it, the world should be grateful, since the result is a fantasy of sustained imaginative quality, which gives a vivid impression of a land and its people, written in a style remarkable for its unselfconscious purity.

Only quotations can do justice to the skill which so completely integrates aspects of the land and its people with the story. Soon after Nils, for his sins, is transformed into an elf, he

> sat and looked at his home. It was a little log house, which lay as if it had been crushed down to earth, under the high, sloping roof. The outhouses were also small; and the patches of ground were so narrow that a horse could barely turn around on them.[1]

As Nils travels from the south to the north, and back to the south, the varying beauty of the Swedish landscape unfolds like a panorama, fields and mountains and forests and water.

> There are solitary rock-columns that spring right up out of the water, and dark grottoes with narrow entrances. There are barren, perpendicular precipices, and soft, leaf-clad inclines. There are small points, and small inlets, and small rolling stones that are rattlingly washed up and down with every dashing breaker. There are majestic cliff-arches that project over the water. There are sharp stones that are constantly sprayed by a white foam; and others that mirror themselves in unchangeable dark-green still water.[2]

Written to achieve a realistic purpose, still the book is animate with the lovely spirit so prevalent in fantasy.

> And then came the gray, dusk-clad birds with plumes in their wings, and red feather-ornaments on their necks. The big birds with their tall legs, their slender throats, their small heads, came gliding down the knoll with an abandon that was full of mystery. . . There was something marvelous and strange about their dance. . . It was as if they had learned it from the mists that hover over desolate morasses. There was witchcraft in it. . . There was wildness in it; but yet the feeling which it awakened was a

[1] Selma Lagerlöf, *The Wonderful Adventures of Nils* (New York, Pantheon, 1947), p. 22.
[2] *Ibid.*, p. 92.

delicious longing. . . Such longing after the unattainable, after the hidden mysteries back of this life, the animals felt only once a year; and this was on the day when they beheld the great crane dance.[1]

It is little wonder that this book, so intensely national in the sense that folk literature and folk music are national, is also universal.

Tribute should be paid the translator, Mrs. Velma S. Howard, Swedish-born and close friend of Selma Lagerlöf, who has retained in another language the unaffected and lucid style of the original, with its quality of serene beauty.

Italy also gave to the world a book so universal in its appeal as to necessitate mention whenever fantasies for children are discussed. In 1880, Carlo Lorenzini (1826–1890), under the pseudonym Collodi, wrote *The Adventures of Pinocchio*. In 1892, Pinocchio was published in English translation in the United States. This story of a puppet brought vividly and realistically to life is a triumphant landmark in the long line of tales which personify inanimate objects. Pinocchio's creator did more than merely endow the little wooden figure with life; he gave to Pinocchio individuality, an irrepressible, heedless, boastful, slightly wicked, and yet lovable individuality. With beautiful inevitability, the other unique qualities of the book stem from the personality of Pinocchio—the stern justice which makes the punishment fit the crime, the pervasive humor which prevents morality from becoming morbidity, the satisfying convincingness of Pinocchio's final and complete transformation.

There is still another sort of fantasy, which has to do with realms that lie beyond life and yet is truer to life than life itself. Confronted with the necessity to describe it, one is frustrated, fettered by the inadequacy of words to capture elusive intangibles. For these books express the inexpressible, attain the unattainable, name the nameless longings of mankind. Each of these books is highly individualistic, the intimate and inimitable creation of a single creative mind, yet all are concerned with the same thing—the search for some plane of existence beyond the material world, where the secret of true happiness will be revealed.

Peter Pan is an expression of eternal youth and of the eternal boy in J. M. Barrie, the boy who loved tales of pirates and tales of wonder and magic, the boy who refused to grow up and lose the joy and wonder of the Never Never Land.

In 1904 Barrie (1860–1937) told Charles Frohman that he had a new play, which he wanted Frohman to produce, although he did not believe it would be a commercial success. If Frohman would produce it, Barrie had a second play written which would make up for loss on the

[1] Lagerlöf, *op. cit.*, pp. 102–103.

first. The first play was *Peter Pan*, which was produced in London in December 1904, the second *Alice-Sit-by-the-Fire*, produced in April 1905. There is a touching quality in the description of Barrie's hesitancy as he made this suggestion to Frohman; there can be no doubt that he was in love with *Peter Pan*. Frohman, too, fell in love with the play, so much so that it is said his last words, as he stood on the deck of the sinking *Lusitania*, were Peter's words, "Death ought to be an awfully big adventure." Frohman apparently had none of Barrie's hesitancy as to production, which speaks volumes for his sense of audience reaction, since the play created a world's record.

The origin of *Peter Pan* goes back to two of Barrie's earlier books. In *Tommy and Grizel* (1900) mention is made of a little boy, happily lost, who fears that if his parents find him he will be compelled to grow up. In *The Little White Bird* (1902) there are six chapters which in 1906 Barrie published separately in *Peter Pan in Kensington Gardens* (1906), with lovely illustrations by Arthur Rackham. This book is Barrie at his best, exquisitely whimsical, delicately imaginative, with that spontaneous captivating charm which is the chief ingredient of all his writing—a charm which, one sometimes suspects, he exerts with an impish, hidden smile, knowing full well the effect it will have upon his audience. In 1911 Barrie made the play into a story, *Peter and Wendy*. In play and story and story-play, the insistence is upon the joy and delight of the world of the ever-young.

William Henry Hudson (1841–1922), English naturalist and a man wonderfully sensitive to the beauty, romance and poetry of the natural world, also wrote about *A Little Boy Lost* (1905); willingly lost, too, but for a very different motive, an instinctive, unreasoning, driving impulse to be at one with the spirit of the universe, to gain utter satisfaction by merging and losing himself in a greater whole. Hudson's book, like Barrie's, is in a certain sense autobiographical. *Peter Pan* is Barrie's remembrance of the play-life of a child, more real than the actual world. *A Little Boy Lost* is Hudson's remembrance of the wonder and mystery that nature held for him, a wonder and mystery that were both frightening and fascinating. Here the resemblance ends. In Barrie, there is the light, delicate humor of whimsy—in Hudson, the almost grotesque humor so often found in folk literature. In Barrie, there is charm and lightness of touch—in Hudson, sternness and powerful drama. In Barrie, there are the delicate pastels of fancy—in Hudson, the darker tones of majesty and grandeur of imagination. In Barrie, there is an intimately and ingratiatingly appealing quality—in Hudson, an awe-inspiring quality. In Barrie, there is a single tone—in Hudson, a richness of variety that defies summation. Together they offer proof positive of the great gift of fantasy; it offers something to every individual, and to many moods of one individual.

Among the loveliest of all the quest books is Walter de la Mare's (1873–1956) *The Three Mulla-Mulgars* (1910), now published as *The Three Royal Monkeys*. There should be little need to stress the shining quality and unearthly beauty of De la Mare's style, with its power of underlining the story with the saving grace of great compassion for the fears and sorrows, the elusive hopes of mankind, and equally with the faith-reviving perception of man's eternal striving and potential greatness.

This is a story of the search of three royal monkeys for the vale of Tishnar, the symbol of all things lovely and hoped for. Once read, it haunts the memory, and one returns to it again and again, each time hoping for new insight into its ineffable secret. It has moments of fear and awe and great drama, but its most lasting impression is of a great capacity for love and tenderness. He who reads is enriched by the sharing of this capacity, especially in the feeling aroused for Nod, the tiny monkey to whom, because there is magic in him, is given the Wonderstone, the talisman for their journey. He is so pitiably anxious, so often sad and lonely and weary, so oppressed by the weight of his burden— and yet so indomitable in the discharge of his responsibility. It is impossible to overpraise this book—it is impossible to praise it adequately.

A Little Boy Lost and *The Three Mulla-Mulgars* are fortunate in having, as illustrator of the American editions published by Knopf, Dorothy Lathrop. The illustrations in *A Little Boy Lost* add much to the book, but those in *The Three Mulla-Mulgars* are almost unbelievably in harmony with the story. In an article published in the May 1942 issue of *The Horn Book Magazine*, Dorothy Lathrop writes of her great joy in being asked to illustrate De la Mare's book; and of her realization of the difficulty of using "concrete lines and forms" to convey the subtle suggestions of the author's poetry in prose. One would indeed doubt that it could be done, had not Dorothy Lathrop done it. In color and in black and white, the pictures have a loveliness of line and detail and imaginative quality akin to the loveliness of the story.

The laughter and beauty of idea and execution with which fantasy has endowed children's literature is for all those, of any age, who recognize two truths, the truth of sound realism and the truth of great fantasy. Because of this, it is probable that no other type of book has done more to give genuine distinction to children's literature than has fantasy.

Bibliography

Berendsohn, Walter. *Selma Lagerlöf, Her Life and Work*. Adapted from the German by George E. Timpson with a Preface by V. Sackville-West. London, Ivor Nicholson and Watson, 1931.

Darton, Frederick Joseph Harvey. *Children's Books in England; Five Centuries of Social Life*. Cambridge, Eng., University Press, 1932.
Fish, Helen Dean. "Book Visits in England and Scotland." *The Horn Book*, Vol. 13 (Nov.–Dec., 1937), pp. 355–358.
Lathrop, Dorothy. "Illustrating De la Mare." *The Horn Book*, Vol. 18 (May–June, 1942), pp. 188–196.
Maule, Harry E. *Selma Lagerlöf, The Woman, Her Work, Her Message*. New York, Doubleday, 1917.
Moore, Anne Carroll. "Review of *A Little Boy Lost* by W. H. Hudson." *The Bookman*, Vol. 48 (Nov., 1918), pp. 328–330.

8

Romance and Actuality

The realities of fantasy know no bounds of time or place. The actualities of realism are largely reflective of time and place. Yet good realism offers insight into ways of life and living as fundamental and permanent as is the more intangible illumination of fantasy. Both are capable of offering greatness to children's literature; but it is a mistake to attempt to compare one with the other to the advantage or disadvantage of either. Each kind must be allowed to have its own place, and each must be evaluated in accordance with criteria that grow out of the nature of the type.

The first book of fiction written specifically for children was realistic, and its realism reflected social, educational, and economic aspects of the period with which it deals. This is *The History of Little Goody Two-Shoes*, the best known of John Newbery's publications.

Realism should have a wide spread, including re-creations of everyday life in this and other countries, of animal life in its natural setting, of the romance and significance of the past in historic fiction, of romance and vicarious experience in the form of adventure. The books written between 1890 and 1920 are indicative of the abundant variety which was to be so strong a mark of the next five decades.

From the time of Louisa Alcott to the present, stories with a background of home life have formed a large part of a children's book collection. The distinctive and distinguishing characteristics of such books published in the late 1890's and early 1900's are serenity and security, the reflection of a way of life that has a simple graciousness and a firm hold on essentials. They are the products of a leisured and happy period, and in comparison with them, certain books of the immediate present have a disturbing undercurrent of restlessness and uncertainty. This is inevitable, since realism concerned with the here and now must, by its very nature, reflect the here and now. It is to be feared, however, that we are in danger of losing sight of the therapeutic values of these books of the past because they have a superficially dated quality; whereas the truth of the matter is that good realism, like good fantasy, is imperishable. This may be objected to as an adult point of view, motivated by a nostalgia for things known and vanished. There is no reason to doubt that children may experience a different sort of nostalgia, for things never known but instinctively longed for.

One of the writers of this period, and one whose long list of books extended into the twenties and thirties, was Eliza Orne White (1856–1947), unexcelled portrait painter of small girls. They step living from the pages of *When Molly Was Six* (1894), *A Little Girl of Long Ago* (1896), *A Borrowed Sister* (1906), *The Blue Aunt* (1918), and the rest of the extraordinarily alive stories. They are intensely feminine, lovable and irritating, now compliant and now willfully stubborn, unpredictable and charming. For adult and child reader, the child characters are the focal points of interest. Adults are there in the background, mothers and fathers and aunts, stepping into the foreground when needed, understanding and sympathetic or firm, as occasion calls. Between children and adults there is a wholly normal, wholly admirable relationship, often touched with humor, as child and adult view each other with temporary misgiving, which never threatens the basic understanding between the two.

Skill is needed to make completely actual activity and incident interesting and stimulating to a child. The writer must first be able to capture and portray the child's fresh enjoyment of experiences of many sorts, the thrills of birthday and holiday celebrations, of a trip, of a book read or a play seen, of a special or unexpected treat, the feel of the changing seasons, the strange excitement of the discovery of the varied beauty of the world. This ability is an outgrowth of a vivid memory of childhood. Skill enters when an author is able to avoid the reminiscent and wistful mood which results in a book about children rather than for them. Eliza Orne White's books have an immediacy which rids them entirely of any retrospective attitude and which gives them an intense reality. This reality, founded on sound character portrayal and objectivity of feeling, is further heightened by her faculty for utterly natural spontaneous conversation, of which there is plenty and all of it good.

It may be worth noting that the span of Eliza Orne White's writing life extended into and past the First World War. In *The Blue Aunt* she does not hesitate to introduce the anxiety and sorrow of that period. She does it without loss of wholesomeness and with appreciation of a child's capacity for sympathy.

It is a temptation to state unequivocally that all writers of such books as these should have the kind of childhood that left upon the minds of Eliza Orne White, Laura Richards (1850–1943), and Kate Douglas Wiggin (1856–1923) such indelible memories. Their books so apparently draw upon enriching remembrances of play and reading, of vivid, life-long associations connected with books and poetry, a well-loved place, happy family experiences, the understanding companionship of an adult. There can be little doubt that in the books in Laura Richards' *Queen Hildegarde* series (1889–) and *Three Margarets* series (1897–) character, incident and situation are drawn from life. Even the delightful anecdotes told in *Queen Hildegarde* may have been heard by the child Laura Howe in summers spent in The Valley, of which she writes with so much love in *When I Was Your Age* (1894). To reread these books as an adult is to gain a deep appreciation of the impression made when they were read as a child; an impression made up not so much of the details of the story, but rather of halcyon days in the country, the delights of wood and stream and planted fields, of a barn with "dusty, golden, cobwebby sunbeams slanting down through the little windows"; of the inherent worth and dignity of simple, virtuous men and women; of the fun and frolic of a large family like the Merryweathers, each of them an individual, and allowed to be so; of the give and take of family relationship; of the joy of good talk, free and spontaneous, permitted to drift as it pleases; and not least of all, the pleasure of meeting an old friend among books, like *Robin Hood*, best beloved of all Hildegarde's books, "by the grace of Howard Pyle made into so strong an enchantment that the heart thrills even at the sight of its good brown cover"; or the equal pleasure of being introduced to a new friend in literature, presented by one of Mrs. Richards' characters with that genuine enthusiasm which so successfully sells a book.

Viewed in retrospect, and in contrast with our own day, the way of life represented by these books seems surrounded by a golden haze. Yet these writers, like their predecessor, Louisa M. Alcott, saw life whole, saw illness and death, sorrow and trouble and poverty as parts of life to be met with normality and courage. Because they saw life constructively and saw it whole, because they knew that children must share in the vicissitudes of life as well as in its joys, their books, individually and as a group, escape the hackneyed and made-to-order quality which can become so unproductive an aspect of realism for children. *Rebecca of Sunnybrook Farm* (1903) came from poverty to a home where there was another kind of poverty, poor in the grace of living and in understanding of a child. The success in the evolution of such a theme depends wholly on the character portrayal of the child and can become a maudlin interpretation of the "little child shall lead them" idea. The great thing about Kate Douglas Wiggin's book is that in it a notable child character is born, a life-full and unforgettable personality, an individual with a strong sense of herself as an individual. Vivid, generous, eager, with tremendous capacity for joy and sorrow and sympathy, timeless in her appeal, she dominates the book. From the time she arrives in Riverboro, a small person who slid around on the leather cushions of the stagecoach, wearing a funny little straw hat and carrying a pink sunshade, the "dearest thing in life" to her, to the close of the book, she is more real than many a person in actual life.

In a lighter vein are the "incomparable Bastables" who take upon themselves the burden of restoring the "fortune of the fallen House of Bastable." Since E. Nesbit is their creator, it goes without saying that their methods are ingenious, occasionally disastrous, and frequently based on ideas gained from their wide reading; like Jo March and Hildegarde Grahame and Rebecca Randall, they are lovers of books, and it is utterly natural for them to send one of their number off on an attempt to achieve a fortune with the cry "good hunting" ringing in his ears. The Bastables are as ingratiatingly real as the children in the author's inimitable fantasies. Bridging the gulf between child world and adult world is one of those delightful uncles whose reason for being in children's books is worth a study in itself. The fact that he is really Albert-next-door's uncle does not prevent the Bastables from staking claim to him. They take a dim view of Albert but recognize his uncle as a kindred spirit and at the same time as one who has a penetrating knowledge of them, a knowledge without illusion. Pervading the books is that amazingly subtle humor, inherent in character and situation, which provokes a loving laughter, free of any taint of condescension or mockery or cynical superiority. The adult's amusement is tempered with the tenderness aroused by the somehow pathetic appeal of childhood; the child's amusement is tempered by the seriousness of the Bastables themselves toward their efforts to acquire a fortune. The three books concerning the Bastables were first published in English magazines. *The Story of the Treasure Seekers* was published in book form in England in 1899, *The Would-Be-Goods* in 1901, and *The New Treasure Seekers* in 1904. In 1928, Coward-McCann issued the three books in an omnibus volume, *The Bastable Children.* In 1931 the same publisher issued the three books in separate form.

The age under discussion is one frequently characterized by our own, usually in accents of scorn, as one inclined toward sentimentality and idealized romanticism, even in its realism. This is too superficial a view, even if it were not for the fact that fair and adequate criticism necessitates an understanding and consideration of the mores of the period in which a book was written. Especially in viewing children's literature we are apt to allow the surface mannerisms of a book to blind us to the permanently truthful aspect of life it presents, and to overrate the contemporary at the expense of the past. The present adult fashion of cynicism leads us as adults to label as sentimental anything that is less than cynical, thereby putting us, as arbiters of children's books, in a dilemma. We are afraid of sentimentality and we may welcome cynicism ourselves but we shun it for our children. The inevitable compromise lies sometimes, fortunately not always, in the shadowy realm of inanity and innocuousness. In any case, it is natural that the realism of the Victorian Age, undergoing the discipline of actuality, should still retain at times the idealization and sentiment characteristic of the period.

The combination of the old and the new is seen in Mrs. Frances Hodgson Burnett's (1849–1924) *The Secret Garden* (1911). The setting and background of the story are highly romanticized; the moors, with their strange beauty and fascination; the old house with its many rooms filled with curious and exotic things; the almost unearthly beauty of the secret garden and the tantalizing quality of the mystery concerning it; the Arcadian simplicity of the boy Dickon and his friendship with animals and birds. In the midst of all this there is a problem more intense and more peculiar than those presented in *Queen Hildegarde* and *Rebecca of Sunnybrook Farm*, a problem, in fact, rarely attacked by writers for children. It is the conversion into mental and physical health of two children, one introspective, withdrawn, inimical to people, and the other a confirmed hypochondriac, ungoverned and hysterical. The conversion is accomplished by a combination of self-development, the healing qualities of the outdoors and the self-forgetting love of growing things, and, of all things, the principles of mental healing. And all of it is more plausible than it may sound, and it is plausible because basically Mrs. Burnett is right. Oversimplified and idealized as her presentation may be, her thesis is the same as that of Laura Richards, of Kate Douglas Wiggin, and of others before and since her time—a happy and normal child must care for something and must be cared for.

Somewhat similar to *The Secret Garden* in type of romanticism, though different in theme, is Abbie Farwell Brown's (d. 1927) story of a boy tumbler, *John of the Woods* (1909). Mistreated by his masters, the boy runs away and is befriended, taught, and trained by a hermit living a lonely but idyllic life in the forest. Like Dickon in *The Secret Garden*, the hermit is the trusted friend of all the animals and birds of the forest. Under his tutelage, John learns to practice the virtues of faith, charity, and love, finally proving himself worthy of learning his true identity. The theme is the age-old one of the ultimate conquest of cruelty and evil by mercy and good. It is a quiet, gently romantic story which accomplishes its thesis without pointed didacticism.

Many doll stories belong to fantasy, since they play on the popular theme that toys, to children who love them, have life and personality. *The Lonesomest Doll* (1901), again by Abbie Farwell Brown, is realistic in its treatment of a little girl's love for her doll, but romantic in a fairy-tale charm which has made the story a long time favorite.

School life constitutes a large part of the contemporary scene, as far as children and young people are concerned. The great original school story is of course, *Tom Brown's School Days*. Whether or not this book influenced writers in America to write about private or boarding schools, it is a fact that most of the earlier school-life stories by American authors were laid in private schools. In the early 1900's, Ralph Henry Barbour's (1870–1944) stories had sure appeal, an appeal which persisted and which tempted many later authors to adopt Barbour's pattern. Having once established it, as in *The Half Back* (1899) and *The Crimson Sweater* (1906), Barbour himself repeated it in book after book. The books are centered on sports and the emphasis is on the right school spirit, good sportsmanship, the triumph of those who are right-minded over those who are not. The plot and action and incident characteristic of Barbour have now become stereotyped through overuse, and this makes it difficult to judge him fairly. Certainly he seems to have a freshness and spontaneity, at least in his earlier books, which is lacking in some of the later writers. Whether this is a retrospective memory, based on childhood reading, fostered by the recognition that he originated the type, is hard to ascertain. At least, of his historical place there is no doubt.

Two English books, whose chief appeal and value are for older young people rather than for children, are nevertheless revealing of the quality which school stories may attain. Kipling's *Stalky & Co.* (1899) is absolutely non-contrived, a natural story enlivened by actuality of incident and strong character personalities. Horace Vachell's *The Hill* (1905) is secondarily a school story, primarily a memorable record of a fine friendship.

Many good things must be said of the majority of these writers of childhood for childhood. They could create plot and character; they could tell enticing stories with charm of incident and with a use of mystery and suspense which was always kept within the bounds of good taste; they had a fine sense of lasting and essential values, and never allowed these values to become distorted or the emphasis to be misdirected; they wrote with authority, as those to whom childhood was a memorable experience; they knew and understood children, with an intelligent and sympathetic knowledge.

This understanding of children included an awareness of the universality of childhood and of the appeal of childhood to childhood the world over. In the early 1900's the term "melting-pot" was coined to describe the mingling of races which was America, and the need for common understanding among people of various races became manifest. Children's literature has been sensitive always to felt needs, and there appeared in this period stories of children in other lands which were prophetic of the outpouring of such books which was to come after the First World War. Gradually a double purpose emerged; on the one hand, to present the heritage brought to America by people of other lands, and on the other hand, to present to the world and to ourselves the heritage of America. Ultimately, this double motive was to have a vital effect upon historic fiction for children.

The two "twins" series by Lucy Fitch Perkins (1865–1937) exemplify concretely this thought and trend. The first series, starting with *The Dutch Twins* (1911), to be followed by *The Eskimo Twins* (1914), *The Japanese Twins* (1912), *The Irish Twins* (1913), and many others, exemplify, too, a fact early recognized and always a motivating element in stories of other lands. If such books are to be interesting to and effective with children, this purpose must be made intimate and personal through stories of individuals. Generalization would be ineffective. Consequently the potential interest and value of this form of realistic fiction is compounded of the alikeness of children everywhere, the alluring quality of strange scenes and customs, and the attraction of a good story strong enough to bear the weight of incidental or intentional information. Mrs. Perkins' stories of other lands have been favorites of generations of younger children because they combine the familiar and the unfamiliar aspects of everyday experiences with simplicity and attention to details. Later Mrs. Perkins used the twin device to write historic tales in *The Puritan Twins* (1921), *The Colonial Twins of Virginia* (1924), and others.

Donkey John of Toy Valley (1909) by Margaret Morley (1858–1923) is a story of atmosphere, owing its vitality to beauty and tradition, rather than to action and incident. And yet to various children it holds various appeals; the exquisite descriptions of Tyrolese mountain and meadow and picturesque village; the friendship between two very different boys, each with his own absorbing interest and ambition; the quaint simplicity of the isolated life of the mountain people; the fairy tale charm of the village of toy-makers, where for generations, members of the same family have carved the same toys; the remote, almost dream-like quality that pervades the book.

The internationalism of good children's books should justify the inclusion here of Dikken Zwilgmeyer's (1859–1913) *Johnny Blossom* and *What Happened to Inger Johanne*. Written in Norwegian, they were translated into English by Emile Poulsson in 1912 and 1919, respectively. The country background *is* background, lending a different and attractive setting to the stories for non-Norwegian readers. It is to be remembered, however, that these were written for Norwegian children. It is, therefore, inevitable that their primary interest lies in the child about whom each story centers, and this fact constitutes their importance. Johnny and Inger Johanne have their counterparts in every race on earth, and are as irresistible to adults everywhere and as understandable by children everywhere as are the Bastables in England and the Moffats in America. They belong to the international order of childhood.

Animal Stories Are Disciplined by Actuality

There comes a time in most children's lives, as librarians know to their sorrow, when animal stories are an obsession. With some children, this interest seems to demand something more than a domesticated story of a domesticated animal. They crave the strong reality, the drama, and with it, the tragedy, of wild animal life, or the story of a domestic animal which escapes the tameness of a typical "pet" story. This craving demands actuality, truth to animal nature and habit, and yet prefers that a sense of personal significance be given to the animal. To accomplish this without humanization is not easy. It is no exaggeration to say that this period produced some books of this kind which are still unsurpassed.

Ernest Thompson Seton's (1860–1946) *Wild Animals I Have Known* (1898), stories of animals in their own environment, are utterly satisfying to children who want animal biographies. The author has a respect for animal life which prevents him from incurring the defects of sentimentalization or exaggeration of their animal instincts. His authenticity, founded on knowledge and observation, is impressive. His imagination and genuine sympathy imbue his facts with feeling and constructive emotional quality.

Buck, in Jack London's (1876–1916) *The Call of the Wild* (1903), is one of the notable dogs in dog literature. In this book, characters of men and dogs are sketched in with few but deft touches, and background and situation have a fine and honest realism.

Because it is something infinitely greater than the term dog story usually implies, Alfred Ollivant's (1874–1927) *Bob, Son of Battle* (1898) is a classic. It has an epic quality in its fatalism, its picture of man and dog inevitably moving toward their doom, impelled by innate qualities within themselves. It has an epic quality in its opposition of dog and human protagonist and antagonist. It has an epic quality in its tremendous sense of impending and realized sorrow and tragedy. It is grand and inexpressibly moving in its depiction of nobility in man and dog.

These three books are utterly realistic, even starkly so. But romance persisted here as it did in other forms of realism. Olaf Baker's (b.187–) *Shasta of the Wolves* (1919), published at the end of this period, is reminiscent of Kipling in its story of an Indian boy left in the forest by enemies and adopted by a wolf. At the same time, there is a feeling for nature and natural life which apparently gives children the same satisfaction as do the stories of Ernest Thompson Seton. In *Dusty Star*, published in 1922, the theme is reversed, in that a wolf cub is brought home to Dusty Star to become his intimate companion. The appeal of the relationship between boy and animal remains the same.

Adventure—the Romance of Incident and Far Places

Adventure is basically realistic and inherently romantic, as Stevenson so convincingly stated in his "A Gossip on Romance" and so effectively proved in his *Treasure Island*. His influence was strong in this period, when authors believed that pure adventure should, and could, be a literature of frank escape, concerned with treasure, and smuggling, and extraordinary experiences, or with strange scenes in far-off romantic places.

John Masefield's (1878–1967) *Jim Davis* (1911) is a book Stevenson would have loved, a book splendid in its quality of story told for story's sake and told with the combined art of a poet and a storyteller. The poet fills the story with the spirit of the Devon coast, and with the salty breath of the sea. The storyteller gives it the zest of mysterious happenings—horsemen galloping in the night, the cry of the owl used as a signal, the discovery of secret passages leading into caves where the smugglers hide their loot. All in all, it is a work of art which rivals Stevenson in its clever manipulation of circumstance and character, in its skillful touches which induce mounting suspense and anticipation, and in its final resolving of the whole situation.

There are touches of Stevenson in *The Aztec Treasure-House* (1890) by Thomas Janvier (1849–1913), a classic tale of a search for an ancient and lost city of the Aztecs and for the treasure it contained. The idea of the quest itself fulfills every requirement of romance, associated as it is with the mystery of the ancient Aztec civilization. The men who undertake the search are as diverse a group of characters as could be devised—the scientist and scholar, impelled by the desire to gain new knowledge; Rayburn, the engineer, and Young, the railroad man, hard-boiled Americans, whose capacities for remaining their irreverent and imperturbable selves under all circumstances give the story the relief of humor; Pablo, the Mexican boy, naive, lovable, and loving; the saintly priest, who sacrifices his life to save the lives of the others. To the human characters must be added that of "The Wise One," the small donkey, whose personality adds much charm to the story, and who plays no small part in determining the final issue. The exciting nature of the search, the reality lent by vivid characterization, the ever changing adventures and hazards of the journey, are supplemented by the strange, romantic beauty of the mountains and valleys through which the men pursue their journey. It is a book which accomplishes what all romance should accomplish; for the time being the real world, to the reader, is the world of the book, and he returns to his own life and surroundings with a sense of shock and unreality.

In *The Aztec Treasure-House* there is companionship in danger. There is one man alone in Janvier's *In the Sargasso Sea* (1898) with only a black cat for company. This is a book of powerful imaginative quality, an imaginative quality akin to Defoe's in *Robinson Crusoe* in its discipline, but pervaded with an awesomeness and horror which lie far beyond the realm of Robinson Crusoe. *In the Sargasso Sea* has scenes that are unforgettable. That sea of the dead is a thing in itself to challenge the imagination, with its central packed mass of wrecked ships of all ages, surrounded by an impenetrable net of sea weed, and over it all a constant golden haze. In the center of the huddled ships, the shipwrecked Stetworth, trying to find his way to the outer ring of ships, comes upon the U. S. Sloop-of-war *Wasp*, lost in the War of 1812, with its captain lying under the American flag in his cabin, and the skeletons of the gunners at their posts. The description of the decadent beauty of phosphorescent light playing at night on the wet and rotting woodwork of the ancient ships, soft and shimmering and unearthly, is so awe-compelling, so fantastic, so dreadful in its implication, that one wonders, as Stetworth did, why he did not go mad, shivering and shaking as he watched it. It is a gripping story, filled with drama and emotion handled with restraint.

It is interesting that these three books use Stevenson's device of the first person narrative and use it as he does—to induce the quality of convincingness; to provide moments of anticipation when the reader is permitted a glimpse of coming events; and to allow a certain degree of relaxed enjoyment of horror and peril, since one is certain that the person telling the story survives in the end, else he could not be telling the tale.

In many of the American adventure tales of this period, certain purely national influences are very apparent. In earlier books, interest in that most stirring aspect of American history, the period of Western expansion, had been apparent. The great movement westward, beginning after the Revolution and continuing for more than half of the nineteenth century, has always exerted strong hold upon the imagination of writers. The uniquely American figure of the pioneer and frontiersman, the hardiness and indomitable spirit of the men and women who followed the frontiersman into the wilderness and established settlements there, have been the inspiration of many books, adult and juvenile, which hover on the border line between adventure and historic fiction, weighted on the side of history due to the interesting fact that many of them are founded on firsthand experience.

Indicative of the interest in the West are Hamlin Garland's (1860–1940) *Boy Life on the Prairie* (1899), with its account of farm life in Iowa, and its descriptions of herding cattle, killing rattlesnakes and hunting wolves; and George Bird Grinnell's (1849–1938) *Wolf Hunters* (1914), based on an original manuscript, telling how three soldiers spent a winter on the plains, hunting wolves.

Grinnell, through his scientific explorations in the West, and his governmental work, had long association with the American Indians. He collected their folk tales and wrote their history. Out of the knowledge of the West and of the Indians there came too a long series of books in which Jack Danvers lives on a ranch, hunting bear and antelope and elk, or joins a cowboy camp and learns to brand cattle, or lives on the prairies with the Indians.

Grinnell and James Willard Schultz (1859–1947) were two of the first three white men to explore what is now Glacier National Park. Schultz lived with the Pikuni tribe of the Blackfeet on the Blackfeet Indian Reservation. His books, *Sinopah the Indian Boy* (1913), *With the Indians in the Rockies* (1912), *Lone Bull's Mistake* (1918), and others, are sound in their depiction of tradition and custom.

The West was not the only frontier to attract attention. The wilderness of the Far North also exerted a hold on the minds of men. Dillon Wallace (1863–1939) was a member of the expedition to Labrador, organized in 1903 by Leonidas Hubbard, Jr. who lost his life on the expedition. Wallace wrote the story in his first book, *The Lure of the Labrador Wild* (1905). This was followed by *Ungava Bob* (1907), *The Gaunt Gray Wolf* (1914), and *Grit-a-Plenty* (1918), stories of trapping in Labrador, which manage to give a good deal of background information in an interesting manner.

The Romance of the Past

Mention has been made of the fact that lines of distinction between historical fiction and other types of story were growing more and more undistinguishable. Stories of family life, regional stories, adventure, recreations of a period, all of these may have an historical aspect. Only sufficient perspective is needed to give historical value to books like Louisa May Alcott's *Little Women,* or Thomas Bailey Aldrich's *The Story of a Bad Boy* or Mark Twain's *The Adventures of Tom Sawyer* and *The Adventures of Huckleberry Finn.* These have the added quality of being stories of specific regions, where the way of life was determined not only by the period as a whole, but also by the individual characteristics of that region at that time. Historical fiction gains much of its romance from adventure and adventure in turn frequently takes its setting and situation from the past. *The Aztec Treasure-House* and *Jim Davis* are merged with history. At the present time, the books of Grinnell and Schultz have become pictures of a past era. Howard Pyle, in his *Otto of the Silver Hand* and *Men of Iron,* had shown clearly and beautifully the power of a period story to interpret for all time the complexion and significance of an age. By the turn of the century the range of historical fiction had broadened to such an extent that any single definition or limitation is impossible. It is necessary only that such a book should depict the sufficiently remote past, in the presentation of an event, a personage, a period, a region, a nation, or a civilization.

By this time also methods of presentation had developed characteristics which were to prove permanent. Romanticism, from the time of Sir Walter Scott to the present, has been, in one degree or another, an ingredient of historical fiction for children. Any reconstruction of the past is essentially romantic, in children's books at least. It is equally true that Sir Walter Scott introduced realism into his stories, particularly in his creation of everyday, ordinary characters. As time went on, the inclination to reveal the effect of history upon the average person became more and more marked in historical fiction. It is interesting to speculate to what extent this trend in fiction influenced the socialized point of view which so thoroughly dominates the histories of recent years. Realism was strengthened by the realization that a sound and authentic basis of thorough and detailed knowledge is essential for the resurrection of any aspect of history in fictional form; and that, being steeped in his subject, as Howard Pyle was in the Middle Ages, an author must be able to select those essential and effectual details which will make his story a living, breathing entity.

The books selected to represent this type of story in the 1890's and 1900's illustrate the merging of various strains into historical fiction and the power of writers to construct a sound and living historical base on which to build a good story.

Among the most intensely and lastingly popular of authors was Joseph Altsheler (1862–1919) with *The Horsemen of the Plains* (1910), *The Guns of Bull Run* (1914), and others. Those of us interested in children's books and reading would be on more certain ground regarding children's reading tastes if we took the time to study the work of writers who have the universal and permanent appeal that Altsheler has. He had knowledge of, belief in, and enthusiasm for the materials, and the significance of the materials, which he used. He felt deeply and earnestly the value of the heritage left us by the history of our country. Being persuaded of the interest inherent in his subject, he felt no necessity for over-straining to create interest. Consequently he tells his story with an almost transparent simplicity and naturalness, and with single-mindedness in the depiction of character and incident. He had a fine sense of the human interest and drama inherent in our history and the ability to point up those aspects which best exemplify the interaction of men on history and of history on men. His respect for his subjects and for his readers led him to keep himself as author in the background and to allow his story to stand on its own feet. Many of his stories, particularly those of the frontier, hold the same fascination that James Fenimore Cooper offered to older generations; the fascination of the wilderness, and of men who had developed to a fine art the craft of forest lore, of tracking and hunting and trailing, of pitting their wit and their courage against the forces of nature and of human enemies. That he should be reminiscent of Cooper is not surprising, since Altsheler owed much to Parkman, and Parkman in turn had been impressed by Cooper.

Taking all these qualities into account, it is completely understandable that the demand for Altsheler's books on the French and Indian Wars, on the opening of the wilderness, and on the Civil War lasted for more than twenty years, and still continues. These three series escape the censure so often connected with many sequels because of their progressive coverage of great and meaningful periods of history. They are more nearly sagas of an age. Indeed, Altsheler made a slight approach to the family saga, in that the cousins of the Civil War series, one fighting for the Union and the other for the Confederacy, are great-grandsons of Paul Cotter and Henry Ware of the frontier series.

Thomas Nelson Page's (1853–1922) *Two Little Confederates* (1888) shows, as do Altsheler's books on the Civil War, that the passage of time had lessened the tension and brought instead realization of the pity and tragedy of a conflict which divided families and friends. It is infinitely slighter than Altsheler's coverage from the secession of South Carolina to the surrender at Appomattox. For younger children, it is a boy's-eye view of the war, a book which quickens sympathy without dwelling unduly on the horrors of war.

John Masefield's *Martin Hyde; the Duke's Messenger* (1910) is one part adventure, one part historical fiction. The adventure element is compounded of elements dear to the hearts of lovers of stories of intrigue —secret papers, disguise, narrow escapes from heated pursuit, a mysterious woman spy, plots and counter plots. The historical element consists of the fact of Monmouth's rebellion of 1685, and of the fine impression of the period. This impression is conveyed by a succession of sharply etched pictures—the description of the old houses in Billingsgate, of the Thames River and its traffic, of the camps of the Duke of Monmouth, and of the moors surrounding the camps. Again Masefield uses the device of the first-person narrative. He uses it with effect, filling the story with a sense of personal experiences and emotions which are unforgettable, lending to the telling that feeling of urgency, as if the teller were driven to tell his tale, which is so compelling a result of the artistic use of the personal narrative form.

If this period had produced no other books than those of John Bennett (1865–1956), still it would be a notable one. His books are distinctive and distinguished; so much so that the only possible regret is that there are not more of them. There were earlier books which had put on record the dominant qualities of a period. There were to be books exceptional in their interpretation of the spirit of a period. But *Master Skylark*

(1897) remains unsurpassed in its enchanting capture and portrayal of the flavor and color of Shakespearian England. It is a book of quickly changing moods, vigorous and zestful, gentle and tender, gay and sad. It is exuberant with the abundant life, exultant with the joy of creative work, delicately responsive to the sense of beauty which made the Elizabethan age glorious. It is crowded with characters and incidents, but never confusing; filled with details, but never exhausting. It is written with a sensitivity that makes the reading of it an experience to be coveted. And through it all breathes the spirit that is uniquely and forever England.

Hardly less notable is *Barnaby Lee* (1902) which builds up to and centers on Peter Stuyvesant's forced surrender of New Amsterdam to the British. Here is the same craftsmanship in the handling of a complex story pattern, the same perceptive appreciation of human values, the same power of character portrayal, the same generosity of feeling and emotion, the same ability to make a past period pulse with life. It is a book tonic in its demonstration of the virtues of honor and loyalty and gallantry, and in its condemnation of dishonor and dishonesty.

These books indicate the faculty of historical fiction to elucidate the past, to combine information, recreation and inspiration, to instill appreciation of character and of great moral values. Events of the future were to enhance these potentialities and were to add to them the ability to illuminate problems of the present by pictures of the past which constitute a pregnant and poignant record of man's continuing opposition to all that threatens his dignity and integrity as a human being.

Bibliography

Eaton, Anne Thaxter. "Laura E. Richards." *The Horn Book*, Vol. 17 (July–Aug., 1941), pp. 247–255.
——— *Reading with Children*. New York, Viking Press, 1940.
Laski, Marghanita. *Mrs. Ewing, Mrs. Molesworth, and Mrs. Hodgson Burnett*. New York, Oxford University Press, 1951.
Mahony, Bertha E. "Salute to Laura Richards." *The Horn Book*, Vol. 17 (July–Aug., 1941), p. 245.

· 9 ·

Events and People

Since 1920 there has been rare and fine development in many types of books for children. This is explicitly observable in history and biography, where there have occurred extraordinary change in presentation, writing, and readability, and equally extraordinary increase in production. In comparison with the present, the early 1900's seem poverty-stricken in these two fields, in regard both to number of books and to significance of presentation.

The radical change in the conception, teaching, and writing of history for children which came after the First World War makes it somewhat difficult to do justice to the few outstanding histories of the opening years of the twentieth century. The present emphasis, and with good reason, is almost completely upon the social values of history, upon its economic, cultural, political, and civic aspects. This is in strong contrast to the point of view of the older histories, which used frequently the legendary approach and which utilized in their presentation the appeal of great heroic and dramatic figures in history, centering their depiction of facts upon the deeds and influence of such personalities. There can be no doubt of the importance and value of socialized history. Yet a rereading of such books as Mary MacGregor's (1876–?) *The Story of Greece* (1913) and *The Story of Rome* (1912), of Henrietta Marshall's (1876–?) *An Island Story* (1905) and *Scotland's Story* (1906) raises a question as to whether the legendary and heroic approach may not also have a place. Certainly these authors were correct in their realization that the tradition, legend, and folklore of a country are part of the history of that country. Certain modern histories, in their combination of political and literary history, show the same realization. Certainly the earlier authors were also correct in their appreciation of the fact that to children, all knowledge is first of all a story, and that the warmth and glamor of a great personality, the drama of central figures of great epochs, enliven the cold remoteness of facts. This should not involve distortion of fact or character, nor does it in the books of Marshall and MacGregor. In the former's *An Island Story* (changed to *Our Island*

Story in a later edition) the picture of Charles I, walking with courage and dignity through the streets of London for the last time on his way to his execution, does not obscure the record of his weakness. By its drama, it impresses permanently on the mind the facts of Charles's reign and its outcome. Indeed, a glance through this book brings the realization that here are all the events and stories which come first to the mind when one thinks of English history—King Alfred and the cakes, Canute and the waves, Richard and Blondel, the Magna Charta, the little Princes in the Tower, Elizabeth and Raleigh, Trafalgar and Waterloo, and Lucknow. Surely all these are part of the rich texture of English history.

The method in these histories of Greece and Rome, of France, Scotland, England and the British Empire, is the same—intensive selection of large events and great figures, concentration on the dramatic nature of the events and characters, and plentiful interpolation of story and legend. The writing reflects the interest and enthusiasm of the authors, and while the style is occasionally over-conscious of a child audience, this is a minor fault redeemed by simplicity and directness and sincerity. The values of these books lie in their power to establish a basic familiarity with names and incidents, to arouse an initial interest, and to stimulate a desire for further knowledge. They do not pretend to be exhaustive and cannot be compared with more detailed histories or with those which lay claim to profound interpretation of the significance of the past. Still their intention to serve as an introduction to the subject of history is a valid and achievable one, and is echoed by a few contemporary books.

One of the fine by-products of the present intense interest in history has been the realization of the importance of certain periods or aspects in the life of the world or of a country. Anticipation of this interest and of the desirability of additional resources in this respect is evidenced by Eva March Tappan's (1854–1930) *When Knights Were Bold* (1911). This book is anticipative, too, in its content, emphasis, and method. In accordance with the purpose stated in the preface, it presents pictures of the ways of life and thought which characterized the Middle Ages and which left their impress upon future periods. The depiction of life in castles, towers, manors and monasteries, of beliefs and customs, of the arts and sciences, gives to this earlier book a lasting quality, equal to that of such recent books as William Stearns Davis' (1877–1930) *Life on a Medieval Barony* (1923) and Gertrude Hartman's (1876–1955) *Medieval Days and Ways* (1937).

The relation between history and biography is a strong one. The new emphases in history undoubtedly helped to stimulate the greatly improved and increased biographical writing for children which is so marked a feature of contemporary juvenile literature. In the early

1900's, however, the situation justified Anne Carroll Moore's comment in *Cross-Roads to Childhood* (1926), that Albert Bigelow Paine's (1861–1937) *Boys' Life of Mark Twain* (1916) "is one of the few readable biographies for boys and girls." Considering the long recognized interest of young people in personality and accomplishment, their tendency toward hero worship, and their aptitude for inspiration by example, it is strange that biography took so long a time to establish itself in the field of children's literature. It is equally strange that the early stress upon the value of an introduction to children of epics and heroic literature did not lead to more profuse writing of biography. Not yet have we fully realized the biographical aspect and technique of the epics, and their consequent potentiality as an introduction and stimulation to the reading of biography. Legendized though they may be, a study of the epics as life-writing reveals a sound and artistic technique, which could well form a basis for an appreciation of pure biography. They rose from the same major impulses that initially give rise to biography, the commemorative impulse, and the intention to inspire by example. They are memorials to achievement of character and deed. They center their narrative upon the life of one person who is unique, and whose uniqueness is clearly defined, so that he is differentiated from his fellow men. They use the biographical method of portraying character by allowing their subject to reveal himself by speech and deed; by describing his effect upon his contemporaries, friends, and enemies; by revealing his reactions under strongly contrasted circumstances. They employ the objective method of narration without sacrificing drama and emotion, as good biography for children should do. Above all, they have the literary power that stems from intense sympathy with and proper emotional interest in their subject, and from an abiding faith in the greatness of which man is capable. It is curious that the years at the turn of the century, which saw so clearly the beauty and significance of epic material and which produced such fine retellings of epics, did not have equal vision as to the similar significance and importance of biography in children's reading.

However, there were biographies written at this time which are worthy of mention because of the biographers' enthusiasm for their subjects, their appreciation of the necessity for authenticity, and the readability of their writing.

Laura Richards' (1850–1943) interest was plainly in women, and she chose her subjects wisely. *Abigail Adams and Her Times* (1917), *Elizabeth Fry; the Angel of the Prisons* (1916), and *Florence Nightingale; the Angel of the Crimea* (1909) are all written with a contagious zest and vigor, which hold interest throughout the book in spite of occasional digressions from the thing in hand, like the sketch of John Foxe in *Elizabeth Fry*. The adult reader, at least, is inclined to be lenient with such wanderings, recognizing that they are due to Mrs. Richards' all-embracing interests. Moreover, such a fault is negligible in comparison to her pleasant, informative habit of linking the period of her subject with world events of the time or with her use of small and telling detail to build a background of the domestic or social or political life of the times. Her extensive use of quotations from letters, diaries, and journals, while it indicates study and research, is unpretentious and succeeds in portraying character as no indirect narrative could. The most delightful qualities of her biographies are the reflections of her warm response to people and of the sincerity of her admiration for her subjects, and the informal style of her writing. It is the degree to which these qualities exist in *Florence Nightingale* that makes this book probably the best of all her biographies.

Mrs. Richards was influenced in her selection of subjects by her interest in the character and achievement of fine women. Eva March Tappan was undoubtedly influenced by her interest in history. She chose as her subjects great historic figures of English history—Alfred the Great, William the Conqueror, Queen Victoria, and Queen Elizabeth. The fact that all her titles begin with the words "In the days of" may have been intentional, since her biographies succeed well in revealing their characters against, and in connection with, a live background of the times. She shares the modern tendency toward a semi-fictional presentation. This, together with an interest in her subjects equal to that of Mrs. Richards, gives to her biographies an appeal comparable to that of historical fiction. Although her style may be a little dated, and she may seem to oversimplify complex personalities and the great events of their eras, her books retain interest and essential truth to the periods with which they are concerned. It is a pity that these biographies seem to be vanishing from children's book collections. This is especially true of *In the Days of Queen Elizabeth* (1902) and *In the Days of Queen Victoria* (1903). No better biographies have appeared of these two rulers in whose reigns such momentous events occurred.

It was a natural thing for Helen Nicolay (1866–1954) to turn to the writing of biography. Her father was private secretary to Abraham Lincoln and co-author with John Hay of the ten-volume life of Lincoln. Due to her father's serious eye trouble, she, with the rest of the family, participated in the monumental task, reading source material, taking dictation, and correcting proof. After her father's death, she was asked to write, for young people, a condensation of her father's work. *The Boy's Life of Abraham Lincoln* was published in 1906. From that date through the 1930's, Helen Nicolay wrote biographies of prominent figures in American history, of Grant and Jackson and Washington and Jefferson, of Hamilton and Franklin and Lafayette. Her work shows a grasp of the requirements of biography, sound and conscientious workmanship, and careful attention to the details necessary to a correct picture of the period and of her subject. She is able to avoid over-idealization without despoiling her characters of their greatness. Her style has a fine dignity and simplicity. She is a better biographer, in the real sense of the word, than are Laura Richards and Eva March Tappan. And yet, one misses, in some of her books, the lovable spontaneity and warmth of feeling which are so characteristic of Mrs. Richards in particular.

It is possible to combine good biographical technique and the quick sympathy with a subject which makes a biography something more than information, which makes it literature. This possibility is made actual in Albert Bigelow Paine's (1916) *Boys' Life of Mark Twain* and *The Girl in White Armor; the True Story of Joan of Arc* (1927). Both these books are condensations by the author of his adult biographies of the same persons. The fact that adaptation for children of adult biographies was fairly frequent at this time is an indication of the need felt for biographies for young people and at the same time of hesitancy in the writing of such books directly for this age.

Paine's life of Mark Twain shows the inestimable value of a close personal relationship between biographer and biographee. The chapters in which Paine describes the beginning of the collaboration between himself and Mark Twain are full of human interest; they are equally interesting in their revelation of Paine's realization of the difficulty involved in the method they were using.

> The creator of Tom Sawyer and Huck Finn had been embroidering old incidents or inventing new ones too long to stick to history now, to be able to separate the romance in his mind from the reality of the past. . . Certainly the dictations were precious, for they revealed character as nothing else could; but as material for history they often failed to stand the test of the documents in the next room.[1]

"They revealed character as nothing else could." Paine had opportunity to listen to the reminiscences of Mark Twain. He had also a sensitive and affectionate appreciation of the rare and lovable personality revealed in the delightful, spontaneous talk. Consequently, the biographer brought to life a man who possessed in utmost degree that most necessary qualification for a humorist, the perception of the mingled pathos and humor of human existence.

The Girl in White Armor, in contrast, is an equally fine demonstration of the potentialities of a biography based on profound and absorbed study of the records of an individual and her period and country. It is a poignant portrayal of that frequent tragedy, the destruction of its best hope by a country too short-sighted to perceive wherein its salvation lay.

[1] Albert Bigelow Paine, *The Boys' Life of Mark Twain* (New York, Harper, 1916), pp. 316–331.

Paine's two biographies deserve characterization by that much abused word, distinctive, and their distinction has given them a lasting place in biography for children.

It is interesting that the age that produced classics in adventure fiction produced, also, classics in actual and personal accounts of voyage, discovery, and exploration, a kind of book often characterized by adventure equal to any fiction can devise.

The impulse which from earliest times has driven men to discover the unknown is stirring testimony to the nobility of curiosity, the height of courage and daring, the extent of hardship and toil and self-sacrifice of which man is capable and which is greatly responsible for the progress of civilization. The record of how "the spirit of man has mastered the earth"[1] has never received so magnificent a presentation as in Margaret Bertha Synge's (d. 1939) *A Book of Discovery* (1912). The book begins with the Phoenician mariners, includes all the great explorers, and ends with the discovery of the South Pole. Extraordinarily comprehensive, it maintains unflagging interest. It is filled with little known, fascinating facts, written with imaginative perception of the romantic aspect of its material, and heightens its sense of reality by permitting many of the explorers to tell their stories in their own words. No small part of the uniqueness of the book lies in its illustrations, reproductions of old maps and charts, of early prints and woodcuts. Particularly effective is the series of maps showing the "unfolding of the world."

From the days of Richard Henry Dana and Herman Melville and Frederick Marryat to the days of John Masefield and Joseph Conrad, the wonder and the mystery of the sea and the struggle of man against the sea have exerted strong hold on the imagination of many writers. Some tales of the sea and of the men who go down to it in ships can be numbered among the great books in the English language. *The Cruise of the "Cachalot"* (1899) by Frank Bullen (1857–1915) is such a book. The superb quality of this story of life on a whaler is so well known as to make further discussion of its merits repetitious and superfluous. One point, however, may well be stressed. Children of certain ages are hungry for realism. This demand is often misinterpreted as a longing merely for the here and now. This is unjust to the child. What he is trying to say is that he wants a reality stark and strong and powerful, a sense of abundant and vigorous life. Such reality is independent of time or place and is found in books written in 1840 and 1851 as well as in books written in 1940 and 1951. It is the distincitve quality of *Two Years Before the Mast*, of *Moby Dick*, and of *The Cruise of the "Cachalot."*

[1] M. B. Synge, *A Book of Discovery* (New York, Thomas Nelson, n.d.), p. 544.

· 10 ·

The March of Picture Books

In the creation of picture books, Randolph Caldecott, Walter Crane, and Kate Greenaway had established all-time precedents. Caldecott in particular set high standards of technical excellent, of imaginative insight, storytelling detail, humor and gaiety, beauty of color and line and background. It is not surprising that the development of the picture book should be a gradual one. Indeed it may be a matter for gratitude that at this point such books did not come in such abundance as to produce mediocrity and thus mar the conception of consistent and harmonious beauty which the three English picture-book makers upheld.

Comparatively few in number though they are, a survey of the picture books of this period reveals interesting and prophetic trends. They show continuation of earlier ideas, an inclination to discover fresh and original material, realization of the need for illustration consistent with the tone and spirit of the text, recognition of the interests of small children and of the power of pictures to tell a story independent of text. They also reveal an appreciation of the work of countries other than England and America. This appreciation ultimately gave distinction to picture-book collections in this country through importation of foreign books and through native books deriving their inspiration from the art forms of many countries.

The note of admonition, presented humorously and by awful example, had been struck before this time, in picture book and in verse. In *Clean Peter and the Children of Grubbylea* (1901) and in *Goops and How To Be Them* (1900) Ottilia Adelborg (1855–1936), a Swedish artist, and Frank Gelett Burgess (1866–1951), an American, strike it again. From the moment of its translation into English, *Clean Peter* has been a favorite. The animated drawings are clear and simple, gay with the unforced humor implicit in the idea of the book, and with the fun of small added touches. The first pictures of the unwashed, unkempt children, splashing in mud puddles, eating like little pigs, are delicious. In the second picture, showing the unmannerly children at tea, there hangs on the wall a picture of a pig eating from the trough, a touch almost worthy of Leslie Brooke. The basins and the jugs, walking together "in friendly talk," with smiles on their faces, is an animated drawing of inanimate objects rivaling those of Caldecott. When *Clean Peter*, whose snowy white garment is in constant contrast to the dirty children, begins his energetic cleaning, the pictures are full of laugh-provoking action and emotion. Particularly delightful is the one where Peter is cutting the hair of a boy tied to a chair, while an awestruck little girl watches, her fingers in her mouth. *Goops and How To Be Them, A Manual of Manners for Polite Infants*, is filled with black-and-white drawings of Goops and of the adults whom the Goops annoy with their unpleasant habits. The fun that children get from books like these is partly due to the ability to laugh at themselves, partly to a kind of superiority at finding culprits like themselves in print. The text of both books is in verse, which raises an intriguing speculation as to why humorous teaching of manners and morals so often takes the form of jingles and rhymes.

If Adelborg and Burgess maintained an older tradition, E. Boyd Smith (1860–1943) introduced a new type of subject matter in his picture books of farm and seashore and railroad. *The Railroad Book* (1913) inevitably has become dated, but *The Story of Noah's Ark* (1909), *Chicken World* (1910), *The Farm Book* (1910), and *The Seashore Book* (1912) have a permanency of appeal. In these books, the pictures are decidedly of an importance superior to the text. In that sense they are true picture books, since the text accompanies the pictures, instead of the pictures illustrating the text. The illustrations stand alone, independent of any explanation, possessing completely satisfying storytelling details. This ability of the pictures to carry the whole weight of story interest is plainly evident in *Chicken World*, one of the best of Smith's books and typical of his work. The pictures spread across the double page, with the black hen and her chicks prominent in every picture. Satisfactorily, there are always ten chicks, even though sometimes just a little tail or head shows. The colors are bright and clear, and there is real beauty in the unobtusive background and decorative details of flowers and trees. "The wheel of chicken life goes round" from April to December and the passing of the seasons is delicately depicted in change of flowers and fruit and trees until the snow comes in November and December. It is an original book, filled with the humor innate in chickens, and with the lovable appeal of small things. In *The Farm Book* the text is more extensive and definitely informational. Again the pictures capture the interest, portraying the fascination of old-time farm life—of plowing and sowing of seed, of milking and churning, of going to market and to church. Comparable in informational intention is *The Seashore Book*, with its pictures of shipyards and sail lofts and ship launchings, of whaling and shipwreck. In *The Story of*

Our Country (1920) and *The Story of Pocahontas and Captain John Smith* (1906), E. Boyd Smith introduced history and biography to the picture-book format.

Another book ahead of its time in "social study" value is *Four and Twenty Toilers* (1900), with verses by Edward Verrall Lucas (1868–1938) and illustrations by Francis D. Bedford. The verses describe twenty-four trades, and for each trade there is a picture, done in colors reminiscent of Caldecott, and frequently with a background of typically English fields and stiles, woods and gabled cottages and village streets, which also calls Caldecott to mind.

Two other illustrators show extreme single-mindedness in their specialization of content. Cecil Aldin's (1870–1935) pictures of dogs in *The White Puppy Book* (1917), *The Mongrel Puppy Book* (1912), and others are full of life, character, and essential doggishness. In later years other illustrators were to make beautiful picture books of horses, cats and dogs, but none has ever exceeded Aldin in his ability to portray realistically animal personality.

To many middle-aged people, the mention of Palmer Cox's (1840–1924) *The Brownies: Their Book* (1887) calls up an astonishingly clear memory of the pages of the picture books which showed the adventures of the brownies at home and abroad. These books had tremendous popularity which must have been due to the pictures, since they are remembered vividly, while the text and its content are forgotten, except for the fact that the text is in verse. Cox took the habits of his brownies from folklore, in that they "delight in harmless pranks and helpful deeds [and] work and sport while many households sleep." He adds a novel touch in the individualization he imparts to them; there is a policeman brownie, and a dude brownie, and a cowboy brownie, a Frenchman and a Chinaman and a Dutchman. It is probable that each child has his favorite and experiences a thrill of satisfaction as he finds that particular brownie in every picture, proof that Palmer Cox was wise in the ways of children. The large pictures and the little merry sketches of single brownies, caught in all sorts of postures and actions, have a fascination difficult to capture in words. It is something akin to the spell exerted by *The Night Before Christmas*, a thrill that only a child can experience. Yet once experienced, the feel of it is never forgotten, and an adult, turning the pages of the Brownie books, comes close to recapturing, for a moment, that lovely excitement which he felt as a child.

High quality and integrity of workmanship distinguish the illustrations of Louis Maurice Boutet de Monvel (1850–1913) and Henriette Willebeek Le Mair (1889–   ). Many people have called Boutet de Monvel's *Jeanne d'Arc* (1897) the most beautiful picture book ever made. That its text, even in the English translation, may not be within the comprehension of the picture-book age is an immaterial factor. More than a few children of many ages have been enthralled by the pictures and have gained an ineradicable appreciation of good art from its pages. The artist was born in Orléans, and much of his life was associated with that city where Joan of Arc defied the English. The book is highly and colorfully authentic in its fifteenth century background, and the pictures, of an indescribable variety in mood and color, never exhaust interest and attention. Some of them are tumultuous in action. In the battle scene, there is utter confusion which is not confusing; the clangor and clash of armor, the shouts of men, and the shrieks of horses are almost audible. No words could describe the pomp and ceremony, the color and ritual, of the period as does the illustration depicting the crowning of the king in the cathedral to the sound of trumpets and the flinging aloft of the swords of the noblemen. In deep and beautiful contrast is the scene of Joan of Arc in prayer before the altar, the background quiet and somber in tone, pricked with the golden flames of candles; or the trial scene, where Joan of Arc's figure in blue stands out against the dark brownish-gray walls of the room, and against the figures of the judges, whose robes repeat, with variations, the tone of the walls. The faces and expressions of the judges are extraordinary studies in thought and character portrayal. Superb in its technique, astonishing in its detail, this book inevitably made and still makes a tremendous impression. Published in 1897 in France, it was issued with English text in this country in 1907 by Century. In *Filles et Garçons* and in *Nos Enfants* by Anatole France, issued in the United States in 1913 and 1917, Boutet de Monvel's illustrations show his close observance of children and his ability to draw them with astounding simplicity and startling lifelikeness. The pictures are as young and fresh, as unspoiled and natural, as the the children who are their subjects.

The association between Boutet de Monvel and Willebeek Le Mair was close, and the results can be seen in her picture books. Born in Rotterdam of artistic parents, she early showed talent in drawing and painting. At the age of sixteen, she went to Paris to consult Boutet de Monvel. For several years she worked according to his advice, studying anatomy and painting children's portraits, submitting her work once each year to him for suggestion and criticism. Her favorite subjects are children and nursery rhymes illustrated by actions and movements and moods of children. *The Children's Corner* (1915) and *Little People* (1916), with verses by R. H. Elkin, have exquisite and lovely pictures of children in everyday activities. *Little Songs of Long Ago* (1912) and *Our Old Nursery Rhymes* (n.d.), with the rhymes set to music by A. E. Moffat, are illustrated in delicate pastel colors with a subtle and poetic imaginative quality in the conception of the pictures. The manner of her imagination frequently gives an individual interpretation of a nursery rhyme, as in the picture for "Mary, Mary, Quite Contrary." The "Little maids all in a row" are dolls each dressed differently, sitting around the walls of a garden. The cockle shells edge the strip of lawn on which the dolls are sitting, and in front of Mary is a tiny circular pool, with miniature bushes around it, linked with ribbons on which hang silver bells. Like Boutet de Monvel, she can use a single tone of color with exquisite effect, as in the illustration for "Twinkle, Twinkle, Little Star," all in gray melting into white; or in "Sleep, Baby, Sleep," in blue of a twilight shade; or in "Girls and Boys Come Out To Play," with the color of the dusk that comes with a new moon. Her use of color and her decorative details make so immediate and so strong an impression that it is easy to assume that there is little or no action in her pictures. This is a misjudgment. Motion and action are there, not in robust or vigorous degree, but suggested with the delicacy which is her outstanding quality. Her children fall into poses which imply that they have been arrested in flight or caught at a moment of suspended motion. At other times, her pictures have a lovely, graceful sense of movement. In all instances, her children have the charm of naturalness and verisimilitude. This achievement is due to the exacting method of study demanded by her Dutch teacher, who required her to draw from models in slow and swift motion. In the *Old Dutch Nursery Rhymes* (1917) the illustration for "Our Baby Prince" has exquisite grace, comparable to the beauty of pose caught and held in a dance; while in "The Little Sailor," one can hear the whistling of the wind and feel the buffeting of the sails and the bending of the masts.

To England belongs the honor of possessing two of the greatest illustrators, not only of this period but of all time. The quality of Beatrix Potter's illustrations and the intimacy of their relationship to her books has been discussed. The name of L. Leslie Brooke (1862–1940) is well known and discerning and deserved tribute has been paid him. There should be no need to stress that he belongs to that fine English tradition to which children's literature owes an immeasurable debt; the tradition of men great in heart and mind and spirit, of Caldecott and Lear and Carroll, of Kipling and Grahame and Milne and Tolkien and others, who have infused children's books with gentleness and tenderness and gaiety, with fundamental goodness and sanity, and with optimism and beauty for all of which the adult, as well as the child, is grateful.

More than most illustrators, Brooke has revealed in his work the charm of his own personality. To be familiar with his pictures is to have an intensely intimate feeling of personal acquaintance with the man who made them, with his geniality and warmheartedness, his quick interest and sympathy, his peculiar power of imagination, his delightfully uninhibited and spontaneous enjoyment of the inner spirit of the stories and rhymes he illustrated. It is possibly this feeling of personal friendship with him which, in part, has made his name so revered on this side of the Atlantic. But the debt which America feels is owed to him is also due to our respect for his knowledge of children, a knowledge founded on genuine interest and sympathy and appreciation of a child's preferences. He knew that whereas an adult, at first sight, gains a general impression of a picture as a whole, and is frequently oblivious to small details, the child begins with the small details and from them achieves a cumulative appreciation of the totality of the picture. The details must be stimulating to the imagination and must have storytelling quality within themselves. They must also be harmonious with the picture as a whole and consistent in their continuity. Leslie Brooke had many great gifts, but his genius for detail is at one and the same time the underlying factor of much of his gaiety and humor and imaginative insight, and the secret of his great appeal. The *Johnny Crow* books are loved as living things, intimately associated with the child, are loved by him, and it is easy to see why, once one has seen what a little child sees in these books. At the end of *Johnny Crow's Garden* (1903) each animal has become a definite personality and a friend with Johnny Crow, the ubiquitous and generous host, the friendliest of all. In *Johnny Crow's Party* (1907) and *Johnny Crow's New Garden* (1935), no change has been allowed to mar the reality of that hospitable garden. All things remain securely and serenely the same; the lion has his "green and yellow tie on"; the bear still possesses his striped pants and tailcoat. Johnny Crow still plies rake and hoe and improves his garden, coping patiently and politely with the troubles and idiosyncrasies of his guests. Every picture tells with graphic and faithful detail the incident described in the accompanying mnemonic and nonsensical verse.

  The Golden Goose Book (1905) is a thing without price in its insight into the appeal such stories as *The Three Bears* or *The Three Little Pigs* have for little children. In one of Leslie Brooke's letters, quoted by Reginald Birch in his article in the Leslie Brooke memorial number of *The Horn Book* (May–June 1941), there is an implication that the illustrator had been taken to task for his personification of animals by some ardent realist. Such prosaic and literal-minded people miss the whole point of the classic appeal of the nursery folk tale. That appeal lies in the combination of the familiar and unfamiliar which only the folk tale and its faithful imitations possess. Bears, as such, are familiar animals, and home life a familiar experience; but bears living in a house, sleeping in beds, sitting in chairs, and eating porridge, constitute a novel and utterly fascinating deviation from the thoroughly realistic and therefore unexciting, commonplace. How well Leslie Brooke knew this, and how thoroughly he entered into the spirit of the little child's response to such stories is eminently revealed in the illustration for *The Three Bears* and *The Three Little Pigs*. The bears live in a typical English cottage, but it is unmistakably clear that this is a bear's cottage. The bed on which Goldilocks takes her nap has tiny figures of bears upright on the footboard. Bears are stenciled about the edge of the coverlet, and bears' heads form the design on the rug. The bedside book is *Tom Bruin's School Days*, and the newspaper lying carelessly on the table is *The Bear Truth*. Statues of bears and small models of beehives form the mantel decorations. The ancestral portrait hanging on the wall is that of Major Ursa, D. SO., and the motto of the framed family tree is "Bear and Forbear." Such delightful whimsy is more than superficial fancy. It is the result of an uninhibited imagination at play within the literature being illustrated. This same quality of imagination enabled Brooke to create additional little side stories which invariably harmonize with the main story, rather than detract from it. In fact, such side issues as the pictorial story of the little bear aiming his sling shot at a robin, and missing it, or that of the family walk, with the little bear turning somersaults down the hill, add immeasurably to the spirit of the story. Incidentally, the emotion of parental complacent pride in offspring has never been more faithfully portrayed than in the faces of the parent bears, as they walk arm in arm, beaming at the antics of their child.

It has been said of Caldecott that he was master of the fine art of leaving out, and that he could express a whole story in a few lines or a single figure. The same thing could well be said of Brooke. Among his most delightful and expressive work are the tail pieces to the stories in *The Golden Goose Book* (1905). The black-and-white sketch of the small bear, parading triumphantly around the garden with Goldilock's big hat, wrong side to, tied under his chin—the utter satiety implied by the back view of the little pig, finishing his dinner of wolf, are not only perfect finales, they are masterpieces of simplicity.

Underlying Brooke's humor and merriment, his story-full detail and the play of his imagination, the fineness of his technical skill and the quiet beauty of his workmanship, is a sustaining quality comparable to that of Beatrix Potter—a quality of old-world peace, of pleasure in the simple and gracious things of life. This is, indeed, a quality which in some kind or degree pervades the best picture books of all times. It constitutes their greatest single gift to children who find in picture books a world which is their own world of wonder and delight—and to adults, who, it may be suspected, find in picture books an anodyne for the confusion and contradiction of the modern world. By its very nature and intention, the picture book is freed, as is fantasy, from any necessity to reflect the present, and like fantasy, the picture book speaks an international language.

Bibliography

The Horn Book. "The Leslie Brooke Number." Vol. 17 (May–June, 1941).

Mahony, Bertha E., Louise P. Latimer, and Beulah Folmsbee, comps. *Illustrators of Children's Books, 1744–1945.* Boston, The Horn Book, 1947.

Poets of Childhood

It is desirable that writers of prose for children should retain, in their maturity, vivid memories of childhood impressions. It is essential that writers of poetry for children should do so. Poetry is inherently a thing of mood and emotion, of response to impression. Except for the straightforward, objective narrative and purely nonsensical types, it is a form of literature innately tended toward the subjective. The subjective either in its retrospective or introspective mood, has no interest for children, who have not lived long enough to know the wistful longing for things once possessed and lost, and who feel intensely, but never analyze their feeling.

The existence of true poetry of and for childhood, rather than about childhood, is therefore an achievement which calls for wonder and gratitude. In the thirty years between 1890 and 1920, the swing toward utter liberality of thought and imagination, which began in the mid-nineteenth century, had created imperishable prose for children. These thirty years saw the same liberating force in poetry for children, a force founded upon intelligent respect for and sympathetic understanding of a child's capacity for appreciation of the fine and the true and the beautiful, and upon the eager willingness of writers to give of their best in writing for children. It is altogether fitting and right that this period should culminate in the work of a genuinely great literary artist, whose poetry for children takes its place among the great poetry of the English-speaking world.

An early successor to *A Child's Garden of Verses* was *Little-Folk Lyrics* (1892) by Frank Dempster Sherman (1860–1916). This collection seems little known or remembered today, though verses from it appear occasionally in anthologies. The lyrics are delicate impressions of the beauty of the natural world, revealed in poems which picture the distinctive, essential qualities of flowers and birds, of the months of the year, of snow and frost and rain and sun. An architect by profession, Sherman had the artist's eye for small and telling detail. Combined with the artist in him was the poet, with his insight into the significance of the beauty of the natural world, and his childlike habit of personification. His nature poems are filled with pretty, childlike fancies—"The Waterfall" with its tinkling of elfin bells; "The Snow-Bird," walking on the snow, prints it with stars; "Wizard Frost," who paints on the window pane a picture "scarcely larger than a hand, of a tiny Switzerland." Occasionally, as in "A Wish" or "Spinning Top," he comes close to Stevenson in his ability to interpret the imaginative play life of a child.

Nursery rhymes should constitute the first introduction to poetry and should be followed immediately by nonsense rhymes, logical successors to Mother Goose in their spontaneous fun and emphatic, regular rhythm heightened by alliteration. It takes a peculiar genius to write nonsense rhymes, as is evidenced by the comparatively small amount of good nonsense verse. In this field, Laura Richards' (1850–1943) work has distinction, even when compared with such classic poems as those of Lear and Carroll.

Mrs. Richards was born apparently with a keen sense of rhythm, developed and strengthened by being raised on Lear, as she herself says, and by the songs which her mother created and sang for all her children. When her own children came, she, in her turn, made verses and songs for them. It has already been told how these first poems appeared in the early volumes of *St. Nicholas*. In 1890 Mrs. Richards published *In My Nursery* and in 1902 *The Hurdy-Gurdy*. In 1932 *Tirra Lirra; Rhymes Old and New*, born of a happy accident so entertainingly described by Mrs. May Lamberton Becker in her Foreword, was published, delightful proof of the life-long hold exerted by true nonsense verse. In this book are the old poems from books long out of print and new ones, written by Mrs. Richards at the age of eighty-one, with the same abandoned joyousness, the same easy fluency, the same rhythmic melody, the same delightful word coinage.

There are verses other than nonsense rhymes in the collections— songs for her children, like "A Song for Hal," with its chorus of "And every little wave had its nightcap on," which inevitably sets itself to a tune; lullabies like "Johnny's By-Low Song," with its sleepy refrain; poems of a child's life, like "A Party," "The Song of the Corn-Popper," "Alice's Supper," and "Pot and Kettle," many of which have a humorous note, easily appreciated by children, in their gentle scolding or their equally gentle laughter at children's idiosyncrasies. But the best loved and the longest remembered are the nonsense verses—the solemnly told ridiculous stories of "The Seven Little Tigers and the Aged Cook," "The Little Cossack" and "An Indian Ballad"; the hilariously absurd word mix-up of "Eletelephony"; the eternal human problem of "Mrs. Snipkin and Mrs. Wobblechin." It is natural that such verses should become family possessions, loved in childhood and recalled in middle-age with affection.

Over the years American literature, adult and juvenile, had evidenced a steadily increasing national flavor in its creation of American character and life and scene. Inevitably, also, the diversity of America in its regional backgrounds was reflected. Washington Irving had made a "country famous with a legend." The New England school had depicted New England scene and character with significant fidelity. Mark Twain and Bret Harte, no less than Washington Irving, had individualized American literature with local color of section and character. The eighties and the nineties were the era of the common man, the man who had pushed his way westward in the pioneer days, and whose descendants, on the farms and in the small towns and villages of the Midwest, formed the backbone of America. It was the common man, with his shrewdness and homely wisdom, his humor and his easily touched sentiment, his humanity and interest in people, who typified America's growing awareness of itself. Eugene Field (1850–1895) and James Whitcomb Riley (1849–1916) were not great poets, but they were highly characteristic of their time and place, and consequently their writing has significance. It is interesting to observe that before 1920 there was plenty of written comment about these two men in books other than histories of American literature, and the major part of it was enthusiastic. Not only the common man for whom they wrote but the man of letters praised their work. Since 1920 they have been little mentioned. Their age has passed, and yet it may be that their flavor persists in the tall tales of America, which are also literature of the people for the people.

Eugene Field was born in St. Louis, reared in New England, and by choice made the West and the Middle West his permanent home. That choice represents the dominant side of his nature. By profession a journalist, he inaugurated newspaper columns, famous in his day, in which he indulged his love of talk, of jests and pranks, and in which much of his verse appeared. James Whitcomb Riley was born and raised in Indiana and spent his life there. Both men had strong strains of humor in their make-up, but while Field's verged on the bizarre and the obvious, Riley's was more complex. He showed real understanding of the peculiar genius of American humor, saying once that it is not the matter but the manner that constitutes the charm of our native humor. Both men had lasting memories of their childhood as a happy period, and consequently a tenderness for childhood as a time of life. Both men had the common touch, the quick and frequently easy appeal to the emotions. Both had a certain gift for the writing of fluent, rhythmical verse which sometimes deteriorates into mere jingles.

Field's *Poems of Childhood* (1904) fall for the most part into three groups. In his poems of children and of child life, one is almost invariably conscious of Field himself, aware of the transitory nature of childhood and of the pathos of parental love. Unlike Stevenson, Field, in this sort of poem, is most frequently writing in retrospect, or as an adult trying to capture that appeal which children have for adults. His humorous poems are usually of the nonsensical order. "The Sugar-Plum Tree" or "The Duel" evidences a certain facility in the construction of nonsensical idea and language which, however, falls short of that solemn, inevitable rightness which marks superb nonsense. Few, however, other than Lear and Carroll, have achieved this. He strikes the note of pure human comedy less often than Riley does, though there is a delightful touch of it in "Grandma's Prayer," tinged with a characteristic pathos. Except for his nonsense verse, his lullabies are his most childlike poems, melodious in their sound and soothing in their rhythm. Occasionally, these are marred by the sentimentality to which he was prone, but it is likewise true that they reflect a sincerity of feeling that gives them a quality his other poems sometimes lack.

Field used dialect only occasionally. In *Rhymes of Childhood* (1890) Riley's use of it was constant, and he used it with assurance. In other ways than dialect, his verses reflect locality in incident and character and tone. He was well acquainted with rural America, with its love of small gossip, its interest in small events, and with the intimacy of its life. He had a stronger sense of character than Field had, so that "The Funny Little Fellow" and "Little Orphant Annie" and "The Raggedy Man" linger in the memory. Although his mood is frequently retrospective, some of his poems have an immediacy of feeling. In "Aunty's House," a child's delight in the novel experience of eating on the porch is clearly portrayed, and the portrayal is made real by the childish habit of association of little extraneous details with the experience—the red birds eating the cherries, the feel of the wind in the child's hair, and the smell of clover. It is in this kind of poem, where he writes of the live pleasure of children in small experiences, that Riley comes closest to writing verses for children—in this, and in his humorous poems, where he is addicted to the note of comedy produced by mingling the frightening and the ludicrous.

In their own day, the personalities of the two men, their representation of aspects of their time, and the novelty of their verse led to an exaggerated estimate of them as poets for children. Viewed more objectively, it is apparent that their reverence for childhood was, for the most part, a nostalgic and personal emotion. Although occasionally they approach a clear-sighted insight into the actuality of a child's viewpoint, chiefly they wrote as adults looking back upon childhood as the happiest period of life. Their personal involvement was too intense and too tinged with sentiment to allow them to capture Stevenson's objectivity or to enable them to see the deeper and universal significance of childhood.

It is impossible to form any transition from other poetry of and for childhood to that of Walter de la Mare (1873–1956). His poetry simply exists in itself, independent of significances and trends and time. There had been others, and would be others, who write for childhood with a sure touch, but none with his penetrating and illuminating insight. There had been others who wrote of the beauty of this world, but none with his sense of the transience of beauty, and at the same time his perception that the evanescent beauty of this world affords a glimpse into a greater and eternal beauty. There had been others who invoked the supernatural, but none in his varied keys—weird, grotesque, mysterious, enchanted. There had been others who were fascinated by sleep and dreams, but none with his feeling of lovely mystery. There were others who had mastery over words and form, but none greater than his. He loves England as Chaucer loved it, as a "land all possessed of faërie," as Shakespeare and Kipling loved it.

It is pleasant to know that it was Andrew Lang who accepted for publication De la Mare's first collection for children, *Songs of Childhood* (1902), published under the pseudonym Walter Ramal. The name of De la Mare is now famous, but a first reading of the *Songs* must have been an unforgettable and not to be repeated experience. It is easy to trace here similarities to William Blake, to the Pre-Raphaelites, to Keats, but there is something more, something indefinably De la Mare. There is his rich, rare power of imagination, which can imbue the eerie, the grotesque, even the gruesome, with a strange beauty; which can give to nursery rhymes an exquisite charm; which can, through perception of the significance of finite beauty, give a momentary glimpse into the infinite. There is in this book the secret life of childhood, the enchantment of the land of faerie, the spirit of England, that "land so witchery sweet." There is in it the liquid loveliness of his lullabies. Indeed, two of these are as exquisite as anything he has ever written. "I Met at Eve" is typical in its weaving of a spell by pure word sounds.

> I met at eve the Prince of Sleep,
> His was a still and lovely face,
> He wandered through a valley steep,
> Lovely in a lonely place
>
> .   .   .   .   .   .
>
> His twilight feet no sandals wore
> His eyes shone faint in their own flame,
> Fair moths that gloomed his steps before
> Seemed letters of his lovely name.[1]

And "Lullaby" demonstrates his mastery of form and line, with the breathtaking, whispering sudden pause of the short line, "O be still!" in the last verse.

[1] Walter de la Mare, *Songs of Childhood* (New York, Longmans, 1926), p. 169.

Sleep, sleep, lovely white soul!
Time comes to keep night-watch with thee,
Nodding with roses; and the sea
Saith 'Peace! Peace!' amid his foam.
'O be still!'
The wind cries up the whispering hill—
Sleep, sleep, lovely white soul.[1]

Eleven years after *Songs of Childhood*, in 1913, *Peacock Pie* was published. To the fullest extent the second collection fulfills the promise of the first. There are nursery rhymes, strongly individualized by the De la Mare touch; verses with rare and unique nonsensical conception; fairy tales that seem to belong to the beginning of time; the strange and haunting mystery of "The Little Green Orchard" and of "Some One"; the twilight spell of "Dream-Song"; the soft, gleaming patina of "Silver." His exquisite melody, his extraordinary facility in varied rhythm, lend to his poems, even those which at first sight seem to be mere objective stories, a haunting sense of ultimate significance. It is just this combination of penetrating and illuminating vision made apprehensible by music of word and line that gives to De la Mare's poetry such distinct and unique loveliness.

A Child's Day (1912) is the writing of a man whose tender understanding of the importance and meaning of childhood is so finely expressed in *Early One Morning in the Spring* (1935), and in the introduction to his anthology *Come Hither* (1923). This long narrative poem surrounds the child with a love that is completely without sentimentality. Simply and objectively, but with moving charm and revealing imaginative quality, it draws a picture of a small child's day; a day of routine experiences, made exciting and novel by touches of nonsense and humor; a day of wonder and dreams and half-seen visions, caught in some of De la Mare's loveliest songs.

In his introduction to *Bells and Grass* (1941) De la Mare writes:

I know well that only the rarest kind of best in anything can be good enough for the young. I *know* too that in later life it is just . . . possible now and again to recover fleetingly the intense delight, the untellable joy and happiness and fear and grief and pain of our early years, of an all but forgotten childhood. I have, in a flash, in a momentary glimpse, seen again a horse, an oak, a daisy, just as I saw them in those early years, as if with that heart, with those senses.[2]

---

[1] De la Mare, *op. cit.*, p. 172.
[2] Walter de la Mare, *Bells and Grass* (New York, Viking, 1942), p. 9.

Such perceptiveness of the vision of a child gives to the poetry of De la Mare an unequaled supremacy in inspiration and high poetic quality, in understanding and interpretation, in abundance of mood and emotion, in diverse but always extraordinary imaginative quality, in pervasive, poignant beauty.

Bibliography

Barnes, Walter. *The Children's Poets*. Yonkers-on-Hudson, N.Y., The World Book Company, 1924.

Bianco, Margery. "De la Mare." *The Horn Book*, Vol. 18 (May–June, 1942), pp. 141–147.

Duffin, Henry Charles. *Walter de la Mare; A Study of His Poetry*. London, Sidgwick and Jackson, 1949.

Eaton, Anne Thaxter. *Reading with Children*. New York, Viking Press, 1940.

The Horn Book. "A Walter de la Mare Issue." Vol. 33 (June, 1957).

Laughlin, Clara E. *Reminiscences of James Whitcomb Riley*. New York, Fleming H. Revell, 1916.

Monahan, Michael. "Our Best-Loved Poet." In *New Adventures*. New York, Doran, 1917. Pp. 169–186.

Nicholson, Meredith. "James Whitcomb Riley." In *The Man in the Street*. New York, Scribner, 1921. Pp. 26–64.

Reid, Forrest. *Walter de la Mare; A Critical Study*. London, Faber and Faber, 1929.

Stedman, Edmund Clarence. "Eugene Field." In *Genius aud Other Essays*. New York, Moffat Yard, 1911. Pp. 183–192.

Thompson, Slason. *Life of Eugene Field, the Poet of Childhood*. New York, Appleton, 1927.

Wyatt, Edith. "James Whitcomb Riley." In *Great Companions*. New York, Appleton, 1917. Pp. 182–190.

· 12 ·

Major Steps Forward

Recognition of the importance of opening to children the resources of a book collection was first evidenced in the early 1800's. In 1803 Caleb Bingham, a bookseller, remembering his own longing for books when he was a boy, gave a library for the sole use of the children of Salisbury, Connecticut, from nine to sixteen. In presenting the library, he suggested that " 'to this small beginning it is presumed the liberality of your fellow-townsmen will induce them to make such additions from time to time, so that at length it will become respectable. . .' The Bingham Library for Youth is perhaps the first library in the United States to have received support from a municipality and is also one of the first libraries for children in the country."[1] In 1805 Dr. Jesse Torrey started a children's library in New Lebanon, New York, with the formidable title, "The Lebanon Juvenile Society for the Acquisition of Knowledge." In Alice I. Hazeltine's *Library Work with Children*, Alice M. Jordan gives a delightful account of a third children's library established in 1835 in West Cambridge, Massachusetts. The collection of books was taken to "its first home in a wheelbarrow." During the week the librarian, "Uncle" Dexter, made hats. On Saturdays he opened the library to children.

By 1876 the public library movement in the United States justified the establishment of the American Library Association. However, at this time, the right of children to public library service and the value of such service were not generally recognized nor admitted. As a result, children had access to books chiefly through three non-public agencies, none of them completely effective. Many states followed the example of New York, which in 1838 passed a law appropriating $55,000 for the establishment of school libraries, with the stipulation that each school should raise an amount equal to that granted by the state. Gwendolyn Rees points out that the books in these libraries were not always suitable, but that most public libraries were closed to children, and that the school

[1] Mary E. S. Root, "An American Past in Children's Work," *The Library Journal*, Vol. 71 (April 15, 1946), pp. 547–48.

libraries at least offset to some extent the popularity of the dime novel.[1] Young people could also obtain books from the Apprentices' Libraries, established for this purpose. The Sunday School library movement, starting in England and spreading to the United States, constituted the third and probably the greatest source of books for children and, through the publications of the American Sunday School Union, had a distinct effect upon the tone and content of children's books.

In the years from 1876 to 1900, there was a change in the attitude of public libraries toward children. This was the result of the vision of certain far-seeing adults, urged on by the insistent demand of the children themselves. In 1877 Mrs. Minerva L. Saunders, Librarian at Pawtucket, Rhode Island, set aside a corner in her library for the use of children, provided special chairs for them, and began lending them books. Mrs. Saunders was a woman far in advance of her age; she also provided rocking chairs for adults, apparently seeing no reason why the pursuit of culture should be associated with physical discomfort. She was also a woman of courage, defying the widespread conviction that the presence of children in a public library would be an unbearable annoyance to adults. Mrs. Root, herself a pioneer in children's library work, used this children's corner as a child in the early 1880's and quotes Mrs. Saunders as reporting, "Such is the quiet the adults are not disturbed and the only children who abuse their privileges are occasionally boys who hide dime novels between the leaves of books."[2] Her method of dealing with such sinners was forceful and vigorous. She made a scrapbook of newspaper clippings, telling of boys who had been instigated to crime by the reading of dime novels. "After reading that they were glad to read something better." There is nothing new under the sun. In the twentieth century, the comic has succeeded the dime novel.

It was apparently Miss Caroline M. Hewins who brought the matter of children's reading before the American Library Association. Miss Hewins was librarian of the Hartford, Connecticut, Public Library, and later the author of *A Mid-Century Child and Her Books* (1926), which gives so charming a picture of the reading of a child at the turn of the century. She was also the compiler of one of the first authoritative book lists for children, *Books for Boys and Girls*. In 1882 Miss Hewins presented to the American Library Association a report on children's work, based on the answers to a question sent to twenty-five leading libraries, "What are you doing to encourage a love of good reading in boys and girls?" It is said that the answers were not encouraging.

It is quite probable, however, that Miss Hewins' report stimulated an interest already existent, but dormant. Public libraries were finding

[1] Gwendolyn Rees, *Libraries for Children* (London, Grafton and Company, 1924), p. 86.
[2] Root, *op. cit.*, p. 548.

it more and more difficult to exclude children, who persisted in staking their claim to free access to books. An instance of the problem libraries were meeting is provided by the Boston Public Library which, in 1895, opened a new building to the public. That public included the inevitable large number of children, with the equally inevitable result that the staff had a situation on their hands, since no provision had been made for children. In less than two months, two thousand books for children were placed on open shelves in a room on the second floor.

In 1894 the American Library Association held its conference at Lake Placid, New York. Before that conference, Miss Lutie Stearns, of the circulation department of the Milwaukee Public Library, read a paper, *Report on Reading for the Young*, which must be counted a landmark in the development of library work with children. It is credited with arousing the librarians present to a clear conviction of the desirability of abolishing age limitations in the public library, and of providing special rooms for children with special attendants designated to serve children.

The first general discussion of library work with children took place in 1897 at the Philadelphia conference, and had to do chiefly with the comparative advantages of library buildings devoted wholly to children and of separate rooms for children in libraries giving service to adults as well as children. That the discussion centered on this point would seem to imply that opinion had reached a point where service to children was considered desirable and even necessary.

All of this indicates that before 1890 the public library did not fully recognize the fact that children form an important part of any community, and that, as such, they deserve specialized services. Between 1890 and 1900, libraries from the East to the West opened children's rooms. In the latter part of this period, articles and reports in *The Library Journal* and *Public Libraries* make it certain that by 1900 children's rooms had been opened in Brookline, Cambridge, and Everett, Massachusetts, in New Haven, Boston, Pratt Institute in Brooklyn, Newark, Buffalo, Pittsburgh, Cleveland, Detroit, Minneapolis, Milwaukee, St. Louis, Omaha, Seattle, and San Francisco. Many of these articles claim that Brookline, opening a children's room in 1890, was the pioneer in this respect. Arthur E. Bostwick, in his *The American Public Library*[1] disputes this. He points out that a children's library, established in 1885 in New York City by Emily S. Hanaway, principal of the primary department of a grammar school, was removed, in 1888, to the third floor of the George Bruce Library, then a new branch of the New York Free Circulating Library, which became the New York Public Library in 1895.

[1] Arthur E. Bostwick, *The American Public Library* (New York, Appleton, 1929), pp. 11–12.

By 1900 it was apparent that library work with children was a vital and permanent part of the whole public library development in the United States. As such, the work needed organization, specialized training, establishment of policies and objectives, determination of criteria for book selection, and development of methods of work. In 1898 Frances Jenkins Olcott organized the children's department of the Carnegie Library of Pittsburgh, developing a pattern for reaching children through the children's rooms of branch libraries, through the schools, and through the homes. In 1903 Clara Whitehill Hunt, who had been a children's librarian in Newark, New Jersey, went to Brooklyn to develop the work there. In 1904 Caroline Burnite, later Mrs. Walker, who had been assistant to Miss Olcott, became Supervisor of Children's Work in Cleveland, where Effie L. Power had already started children's work. In 1906 Anne Carroll Moore, who had been in charge of the children's room opened in 1896 in the Pratt Institute Library, was asked to organize the children's department of the New York Public Library. In Milwaukee Mary E. Dousman gave notable service to children.

There are many others whose names recall high achievement in the development of library work with children—Jessie Carson, famous for her establishment of children's libraries in France after the First World War; Alice Hazeltine, of Pittsburgh, St. Louis, and the School of Library Service at Columbia University; Alice Jordan of Boston; May Massee, Children's Editor at The Viking Press; Effie L. Power, of Cleveland, St. Louis, and Pittsburgh; Mrs. Root of Providence; Carrie Scott of Indianapolis; Elva S. Smith of Pittsburgh; Anna Cogswell Tyler, who did pioneer work in storytelling in New York. A few years later, another group, graduating from the library schools and training classes added honor to the roll of names—Nina Brotherton, Julia Carter, Louise Latimer, Helen Martin Rood, Louise Singley, Lillian Smith, and Jessie Gay Van Cleve.

Simultaneous with the trend toward the organization of children's work on a departmental basis was the recognition of the need for specialized professional education. In 1898 Anne Carroll Moore, at the Chautauqua conference, presented arguments for such education and described its nature. Two years before, she had instigated lectures on library work with children at Pratt Institute, where, in 1898, a course in this field was started. Miss Olcott "found it imperative" in 1900 to establish a training class to provide children's librarians for the Carnegie Library of Pittsburgh. The need for children's librarians in various parts of the country was so great that in 1901 the training class became The Training School for Children's Librarians, accepting students from outside Pittsburgh and placing its graduates in cities and towns throughout the country. Until 1917 this school trained exclusively for children's library work. In 1909 a training class for children's librarians was started by Caroline Burnite in the Cleveland Public Library.

Full professional standing was given to children's work by the formation, in 1900, of the Section for Children's Librarians of the American Library Association, which in 1941 became the Children's Library Association of the Division of Libraries for Children and Young People. The Section held its first Conference meeting in 1901, with Anne Carroll Moore as chairman. From that year until the 1920's, the reports of Section meetings in the Conference numbers of *The Library Journal* make exciting reading, recording the names of women famous in the development of children's work and reflecting their vigor and enthusiasm. Those who followed them as officers and committee members of the Section and of the later Children's Library Association for the last thirty or more years have been able successors.

Sufficient tribute has never been paid to the pioneers in this work and to the early graduates of the library schools at Pittsburgh and Pratt Institute and of the training classes in public libraries. Children's librarians, children's library work, and children's literature owe them an immeasurable debt for their vision and wisdom, their vitality and initiative. They dignified and professionalized library work with children; they formulated and stated fundamental and permanent aims and objectives; they developed and established sound methods of work; they instigated specialized professional education; above all, they recognized literature for children to be a vital part of all literature, and they evolved criteria for the selection and use of children's books which are eternally valid. They made the years from 1900 to 1920 remarkable for the swift progress and broadening influence of library work with children. The children's librarians of later years have maintained, individually and collectively through the Children's Library Association, the precedent set. As a result, the children's departments in public libraries are a unique American institution, deserving the famous tribute paid by Paul Hazard in his *Books, Children and Men*, and Dr. Leigh's statement, "children's rooms and children's librarians have been the classic success of the public library."[1]

As the twentieth century approached the end of its second decade, library work with children had become an important and established phase of public library work. By this time, also, children's books formed a body of literature which had importance and significance. Dr. Richard Darling, in his book *The Rise of Children's Book Reviewing in America, 1865–1881*,[2] demonstrates that there had been, in America, reviewing

[1] Robert D. Leigh, *The Public Library in the United States* (New York, Columbia University Press, 1950), p. 100.
[2] Richard L. Darling, *The Rise of Children's Book Reviewing in America, 1865–1881* (New York, R. R. Bowker Co., 1968).

of children's books in a variety of periodicals during the years covered by his study. What is needed now is another study covering the years 1881 to 1918, when Anne Carroll Moore was asked to contribute an article on children's books of the year to *The Bookman*. In an article concerned with contemporary criticism of children's books, Miss Moore wrote

> Standards of appraisal consistently applied to the consideration of children's books as holding a place in contemporary criticism were unknown in 1918 when I was invited to contribute a general article on the children's books of the year to *The Bookman*. I had long felt the need for such recognition of children's books but I had looked in vain for a seasoned critic to appear and carry forward such leads as Horace E. Scudder and Mary Mapes Dodge had given while editing the *Riverside Magazine* and *St. Nicholas*.[1]

The article referred to by Miss Moore was published in the November, 1918, issue of *The Bookman*, and contained a review of William Henry Hudson's *A Little Boy Lost*. This review is a fine example of the technique of comparison, which is highly effective when the critic has a knowledge of literature and literary effects sufficient to enable him to make an exact and telling comparison of one book with others.

Until 1927 Miss Moore contributed articles to *The Bookman*. Eventually, these articles, together with additional material, were published by the George H. Doran Company in three volumes, *Roads to Childhood* (1920), *New Roads to Childhood* (1923), and *Cross-Roads to Childhood* (1926).

The importance of valid literary criticism of children's books cannot be overestimated. There is always danger that this form of literature may be invaded by the inane rather than the significant, by artificial and contrived writing for didactic purpose, rather than by writing inspired by deep conviction. Miss Moore's wisdom and ability demonstrated at a crucial time that criticism can establish the distinction between the merely average and the genuinely great; that it can discover books of quality and can define the quality; that it can stimulate creative writing and creative illustration. There is still need for more penetrating and knowledgeable criticism, which estimates the quality of a book in relation to what it is rather than what it is not; which dwells upon significances, not upon trivialities; which considers a book in its totality, rather than allows a minor aspect to distort the whole; which is authoritative in its perspective of the past and its knowledge of the present.

The organization of children's departments at the beginning of the

---

[1] Anne Carroll Moore, *The Three Owls; Third Book; Contemporary Criticism of Children's Books, 1927–1930* (New York, Coward-McCann, 1931), p. 2.

twentieth century and the initiation of true literary criticism at the end of the second decade of the century are major steps forward into the next fifty years of progress.

Bibliography

American Library Association. "Section for Children's Librarians." *The Library Journal*, Vol. 26 (Conference No.) (Aug., 1901), pp. 163–170.

Bostwick, Arthur E. "The Library and the Child." In *The American Public Library*. New York, Appleton, 1929. Pp. 87–106.

Darling, Richard L. *The Rise of Children's Book Reviewing in America, 1865–1881*. New York, R. R. Bowker, 1968.

Hazeltine, Alice Isabel, ed. *Library Work with Children*. New York, H. W. Wilson, 1917.

Leigh, Robert D. *The Public Library in the United States*. New York, Columbia University Press, 1950.

Mahony, Bertha E. "Anne Carroll Moore—Doctor of Humane Letters." *The Horn Book*, Vol. 18 (Jan.–Feb., 1942), pp. 7–18.

——— "Criticism of Children's Books." *The Horn Book*, Vol. 22 (May–June, 1946), pp. 175, 224.

Moore, Anne Carroll. "Review of *A Little Boy Lost* by W. H. Hudson." *The Bookman*, Vol. 48 (Nov., 1918), pp. 328–330.

——— "Viewing and Reviewing Books for Children." *The Bookman*, Vol. 50 (Sept., 1919), pp. 29–37.

Powell, Sophy. "Early Libraries for Children." In *The Children's Library—A Dynamic Factor in Education*. New York, H. W. Wilson, 1917. Pp. 33–46.

"Reading Rooms for Children." *Public Libraries*, Vol. 2 (April, 1897), pp. 125–131.

Rees, Gwendolyn. "United States of America." In *Libraries for Children*. London, Grafton, 1924. Pp. 85–138.

Root, Mrs. Mary E. S. "An American Past in Children's Work." *The Library Journal*, Vol. 71 (April 14, 1946, Oct. 15, 1946), pp. 547–551, 1422–1424.

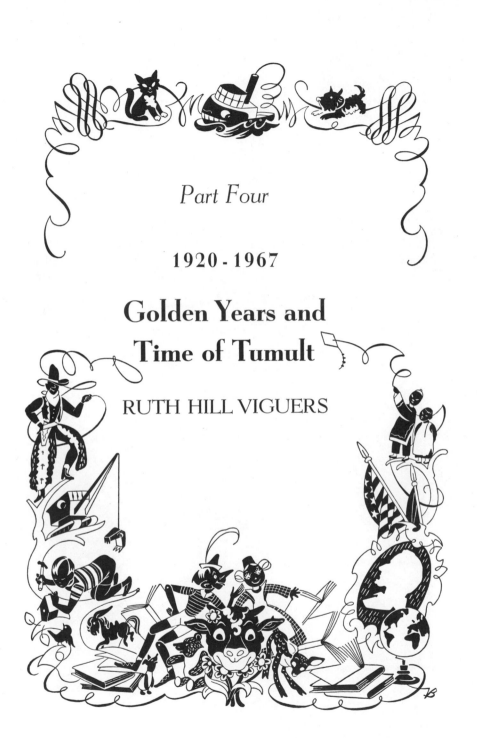

Part Four

1920 - 1967

Golden Years and Time of Tumult

RUTH HILL VIGUERS

· 1 ·

Childhood's Golden Era and After—
An Introductory Survey

Among the many sentiments that have stood the test of time
and mingling of races, the men on the *Mayflower* took over with
them the respect and love for childhood, and this respect and love
have borne fruit in a new soil.—PAUL HAZARD[1]

Looking back over the children's books published during the early
years of our country, the expression of that respect and love for childhood would often seem to have taken strange forms. Shadowed by the
stern doctrines of Puritanism, those first children's books were an expression of their times, even as later children's books reflected a period
of class consciousness, and still later ones showed the influences of extraordinarily rapid scientific developments and radical social changes. The
mere fact of the existence of those early children's books was evidence
of a new awareness of a special responsibility to childhood.

With the growth of the country and the arrival of peoples from
many parts of the world, people who had left behind all ties with the
past, the predominating emphasis was on the future—on childhood.
It was natural that this ideology, in a country abounding in natural resources and growing in the variety and richness of its human resources,
should take concrete form in widespread programs for the welfare of
children, and that when Paul Hazard came here to teach at Columbia
University in 1932 he should see the fruit of that deeply planted respect
and love for childhood.

Concern with the condition of children in the United States was evident in 1909 when President Theodore Roosevelt called a conference to
consider the needs of dependent children, setting a precedent for the
White House Conference on Children and Youth held every decade.
Preoccupation was at first with the physical and economic needs of children, but the range of later conferences was widened to include "those
social and environmental factors which are influencing modern childhood." To the 1950 conference were invited not only educators, doctors,

[1] Paul Hazard, *Books, Children and Men* (Boston, The Horn Book, 1944), p. 87.

nurses, and social workers, but librarians, children's book editors, and others working specifically with books for children.

To the Golden Anniversary Conference in 1960 came representatives of still other groups: religious leaders, philosophers, psychologists, economists, sociologists, recreational workers, publishers; and motion picture, television, and radio producers, writers, and performers. The theme of the conference was "To promote opportunities for children and youth to realize their full potential for a creative life in freedom and dignity." Mass communication was considered in all its aspects. Workshops dealt with the effects on children of radio and television, films and plays, books, magazines, and newspapers, comic books and comic strips. Resolutions presented to the forum at the conclusion of the conference showed an awareness of the significance of books in young people's lives and of the need to make library services available to everyone.

The importance of books in childhood was recognized but the shining peak that children's *literature* had already reached was often obscured by the many other concerns. Anne Carroll Moore, whose first contributions to children's book criticism have been mentioned, called attention to that Golden Age of children's literature of the nineteenth century, and set astir a renaissance of children's book criticism in the twentieth.

In 1924 she began to edit "The Three Owls," a page of criticism of children's books in the *New York Herald Tribune Books*, which ran weekly for six years and included contributions from writers, illustrators, critics, and librarians. The material published in those pages was collected in book form, under the title *The Three Owls*, in three volumes—the first published by Macmillan and the others by Coward-McCann. These books, together with the earlier *Roads* books, constitute an invaluable record of publications and of criticisms for the years 1918 to 1930. Selections from the three *Roads* volumes, with a new section, "High Roads to Childhood," were published in one volume by Doubleday, Doran, *My Roads to Childhood* (1939).[1]

Others who also had an instinctive ability to recognize excellence and a natural respect for children's intelligence, tastes, and interests followed Anne Carroll Moore. In 1930 Anne Thaxter Eaton began writing the page, "Books for Younger Readers," in *The New York Times Book Review*, at first biweekly but soon a weekly feature, which she carried for fourteen years. In 1932 May Lamberton Becker began to conduct the weekly page of children's book reviews in the *New York Herald Tribune Books*, and was followed a few years later by Louise Seaman Bechtel. Mrs. Marion Canby edited a children's book review column in *The Saturday Review of Literature* (later to become simply *Saturday*

---

[1] In Part IV the dates following titles are dates of first publication in the United States, unless otherwise indicated.

Review) in 1927 and 1928, but children's book reviewing did not become a regular monthly feature of that magazine until 1943 when Mary Gould Davis edited its column, "Books for Young People."

In 1924 the first issue of *The Horn Book Magazine* was published by the Bookshop for Boys and Girls in Boston under the editorship of Bertha Mahony and Elinor Whitney, a magazine devoted entirely to the books and reading of children and young people. In 1916 the Women's Educational and Industrial Union had enlarged its educational work to include the Bookshop for Boys and Girls, thus making possible the realization of Bertha Mahony's dream of a shop that would emphasize the best kinds of literature for children and give to customers intelligent help in book selection. The Bookshop rapidly became a place of delight where children could make their own discoveries among books. It became a goal for librarians and parents who felt the need to browse in a collection selected with as much care as that of a model library of children's books. Alice Jordan, the Supervisor of Work with Children of the Boston Public Library from 1917 through 1940 and for many years a contributing editor of *The Horn Book Magazine*, knew the Bookshop as "a center for those who choose to take children's books seriously as a branch of literature." *The Horn Book Magazine* was an outgrowth of lists that had been compiled by Bertha Mahony and Elinor Whitney in connection with the Bookshop. Bertha Mahony Miller retired as editor of the magazine in 1951 and was followed by Jennie D. Lindquist, who was succeeded by Ruth Hill Viguers in 1958. At the end of 1967 Paul Heins became editor.

A growing consciousness of the importance of books for children was evident among publishers of trade books throughout the twenties. It was obvious at this time, when children's literature was rapidly becoming a distinct field of publishing, that specialists were needed to stimulate and direct it and relate it to the widening world of childhood. The Macmillan Company in 1919 had already pioneered in creating a separate Children's Book Department with Louise Seaman at its head. In 1922 Helen Dean Fish became the first children's book editor at Frederick A. Stokes and Company, and, in 1923, May Massee at Doubleday, Page and Company. Ten years later Miss Massee went to the new Viking Press to create their children's book department. Other publishers followed, establishing children's book departments with specialists in charge. In 1967 the Children's Book Council, whose membership is limited to publishing firms with specific departments for children's books, had eighty members.

Children's Book Week, which has had a nation-wide observance each year in libraries, schools and bookstores since 1919, received its first impulse from Franklin K. Mathiews. He became Chief Scout Librarian in 1912, and, in his determination to raise the level of boys' reading, toured the country in the promotion of a Good Book Week. In 1919, when the close of World War I permitted new efforts, Mr. Mathiews' idea of a Week for books was given wider significance when the American Booksellers Association, with Frederic G. Melcher as chairman, organized a committee to inaugurate Children's Book Week. The committee included booksellers and publishers, public and school librarians, representatives of the Scouts, and members of the press. Children's Book Week has steadily increased in influence, gaining a firm place in library programs, school calendars, and bookstore activities, with the Children's Book Council, originally organized for the purpose, taking over publicity and publications relating to it.

That he should have been among the first to sense the possibilities of a Children's Book Week was early evidence of the vision behind the encouragement that Mr. Melcher was to give through the years to those involved in the many and varied activities in the field of children's reading. His appreciation of the importance of books in children's lives had stemmed from a childhood enlivened by books and by the regular advent of *The Youth's Companion*. As the editor of *Publishers' Weekly*, he was well aware of the practical issues and problems of publishing. There is no doubt that the fortunate relationship between children's librarians and children's book editors, between the readers of children's books and the publishers of them, and the strides made in the publication of children's books in America over more than forty years were accomplished largely because of the existence of such a unifying factor as the warm personality of Mr. Melcher, a great publisher who never lost the viewpoint of the reader—of any age.

In 1922 another landmark in the recognition of children's books as literature was envisaged and established by Frederic Melcher. He proposed at the American Library Association Conference, held in Swampscott, Massachusetts, in 1921, that a medal be awarded each year by the Children's Librarians Section of the American Library Association for the most distinguished book for children, an original work, reprint and compilations not to be eligible, written by a citizen or resident of the United States and published during the preceding year. He believed that children's librarians could encourage the writing of more worthwhile books for children by really able authors, and that such an award might be one means of accomplishing this aim. Mr. Melcher's offer to present such a medal was accepted enthusiastically and thus the "John Newbery Medal for the Most Distinguished Contribution to American Literature for Children," awarded annually since 1922, came into being. Later Mr. Melcher made a similar suggestion in regard to important picture books. Since 1938 the Caldecott Medal has been presented annually to the illustrator of the most distinguished picture book of the preceding year.

In his *Books, Children and Men*, Paul Hazard pays tribute to America's interest in children's reading and marvels at her vast production of children's books.

Do many people know how many books are printed in the United States, for the use of children? In 1919, twelve million; in 1925, twenty-five million, two hundred thousand; in 1927, thirty-one million. In 1919 appeared four hundred and thirty-three new works intended for young people; in 1929, nine hundred and thirty-one . . . Queer country where they do not seek to make sordid economies in everything, and especially in books. Where they do not disdain to make works cheaply, but where they do not think either that cheapness is necessarily and always the last word in perfection; where they will permit neither poor paper nor worn-out type, nor faded ink, nor insufficient binding, nor misprints shamefully displayed. Where they seek to arouse not only the love but the habit of beauty from early childhood.[1]

In *The Three Owls, Third Book*, Anne Carroll Moore commented, "Children's books published in the decade between 1920 and 1930 reveal more new forms, both outward and inward, than at any other period in their history" and in the years following, the new forms introduced in the twenties have been the inspiration for further developments and other new forms. A mountain of literature for children has arisen, its sides carpeted with a varied and often beautiful flowering. No such rapid upthrust could have come about without the appearance of much that is mediocre and poor; the publication of every hundred good books has been accompanied by a thousand that would serve children better by not existing to overshadow the scores of fine books. The trend to encourage authors to meet specific needs has sometimes discouraged the author's writing out of his own deep incentives. But, as one gains perspective on nearly fifty years of children's books, the indifferent publications drop out of sight and the problem of knowing which of the many good books to accent in our discussion has been difficult indeed.

A panoramic view of the children's books published from 1920 through 1967 and of the trends that influenced the writing and publishing of them may throw light on the literature that has emerged.

1920 to 1930—Experimentation with New Methods and New Forms

Before looking at the twenties to see some of the books which reveal the new forms, it may be well to mention a few of the people writing then who had already begun their writing careers before 1920. Their

---

[1] Hazard, *op. cit.*, p. 87.

work, like the best of earlier generations, foreshadowed future developments and was to have an important influence on children's books in
the years ahead. These writers became a company of deans for a new
era of children's books.

Padraic Colum was one of them. He had already shown his special
genius in dealing with heroic and legendary material and in his sensitive
interpretation of the world of fancy. Others were Seumas MacManus
and Parker Fillmore, who set high standards for the retelling of folk
tales; Cornelia Meigs, whose *Master Simon's Garden* (1916) was an
important forerunner of American historical fiction for boys and girls;
Elsie Singmaster, who had introduced to young readers the Pennsyl-
vania-German people and the history-packed region around Gettysburg;
Caroline Dale Snedeker, who had been recognized for her living story
of ancient Greece; Lucy Fitch Perkins, who had re-created other lands
and people with imagination and vitality; Eliza Orne White, who had
shown that the children in books could be as real as the children next
door; and Walter de la Mare, whose poetry and strange, enchanting
stories have no period limitations.

Between 1920 and 1930 many new authors began writing books that
children claimed for their own and continued to enjoy for almost half
a century. The era was marked by a fluidity of expression that, by
the end of the decade, would show itself in new trends, interesting
experimentation, and widening opportunities. Brief attention to some
of the books will give a better idea of the richness of this period.

The trend to collect folk tales from many countries, from oral as well
as written sources, was gaining momentum, and every year of this
decade a number of good folk tale collections appeared as well as retellings of ancient hero tales. The New World had been discovered as a
fascinating source of folklore, with many new collections of American
Indian tales being published.

Modern fairy tales predominated in this decade just after the First
World War. At the beginning of the period came such unusual books
as W. W. Tarn's tale of search for fairy treasure, *The Treasure of
the Isle of Mist* (1920), a reaffirmation of the goodness of life and faith
in fundamental truths, Carl Sandburg's *Rootabaga Stories* (1922) and
Hugh Lofting's *The Story of Doctor Dolittle* (1920). Margery Bianco
began writing her nursery fantasies, Arthur Chrisman his Chinese fairy
tales, Anne Caserly her stories out of Ireland; and the modern mechanical world made its entrance into fantasy.

In 1924 appeared the work of a new poet of childhood, *When We
Were Very Young* by A. A. Milne. There were other poets whose
verses are true expressions of children's thoughts and feelings. *Silver
Pennies* (1925) was one of the earliest anthologies with strong appeal
to young children, selected by Blanche Jennings Thompson chiefly from

the work of contemporary poets. Poetry, distinctly American in flavor, appeared in Vachel Lindsay's *Johnny Appleseed and Other Poems* (1928) and in Mary Austin's *Children Sing in the Far West* (1928), which grew out of her experiences while teaching in the Southwest and which was expressive of the region and of the universality of childhood.

The first sea story of Charles Boardman Hawes, *The Mutineers*, was published in 1920, setting a high standard for adventure stories. During this decade interest in the sea was expressed also in a number of factual adventures, among them A. J. Villiers' story of the last clipper ship race around Cape Horn, *Falmouth for Orders* (1929), and two accounts of the raising of the *S-51*—Tom Eadie's from a professional diver's point of view, *I Like Diving* (1929), and Edward Ellsberg's from a commander's point of view, *On the Bottom* (1929).

Among the distinguished historical fiction in this period were Caroline Dale Snedeker's two stories of ancient Greece, and Eric Kelly's tale of fifteenth century Poland, *The Trumpeter of Krakow* (1928). American period fiction was represented by Elsie Singmaster's *Boy at Gettysburg* (1924), Mrs. Snedeker's *Downright Dencey* (1927), and the works of such new authors as Constance Lindsay Skinner, Marjorie Hill Allee, and Rachel Field.

We find in the twenties expression of the need of the young pre-school child for stories of things within his everyday experience, with Lucy Sprague Mitchell the chief exponent of this type of writing.

Though many writers would not discover for another twenty years the opportunity for drama in American settings and though as yet there was no conscious intent to create regional stories, there was, in a few of the realistic stories of this decade, a hint of the variety to be found in American backgrounds: Grace Moon's *Chi-Wee* (1925), a simple story of the everyday life of a little Pueblo Indian girl that gives an appealing picture of the Southwest and the desert; Evelyn Scott's *Witch Perkins; A Story of the Kentucky Hills* (1929), and, most important, Will James's *Smoky* (1926). These were stories that grew naturally out of their backgrounds.

The first five years of the twenties produced books of romantic adventure, such as Charles Nordhoff's *Pearl Lagoon* (1924), Dhan Gopal Mukerji's stories out of his own heritage, and historical tales with foreign settings. With the exception of the books by Lucy Fitch Perkins, there were, however, few realistic stories of everyday children set in other lands. Beginning in 1926, with Evelyn and C. Kay Scott's story of the adventures of two children on the Sahara and Dorothy Rowe's first collection of stories of Chinese children, the number of foreign background stories increased until, by 1929, there were many.

New forms and approaches were not limited to the story books of this period. History was brought to fresh life by Hendrik van Loon in his *Story of Mankind* (1921), and a few years later V. M. Hillyer succeeded in giving young children a comprehensible and delightful introduction to history and geography in his first two books, *A Child's History of the World* (1924) and *A Child's Geography of the World* (1929).

Charles Lindbergh's flight across the Atlantic in 1927 was the spark that touched off the tinder of children's interest in aviation. The scientifically minded child and the fancifully minded child had enjoyed the idea of flight for years. There had been some few informational books on aviation, but "flying machines" and balloons had seemed more at home in imaginative tales. Now the dramatic accomplishment of a quiet young man made aviation a possibility for every boy. Books for young people promptly reflected this wide and sudden interest. Commander Richard Evelyn Byrd's *Skyward* (1928), giving accounts of his North Pole and transatlantic flights, and his plans for flights to the Antarctic, was a thrilling book for the air-minded child; and *Sky High* (1929) by Eric P. Hodgins and Frederick A. Magoun was the first important young people's history of aviation from its beginning to the building of the *Graf Zeppelin*.

One of the most important events of the period came at the end when story-telling picture books, which before this had largely been imported from Europe, began to be published in America. *Clever Bill* (1927) by William Nicholson was the first, followed in 1928 by Wanda Gág's *Millions of Cats*.

Illustration had always been recognized as an important, though not always possible, adjunct to children's books, but by 1920 many more artists than ever before began exploring children's book illustration as a medium of expression. The American artist began breaking away from Old World traditions and constraints to experiment in different and original techniques and methods. With the improvements in graphic processes, which made book illustration practical, a new field opened for the artist. He recognized the special problems of book illustration, which required not only appropriate pictures, but understanding of design, typography, physical make-up of the book, and ability to integrate all these elements. Like the great writers, the great book artists had faith in the ability of children to enjoy varied techniques, originality, the best that each artist had to give.

Boris Artzybasheff was one of the first of the young artists of the twenties who felt the challenge of children's book illustration. Since 1925 he had been decorating children's books with distinctive drawings. In 1928 he made a book of his own in concept, though the words belonged to familiar poets, using a new technique with an effect much like wood blocks. The result was *The Fairy Shoemaker and Other Fairy Poems*, a beautiful book expressing lightness and gaiety although the pictures were entirely in black and white.

The republication of old favorites with new illustrations and unusual format became typical of this period of experimentation, and without doubt this reissue of books in attractive new forms brought new vitality and fresh interest to many titles. James Boyd's *Drums*, for instance, a well written, historical novel published in 1925, was not acclaimed by young people until it reappeared in 1928 with exciting illustrations in color by N. C. Wyeth.

Heroes from Hakluyt (1928) was an example of excellent collaboration. The skill of Charles Finger in selecting, editing and, when necessary, rewriting, matching his own style with that of the Elizabethan prose of the original, was successfully combined with Paul Honoré's wood cuts, strong and decorative and interpretive of the vigor of the tales. There were many more new editions of old favorites with pictures by James Daugherty, Arthur Rackham, Edmund Dulac, Pamela Bianco, Dorothy Lathrop, and other artists who brought new interpretations to classic stories.

This was a period of experimentation. By the next decade, the popularization of new methods of reproduction would become complete and the artist, who in his reinterpretation of old favorites and classic stories had a solid support to lean on, would now be able to launch forth on his own.

Important publications of the nineteenth century had shown that books for children could be literature; in the first twenty years of the twentieth century the concept of children's literature reached maturity. No longer were children limited in their reading to the few books which by fortunate accident held something that they could enjoy. No longer were books seen as merely teaching tools, nor children as immature people who must quickly be transformed into the pattern of their elders. Children were individuals, worthy of special attention. By 1920 writers and, a little later, artists appreciated this changing attitude, and the rapid increase in quantity of children's books published each year, as well as the variety of literary forms, subjects, and approaches, gave proof that many creative writers were aware of this responsive audience.

1930 to 1940—Popularization of New Printing Processes and Recognition of the Need for Books for "Young Adults"

In an essay on the children's books between 1930 and 1935, Bertha Mahony gives three reasons for the tremendous, but at the same time varied, rich and colorful output of children's books in America; the first being the great variety in the country itself—in its land, climate and people; the second, the public library children's rooms, which had not only created a demand for children's books, but from which had come articulate and careful criticism of them; the third being the organization of children's departments in publishing houses.

By this time, also, were appearing writers who, growing up in that first golden era of children's literature, had read *St. Nicholas* and the books of Howard Pyle, Rudyard Kipling, Frank R. Stockton, Kenneth Grahame, Beatrix Potter, and the fairy tales of Joseph Jacobs and Andrew Lang. Writers, artists, critics, and librarians combined to form a bridge across years of economic depression when the publication of books for children might very easily have received a shocking set-back. During that discouraging period people working with children's books were most certainly aware of curtailments and drastic reductions in plans and programs, but in looking back over the thirties, there is strong evidence of the recognition of values and of a consistent maintenance of high standards. Publishers, writers, artists, and designers made the most of improved methods and techniques, and, as never before, children's books kept pace with widening interests, rapid scientific developments, and educational trends toward the integration of the child and his world. Perhaps the very necessity for careful weighing and measuring, because of the limitations of severe economic depression, helped rather than hindered the maintaining of values.

By 1930 new developments in photo-offset lithography were available in America, making possible large editions of illustrated books at much lower cost than before. From this time on, the importance of illustration in children's books has been granted, and the true picture book, that is, the book in which the pictures tell the story without the need of text, or in which the story can be told only by the complete integration of pictures and text, came into its own in America.

The most spectacular development then, between 1930 and 1940, was the great number and variety of picture books, and the profusely illustrated story books. There was no precedent for the latter, the very original picture-story books published during the first decade of lower reproduction costs. In a very few years, in the field of books for the younger children, the artist attained a place of equal importance with the writer. In many cases this necessary partnership of artist and author stimulated an artist to experiment in writing his own stories.

An avalanche of merchandise, in lieu of literature, was to come, but not until after 1940. The popularization of the printing processes had followed upon such a short period of experimentation that the picture books and illustrated books of the thirties show the respect that is usually accorded a significant new development. It was not until a few years later, after the new developments were taken for granted, that sometimes a printer "turned publisher," and the mass production of picture books followed—bright in color, cheaply put together, with pictures and stories made to specific order.

With the growing emphasis on the appearance of the book, traditional literature, the children's oldest heritage, was to take on new outward forms. Wanda Gág's retellings of European folk tales, including a number of stories from the Grimm Brothers, were the work of a master story-teller who could enhance the true folk quality of her stories with her remarkable drawings. Throughout the decade folklorists were bringing to American children the folk tales of many lands, some of which were to be translated from oral to printed literature for the first time in these American editions. For the first time also the legendary stories of the American folk hero, Pecos Bill, were set down for children by James C. Bowman, and Paul Bunyan had at least two new interpreters.

There was a sharp decline in the number of new books of fantasy in this decade but among a few literary fairy tales of unusual originality J. R. R. Tolkien's *The Hobbit* (1938) is a milestone.

Poetry publications included selections of interest to children from the work of Sara Teasdale, Carl Sandburg, and Eleanor Farjeon. *Pool in the Meadow* (1933) was Frances Frost's first collection of poetry out of the child's world of nature. Rosemary and Stephen Vincent Benét gave vitality to American history by their satirical and poignant insights into famous personalities, *A Book of Americans* (1933).

Historical fiction of the decade had variety and color, and more distinguished American period stories were published than ever before: Elizabeth Janet Gray's three adventure stories, with settings in Scotland and the Carolinas; Rachel Field's *Calico Bush* (1931), with its background in colonial Maine; Marjorie Hill Allee's stories of Indiana Quakers in the nineteenth century; and Florence Crannell Means' pioneer stories. Elizabeth Coatsworth introduced her well-loved heroine Sally in the first book of a series. Emma Gelders Sterne wrote *Loud Sing Cuckoo* (1930), a story of England in Chaucer's time. Ethel Parton began her nineteenth century New England stories, Laura Ingalls Wilder wrote the first books in her American pioneer series, and Lois Lenski the first of her historical stories. Ruth Sawyer's *Roller Skates* (1936) joyously re-created New York at the end of the nineteenth century. Caroline Dale Snedeker, Cornelia Meigs, Stephen Meader, and Constance Lindsay Skinner continued to write books with American period settings.

It was natural that the closing in of the world should have its effect on children's books. Travel in the nineteenth century was serious business, and the travelogue story books of that period were conscientious attempts to pass on to the stay-at-homes the advantages of travel. Differences of other lands and cultures were emphasized because they were what the traveler went abroad to see. By the end of the first quarter of the twentieth century, two forces were changing the attitude of Americans toward people in other lands. The first was the rapid development in transportation, particularly air transportation, which had been stimulated by the First World War. The second was the emphasis on understanding other peoples, a reaction to the war. In the thirties the good realistic stories of children of other countries greatly outnumbered the stories of everyday American children that were in any way unusual or original.

For every piece of American realism, such as Margery Bianco's *Street of Little Shops* (1932) or Evelyn Scott's *Billy the Maverick* (1934), there were many stories of children in faraway lands, learning the meaning of courage or taking their places in their tribes. There were warm family stories of Norway and Ireland, exciting tales of the African veldt, colorful stories of Bulgaria, Spain, Italy, Mexico, and Guatemala. Elizabeth Cleveland Miller wrote of family life in Albania. Eleanor Frances Lattimore, Elizabeth Foreman Lewis, and Mary Brewster Hollister began to write of China. Memories of her own childhood made vivid Kate Seredy's first story of Hungary. American children found much in common with the English children of Arthur Ransome's stories, whose play life could become complete reality.

Awareness of other lands sharpens awareness of people at home who have special problems. Along with Grace Moon's stories of the happy everyday life of American Indian children were other sympathetic stories of Indians who face the problem of adjustment to two widely different cultures. Arna Bontemps wrote with sensitive humor of Negro children. Florence Crannell Means and later John Tunis began their championship of minority groups in some absorbing novels for young people.

The audience for these junior novels was steadily growing. With the general improvement of child labor laws and, in many states, compulsory education to the age of sixteen, large numbers of adolescent children were suddenly in evidence. Libraries felt the presence of these "young adults" with leisure time on their hands, and from 1930 began the trend to develop in libraries special departments for work with young people. Here was added stimulation for the writer whose natural audience was the older children. The many acute problems that accompany the process of growing up found their places in the stories of adolescent boys and girls, giving the readers a sense of relationship with the characters.

Stephen Meader, Margery Bianco, Mabel Louise Robinson, Elsie Singmaster, Marjorie Hill Allee, Hubert Skidmore, and many others wrote with sympathy of young people facing problems of adjustment to new environments, choosing careers, achieving ambitions in spite of opposition, along with the often painful process of finding one's niche in adult society. The young people's novel—the psychological story as well as the story of action—became an actuality in the thirties.

A handful of outstanding biographies for children had appeared in the twenties. In the thirties biographies were published "to fill a need," but among the great number written to order appeared some that emerged as literature. Among them were such books as Elizabeth Janet Gray's *Penn* (1938) and *Young Walter Scott* (1935), Cornelia Meigs' *Invincible Louisa* (1933), and James Daugherty's *Daniel Boone* (1939).

In this decade those books that had not before been considered in the category of creative writing—informational books—became a branch of "children's literature." Science was suddenly a "great field of adventure."

The rapid strides made in aviation in the thirties, the opening of the planetariums, developments in radio, all the new inventions and scientific discoveries were reflected in the books of the period. Maxwell Reed saw the universe through the wondering eyes of a boy and, beginning with his *The Earth for Sam* (1930), presented scientific knowledge in a literary form that enhanced rather than explained away that wonder.

1940 to 1950—The Reflection of Great Events in Children's Books

By 1940 the road ahead was wide and well traveled. Children's books were taken for granted; they were considered important to modern education and accepted as a branch of current literature. New and original methods for the promotion of children's books were found in radio and television. Suddenly children's books became profitable business, became, in some cases, big business. Mass production made possible large editions of elaborately illustrated books at small cost, with selling outlets not only in book shops but in ten cent and variety stores, drug stores, and even chain grocery stores. Children's books had become a commodity.

Many, looking at the bright, innocuous books so easily available, felt that they were the answer to the problem caused by the wide distribution of the so-called comics. Forgetting that each era has had its sensational reading matter, parents and educators were slow to realize that there was little in these mass-produced books, intended primarily for the young child, to develop creative imaginations and appreciation of good drawing, good writing, and genuine humor, and so to build up resistance to cheapness and mediocrity.

Books for children that had the power of enrichment were still being published, in larger numbers probably than ever before, but to cope with the flood of "juveniles," thoughtful and critical evaluation of children's books, always important, became essential.

Like a steadying keel in turbulent waters, *The Horn Book Magazine* maintained its same high standard and fine perspective through the years. *The New York Times* and the *New York Herald Tribune* continued their weekly columns devoted to children's books, but few other daily papers recognized the importance of such a column. *The Satur-*

day Review of Literature continued to run a department devoted to children's books and reading once a month, and the book trade's *Publishers' Weekly* consistently emphasized children's books as an important field of publishing.

The problem, once of not enough books for children, became suddenly the problem of too many, with the combined voices of critics making too small a sound to be heard very widely above the roar of the 1940's. Within a few years, however, the lesser books were forgotten.

The consciousness of a need for devices to encourage the search for good books among the many publications was evidenced in the establishment of new awards. Several children's book awards were created in the forties by associations and foundations, usually to emphasize social and moral values in children's books. Others, chiefly those formed by regional library associations, reflected the children's own responses to books. The first of these was the Young Readers' Choice Award, initiated in 1940 by the Pacific Northwest Library Association.

The *New York Herald Tribune* had started a Children's Spring Book Festival in 1937 to encourage publication and sale of children's books between January and June. A money prize was given to the author of an outstanding book, published in the first six months of the year, in each of two different age groupings, and to the artist of an outstanding picture book. Whether or not the Festival stimulated the spreading of children's book publication throughout the year, it did bring early recognition to important new books. The Spring Book Festival continued under the sponsorship of the *New York Herald Tribune* until the newspaper ceased publication in 1967, when *Book World*, a publication of the *Washington Post* and the *Chicago Tribune*, carried on the Festival.

Throughout the forties new author-artists entered the picture-book field, showing originality, new techniques, and great variety in characterization and style: Robert McCloskey, Virginia Lee Burton, Leo Politi, Marcia Brown, and Louis Slobodkin, to mention but a few. There were new collections of poetry by well-loved poets and a few new poets showing sensitive insight into the child's world. The nonsense rhymes and pictures of Dr. Seuss, appearing through the decade, had much of the spontaneity and inventiveness of the early ones. American folk songs and ballads and everyday rhymes, inherent with American children, came into their own as a part of our traditional literature.

Widening perspectives were revealed in the publication of folklore from faraway regions: East Africa, West Africa, South Africa, Puerto Rico, Mexico, and Haiti; and from the Eskimos of Alaska and the Indians of the Pacific Northwest.

New selections from familiar sources continued to appear, bringing fresh points of view on well-loved stories. Notable among them is Sigrid

Undset's selection from the stories of Asbjörnsen and Moe, *True and Untrue* (1945), prefaced with a scholarly essay, "The Adventure Story of the Folk Tale."

The few outstanding modern fairy tales and fantasies of the thirties were followed in the next decade by many. In this development is seen a resemblance to the twenties. Perhaps the closeness of a great war in each of these periods was a reminder of the fundamental, changeless values in great literary fantasy. *The Little Prince* (1943), *Rabbit Hill* (1944), *The Quaint and Curious Quest of Johnny Longfoot* (1947), and *The Little White Horse* (1946) have imaginative strength. A number of books bridged the chasm between reality and the world of the unseen, like Walter de la Mare's *Mr. Bumps and His Monkey* (1942) and Enys Tregarthen's *The Doll Who Came Alive* (1942), both characterized by mysticism and tenderness. John Buchan in *Lake of Gold* (1941) and Julia Sauer in *Fog Magic* (1943) showed how thin the veil is between the past and the present for imaginative children. Dolls came to life through the magic of Rumer Godden, Carolyn Sherwin Bailey, and Elizabeth Orton Jones.

There was still an interest in foreign backgrounds, but with the exception of Hilda Van Stockum's stories of Ireland and Holland, Jean Bothwell's stories of India, and a few appealing stories of South America, all of which point up family relationships in those countries, the emphasis in the foreign background stories was on unusual settings and dramatic situations. Louise Rankin's story of a Tibetan child, *Daughter of the Mountains* (1948), was typical.

A number of writers found within the United States of this period situations and problems quite challenging enough for exciting, often moving, stories. The 1940's were not good years for foreign travel and writers of realistic and family stories turned naturally to American settings. The movement to know-your-own-land had an enlivening effect on American children's literature in those ten years and resulted in John Tunis' sport stories, with emphasis on tolerance in a democracy; Florence Crannell Means's stories of minority groups, and her poignant understatement of the status of Japanese-Americans during the war, *The Moved-Outers* (1945); Doris Gates's story of a migratory worker's child, *Blue Willow* (1940); and Eleanor Estes' simple, unforgettable story, *The Hundred Dresses* (1944). This same movement emphasized the regional story of the forties, which owed its actual classification to its chief exponent, Lois Lenski. Surviving beyond the period were a few stories marked by a strong sense of region that was not the result of purposeful study but of a writer's long acquaintance with a section of the country and a special love for it.

Of the family stories of this period, few possessed more warmth of family relationships, humor, or understanding of childhood than Eleanor

Estes' three books about *The Moffats* (1941–1943). Another highlight was Robert McCloskey's irresistible extravaganza on the American scene in general and small boys in particular, *Homer Price* (1943).

American writers rediscovered American history as a rich source for adventure, with *Johnny Tremain* (1943), *The Matchlock Gun* (1941), and *Tree of Freedom* (1949) outstanding examples of vitality of treatment of American historical periods. The issuing by different publishers of various series of books with American backgrounds was typical of this emphasis on American settings and tradition.

Technological developments stimulated the writing of science fiction, a genre that became more popular with every succeeding year.

Although social mores and economic trends have always been reflected in children's books, never were these reflections so obvious as they were during the forties when books for children were published in such large numbers. Long before the Second World War children's literature had begun to show the influence of every major event, every social attitude or scientific advancement. Apart from the changes that war was bound to cause, the possibilities for adventure that it afforded could not be overlooked in fiction. Every day children were taking part in events far more exciting than any to be found in realistic books of the past. Tales of escapes from Nazi-occupied countries were only slightly more dramatic than stories of people who remained in them. There were stories in which dogs were trained for war service, stories of the war in terms of childlike experience, stories of children's adjustments to a new ideology, of children playing their part in defending their homes against invasion, of children transplanted to America for the "duration," and many stories of refugees and other displaced persons.

The popularity of animals in literature has never wavered, from the days of the crude woodcuts in the *New England Primer* to the present. Animals in fantasy have remained much the same, but realistic animals received a radical change of treatment in the thirties and forties. The sentimental books in which animal heroes reacted with human emotions gave way to more objective accounts. The refreshing new approach encouraged the writing of animal books by authors who could make interesting the natural patterns of animal life.

Informational books bore out the high promise of the thirties, including not only scientific information but the history of different aspects of science. Katherine Shippen told the story of electricity, making it understandable and showing it as an opportunity for adventure.

Biographers were writing less from a sense of purpose than from a sincere interest in their subjects. New names quickly became familiar: Nina Brown Baker, Mabel Leigh Hunt, Louise Hall Tharp, Covelle Newcomb. There were lively atmospheric portraits of Fannie Burney, Jane Austen, and Harriet Beecher Stowe. And among the biographies of writers, musicians, scientists, and pioneers were the less familiar stories of Sun Yat Sen and Nehru.

At this time Genevieve Foster wrote the first of her parallel histories, *George Washington's World* (1941). There was a growing trend in the period to publish history and geography books in series: The Land and People Series, The Landmark Books, series of American regional picture histories, "Made in" books, picture histories, and picture geographies of one country after another, and many more.

1950 to 1967—Children's Books in a Technological World

During the next decade the most dramatic events reflected in children's books were the advancements in science and technology. Even children's pleasure reading was affected by a preoccupation with making the many aspects of science and technology understandable.

The successful launching of Sputnik on October 4, 1957, was no surprise to scientists, but, as the first visible evidence to the non-scientific world of one direction scientific progress was taking, it became a focus for world-wide attention. Few people were mindful of the developments in other countries that paralleled those made in the Soviet Union. Russia had the first successful launching of a satellite. Why? For some years the voices of outstanding American educators, aware of needs for change and improvement in the country's schools, had received little attention. Suddenly education in the United States became the target for criticism and analysis, and informational books of all kinds inundated bookshops, libraries, and schools.

The children's story as an art form was a literate concept that had been realized early in the nineteenth century and steadily developed through the first fifty years of the twentieth. The informational flood almost quenched it. Children were again the victims of the good intentions of grownups.

John Newbery, in the eighteenth century, had proved that there was profit in publishing attractive books for children's pleasure, but not until the 1940's did books for children become big business. By the late 1950's children had become the most important market for products of many kinds. An apex in the juvenile population coincided with a peak in advertising ingenuity and techninques, making businesses involved with products for children more lucrative than any gold rush of the past. In the publishing field "educational materials"—first, elementary-school textbooks, and then books for children's pleasure reading—became the most profitable and the most competitive branch of the industry. By the early 1960's several mergers of text- and trade-book publishers had been completed and their stock placed on the open market. Good business demanded more attractive textbooks and more informative trade books. The result was less difference than ever before, in both appearance and content, between schoolbooks and books for children's leisure reading. The idea of children's books as a branch of literature tended to be forgotten by many people in the obsession with children's books as a gainful product.

Federal programs, unprecedented in United States history, began to affect book publishing and distribution. The Head Start Program begun in 1965 concentrated attention on the educational and cultural needs of young children in underprivileged areas. The passing by the Federal Government of the Elementary and Secondary Education Act of 1965, making available under Title II of the Act $1,000,000,000 for school library materials, textbooks, and other instructional materials, revealed the complete lack of libraries in nearly half of the elementary schools in the country, and inadequate library service in others and in many secondary schools. The sudden awakening of many communities to the importance of libraries in their schools was astonishing and the availability of money for books of all kinds accelerated the production of trade books as well as texts. Spending for books was often more rapid than wise and it encouraged indiscriminate publishing, but the sudden awareness of the importance of school libraries was a big step in the direction of making good books available to all children.

In the unique excitement of spending more money for books in a shorter time than ever before, and in the rush to produce books fast enough to meet the demand, librarians, teachers, and publishers could easily forget the intrinsic purpose of books and libraries for children. But seemingly undisturbed, the best of the authors and artists continued writing and drawing. Genius thrives despite circumstances. Neither poverty, indifference, nor affluence can wholly extinguish it.

With his powerful *Tower by the Sea* (1950) Meindert DeJong became recognized as an important writer for children. Mary Stolz's first of many books that seemed to have truly grown out of the adolescent's uncertain world appeared in 1950. Elizabeth Yates turned from retelling old stories and adapting the work of others to the writing of distinguished biographies and stories of her own. In the fifties Edward Eager, Natalie Savage Carlson, Lavinia Davis, Leonard Wibberley, André Norton, William O. Steele, Elizabeth George Speare, Joseph Krumgold, Eleanor Cameron, Beverly Cleary, E. C. Spykman, Eloise Jarvis McGraw, William Corbin, Annabel and Edgar Johnson, and Olivia Coolidge began writing for boys and girls. These and others were making places for themselves as writers of influence in the United States. The work of some of them began to be known abroad.

Books emerged from the hundreds of commonplace titles and came to be thought of as "modern classics" within a few years: *Charlotte's Web* (1952) by E. B. White, *The Secret River* (1955) by Marjorie Kinnan Rawlings, *Banner in the* Sky (1954) by James Ramsey Ullman,

Gone-Away Lake (1957) by Elizabeth Enright, *My Side of the Mountain* (1959) by Jean C. George.

From England in this period came all seven of C. S. Lewis's stories of the mythical land of Narnia, Mary Norton's four books about the Borrowers, Lucy Boston's Green Knowe stories, Joyce Collin-Smith's *Jeremy Craven* (1958), several doll stories by Rumer Godden, unusual books by Philippa Pearce, and Barbara Leonie Picard's retellings of legendary tales and the first of her own stories. Throughout the period Rosemary Sutcliff showed an unmatched ability to bring the past to life in absorbing historical novels.

The productiveness of the fifties continued into the sixties as more writers with a great deal to say and the ability to say it well caught the imaginations of children: Madeleine L'Engle, Jean Merrill, Jean Fritz, Erik Haugaard, Lloyd Alexander, Robert Burch, Sorche Nic Leodhas, Sid Fleischman, Elizabeth Borton de Treviño, and Aileen Fisher in the United States; and Madeleine Polland, Hester Burton, Barbara Willard, K. M. Peyton, William Mayne, and Alan Garner in England. Eilís Dillon wrote numerous stories set in the Irish Islands, Margaret MacPherson on the Isle of Skye, and Joan Phipson in Australia. Mary Stolz and Rebecca Caudill, well known for their novels for older boys and girls, began writing stories for younger readers. Certain very original books shine out: *The Animal Family* (1965) by Randall Jarrell, *Island of the Blue Dolphins* (1960) by Scott O'Dell, *The Incredible Journey* (1961) by Shiela Burnford, *Shadow of a Bull* (1964) by Maia Wojciechowska, *The Return of the Twelves* (1963) by Pauline Clarke, *The Faraway Lurs* (1963) by Harry Behn, *Rascal* (1963) by Sterling North, *The Bushbabies* (1965) by William Stevenson.

Rebellion against the dull primers, almost the only books simple enough for beginning readers, suggested an experiment—*The Cat in the Hat* (1957) by Dr. Seuss. Almost simultaneously was published *Little Bear* (1957) by Else Holmelund Minarik, illustrated by Maurice Sendak. A rash of easy-to-reads followed.

All during the fifties and well into the sixties, poets Harry Behn and David McCord in the United States and James Reeves and Robert Graves in England were writing not only engaging verse, but poetry for children.

New artists, using many different media and techniques, discovered the satisfaction of working for children: Taro Yashima, Ezra Jack Keats, Maurice Sendak, Juliet Kepes, Antonio Frasconi, Evaline Ness, Leo Lionni, Symeon Shimin. Among artists beginning in the sixties were Beni Montresor, Nonny Hogrogian, Blair Lent, Ed Emberley, Uri Shulevitz. Artists known in the thirties and forties continued illustrating and creating books: Roger Duvoisin, Leonard Weisgard, Marcia Brown,

Barbara Cooney, Marie Hall Ets, and Robert McCloskey demonstrated unusual versatility as they fulfilled the earlier promise of their talents. From England came the brilliant color work of Brian Wildsmith and the beautiful color and viable line of Raymond Briggs's picture books.

In 1964 Morton Schindel, whose Weston Woods Studios in Connecticut had for a number of years been producing picture-books films completely faithful to the originals, was commissioned by the Children's Services Division of the American Library Association to make a motion picture about picture books. Joanna Foster wrote and directed the film, which was photographed and edited by William D. Stoneback. It presented John Langstaff, as Master of Ceremonies, who discussed picture books, showing examples of a wide variety of work by many different artists, and interviewed three guest illustrators in their studios: Robert McCloskey, Barbara Cooney, and Maurice Sendak. The result was a stunning testimonial to picture books at their best, exciting encouragement to those working with children and books, and a milestone marking the progress of picture books in the United States.

Not all books have been served so well by film producers. Literary style and the subtle nuances of many stories do not translate to the screen; too often sensitivity is turned into sentimentality, humor to slapstick, and whimsy to sugary condescension. And a frequent unfortunate by-product has been the retold and watered-down "film edition" of stories well loved in their original forms.

Had L. Frank Baum possessed stylistic genius along with his lively imagination, he might have succeeded in being the first American to write great fantasy for children. But, inventive though it was, *The Wizard of Oz* (1900) was told in such lifeless prose that rereading it in adulthood is a disappointment. Because there is no grace in the style, no subtlety in the storytelling to give conviction to the fantastic people and incidents, it lost nothing in translation to the screen. It is probably one of the few children's book to be successfully filmed. Later liberties taken by film producers, notably Walt Disney, with fantasies of literary quality—*The Wind in the Willows*, *Winnie-the-Pooh*, and *Mary Poppins* among them—destroyed the integrity of the original books, making widely available the mediocre and tasteless.

Although during the first half of the century more literary fairy tales were written in Britain than in the United States, by the fifties American writers were beginning to find their way into imaginative realms. In the sixties there was an exciting burgeoning of fantasy in the United States.

The awakened appreciation of fairy tales and fantasy was marked by new editions of important earlier books. In 1960 appeared a new translation by Pat Shaw Iverson and Carl Norman of the classic *Norwegian Folk Tales* (1961) by Peter Christian Asbjörnsen and Jörgen Moe, illustrated with many of the original pictures by Erik Werenskiold and Theodor Kittelsen. In the fifties and sixties not only were new editions of Andersen being published, but numerous picture-story books were made of individual Andersen tales, illustrated by different artists in various moods and techniques. *Seven Tales by H. C. Andersen* (1959), a very beautiful book with illustrations in color by Maurice Sendak, included stories selected and newly translated by Eva Le Gallienne. In her harmonious drawings for *The Wild Swans* (1963), one of Andersen's most dramatic tales, Marcia Brown gave worthy tribute to the master storyteller. Two of Frank R. Stockton's stories—too long neglected—were published as separate books with Mr. Sendak's illustrations: *The Griffin and the Minor Canon* (1963) and *The Bee-man of Orn* (1964). Kathleen Lines skillfully edited Charles Kingsley's *The Water Babies* (1961) to make the feeling of the underwater world and the adventures of Tom clearer for modern children. Not only were the favorite fairy tales of George Macdonald reissued in new editions, but two little-known ones were published: *The Lost Princess* (1966) and *The Golden Key* (1967).

Informational books most characteristic of the period were profusely illustrated ones. Some were useful, many were obviously made to attract the adult buyer in search of informative material for reluctant readers. Most became outdated within a short time. A few were of enduring quality. These were sometimes the result of artist and writer working closely together, or of an artist successfully writing his own text. Edwin Tunis wrote, and illustrated with meticulous drawings, a series of beautiful books: *Wheels* (1955), *Colonial Living* (1957), *Frontier Living* (1961), and others. Miroslav Sasek began his picture books about cities with *This Is Paris* (1959) and *This Is London* (1959). Anthony Ravielli wrote and illustrated *The Wonders of the Human Body* (1954) and *An Adventure in Geometry* (1957). Virginia Lee Burton's *Life Story* (1962) was a most original presentation of the earth's changes.

By the mid-sixties changes came about in the publishing scene that were even more drastic than the merging of text and trade-book publishing concerns, major business corporations began buying old prestigious publishing companies. Book publishing, so long carried on by small family firms, evolved into multibillion-dollar businesses controlled by vast industrial corporations. The publishing gold-rush fever did not affect all the old companies, however. Joining those that survived as independent firms were new companies made up of book men whose concern with profit was secondary to their interest in publishing good books.

Among the unfortunate results of the annual publication of great numbers of new children's books was the blow dealt to the reviewing and serious criticism of them. Beginning in the forties and continuing through the fifties and sixties, the regular and consistent reviewing of children's books deteriorated to little more than descriptive notes, and, with very few exceptions, was limited to library and education periodicals. Space for reviews did not increase to accommodate adequate consideration of the many books published. Nor did many magazine publishers show interest in giving children's book reviews priority over other material. Reviewers of the fifties and sixties rarely had the opportunity, even if they had the ability, to write cogent essays like those that appeared in *The Bookman*, the *New York Herald Tribune Weekly Book Review*, and *The Saturday Review of Literature* during the twenties by Anne Carroll Moore, Margery Bianco, May Lamberton Becker, Henry Beston, Louise Seaman, and Dorothy Lathrop.

At a time when consistent reviewing was more necessary than ever before, fewer general magazines included regular consideration of children's books in their pages. The state of reviewing revealed neither the enthusiastic attention to children's books characteristic of the late nineteenth century nor the literary criticism that reached a high level in the twenties and thirties. Criticism of children's book criticism began to be heard, however, from a few literate people interested in good books for boys and girls.

Although in the fifties paperback publishing was flourishing, children's books in paper bindings were few. By 1967, however, so many different titles were available at low cost that paperback book fairs were held in schools, wide use was made of paperbacks for supplementary reading, and children were encouraged to buy them to start their own libraries.

People influenced by the writings of Marshall McLuhan referred to the sixties as the "post-literate age," marking the move of civilization away from books. In contradiction were statistics showing that more books were published and sold than ever before, and more people were using libraries.

All during the fifties interest in the Newbery and Caldecott Medals was growing. In many cases award-winning books were the first ones read by people newly interested in the field of children's literature and they inspired spirited discussion. Although emphasis was sometimes given to winning books, to the exclusion of other equally important ones, the existence of awards created stepping stones to wider book experiences. They also stimulated the founding of other awards.

Of special significance was the creation in 1954 of the Laura Ingalls Wilder Award by the Children's Services Division of the American Library Association, with Mrs. Wilder herself the first recipient. Its purpose is to give recognition, at five-year intervals, "to an author or illustrator whose books published in the United States have over a period of years made a lasting contribution to literature for children."

In 1960 the Wilder Award went to Clara Ingram Judson, and in 1965 to Ruth Sawyer.

Children's book awards had also been founded abroad. The British Library Association established its Carnegie Medal in 1936 and twenty years later the Greenaway Medal for distinguished work in illustration. In 1947 The Canadian Library Association gave two medals for the Book of the Year for Children, honoring the authors of two outstanding children's books—one in English and one in French. Most European countries had created children's book awards before the mid-sixties.

During the fifties so many children's book awards and citations were created that they became almost commonplace, but they demonstrated a growing concern with the need to make people aware of good books for boys and girls.

England, the first source of books for American children, continued as a major source for so many generations that, even after the United States began publishing its own children's books, young readers made no distinction between British and American books. Books translated into English have had the same natural acceptance. Children's stories have been traveling from country to country for hundreds of years, children's books for many generations. American children would have been deprived indeed without the fairy tales of the Brothers Grimm and Hans Christian Andersen, without *Pinocchio* or *Heidi*, *The Wonderful Adventures of Nils*, *The Little Prince*, or Elsa Beskow's picture books.

By the fifties the closing in of the world stimulated an even wider exchange of children's books. In many countries people knew that children's books had an important role to play, not only in education, but in the stimulation of the mind and imagination of the young post-war generation.

In Zurich in 1953 was held the first General Assembly of the International Board on Books for Young People, established through the efforts of Mrs. Jella Lepman, the founder of the International Youth Library in Munich. The most important aim of the IBBY was to serve "as a world conscience for international children's literature." One of its major functions was the bestowing at two-year intervals of the Hans Christian Andersen Medal: to be "awarded to a living author who, by an outstanding work (after 1960, by his complete work) has made an important international contribution to juvenile literature."

Two Hans Christian Andersen Medals were awarded at the Stockholm Congress in 1956: to Jella Lepman in recognition of her work to further international understanding through children's books; and to Eleanor Farjeon for *The Little Book Room*. Later recipients of the award were Astrid Lindgren (1958), Erich Kastner (1960), Meindert DeJong (1962), René Guillot (1964), and Tove Jansson (1966).

The establishment of the IBBY and the Andersen Medal gave increased impetus to an already growing movement. In the ten years following the Stockholm Congress many American books were translated, and in return books from other countries greatly strengthened children's book collections in the United States. Among many books from Sweden came *Pippi Longstocking* (1950) by Astrid Lindgren, *Spettecake Holiday* (1958) by Edith Unnerstad; from Norway *The Road to Agra* (1961) by Aimée Sommerfelt; from Germany *Big Tiger and Christian* (1952) by Fritz Mühlenweg and a number of books by Margot Benary-Isbert and Hans Baumann; from France *Tistou of the Green Thumbs* (1958) by Maurice Druon, several stories by Paul Berna, and many by René Guillot. Beautiful picture books came from abroad, including those by Bruno Munari in Italy, Hans Fischer and Celestino Piatti in Switzerland, Rainey Bennett in France, and Felix Hoffmann in Germany.

Many other books of high literary and artistic quality came from abroad but inferior ones came also. With the tremendous growth of the book market, publishers left no foreign source unexplored, with the result that some of the translations increased even further the great bulk of mediocre publications for children in the United States.

An impetus to the publishing of the best of foreign children's books was the Mildred L. Batchelder Award established in 1967 by the Children's Services Division of the American Library Association: to be presented annually to the publisher of the book "Selected as the most outstanding of those books originally published in a foreign language in a foreign country and subsequently published in English in the United States of America."

Only superficially has been traced the panorama of changes and trends in publications for children through forty-seven years spanning wars and economic depression, unparalleled scientific development, and unprecedented government expenditures for education. Form after form of mass entertainment has usurped children's free time; but between 1950 and 1967 many new libraries were built where libraries had not existed before, and new library buildings replaced old ones to meet the demands of communities throughout the United States. Although modern marvels of communication have seemed at times to displace books in schools and in homes, books still remain the most convenient and the most private way to find answers to questions and to satisfy the human longing for "escape into experience."

In the chapters that follow will be discussed, in groupings by subject or literary types, representative books of nearly half a century. Good books cannot be satisfactorily categorized any more than children can be, and book discussions that cut across arbitrary dividing lines are far more interesting and illuminating than those which treat books in neat groups. The consideration in so brief a space of the children's books published during this time is so stupendous a task, however, that divisions must be made if only to chart a way.

The books mentioned in the pages that follow are only a small per cent of the many that could have been discussed if more space and time had been available, but they give some indication of the growth of literature for children during the forty-seven-year period. Attempt has been made to include books written with special distinction and those indicative of trends and influences, but many popular and useful titles, and many competent writers and artists could not be mentioned within practical space. It is quite possible also that in such a vast outpouring some books may not have reached this writer's attention. All of the books included, however, are fragments in the colorful mosaic. More time must pass before we can see whether they continue to show gleam or color in the pattern.

Bibliography

Arbuthnot, May Hill. *Children and Books*. Chicago, Scott, Foresman, 1947.

Barry, Florence V. *A Century of Children's Books*. New York, Doran, n.d.

Becker, May Lamberton. *Adventures in Reading*. New York, F. A. Stokes, 1927.

Burgess, E. W., and Others. Symposium on "The American Family." *American Journal of Sociology*, Vol. 53 (1948), pp. 417, 495.

Conference on the Care of Dependent Children, Washington, January 25, 26, 1909. *Proceedings*. Washington, Government Printing Office, 1909. (State Documents, Vol. 13.)

Dalgliesh, Alice. *First Experiences with Literature*. New York, Scribner, 1932.

Eaton, Anne Thaxter. *Reading with Children*. New York, Viking Press, 1940.

—— *Treasure for the Taking*. Rev. ed. New York, Viking Press, 1957.

Eyre, Frank. *20th Century Children's Books*. Published for the British Council. London, Longmans, Green, 1952.

Ferris, Helen, ed. *Writing Books for Boys and Girls*. New York, Doubleday, 1952.

Fisher, Margery. *Intent upon Reading*. New York, Watts, 1962.

Ford, Ford Madox. *The March of Literature*. New York, Dial Press, 1938.

Frank, Josette. *What Books for Children?* New York, Doubleday, Doran, 1937.

Fuller, Muriel, Editor. *More Junior Authors*. New York, H. W. Wilson, 1963.

Ginzberg, Eli, Editor. *The Nation's Children*. 3 vols. 1: *The Family and Social Change*. 2: *Development and Education*. 3: *Problems and Prospects*. Golden Anniversary White House Conference on Children and Youth. New York, Columbia University Press, 1960.

Hazard, Paul. *Books, Children and Men*. Translated by Marguerite Mitchell. Boston, The Horn Book, 1944.

Hohman, Leslie B. *As the Twig Is Bent*. New York, Macmillan, 1940.

Horn Book Magazine, The. Boston, The Horn Book, 1924–1968.

Kingman, Lee, ed. *Newbery and Caldecott Medal Books: 1956–1965*. Boston, The Horn Book, 1965.

Kunitz, Stanley J. and Howard Haycraft, eds. *The Junior Book of Authors*. New York, H. W. Wilson Co., 1934.

—— 2d ed., rev. 1951.

Levy, John and Munroe, Ruth. *The Happy Family*. New York. A. A. Knopf, 1938.

Lines, Kathleen M. *Four to Fourteen*. Published for The National Book League. Introduction by Walter De la Mare. Cambridge, Eng., University Press, 1950.

Mahony, Bertha E. and Elinor Whitney. *Contemporary Illustrators of Children's Books*. Boston, Women's Educational and Industrial Union, 1930.
—— *Five Years of Children's Books*, A Supplement to *Realms of Gold*. New York, Doubleday, Doran, 1936.
—— *Realms of Gold in Children's Books*. New York, Doubleday, Doran, 1929.
Miller, Bertha Mahony and Elinor Whitney Field, eds. *Caldecott Medal Books: 1938–1957*. Boston, The Horn Book, 1957.
—— *Newbery Medal Books: 1922–1955*. Boston, The Horn Book, 1955.
Montgomery, Elizabeth Rider. *The Story Behind Modern Books*. New York, Dodd, Mead, 1949.
Moore, Anne Carroll. *Creation and Criticism of Children's Books*. Reprint of a paper read at the meeting of the Section for Library Work with Children in Montreal in 1934. Chicago, American Library Association, 1934.
—— *My Roads to Childhood*. New York, Doubleday, Doran, 1939.
—— *The Three Owls*. New York, Macmillan, 1925.
—— *The Three Owls, Second Book*. New York, Coward-McCann, 1928.
—— *The Three Owls, Third Book*. New York, Coward-McCann, 1931.
Robinson, Evelyn R. *Readings About Children's Literature*. New York, McKay, 1966.
Smith, Irene. *A History of the Newbery and Caldecott Medals*. New York, Viking Press, 1957.
Thom, Douglas. *Everyday Problems of the Everyday Child*. New York, D. Appleton, 1927.
Townsend, John Rowe. *Written for Children*. London, Garnet Miller, 1965.
Van Doren, Mark. *Liberal Education*. New York, Henry Holt and Co., 1943.
Washburn, Ruth Wendell. *Children Have Their Reasons*. New York, D. Appleton-Century Co., 1942.
White, Dorothy Neal. *About Books for Children*. New Zealand Council for Educational Research in Conjunction with the New Zealand Library Association. Christchurch, Whitecombe and Tombs Ltd., 1946.
White House Conference on Child Health and Protection, 1930. *Addresses and Abstracts of Committee Reports*. New York, Century Co., 1931.
—— *Preliminary Committee Reports*. New York, Century Co., 1930.
White House Conference on Children in a Democracy, January 18–20, 1940. *Final Report*. Washington, U.S. Government Printing Office, 1942. (Children's Bureau Publication no. 272. U.S. Department of Labor)

Treasure from the Past

Folk and Fairy Tales—New Collections of Folklore

Many of the collections of folk and fairy tales available today to English-speaking children are the result of the growing interest between 1930 and 1950 in folk music, folk tales, and folk arts of all kinds. Folklore societies in the days of the brothers Grimm were made up of scholarly men whose interest was in the historic and philological aspects of folklore. By the mid-twentieth century these societies included people of many backgrounds interested in folk arts because of their universal humanness. Many a traveler has turned folklorist because of his interest in a people whose traditional stories happen still to be an evident part of their culture. With the impetus that writing for children received after 1930, it is not surprising that the making of books from this oldest of all sources should be stimulated as well.

Parker Fillmore became interested in Czech folklore during the First World War while living and working on the upper East Side of New York in a Czech settlement. Two books grew out of this interest: *Czechoslovak Fairy Tales* in 1919 and *The Shoemaker's Apron* in 1920. First hearing many of these stories from Czechoslovak storytellers, he afterwards searched them out in old books, comparing versions and putting himself in the role of storyteller, rather than translator, in his final presentation of them. The resulting stories have the grace and humor of the best oral storytelling while they keep the spice and color of their Czech, Moravian, and Slovak origins. The tales in *The Laughing Prince* (1921) he drew from Yugoslav sources; and, renewing his boyhood enthusiasm for the *Kalevala*, he drew directly from some of the stories in the Finnish epic for *The Wizard of the North* (1923).

The stories in *Tales from Silver Lands* (1924) were based on those that Charles Finger had heard directly from the Indians he met in his wanderings through South America. The background of each story is vivid, there is great variety in setting and plot and, in the telling of them, Mr. Finger succeeded in pointing up the individual flavor of the different countries. The stories have extraordinary power and dignity, are full of magic—strong magic that accomplishes mighty changes. The supernatural beings are witches and giants, yet the flowers and birds and animals have important place in the stories as well: the hummingbird and condor, the flamingo and ostrich, the iguana, the deer, and the gentle, proud huanaco—"where dies a huanaco there springs up a flower blue as the sky, its petals all gold tipped." *Tales from Silver Lands* was awarded the Newbery Medal in 1925.

Lucia Borski, in a New York library, had been telling Polish stories in Polish to groups of Polish children and in English to groups of American children. She worked over the stories with Kate B. Miller until their form seemed right for telling. Published in 1925 as *The Jolly Tailor and Other Fairy Tales*, they are jolly indeed and fast-moving, the style simple, the English words apt and colorful, and they possess the special flavor of Polish folklore.

From Russia, in the twenties, came two books in marked contrast. The first was a collection of homely beast tales and fables, illustrated with simple but humorous line drawings, Valery Carrick's *Picture Folk Tales* (1926); the second was Ida Zeitlin's *Skazki, Tales and Legends of Old Russia* (1926), lavish in format and distinguished in writing.

There were two collections of African folk tales at this time. Erick Berry's *Black Folk Tales* (1928), retold from the Haussa of northern Nigeria, grew out of her experiences in West Africa. The characters are animals as well as humans. The lion, gazelle, elephant, hippopotamus, monkey, spiders, goats, and frogs give the stories a strong sense of locale. Blaise Cendrars' *Little Black Stories*, very ably translated from the French by Margery Bianco in 1929, was an unusual collection that transmitted through its rhythm, humor, and concise style the dense jungle, the deep river filled with crocodiles and hippopotami, the wind on the mountain, and the fears and superstitions of the people.

Constance Smedley's book of folklore from Africa and Asia, *Tales from Timbuktu*, appeared in 1923. Translated for the first time into English were Luigi Capuana's sparkling *Italian Fairy Tales* (1929); Zacharias Topelius' fairy tales, legends, and simple stories of child life in Finland and Lapland, *Canute Whistlewinks* (1927); and Gottfried Keller's romantic and humorous Swiss fairy tales, freely translated and adapted by Louis Untermeyer in *The Fat of the Cat* (1925).

Rich indeed was the folk inheritance passed on to English-speaking children from the twenties. And, during the next forty years, many new translations of old tales and new adaptations from recorded sources were published. More significant, however, were collections of stories by folklorists who traveled far to gather stories directly from the people of distant lands.

Sybille Noel's childhood had been spent largely in the Orient and she grew up well acquainted with Oriental life and thought. As the wife of Captain John Noel, Tibetan-Himalayan explorer and author, she came to know intimately the land and lore of Tibet. The dramatic and beautiful stories in *The Magic Bird of Chomo-Lung-Ma* (1931) were chiefly gathered when she directed an artist expedition on horseback into the interior of Tibet.

Early in the thirties Ruth Sawyer went to Spain in search of folk tales. In her college years she had been a student of folklore. She knew the richness of Spain's inheritance from the different peoples who had occupied the land and she hoped to find there storytellers as gifted as those she had found in Ireland. Out of her Spanish journey came *Picture Tales from Spain* (1936) and other stories published eventually in *The Way of the Storyteller* (1942), *The Long Christmas* (1941), and *Joy to the World* (1966). Typically Spanish in their humor and in the rhymes sprinkled through them, the stories seem to have caught the spirit of the storytellers from whom she had heard them. Many years later in *My Spain* (1967) she told the story of that year of journeying and of finding that a search for stories in La Coruña, Madrid, Barcelona, Granada—wherever her quest took her—unfailingly opened the way to friendships as well as stories. Her tales glow with her love for the country and the people who welcomed her and exchanged stories with her.

Also from Spain came some colorful, romantic stories collected there by Ralph Steele Boggs, *Three Golden Oranges* (1936). Mary Gould Davis, who collaborated with Mr. Boggs in putting the tales in form for American children and American storytellers, went to Spain so that she herself could hear them told, taking with her the illustrator and editor, the three of them absorbing the atmosphere as well as the stories of Spain.

Out of Spain, too, came *Padre Porko* (1939) by Robert Davis. For years Mr. Davis had heard references to that gentlemanly pig, but in 1938, when communications were difficult in Spain, he was traveling on a slow train with an elderly woman who told stories out of her great fund of local superstition, custom, legends, and fables, and by the end of the journey the genial character and many exploits of the fabulous pig had emerged complete and unforgettable. While the king was ruler of the people, Padre Porko ruled the animals, and it was his belief that all animals should work together and be like brothers to each other. He came to Spain with the Irish hundreds of years "before the Romans and the Arabs and such quarrelsome people," and there he has lived ever since, "as the best friend of every Spaniard."

Anita Brenner heard in childhood many of the stories in *The Boy Who Could Do Anything and Other Mexican Folk Tales* (1942) and, in her retelling, kept the lively touches of the native storyteller. The tales show the influences of the twentieth century, continuing to grow and change in the midst of planes, motors, railroads, and all the practical wonders of the present. Jean Charlot's strong, humorous line drawings illustrate the stories.

Growing up in Puerto Rico in a family of storytellers, Pura Belpré had long known and later told to the children in an American public library the stories she collected in *The Tiger and the Rabbit* (1946). Influenced by both the folk culture of Spain and the ways of American life, the stories remain, nevertheless, essentially an expression of the people of the beautiful island.

Many folk-tale collections have grown out of story-listening childhoods. Lucky the children who inherit the good fortune those writers have passed on. As a child in Jamaica, Philip Sherlock listened to the tales of Anansi who was sometimes a man and sometimes a spider. "When things went well he was a man, but when he was in great danger he became a spider, safe in his web high up on the ceiling." Originating in West Africa, the stories in *Anansi the Spider Man* (1954) had come with the people who many years ago migrated to the islands of the Caribbean. Philip Sherlock, Vice-Principal of the University College of the West Indies at Jamaica, told the stories at a meeting of the American Library Association, where a children's book editor heard him and persuaded him to make them into a book. Anansi is important in several stories in *West Indian Folk-Tales* (1966), also by Mr. Sherlock.

Anansi appears also in many of the stories of the Ashanti people collected by Harold Courlander in *The Hat-Shaking Dance and Other Tales from the Gold Coast* (1957). Mr. Courlander, a novelist, musicologist, and student of folklore, made several important collections of hitherto unpublished stories. His first collection of tales for children, *Uncle Bouqui of Haiti* (1942), tells of Bouqui who is always in trouble, and Ti Malice, who is always thinking up new schemes, who "works in the fields like everyone else but who prefers to live on his intellect." Mr. Courlander collected the tales from native storytellers in the mountains of Haiti, a country that has been his special interest for over thirty years. The original stories were old when they were brought by the first slaves from Africa, but there is a strong sense of the present about them, too, as though one would certainly meet blundering Uncle Bouqui and his evil genius Ti Malice if one were to climb into the hills of Haiti.

Other books of folk tales came out of Mr. Courlander's experiences in West Africa, Ethiopia, Indonesia, Asia, and islands of the Pacific, each one presenting stories of great freshness and originality. Recording the folk music of native musicians and the storytelling of native storytellers to help him with the subsequent study of the material, he retained the atmosphere of the region and the flavor and living quality of the original stories. The tales in *The Terrapin's Pot of Sense* (1957) were told to him by Negro storytellers in Alabama, New Jersey, and Michigan. Concluding notes show the relationship of the tales to African variants.

The stories in *Wakaima and the Clay Man* (1946) belong to the Baganda tribe of East Africa, where Ernest Balintuma Kalibala heard them as a child. He retold them in English, assisted by Mary Gould Davis. Animal stories full of life and humor, they have evident kinship to the Uncle Remus stories.

Russell Davis and Brent Ashabranner, working as a team for the International Cooperative Administration, spent two years in Ethiopia. Gathering materials for textbooks for the schools of Ethiopia and testing what they gathered, they journeyed all over the country and came to know both people and stories. From thousands of tales they selected for *The Lion's Whiskers* (1959) those representative of the nine major tribes of Ethiopia, weaving them together with accounts of the authors' experiences as they traveled. A year later was published *Ten Thousand Desert Swords* (1960), a selection, retold in English for the first time, of the most characteristic of the stories, songs, and poems of the Bani Hilal, one of the most powerful of the ancient desert tribes. The tales are colorful and exciting, told with swiftness and dignity.

No region was too remote for the folklorists of this period. The South African velt, the Dead Heart of Australia, the Philippines, and other lands have yielded up their stories to enrich the literature of English-speaking boys and girls.

The treasure store of Chinese legendary and folk stories that has frequently been tapped to bring pleasure to Western children seems inexhaustible. For *The Magic Spear* (1938) Louise Crane selected legendary stories of China's heroes, many of which had been adapted for the theater and were favorites with Chinese children. Arthur Waley translated the first seven chapters of the Chinese children's classic *Monkey*, calling his book *The Adventures of Monkey* (1944). For its humor, nonsense, and satire the story is surely as delightful and surprising today to Americans as it was more than three hundred years ago when the story was first written by Wu Ch'eng-en for Chinese children.

For ten years a Chinese writer from the province of Fukien, Lim Sian-Tek, gathered, from many different Chinese sources, a representative group of myths, legends, fairy and folk tales, romance and historical legends to introduce ancient Chinese literature to Western boys and girls. The result was *Folk Tales from China* (1944), a rich and varied collection. Most of the stories are short, and where several variants exist, the writer used the version current in Fukien, "for where is the man who can forget the stories told to him in his enchanted childhood?" *More Folk Tales from China* (1948) published a few years later is an equally carefully selected and interesting collection.

The daughter of Mme. Sugimoto, Chiyono, born in Japan, grew up and received her education in the United States. Returning to Japan as a grown girl she was as fascinated as a stranger might have been with hearing the old stories in their proper setting. With her American background she was well able to make interesting selections of stories that would interest Western children in her *Picture Tales from the Japanese* (1928) and *Japanese Holiday Picture Tales* (1933). The tales of the second are tied together with the story of a Japanese girl and her grandmother, through which bits of home life and holiday customs are woven, reminding one of Frances Carpenter's framework of family and national customs in her *Tales of a Korean Grandmother* (1947) and her other "Grandmother" collections. Yoshiko Uchida told the favorite stories of her childhood in *The Dancing Kettle and Other Japanese Folk Tales* (1949). Some of the stories are familiar, but all reflect the special enjoyment of long, happy association. With the same authenticity and good direct style she adapted other old Japanese tales in *The Magic Listening Cap* (1955) and *The Sea of Gold* (1965).

From many published sources Eleanore M. Jewett gathered the threads of stories to make *Which Was Witch? Tales of Ghosts and Magic from Korea* (1953). Sometimes choosing from several variants she changed, elaborated, and, where necessary, reconstructed the stories, keeping true, however, to Korean thought and to the ancient Korean culture.

The stories in *The Beautiful Blue Jay and Other Tales from India* (1967) compiled by John W. Spellman, unlike most collections of tales from India, are drawn from none of the classical stories but from oral sources throughout India. Closely related to European stories in their themes and plots, they illustrate the universality of folk tales and the "distinctiveness of India within that universality. . . . They reflect the humor, the struggles, the concerns and the behavior of the common folk of India."

Enys Tregarthen, who lived in the shipping town of Padstow on the north coast of Cornwall, did not want the Cornish legends to be lost. Though an invalid most of her life, she collected many of the legends. Some were published and found their way into the hands of storytellers and other lovers of folklore. Elizabeth Yates was one of these. When she and her husband were traveling in Cornwall in 1939 they were given access to a little trunk filled with scrapbooks, letters, and stories. *Piskey Folk* (1940) is their selection of these hitherto unpublished legends and tales of Cornwall. The windswept moors, the rugged hills, the quiet harbors and the ragged cliffs, the small villages and the neat cottages, the downs "green and sweet with thyme," are as much a part of the stories as the strange, small creatures that people them. These Cornish fairy tales with their brittle charm and delicacy are a marked contrast to the robust stories of giants and heroes characteristic of many other parts of England.

Of the stories in *Tales from a Finnish Tupa* (1936) by James Cloyd Bowman and Margery Bianco, some were selected and translated from two of the earliest of printed collections of Finnish folk tales and others were told to the authors by old Finnish storytellers. All of the stories have vitality that makes them seem as though they are coming directly from the storytellers without any medium of translator or collector. The book is divided into "Tales of Magic," "Droll Stories," and "Fables," but all are filled with the special "magic of words" so familiar in the *Kalevala*; marvels are accomplished by the singing of magic runes. Humor and lively action and good, hard, peasant common sense abound.

Alice Geer Kelsey was the first to introduce to American children the hodja of Turkey and the mullah of Persia in *Once the Hodja* (1943) and *Once the Mullah* (1954). The hodja and the mullah are closely related. Each is the Moslem priest-teacher-judge for his village. Good natured and simple minded, posing as very wise, they both have great talent for getting into trouble and even greater talent for getting out of it.

Anne Sinclair Mehdevi's many nieces and nephews had collected stories told to them in childhood by their nurse Nana Roosie. In *Persian Folk and Fairy Tales* (1965) Mrs. Mehdevi retold the stories in a lively, informal style. Themes and plots are familiar but the flavor of the telling and the drawings by Paul E. Kennedy have the atmosphere of Mrs. Mehdevi's adopted country.

The stories from Armenia in *Once There Was and Was Not* (1966), modern retellings by Virginia Tashjian of tales recorded by Hovhannes Toumanian, are closely related to the tales of Turkey and Persia. The opening of each "Once There Was and Was Not" is common to Majorcan and Spanish lore. The Armenian flavor and humor, however, give them their own distinction as does the good, storytelling style; and the handsome illustrations by Nonny Hogrogian, also of Armenian descent, give the book a beautiful unity.

Rose Laura Mincielli selected and retold ten stories and a framework story from *Il Pentamerone* in *Old Neapolitan Fairy Tales* (1963). Gathered by Giambattista Basile and published in 1674 in Naples, *Il Pentamerone* was the earliest collection of European folk tales and had an influence on stories told throughout Europe. Among the stories best known and loved today are variants of those tales which have been honed down by successive storytellers to their simple, direct forms.

In *Tit for Tat* (1967) Latvian folk tales were adapted by Mae Durham from the translation of Skaidrite Rubene-Koo, with line drawings by Harriet Pincus, and notes by Alan Dundes.

Folk and Fairy Tales—Distinguished Retellings

The Irish Renaissance was a vital movement in Ireland when Padraic Colum was a young man living in Dublin. Stories and poetry heard in his childhood had given him an early interest in the legends and traditions of Ireland, further stimulated by the Celtic Revival. He was drawn into all the activity that was being carried on by the young Irish intellectuals. He became active, with William Butler Yeats, Lady Gregory, "A. E." and J. M. Synge, in promoting the Irish Theatre, and with James Stephens and Thomas McDonagh he founded the *Irish Review*. When he came to America in 1914 he began translating passages from a long Irish folk story (which was the only text he had at the time in Gaelic) to keep from forgetting the language. His translation found its way to the children's page of the New York *Tribune*, where it caught the interest of the Hungarian illustrator Willy Pogány, who suggested that Mr. Colum write a book that he would illustrate. Mr. Colum took his translation, added to it and wove it into the long romantic story full of adventures and enchantment, *The King of Ireland's Son* (1916).

The Forge in the Forest (1925) has the same poetry and high imagination, borne out in the illustrations by Boris Artzybasheff. It includes a story for each of the elements that the forest blacksmith used in his trade—fire, water, earth and air—the stories being told in payment for shoeing a wild horse.

The stories in *The Big Tree of Bunlahy* (1933) are, many of them, familiar in their themes, but told under the big elm tree in the little village that was "all on one side—there never was, and there never will be two rows of houses in Bunlahy—" they are as new to the reader as though he were hearing them for the first time.

Early in the century several collections of stories by the Irish poet, playwright, and storyteller Seumas MacManus (1870–1960) had appeared. Late in his life he collected and revised some of his favorites among his stories for *Hibernian Nights* (1963), published three years after his death at ninety—the last of the "true Irish shanachie."

Wanda Gág grew up in an American town but in the folk traditions of the Old World. Though she entered children's literature as the first great American picture-book artist-author, it was natural that she should also retell in words what she could tell so skillfully with her drawings. She speaks of making a Hansel and Gretel drawing at one time, and "the old *Märchen* magic gripped me again and I felt I could not rest until I had expressed in pictures all that *Märchen* meant to me." In selecting stories which were, no doubt, her own favorites, she delighted most children, and in her retelling of them proved that the magic must have held her tight again and shown her how to write down stories so that they hold all the charm of the story told. *Tales from Grimm* (1936), *More Tales from Grimm* (1947), and other retellings became wonderful new books as Wanda Gág interpreted them.

Rachel Field took the fairy tales of the Comtesse d'Aulnoy as they had been translated by Monsieur Planché, arranged and edited them, and Elizabeth MacKinstry illustrated them most appropriately to make a very beautiful book, *The White Cat and Other Old French Fairy Tales* (1928).

In 1923, on the invitation of the Hawaiian legislature, Padraic Colum went to Hawaii "to make a survey of traditional stories of the islands and reshape them into stories which could be used to bring the imaginative past of the Polynesian people to the newer groups in the Islands." The result was two collections of Hawaiian stories: *At the Gateways of the Day* (1924) and *The Bright Islands* (1925).

With the accession of Hawaii to statehood in 1959 and a widening interest in the islands, many publications about Hawaii began to appear, but they were primarily fiction and informational books. Little interest was evident in exploring and taking advantage of traditional resources for books for boys and girls. Marcia Brown, while traveling in the islands, found a legend that excited her interest as a heroic tale, rooted in tradition and in early Polynesian life, which she believed had meaning for young people anywhere. She based her telling of *Backbone of the King* (1966) on a literal translation by Dorothy M. Kahananui. The story is chiefly of Paka'a, who lost his place of power because evil men coveted his honors; and of his son Ku, who by cleverness and courage overcame his father's enemies and brought about the restoration of Paka'a as an honored chief and "the backbone of the king." Chants woven throughout add to the flavor and rhythmic flow of the exciting tale. Miss Brown's illustrations, linoleum block prints in olive green, have great strength and feeling in harmony with the atmosphere of the story.

Little Magic Horse (1942) is a translation of the old tale of the humpbacked horse which had been made into a long narrative poem by Peter Ershoff when he was a young student in Petrograd. In this form it has been a favorite children's story in Russia for well over a hundred years. Tatiana Balkoff Drowne, who had loved the story as a child and could, like many Russian children, recite long passages of it by heart, saw her own American daughter growing up without the pleasure of knowing the tale, and so was inspired to translate it for her, retaining as much of the original rhyme and meter as possible. This story had also been a favorite in the Russian childhood of Vera Bock who brought affection, as well as skill and imaginative quality, to her illustrations for it.

The Quaint and Curious Quest of Johnny Longfoot, the Shoe King's Son (1947) is an expansion of an old Polish folk tale by Catherine Besterman. The book has unusual vigor and humor, marvelous events, and exciting characterizations including self-sufficient, ingratiating Johnny, his miserly uncle, and some amazing cats, bears, and dogs.

Once in France (1927), by Marguerite Clement, is a collection of legendary stories of different provinces that seem almost to tell themselves, they have so much spirit and humor. Very apparent is the author's love of France and her appreciation of the special charm of each province. Dorothy Lathrop retold and illustrated with great beauty the story of the holy man of the Hindus, Kirpalu the friend of the animals, from the text of Sant Ram Mandal, calling her book *The Happy Flute* (1939). In *The Sky River* (1950) Chang Fa-shun told the long, fascinating legend of the Milky Way, an appealing version of a story long loved in China.

In 1960 Leclaire Alger, a Pittsburgh children's librarian, writing under a Scottish name, Sorche Nic Leodhas, delighted all who value good stories and superior storytelling. *Heather and Broom* (1960) contains seanachie tales told by the wandering storytellers in the Scottish Highlands. They are full of humor, romance, and magic. Although the tales were told to Miss Nic Leodhas in America long ago, she remembered so clearly "the echoes of the telling" that she caught on the printed page their natural rhythm and cadence. Hers was the clear voice of a storyteller giving new vitality to old tales. *Thistle and Thyme* (1962) includes several kinds of stories: legends, folk or cottage tales, seanachie stories, and sgeulachdan—stories created for important occasions by a special story maker-and-teller. Later two collections of ghost stories appeared: *Gaelic Ghosts* (1963) from the Scottish Highlands and *Ghosts Go Haunting* (1965), made up chiefly of stories heard at clan gatherings in many large cities in the United States, outings that were all the more intensely Scottish in compensation for the foreign surroundings. The history tales in *Claymore and Kilt* (1967) are as fresh and well told as her other stories. Miss Nic Leodhas used old songs for the story lines in two picture books, *All in the Morning Early*, illustrated by Evaline Ness (1963), and the Caldecott Medal winner *Always Room for One More* (1964), illustrated by Nonny Hogrogian.

Isaac Bashevis Singer, one of the last great Yiddish authors, came to the United States in 1935. He was well known for his novels of Jewish life (the first, *The Family Moskat* appeared in 1950) and for his autobiography, *In My Father's Court*, when his first children's book was published. *Zlateh the Goat* (1966) includes seven tales, six of which had their beginnings in middle-European Jewish folklore and legend. Devils as well as ordinary people inhabit the stories, and many fools, chiefly from Chelm, a village of fools. The title story, however, must have grown more from memories of life than of legend. It tells of a terrible snowstorm just before Hanukkah when his beloved pet goat saved the life of twelve-year-old Aaron. The illustrations by Maurice Sendak, whose family roots reach back, like those of the author, to the village life of pre-war Poland, underline the atmosphere and humor of the timeless book.

In the illustrators of his next two children's books, Mr. Singer was also fortunate or, perhaps, the unusual atmosphere of his stories was a special challenge to each artist's originality and skill. Humor underlies the eloquent boldness of Nonny Hogrogian's illustrations for *The Fearsome Inn* (1967), a tale of three girls and three young men who outwit a devil and a witch. Margot Zemach's pictures for an old folk tale, *Mazel and Schlimazel* (1967), have her characteristic lively, amusing people and exhibit more genuine warmth and atmosphere than her earlier picture books showed.

American Folklore

American folklore can be divided roughly into three groupings: the lore of the Indians, folk tales that came with the settlers and slaves from Europe and Africa and have been colored by the new environment, and the stories of American legendary heroes.

That the Indians had a wealth of oral literature had been recognized early, but not until the twenties did many writers begin to show interest in exploring the mine of legendary material indigenous to America.

Arthur C. Parker, an Iroquois Indian whose tribal name is Gawaso Wanneh, told in *Skunny Wundy and Other Indian Tales* (1926) two groups of stories: Seneca tales, heard in childhood from his grandfather and visiting chieftains, and other stories, heard as a young man from other great tribal storytellers. Elizabeth De Huff's *Taytay's Tales* (1922) has animal folk tales of the Pueblo Indians, collected from the Indian children themselves. Aileen Nusbaum, who had lived in the Southwest, included in her *Zuñi Indian Tales* (1926), based on Frank Hamilton Cushing's *Zuñi Folk Tales*, stories she had heard from old tribesmen.

Alice Marriott's *Winter-Telling Stories* (1947) tells the "how" stories of the Kiowas, a Plains tribe. Many of these have for their hero the trickster Saynday. In *When Coyote Walked the Earth* (1949), drawn from authentic source material recorded by Professor Melville Jacobs for University of Washington publications in anthropology, Corinne Running told stories of the animal world before the first Indians came. The Alaskan Eskimo animal tales in *Beyond the Clapping Mountains* (1943) were heard by Charles E. Gillham from the Eskimos and, in his telling, retain a great deal of atmosphere and humor.

Jaime de Angulo, linguist, ethnologist, and anthropologist, lived for forty years among the Pit River Indians of California, but the writing of his *Indian Tales* (1953) gives evidence that he was both a poet and scientist. In an appreciative foreword Carl Carmer spoke of the time of the action of the tales as "that prehistoric dawn when men and animals were not so distinguishable from each other as they are today." The world he wrote of:

is a triumph of a poet's fancy, one in which he may indulge his knowledge of the past, his feeling for the present, his intuitive prophesies of the future. It is fundamentally a human world. . . . It is also an *American Indian* world and no writer of a language other than Indian has understood it so well. Here is all the ingenuous wonder, the experienced wisdom, the rollicking humor of the Indian presented with a sureness and clarity seldom if ever achieved.[1]

The adventures and folklore, tall tales and songs, allegories, jokes, and games are united with the structure of the journey of Bear and Antelope —with the baby Quail strapped on a cradleboard—and argumentative, little boy Fox trotting or dashing or playing games beside them.

The animal tales of the California Indians are more conventionally presented but very well told in Jane Louise Curry's *Down from the Lonely Mountains* (1965) and Anne B. Fisher's *Stories California Indians Told* (1957).

Christie Harris became interested in the coastal Indians of the Pacific Northwest when her husband was officer in charge of Canadian Immigration in British Columbia. As she came to know them, visit them in their villages, and listen to their tales, her interest was heightened. The legends she told in *Once upon a Totem* (1963) have the complexities of all great hero stories and reflect the mythology, history, and intricate social systems of a once proud people.

In *John Rattling-Gourd of Big Cove* (1955) Corydon Bell told legends of the Cherokee Indians of the Great Smoky Mountains of North Carolina. In *The World of Manabozho* (1965) Thomas B. Leekley collected tales of the Chippewa and Ottawa tribes of Ontario, stories related to the mythology of the Blackfeet and Cree Indians.

The Dancing Horses of Acoma (1963) by Helen Rushmore and Wolf Robe Hunt (whose striking pictures in full color illustrate the book) is a first recording of the legends of the Acomas, a tribe of Pueblo Indians whose adobe dwellings rest on a high mesa in New Mexico. Called "The Island in the Sky" by the Spanish explorers, it is the oldest continuously inhabited town in North America, built well before Columbus came to the New World. The stories are complex legends of gods and heroes. They reflect the customs and tribal rites and ceremonies and preserve the ancient tradition, which otherwise might be forgotten.

Washington Irving and Joel Chandler Harris had both recorded stories American in character but derived from other parts of the world. Not until the forties, however, were other stories of this kind collected and published for boys and girls. Richard Chase then discovered com-

---

[1] Carl Carmer, Foreword to *Indian Tales* by Jaime de Angulo (New York, Hill and Wang, 1953), pp. v, vi.

munities in America where storytelling as a folk art still flourished. Traveling widely in North Carolina, Virginia, and Kentucky (and he acknowledged that a bit of one story came from Maine), he heard and told a variety of stories. The tales he found were obviously derived from English folklore, but their environment had changed them, and the tellers of them, cut off from original sources, were unrestricted in their own embroidering on the old themes. The stories that emerged were completely different from their ancestors in setting, mood, and atmosphere. *The Jack Tales* (1943) was followed by *Grandfather Tales* (1948) and the American version of "The Three Sillies," *Jack and the Three Sillies* (1950).

In *The Talking Cat* (1952) Natalie Savage Carlson retold stories of French Canada heard by her mother as a child. Years ago during the long winter evenings in Canada anyone who could tell a good story was a welcome guest. Such a one was Michel Meloche, a *coureur de bois*, who, when he came out of the woods and visited his village friends in their firelit kitchens, told these lively tales of strange happenings to the people and their animals.

Less specifically regional are the stories in *The Golden Phoenix and Other French Canadian Fairy Tales* (1958) collected by Marius Barbeau directly from French Canadian raconteurs and retold by Michael Hornyansky. Brought to Canada by French colonists three hundred years ago, the tales now have a flavor quite different from the European roots from which they sprung.

Carl Carmer accounted for the creation of the fabulous heroes of American folklore by the almost superhuman challenge of the great jobs that awaited newcomers in making homes or merely surviving in the wilderness.

> And after the day's work was done and they saw how little of the great woods had been cut, they went home at night to rest and to make up stories after supper, about a hero so big and strong he could clear whole forests all by himself in a day. Each swing of his axe, they would say, opened up an acre of sunshine in the dark woods.[1]

The numberless cattle, grazing on the vast, treeless plains, inspired the cowboys when they sat by their campfires at night to tell stories about a great cowboy who could do easily what was impossible for ordinary men. And so it went; out of the imaginations of the hardworking men in America's great industries, one after another gigantic heroes emerged, and a new type of folklore, typically American, began—big as the country was big and robust as were the men who helped America grow.

[1] Carl Carmer, *America Sings* (New York, A. A. Knopf, 1942), p. 8.

Paul Bunyan, the super-lumberjack, was the first of these fabulous heroes to enter children's literature and Esther Shephard the first to record his feats. Most of the stories in her *Paul Bunyan* (1924) were collected from loggers in Washington, Oregon, and British Columbia, many of whom had followed the logging industry from the East and had brought with them stories that they had heard in Canada, Michigan, and the logging areas of the Middle West. She used the vernacular of the lumberjacks and kept the stories essentially just as the men in the lumber camps told them. Dell J. McCormick told more stories of Paul Bunyan in *Paul Bunyan Swings His Axe* (1936) and *Tall Timber Tales* (1939). In the telling of all these tales each logger speaks from "personal experience" or from the experience of a friend or relative and he sticks to the "truth" in recounting the incredible exploits. In his *Ol' Paul the Mighty Logger* (1936), Glen Rounds is another lumberjack relating a "true account" and illustrating his account with drawings "made at the scene." These are not tales of the past only, but living, growing folklore.

James Cloyd Bowman was the first to recount the fabulous adventures and deeds of *Pecos Bill, the Greatest Cowboy of All Time* (1937), and no other book about Pecos Bill has superseded this, though there have been other good accounts by Harold Felton and Leigh Peck.

Out of the South came the great Negro railroad-construction worker, John Henry. Irwin Shapiro gave a full-blooded, robust accounting of his exploits in *John Henry and the Double-Jointed Steam-Drill* (1945), and Harold Felton told another version in *John Henry and His Hammer* (1950). *Big Road Walker* (1940) is a less well-known but equally fabulous Negro hero. His story is told by Eula G. Duncan, who heard tall tales about him from a Negro cook in North Carolina.

James Cloyd Bowman wrote *Mike Fink* (1957), the first significant book about the "great hero who was King of the Mississippi before Paul Bunyan even got around to digging the river," and who was known also as Snapping Turtle of the O-hi-o-o, and Snag of the Massassip. Mr. Bowman's imagination had been kindled by stories his mother had told him of his grandparents and their trek across the Alleghenies and down the Ohio. In filling in the background of his story about Mike Fink he delved into old diaries and records of the westward march of his pioneering forebears.

Two books of distinction, worthy to represent America in the mythical but great League of Nations of folklore from all the world are Carl Carmer's *America Sings: Stories and Songs of Our Country's Growing* (1942) and Anne Malcolmson's *Yankee Doodle's Cousins* (1941), in which are collected stories of well-known American legendary heroes and others not so well known but equally fascinating to read about.

In unrhyming tetrameter Ennis Rees gave surprise and punch to a new version of stories about two of the work giants. In *The Song of*

Paul Bunyan and Tony Beaver (1964) he invented a meeting of the great lumberjacks—Paul Bunyan from the north and Tony Beaver from West Virginia—rounding off the two stories as one in an ingenious and pointed way.

William O. Steele developed a new genre: the germ of a folk tale, allowed to grow in his fertile imagination, became a hilarious and convincing tall tale. Among several are *Davy Crockett's Earthquake* (1956) and *Daniel Boone's Echo* (1957).

The vein of stories in America's past has not been exhausted. Books of folk tales have continued to appear, among them *The New England Bean-pot* (1948) by Moritz A. Jagendorf; stories of the Carolina mountains by Ellis Credle, *Tall Tales from the High Hills and Other Stories* (1957); and Conrad Richter's haunting tale of the Pennsylvania Dutch country, *Over the Blue Mountain* (1967), in which mystery, piety, and superstition are closely mingled.

The Art of Storytelling

From the very beginning of organized work with children in public libraries storytelling has had its place. The field was ready for sowing when Marie Shedlock, an English storyteller, came to America at the beginning of the century to give a series of programs of stories in French and English. To one of these matinées came Mary Wright Plummer, of the Pratt Institute Free Library, who was an important force in the developing field of library service and a great and forward-looking person. She became the link that drew Marie Shedlock into that new circle of librarians who wanted to bring books and children together, and Marie Shedlock revived storytelling as an art in America. Her book *The Art of the Story-teller* (1915) has not been surpassed as both a practical and inspiring aid to the storyteller. There is no place here for consideration of the many people who became storytellers as a result of Miss Shedlock's influence, or whose lives were affected directly or indirectly. Certainly the recognition of storytelling as an art had its effect on the whole field of traditional literature of the first half of the twentieth century, that literature which has its roots in the oral tradition, and it has been seen that many folklorists were, first of all, storytellers and many storytellers arrived at the art through the study of folklore.

This development of storytelling as an art resulted in some collections of stories especially significant because they were made by gifted storytellers, who saw the material from the point of view of the oral presentation and brought together from many sources stories of unusual quality.

Ruth Sawyer was one of the young women whose life Miss Shedlock changed. She had grown up knowing the joy of the story told; she had traveled in Ireland and listened to the native storytellers; she had thought of storytelling as folk art, but Miss Shedlock showed it to her as a "living and a creative art," an art she chose to master though she was aware of the long road ahead. Ruth Sawyer's *The Way of the Story-teller* is conclusive proof that she made the art her own, and that she succeeded in her ambition to fuse the folk art that Johanna of her childhood had given her with the creative art that Marie Shedlock showed her in her college days. Eleven splendid stories, which Ruth Sawyer found in several parts of the world, are included in *The Way of the Storyteller* (1942). Her *The Long Christmas* (1941) and *Joy to the World* (1966) are made up of little-known Christmas tales gathered largely from the people of Ireland, Spain, Austria, France, Arabia, and the Isle of Man, and from the Finnish gypsies, and retold with so much wisdom and beauty that the stories glow with the abiding miracle of the Christmas season.

The emphasis on the "tellable" quality in stories, as they are retold and as they are collected in anthologies, shows the completion of the cycle. The oral story has been imprisoned in books, but it has found wings again on the voice of the storyteller.

Hero Stories

Among the early contributions that Padraic Colum made to literature for children was his vigorous retelling of the Iliad and the Odyssey, *The Children's Homer: the Adventures of Odysseus and the Tale of Troy* (1918). He wove the two epics into one account while preserving the unity of each. His *The Voyageurs* (1925) tells the stories of the lost Atlantis, of Maelduin, St. Brendan, and Eric the Red and his sons, as well as the voyages of Columbus, Ponce de León, Vespucci, and the settlers of Virginia. His *The Island of the Mighty* (1924) is a beautiful version of the Mabinogion.

The glimpses Padraic Colum has given of his childhood show the influences that led to the writing of these and others of his distinguished books. He was born in a small Irish town, where his father was master of a workhouse. As a child he had the run of the institution and was often entertained by the gossip and stories of the old people, survivals from an Ireland that no longer existed. He was more interested, though, in the transients who stopped for a night's shelter—wayfarers and tramps, itinerant artisans, ballad singers and pipers.

> As I watched them taking the road of a morning, going I knew not into what mysterious region, the romance of the road was brought home to me and I think it has never quite left my mind. It is on account of these early impressions, I think, that so many of my poems and stories are about wandering people.[1]

[1] Stanley J. Kunitz and Howard Haycraft, eds. *The Junior Book of Authors*, 2d ed., rev. (New York, H. W. Wilson, 1951), p. 76.

In *The Golden Fleece and the Heroes Who Lived before Achilles* (1921) Mr. Colum cast the Greek myths within the framework of the story of Jason and the heroes who set forth in the Argo to seek and find the golden fleece. The skill of the oral storyteller in tightening the stories and often weaving them around a central thread is evident in these stories and in his retellings of the Norse myths, *The Children of Odin: The Children's Book of Northern Myths* (1920).

Ella Young was born in a little village in County Antrim, Ireland. She was a storyteller who had learned the art from the professional storytellers, the *shanache*. She was a scholar working for a distinct Irish culture who knew both the literature of her people and the heroic literature of other lands. And she was a poet. Frances Clarke Sayers spoke of her prose as having a spell upon it, "a real enchantment, that echoes through the mind like remembered music." Ella Young came to the United States as a lecturer in 1925, some years later holding the Phelan Memorial Lectureship on Celtic Mythology and Literature in the University of California at Berkeley. In an appreciation Padraic Colum called her a "druidess":

> For she must have belonged to some such order. She speaks of Celtic times as though she were recalling them. The meaning of certain passages in mythology becomes clear when she speaks of them. From the first time I knew her I have thought of her as one whom some seeker in ancient Celtia would find beside a well on which the sacred hazels dropped and from whom he would learn some of the mysteries.[1]

Her first book, *Celtic Wonder Tales* (1923), embodies the Celtic myth of the Creation. These were classic renderings but did not reveal what Mr. Colum calls her "distinctive way of writing." That, the poetry and rhythmic beauty, her humor, the exquisite descriptions of places, the "pattern that carries the sense of something told to a responding audience, not something written for readers whose presence is not felt," are very present in her two hero stories. *The Wonder Smith and His Son* (1927), the story of the Gubbaun Saor and his son and daughter-in-law, was taken from a minor cycle of Irish storytelling. *The Tangle-Coated Horse* (1929) is the story of the childhood and youth of Fionn Mac-Cumhal, the hero of the Fionn Saga, one of the world's great hero stories. Of these two books Mrs. Sayers wrote:

> They are immediate, not lost in the antiquity of the folklore and legend from which they come. They are filled with the matter of common life: eating and drinking; the conversations of living people; the texture of cloth; the flavor of food; and above all, they

[1] Padraic Colum, *Ella Young, an Appreciation* (New York, Longmans, Green, 1931), pp. 3–4.

are filled with color, the color of jewels, of birds, of flashing fish. Events and people are described as if she watched them from her own doorway, as if she fought with them, as one of them, spear in hand.[1]

In *The Book of the Three Dragons* (1930) Kenneth Morris told stories of gods and men of ancient Wales, particularly of the wanderings of Manawyddan, who won back the stolen treasure of the gods. Based on the Mabinogion, the account here of Manawyddan is much fuller than that in other renditions of the Welsh tales.

Two other important retellings of the great myths are Edith Hamilton's *Mythology* (1942), a presentation of Greek and Norse myths that is both alive and scholarly; and *Stories of the Gods and Heroes* (1940) by Sally Benson, who based her collection on Bulfinch's *The Age of Fable*, selecting the most famous stories and those most appealing to children, skillfully editing or rewriting to give the stories clarity, and managing to keep much of the flavor of the famous book.

Among later retellings of Greek and Roman tales, those by Barbara Leonie Picard stand out for clear, heroic prose. Her *The Odyssey of Homer* (1952) and *The Iliad of Homer* (1960) are among the most immediately appealing to boys and girls of the many retellings. Events move swiftly and with dramatic feeling without sacrificing the power and dignity of the classic translations. Her *Tales of the British People* (1961) and *Celtic Tales* (1964) also show her understanding of the great legends.

In her retelling of the Norse myths, *Thunder of the Gods* (1952), Dorothy Hosford retained the power of the terse stories, yet gave them substance through her strong imaginative re-creation of events. Lillian Smith spoke of the demands such successful re-creation makes on the writer:

> It asks for more than a surface familiarity with the events of the stories. The reteller must also understand the world of ideas in the Eddas, their vast conception of the creation of the world and its ultimate destruction, their powerful dramatic atmosphere which is alive with tremendous events.[2]

She spoke of Mrs. Hosford's telling the stories in the direct manner of the folk tale but also "in a heightened language which recreates the dramatic form of the original stories."[3]

---

[1] Frances Clarke Sayers, *Summoned by Books* (New York, Viking, 1965), p. 133.
[2] Lillian H. Smith, *The Unreluctant Years* (Chicago, American Library Assoc., 1953), p. 75.
[3] *Ibid.*, p. 76.

Dorothy Hosford in 1932 adapted the first two books of William Morris' epic poem, *Sigurd the Volsung*, in her *Sons of the Volsung*, a beautiful prose rendering of the story of the noble king Volsung, of his son Sigmund to whom Odin gave the sword of the Branstock, and of Sigmund's son Sigurd, the greatest of all, who eventually braved the ring of fire to wake Brynhild from her long sleep.

Merriam Sherwood was the first to bring the Spanish romance of *The Cid* to English-speaking children. Her *The Tale of the Warrior Lord* (1930) is based on the edition *El cantar de mio Cid* by Ramón Menéndez Pidal. She deviated from the text only in a few minor instances. In a smooth, clear translation, she presented the color and excitement of the days of romance and chivalry, when Don Rodrigo Díaz de Bivar, although sent into exile by the king, could still fight the Moors in the king's name, and whose friends would help in avenging the insults to his daughters.

Merriam Sherwood's rhythmic translation of *The Song of Roland* (1938) was based on the Oxford Manuscript and tells of the treachery of Ganelon, the death of Roland and Oliver, and the final triumph of Charlemagne over the Saracens.

Mark Powell Hyde in *The Singing Sword* (1930) told the story of Sir Ogier the Dane, of his quarrels with Charlemagne, and of his love for the Princess Clarisse of Britain. Weaving around his heroes imaginary events based on old songs and stories that cluster about the figure of Charlemagne, Mr. Hyde succeeded well in re-creating the atmosphere of the time.

One of the little-known stories of the Charlemagne saga tells of Huon, the Duke of Bordeaux, exiled from France, who after many heroic deeds won his right to return. There is more fairy magic in Huon's story than in most of the romances of chivalry. In *Huon of the Horn* (1951) André Norton told a swiftly moving tale while keeping the flavor of the medieval legends.

The epic of Beowulf has been told numerous times for children, but *The Story of Beowulf* (1933) by Stafford Riggs, with its smooth, beautiful prose, was the first important retelling for children. Dorothy Hosford (1900–1952), in *By His Own Might* (1947), also retold the Beowulf epic with directness and simplicity while maintaining the strength and dignity of the great story.

Rosemary Sutcliff's ability to bring the past to life is evident in her epic stories as well as in her historical fiction, which will be discussed later. Her *Beowulf* (1962) is a brilliant re-creation that gives the story new appeal. Her retelling of the Cuchualin Saga, *The Hound of Ulster* (1963), is equally powerful, but as different in feeling as are the two peoples from whom the stories have sprung. In a note Miss Sutcliff wrote:

However wild the happenings in the Saxon story, its feet remain firmly on the ground; and Beowulf and his companions are recognizably human beings grown to hero-size. But the Celtic tale leaps off into a world completely of the imagination, and the Red Branch Heroes have the blood of the Gods and the Fairy Kind . . . running fiery in their veins.[1]

In *The High Deeds of Finn Mac Cool* (1967) she told the stories of the Fianna that belong to a later period in Ireland:

. . . stories made simply for the delight of story-making, and I have retold them in the same spirit—even adding a flicker or a flourish of my own from time to time—as everyone who has retold them in the past thousand years or so has done before me.[2]

The English poet Ian Serraillier made his own poetic version of the medieval poem *Sir Gawain and the Green Knight*. His *The Challenge of the Green Knight* (1967) is a vigorous re-creation of legend and setting and a subtle portrayal of Gawain.

In her *Deirdre* (1967) Madeleine Polland gave the substance of a novel to the sorrowful tale without losing the atmosphere of legend. She read seven versions of the Celtic legend, seeking "the vein of constancy that runs through every version" on which to base her tale. Deirdre is a completely realized character—cheerful, loyal, deeply loving, with a wisdom and sturdy humor that give credence to her unearthly beauty. The reality makes the tragedy all the more eloquent.

The Story of Gudrun (1967) by E. M. Almedingen is based on the third part of the Epic of Gudrun that was probably composed during the late twelfth and early thirteenth centuries. It is unusual in that there are few magical elements—none in the part retold here—and the love story has a happy ending. Miss Almedingen called it "The most tender of all the Medieval German epics" and probably "one of the very first attempts to introduce realism into romantic literature."

In *Taliesin* (1967) Robert Nye, an English poet and novelist, made comprehensible and often beautiful one of the strange stories of the Mabinogion. The legend of the poet whose origin was magical has in this retelling, humor and beauty. The tales in Mr. Nye's *March Has Horse's Ears* (1967) are fresh, lively retellings of Welsh legends.

Another figure, well known and loved in the Austrian Tyrol but unfamiliar to American boys and girls, was the German folk-tale hero Dietrich of Berne, known in history as Theodoric the Great, king of the Ostrogoths, a controversial figure of the fifth and sixth centuries. While searching for stories in Austria Ruth Sawyer had become interested in

---

[1] Rosemary Sutcliff, *The Hound of Ulster* (New York, Dutton, 1963), p. 7.
[2] Rosemary Sutcliff, *The High Deeds of Finn Mac Cool* (New York, Dutton, 1967), p. 6.

Dietrich as she found him appearing and reappearing in the folk tales of the region that Emmy Mollès translated for her from the Middle High German. Eventually he became the focal figure in *Dietrich of Berne and the Dwarf King Laurin* (1963). Each incident in the book is a complete, well-told story, and the central heroic figure gives sequence and cohesion to the narrative.

From the point of view of oral tradition, the Finnish saga the *Kalevala* is one of the oldest of all, but it was not recorded in print until 1835. Because he loved the old ballads so much, Dr. Elias Lonnrot traveled throughout Finland, visiting the people who remembered them, and collecting a great wealth of traditional material. Out of this he selected the stories that formed a continuous whole for *The Kalevala*, or *The Land of Heroes*, made up of fifty cantos. James Baldwin had used some of the stories with other material for his *The Sampo* (1912), but the first person to give the story of the *Kalevala* to American boys and girls, retaining as far as possible in a prose narrative the character of the original runes, was Babette Deutsch. In *Heroes of the Kalevala* (1940) she told of the great singer and magician Vainamoinen and of his brother, the smith, Ilmarinen, who forged the magic sampo to win the hand of the Maid of Beauty. Her telling is lusty, humorous and swift; it emphasizes the unique atmosphere and vigor of the original and is an important contribution to heroic literature for children.

Although several of the epic stories of the East had been retold for children, Mabel Ashe Beling, in *The Wicked Goldsmith* (1941), was especially successful in bringing them within the understanding of young people without destroying their atmosphere and mystery. Her book is a free rendering of old Hindu legends including two long tales from the epics *The Ramayana* and *The Mahabhárata*. She selected only the main events in the central story of *The Ramayana* to tell "Half a God and All a Hero." "This Hound Hath Loved Me"—one of the world's most beautiful stories—is a selection of such episodes of *The Mahabhárata* as provide enough background to interpret the story of the most heroic of the sons of Pandu, Yudhisthir, and his hound.

Elizabeth Seeger's *The Five Brothers* (1948) is an adaptation of the central story out of *The Mahabhárata*, which tells of the five sons of Pandu and their fight for their kingdom. It is a straightforward rendering of the story and retains much of the atmosphere and quality of the original.

Joseph Gaer's simple, vivid retelling of the stories from the Hindu epic *The Adventures of Rama* (1954) is a dignified introduction to *The Ramayana*. His *The Fables of India* (1955), from *The Panchatantra*, *The Hitopadesa*, and *The Jatakas*, are especially good versions of the ancient "beast fables" for the storyteller.

Anita Feagles' *He Who Saw Everything* (1966) was probably the

first retelling for children—certainly the first in attractive format—of
the ancient story of Gilgamesh, written down in Sumerian cuneiform
three thousand years before Christ. Illustrated with reproductions of
paper sculpture by Xavier González, it is a simpler, more direct, and
less sophisticated telling than Bernarda Bryson's *Gilgamesh, Man's First
Story* (1967). Miss Bryson's style has power and her illustrations are
warm with feeling, glowing with color, and reflect her rich archaeological background.

The White Stag (1937), based on the old tale of the legendary
founding of Hungary, is told by Kate Seredy in dramatic prose and
magnificent drawings. It is the story of the migration of the Huns
and Magyars, led by Bendeguz and his son Attila, to their promised
land. Miss Seredy won the Newbery Medal for *The White Stag*.
Eunice Tietjens told the hero legend of the great Arab chief in *The
Romance of Antar* (1929). Alan Lake Chidsey retold selections from
the ancient Persian epic, the *Shah Namah* of Firdausi in *Rustam, Lion
of Persia* (1930), welding into a connected account those parts of
the epic that deal with Rustam.

Composed not for children but for grownups, often for kings and
nobles, the epic and hero stories possess magic, idealism, romance,
tragedy, and all the complexities of human personality and behavior.
Such stories can be mighty experiences if they reach boys and girls at
the time when heroic drama makes lasting impressions.

Bible Selections

No book has been retold so many times as the Bible, and each period
has had its particular approach to retellings and editions. Although
between 1920 and the mid-sixties many Bible story books were published, probably more "arrangements" were produced in that time than
in any corresponding period. In most of these can be noted the recognition that writers have made of the special beauty of the King James
version as literature for children.

The trend was to select and rearrange sections without changing the
actual text, omitting irrelevant passages so that a continuous whole
might result. The *Little Children's Bible* (1924) and *The Older Children's Bible* (1927), edited by Canon Alexander Nairne, Sir Arthur
Quiller-Couch, and T. R. Glover are good examples of these. *Book of
Books: The King James Version of the English Bible* (1944), abridged
and arranged with editorial comments for younger readers by W. O.
Sypherd, is a distinguished and beautiful book. An excellent reminder,
in this era of new artistic trends, of the unsurpassed contributions of the
Renaissance to interpretations of the Bible are *Seventy Stories of the
Old Testament* (1938), compiled by Helen Slocum Estabrook, and
Scenes from the Life of Jesus in Woodcut (1947) by Susan Nichols
Pulsifer. Both books are illustrated with reproductions from woodcuts

of the fifteenth and sixteenth centuries. The text of *Jesus' Story; a Little New Testament* (1942)—a small book that a child can hold with a sense of loving possession—was selected from the King James version, and the illustrations in color by Maud and Miska Petersham were done with both tenderness and authenticity. *Joseph; the King James Version of a Well-Loved Tale* (1947) was arranged by Elizabeth Yates and illustrated with wood engravings by Nora Unwin to make a distinctive book.

For a handsome book *God and His People* (1966) illustrated by Clark B. Fitz-Gerald with line drawings washed with a golden tan, Harold Bassage selected the more colorful and important stories from the Old Testament, setting the King James text in short lines like poetry. Brief prefaces and transitional paragraphs give the chronicle cohesion so that the reader can know the impact of the majestic story and perhaps be led to the complete Bible.

Characteristic of this period are retellings by artists rather than by writers and theologians. The King James text was used in each instance in the following books unusual for their illustrations: Helen Sewell's *A First Bible* (1934), a selection of the stories that have always been favorites with children, with dignified, beautiful illustrations; Dorothy Lathrop's *Animals of the Bible* (1937), with authentic pictures of the flora and fauna of Bible lands that reveal the artist's love of animals; Maud and Miska Petersham's *The Christ Child* (1931), made after several months spent in Palestine. The reverence and beauty of their pictures, many of them in full color, make this one of the loveliest of interpretations of the Christmas story for little children.

In *The Lord Is My Shepherd* (1949) Nancy Barnhart deviated only slightly from the King James text to tell seventeen carefully selected stories from the Old Testament and a short version of the New Testament. Her many striking drawings were made of the actual scenes in Egypt and Palestine and offer an inspiring invitation to the Bible stories.

To his *Stories from the Bible* (1929), Walter de la Mare brought deep appreciation: "remembrance of what the matchless originals in the Bible itself meant to me when I was a child is still fresh and vivid in mind, and these renderings are little more than an attempt to put that remembrance as completely as I can into words."[1] His endeavor was to remove some of the difficulties, while keeping as close to the text as possible.

Saints and Biblical Heroes

Eleanor Farjeon told the stories of the lives of some well-known saints and others less familiar in her *Ten Saints* (1936), giving them human-

[1] Walter de la Mare, *Stories from the Bible*, Introduction to the American edition, p. 10.

ity as well as saintliness. Following each story is a poem that expresses the essence of beauty, humor, and drama in each life. Lucid, strong illustrations by Helen Sewell reflect the sunny clarity of Miss Farjeon's storytelling.

Padraic Colum's *The Legend of Saint Columba* (1935) reads with the flow of poetry and the drama of a hero tale. It is a story of sixth century Ireland caught in the tide of change from barbarism to civilization, and of Colum-cille who played a part in this change. Mr. Colum drew his story from the voluminous sixteenth century work of Manus O'Donnell, who had collected everything written about the saint in Latin or Irish and all the poetry attributed to him. Irish folklore, the rigorous precepts of the early church, humor, heroism, and sacrifice are woven through the story.

There have been many biographies of biblical characters but few achieve the stature of Katherine Shippen's *Moses* (1949). She realized in it the full dignity and beauty of the Old Testament story of the Exodus and the reality of the character of Moses. *Luke's Quest* (1947) by Caroline Dale Snedeker tells of the adventures of the young Luke and shows his spiritual growth as he embraced Christianity. Mrs. Snedeker used Luke's decision to write the life of Jesus and his search for information from the people who had known Him, to illuminate the times in which Jesus lived.

The Literature of the Religions of the World

Ruth Smith, who worked with Robert Ballou on *The Bible of the World* (1939), compiled *The Tree of Life* (1942), a book of extraordinary power and beauty, made up of selections from the literature of the world's religions. In them are to be found the ethical concepts of mankind—the source from which have flowed the streams of traditional literature: folklore, homely, wise and human; mythology and legendary and epic tales, grand and heroic, fed by the wisdom, philosophy, and deep religious feeling of all the ages.

A number of anthologies of selections from the world religions followed *The Tree of Life*, but none was so comprehensive. Most of them combined unusual illustrations with brief quotations to point up the diversity of expression of unusual religious and ethical thoughts. Such a book is Natalia Belting's *The Sun Is a Golden Earring* (1962), containing the thoughts of men in many parts of the world when they first looked in wonder at the heavens. Poetic drawings, rich with emotion and atmosphere, by Bernarda Bryson fill the pages. "Tales of Beginnings" from Siberia, India, Africa, Burma, the Philippines, and Indian tribes of North and South America make up *The Earth Is on a Fish's Back* (1965) by Miss Belting with harmonious line drawings by Esta Nesbitt.

Attempts of numerous artists to illustrate abstract religious concepts have resulted in interesting, sometimes striking, books, introducing readers through the attractive presentations to the stimulation of philosophical thoughts and, perhaps, inviting them to explore further.

Introductions to Great Literature

Marchette Chute wrote *Stories from Shakespeare* (1956) in the hope of preventing young people from dismissing Shakespeare's plays as too difficult to read for pleasure. The book includes a synopsis of each of thirty-six plays with explanations of the intentions and points of view of the characters. Brief though the story summaries are, they carry a great deal of the humor and emotion. Quotations are interspersed to give a hint of the beauty and strength of the language. In her introduction alone, Miss Chute did a service to young people. Her enthusiasm for Shakespeare and her explanation of why "in all the world of storytelling, his is the greatest name" is an invitation to read her book, which, in turn, is a nearly irresistible invitation to read the plays.

Don Quixote by Miguel Cervantes Savaadra, Shakespeare's contemporary, was surely as quickly found by children as were such other books, not written for them, as *Robinson Crusoe* and *Gulliver's Travels*. Many retellings of the great novel have been made for children, one of the most inviting being *Exploits of Don Quixote* (1959), retold by James Reeves, with illustrations by Edward Ardizzone. The book is closer to the original Spanish text than some others and the twenty-one chapters representing as many exploits are well selected from the large number in the original. Mr. Reeves's enjoyment of *Don Quixote* and his appreciation of Quixote's embodiment—even though an exaggeration— of a great idea, are evident in the vitality, humor, and integrity of the retelling. In his introduction, Mr. Reeves writes:

> Knight and squire represent two sides of human nature—the desire to lead and the desire to serve; the need for a spiritual aim and the need for material well-being; the balance between madness and common sense, illusion and reality, courage and prudence. Cervantes, in creating these two complementary figures, not only invented a tale of lasting charm, pathos and humor, he made a unique contribution to humanity's knowledge of itself.

Anne Malcolmson, concerned by the numbers of well-read people who never became acquainted with Chaucer's writing, provided *A Taste of Chaucer: Selections from The Canterbury Tales* (1964). Excerpts from the Prologue and Tales in modern poetic transcription retain rhythms, rhymes, and cadences of the original. Commentaries introduce the selections, and notes and glossary give explanations of vocabulary and allusions. The result proved of interest to many young people and their elders and dispelled any illusion that Chaucer did not belong to the present.

In *Saint George and the Dragon* (1963) Sandol Stoddard Warburg presented a translation, only very slightly shortened and simplified, of the legend of the Red Cross Knight from Edmund Spenser's *The Faerie Queene*. In her introduction Mrs. Warburg spoke of hoping not only to share the magnificent old legend with many new readers but to show that:

> poetry itself cannot be translated. It has worlds and worlds of special meanings in its sounds and its silences, in its shapes and arrangements and rhythms. Only the poet can tell us all he knows; we must learn how to hear it. Therefore I have tried in this book to move very gradually from the sounds and rhythmic patterns which are already familiar to us all toward those special and much more beautiful constructions which are Spenser's own.

Handsome in format, with initial letters of the stanzas and Pauline Baynes's appropriate, magnificent drawings in red, the book is an example of a distinguished, exciting invitation to great literature.

Such books as the two above, considered experimental at the time of their publication, introduced to children and adults pleasure they might easily have missed. In a period when the inferiority of mass publications often insulted the taste and intelligence of young people, introductions to great literature were especially important and very encouraging.

Bibliography

Botkin, B. A., ed. Introduction to *A Treasury of American Folklore*. New York, Crown, 1944.

Carmer, Carl. Introduction to *America Sings*. New York, A. A. Knopf, 1942.

———— Foreword to *Indian Tales* by Jaime de Angulo. New York, Hill and Wang, 1953.

———— and Mary Gould Davis, *Folklore, Two Articles Reprinted from Comptom's Pictured Encyclopedia*. Chicago, F. E. Compton, 1950.

Colum, Padraic. *Ella Young, an Appreciation*. New York, Longmans, Green, 1931.

———— *Story Telling, New and Old*. New York, Macmillan, 1961.

Colwell, Eileen H. *Eleanor Farjeon*, a Walck Monograph. New York, Henry Z. Walck, 1962.

Gág, Wanda. *Growing Pains*. New York, Coward-McCann, 1940.

Haviland, Virginia. *Ruth Sawyer*, a Walck Monograph. New York, Henry Z. Walck, 1965.

Jakobson, Roman. "Folkloristic Commentary" in *Russian Fairy Tales*. Translated by Norbert Guterman. New York, Pantheon, 1945.

Reeves, James. Introduction to Cervantes' *Exploits of Don Quixote*. Retold by James Reeves. New York, Henry Z. Walck, 1960.

Sawyer, Ruth. *The Way of the Storyteller*. New York, Viking Press, 1942.

Sayers, Frances Clarke. *Summoned by Books*. New York, Viking Press, 1965.

Scott, Alma. *Wanda Gág, the Story of an Artist*. Minneapolis, University of Minnesota Press, 1949.

Shedlock, Marie L. *The Art of the Story-teller.* 3d ed. New York, Dover, 1951.

Undset, Sigrid, ed. "The Adventure Story of the Folk Tale" in *True and Untrue and Other Norse Tales.* New York, A. A. Knopf, 1945.

Warburg, Sandol Stoddard. Introduction to *Saint George and the Dragon.* Retold by Sandol Stoddard Warburg from "The Legend of the Red Cross Knight" by Edmund Spenser. Boston, Houghton Mifflin, 1963.

Young, Ella. *Flowering Dusk: Things Remembered Accurately and Inaccurately.* New York, Longmans, Green, 1945.

· 3 ·

Worlds Without Boundaries

Fancy is to the imagination what the seed is to the tree. Let it lie in barren ground and it will not grow. But nourish it and care for it through the years and it will grow into imagination, as dear a possession for the man as fancy is for the child. He who lacks imagination lives but half a life. He has his experiences, he has his facts, he has his learning. But do any of these really live unless touched by the magic of imagination? So long as the road is straight he can see down it and follow it. But imagination looks round the turns and gazes far off into the distance on either side. And it is imagination that walks hand in hand with vision.

—PAUL FENIMORE COOPER[1]

The goal of storytellers . . . consists of fostering in the child, at whatever cost, compassion and humaneness—this miraculous ability of man to be disturbed by another being's misfortunes, to feel joy about another being's happiness, to experience another's fate as one's own . . . to teach the child in his early years to participate with concern in the lives of imaginary people and animals, and to make sure that in this way he will escape the narrow frame of his egocentric interests and feelings.

—KORNEI CHUKOVSKY[2]

The great modern fairy tales, even those that are most original in concept and style, have been, almost invariably, written by people deeply imbued with traditional lore. A firm grounding in the old tales is evident in the stories that follow the patterns and use the devices of traditional fairy tales. But the writers of all the most distinguished fairy tales—fantasies, wonder stories, or whatever one chooses to call them—are wise in the authentic lore of the ancient storytellers.

[1] "On Catching a Child's Fancy," *The Three Owls, Third Book* by Anne Carroll Moore (New York, Coward-McCann, Inc., 1931), pp. 56-57.
[2] Kornei Chukovsky, *From Two to Five* (Berkeley and Los Angeles, University of California Press, 1963), p. 138.

Fantasy is probably the field of writing for children in which more people try and more fail than any other. A merely superficial acquaintance with a few of the familiar fairy tales invites a writer new to children's books to try his hand, and the seeming lack of restraint while taking off on imaginative forays is tempting. The results are often dull, unconvincing parodies. Wisdom that has drawn nourishment from the deep consciousness of the human race and wide knowledge and understanding of the "real" world, linked with a vital imagination and storytelling skill, are requisite for the writing of successful fantasy. Its theme is built around fundamental truths, but its protagonists are often creatures of another world, the settings are over the border of reality, and time, as measured in our everyday lives, does not exist; yet the stories must be logical, events must follow in proper sequence, the plot must build up to a climax, and the outcome must be reasonable.

Margery Bianco, in an essay, "Our Youngest Critics," is very much to the point:

> Whereas if true invention lies anywhere it lies in making the utmost use of very definitely limited means, and imagination which does not spring from some correlation of ideas is apt to be just about as interesting as delirium.[1]

And in her tribute to Walter de la Mare she said,

> Imagination is only another word for the interpretation of life. It is through imagination that a child makes his most significant contacts with the world about him, that he learns tolerance, pity, understanding, and the love for all created things.[2]

It is not surprising then that authors of great fantasy are so often poets, the writers who are at once the most perceptive and the most disciplined.

Some Poet-Storytellers

The work of two great English storytellers, Walter de la Mare and Eleanor Farjeon, spans most of the first half of the twentieth century. Both were poets, story writers, anthologists. Both had rare understanding of children. But their poems and stories for children were drawn from the depths of their own natures, each unique and unmistakable.

In addition to his long fairy tale, *The Three Mulla-Mulgars*, discussed earlier, Walter de la Mare (1873–1956) wrote twenty original stories and retold sixty folk and fairy tales. Most of his original

---

[1] Margery Bianco, "Our Youngest Critics," in Anne Carroll Moore and Bertha Mahony Miller, eds., *Writing and Criticism* (Boston, The Horn Book, 1951), p. 50.
[2] Margery Bianco, "De la Mare," in *Writing and Criticism*, pp. 70–71.

stories are to be found in his *Collected Stories for Children*, published in England in 1947. In the United States the stories were published in *Broomsticks and Other Tales* (1925) and *A Penny a Day* (1960). The stories contain witches, wizards, and ghosts, enchantments, transformations, and spells of many kinds; but, besides the fairy-tale devices they have elements that turn them into experiences that are more mystical than magical. Some of the stories are eerie, all of them have shadows that make the light places all the more dazzling. They demand of their readers imaginations strong enough—to paraphrase one of his characters—to know that real stories are better than true.

One of the most beautiful of his original tales, "The Old Lion," was published as a single book and called *Mr. Bumps and His Monkey* (1942), illustrated by Dorothy Lathrop. It expresses more warmly than any other, perhaps, his appreciation of "living creatures of every estate that during our own brief stay on this earth share it with us—their life, wonder, mystery, and benefactions."[1] In her pictures Dorothy Lathrop showed how truly she shared the storyteller's perfect understanding of the wistful spirit of "the little captive monkey in the alien world of man." Her introduction closes with:

> I wonder if this perfect story, this humorous and poignant tale of a little super monkey, is not as well a clearsighted glimpse of the spirit of any creature as it tries without bitterness to adapt itself to our wishes and our strange, incomprensible ways.[2]

Most of the tales in *Animal Stories* (1940) and all of them in *Told Again* (1927)—published in 1959 under the title *Tales Told Again*—are retellings of traditional stories. Mr. de la Mare's introduction to *Animal Stories* is both scholarly and delightful, full of information and insight into old stories of all kinds, especially animal tales, and into human imaginations and feelings, as well.

> Marvellous, indeed, is man's Imagination. It ranges this way and that in Time, and to the very ends of the universe. With love and faith to aid him, it would save him from most of his miseries. With it, and with his own desire for goodness, he could, by the mercy of God, build his world anew. In their own primitive, queer, various, exquisitely simple, or rich and fascinating fashion, these ancient tales build *their* world anew. But not a syllable of their magic will be audible unless the right kind of ear is bent to attend to their spell.[3]

---

[1] Leonard Clark, *Walter de la Mare* (New York, Henry Z. Walck, 1961), p. 70.
[2] Dorothy Lathrop, Introduction to *Mr. Bumps and His Monkey* (Chicago, John C. Winston, 1942), p. v.
[3] Walter de la Mare, *Animal Stories* (New York, Scribner, 1940), p. lvi.

Tales Told Again includes many of the most graceful and romantic of the old fairy tales. In retelling them, Mr. de la Mare altered none of the essentials of plot or character but by filling in some of the backgrounds, giving more personality to the people, whether princesses or swineherds, he added sparkle and humor to make them seem like new stories. His writing always has life, whether in a retelling of an original tale, an essay, or merely notes in his remarkable anthologies.

Leonard Clark wrote in his monograph on the poet-storyteller:

Walter de la Mare was a writer whose voice was so personal and whose style so wonderfully matched that voice, they cannot accurately be torn apart. But the craftsmanship is there as well as the shining quality and unearthly loveliness; the glow of the fire as well as the fire itself.[1]

Eleanor Farjeon (1881–1965) was born in England to an exciting, talented family. Her father was Benjamin Farjeon, a successful novelist; her mother was Margaret Jefferson, daughter of the great American actor, Joseph Jefferson. She claimed that she had no education except what her father's library provided, but that library was extensive. She and her three brothers were surrounded with music as well as books. The theater was an important part of their lives even in early childhood, and continuously in and out of their home were family friends and acquaintances—clever, famous, vital people. Throughout her childhood, writing was as natural an occupation as reading, almost as unconscious as breathing, and she was stimulated by the encouragement and criticism of her father.

The story of her rich childhood and much about her remarkable parents are told in the beautiful first volume of her autobiography, *A Nursery in the Nineties* (1935). She never gave up this self-indulgence, as she referred to her writing. Not to write was a privation. All manner of creations poured joyously from her imagination. Among them were rhymes and singing games, poetry, plays, retellings—of Canterbury tales (*Tales of Chaucer*, 1932), of heroic stories out of history and legend (*Mighty Men*, 1926), an introduction in prose and poetry to saints (*Ten Saints*, 1936), and many stories, especially fairy tales. She was a radiant person. Warmth, sunshine, and gaiety fill her stories and touch everything she wrote.

The Little Book Room (1956), a collection of Eleanor Farjeon's favorites among her own stories, is an excellent introduction to her work. The book is called by the name she gave as a child to the dusty little room that "gathered to itself a motley crew of strays and vagabonds, outcasts from the ordered shelves below," where she used to

[1] Leonard Clark, *op. cit.*, p. 75.

love to go to read "old plays and histories, and old romances; superstitions, legends and what are called the Curiosities of Literature."

> No wonder that many years later, when I came to write books myself, they were a muddle of fiction and fact and fantasy and truth. I have never quite succeeded in distinguishing one from the other, as the tales in this book that were born of that dust will show. Seven maids with seven brooms, sweeping for half-a-hundred years, have never managed to clear my mind of its dust of vanished temples and flowers and kings, the curls of ladies, the sighing of poets, the laughter of lads and girls: those golden ones who, like chimney-sweepers, must all come to dust in some little bookroom or other—and sometimes, by luck, come again for a moment to light.[1]

In a foreword to the first American edition of *Martin Pippin in the Apple Orchard* (1922) J. D. Beresford wrote of reading the book in manuscript and being "transported into a world of sunlight, of gay inconsequence, of emotional surprise, a world of poetry, delight, and humor."[2] Anne Carroll Moore of the New York Public Library knew and admired Miss Farjeon and had written with great appreciation of the book. Not, however, until *Martin Pippin in the Apple Orchard* was reprinted in 1952 was it considered in England as a children's book. *Italian Peepshow and Other Tales* (1926) was the second of Miss Farjeon's books to be published in the United States. *Martin Pippin in the Daisy Field* (1938) was unquestionably written for children. In it Martin Pippin tells stories to the six children of the six milk maids to whom he had told stories in *Martin Pippin in the Apple Orchard*—sunny stories also, full of humor and poetry, and the springtime freshness of Sussex meadows. Yet each story is remarkably different from the others, with characters who remain in the memory: Elsie Piddock, skipping forever on Mt. Caburn; Tom Cobble and Ooney, making use of their fairy tricks in a circus; the Long Man of Wilmington, who still gleams white on a Sussex hillside; and a number of others quite as strange or mysterious, as well as the little girls of the daisy field.

For all their "gay inconsequence" the import of the stories is never literal; sometimes it is so elusive that the reader's pleasure is less in the sense than in the essence. In a tribute to Eleanor Farjeon Naomi Lewis wrote, "The best of her poetry possibly lay in her prose which—though

[1] Eleanor Farjeon, *The Little Book-Room* (London, Oxford University Press, 1956), pp. viii, ix–x.
[2] J. D. Beresford, Foreword to *Martin Pippin in the Apple Orchard* by Eleanor Farjeon (New York, F. A. Stokes, 1922), p. vii.

she claimed to know no rules—had something of the inner tensions, the design and swift moves of poetry."[1]

Less rarefied and sparkling with nonsense is her novel-length dilation of "Tom-Tit Tot," *The Silver Curlew* (1954). That and *The Glass Slipper* (1956), a tender, magical expansion of "Cinderella," were written first as plays, and in the rewriting they retain the continuing movement and the lively, and in the case of the first, the comic, conversations. Frances Clarke Sayers characterized Eleanor Farjeon's world as having "little whimsy in it, but great magic and stout humor, wit, and free-running nonsense," and a "comfortable practicality" to the whole of it.[2]

The New Book of Days (1961), first published in London in 1941, is an example of Eleanor Farjeon's powers as an anthologist. It is not, however, a collection of pieces from other authors. Verse and proverbs are her own, and brief essays and stories and bits of history from many sources were retold, transfigured by her imagination and her exuberance. "A moment of interest may create a lifetime of curiosity," she wrote, and gave to children in this book three hundred and sixty-six "moments of interest." Until her death at eighty-four she stayed in tune with life, enjoying her friends, conversing, reading, discovering, and writing. Two anthologies collected and edited with the collaboration of William Mayne, *A Cavalcade of Kings* and *A Cavalcade of Queens* (both 1965), are unconventional, creative works in arrangement, selection, and the brief introductions to the stories. Her last book, *Mr. Garden* (1966), shows unabated her imagination and her ability to tell a subtle story and reaffirms her abiding joy in life.

Ella Young's *The Unicorn with Silver Shoes* (1932) is the tale of Ballor's Son, who wanted the things that belong only to fairyland, of Angus the ever young, of the Pooka, the tricky little spirit that could take any shape it fancied, and of Flame of Joy, who guided Ballor's Son through fairyland. Miss Young told the story to children who liked tales about "Ogres and Magicians and Strange Beasts," and Ballor's Son delighted them because of his very human willfulness. It should be shared orally to reveal in full the poetry in it, the freshness and wit.

To Carl Sandburg (1878–1967), who found poetry in all aspects of America—its vast plains, high mountains, blue seas, and its tall, smoky cities—American folklore was an absorbing interest. His fairy tales are a child-hearted poet's response to America, colored by his native enjoyment of absurdity and his desire to give pleasure to his own children. In *Rootabaga Stories* (1922) are tales like no others. They are nonsense

---

[1] Naomi Lewis, ed., Introduction to *A Book for Eleanor Farjeon* (New York, Henry Z. Walck, 1966), p. 8.
[2] Frances Clarke Sayers, *Summoned by Books* (New York, Viking, 1965), p. 126.

and they are poetry. They are full of words that sputter and splash and roll and pop. The characters are as graceful as the White Horse Girl and the Blue Wind Boy, as pretty as Wing Tip the Spick from the Village of Cream Puffs, and as absurd as Jason Squiff, the Cistern Cleaner, with his popcorn hat, popcorn mittens and popcorn shoes, or Henry Hagglyhoagly, who stood under Susan Slackentwist's window and played the guitar with his mittens on. They are stories that should be told or read aloud to keep from losing the fun of the alliteration or the response of the audience, for, like poetry, they stimulate creative listening. These stories showed that by a poet's alchemy familiar scenes and things out of the heart of America, as well as those out of distant times and places, possessed fun and enchantment.

Monica Shannon showed this, too, in her *California Fairy Tales* (1926) that drew their magic from the sunlight and color, the mountains and deserts of California.

Elizabeth Coatsworth's work spans more than forty years. Hers was one of the careers influenced by the first director of a department for children's books in a publishing house. Miss Coatsworth had published several volumes of poetry when Louise Seaman of Macmillan, a Vassar College classmate, interested her in writing for children. Her first story, *The Cat and the Captain* (1927), gave little indication of her potential craftsmanship as a writer, her creative strength as a storyteller, or the rich sources from which she could draw. Slight though the book was, it was the beginning of her career as a writer for children. Only three years later *The Cat Who Went to Heaven* (1930) was published. In her childhood she had traveled with her family through Egypt and much of Europe, as a young woman she had lived in the Orient. With her husband, Henry Beston, she traveled in Mexico and Yucatan and was well acquainted with the southwestern United States. Although later she became identified especially with New England, her imagination has been illumined also by her memories of many far places. *The Cat Who Went to Heaven* glows with the serenity of Japan and sympathy for a religion that esteems even the lowly animals. In it Elizabeth Coatsworth's power as a storyteller declared itself and for it she received the Newbery Medal. Also drawn from her knowledge of the Orient are the tales in *Cricket and the Emperor's Son* (1932), which have the atmosphere of Chinese and Japanese legends.

Many books followed, proving her an able as well as a prolific writer: adult books and poetry, simple stories with familiar settings for the youngest readers, novels for older boys and girls, and historical fiction with various settings. The least of them are well-constructed, lucidly written, appealing stories. The best are extraordinary literary creations. One of the most beautiful of these is *The Enchanted, an Incredible Tale*

(1951). In northern Maine is a region where a stream, known as the Upper and Lower Enchanted, flows through the forest, disappears underground, and then appears again. Here young David Ross came to know the lighthearted Perdry family, and here he had to accept enchantment with his love for Molly Perdry. The story has a mysterious magic yet it is entirely natural. The Maine woods and villages are clearly seen, and the atmosphere is pervaded by joy in the simple act of living, in the continuity of the cycle of seasons, and in life itself. The measure of the book's appeal is not by age or background but by the freshness of the reader's imagination.

From France came Antoine de Saint-Exupéry's *The Little Prince* (1943) at a time when the world had suffered great spiritual as well as material devastation. It is wise, simple, as uncluttered as the landscape of the African desert with the one star over it where the little prince was first, and where he was last seen. It speaks to every age with an individual message for each reader. " 'All men have the stars . . . but they are not the same things for different people.' " And it must be read with the heart as well as the mind. It has been called a fairy tale for grownups, but children are often more capable of catching its elusive message than are grown people:

> I raised the bucket to his lips. He drank, his eyes closed. It was as sweet as some special festival treat. This water was indeed a different thing from ordinary nourishment. Its sweetness was born of the walk under the stars, the song of the pulley, the effort of my arms. It was good for the heart, like a present. When I was a little boy, the lights of the Christmas tree, the music of the Midnight Mass, the tenderness of smiling faces, used to make up, so, the radiance of the gifts I received.[1]

Randall Jarrell (1914–1965) was well known as a poet and literary critic when he turned to writing for children: *The Gingerbread Rabbit* (1963) and *The Bat-Poet* (1964). *The Bat-Poet* is a gentle, satiric commentary on poets and their audiences, but the author's conscious effort to write for children is evident. The book does show, however, his tenderness and graceful style that make *The Animal Family* (1965) one of his most poetic achievements.

The Animal Family has been compared with *The Little Prince* because it too has the beauty and impact of poetry in the art form of the fairy tale, and because each reader finds an individual import in a story that is universal in emotion, yet personal in meaning. It tells of the hunter who lived alone in his log house near the sea.

---

[1] Antoine de Saint-Exupéry, *The Little Prince* (New York, Harcourt, 1943), pp. 78–79.

And when at evening, past the dark blue shape of a far-off island, the sun sank under the edge of the sea like a red world vanishing, the hunter saw it all, but there was no one to tell what he had seen.[1]

In time the mermaid came to live with him, and then a bear cub, a lynx kitten, finally a little boy whom the sea had cast ashore, and the family was complete. It is a story warm with the need of earth's creatures for each other; disparities and adjustments are only hinted at; in the concept of wholeness they are of little importance. But very clear is the mosaic of realities—clumsy, clever, humorous, tender—that make a home where each member, often startlingly different from the others, finds completeness, as though life without the others would not be life at all.

Tistou of the Green Thumbs (1958) by Maurice Druon, a distinguished French writer, translated by Humphrey Hare from the original French edition of 1957, is an allegory laced with humor and satire. Tistou's father, an eminent manufacturer, was dismayed when the little boy came home from school with a note, "Sir, your son is not like other people. We cannot keep him here." But Tistou had a wonderful talent; he could make flowers grow anywhere—in a hospital, a zoo, even among the guns of his father's armaments factory. Very young children recognize Tistou as a believable and enchanting companion, but there are no age limits to the appreciation of the humor and surprise of the unusual story.

A more somber tale, *Knee-Deep in Thunder* (1967) by Sheila Moon, takes the reader on a mysterious journey into another world. Accompanying Maris are two beetles, a red ant, a caterpillar, and a mouse (all of a size to be companionable), and, eventually, a boy. "Each one seemed to have been mysteriously drawn from his usual struggle toward some unknown goal." The author is a poet, a writer on Navajo mythology, and has been a student at the C. G. Jung Institute in Zurich. Her knowledge of young people as a practicing psychotherapist and as a teacher might have overburdened the adventures with symbols and purpose. But the story is a strong one. It is told in the first person, almost as though Maris were relating the adventures years later with the perspective of time giving her clear insights into the importance of the events and the reason for her need to realize her identity. "You cannot know who you are unless you are contained in some way that gives you shape." The story may make the thoughtful young person more patient with his own needs and his sense of inadequacy.

[1] Randall Jarrell, *The Animal Family* (New York, Pantheon, 1965), p. 8.

Other Worlds

J. R. R. Tolkien has spoken of the writer of fantasy as a "sub-creator," not making "a comment on life" but making a "Secondary World" which your mind can enter. Inside it, what he relates is "true"; it accords with the laws of that world. You therefore believe it, while you are, as it were, "inside." Probably no writer of fantasy has created more completely—in every detail—another world. J. R. R. Tolkien is a British philologist, retired Merton Professor of English Language and Literature at Pembroke College, Oxford, and a former teacher at the University of Leeds. His essay "On Fairy-Stories" is, according to C. S. Lewis, "the most important contribution to the subject that anyone has yet made."

His first book, *The Hobbit*, was published in the United States in 1938. Like many before and since, Professor Tolkien told his story to entertain a young family, but his children were much more fortunate than most. His lifetime study of the literature and legend of the early Middle Ages and before had deepened his imagination and given him a rich store of knowledge of traditional lore and, through that, of man himself in the times when his thoughts were expressed in song and story instead of books.

The hobbit is a small, home-loving creature ("smaller than dwarves . . . but very much larger than lilliputians") but the hero of this story, Bilbo Baggins, is a hobbit with a slight strain of fairy in him, for his mother had been a Took. ("It had always been said that long ago one or other of the Tooks had married into a fairy family . . . certainly there was still something not entirely hobbitlike about them, and once in a while members of the Took-clan would go and have adventures.") It is because of this ever so slight leaning toward adventure that Bilbo is persuaded to leave the comfort of his hobbit-hole to join the dwarves in their attempt to regain the treasure that Smaug, the dragon, had stolen from their forefathers. The quest is fraught with danger and adventures of all kinds, the characters reach heights—and depths—of nobility and selfishness, courage and greed, and set against the drama of heroic emotions is the commonplace little hobbit, matter-of-fact, often thoroughly tired of battles and adventures but decent, brave when he has to be, and never one to let his friends down, no matter what it might cost him.

The Hobbit is as convincing as though it were a bit of history out of a time when the world was younger—"in the quiet of the world, when there was less noise and more green. . . ." Of it M. S. Crouch in *The Junior Bookshelf* said, "I know of no children's book published in the last twenty-five years of which I could more confidently predict that it will be read in the twenty-first century." And later,

Warmth and nobility and lofty imagination are not common qualities of modern writers of fantasy, most of whom prefer to chase the frail moth of whimsy. These qualities, however, produce in *The Hobbit* a story which is profoundly imaginative and yet firmly based on truth. It is a convincing answer to those who find fantasy "escapist." Here is no escape from, but an interpretation of reality.[1]

Soon after *The Hobbit* was written, Professor Tolkien began a sequel, but as it progressed, "the story was drawn irresistibly toward the older world, and became an account, as it were, of its end and passing away before its beginning and middle had been told." There were some references to the older matter in *The Hobbit* and glimpses,

> that had arisen unbidden of things higher or deeper or darker than its surface. . . . The discovery of the significance of these glimpses and of their relation to the ancient histories revealed the Third Age and its culmination in the War of the Ring.[2]

The composition of the trilogy *The Lord of the Rings* went on slowly and intermittently over a period of thirteen years. The chapters telling of the journey of Frodo to Mordor, which eventually became Book IV, were written and sent as a serial to Professor Tolkien's son, then in South Africa with the R.A.F. Because the Second World War and major world changes had been taking place at the same time that work was progressing on the three books, many people tried to find inner meaning in the trilogy. Its author refuted any such intention:

> It is neither allegorical nor topical. As the story grew it put down roots (into the past) and threw out unexpected branches; but its main theme was settled from the outset by the inevitable choice of the Ring as the link between it and *The Hobbit*.[3]

Although *The Fellowship of the Ring* (1954), *The Two Towers* (1955), and *The Return of the King* (1956), which make up the trilogy *The Lord of the Rings*, were written for the author's own satisfaction with "little hope that other people would be interested" in it, other people were interested in it, adults chiefly, until it was discovered by the children who had enjoyed *The Hobbit* and who wanted to know more about these ancient people who had only the "everyday sort" of magic about them. As growing-up children read and reread the trilogy, word

---

[1] M. S. Crouch, "Another Don in Wonderland," *The Junior Bookshelf*, Vol. 14, No. 2 (March, 1950), pp. 51, 52.
[2] J. R. R. Tolkien. Foreword to *The Fellowship of the Ring* (New York, Ballantine Books, 1965), p. viii.
[3] *Ibid.*, p. x.

of its fascination spread to college campuses where young people may have found in it, besides excellent storytelling, what Edmund Fuller spoke of as a special quality of fantasy:

> The integrity and courage of imaginary beings in their world may sustain our integrity and courage in the face of mundane, pressing dilemmas in our own living.[1]

In an appreciation of Mr. Tolkien's work, Loren Eiseley wrote:

> Beginning with *The Hobbit* . . . , we pass from the fascinating child's tale to the great orchestra of *The Lord of the Rings*, in which a whole Secondary World is created and successfully sustained through three large volumes.
>
> These are sure to remain Tolkien's life work, and are certainly destined to outlast our time. They stand as a major creative act, and it is not without significance that Tolkien tells us in *Tree and Leaf* that his full taste for fairy stories, using the term in its highest sense, arose during the war. He knows better than most that the adult mind has, if anything, greater need of fantasy than that of the child, greater need of consolation . . .[2]

Long after Clive Staples Lewis (1898–1963) had become famous as England's distinguished Christian apologist, as a poet, and as author of scholarly literary, philosophical, and religious books, and powerfully written fantasies for adults, he referred to a children's book he was writing "in the tradition of E. Nesbit." At that time he was at work on *The Lion, the Witch and the Wardrobe* (1950), which had been in his mind as early as 1938. It was followed by six other books. Except that ordinary children of the first book step over the border of reality into an imaginary world, the stories have little resemblance to those of E. Nesbit. Nor do they reflect the atmosphere in the fairy tales of George Macdonald, whose *Phantastes* Mr. Lewis had read as a young man and whose writings from then on profoundly influenced his religious and literary development. All his life C. S. Lewis was an omnivorous reader and undoubtedly events and scenes out of his reading etched themselves on his memory. But any of his ideas, whether drawn from memory, imagination, or intellect, were, in his own writing, transmuted into something new with his distinctive mark upon them.

In a definitive essay he spoke of "writing a children's story because a children's story is the best art form for something you have to say."

---

[1] Edmund Fuller, "Speaking of Books," *The New York Times Book Review*, Jan. 12, 1964.

[2] Loren Eiseley, "The Elvish Art of Enchantment," *The Horn Book*, Vol. 41 (Aug., 1965), p. 365.

Indeed everything in the story should arise from the whole cast of the author's mind. We must write for children out of those elements in our own imagination which we share with children. . . . The matter of our story should be a part of the habitual furniture of our minds . . . We must meet children as equals in that area of our nature where we are their equals. Our superiority consists partly in commanding other areas, and partly (which is more relevant) in the fact that we are better at telling stories than they are. The child as reader is neither to be patronized nor idolized.[1]

In his seven children's books the world of Narnia is created, a world not of our own universe but one just as clearly seen. The reader lives within it. Each book is a complete story, each has its own plot and landscape, yet each is an essential part of a larger epic story. The sequence of time in Narnia does not follow the order in which the books were published. Although the first book written is usually agreed to be the child's best introduction to Narnia, the creation of Narnia is described in *The Magician's Nephew* (1955). Centuries of Narnia time have passed when in *The Lion, the Witch and the Wardrobe* four human children find themselves in a Narnia wrapped in snow and ice, to which warmth can never come until the spell of the wicked White Witch is broken. *The Horse and His Boy* (1954) is an episode in the reign of one of the four children who become kings and queens in Narnia. Several more years pass before, in *Prince Caspian* (1951), the war of liberation from the Telmarines takes place. *The Voyage of the Dawn Treader* (1952) is a series of adventures in the reign of Caspian the Seafarer. Events of *The Silver Chair* (1953) are laid at the end of Caspian's reign. *The Last Battle* (1956) takes place many generations later, long after Aslan had ceased to walk through his world and the powers of evil were slowly undermining it to bring eventually the destruction of Narnia.

Marcus Crouch found flaws in the characterizations of the children and sometimes in the language, but followed his criticism with the thought that what makes the Narnia stories important is not style, not even superb storytelling, but the fact that the author had something to say. "His opinions and faith stand out on every page."

Children read the books for the fast-moving, exciting narratives, for the vivid, beautiful pictures in the storytelling, for the scenes of valiant action, the Norse eddas of Mr. Lewis's childhood yielding their heroic influence. Evil takes various forms in the different stories, but through them all the great lion Aslan represents good.

Lillian Smith wrote:

[1] C. S. Lewis, "On Three Ways of Writing for Children," *The Horn Book*, Vol. 39 (Oct., 1963), p. 469.

We may call these books fairy tales or allegories or parables, but there is no mistake about the significance of what C. S. Lewis has to say to the trusting, believing, seeking heart of childhood. But C. S. Lewis knows well that if children are to hear what it is he has to say to them, they must first find delight in the story he tells. And so the fresh and vigorous winds of his imagination carry his readers exuberantly through strange and wild adventures, adventures that, half consciously, they come to recognize are those of a spiritual journey toward the heart of reality. This is the final quality, I think, of C. S. Lewis' writing about the country of Narnia; that above and beneath and beyond the events of the story itself there is something to which the children can lay hold: belief in the essential truth of their own imaginings.[1]

The world of Mary Norton's Borrowers is linked to the human world by things—needles and hatpins, empty spools and matchboxes, bits of string and scraps of cloth that are so practical for making tools and clothes and furnishings for living quarters, things that human beings lose and seldom miss. The two worlds are linked also by fear—the Borrowers' fear of the great, clumsy people who have tiny creatures at their mercy and are much too ready to tread on or exterminate them, or to make use of them as money-yielding curiosities. But, except for these links, the world of the Borrowers is foreign to most human beings. A shortsighted child, watching "wood violets quivering on their massed roots from the passage of some sly, desperate creature pushing its way to safety," wondered what it would be like to be so small and vulnerable yet, for all the smallness, to be essentially human. Out of her childhood memories evolved the race of tiny people in a world of their own discovery and creation. In *The Borrowers* (1953) Pod, Homily, and Arrietty—father, mother, and daughter—lived under the kitchen of an old house until evil Mrs. Driver discovered them and drove them out. In *The Borrowers Afield* (1955) they escaped to the wild outdoors of a very different life, made a snug home in an old boot, and became acquainted with the enterprising young Borrower orphan, Spiller, who gave the family help in the matter of food—which had been no problem in an old house where appetizing leftovers were plentiful—and encouraged Arrietty in her enjoyment of life outdoors. For a brief period they found a haven again among lath and plaster and then, in *The Borrowers Afloat* (1959), had to flee to the river. Afloat in a tea kettle, they escaped from a human enemy and were rescued by Spiller in a knife-box boat—"very long and narrow, with symmetrical compartments for varying sizes of cutlery," operated by means of an amber-

[1] Lillian H. Smith, "News from Narnia," *The Horn Book*, Vol. 39 (Oct., 1963), p. 473.

colored knitting needle for punting and "a wafer-thin butter knife of tarnished Georgian silver" for paddling. In *The Borrowers Aloft* (1961) the family found a charming home in Little Fordham with Vine Cottage for their own, a railroad to ride on, and stores, a church, and an inn. But in a model village they were bound to be seen sooner or later and a Borrower, once seen, must move away. Kidnaped by the Platters, who also had a model village and wanted live inhabitants for it, they ingeniously managed to escape by toy balloon. They could not return to Vine Cottage for they knew there was no real security for them in Little Fordham. The reader is left with the assurance that, because they must move again, their story never ends. Somewhere Pod, Homily and Arrietty, and Spiller are living, forever trying to avoid the eyes of human beings.

Mary Norton's writing is consistent in every detail and very beautiful.

> [The rain] was coming down in torrents; but the mouth of the boot faced out of the wind and there was a little dry patch before it. Arrietty filled the tin lid [of the aspirin bottle] quite easily by tipping a large pointed fox-glove leaf toward it so the rain ran off and down the point. . . . There was a smell of wildness, of space, of leaves and grasses and, as she turned away with the filled tin lid, another smell—wine-y fragrant, spicy. Arrietty took note of it to remember it for morning—it was the smell of wild strawberries.[1]

Two earlier books by Mary Norton, *The Magic Bed Knob* (1945) and *Bonfires and Broomsticks* (1947), published together in 1957 under the title *Bed Knob and Broomstick*, tell of two children who have adventures in far places and distant times through their friendship with the demure Miss Price, who was actually a witch. Humor and inventiveness mark the stories, which, in their mixture of magic and reality, are reminiscent of books by E. Nesbit and her American follower Edward Eager.

It is for her stories about the Borrowers, however, that Mrs. Norton's place in literature is secure. The logical development of a completely original idea, the conviction of characterizations of both Borrowers and human beings, and the clean, beautiful strength of her style make the books as nearly perfect literary creations as have been produced for children in the English language within the past fifteen years.

American Carol Kendall was no doubt inspired by J. R. R. Tolkien's *The Hobbit* in her creating of the Minnipins of *The Gammage Cup* (1959) a sober, conservative people living in twelve villages "completely surrounded by unclimbable mountains." Among the villagers of

---

[1] Mary Norton, *The Borrowers Afield* (New York, Harcourt, 1955), p. 57.

Slipper-on-the-Water a few still retained a spark of the independence and adventuresomeness that had brought the early settlers to the Land Between the Mountains. Mrs. Kendall made a new world, complete with its own history and tradition as Mr. Tolkien did. But, although a follower, she was not an imitator. Her book is richly original. The characters are not so much like another race of people as they are like cousins who have been long isolated in their own small world. The emergence of rebellion or fresh ideas is therefore more sharply evident against the changeless complacence of the inhabitants of most of the villages. The characterizations are exceptionally good, especially those of the six exiles who eventually saved the village from an ancient enemy. Six years passed before Mrs. Kendall's second book about the Minnipins appeared. In *The Whisper of Glocken* (1965) certain of the inhabitants of flooded villages sought refuge in Slipper-on-the-Water. There the refugees met the five Outlaw Heroes of the earlier book, who had achieved almost legendary fame, and found that they themselves had the chance to prove that heroism is not limited to history. The books have a great deal of engaging humor and play on words.

Lloyd Alexander's chronicles of the Land of Prydain have strong roots in traditional tales, particularly in legends of ancient Wales. Mr. Alexander told of the happy accident that made him aware of the rich treasure trove of Welsh mythology. He had thought to include a Welsh episode in *Time Cat* (1963), a story of a cat that had the magic ability to take his young master into different eras of the past. He found research into the ancient legends so exciting that he used an Irish episode in *Time Cat* and resolved to draw from the vast store of Welsh legendary material for a larger theme. His framework for *The Book of Three* (1964) was given him by a brief passage from the *Myvruan Archaiology*.

It describes a certain battle in only about half-a-dozen lines that go, in part, like this: *And Arawn King of Annuvin fought. And there was a man in that battle, who unless his name were known, could not be overcome . . . And there was a woman called Achren . . . and Gwydion ap Don guessed the name of the man.*[1]

Thus what had begun as an episode became eventually five volumes, the books all linked by characters and background but each an independent story. The characters who stem from legendary figures have had a rebirth in the writer's mind to be integrated components of a completely new tale. Knowing nothing of his own heritage, Taran, Assistant Pig Keeper, has grown up under the tutelage of Dallben, who has taught him from the *The Book of Three* about the many kingdoms

[1] Lloyd Alexander, "The Truth About Fantasy," *Top of the News*, Vol. 24 (Jan., 1968), p. 172.

that make up Prydain, about the might and stolen wealth of King Arawn, lord of the land of death, and about the ever-present danger to their peaceful country from the forces of evil. By the end of the story Taran has been through danger and seen the heroism of others but he knows he himself has not yet learned the meaning of courage.

In *The Black Cauldron* (1965) Taran and his faithful companions destroy the cauldron in which are created the "mute and deathless warriors" who serve the evil Lord of Annuvin, and in *The Castle of Llyr* (1966) they rescue the Princess Eilonwy from an enchantress. Although in *Taran Wanderer* (1967) Taran does not learn the secret of his parentage, he comes to realize how unimportant was his hope of noble birth. He is at last growing up; his personality is more nearly realized and the mature, thoughtful ending is satisfying. In the final book, *The High King* (1968), winner of the Newbery Medal, Mr. Alexander showed the wholeness of his concept. In all the books, courage and sacrifice give meaning to the adventures, but lightening the stories are gleams of nonsense in the speech of the grotesque, fiercely loyal Gurgi, and in the character of Fflewddur Fflam, the minstrel prince whose harp strings break whenever he stretches the truth. Like most good fantasies, the books are related to humanity; the characters have failings but they also have potentialities for greatness. Inner meanings do not distract from the excitement of the adventures. The books succeed because they entertain and because the child who enjoys them has something more to keep than he had before he read them.

Elizabeth Enright's (1909–1968) mood in writing fantasy is light but her *Tatsinda* (1963) is a many-faceted story. In it she created a mountaintop kingdom of Tatrajan where live a race of beautiful people with glittering white hair and ice-blue eyes, among whom Tatsinda is pitied for her golden hair and dark eyes. Glowing pictures by Irene Haas add to the beauty of the book, which has much to delight children: the careful descriptions of the Tatrajanni, their homes, their customs, their animals—all beginning with "ta," and the romance and magic of Tatsinda's rescue from enemy giants.

Fairy Stories in Traditional Patterns

Arthur Bowie Chrisman's first acquaintance with the Chinese was made when he stopped in a Chinese shop to enquire about the foods appropriate for a Chinese character that he was putting into a story. This led to an acquaintance with a Chinese gentleman, who not only aided him with his particular problem, but started him on a study of Chinese history and the writing of the stories that seven years later made up *Shen of the Sea* (1925), for which he received the Newbery Medal. So steeped was Mr. Chrisman in the lore of China, the wisdom of her proverbs, and Chinese history and life, that his stories were thought at first to be direct translations of Chinese folk tales.

Alice Ritchie's *Treasure of Li-Po* (1949) is a book of unusual spirit and quality. All are stories laid in China, some have magic, some, like the title story, have only the magic of wisdom and kindliness. They are told simply but with vivid atmosphere; there is a great deal of gentle, understated humor that leaves the reader warmly content.

James Thurber's *Many Moons* (1943) is a perfect, modern fairy tale. Its magicians are pretenders and its magic is nonsense, but achievement is the result of childlike wisdom and the heroine is an appealing little princess who wears her crown in bed. Very satisfying to children is a story that expresses so completely a child's imaginings (Louis Slobodkin received the Caldecott Medal for the illustrations, which are in perfect accord) yet is lightened by the kind of nonsense that children look to grownups to provide. Mr. Thurber used an old fairy-tale theme to make a new story in his *The Great Quillow* (1944). The hero is the little toy-maker who put to rout the terrible giant Hunder and saved his village. There was no question about Mr. Thurber's grounding in folk and fairy lore; he knew the rules and could tell a story with conviction as well as with imagination and humor.

Katharine Gibson related in *Cinders* (1939) the story of Cinderella's coachman who did not turn back into a mouse. The opening scene at the palace gate creates mystery and atmosphere that is maintained throughout the fantasy: we see, through the darkness, the little man dressed in gray with the wide-brimmed hat, the long pointed nose, the coattails flapping in the wind, and catch a glimpse of a ragged girl slipping away into the night.

Maurice Dolbier, a Rhode Island journalist and critic, wrote some very amusing tales in *The Half-pint Jinni* (1948). The title story is an account of the complications that develop because the jinni's magic is only half as powerful as the magic of a full-sized jinni, a theme used to advantage also by Edward Eager. All the stories are fresh and ingenious with appeal to children older than those who enjoyed his *The Magic Shop* (1946).

In 1950 appeared the first of Barbara Leonie Picard's books of her own fairy tales, *The Mermaid and the Simpleton*, published in England the year before. Marcus Crouch referred to Miss Picard as possessing "a little of de la Mare's strong and delicate fantasy and his easy mastery of words,"[1] and of her being a writer who "seemed able to share the thoughts of the primitive anonymous storytellers of the remote past."[2] In the United States she had been known for her retellings of epic and legendary hero stories, but her place as a writer of original fairy tales in the spirit of the stories of the past was not recognized until the publication of *The Lady of the Linden Tree* (1962) and *The Faun*

[1] Marcus S. Crouch, *Treasure Seekers and Borrowers* (London, The Library Assoc., 1962), p. 102.
[2] *Ibid.*, p. 115.

and the Woodcutter's Daughter (1964), both of which had been published in England in the early fifties. *The Goldfinch Garden* (1965) followed. Miss Picard's stories are told in the style and mood of the old fairy tales and contain many of the traditional elements: witches, magicians, the crafty fox, courageous knights, imprisoned princesses, finger rings that need only to be turned to accomplish magic, fortunes sought and won, and wishes granted. Although the stories often have the same central theme—the triumph of love and selfless courage—each is remarkably different from the others. All are written in the smooth, economical prose and have the directness and closely knit plots of traditional tales, making them excellent for reading aloud and story-telling. As literary fairy tales, they have an extra dimension—the wisdom and certainty characteristic of stories by writers who have been deeply immersed in the ageless stories of the past.

A reference question in the Massachusetts library, where she was a librarian, started Elizabeth Hodges on a quest for the source of the tale, *The Three Princes of Serendip*, that had inspired Horace Walpole to coin the word "serendipity." Her search led her to an English translation of *Peregrinaggio di Ire Giovani Figliuoli del Re di Serendippo*, published in Italy in 1557, and to a translation of the French version published in 1721, which is believed to have been the one read by Walpole. The two versions were different in many respects, and although neither was written in a style or with plot and characterizations to interest children, they included the adventurous episodes and magical elements that children do enjoy. The book that resulted from her quest and from much further research, *The Three Princes of Serendip* (1964), had its roots in the old tale but was a new story, a "historical fairy tale." At the end of each chapter of the first book and ornamenting each story in the second, *Serendipity Tales* (1966), is a poem by the author—a *pantoum*, a poetic form derived from the *pantun* of Malaya. The adventures of the princes and the stories are gracefully told and Oriental in feeling.

The *kappa*, a water sprite of Japanese folklore, was quite unknown to American children until Betty Jean Lifton wrote *Kap, the Kappa* (1960), illustrated by Eiichi Mitsui. Kappas are elves who live in ponds and streams, have shells like those of turtles, heads concave on top to hold water, and are extremely mischievous. Mrs. Lifton lived for a number of years in Japan, where her husband was a research psychiatrist. Her appreciation of the country, the people, and their art and legends is evident in her several books set in Japan. She became well acquainted with kappas through artist and writer acquaintances, and had, indeed, made a special search for them, not only in literature—they have appeared in many Japanese tales for adults—but had journeyed to one of the southernmost islands to attend the annual midsummer kappa festival. Also rooted deeply in Japanese culture and tradition was one of her most beautiful books, *The Dwarf Pine Tree* (1963), with illustrations by the Japanese painter Fuku Akino.

The feeling of region is often stronger in fantasy than in realistic stories. It is very strong in Eleanor Hoffman's *Mischief in Fez* (1943) with its djinns, date gardens, market places, and minarets; and it is vivid in two later stories: *Tal and the Magic Barruget* (1965) by Eva-Lis Wuorio, laid in a Balearic fishing village, and *The Kelpie's Pearls* (1966) by Mollie Hunter, a story of the Scottish Highlands.

Dolls and Toys in Fantasy

Margery Bianco's first children's book, *The Velveteen Rabbit*, was written while she was living in England and originally published there in 1922. She had written several novels, but had become dissatisfied with her work and wanted to do something quite different. Her own two children were young, at an age when toys meant much to them, and she had vivid memories of the toys she had loved as a child. Her thoughts and memories suddenly brought them to life. In two stories, *The Velveteen Rabbit*, which introduced the English portrait painter William Nicholson to the field of children's books, and *The Skin Horse* (1927), which her own daughter Pamela illustrated, she revealed a memory of well-loved toys and a deep understanding of children's feelings toward their playthings. Two longer stories of nursery friends followed, *The Adventures of Andy* (1927) and *Poor Cecco* (1925), and a third, an unpretentious little book *The Little Wooden Doll* (1925). This last, with illustrations by Pamela Bianco, was especially successful. In its simplicity it is completely childlike, unsophisticated, and endearing: a tiny book that fits a child's hands.

Perception of the child's world, of his imaginative play, caught and enchantingly expressed in A. A. Milne's poetry of childhood, is the substance of his whimsical tales, *Winnie-the-Pooh* (1926) and *The House at Pooh Corner* (1928). The teddy bear, Winnie-the-Pooh, had been an important member of the Milne family since the first birthday of Christopher Robin, and was for years the little boy's inseparable companion. He and Piglet, Eeyore the old gray donkey, Kanga, Roo, and other nursery animals are imbued with the personalities that only a child could give them and a poet could express. Distinguished as was Mr. Milne's record as an editor of *Punch*, a novelist, and playwright, it is likely that it will be for his poems and fantasies of childhood that his name will survive.

The stories in Crockett Johnson's *Ellen's Lion* (1959) are made up of conversations between Ellen and her stuffed lion. They are refreshingly devoid of whimsy, are sensibly funny, and real; they can please at one time the young imaginative child and the most practical adult.

In a number of books that are easy to read but never condescending Mr. Johnson has been uniquely successful in combining reality and imaginative play.

Anne Parrish, who with her brother had been inventing fantasy since their childhood and who had already been recognized for her novels, published in 1930 *Floating Island*, her very original story of a dollhouse family shipwrecked on a tropical island. In that year Rachel Field's *Hitty* won the Newbery Medal. Although focused on a doll, the story has the dimensions of a historical novel (it is discussed in Chapter V, page 512). *Floating Island* gives a doll's-eye view of the world, yet by the very smallness of scale the reader has insight into special beauty—a blossom that can be turned upside down for a hat, the dense jungle of the ferns, the dramatic colors of a seashell. The writing is touched by that delicately satirical humor so evident in Miss Parrish's novels. There is also indication here of her knowledge of the pleasure children get from picturesque, many-colored words, given such delightful scope in her later book, *The Story of Appleby Capple* (1950).

For many years after *Floating Island* few, if any, doll stories of literary significance were published. Perhaps the same matter-of-fact school that from time to time discourages the reading of fairy tales was in the ascendance. Then in 1946 came *Miss Hickory*, who was certainly of the doll family, although it is doubtful that she would ever have got on well with conventional dolls. Carolyn Sherwin Bailey created a unique personality in this country doll made of an applewood twig and a hickory nut. Miss Hickory has the common sense and the forthright qualities that her name implies. They keep her from succumbing to adversity—they even help her to turn it into adventure—but they also keep her from witnessing a miracle. The story is set against the panorama of the New Hampshire countryside through the changing seasons—vivid on every page and pointed up in Ruth Gannett's illustrations—and the writing has great humor and zest. The story is fanciful and lighthearted but firmly planted among the good things of the earth. Carolyn Sherwin Bailey received the Newbery Medal for *Miss Hickory*.

Suddenly dolls came into their own. Elizabeth Orton Jones's memory of childhood was very clear and her understanding of the emotions of children sure. Her *Big Susan* (1947) is the story of a doll house on Christmas Eve during the short, magical moments when the dolls can speak and act for themselves without the help of the child, Big Susan.

In 1947 in England—the next year in the United States—*The Dolls' House* by Rumer Godden was published. Written by a novelist, recognized for her style and perception, with the same discipline she brings to her work for adults, the seemingly simple story is a perfect novel in miniature. The plot was constructed with the greatest care and the characters warmly portrayed, but they remain dolls throughout. Only the scale is small. The problems and emotions are as large as humanity.

> This book [said Lillian Smith] reaches out beyond its doll characters into the fundamental questions of human life: good and bad; right and wrong; the recognition of true as opposed to ephemeral values. These are questions that are universally important. They are themes found in all great literature. To find them treated in this microscopic way does not lessen their importance; perhaps it even clarifies them and brings them into perspective.[1]

It cannot be assumed that such inner meaning will elude the child who reads doll stories. Adults seldom recognize the child's impressionability nor the penetration of feeling, if not comprehension, when a story gives real enjoyment. The children, Charlotte and Emily, are important to the framework and the manipulation of events, but not to the emotion that gives the book life. In each of later doll stories—*Impunity Jane* (1954), *The Fairy Doll* (1956), *The Story of Holly and Ivy* (1958), and *Candy Floss* (1960)—the story of a person and the story of a doll overlap and finally unite in one satisfying conclusion. In *Miss Happiness and Miss Flower* (1961), *Little Plum* (1963), and *Home Is the Sailor* (1964) dolls are the catalytic agents. Their stories are closely related to those of the human beings through events explosive or calm; dolls and children give and receive, and lives are happier for the interweaving of human and doll destinies. In these last three books particularly, Miss Godden's remarkable insight into the workings of children's hearts and minds, so clear in her novels for adults, gives the stories poignance, special vitality, and humor.

A most original story of toys is Pauline Clarke's *The Return of the Twelves* (1963), published in England as *The Twelve and the Genii* (1962). The twelves were the wooden soldiers that the Brontë children had played with, and about whom Branwell Brontë, at the age of twelve, had written *History of the Young Men*. Max had heard them drilling in the attic of the old farmhouse to which his family had just moved but as soon as they saw him they "froze." With great patience and quietness Max discovered that the little men could be warmed to life by affection. In time he revealed the secret to his sister and brother, and the three children were called Genii by the little soldiers. The very individual personalities of the little men and their strange names—Crackey and Tracky, Monkey and Cheeky, Bravey and Gravey, Sneaky and Stumps, Parry and Ross, the Duke of Wellington and the patriarch Butter Crashey—follow the old account, but the book

[1] Lillian H. Smith, *The Unreluctant Years* (Chicago, American Library Assoc., 1953), pp. 151–152.

has present-day conviction and reality. The careful development of the plot and excellent writing give the story excitement and immediacy.

Animals in Fantasy

Hugh Lofting (1886–1947), in fact as well as spirit, belonged both to England and America. He had come from England to attend the Massachusetts Institute of Technology in 1904. He completed his technical education in England but returned a few years later to make his home in the United States. With the outbreak of the First World War he enlisted in the British army, and commissioned by his children to write illustrated letters to them, he wondered what he could write them from the front that would be neither horrible nor censorable. He noticed the animals that were playing their part in the war, or merely caught in it, taking the same chances as humans but receiving none of the benefits of surgery when needed as the humans did. He began to speculate on the complications of giving proper medical care to animals. A knowledge of animal languages would certainly be necessary, as well as animal anatomy. That was the beginning of an idea—an eccentric doctor with a great love for pets and a bent for natural history who would finally decide to give up his conventional practice and devote himself to the therapy of animals. Thus Doctor Dolittle found his way into the letters that Mr. Lofting sent home to his children, and later into ten books for boys and girls. *The Story of Doctor Dolittle*, published in 1920, starts the good doctor on his new career and into the complications of learning animal languages with the help of the parrot Polynesia. She takes him off to Africa to cure the monkeys of a terrible disease and introduces the rare pushmipullyu. Each succeeding volume is full of the adventurous travel that Hugh Lofting dreamed of as a little boy. The second book, *The Voyages of Doctor Dolittle* (1922), won the Newbery Medal. One of the great charms of the books is the scrupulously logical development of each idea and adventure. Every project is worked out in careful detail, faithful to science as it has been developed by John Dolittle. The nonsense is logical nonsense. Mr. Lofting had respect for children's intelligence and for their imagination: within the framework of his fantasy everything that happens is possible, yet it is never dull. Doctor Dolittle himself is a personality that children do not forget. Kind, wise and patient, never flurried, equal to any emergency, he loves his home in Puddleby-on-the-Marsh but is always ready for adventure. Children are at ease and happy with such a hero.

Recognition of the delight that stories about talking animals have always given children is evident in every period. The weakest efforts in imaginative writing, however, are in animal fantasy. Difficult though it is to interpret an animal in human terms without destroying its integrity as an animal it is a constant temptation to new writers for children.

Beatrix Potter's many imitators have never approached her skill either in telling a story or in presenting, against the incongruity of human concepts, animals that are endearing and humorous but that remain animals.

Robert Lawson, (1892–1957), one of the great originators in this genre, told in *Rabbit Hill* (1944) a tale so spontaneous and natural that it seems to have reached the printed page without effort. Story and illustrations, both by Mr. Lawson, and humorous as well as beautiful, are set against Connecticut meadows, farms, and woods, which the author-illustrator presented with the kind of affection that Beatrix Potter brought to her stories of the English countryside. Mr. Lawson received the Newbery Medal for *Rabbit Hill*. In *The Tough Winter* (1954), the same animals appear, each a personality yet each his animal self though he speaks in the language of men.

In his first book to be both written and illustrated by himself, *Ben and Me* (1939), Robert Lawson interpreted the events of Benjamin Franklin's life through his closest friend, advisor, and constant companion, the good mouse Amos, touching history with nonsense in a way that would probably have delighted the genial Mr. Franklin himself. The author-artist had similar fun with history in *Mr. Revere and I* (1953), the tale of events in Boston before the Revolution told through the experiences and words of Paul Revere's horse.

In every period animal characters have been the vehicles for the presentation in stories of adult philosophy or homely wisdom. The resulting whimsey is attractive to adults but often too lacking in action or suspense to satisfy children. Whatever philosophy emerges from the pages of Walter Brooks' *To and Again* (1927) is balanced by the amusing adventures and unique individualities of the enterprising animals of Mr. Bean's farm. The satire of *High Water at Catfish Bend* (1952) and *Seven Stars for Catfish Bend* (1956) by Ben Lucien Burman is appealing to adults, and children are engaged by the personality of Doc Raccoon who tells of the adventures and ingenuity of the animals who traveled down the Mississippi accomplishing what people did not— the repair of the levees near Catfish Bend. At times the humor is reminiscent of Joel Chandler Harris's Uncle Remus stories.

Like the ancient fabulist, some writers use animals to tell a human story. The animals of these tales are usually people in animal form in human dress, a complex situation, certainly, but not one that bothers young children who see personality in every creature and accept as natural human personalities in animal characters. Such anthropomorphism, however, to be successful demands humor, imagination, and stylistic genius. A prototype of such a book—a moral fable for adults that children recognize only as a very funny animal story—is *A Lion in the Woods* (1955) by Maurice Dolbier. In the same category, but in marked contrast is *Emily's Voyage* (1966), Emma Smith's story of the "guinea pig who loved to travel." So well written is the story that adults enjoy the humanization and see it as a commentary on human foibles, while young children take it to their hearts as a good story about someone they like—Emily, the guinea pig.

Another successful example of anthropomorphism is *Owlglass* (1964) by Will Nickless. The small animals of a wood near an English village realized that their venerable colleague, the owl Old Beak and Claws, needed glasses to correct his failing vision. In his shortsightedness he could easily mistake one of them for his next meal. Relaxed and truly humorous, the story is in the tradition of the best English animal fantasy.

E. B. White's *Stuart Little*, described by Alice Jordan as "a mouse, two inches long, a gentle and heroic human figure," received a mixed response in 1945. Certain literal-minded grownups objected to the idea of a mouse child in a human family. Others were entertained by the satire. Many children found Stuart Little endearing and his adventures amusing. Even more successful among boys and girls, however, was Mr. White's *Charlotte's Web* (1952), the story of Wilbur, a pig, whose life was saved by the remarkable spinning of Charlotte, a spider. The eight-year-old girl Fern, friend of Charlotte and Wilbur, gives children a human focus for identification and emotional involvement with the fate of the two creatures often despised by people. The situation, congenial to the commonplace earthiness of the setting, is imaginative, but it is nonsense and a fragile fabric to burden with so much emotion. But Mr. White triumphed. The style and wit of his writing, his wisdom, and his remembrance of a child's rapt concern with the things he loves strengthened the slender thread of story. Few books of the period had so widespread and enthusiastic a reception from children, and such lasting appreciation.

The Cricket in Times Square (1960) by George Selden is original in setting and in combinations of characters, including a human hero, which gives the book wider age appeal than that of most talking animal tales. The story is laid chiefly in the Times Square subway station where Tucker Mouse and Harry Cat share their home with a cricket from Connecticut, proving that New Yorkers can be friendly indeed. The book has spontaneity and is full of surprising events and convincing nonsense.

In quieter mood is Rumer Godden's *Mousewife* (1951), based on an account in Dorothy Wordsworth's journal, that tells an allegorical tale of the friendship of a mouse and a dove.

The story in *An Edge of the Forest* (1959) by Agnes Smith is a simple one—of an orphaned black lamb who makes friends in an alien forest but who, because she is "the shepherd's lamb," eventually finds her way back to the fold. It is a rare and subtle book that Julia Cunningham found can "bring a sudden magical understanding of the truth at the core of every person and every thing."[1]

Two mice play more than heroic roles in *Belling the Tiger* (1961) by Mary Stolz, with pictures by Beni Montresor, the first of a series of illustrated storybooks by Mrs. Stolz. They are adventure tales for young children, but modern fables for adults. The same qualities characterize Margery Sharp's *The Rescuers* (1959) and her other tales about a company of indefatigable mice actively working for a venerable mouse organization, "The Prisoner's Aid Society."

Island Mackenzie (1960) by Ursula Moray Williams is a story of shipwreck and castaways on a desert island, and of Mackenzie, one of the most engaging little cats in fiction. He survived the dangers of sharks and crocodiles and found plenty of good food, but almost did not survive the enmity of Miss Mary Pettifer, his only companion on the tropical island.

Edgar Parker used the folk-tale motif in *The Duke of Sycamore* (1959) and several other books, all handsomely produced, with his own unusual, beautiful illustrations. Such books as the above, told with wit and style, appeal to adults and children on different levels. Because, however, they are often difficult for beginning readers to read for themselves, the children to whom talking-animal stories give the greatest pleasure are likely to miss them, unless they are read to the child.

Animals have always been important in fairy tales, traditional or new. Not to be forgotten are the colorful adventures of Paul Fenimore Cooper's orphan boy *Tal* (1929) with the old man Noom-Zor-Noom and his snow-white donkey Millitinkle, and the surprise and gentleness of Mairín Cregan's *Old John* (1936) and his little fairy cat, and the fun of riding behind Patricia Lynch's *The Turf-cutter's Donkey* (1935), catching sight of a leprechaun, and seeing real magic at the fair.

Tall Tales and Nonsense

Much imaginative writing abounds with humor but the fantasies that possess the kind of incongruities, ridiculous situations, and earthy funniness that make children laugh spontaneously have always been rare. Many talking-animal tales have it to some degree. *Rabbit Hill* (1944) certainly does. *Robbut* (1948) also by Robert Lawson has more sheer nonsense. The humor rollicks in Betty Babcock's *The Expandable Pig* (1949) in which a farm pig inflates himself like a balloon to transport Gary and his pets to England (where, since it is war time, pork is scarce!) to see Gary's dear friend Howard. Ruth

[1] Julia Cunningham, "From Another Edge of the Forest," *The Horn Book*, Vol. 42 (June, 1966), p. 291.

Gannett's *My Father's Dragon* (1948) is childlike in its imaginings and nonsense and satisfying because Elmer Elevator's adventures on Wild Island are both exciting and funny. Dancing animals have always made children laugh, and Elizabeth Baker's *Sunny-boy Sim* (1948) wafts the fragrance of the piny woods while the deer and bears and black-faced raccoons dance to the tune of grandpappy's fiddle. James Playsted Wood introduced a most satisfactory playmate when the three children of *An Elephant in the Family* (1957) accepted without question the talking elephant who came to live with them and with whom they carried on normal conversations and traditional activities. This talent for exaggeration combined with understatement—so frequently demonstrated in the tall tales of American folklore—has resulted in other stories with hilarious implications. The matter-of-fact restraint in Arna Bontemps and Jack Conroy's *Fast Sooner Hound* (1942), interpreted so well by Virginia Lee Burton's pictures, makes that story exceedingly droll. And the completeness and the logic of the exaggeration in Sam and Zoa Swayne's *Great-Grandfather in the Honey Tree* (1949) give it a place with the classic tall-tales. There is very definite American flavor in these two stories. Theodor Geisel, better known as Dr. Seuss, joined the suspense and magic of a highly original fairy tale with irresistible nonsense in his *The Five Hundred Hats of Bartholomew Cubbins* (1938).

Many nonsense stories begin with the commonplace. It is as though a child, in momentary rebellion against his own sensible way of life and the well-known things around him, suddenly said, "What if?" And from that "if" grow all the adventures and the fun. The setting for Richard and Florence Atwater's *Mr. Popper's Penguins* (1938), for instance, is familiar, almost dull until Mr. Popper's letter about penguins sent to Admiral Drake in the Antarctic sets the tale alight. Oliver Butterworth carried on the tall-tale tradition in *The Enormous Egg* (1956), when Nate Twitchell's ordinary hen laid an egg that hatched a baby dinosaur. In *The Pushcart War* (1964) Jean Merrill gave a straight-faced account (including newspaper items, police reports, and quotes from "new math" books used in the New York schools) of events that began in 1976 when a truck demolished a pushcart laden with daffodils, and blossomed into full scale war between the multitude of trucks that jammed New York streets and an invincible pushcart-city-children combination. Satire and nonsense were successfully combined to delight a wide range of ages.

In 1950 *Pippi Longstocking* by Astrid Lindgren came to the United States from Sweden, where it had had tremendous popularity. Pippi, a harum-scarum tomboy, lived alone, except for a monkey and a horse, in a little house at the edge of the village. Her wildly imaginative adventures, related in a most matter-of-fact way, are very funny to children who often enjoy in dreams, at least, such an uninhibited life as Pippi's.

Joan Aiken's books *The Wolves of Willoughby Chase* (1963), *Black Hearts in Battersea* (1964), and *Nightbirds on Nantucket* (1966) are exciting or funny—depending on whether a child or adult is reading them. They are takeoffs on nineteenth century melodrama, consistent in every detail. Events move with great speed, people are either very good or very wicked—mistreated children are inevitably fleeing from the one kind to the other—and the storytelling is so matter of fact that even such preposterous sights as the pink whale of the third book seem, for the moment, real.

Higglety, Pigglety, Pop! or There Must Be More to Life (1967) by Maurice Sendak is funny, mystifying, childlike, and original. Jennie, a little Sealyham terrier, who had everything she wanted, wanted something else. "There must be more to life than having everything." So she packed her bag and went out into the world to search for the experience necessary to get a job acting in the World Mother Goose Theater. The book ends with a play within the story—a series of pictures showing the new production of the play "Higglety, Pigglety, Pop!" with Jennie as the leading lady. It is a book to be read aloud, and more than once. Many children found it hilarious; many adults found it puzzling. Time will prove the significance of Mr. Sendak's nonsense, as it has done for the work of other original talents.

An American writer expert in using the familiar as a springboard to fantastic adventures is William Pène du Bois. His childhood love had been Jules Verne and from this enthusiasm had developed his interest in all types of inventions, new methods of transportation, and particularly balloons. The excursions of his imagination are governed by science and controlled by his strong love of order, for which he expressed gratitude to the discipline of the Lycée in Versailles, which he attended between his eighth and fourteenth years, and his Saturday night visits to Paris to the circus. Here was discipline clothed in glamour. The childhood love of the circus was to emerge from time to time in his stories, notably *The Great Geppy* (1940), the story of the red-and-white striped horse of extraordinary intelligence. The idea for *The Twenty-one Balloons* (1947), for which Mr. du Bois received the Newbery Medal, had been in his mind before he went into the Army in the Second World War; little segments of it had grown up with him, and after the war the book took form. The appeal of the story is ageless. Anyone who enjoys having his curiosity piqued, who delights in scientific logic and inventiveness, who has speculated on the Utopian state that would most perfectly fit his dreams, finds much in this story to engage him. The beginning tells of Professor William Waterman Sherman, who, after forty years of teaching arithmetic to small boys, sets off on his great adventure, a trip by balloon from the Pacific Coast, and three weeks later is picked up in mid-Atlantic among the wreckage of twenty balloons, setting the whole world agog with amazement and curiosity.

Mr. du Bois's *Peter Graves* (1950) who had some incredible adventures with an anti-gravity compound might be any inventive American boy. And *The Giant* (1954) is El Muchacho, a Spanish boy who, being seven stories tall, could not have the life and pleasures of ordinary children and was welcome nowhere. The humor and suspense of all of Mr. du Bois's tales owe as much to the smoothness and clarity of his style as to careful attention to every detail.

Worlds Without Boundaries

In *The Wonderful Locomotive* (1928), a story of a little boy's love for steam engines and his record run on battered old Number 44, Cornelia Meigs showed how finely drawn in the small child's world is the line between realism and fantasy. The fox, in *The Little Prince*, tells this secret. "It is only with the heart that one can see rightly; what is essential is invisible to the eye." Hans Christian Andersen, George Macdonald, and all the great writers of fantasy have said the same in their own way, and for children the meaning is clear. Grown-ups must step beyond the wall that separates the real and the unreal to enter the world of the imagination. For many children there is no wall.

Billy Barnicoat (1923) by Greville Macdonald is a fantasy full of mystery and tenderness, and true to Cornwall, its countryside, its cliffs and cottages, and its godfearing village folk. Like the fairy stories of the author's father, George Macdonald, this one too took a strong hold on growing imaginations.

Mary Poppins (1934) by Pamela Travers is as fresh as the east wind on which the extraordinary nursemaid blew into the lives of the Banks family just when she was needed most. To most people she appeared prim, vain, self-sufficient; but the children knew her for what she was, and found life with Mary Poppins full of wonderful tricks and amazing adventures. Pamela Travers, Australian-born writer living in England, once claimed that Mary Poppins came to amuse her when she was convalescing from an illness. So saturated with fairy tales was Miss Travers's childhood that her imagination was ready to launch Mary Poppins forth on a busy career. *Mary Poppins Comes Back* (1935), *Mary Poppins Opens the Door* (1943), and *Mary Poppins in the Park* (1952) are consistently ingenious and funny. The Banks family increased in size but Mary Poppins remained the same, never stepping out of character, equal to any emergency; to the outer eye, stern and opinionated, but to the children, secret and magical.

John Buchan wiped out time, as it is measured in reality, in *Lake of Gold* (1941), which brings the dramatic story of Canada's past into the life of a modern boy. In *The Magic Walking-Stick* (1932) a boy had wonderful adventures in other times and far parts of the world while, to family and friends, he appeared to be an ordinary English school boy.

Elizabeth Goudge's stories, although in no way patterned after George Macdonald's, have qualities that are reminiscent of his: strong faith in people, children particularly, warmth in human relationships, and the successful weaving together of the two worlds in which the child lives. Vigor and humor keep her stories from verging on sentimentality. Her writing is wonderfully pictorial, and her plots inevitably satisfying to girls who love traditional fairy tales and are growing toward longer stories. Probably of her children's books, *The Little White Horse* (1946) is most widely appealing.

Enys Tregarthen's *The Doll Who Came Alive* (1942) is the story of a sensitive, intense child who had no one on whom to pour her love until the strange sailor man put into her arms a doll that she loved to life. Greta of Julia Sauer's *Fog Magic* (1943) loved the fog. Whenever it settled on her Nova Scotia home, and as long as it obscured her ordinary world, she could live happily in Blue Cove, a hundred-year-old village that no one else could see.

Edward Eager (1911–1964) was a lyricist, librettist, and playwright who discovered E. Nesbit's books when he was reading to his son. He referred to them as "the best children's books, I am quite sure, in the world," and frequently paid tribute to them as the inspiration for his own children's books. E. Nesbit is mentioned at the beginning of *Half Magic* (1954) when the four children of the book express their discontent over not having the magical adventures that the Nesbit-book-children had. Then, amazingly, they found a coin with the power to grant them half wishes that projected them into some amusing situations. The lively, natural children and the fantastic adventures in past and present, near and far, make a very funny book that called for a sequel. Six books followed: *Knight's Castle* (1956), *Magic by the Lake* (1957), *The Time Garden* (1958), *Magic or Not?* (1959), *The Well-Wisher* (1960), and *Seven-Day Magic* (1962). Adults sometimes found the child characters tiresomely pert but the popularity of Mr. Eager's books has been constant with the children. And the play on words, the puns, the light-hearted mixture of realism and fantasy, and the wit and insight make the books delightful for reading aloud.

Although Lucy Boston's first two books, one a novel and the other a children's book, were not published in England until 1954 when she was sixty-two years old, her writing had its deepest beginning in 1939. In that year she bought the nine-hundred-year-old manor house at

Hemingford Grey, near Cambridge, England. It was the inspiration for almost all of her books and the prototype of Yew Hall and Green Knowe, to which Tolly came to live with his great-grandmother Oldknow. During the Second World War British and American soldiers listened to music and enjoyed Christmas festivities in the music room of the old house, and after the war there were concerts at which refugees from the Latvian army were entertained. Then suddenly the village was quiet again, and Mrs. Boston was alone. To fill the house, she wrote,

> I invented Tolly and his friends, the idea originating from a fancy I had while sitting alone on a winter evening in one of the ingle nooks, that from the one opposite me, across the vigorous hissing and crackle of the wood fire, I was getting snatches of a child's voice singing below his breath, for himself, a song of joy. . . . How wonderful it would be to look up and see, where a moment ago there was an empty nook, an enquiring fire-lit face and the pompous costume of our history books worn crooked and crumpled as only a child can.[1]

At the time of its publication critics spoke of *The Children of Green Knowe* (1954) as a book *of* children rather than *for* them. Marcus S. Crouch suggested that it should be made obligatory reading for all parents, teachers, and librarians. Literate children, however, would have kept it alive without help from adults.

The children whom Tolly came to know and play with had lived at Green Knowe three hundred years before. They were as real to Tolly as the house itself. Past and present were one. The relationship between Tolly and his great-grandmother is sturdy and natural, a strengthening fiber uniting the poetically conceived incidents. *The Treasure of Green Knowe* (1958)—published as *The Chimneys of Green Knowe* in England—brought back other children from the past and related another segment of the history of the house, with Tolly taking part in dramatic events that had happened one hundred and sixty years before. *The River at Green Knowe* (1959) was less convincing, but it did introduce an important person—Ping, a Chinese boy. In *A Stranger at Green Knowe* (1961), Ping befriended Hanno, an escaped gorilla, and kept secret, even from Mrs. Oldknow, the animal's hiding place in the bamboo thickets at Green Knowe. In that book the past did not enter, but the revelation of Ping's courage and integrity is remarkably accomplished. Evil reached Green Knowe in *An Enemy at Green Knowe* (1964), a book in very different mood from the others. The ancient folklore of

---

[1] Lucy M. Boston, "Christmas at 'Green Knowe,'" *The Horn Book*, Vol. 31 (Dec., 1955), p. 473.

witchcraft was woven through the story, blending the periods—remote and contemporary—and building up to a tremendous climax.

Few writers have so successfully interwoven past and present as Mrs. Boston has done, and few have shown a more sensitive understanding of children. When Tolly was with Mrs. Oldknow, "he forgot at once about being a schoolboy. He and she were just two people." Certainly the Green Knowe stories are of children but they have proved to be *for* them also.

In Philippa Pearce's *Tom's Midnight Garden* (1959) the idea that time has no barriers was embodied in nearly perfect literary form. No loose ends, no inconsistencies mar the book. Miss Pearce can explain with few words but great conviction such supernatural events as Tom's passing through a closed door or the actual process of a room's transformation from its unfamiliar past appearance to its familiar present. Tom's acceptance of the fact that he can enjoy a garden that had existed long before his birth and friendship with a girl who had played in the garden more than half a century before is wholly believable. The book is a model of what can be done with an intricate theme by a writer endowed with literary style, understanding of children, and a clear insight into her own vision. John Rowe Townsend wrote:

> The book has a profound, mysterious sense of time; it has the beauty of a theorem but it is not abstract; it is sensuously as well as intellectually satisfying. The garden is so real that you have the scent of it in your nostrils. . . .[1]

Penelope Farmer's *The Summer Birds* (1962) is an account of the summer that a strange boy came to the school in a depressing little English village and taught Charlotte and Emma, and finally all the children in their class, to fly. Despite the wonderful picture the book brings to mind of a great flock of children flying as easily as birds but without the need of wings, the overtones of the book are somber and meanings below the surface leave readers thoughtful. Miss Farmer's second book, *The Magic Stone* (1964), tells of two girls with very different backgrounds who share a strange stone in which is embedded a piece of metal (Could it be a fragment of King Arthur's sword?) that has mystical properties. As the story progresses the reader wonders if perhaps it is the accord of the two personalities that is mystical, and not the stone at all.

Alan Garner had been much acclaimed in England before his *Elidor* (1967) was published in the United States. From a demolition area in an English city four children are projected into a strange land and

---

[1] John Rowe Townsend, *Written for Children* (New York, Lothrop, Lee and Shepard, 1967), p. 128.

mysterious, headlong adventures. Because characterizations are second-ary to action, what remains in the memory are swift movement and dramatic contrasts: the drab realistic setting with the fearsome majesty of Elidor; the treasured pieces of junk with the jeweled sword, glowing stone, and a light-filled cauldron; the blazing last glimpse of Elidor with the demolished slum. Philippa Pearce called *Elidor*,

> realistic-apocalyptic, comic-sublime: the author's art held his two worlds together in exact balance, in a perfection of narrative ten-sion. Here is a splendid achievement.[1]

William Mayne's work will be discussed later but mention should be made here of *Earthfasts* (1967) in which he attempted a more complex story than he had done before. It is a brilliant effort but, as a children's book, not entirely successful. The encounter of two English country boys with a drummer boy of two hundred years before is not confusing but the rationalization of the supernatural events is. The boys are believable but the disasters and sometimes terrifying events are not always comprehensible. Complete understanding has never been en-tirely necessary, however, to children with the patience to enjoy an obscure story.

The entrance of King Arthur into *Earthfasts* links the book with several other fantasies of the same period. Susan Cooper's *Over Sea, Under Stone* (1966) is a story with allegorical overtones that reaches a climax of high excitement. Children spending a summer holiday in a seacoast village of Cornwall find an old map that leads them to clues to a long-sought relic of Arthurian times.

Another American, André Norton, told in *Steel Magic* (1965) a story of modern children who find themselves in Avalon and are be-sought by Huon of the Horn to search for the lost talismans that have the power to overcome evil: Arthur's sword, Huon's horn, and Merlin's ring.

American writers of fantasy in which the real and imaginary worlds are mingled are inclined to show more humor than are English writers in the same genre. The American stories range in kind of humor from the playfulness and unpredictability of Eleanor Estes' *Witch Family* (1960) and her three inventive stories in *The Sleeping Giant* (1948), to the humor of E. B. White's *Charlotte's Web*, Carolyn Sherwin Bailey's *Miss Hickory*, and the subtle wit of Elizabeth Marie Pope's *The Sherwood Ring* (1958).

In Miss Pope's novel two love stories are unfolded and skillfully interwoven—one in the present and the other in the American-Revolu-

---

[1] *Children's Book News* (London, Children's Book Centre), Vol. 2 (July–Aug., 1967), p. 164.

tionary-War past. Transitions are facile and the story sparkles with humor.

In a realistic story *The Majesty of Grace* (1961) Jane Langton demonstrated quick wit, understanding of children, and ability to create memorable personalities. In *The Diamond in the Window* (1962) and *The Swing in the Summerhouse* (1967) she ventured into time without barriers and introduced some endearing, often funny, characters into stories that have romance, excitement, symbolism, and comedy. Both books are laid in a uniquely American town, Concord, Massachusetts, a perfect setting for imaginative tales in which past and present mingle.

In lightness of touch Edward Ormondroyd's *Time at the Top* (1963) resembles Edward Eager's books. In its convincing glimpse of another setting it reminds one of *Tom's Midnight Garden*, but it is much more humorous. When Susan Shaw took the elevator to the top floor of her apartment house the elevator went well beyond the top before it stopped, and she found herself in an ornate Victorian house in 1881 instead of 1960. The interweaving of periods is skillful and the end of the story surprising and original.

In *The Cat and Mrs. Cary*, (1962) Doris Gates, well known for her excellent, realistic stories, took a careful step into the world of fantasy and managed so well that the reader is as surprised and convinced as are all the children of the story. The Cat is a memorable feline of great conceit, dignity, and enterprise.

It was natural that in the age of invention the world of fancy should embrace machines and skyscrapers. Poets and artists had already found beauty in modern cities and machines. Early in the twenties writers began experimenting with fanciful tales of airplanes and buses and other mechanical things. *Little Machinery* (1926) by Mary Liddell was a picture-story book worked out with careful attention to mechanical details, demonstrating the importance of accuracy and consistency in fantasy. Soon afterward came Hildegarde Hoyt Swift's *Little Blacknose* (1929), the story of the tiny DeWitt Clinton engine, the first ever built for the New York Central Railroad; May McNeer's story of a runaway automobile, *Stop Tim* (1930); Hardie Gramatky's tale of a tug boat, *Little Toot* (1939) (*Little Toot on the Thames* appeared in 1964); Virginia Lee Burton's *Mike Mulligan and His Steam Shovel* (1939); and William Pène du Bois's *Flying Locomotive* (1941). These, suggestive of the many ways in which fancy and scientific invention meet on common ground, show the importance of pictures as well as words in interpreting the story.

It was only a step from creating machines with personality that could have fantastic adventures, to creating machines that were in themselves fantastic. Science fantasy had begun. Author-artist Louis Slobodkin's inventiveness was given full play in *The Space Ship Under the Apple Tree* (1952). Eleanor Cameron, to satisfy the wishes of a young son, wrote *The Wonderful Flight to the Mushroom Planet* (1954), a story of the adventures of two ingenious boys who, in answer to a newspaper ad, built a space ship out of "materials found at hand," met the mysterious Mr. Tyco Bass, and took off in their space ship to bring help to the inhabitants of the planet Basidium. Mrs. Cameron succeeded so well in her wish to create a story that had facts as well as wonder and magic that the book was immediately popular, and boys were eager for more about the mushroom planet. Four other stories about David and Chuck followed, their friendship with Mr. Bass growing, and their adventures maintaining—and sometimes surpassing—the excitement of the first.

The distinction between science fiction and science fantasy is often obscure. Much science fiction is written for adults, but so is science fantasy—C. S. Lewis's *Out of the Silent Planet* (1943) for instance. Children with strong scientific interests, however, enjoy many stories that might seem too complex for them. A burgeoning of science-fiction and science-fantasy writing began in the forties, the concern with rocket ships and pioneering on other planets at first a natural expression of man's love for scientific prophecy. Developments in science today, however, can outstrip the most agile imaginations and it is not surprising that scores of writers, good, mediocre, and bad, have dealt with interplanetary travel and similar mysteries, and interpreted life in the distant future. In the forties Robert Heinlein began writing for young people, with conviction and disturbing plausibility, of adventures on other planets. Among his many titles are *Farmer in the Sky* (1950), *Star Beast* (1954), and *Have Space Suit—Will Travel* (1958). John Kier Cross's *The Angry Planet* (1946) is more eerie, and has more qualities of fantasy than Heinlein's books. André Norton, the pen-name of Alice Mary Norton, had written a number of young people's books based on history and legend when she wrote her first science fiction, *Star Man's Son* (1952). Many others followed, among them *Galactic Derelict* (1959) and *Judgment on Janus* (1963). These are a few representative books by three science-fiction writers that children especially enjoy.

Science opened new paths for creators of fantasy. They wrote of space travel and life on other planets but made use also of the unlimited variety of new devices and problems, some of which gave rise to philosophical themes and concepts that had seldom if ever been introduced into children's books. Some of the concepts in science fantasy may be as frightening to children today as were the subtle terrors imposed on them at times in mid-nineteenth century moral tales. The struggle between good and evil in its many variations, fundamental to the old tales, was given more sophisticated form in the new. Following are brief descriptions of three very different examples.

Patricia Wrightson's *Down to Earth* (1965), a book from Australia, is an ingeniously worked out story of a boy from Mars found in a partially demolished house by two children who tried to protect him from the unbelieving adult world. The book is shrewd, often funny—a wonderful combination of sage observance of human attitudes, exciting events, and convincing fantasy.

In *The White Mountains* (1967) John Christopher told a gripping story of a small group of rebels trying to save their minds and individualities in a world controlled by the monstrous Tripods, vast machines that stalked the earth rendering docile everyone over the age of fourteen.

Bruce Clements created a tense situation that stimulates thought in his beautifully written *Two Against the Tide* (1967). It tells of a brother and sister kidnaped and taken to an island inhabited by a group of people who have the secret of continuing life indefinitely. Believing that the presence of children will relieve the unchanging monotony, one of them brings Tom and Sharon to the island, gives them the miraculous pill that prevents any physical changes, and promises that at the end of the summer they may choose their future: to stay on the island and remain just as they are, or to return to their own world where they will grow old and die.

A book that combines devices of fairy tales, overtones of fantasy, the philosophy of great lives, the visions of science, and the warmth of a good family story is an appropriate one with which to end this chapter. Before she wrote *A Wrinkle in Time* (1962), which won the Newbery Medal, Madeleine L'Engle had written novels for adults and two perceptive realistic stories for girls. *A Wrinkle in Time* tells of the adventures of three children in search of the father of two of them, who had disappeared while engaged in scientific work for the government. By means of "tessering," which proves that in space a straight line is not the shortest distance between two points, the children and their protectors travel to several planets, even through the Dark Thing, which shadows the earth and in which some planets have been lost, and finally reach one of the lost planets, where the father is prisoner. The scene in which the children manage to resist the evil brain that all but absorbs them is tense and powerful; the ending triumphant. It is an exuberant book, original, vital, exciting. Funny ideas, fearful images, amazing characters, and beautiful concepts sweep through it. And it is full of truth.

The broader the foundation of knowledge from which the imagination can reach forth, the wider the base for the creator of literary fantasy.

Fantasy [said J. R. R. Tolkien] is a natural human activity. It certainly does not destroy or even insult Reason; and it does not either blunt the appetite for, nor obscure the perception of, scientific verity. On the contrary. The keener and the clearer is the reason, the better fantasy will it make. If men were ever in a state in which they did not want to know or could not perceive truth (facts or evidence), then Fantasy would languish until they were cured. If they ever get into that state. . . Fantasy will perish, and become Morbid Delusion.

For creative Fantasy is founded upon the hard recognition that things are so in the world as it appears under the sun; on a recognition of fact, but not a slavery to it.[1]

[1] J. R. R. Tolkien, "On Fairy Stories," in *Tree and Leaf* (Boston, Houghton Mifflin, 1965), pp. 54–55.

Bibliography

Alexander, Lloyd. "The Truth About Fantasy." *Top of the News*, Vol. 24 (Jan., 1968).

Beresford, J. D. Foreword to *Martin Pippin in the Apple Orchard* by Eleanor Farjeon. New York, F. A. Stokes, 1922.

Boston, Lucy M. "Christmas at 'Green Knowe.'" *The Horn Book*, Vol. 31 (Dec., 1955).

Chukovsky, Kornei. *From Two to Five*. Translated by Miriam Morton. Berkeley and Los Angeles, University of California Press, 1963.

Clark, Leonard. *Walter de la Mare*, a Walck Monograph. New York, Henry Z. Walck, 1961.

Cooper, Paul Fenimore. "On Catching a Child's Fancy." In *The Three Owls, Third Book* by Anne Carroll Moore. New York, Coward-McCann, 1931.

Crouch, Marcus S. "Another Don in Wonderland." *The Junior Bookshelf*, Vol. 14, No. 2 (March, 1950).

―――― *Treasure Seekers and Borrowers*. London, The Library Assoc., 1962.

de la Mare, Walter. *Animal Stories*. New York, Scribner, 1940.

Eiseley, Loren. "The Elvish Art of Enchantment." *The Horn Book*, Vol. 41 (Aug., 1965).

Farjeon, Eleanor. *The Little Book-Room*. London, Oxford University Press, 1956.

Fuller, Edmund. "Speaking of Books." *The New York Times Book Review*, Jan. 12, 1964.

Green, Roger Lancelyn. *C. S. Lewis*, a Walck Monograph. New York, Henry Z. Walck, 1963.

Jarrell, Randall. *The Animal Family*. New York, Pantheon, 1965.

Lathrop, Dorothy. Introduction to *Mr. Bumps and His Monkey* by Walter de la Mare. Chicago, John C. Winston, 1942.

Lewis, C. S. *An Experiment in Criticism*. Cambridge, Eng., University Press, 1961.

―――― "On Three Ways of Writing for Children." *The Horn Book*, Vol. 39 (Oct., 1963).

Lewis, Naomi, ed. Introduction to *A Book for Eleanor Farjeon*. New York, Henry Z. Walck, 1966.

Masefield, John. *So Long to Learn*. New York, Macmillan, 1952.

Moore, Anne Carroll and Bertha Mahony Miller, eds. *Writing and Criticism, a Book for Margery Bianco*. Boston, The Horn Book, 1951.

Norton, Mary. *The Borrowers Afield*. New York, Harcourt, 1955.

Pearce, Philippa. Review of *The Owl Service* by Alan Garner. *Children's Book News*, Vol. 2 (July–Aug., 1967).

Rose, Jasper. *Lucy Boston*, a Walck Monograph. New York, Henry Z. Walck, 1966.

Saint-Exupéry, Antoine de. *The Little Prince*. New York, Harcourt, 1943.

Smith, Lillian H. "News from Narnia." *The Horn Book*, Vol. 39 (Oct., 1963).

—— *The Unreluctant Years*. Chicago, American Library Assoc., 1953.

Tolkien, J. R. R. Foreword to *The Fellowship of the Ring*. New York, Ballantine Books, 1965.

—— *Tree and Leaf*. Boston, Houghton Mifflin, 1965.

Townsend, John Rowe. *Written for Children*. New York, Lothrop, Lee and Shepard, 1967.

Walsh, Chad. *C. S. Lewis: Apostle to the Skeptics*. New York, Macmillan, 1949.

4

Quests, Survival, and the
Romance of History

The Lure of Adventure

The adventure story, after the folk tale, was probably the first form of literature that children took for their own. By its very nature it spoke to every age. The narrator of exciting action is not diverted by consideration for age levels.

"A bold undertaking in which hazards are to be met and the issue hangs upon unforeseen events," the definition of *adventure*, might well be the definition of a good children's story. Dull books, ordinary ones, lack the boldness and the perils. The issue can sometimes be guessed, if not foreseen, the enterprise may be entered upon unwillingly, and in children's stories it often is, and the hazards may be spiritual; but unless they are met with valor the book is lacking in what children most enjoy and what they have a right to expect in their stories.

Books of fantasy—adventures outside the limitations and logic of the physical world—have been discussed. Except for them most adventure fiction has a historical setting. Yet, even in some of these, the romance of the setting, the extraordinary situation, the special vitality of the characters, so dominate the story that the reader has little concern with historical period. In such books events are related to conditions of the real world but the essence of *story* transcends time and place. As literary experiences, they stimulate the creative imagination much as fantasy does.

The increasing number of pure adventure stories is evidence of the growing literary maturity of children's literature. Elizabeth Nesbitt has shown how Robert Louis Stevenson's "conception of the true nature of romance" furthered the development of children's literature in the nineteenth century, and Rudyard Kipling, "the great originator," carried it forward at the beginning of the twentieth.

Eventful Journeys

The best adventure stories do not fit into any one category, but they often take the form of a journey. Outstanding among adventure stories of the thirties was *Yinka-Tu the Yak* (1938) by Alice Alison Lide, the first vivid story of Tibet for children. It tells of the hard, adventurous journey of the boy Sifan and his pet yak when they carried a secret message to the great monastery of Mombasa. Just ten years later appeared another account of the journey of a Tibetan child—*Daughter of the Mountains* (1948) by Louise Rankin. When her beautiful Lassa terrier was stolen, Momo set off to search for him, leaving her home far up in one of the highest passes to follow the caravan route down through the mountains, through lonely stretches and crowded villages in the vast rainy valley to the frightening city of Calcutta. Momo is so indomitable and so completely realized as to win for herself a place among the best-loved characters of children's fiction.

The India seen through Christine Weston's eyes in *Bhimsa the Dancing Bear* (1945) has great beauty, and fantastic though the adventures are, the story carries conviction. David, running away with Gopala and his wonderful bear, is rushing into the fulfillment of a dream that is common to children everywhere: the freedom to roam where they will, to eat what they will, and to sleep where they will, to enjoy perfect, unchecked freedom, with surprise and adventure around the bend in the road. The atmosphere created by the fluid, beautiful writing is unforgettable.

One of the most extraordinary journeys in fiction and a unique literary experience is *Big Tiger and Christian* (1952) by Fritz Mühlenweg, skillfully translated from the German by Isabel and Florence McHugh. A long book, its bulky appearance offset by pages alive with conversation and many motion-filled drawings by Rafaello Busoni, it relates the adventures of two boys, Chinese and English, who, in search of a wide open space to fly their kite, found themselves prisoners of war. The time was the early twenties, "the days of the civil wars or 'generals' wars,' of bandit chiefs who prospered, and of presidents of the Chinese Republic who were powerless." But most readers are caught in the immediacy of the events and do not stop to wonder, What war?

Big Tiger's courage and common sense had been well fortified by the wisdom of his old grandfather; Christian, born in Peking, the son of a doctor, could speak Chinese as well as English and was enterprising and quick witted. Their friendship was strong, supporting their courage and their natural ability to make the best of extraordinary situations. Through events that led from disappointment, to trouble, to disaster, the comment was apt to be, "It can't be helped."

The author, a painter and lecturer living in southern Germany, told the story to his seven children. He had once been a caravan leader in the Gobi desert and knew many of the people personally. "In those times," he wrote in his brief foreword, "one came across many splendid people, but also many not so creditable characters. They appear in this tale, good and bad, just as they really were." The setting in Mongolia is very clear and the backgrounds and culture of the many different people are evident in attitudes and conversation.

> "How sad it must be," said the woman, "not to be born a Mongol!"
> "It is certainly a misfortune," agreed the old man, "but what luck he has found the way to us!"[1]

The story is rooted in actuality, but the strangeness of the situations, the extraordinary vitality of the conversations, extend the experience beyond factual authenticity. The reader is wholly unaware of acquiring information. Six hundred pages of edification could not have survived for fifteen years, even as "required reading." The intense delight that book-loving children have found in the adventures—in a period when vicarious excitement can be had with no effort at all—is rather strong evidence that *Big Tiger and Christian* will give pleasure well into the future.

Banner in the Sky (1954) by James Ramsey Ullman is a perfect example of a book for young people that is successful both as a literary accomplishment and as a story wholly satisfying to boys and girls whatever their interests. The story itself is simple, and its theme familiar— a boy accomplishes a great physical feat despite his youth, ridicule, and his mother's determination to keep him from danger. Rudi Matt's dream was to climb the Citadel, the greatest mountain in Switzerland, which no one before had succeeded in conquering—the mountain that had taken the life of his father, the most practiced and skillful guide ever to attempt the ascent. The climax of the story is even more triumphant than the successful conquering of the peak. Mr. Ullman writes out of the excitement and enthusiasm of an experienced mountaineer. In writing for young people he adds to the background and knowledge, so significant in all his work, a keen understanding of boys and of what makes an absorbing story. Rudi's personality is as memorable as his accomplishment.

In 1954 appeared another story of a boy's devotion to a dream, *High Road Home* by William Corbin. Nico, a French orphan, had come to the United States ostensibly to be adopted into an American home, but he had other plans. He refused to believe that his father was dead and, from the moment in Cleveland when he jumped from the train, he was off on his own quest. The humor and the excellent characterizations make the story completely real. It is not only an exciting adventure but as honest a view of the United States as is to be found in a book for young people.

Marchette Chute's *The Innocent Wayfaring* (1943) is a midsummer

---

[1] Fritz Mühlenweg, *Big Tiger and Christian* (New York, Pantheon, 1952), p. 189.

journey through fourteenth century England, a lighthearted journey despite the dangers that beset the travelers. In a brief foreword, Miss Chute, the author also of *Geoffrey Chaucer of England* (1946), explains her inspiration for the sunniness of this engaging love story:

> As for the mood, no century is one of unrelieved sobriety, least of all the fourteenth. It produced Geoffrey Chaucer, and he was the greatest comic poet England has ever known.[1]

Her knowledge of the period gives her authority and freedom in her storytelling, but only a writer with a rich understanding of people can weave the accurate details into so graceful a story as this.

Elizabeth Coatsworth wrote many stories of journeys. Two of them are unique in the strangeness of the adventures. *Ronnie and the Chief's Son* (1962) has a haunting quality in its description of the animal herds drifting and flowing across the African plains, and in the account of Ronnie escaping from captivity in the midst of a herd of great antelope. *The Princess and the Lion* (1963) is the other. There is basis in historical fact for the Prison of Princes of about two hundred years ago. There, to avoid any quarreling over succession to the throne, the many sons of the king of Abyssinia were required to live out their lives, with only one exception—the son whom the king would choose as his successor. The journey is that of Mariam, daughter of the king, who disguised herself and her donkey and, with the palace lion beside her, set off to the Prison of Princes high on Mt. Wachni to take a message to her brother that would save his life.

Herbert Kaufmann's *Adventure in the Desert* (1961), translated from the German by Stella Humphries, is the tale of Mid-e-Mid, a young wandering troubadour of the Sahara. The book, in which the feeling of the desert is strong, grew out of the author's first-hand knowledge of the Tuareg people. The story is fast paced and dramatic, and Mid-e-Mid's success is not overdrawn: a mere boy of the desert tribe, gifted as a singer and a song maker, can become famous.

The main characters of Sid Fleischman's *Mr. Mysterious and Company* (1962) are an ingenious family who travel across badlands and prairies, through cactus, mesquite, and greasewood in a red covered wagon, putting on magic shows whenever they stopped at a town. They coped successfully with marauding Indians, an outlaw, and a band of ruffians, and they gave pleasure and met new friends wherever they went. In *By the Great Horn Spoon!* (1963) Praiseworthy, an urbane butler, traveled with Jack, his employer's son, on a fifteen-thousand-mile voyage—which they started as stowaways because their passage

---

[1] Marchette Chute, *The Innocent Wayfaring* (New York, E. P. Dutton, 1943), p. vii.

money had been stolen—to reach the gold fields of California. These and other books by Mr. Fleischman have a tall-tale quality, and situations recounted with skill, liveliness and great good humor.

Elizabeth Borton de Treviño's *Nacar, the White Deer* (1963) tells of the journey of a mute shepherd boy and a rare white deer across Mexico and is no less penetrating in its knowledge of human beings than her Newbery Medal winner *I, Juan de Pareja* (1965). The story of Nacar is based on historical records of the seventeenth century that tell about sending a white deer as a gift from the Viceroy in the New World to the King of Spain. Especially appealing are Lalo's understanding of animals and the poetic harmony that exists between boy and deer.

The Bushbabies (1965) by William Stevenson, a Canadian journalist, is unusual for its background, the diversity of the hazards to be overcome and the problems to be solved. It is the story of the journey taken by an English girl and her tiny pet tarsier, or bushbaby, with an African headman as her friend and protector from Mombasa to Ndi in Kenya, through bush fires, drought, and flood. Although many of the hazards are physical, the danger resulting from bigotry and spiritual blindness is even greater. The writing creates tremendous suspense and brilliantly evokes the setting.

> Wherever the flood had left the land exposed, there sprang a carpet of gay flowers and green shrubs. Where once there had been gnarled thorn and withered scrub, there now appeared green buds and lush grasses. For two weeks this transformation had been in secret preparation. Millions of plants and trees had come unobtrusively into bud, sensing the approach of the rain that within hours would splash color across the landscape like a child's brush on a magic paintbook.[1]

Lonely, wandering, and displaced children have been the natural subjects for children's books for generations. Many of them have led their authors into the trap of sentimentality. In *The Little Fishes* (1967) Erik Haugaard's story of the beggar children of Naples, and in those that follow, the conviction of the characterizations and the disciplined restraint of the writers give the books great emotional depth. Aimée Sommerfelt's *The Road to Agra* (1961), translated from the Norwegian, is laid in India and tells of a brother and sister who make the three-hundred-mile journey on foot to get medical care for the seven-year-old girl who is losing her sight just when she has won a coveted place in the village school. *The Orphans of Simitra* (1962) by Paul-Jacques Bonzon, translated from the French by Thelma Niklaus, is the story of a Greek boy's search throughout Europe for his little sister.

[1] William Stevenson, *The Bushbabies* (Boston, Houghton Mifflin, 1965), p. 269.

John and Patricia Beatty, very competent writers and collaborators on historical fiction, moved away from their usual settings, seventeenth and eighteenth century England, to tell in *A Donkey for the King* (1966) a story of first century Israel. The mute orphan Jesse had found work in a traveling circus. Among the wretched human beings and animals, Jesse found one he could love—Belshazzar, a white donkey who delighted the audience with dancing steps. Story and historical setting are so well integrated that the family from Nazareth, the great star that disturbed the visitors to Bethlehem, and the strange, kinglike men riding their camels into the city are seen from the perspective of their time and place.

In *North to Freedom* (1965) by Anne Holm, David's journey leaves the reader with a heightened sense of the value of life. David had reached the age of twelve without having had any first-hand experience with life outside the walls of an eastern European concentration camp. The story tells of his escape into a world for which he was completely unprepared, of his discoveries of all the wonders that are an unnoticed part of ordinary living, and of his experiences with insensitivity, cruelty, and kindness. The many adventures and the happy ending that seems right and inevitable make a compelling, satisfying story, but its unique achievement is in arousing the reader to see life, people, and the world about him as if for the first time.

Survival

Ever since children first took Daniel Defoe's masterpiece as their own, it has been considered the archetype of the successful children's story. Countless books for children have followed the pattern of *Robinson Crusoe*: children, thrust upon their own resources, using all their knowledge and ingenuity to survive, and succeeding. Settings and number of characters have varied, but the idea of staking one's life on the ability to solve problems that seem all but unsolvable has irresistible appeal.

Robert C. Dusoe's *Three Without Fear* (1947) is a gallant Robinson-Crusoe-like story. A boy shipwrecked off the coast of Baja California drifted to shore and met up with two orphaned Indian children. With great courage and resourcefulness they made their way up the coast.

A situation demanding courage to face the desolation of complete loss as well as fear for the future was the lot of a Japanese boy in *The Big Wave* (1948) by Pearl Buck. There is strong folk feeling in the story of the lone survivor of a fishing village swept away by a tidal wave.

From the fifties on, survival stories often reflected the modern world. Survivers of plane crashes sometimes experienced even greater challenges to inventiveness and courage than did any desert-island castaway.

After the mid-twentieth century, children were apt to consider the favorite old survival tales as remote as fantasy. Such adventures seemed no longer possible with so few remaining unpopulated areas where a castaway would have to depend solely on his wits and ingenuity to live. Then Bianca Bradbury in *Two on an Island* (1965), a story of two children whose boat drifted to an uninhabited island in Maine, reminded readers that unexpected adventures can still happen.

To meet the castaway test because it is thrust upon one demands stamina, courage, and ingenuity. To put oneself deliberately to the test of survival demands in addition the most daring sense of adventure. It is not surprising that Sam Gribley's story of his year of complete self-sufficiency spent in the Catskill Mountains had immediate popularity. *My Side of the Mountain* (1959) by Jean George made possible an extraordinary vicarious experience. Sam's descriptions of the making of his home in a hollowed-out tree, his tools, his clothes; of the gathering and preparing of his food, and the careful planning to survive the winter have the fascination of detail that children appreciate. From the diary record of his mountain-forest year Sam's personality emerges clearly—his intelligence, his pleasure in animals and birds, his perseverance, and even his growing enjoyment of people, though he had chosen to separate himself completely from them to carry out his experiment. The book brings a great deal to its readers—an unforgettable year in the heart of nature.

Among the many stories about survivors of air disasters Marjorie Phleger's *Pilot Down, Presumed Dead* (1963) is outstanding. Caught in a hurricane Steve Ferris was forced to land on the beach of a small, uninhabited island off the coast of Baja California. Thirty days after his crash landing, with a crude raft he had built, Steve managed to reach a Mexican town on the mainland. Until then no other human beings entered the story but never does the interest lag, so intense is the drama of courage and resourcefulness.

Originally published in French in 1888, Jules Verne's *Deux Ans de Vacances* was translated by Olga Marx under the title *A Long Vacation* and published for the first time in English in 1967. An exciting account of shipwreck, on an uninhabited island, of fifteen boys between the ages of eight and fourteen, it reminds one of the beginning of William Golding's *Lord of the Flies*. The emotional maturing of the boys on their long "vacation" is typical of most survival tales of and for children. The challenge of adversity is such an obvious device to show character development that disasters of all kinds have inspired children's stories, thus satisfying at one time the adult's sense of purpose and the child's wish for an exciting tale. Life-or-death struggles against disaster have given variations on the survival theme. A number of these have come from abroad, including three from the French: *The Village that Slept*

(1965) by Monique Peyrouton de Ladebat, which tells of two children and a tiny half-starved baby stranded in the wasteland of the Pyrenees; *Flood Warning* (1963) by Paul Berna, the story of five boys and their schoolmaster hopelessly marooned in the school during flood; and *Landslide* (1963) by Veronique Day. From the Dutch is *The Tide in the Attic* (1962) by Aleid Van Rhijn, based on the 1953 flood in Holland; and, from Australia, Ivan Southall's stories of storm and bush fire, *Hills End* (1963) and *Ash Road* (1965).

Most unusual of all the survival stories, both for subject and for beauty of literary style, is *Island of the Blue Dolphins* (1960), for which Scott O'Dell received the Newbery Medal. The author, a Californian and authority on California history, was inspired to tell his story by the few existing facts about a girl who had lived alone upon the island of San Nicolas from 1835 to 1853 and was known to history as "The Lost Woman of San Nicolas." He has Karana tell her own story of being left behind when her people evacuated the island, making her own weapons for protection and obtaining food, building a house, and finally making friends of the animals and birds. Her strange, beautiful account reveals courage, serenity, and greatness of spirit, and is a lasting experience for children who have the chance to know her.

Rogues, Spies, and Hidden Treasure

Danger assumes different guises during the changing years between infancy and adulthood and in stories it always has great allure—from the foxy gentleman with designs on Jemima Puddleduck to the sophisticated enemy agents of Lockhart Amerman's witty suspense tales. If adventure stories have no substance beyond plot and action, they are read and forgotten and new ones take their places. Not so quickly forgotten is a book about pirates or spies or hidden treasure in which the story is integral to an unusual setting, or which has strong characterizations that give it exceptional depth.

Eilís Dillon, whose first book, *The Lost Island*, was published in the United States in 1952, can tell a suspense story so rich in atmosphere and stout Irish humor, and peopled with such diverse and well realized characters that the books are long remembered and often invite rereading. Eilis Dillon is an Irish woman, steeped in Irish legends and superstitions, so well acquainted with the rugged coast of Ireland and its proud little islands, that her books are vivid experiences. She has such eloquence in the portrayal of people that her characters, from small boys to the crones and patriarchs, are individual and authentic. Viking relics are found to be the treasure of *The Singing Cave* (1959) and Spanish coins the treasure of *The Fort of Gold* (1961).

An outstanding English writer of the sixties is Leon Garfield, whose books have pace, humor, and unusually good characterizations. In each of his books mystery is focused on a strange, dominating figure. His first one, *Jack Holborn* (1965), tells, in the Stevenson tradition, of an orphan boy who falls into the hands of pirates. *Devil-in-the-Fog* (1966) has a set of ingratiating characters in Mr. Treet's family of strolling players. *Smith* (1967), the tale of a small pickpocket of the eighteenth century, is a triumph of story telling, characterization, and suspense. Few present-day writers combine the attributes that seem so effortless in Mr. Garfield's work: well-built plots, suspense, a writing style suited to the mood of each book, and characters that come to life.

The Arm of the Starfish (1965) by Madeleine L'Engle is a story of spies and international intrigue, of family devotion, and the development of a boy's sense of values. Woven through it is the fascinating thread of prophetic advances in the biological sciences. Each of Madeleine L'Engle's books has been a testimony to her originality, breadth of knowledge, and her great resources of imagination and spirit.

Sea Adventure

Charles Boardman Hawes (1889–1923) did not write with any special audience in mind. He had his stories to tell and he told them to the best of his ability, giving back in them the pleasure he had all his life received from his absorbing interest in ships and the sea. At the beginning of a period when books for children were considered apart from the general stream of literature, the influence of a writer like Charles Boardman Hawes was a reminder that, while literature might have many branches, one of them being books for children, the best children's books were still *literature*.

The first of his three adventure stories, *The Mutineers* (1920), is the story of sixteen-year-old Benjamin Lathrop, who put out from Salem Harbor as a green hand on the *Island Princess* bound for Canton, China, and returned eighteen months later a man grown in wisdom and courage.

The Great Quest (1921) is a tale of the adventures of another New Englander, but of the three stories this seems the least whole, possibly because the African setting is less maturely conceived than any of his other backgrounds. The third book, *The Dark Frigate* (1923), for which the Newbery Medal was awarded posthumously to Charles Boardman Hawes, tells of a young English seaman in the time of King Charles. It is full of action and excitement with historic accuracy and authentic seamanship, and gives a glimpse of Devonshire three hundred years ago.

Again and again in sea adventure stories the plot involves a young apprentice or cabin boy who must make his way among seasoned, often cruel, seamen, his world circumscribed by the sea and weather. As this was the story lived so often in real life it is not surprising to find it often in fiction. It never loses its appeal in the hands of an able storyteller.

For its vitality and feeling of truth, Charles Nordhoff's *Pearl Lagoon* (1924) has much in common with the Hawes adventure tales. *Pearl Lagoon*, with its setting in the South Seas, was written after Mr. Nordhoff had lived for some years on Tahiti. The book has reality in the warmth and the companionship of Charlie and Captain Harry Selden with the natives, in the pleasures of fishing in unspoiled waters, in the desperate thrills of fights with great man-eating fish, and the excitement of pearl diving in the magical beauty of the undersea world.

Charles Finger's *Courageous Companions* (1929) is the story of an English boy who sailed with Magellan around the world. Dick Osberne had a talent for friendship, and no doubt it is Charles Finger himself looking at the world through the eyes of Osberne and remembering, not the hardships and dangers of the adventure, but the companionship. Throughout the journey, with all its tragedies, the result often of avarice and treachery, Osberne never lost his idealism, his sense of fairness, nor the courage to hold to the course he had set himself. The classic rhythm of the style gives evidence of Mr. Finger's lifelong pleasure in great books as well as in adventure.

Two years later appeared John Fabricius's *Java Ho!* (1931), the adventures of four boys amid fire, storm, and shipwreck. Originating in Dutch, it was abridged and translated from the German by M. C. Darnton. This story was based on the log of a real Dutch seafarer, Willem Brontekoe, a kindly, generous man and a courageous captain, whose voyage was so beset with dangers and misadventures as to have been the most unlucky passage on record in Holland's golden era of adventure to the Indies. A sense of contemporary reporting is achieved by the skillful characterizations, particularly in the humanity of the skipper and the individualities of the cabin boys, and by the humor woven through the astounding adventures and pointed up by the author's own excellent illustrations.

With a happy childhood spent in Syria and her first language Arabic, it was natural that Agnes Danforth Hewes's first book, *A Boy of the Lost Crusade* (1923), should reflect her interest in the Middle East. In books that give life to the history of trade, however, she made her most significant contribution: *Swords on the Sea* (1928), *Spice and the Devil's Cave* (1930), and *Glory of the Seas* (1933). Although inclined to romanticize human relationships, she, nevertheless, filled the roads out of the past with believable people and gave unity to the far-flung story of discovery and trade.

Other important stories of sailing ships appeared in 1933, notably John Masefield's *Bird of Dawning* and George Grant's *The Half Deck*.

Frequent travel from childhood on had interested Alida Simms Malkus in the early civilizations of the Americas: the Indians of New Mexico, the Mayans of Yucatan, the Incas of Peru, and it was just another step backward in time to have her interest kindled in the Polynesian explorers. In *Eastward Sweeps the Current* (1937) she brought to life members of a race who lived a thousand years before Columbus. The integration of her research is so skillfully accomplished that the story flows with the sweep of the ocean currents. To reread the book after many years is only to have the lines of the portraits sharpened; the personalities of the characters had not been completely forgotten.

Armstrong Sperry had been writing informational books about South Sea Island life when, in 1935 he wrote *All Sail Set*, a story about the famous clipper ship *Flying Cloud*. Through the next three decades he wrote numerous books for young people, including adventure stories— some tales of the sea, others laid in the jungles of South America. He is known best, however, for *Call It Courage* (1940), which received the Newbery Medal and has become recognized as a "modern classic." *Call It Courage* is a tale of the early Polynesians among whom there was no place for the man who was afraid. Based on legend, the story of a boy who, to conquer his fear of the ocean, set forth in his canoe alone, met with every sort of danger and returned to be known as Mafatu, "Stout Heart," has great conviction. Armstrong Sperry's interest in Polynesia grew out of listening to his great-grandfather, who had followed the sea all his life, tell tales of his adventures, especially those on the island of Bora Bora where his great-grandfather had been shipwrecked. Later, on his own travels, Mr. Sperry discovered the islands for himself. As an assistant ethnologist on the Kaimiloa expedition of the Bishop Museum of Honolulu, he became acquainted with the least known islands of the South Pacific, learned the languages, legends and music, storing up background that found expression in his books.

Jean Lee Latham's biographical novel, *Carry On, Mr. Bowditch* (1955) which won the Newbery Medal, moves as fast as the best sea adventure. Nathaniel Bowditch, author of *The New American Practical Navigator* before he was thirty, had packed into his life a great deal of learning, sailing, adventure, and enjoyment of unfamiliar lands and people.

Henry Treece (1912–1966) was a poet and author of criticism and short stories before he found his place as a writer of children's books. Even though much of his adult life he taught at a grammar school in Lincolnshire, England, his output of books was tremendous and most of them were crowded within his last twenty years. As a teacher he was well acquainted with the kinds of writing children enjoy, he was interested in bringing to life periods and peoples that might otherwise have little appeal to children, and he knew the importance of the strictest accuracy. Ancient and medieval Britain were frequent backgrounds for his stories, but in the United States he became best known for his tales of the Vikings, particularly his trilogy dealing with Harold Sigurdson: *Viking's Dawn* (1956), *The Road to Miklagard* (1957), and *Viking's Sunset* (1960). The stories have the violence and brutality of a ruthless period but the style, which shows evidence of Mr. Treece's enjoyment of the Icelandic sagas, gives dignity to the telling.

K. M. Peyton is a British author whose unusual knowledge of sailing and the sea stems from her own experience. She and her family are well acquainted with Essex ports and fishing villages and have sailed the rugged coast. Three of her books for which she is known in the United States are *Sea Fever* (1963), *The Maplin Bird* (1965), and *The Plan for Birdsmarsh* (1966). Each is entirely different from the others but each has a vividly realized Essex setting. The first and last are contemporary stories of boys; *The Maplin Bird* takes place a hundred years ago and has an unusual heroine, spunky, enterprising and appealing. All three tell exciting, original stories, with absorbing plots, and alive people whose characters develop naturally and realistically.

First published in book form in Petrograd in 1923, *Scarlet Sails* has continued through the years to be one of the most popular stories in Russia. Alexander Stepanovich Grinyevsky, under the foreign-sounding pen name of Alexander Green, wrote stories of ships and the sea, yet he himself had only one brief and unsuccessful experience as a seaman. Translated skillfully by Thomas P. Whitney and illustrated by Esta Nesbitt, who also designed the stunning format, *Scarlet Sails* (1967) is the only one of Alexander Green's books thus far to be published in English. It is a remarkable combination of fairy tale and reality with a Cinderella-like theme, the story of a despised and taunted child for whom a charming prophecy comes true.

A sea story with a contemporary point of view was *Sea Hawk Calling* by Hild Henriksen (1962), translated from the Norwegian by Holger Lundbergh. The heroine is a radio operator on a Norwegian freighter determined to get her own sea legs while she waits for the return of her fiancé, an officer on another ship. Of genuine interest is the picture of life at sea through the eyes of a mature young girl deeply in love but thoroughly practical and determined to get the most from her experience.

Three refreshingly original sea stories that were published in 1967 should be mentioned here although the authors are discussed in other chapters. *Cross Currents* by Joan Phipson of Australia shows the development of the personalities of two teen-age boys during an extraordinary sailing experience. The Irish writer Eilís Dillon with her warmth and feeling for people makes the human story as interesting as the sea adventure in *The Cruise of the Santa Maria* and unites an Irish island with a Spanish fishing village, when three boys set off in a new boat that the villagers had marked for disaster. Scott O'Dell's *The Black Pearl*

(1967), laid in Baja California, is a story of pearl diving, gripping and memorable with a strong feeling of authenticity and the overtones and symbolism of legend.

Erik Haugaard's *Hakon of Rogen's Saga* (1963) introduced one of the most important writers of the sixties to the United States. Although a Danish poet, his children's books have been written in English and first published in the United States. *Hakon* and *A Slave's Tale* (1965) are laid in Norway and in the seas about her islands at the end of the Viking period. Although the action is violent, brutal, and tragic, the stories are moving and often beautiful. Mr. Haugaard's third book, *Orphans of the Wind* (1966), is a thrilling adventure story laid at sea, in the Carolinas, and in Virginia during the first Battle of Bull Run. It is narrated by Jim, a deck boy on a British blockade runner, whose awakening to the meaning of slavery and of civil war is sharp and unforgettable.

Mr. Haugaard sets a high standard for books for today's young people. Always he has a story to tell, a powerful story that touches emotions and shows respect for his readers. And, deeply and completely integrated in his story, he has something to say that transcends didacticism, that leaves a residue of wisdom and compassion in the hearts of his readers. He accomplishes what is expected of the best novelists—a reflection of life that throws light upon humanity and the needs and desires of the human spirit.

Before History

No period is too remote to excite the storyteller. Even Lucy Fitch Perkins as early as 1916 set one of her stories of twins among the cave dwellers, but the flavor of her book is more contemporary than prehistoric. Most stories set in prehistory appear to have been written to supplement school assignments; few have life. Among the most convincing is D. Moreau Barringer's *And the Waters Prevailed* (1956) in which the hero dares to think beyond the accepted pattern of existence. Margherita Fanchiotti's *A Bow in the Cloud* (1954), an account of two children who join the company on Noah's Ark, is delightful in its humor and portrayal of people and incidents, important as a well-written, imaginative story, inspired by the Biblical record but that does not attempt to re-create a period.

Harry Behn's *The Faraway Lurs* (1963) rings with the truth of great fantasy. Told by an archaeologist who is also a poet, its roots are deep in history and its characters live. Mr. Behn's journey to Denmark to visit the birthplace of his mother resulted not in a story based on her life but one inspired by the archaeological discovery of the grave of a girl who had lived probably three thousand years ago. It is a tale of intrigue, taboos, and tragedy; but beauty shines through. It gives life to the past and makes the reader feel a part of the long human story.

The Ancient World in Fiction

Caroline Dale Snedeker (1871–1956) was born in New Harmony, Indiana, the great-granddaughter of the Utopian Socialist, Robert Owen, who had founded the town of New Harmony. Her growing years in Indiana and later in Cincinnati were filled with an appreciation of the good things from the past, particularly music which the whole family enjoyed sharing. It was natural when, after their father's death, the four Parke daughters should take an adventurous way to improve the family finances and help their brother through school. They gave concerts, touring Ohio, Illinois, Michigan, North Dakota, and Nebraska. The "hardships we took with a merry heart. . . . We were young and it seemed wonderful to 'be on the stage.'"

After her marriage her husband, Charles Snedeker, dean of St. Paul's Cathedral in Cincinnati, encouraged her to write. When she remarked that only a Greek scholar could write the story she had in mind, he replied, "Well, then, make yourself a Greek scholar." With his help she began to write under her husband's critical discipline. Later she traveled in Greece and Rome, to follow up the legends of the British saints whom she discovered in Ilfracombe and Tintagel, searching out not only literary sources, but the "spiritual sources" of her story backgrounds.

It had not occurred to Mrs. Snedeker that she would find her widest audience among young people when in 1911 her first book, *The Coward of Thermopylae*, was published. The book did not receive the recognition it deserved until the next year when it was republished in a format to appeal to younger readers under a new title, *The Spartan*. Telling the thrilling story of the battle against the army of Xerxes and the hero who returned alone from Thermopylae, she re-created the life of Sparta and opened her first window upon the culture of ancient Greece. Not until many years later did another book follow, *The Perilous Seat*, the story of Theria, priestess of Delphi, a moving love story in which is shown the influence of the Temple of Apollo on people and government. Her third book, *Theras and His Town* (1924), tells of an Athenian boy, who, taken against his will to Sparta, experienced many adventures before he finally found his way back to Athens.

Had she written no more than these three books she would have contributed significantly to the widening span of historic periods interpreted in books for children. But other fine books followed, among them *The Forgotten Daughter* (1933), the story of Chloe, a Greek slave in Rome, and *The White Isle* (1940), the story of a Roman patrician family exiled from Rome. Into *The White Isle* are woven traditions of early British Christianity that rose independent of Rome. The description of the first century Christian service has been cited by church scholars as a reliable description of an early Christian service. Mrs. Snedeker's scholarship gave her books authenticity; her integration of material and plot and her ability to see her characters clearly gave them vitality.

In contrast to the glimpse of the first century of Mrs. Snedeker's book is one of Roman-occupied Israel in *The Bronze Bow* (1961) for which Elizabeth George Speare received the Newbery Medal. The protagonist is Daniel bar Jamin, a proud young Galilean who had seen his father die at the hands of the Romans and was filled with bitterness and passionate purpose—to drive the Romans out of Israel. For five years he had hidden in the hills with outlaws waiting for the day when they could strike. From time to time he saw Jesus and witnessed some of his miracles, but felt only bewilderment. He could not subdue his impatience with those who did not believe in fighting for freedom. He had to see all his hopes crash before he could understand a power stronger than that which can bend a bow of bronze. Written with compassion and restraint, the story is intensely dramatic and moving.

Despite the discovery in 1922 of Tutankhamon's tomb and the golden relics that made the last rulers of the eighteenth dynasty seem astonishingly near, not until 1937 did a book about ancient Egypt appear that had reality for young people. *The Lost Queen of Egypt* (1937) by Lucile Morrison brought to life the boy and girl who had sat upon the throne of the Pharaohs more than thirteen hundred years before the birth of Christ. The story is chiefly about Ankhsenamon, daughter of Ikhnaton and wife of Tutankhamon, about whom, after her husband's death, nothing is known. Lucile Morrison worked out a solution to the mystery of the disappearance of the young queen that is logical and satisfying and rounds out an absorbing novel.

The same period was the setting for Erick Berry's *Honey of the Nile* (1938), a story of intrigue and danger following the reign of Ikhnaton. Eloise Lownsbery's *A Camel for a Throne* (1941) told of the travels of an Egyptian princess who learned by her own experience of the hardships of the common people. Woven through Eloise Jarvis McGraw's *The Golden Goblet* (1961), a swift-moving tale of the pursuit and capture of grave robbers, are details of the goldsmith's craft. In *Egyptian Adventures* (1954) Olivia Coolidge told twelve stories about different kinds of people—pharaohs, soldiers, traders, slaves—in the New Kingdom.

Olivia Coolidge came to America after she had received a classical education at Oxford and taught briefly in London, and here she has stayed. Her classical background and wide reading stimulated her interest in retelling the great myths and epic stories. She advanced considerably beyond retellings in *Roman People* (1959), *Men of Athens* (1962), and *Lives of Famous Romans* (1965), creating incidents and developing characters to give excitement and a strong sense of immediacy, always maintaining historical accuracy. *The King of Men* (1966) is an original novel based on the legend of Agamemnon from his youth until his marriage to Clytemnestra, sister of Helen. In *Marathon Looks on the Sea* (1967), Metiochos, son of the Greek general Miltiades, is the protagonist. Mrs. Coolidge has given flesh to ancient heroes and vitality to their stories, an important accomplishment in any time, but especially significant in a period when classical studies are giving way to scientific, and young people can easily miss any acquaintance with the ancient heroes.

Rosemary Sutcliff and Ancient Britain

Rosemary Sutcliff has been called an "intuitive historian." Her research is thorough, but so great is her ability to think herself completely back into the period of her story that her research is never felt. It is transformed into living experiences. Her first book, *The Queen Elizabeth Story* (1950), was gentle and very appealing but gave little idea of the power that she was soon to gain in her writing. Her books about Roman Britain—*The Eagle of the Ninth* (1954), *The Outcast* (1955), *The Silver Branch* (1957), and *The Lantern Bearers* (1959)—made and established her reputation as one of the most outstanding writers of historical fiction for young people. Afflicted in early childhood with a crippling disease, Miss Sutcliff's physical movement has always been severely restricted, but the vigor of her storytelling gives no hint of any restraints. Her mother read a great deal to her in her childhood and gave her much of her education. She wrote:

> From the age of five I was reared on Dickens, Thackeray and Trollope, on Kingsley's *Westward Ho!* and Lord Lytton's *Last Days of Pompeii*, and other strong meats including two fat and fascinating books of Father's: *Myths of Greece and Rome* and *Hero Myths and Legends of the British Race*. And in this last was the story of Beowulf, which I demanded more often and loved better than all beside.
>
> Some children's books I did have: Hans Andersen, of course, and several of Beatrix Potter's small gems. . . . But these, much loved though they were, were the outer circle of our reading, whose center was Dickens and Beowulf.[1]

The people of books filled her imagination but did not keep her from noticing with special shrewdness the real people she met. The keenness

[1] Rosemary Sutcliff, "Beginning with Beowulf," *The Horn Book*, Vol. 29 (Feb., 1953), p. 36.

of her observation of the world around her—trees, hills, landscapes, and changing seasons—is strongly evident in her story settings, which are as clear as the plots and the characters. *The Shield Ring* (1957) is a story of the last stand of the Viking settlers in the Lake District against the Normans. The hero of *Dawn Wind* (1962) has lost his family to the Saxon invaders and becomes a Saxon thrall. *Simon* (1954) is laid during the Civil War in England, *Warrior Scarlet* (1958) in the Bronze Age, *Knight's Fee* (1960) in Norman England, and *Mark of the Horse Lord* (1965) in second century Britain. Reading the books in the sequence of their periods gives a remarkable sense of the continuity of history. *Brother Dusty-Feet* (1953) and *The Armourer's House* (1952) are referred to by Margaret Meek as "domestication of the past" rather than historical fiction. In *Brother Dusty-Feet*, a tale of strolling players in medieval England, and her first story with a boy protagonist, she appeared to be learning her craft. *The Armourer's House* may seem overly gentle but the charm of the armourer's household, the family's warm inclusion of little Tamsyn among them, the festive events of the year—especially Christmas—and the understanding of the joys of a responsive young girl make the book a happy experience for children younger than those who appreciate Miss Sutcliff's later historical fiction. It is a book with life and spirit and not to be overlooked.

Medieval and Early Modern Europe in Fiction

Eloise Lownsbery's knowledge of other lands and times had been evident in several stories of France in medieval and early modern periods. The most notable of these is her *Boy Knight of Reims* (1927), a story of the building of the cathedral of Reims. It was a natural expression of her love for a city and a cathedral that she had learned to know well after the First World War, when she had worked in France with the Quakers.

Other young Americans went to Europe in civilian capacities to serve during the First World War and became absorbed in the history and the current problems of the peoples. One of these was Eric Kelly (1884–1960). Polish exiles whom he had met in the French organization Foyer du Soldat urged him to go with them to Poland to help in establishing the same type of organized welfare there. Shortly after the armistice he was able to help in the distribution of food and supplies to Poland. He learned the language, traveled widely, and became well acquainted with the people. After his return to America he wrote stories for *St. Nicholas Magazine* and taught at Mercersburg Academy and Dartmouth College. When in 1925 he returned to teach and study at the University of Krakow he wrote *The Trumpeter of Krakow* (1928) within sight of the old church tower where he could hear the trumpeter day and night. The story is laid in fifteenth century Poland, a time of much poverty and suffering, of faith in magic and sorcery, and shows the political and social issues at stake in a colorful, turbulent period. For the book Eric Kelly received the Newbery Medal. His sense of adventure found expression in stories of other lands and times, but in his tales of Poland he made a unique contribution to children's literature.

In the early years of the century there were few convincing historical novels; by the sixties there were many with good characterizations that give immediacy and truth to the adventure.

In the twenties and thirties Allen French's excellently plotted stories of castles and feudal knights were outstanding for good writing and the clear evidence of the social and economic problems behind exciting events.

During the forties certain stories of medieval Europe derived their spirit from contemporary events, though their setting was in the past. With the complete reversion of the concept of the value of human life expressing itself in slaughter and invasion, the sensitivities of writers were shocked into expression. The passion for liberty and the theme of tolerance are ever present in Catherine Coblentz's *Beggars' Penny* (1943), a story of the siege of Leyden that shows how people of different religions and social stations worked together to save their city. Meindert DeJong's *The Tower by the Sea* (1950) is a powerful story based on a North Sea legend that shows the tragedy wrought by misunderstanding and intolerance. Modern parallels were easy to find for Loring MacKaye's *We of Frabo Stand* (1944), the tragic story of the invasion of Gottland by Waldemar of Denmark.

Hans Baumann's *Sons of the Steppe* (1958), translated from the German by Isabel and Florence McHugh, is a cogent story of the grandsons of Genghis Khan, and a vivid re-creation of the Mongolian steppe when the boys were growing up and longing to ride forth with their grandfather as conquerors. Arik-Buka did not change, but Kublai, gradually influenced by his teacher, a wise Chinese philosopher, began to reject bloodshed and cruelty, unknowingly preparing himself to become "the gentle conqueror."

Very eloquent is the unfolding of the brilliant first half of the seventeenth century in Spain and of its people—from the most humble dwarf to King Philip—in *I, Juan de Pareja* (1965) by Elizabeth Borton de Treviño. Rooted in history, it is the story of the Negro slave, inherited by Velázquez, who became the artist's assistant and friend. Mrs. Treviño made the most of the rare written sources and with keen study and imagination gathered from their own paintings much about the artists who appear in the story. The book, which won the Newbery Medal, was strong enough to stand without any apologies or explanations but its relationship to the period in which it was written may be noted in the author's comment in an afterword: "It will appeal, I hope, to young people of both white and Negro races because the story of Juan de Pareja and Velázquez foreshadows, in the lifetime of the two men, what we hope to achieve a millionfold today."

Great Britain in Period Stories

When *Adam of the Road* (1942) was published Elizabeth Janet Gray had already been recognized as an important writer for young people. In her story of England in the days of minstrelsy she brought to a different subject a genius that had been exhibited in other fine books, showing that against a scrupulously accurate historical setting she could create living people. Her own background stimulated interests out of which her books have grown: a home in Pennsylvania and a Quaker heritage from her mother, her Scottish father's contacts with his homeland, and her happy years in North and South Carolina out of which came her delightful stories of colonial days, *Meggy MacIntosh* (1930) and *Beppy Marlowe* (1936). When, after the Second World War, she was chosen to fill an unprecedented post as teacher of English to the Crown Prince of Japan, and "open windows on the world" for many Japanese besides the imperial family, she gave proof of her love for people and her spiritual reserves. This oneness with people of all times and places is the secret of her vivid stories and biographies and the notable contributions she has made outside the field of children's books, where she is better known as Elizabeth Gray Vining. *Adam of the Road*—the book won the Newbery Medal—takes the reader across the length and breadth of England. Tournaments and battles, cruelty and power, are not important here. In a less familiar view of the Middle Ages the reader sees ordinary people experiencing the fair, the busy inn, the excitement around castle and manor house. The view of nobles and peasants, priests and minstrels, students, peddlers, smiths and millers—all the variety of life of any era—is sharpened by the dramatic contrasts of feudal times. The pattern is that of a medieval tapestry, but the lines are sunny and alive. Elizabeth Janet Gray's *I Will Adventure* (1962) also lacks the grim aspects of the middle ages, but the personality of the young hero and the pattern of life are clear.

Judith of France (1948) by Margaret Leighton tells the story of the great-granddaughter of Charlemagne who was married to the aged Saxon King Aethelwulf; and Marguerite de Angeli's first historical story with a European setting and winner of the Newbery Medal, *The Door in the Wall* (1949), is about a crippled boy in thirteenth century England who found his own special way to serve his king.

Geoffrey Trease, a prolific and accomplished author, has been recognized in England since the early thirties for school stories, mysteries, books about everyday children, and historical fiction. In the United States he is known for his historical tales. They move with sweep and excitement, making the most of colorful periods and unusual problems, and fulfilling Mr. Trease's own stipulations for a good children's book: it is one which "uses language skillfully to entertain and represent reality, to stimulate the imagination, or to educate the emotions." His first book to be published in the United States was *Cue for Treason* (1941), laid in Elizabethan times with a hero who became involved with strolling players. Several books followed, one of his best being *Victory at Valmy* (1960), a thrilling tale of the French Revolution and of a gifted boy of the common people who had been taken into the home of an aristocrat. E. K. Seth-Smith wrote an exceptionally good story of traveling players, *Vagabonds All* (1946), and Marchette Chute's *The Wonderful Winter* (1954) employs her excellent Shakespearean background in telling an appealing story of a young boy who acts with Shakespeare in the Burbage Theater.

Patricia Gordon's *Rommany Luck* (1946) is based on the plight of the gypsies during Queen Elizabeth's reign. It tells of the Rommany boy Orlando, who journeyed from Exeter where over a hundred of his people were imprisoned, to Twyford where he hoped to enlist the help of a friendly nobleman to plead the Rommany cause with the "gorgio queen." The story has wisdom and beauty, the joy of the open road, and the vitality and grace of the gypsy people.

Patricia Gordon knew what it was to be footsore and bone-weary. After graduation from the University of Washington she had walked from Seattle to San Francisco. With an imagination, fed by omnivorous reading in her father's library and by wide travel from childhood on, it was not difficult for her to translate her emotions from the setting of West Coast America to those of a gypsy boy in Elizabethan England. Another young adventurer is Miss Gordon's *The Boy Jones* (1943), the cockney ragamuffin found in Buckingham Palace. Patricia Gordon did not confine herself to dates, and ignored the possibility of the incident having any political implications, but the picture of Victorian England is real, the story is complete and satisfying and Jones himself is a flesh-and-blood boy, full of spirit and a sense of adventure.

The success of Cynthia Harnett's historical fiction rests partially on the exactness of details in both text and pictures, making everyday living in the periods of her stories clear. *Nicholas and the Wool Pack* (1953), published in England as *The Wool-Pack* (1951), tells a story of fifteenth century English life, especially of the Cotswold wool center; *Caxton's Challenge* (1960), called in England *The Load of Unicorn* (1959), laid in fifteenth century London, is involved with the antagonism of the scriveners for Caxton because of his introduction of the printing press.

Marcus Crouch has compared Barbara Leonie Picard's first essay into historical fiction, *Ransom for a Knight* (1956), to Rosemary Sutcliff's best work, which "gives the past a sudden radiance." It tells the story of ten-year-old Alys, whose father and brother had been captured by the Scots at Bannockburn and who with her brother's squire traveled from Sussex to pay the ransom. The journey, crowded with incidents and people against the colorful background of fourteenth century England, is convincing and the story is alive. Miss Picard's *Lost John* (1963) is the tale of a young outlaw in the Forest of Arden, and *One Is One* (1966) is a very moving story of a misfit in fourteenth century England.

The fifties was a rich period for historical fiction. Hilda Lewis wrote *The Gentle Falcon* (1957), a beautifully realized tale of the Princess Isabella of France, who, at the age of seven, was brought to London to marry Richard II. In *The Book of Hugh Flower* (1952) Lorna Beers gave an unusually interesting picture of the guild system and the work of craftsmen and artists in fifteenth century England in a story of the rise of a young man from journeyman to master mason. In *Pepys' Boy* (1955) Rachel M. Varble created the lively character of Toby, mentioned with despair in Pepys' *Diary*, with glimpses of Samuel Pepys himself and some colorful aspects of seventeenth century London. In *The Yellow Hat* (1958) Nancy Faulkner told an exciting story of Chaucer's London at the time of the Peasants' Revolt.

Madeleine Polland knew from childhood the part of Galway where the Red King lived, and his family name was hers. It was natural that her first book, *Children of the Red King* (1959), should be about thirteenth century Ireland and the part played by the daughter and the son of the King of Connacht in the reconciliation of their father with the Normans. *Beorn the Proud* (1961) tells of a young girl taken as a slave when the Vikings invaded Ireland. *The Queen's Blessing* (1964), a story of eleventh century Scotland, has a more somber theme than the earlier books. It tells of Merca and her young brother, left as homeless orphans when the forces of Malcolm III swept through Northumbria, and of Merca's inner conflict when she discovered that their deliverer and benefactor was Malcolm's wife. So well developed are the characters that they make very moving the story of a young girl's groping through darkness until at last her burden of hatred is lifted.

Mrs. Polland's books are often enjoyed by younger children than are books by Rosemary Sutcliff and Barbara Leonie Picard, for her settings are less detailed and the plots less complex. Her integration of story and historical background is complete, however, and accuracy and a strong feeling for the times about which she writes are marked characteristics. Grainne O'Malley is the pivotal character in Mrs. Polland's *Queen Without Crown* (1966), but the bold sixteenth century Irish chieftainess was more vividly realized in Edith Patterson Meyer's *Pirate Queen* (1961).

In the sixties came Elizabeth Kyle's *The Story of Grizel* (1961), which takes place during the rebellion against James II when certain Scots were forced to live in exile in Holland. The story is based on events in the life of an actual Scottish heroine. Sally Watson wrote with a refreshingly light touch some very lively stories. *Witch of the Glens* (1962) tells of a gypsy girl in Scotland who had always lived by her wits and nimble fingers and who became, surprisingly, involved with the MacDonald clan during the struggle between Royalists and Covenanters. *The Namesake* (1964) by Walter Hodges is a strong, moving story of King Alfred told by Alfred the One-Legged, the King's scribe.

Castors Away! (1963) introduced an important new English writer, Hester Burton. The battle of Trafalgar forms the climax of the story, which has three facets, each involving one of the three children of a small town doctor. *Time of Trial* (1964) is a story of early nineteenth century London, of the family of an old bookseller in the slums whose strong social conscience made him a victim of the very people he was trying to help and plunged his daughter and godson into danger and excitement. The characters are completely realized and the period so real that the book is a living experience. Mrs. Burton's re-creation of nineteenth century England is as intuitive as Rosemary Sutcliff's of ancient Britain. *No Beat of Drum* (1967) takes its characters from the turbulence of mid-nineteenth century England to pioneering in a penal colony in Tasmania.

The World Wars in Fiction

Wars have stimulated the writing of many exciting stories of action, human relationships being often secondary to dramatic events. Yet it is the attitudes of human beings toward each other that touch off the political or economic triggers to start wars and keep them going. Much also has been said and written about the importance of the indoctrination of children with ideals that will mold the future, but few writers of children's books have shown two conflicting ideologies so dramatically as did Constance Savery in *Enemy Brothers* (1943).

This absorbing story of human relationships in wartime tells of an English boy brought up as the son of a German couple but restored to his English family in the middle of the war. There are revealing glimpses of life in England during the war, but the real excitement and pull of the story is in Tony's very gradual change and the breakdown of his antagonism toward the varied and definite personalities of his English family.

Among the many abortive escapes from the Nazis, some were bound to be successful, and these journeys have given material for stories that have all the excitement of adventures of the distant past, with added thrill because of their near-contemporary settings.

Kitty Barne's *We'll Meet in England* (1943) tells of Hertha Larsen, who, when she was fifteen, found hidden away in an isolated little bay in Norway a seemingly abandoned sailboat, which aroused her heretofore unexpressed determination to escape to England. The Norwegian setting and customs are perfectly integrated, and the characters are remembered long after the book is finished. There is no drop in suspense during the preparations for escape, the escape itself, and the surprising outcome.

Little attempt was made during and after the Second World War to thrust upon the very young and happily unaware American children in their story books the experiences of children whose lives were devastated by the war. Where a good story existed, however, dealing with events within the child's grasp, no effort was made to protect him from such vicarious experience. *Little Girl from the City* (1948) by L. Voronkova, translated from the Russian by Joseph Borger, is the story of an orphan who saw her home bombed and her parents killed and was adopted by a family living on a collective farm in Russia. To the average young American reader the tragic loss of Valentina's parents has less reality than her adjustment to life in the country and the thoughtless cruelty of the other children, who have no patience with the "ignorance" of a city girl. Her delight in the beauty around her, her wonder over the growing of seeds, the show of spring, and the young animals, and her response to the woman who had befriended her are the things that give the story its appeal to children untouched by war. Claire Huchet Bishop's *Pancakes-Paris* (1947) may have tragic overtones for the adult, but the average child enjoys it for the reality of the children, who might be their friends, and who, in spite of the bogey of war and poverty, know how to rejoice in unexpected delights. A companion to *Pancakes-Paris* was Mrs. Bishop's *Twenty and Ten* (1952), a true story of wartime France.

Marie McSwigan wrote two thrilling stories of escape. *Snow Treasure* (1942), based on a true incident, told how a band of children smuggled Norway's store of gold to safety on their sleds within view of the Nazi invaders. *All Aboard for Freedom!* (1954) was based on the Freedom Train's famous dash from Communist Czechoslovakia over the border into Germany. Both are pure adventure with emphasis on suspense rather than characterization and philosophical overtones.

A Norwegian, Sigurd Senje, who was himself an active member of the Norwegian resistance during the Nazi occupation wrote *Escape!* (1964), a tense story of two sixteen-year-olds, a boy and girl, who successfully brought off a bold plan to free a young Russian from a German prison camp. The story is well translated from the Norwegian by Evelyn Ramsden, and the spare, direct writing creates powerful suspense.

Of stories dealing with lives of everyday people during the Nazi occupation, few achieve the reality of four laid in Holland. In Dola de Jong's

The Level Land (1943) each member of the Dutch doctor's family meets the frightening change in his own way and becomes a friend to the reader, who shares in the sense of disbelief that war could actually touch them. *Return to the Level Land* (1947) gives an equally moving picture of Holland after the war and of the same family's return to their home and their efforts to rebuild happy, creative lives.

The Winged Watchman (1962) by Hilda Van Stockum tells of a family in Holland whose home was a windmill. The father, a miller, proved the value of his wind-driven mill in time of crisis; the mother fed countless refugees and took in three homeless little girls as her own. The boys found ways of helping their uncle in activities of the Underground. It is a compassionate story, the tragedies lightened by the author's humor and wisdom and her genius for capturing the ways of people of all ages in small incidents and bits of conversation.

The fourth story of Holland during the German occupation is Margaretha Shemin's *The Little Riders* (1963). From her room in her grandparent's house Johanna could see the little riders, lead figures of crusaders, as they rode around the church steeple whenever the big clock struck the hour. When the Germans requisitioned the riders to be melted down for munitions they could not be found. In her hatred of all Germans Johanna would not even speak to the officer who occupied her room. Yet because of that young captain the little riders were saved. A simple lesson in humanity is perfectly integrated in the poignant story, based on experiences of the author, who was born and lived in the medieval town of Alkmaar, where little figures still ride around the clock tower.

Many stories have been built around the dread circumstances of children being separated and lost from their parents. In time of war such separations are more tragic than ever. Meindert DeJong, serving in the air force during World War II and sent to interior China, found there the inspiration for his deeply felt story, *The House of Sixty Fathers* (1956). Tien Pao, alone with his pet pig, Glory-of-the-Republic, in the family's sampan, had been swept away into Japanese territory. The sixty fathers were American soldiers who helped him in his agonizing search for his parents. The book moves with mounting tension and excitement and ends with a reunion that is almost heartbreaking in its joy.

Ian Serraillier's *The Silver Sword* (1959) tells of four Polish children who toward the end of World War II fled from Warsaw and eventually reached Switzerland. Based on fact, the story is told quickly and dispassionately, the touches of humor and the understatement making the account especially gripping. Jan, the orphan who joined the three Balicki children in search of their parents, reminds one of Guido of Naples in Erik Haugaard's *The Little Fishes*. Whatever their country or time, the lost children of wars have much in common. The Balicki family suffered grievously and their courage was challenged constantly but they were among the fortunate whose story ended happily.

A remarkable thing about the best of the stories of the war is their objectivity and lack of bitterness. Even written in a period of intense feeling, the universality of their themes gives the books value in any period.

It is natural that the war stories of the late fifties and the sixties should have more perspective than the earlier ones. The overtones of many of them are mature, giving them meaning for older boys and girls. Some of them told tragic stories of anti-Nazis in war-time Germany, of people innocent of everything except of being German. Margot Benary-Isbert grew up in Frankfurt am Main and as a young woman worked in the Museum of Ethnology there. After her marriage she and her husband settled in Erfurt, the center of the German seed-growing business, where her husband's family had owned a seed farm for over a hundred years. They were very happy and she was busy with her daughter, with writing, traveling, and raising Great Danes until the Nazis came into power. Suddenly their lives were completely changed. In the little town near the University of Göttingen, where they went to live after the war, Mrs. Benary wrote *The Ark* (1953), published in Germany in 1948. It is the story of post-war Germany and of the Lechow family who converted an old railroad car into a home and named it The Ark because of the many animals the daughter Margret was continually bringing home to care for. *Rowan Farm* (1954) continued the story of the Lechows after the father had returned to them from a Russian prison camp. The two books make a lively, courageous family chronicle.

Mrs. Benary wrote several books of special interest to older girls. *Castle on the Border* (1956) tells of Leni, orphaned and homeless in postwar Germany, living with a relative just over the East-West border in an ancient family castle that became the headquarters for the Castle Theater Company, a group of oddly assorted young people. It is a story filled with life and variety and people of all kinds.

Dangerous Spring (1961), a grim, realistic story, but an absorbing one, of the last days of the war and the beginning of the American occupation of Germany, has the beautiful medieval village of Eberstein for its setting.

John Tunis's moral sense and social conscience have invariably been felt in his books for young people, giving his sports stories extra meaning and depth. By its obviousness, however, the moral sometimes seemed more important than the story. In two books with World War II backgrounds Mr. Tunis told stories powerful enough to support the strong sense of purpose. *Silence Over Dunkerque* (1962) is a realistic picture of war in all its horror and a story of heroism that cannot be labeled with the name of any nationality. *His Enemy, His Friend* (1967) is the story of a Nazi officer in Normandy whose conscience would not permit him to carry out the order to execute six hostages. Condemned after the war as a war criminal, he served his sentence, returned to Germany, and took up again his athletic career as a soccer player. The terse style of the story, the concise structure in three major episodes, and the understatement of the human dilemma inherent in the story make the book unforgettable.

One of the most powerful books of Germany during World War II is Martha Bennet Stiles' *Darkness over the Land* (1966). Through the eyes and experiences of Mark Elend, eight at the beginning of the book, the story is told of Munich during the desperate, hungry years of war and the grim, disillusioning years afterward. Terrible events are neither glossed over nor dwelt upon, but their impact is strong. The reader feels them through Mark's anguish over the persecution of those he loves and through the emotional shocks that devastate him and tear apart his loyalty.

The setting of *Thunder in the Sky* (1967), chiefly on the waterways of Britain, is familiar to readers of K. M. Peyton's other books. Mood and plot, however, are very different. It is the story of the Goodchild brothers, all three of whom, had it not been for the First World War, would have been working on barges, carrying on a family tradition. The skillful writing, quick pace, and excellent characterizations make a gripping story with an important theme.

Eventful journeys, survival on land and sea, danger faced and hazards overcome to gain treasure, power, freedom—these have always been the substance of adventure tales. Most creative people writing for children know that in almost every story a significant theme is felt, an important cause espoused, a fundamental truth expressed. The best writers give the story its unhampered way, never spotlighting the truth inherent in it.

The great writers of historical fiction have been so steeped in the period that they can move about in it freely, seeing and hearing the people who live within it. Then, in Leonard Wibberley's phrasing, the writer gives them back their voices "so they can speak across the centuries of their time on earth."

Bibliography

Chute, Marchette. *The Innocent Wayfaring*. New York, E. P. Dutton, 1943.
Crouch, Marcus S. *Treasure Seekers and Borrowers*. London, The Library Assoc., 1962.
Egoff, Sheila. *The Republic of Childhood*. Toronto, Oxford University Press, 1967.
Meek, Margaret. *Geoffrey Trease*, a Walck Monograph. New York, Henry Z. Walck, 1964.
——— *Rosemary Sutcliff*, a Walck Monograph. New York, Henry Z. Walck, 1962.
Mühlenweg, Fritz. *Big Tiger and Christian*. New York, Pantheon, 1952.

Snedeker, Caroline Dale. "The Trilobite Door." *The Horn Book*, Vols. 23–24 (Sept., 1947–July, 1948).
Stevenson, William. *The Bushbabies*. Boston, Houghton Mifflin, 1965.
Sutcliff, Rosemary. "Beginning with Beowulf." *The Horn Book*, Vol. 29 (Feb., 1953).

5

Adventure in the New World

Pilgrims, Puritans, and Pioneers

Master Simon's Garden by Cornelia Meigs, published in 1916 before many stories with American historical backgrounds had been written and few of any literary quality, was recognized as a landmark in children's literature. The story is told through three generations beginning with life in an early colonial village and ending in the years of the Revolution, with the return of the first great trading ships from China. Through it are woven the basic principles of the founding of America and the flowering of freedom and tolerance, symbolized by the garden that Master Simon had persisted in creating in an austere Puritan settlement, and which was cherished by succeeding generations. It is a book with appealing characters, exciting events, but also a maturity seldom before recognized as important in historical fiction for young people. In later books the author showed more skill in characterization, but her early awareness of the compatibility of children's intelligence with good writing and with the thoughtful interpretation of the fundamental principles of democracy shown in *Master Simon's Garden* has been maintained through a long and varied list of distinguished books.

Cornelia Meigs began to write for children first because of her childhood preparation in a large family where storytelling was taken for granted, and later, when she began to teach young people, because she became aware of the need for more good books for boys and girls. It was natural that the field of historical fiction should appeal to her. Her mother's family had pioneered from Vermont to Illinois, her father's relatives had been, in long succession, officers in the army and navy. Family life was full of stories of the settlement of the Middle West and tales of adventure on sea and land. While she grew up in Iowa, there were always relatives to visit in New England where she could satisfy her thirst for colonial history and sea adventure. Her life has had three important facets, each adding light and color to the others: the writing of her children's books, her teaching (in addition to other positions, for nearly twenty years she taught English and creative writing at Bryn Mawr College), and her long and close association with her twelve nieces and nephews, some of whom grew up in her home.

The majority of her books are American period stories, some based on actual events and all written with careful attention to historical accuracy. In *The New Moon* (1924), she introduced one of her most winning characters, Dick Martin, who came from his tumbledown cottage in Ireland to find his luck and make friends in the American wilderness. *As the Crow Flies* (1927) is the story of Zebulon Pike and the exploration of the Mississippi. *Trade Wind* is a sea adventure laid in the early nineteenth century, when American maritime glory was at its height. *Swift Rivers* (1937) takes place in the newly acquired Louisiana Purchase and gives an exciting picture of the early days of the lumbering industry.

Some of her period stories have an appeal for children under ten, as well as over. Among these is *The Willow Whistle* (1931), a frontier story that includes a visit to a friendly Sioux tribe, a fine introduction to pioneer life for little children. A few of her books have been laid in contemporary times, but those stories are closely tied to tradition and events of history, and often tales of the past are woven through the modern story.

Among her many books, *The Two Arrows* (1949) is outstanding. It tells of two English brothers banished to Maryland in the reign of George II. The settings, both in England and the unsettled country along the Chesapeake Bay, are vivid and the characters are drawn with subtlety and understanding. It is an absorbing story, written with restraint and the excellent style characteristic of her work.

Rachel Field (1894–1942) was already known for her childlike verses and attractive little picture-story books when she and the artist Dorothy Lathrop made the discovery of an old doll in a Greenwich Village antique shop. "Hitty" immediately became a personality to them and her "memoirs" became *Hitty, Her First Hundred Years* (1929). Author and artist worked closely together to make a perfect whole. "Dolls can live, with luck, such a satisfying long time," Miss Lathrop had written to a friend, and resolute little Hitty lived a life of tremendous changes without the loss or even the dulling of the sturdy characteristics. Old Peddler had carved her from mountain-ash wood for little Phoebe Preble one stormy winter day in the State of Maine, and few woods are more sturdy. Time and exposure mellowed her paint but her amiable expression did not change through a century of adventures. This is no doll fantasy, though the story is carefully kept within the framework of Hitty's experiences. It is an exciting period adventure story. People of all kinds pass through the pages and even the most briefly known becomes a complete character. The changes that a century brought to the American scene are arrestingly portrayed, and the adventures themselves reach heights of excitement. There are strong emotional scenes, such as willful Sally's repentance, and in few sea stories are fire and shipwreck more graphically described, yet Miss Field attained the ultimate artistry in the restraint that keeps this Hitty's story.

Rachel Field received the Newbery Medal for *Hitty, Her First Hundred Years* which one critic called "the only true juvenile classic written in America in a generation."

From the time she was fifteen Rachel Field had spent each summer in Maine, enjoying particularly a small wooded island off the coast. *Calico Bush* (1931) derives from Miss Field's love and knowledge of Maine: the rocky cliffs, the pine woods, the pasture thick with the "green and springing" bayberry bushes, the cove at high tide where the spruces "seemed to be wading in their own dark reflections." Early in Rachel Field's writing career editors discussing a novel that had been turned down, remarked about her success in dealing with childhood. It was this encouragement that had started her trying to write for children, but she never could follow the suggestion to make her words as young as her ideas. She kept her artistic integrity and *Calico Bush*, which tells the story of a year in the life of a twelve-year-old French "bound-out" girl, has a nearly flawless structure that was not surpassed even in her widely successful adult novels.

In *Hepatica Hawks*, published in 1932, Rachel Field further tested her skill. Hepatica was fifteen years old and six feet four and a quarter inches tall. Her father was a giant and her only friends were the other members of Joshua Pollock's "Famous Freaks and Fandangos," a traveling circus of the 1890's. Her story could easily have been melodramatic or at least sentimental but it is understated, moving, and beautiful. Rachel Field could see the people inside the odd-sized characters and handle an uncommon and difficult theme with delicacy and perception.

In the decades since Miss Field was writing for young people, new children's books by the hundreds have been published each year, yet her three novels stand out as colorful Americana and as living literature.

Elizabeth Coatsworth also recaptured for children the enchantment she has long felt for Maine. She was not born there but came to know the state after she had lived and visited in many other parts of the world. Her first period story, *Away Goes Sally* (1934), made the most of the entrancing idea of living in a little house on runners, slowly sliding through the snowy New England roads and forests, drawn by twelve strong oxen, to transport its occupants from Massachusetts to a new home in Maine. A great deal of kindly humor is woven throughout the story of Sally and her aunts and uncles and with the many lively events are glimpses of the quiet beauty of the New England winter. Some of Miss Coatsworth's loveliest poetry is to be found between the chapters of this and other books, but her prose, too, is that of a poet, lucent and concise. Four other books about Sally followed as her heroine grew up: *Five Bushel Farm* (1939), *The Fair American* (1940), *The*

White Horse (1942), and *The Wonderful Day* (1946). There is no sacrifice of reality in the more colorful plots and settings of these stories. The clarity of style carries conviction, and, with no extra words the reader is kept aware of the excitement in beauty everywhere, the friendly comfort of life on the well-loved Maine farm, the joy of being aboard a trim ship with the salt wind on one's face, the strange magic of North Africa and alien ways.

Here I Stay (1938) was actually written as an adult novel, but because of its directness and clear plot it was enjoyed by older children also. A quiet story but one that has unusual power, it tells of a girl who, alone of all the villagers, chose to remain in her home when everyone else moved on to another settlement. With its cast of only one important human character, it has nevertheless great variety and is full of the love of gardens and animals and pleasure in all nature.

Miss Coatsworth can turn with apparent ease from the writing of simple, everyday events to the powerful drama of such a book as *Door to the North* (1950), a story of a Norse expedition to America in the fourteenth century, which gives courageous life to voyagers who left scant trace of their heroism.

In the early fifties Miss Coatsworth wrote seven short books with American period settings, each one telling, through a child's experience, of an exciting event of the time. As a writer who can tell stories without condescension but within the ability of the youngest readers, Elizabeth Coatsworth was a forerunner of the authors who, in the late fifties, promoted more conspicuously radical changes in books for beginning readers.

In the fifties also appeared three books by Alice Dalgliesh written with simplicity, dignity, and, in very few pages, telling suspenseful stories and bringing characters to life. *The Bears on Hemlock Mountain* (1952) and *The Thanksgiving Story* (1954) were distinguished by Helen Sewell's beautiful illustrations, but the stories have substance in themselves. Best of all was *The Courage of Sarah Noble* (1954) with wonderfully harmonious illustrations by Leonard Weisgard. It is a true pioneer adventure tale of eight-year-old Sarah, who accompanied her father on a dangerous journey to build a new home in the Connecticut wilderness. When her father returned for her mother and his other children, Sarah stayed behind with an Indian family, remembering her mother's words, "Keep up your courage, Sarah Noble," and her father's, "To be afraid and be brave is the best courage of all."

Rebecca Caudill—the pen name of Mrs. James S. Ayers—in *Tree of Freedom* (1949) told of a family's journey from North Carolina to Kentucky to establish a home there when the country was still under British rule and conflicting issues affected even new homes in the wilderness. At a time when merely to live required the most arduous labor, physical strength, endurance, and industry were the qualities Jonathan Venable fostered in his children. Thirteen-year-old Stephanie and her brother Noel sought to bring something more to their new home. The story shows the patience of the pioneer who began with nothing but a patch of uncleared land. " 'It takes a sight of time to make bread,' Bertha told Willie, patiently, 'and a passel of hands. . . . It takes a heap of sun and rain, workin' at corn sprouts, to turn 'em into bread. . . It takes a sight of patience on the part of humans to make bread.' "[1] The characterizations are unusually strong and viable.

The Far-off Land (1964) is another re-creation of eighteenth century pioneering. It grew out of Miss Caudill's fascination with the journal of Colonel John Donelson, written during the winter of 1779–1780 on board his flatboat the *Adventure*. Sixteen-year-old Ketty had lived for eight years with the Moravians when a much older brother, whom she did not even remember, brought her to join his family traveling by flatboat down the Holston and Tennessee rivers to French Lick. Trying to explain his long absence, her brother expressed what many pioneers have felt; "But the West—it's a wraithy thing, Ketty, part rich level land and part notion, always a-motioning a body to climb the steep mountains that wall it off and come closer."[2] Ketty adjusted to primitive discomfort and constant fear, but the influences of her early years were strong and she could never reconcile herself to hatred of the Indians.

In many of her books Rebecca Caudill used for background eastern Kentucky, where she was born, and rural Tennessee, where her family, including eleven children, moved when she was five. *Barrie and Daughter* (1943) takes place in Kentucky mountain country at the beginning of the twentieth century, *Susan Cornish* (1955) among the bleak lives of the sharecroppers of another southern Appalachian community. Fundamental values are strong in all of Mrs. Caudill's books, coming through the responses of sharply individualized characters. She too is an intuitive historian, hearing out of the past the voices of ordinary people.

The Witch of Blackbird Pond (1958), the second book by Elizabeth George Speare (her first was *Calico Captive*), catches the reader's immediate attention by the interesting contrast between the young heroine's earlier, pleasant, relaxed life in Barbados and her new one in Wethersfield, Connecticut in 1687, when anyone who deviated from the accepted pattern of life or thought was in danger of the charge of witchcraft. The splendid characterizations, careful integration of authentic details of setting and history, and the suspenseful plot make the book outstanding. It won the Newbery Medal for Mrs. Speare, who enjoyed the rare distinction of winning the Newbery award twice, the second time for *The Bronze Bow*.

---

[1] Rebecca Caudill, *Tree of Freedom* (New York, Viking, 1947), pp. 70–73.
[2] Rebecca Caudill, *The Far-off Land* (New York, Viking, 1964), p. 24.

In the same period, also from Barbados, came the Negro slave Tituba, sold to the Reverend Parris and brought eventually to Salem, Massachusetts, to look after her master's sickly wife and to be one of the first three "witches" condemned in the dreadful witch trials. In *Tituba of Salem Village* (1964) Ann Petry brought to life the sensitive, intelligent women, driven by the frenzy of hysteria and superstition that gripped the people of Salem. It is a mature, enthralling story that puts in focus the confusion and dementia of the time and place and is representative of the best of the thoughtful books published for the young people of another confused and troubled period.

The American Revolution

James Boyd's *Drums* (1925), a novel with a wide scope and splendid characterizations, has its setting in North Carolina at the beginning of the Revolution. Other books about the period followed but not until the publication of *Johnny Tremain* (1943) by Esther Forbes was Revolutionary Boston given complete life in a story book.

While working on *Paul Revere and the World He Lived In* Esther Forbes's imagination had been caught by the apprentice boys of Boston and the parts they had played in the Revolution. Although they may have changed the tide of events many times, history has paid them neither honor nor blame and they have been lost in the crowds of ordinary unknown people for whom and by whom wars are fought. But having seen them Miss Forbes could not let these boys slip back into obscurity. When *Paul Revere* was completed and she felt she was free to "make up" something she wrote *Johnny Tremain*. So alive is Johnny, so real Boston of Revolutionary times, that it is difficult to believe that Esther Forbes "made up" anything at all. Here is truth.

Born in Westboro, Massachusetts, surrounded all her life with books, possessing parents who were enthusiastic historians, and ancestors who played exciting roles in many events of New England history and whose stories were a part of family tradition, Esther Forbes early possessed a sense of history. Her entrance into children's literature was made only after recognition as a novelist and after she had received the Pulitzer Prize for History in 1942 for *Paul Revere and the World He Lived In*. *Johnny Tremain*, her first book for young people, won the Newbery Medal. No doubt it was because of the depth of research done on *Paul Revere* that she was able to forget the period as history and live within the setting, clearly evoking place and people.

John Hancock, Sam Adams, Josiah Quincy, Paul Revere, are no longer mere names in a history lesson. They are living people with all the faults and failings of humans but who have made the discovery that " 'We are lucky men . . . for we have a cause worth dying for. This honor is not given to every generation.' " It is easy for the reader to identify himself with Johnny; he has so many faults but is at the same time lovable. He could have been a friend to miserable, lonesome Dove, but he bullied him. He made promises to Cilla, but failed her often; he was both deeply loyal to Rab and jealous of him. His tongue was too quick and his courage often failed him, but the core of his being was strong and idealistic, and it took only Rab's unspoken faith in him to tip the scale on the right side, making it possible for him to accept the bitterness of his first great defeat as a challenge and a new beginning. The novel reaches a peak of revelation when at a meeting of the Observers, James Otis speaks, putting into words what Johnny and Rab could only feel:

"We give all we have, lives, property, safety, skills . . . we fight, we die, for a simple thing. Only that a man can stand up."[1]

Johnny Tremain is already at home with those other classics that young people may call their own, but which their elders can read with absorption and delight.

American history began to interest Leonard Wibberley after he had come as an adult to the United States. He saw the American Revolution as the "most important struggle in the history of what we call Western Man . . . a war for the rights of *all* men."

The more one examines the effect of the Revolutionary War not merely on Americans but on all peoples, the more one is amazed by the enormity of that effect. The shot was indeed heard around the world and is still heard today.[2]

He found that Americans seemed to know little about "this most astounding of all wars" and as he studied it he realized how much more there was to it than is to be found in textbooks. Much was confusing, "But at the bottom of it all, there was a basic dedication to the concept of a freedom that permitted a man to speak his mind even against his own government, his own congress, his own rulers." Out of his desire to bring to the attention of others those elements that had so interested him his series of books about the Treegates developed. *John Treegate's Musket* (1959), *Peter Treegate's War* (1960), *Sea Captain from Salem* (1961), and *Treegate's Raiders* (1962). They are stories with muscle and spirit and make up the large mural that Mr. Wibberley wanted to paint embracing many of the historic figures of the Revolution, and including others, creatures of his imagination.

These latter came to life as I wrote, standing as it were by my elbow and telling me of the weight of their muskets and how the

[1] Esther Forbes, *Johnny Tremain* (Boston, Houghton Mifflin, 1943), p. 180.
[2] Leonard Wibberley, "The Treegate Series," *The Horn Book*, Vol. 38 (April, 1962), p. 200.

birds sounded in the boding woods at Saratoga and how sharp
was the January frost at Morristown. This of course is the work
of the novelist in the field of history—not to instruct but to enrich
that which is already known; not to distort but to listen to the insistent whisper of forgotten voices penetrating the centuries.[1]

Mr. Wibberley is the author of many books for adults, *The Mouse
that Roared* for all ages, and numerous books for children—fantasy,
biography, fiction. His Treegate books rank with *Johnny Tremain* in
the eloquence with which they reveal the Revolutionary period and its
people, known and unknown.

Period stories by Jean Fritz, published in the sixties, are distinguished
by the remarkable reality of the characters. Each one was built around
an adolescent boy and his responses to the special challenges of his
time and place. *Brady* (1960) has interesting background of farm life
in the mid-nineteenth century and tells of a boy who became involved,
accidentally, and at first unwillingly, in the Underground Railroad. *I,
Adam* (1963) also has a farm background, in 1850, but is primarily
the story of a boy's growing up, a book that is both thoughtful and
exciting. *Early Thunder* (1967) takes place in 1774–1775 in Salem,
Massachusetts, which for a brief period was the capital of the colony.
Actual historical events and the clearly evoked pre-Revolutionary background relate the book to *Johnny Tremain* and the Treegate series,
but the center of interest is in Daniel's reactions to the events and his
painfully worked out solutions to his own inner conflicts.

An absorbing story is woven around eighteenth and early nineteenth
century politics in Joanne Williamson's *The Glorious Conspiracy*
(1961). Benjamin Brown tells of his cruel indentures, his work in the
airless cotton mills of Liverpool, and his escape to the New World,
to find that inhumanity existed even there. The somber events of the
first part of the story give way to excitement after Ben finds a new
career and becomes involved in the conspiracy against the Federalists
that won the presidency for Thomas Jefferson. Washington, Hamilton,
Jefferson, and Burr are seen as fallible human beings, who then, as
today, could not always see a clear road ahead, were ruled by their
prejudices, often misunderstood, and could make disastrous mistakes.
Miss Williamson did not always trust her characters to convey her
message, but her storytelling here as in other books is absorbing.

Frontier Adventures

The Revolutionary War extended far beyond New England. Echoes
of its drums were heard in the wilderness, where the frontiersmen were
claiming new lands from the Indians, where trappers were taking

---

[1] Wibberley, *op. cit.*, p. 200.

game that had always belonged to the Indians, and where it was easy to fan the flame of hatred between the two peoples. *Silent Scot* (1925), Constance Lindsay Skinner's first frontier story, tells the adventures of Andy MacPhail and his Indian friend, Runner-on-the-Wind, as they outwitted the enemy and carried messages over the Tennessee mountain trails. In her later books Miss Skinner's plots were more skillfully developed, but this first, even though it loses in suspense by being told as a series of separate incidents, is a landmark among frontier stories.

Constance Lindsay Skinner (1882–1939) was born in the northern interior of British Columbia and grew up at her father's trading post; she knew the wilderness of mountains, forest and rivers, populated by many Indians and few whites and abounding in wild animals. She grew up playing with Indian children. Her early schooling was in the hands of her mother and father and the living room of their big log house was lined with books. She knew and loved the old Indian Tselistah, who had been as her father's father, who had taught him the ways of the wilderness and the wisdom of the Indians, which he passed on to his daughter. So she grew up loving and understanding the forest, the Indians and the fur traders—that "race apart." The knowledge of them gained in childhood was but the beginning of a lifelong study of American Indians. Her books are characterized by a feeling of freedom and space drawn from those growing-up years in the Northwest.

For more than forty years Stephen Meader wrote books of adventure, many of them historical and period stories. His first twelve years, spent in Providence, Rhode Island, were filled more with books than activities but after the family's move to New Hampshire he lived an active outdoor life, had his own horse to care for, and often visited the lumber camps where his father was cutting the timber. These childhood influences—books and the outdoors—prepared him well for his writing. Experiences after college doing social work in Newark, New Jersey, with the Children's Aid Society and the Big Brother Movement no doubt gave him added insight. Uncles and aunts in New Hampshire, able storytellers, passed on to him tales that had been handed down through generations of his family. Many of these were grim stories of dangers that had swept down from Canada—wolves that had slaughtered the sheep and Indians who had raided the settlements and killed the people or made prisoners of them. *River of the Wolves* (1948) is the story of a boy captured by Indians and taken to Canada after a raid on a New Hampshire settlement during the French and Indian War.

A historical treatise on the Carolina pirates gave material and inspiration for Mr. Meader's first book, *The Black Buccaneer* (1920). Other period adventure stories followed, including two other sea stories. One of his best books, *Boy With a Pack* (1939), tells of a New Hampshire boy of 1837 who set off on foot with his tin trunk full of

"Yankee notions" to make his living, and who had adventures of all kinds, including experiences helping out on the Underground Railroad. The plots of many of his stories are concerned with nineteenth century transportation as well as long journeys on foot, among them the story of Jonathan, of *Jonathan Goes West* (1946), who traveled from Maine to Illinois by schooner, rail, steamboat, and in a bookseller's caravan.

Like his adult novels, Walter D. Edmonds' children's books are chiefly laid in northern New York state, where he was born. His first three are excellent examples of the short story form, brief, with closely knit plots. They are illustrated profusely and dramatically, appearing at first glance to be picture-story books. The stories themselves, however, are too full of excitement and too well written to depend on illustration, though the telling is heightened in each case by the unusual pictures. His first book for children, *The Matchlock Gun* (1941), won the Newbery Medal. It tells of a tragic incident in the life of a colonial family when a ten-year-old boy drove off marauding Indians with an ancient Spanish gun. Written with dramatic simplicity, it rises to almost intolerable heights of excitement with Paul Lantz's lithographs augmenting the horror and the desperate courage.

Wilderness Clearing (1944) is a novel concerned with the border warfare at the beginning of the Revolution, and the reactions of the settlers in a little community in northern New York state when they received the news that the Indians had turned against them. The tenseness of the story is relieved by the sensitive characterizations of Maggie Gordon and Dick Mount, who grew to maturity in the crisis, and by their quiet romance in a time of such urgency and terror. The book is based on an actual raid and peopled with historical characters. *Cadmus Henry* (1949) is a story of the Civil War in which a young Confederate finds himself set aloft as a military observer in a circus balloon that escapes its moorings and carries him into Union territory. Time and place are evoked so convincingly as to make the story seem to have been written out of personal experience.

Although the Tennessee town where William O. Steele grew up was no longer in Indian country, he discovered that the frontier was not entirely gone. Indian arrowheads could still be found in the plowed fields, the old log cabins had been turned into smokehouses, the old pioneer speech could still be heard, and old superstitions were still believed. His interest in sharing his enthusiasm for Tennessee history resulted in *Wilderness Journey* (1953), *Winter Danger* (1954), *Tomahawks and Trouble* (1955), *Flaming Arrows* (1957), *The Far Frontier* (1959), and other very exciting, credible pioneer adventure tales. The clear, direct style, well-realized characters, and brief but suspenseful storytelling made his books readable for children of eight and nine years, and interesting to a wide age range.

Old chronicles of the settling of America, of its exploration, the struggles with Indians, and the conflict between the various nations laying claim to the New World, tell repeatedly of Indian captives. It was a familiar story, one that was lived over and over during the bitter years when white men used the Indians to promote their wars with each other. Many writers of books for young people have been unable to resist the drama of the white child captured by Indians, surviving by sheer courage and determination. It is an arresting story in the hands of an able writer.

Among Lois Lenski's several stories with American historical backgrounds, her *Indian Captive* (1941) stands out for its good integration of historical background, incident, and characterizations. It is the story of Mary Jemison, who was captured by Indians in 1758 and taken from her Pennsylvania home to a Seneca village in New York state. When, after two years, the chance came for Mary to return to live with the white people, she chose to remain with the Indians. Mary Jemison's story is not unique; for every child captive who was redeemed or was able to escape, there were some who, adopted into the tribe, could not be reconciled to another change, and lived out their lives as Indians. In Miss Lenski's book, however, the child's adjustment to the tragic loss of her family and to a strange way of life is shown with unusual understanding.

Elizabeth George Speare's *Calico Captive* (1957) was based on a journal published in 1807 by a woman who, with a younger sister, had been captured by Indians during the French and Indian War. The story follows the captives on their long agonizing trek to Montreal to be sold as hostages to the French, and tells of Miriam's life until her release.

Journeys Westward

Covered-wagon days and the hardships of the pioneers who set forth to make homes ever farther to the west is another theme so full of drama and courage that it is not surprising that writers have frequently used it. Old letters and diaries kept during the long overland journey continue to yield inspiration and information for new books.

Honoré Willsie Morrow's *On to Oregon*, published in 1926, was, for that time, an unusually realistic treatment of adventure westward. It is a stark, moving story, based on the tragic journey of the seven Sager children, who after their parents' death became lost from the rest of the company, and under the leadership of thirteen-year-old John, traveled a thousand miles to the haven of the Whitman mission in the Oregon Territory.

Journey Cake (1942) by Isabel McLennan McMeekin has distinctive flavor and fine characterizations, with the Negro serving woman Juba standing out as an unforgettable personality. It tells of the trek of the six Shadrow children from North Carolina to join their father in their new home in Kentucky. Their mother had died after their father's departure, but Juba, in spite of every opposition, succeeded in carrying out the father's plans, getting his children to him at the appointed time.

Song of the Pines (1949) by Walter and Marion Havighurst is another unusual pioneer story. It tells of a fifteen-year-old Norwegian boy who emigrated to America and journeyed west to what is now Wisconsin to seek his fortune in the lumbering industry. Nils is an engaging boy, ingenious and enterprising, who inevitably finds his fortune and sends back to Norway as a testimony of the goodness of the New World the little bag of American earth that had been given him in Norway by a returned traveler and that had fired his dreams of adventure. Humor gleams through the story, and there is a keen sense of the magnificent forests and of the men who worked in them.

Especially appealing are the strong family feeling and the individuality of each of the eight children in Dale White's *The Singing Boones* (1957). On the long trek by wagon train from the Missouri River country to California in 1852, their singing talent sustained them more than once and in different ways. *Carolina's Courage* by Elizabeth Yates (1964) is the story of a little girl and her family on their journey by oxcart and covered wagon from New Hampshire to a new home in the Nebraska territory, and the part played by Carolina's precious doll Lydia-Lou in insuring safe passage through the Indian country.

Annabel and Edgar Johnson began their writing partnership when they were married in 1949. Their books have great vitality, characters with strong individualities that grow within their stories, and accuracy in all details of history and locale. *The Black Symbol* (1959) is a story of a medicine show that traveled through the Montana mining fields before the advent of the railroad, seen through the experiences of Barney Morgan, an unwilling member of the troupe. *Torrie* (1960) is another tale of the strangeness and hardships of a covered-wagon journey, added to the problems of a girl already suffering through the agonies of growing up and learning how to take responsibility. *Wilderness Bride* (1962) treats ideological and religious conflicts with great sensitivity in telling the story of two young people on the courageous westward trek of the Mormons from Nauvoo, Illinois, in search of the New Zion. The excitement in *The Bearcat* (1960) grows from the tensions in a coal-mining community when labor unions were first springing up around the country. *A Golden Touch* (1963) is full of mystery and suspense and the fascinating mixture of people of a

Colorado gold-mining town. These and other stories by the Johnsons bring the varied history of western United States brilliantly to life.

The Underground Railroad and the Civil War

Elsie Singmaster (1879–1958), whose father was a Pennsylvania German and mother a Quaker, grew up with the battlefield of Gettysburg all about her and early discovered that she had abundant material at hand for stories. She wrote many books, most of them set in the region she knew so well. Early in the century *When Sarah Saved the Day* (1909) and its sequel proved her skill in interpreting the people and speech of the locality. *A Boy at Gettysburg* (1924), the first important story of the Civil War and the Underground Railroad, is also a poignant portrayal of a courageous boy. Lincoln appears briefly, but memorably. Nine years later appeared Miss Singmaster's second book about the Civil War, *Swords of Steel* (1933), in which again her characterizations give the story reality. Miss Singmaster never rested on her skill in characterization or her ability to create local atmosphere. She once spoke of learning from her father that a story should have a point to be worth telling, and his teaching is evident in the well-developed plots of all of her books.

Marjorie Hill Allee's *Susanna and Tristram* (1929), woven about Quaker activities on the Underground Railroad, was one of the early books to make significant use of this exciting movement in American history. In the thirty years between that book and *Brady* (1960) by Jean Fritz, most of the children's stories set between 1840 and the Civil War had incidents relating to the Underground Railroad. The struggle for the basic rights of human beings, whatever form it takes, is a fundamental theme, charged with excitement and emotion.

The dramatic story of Harriet Tubman, who escaped to freedom on the Underground Railroad and who helped so many others to escape that she was called the "Moses of her people," was given great vitality in 1932 by Hildegarde Hoyt Swift. Her *The Railroad to Freedom* (1932) was the first important account of Harriet Tubman's life for young people. Although fictionalized, it was entirely authentic in the essential facts and true to the spirit of its heroine.

Emma Gelders Sterne in *No Surrender* (1932), *Amarantha Gay, M.D.* (1933), and *The Calico Ball* (1934), laid in the South at the end of the Civil War, told romantic stories about appealing heroines who adjusted to the end of one way of life and the beginning of a new. In the forties there were books laid in the post Civil War period that were presented with more realism and brought events sharply within the reader's focus. A good example was Jere Wheelwright's *Gentlemen Hush* (1948) about three young Confederate officers, immediately after

Lee's surrender, who met with courage and humor the challenge to make a new life out of the ruins of the old.

When Harold Keith was doing research for a life of Will Rogers he discovered his subject's father, Clem Rogers, a wealthy part-Cherokee soldier and politician who during the Civil War in the Cherokee country rose to a captaincy in the rebel Cherokee force commanded by General Stand Watie. Further research on the Civil War in Oklahoma held so much fascination for him that Mr. Keith spent the summers of 1940 and 1941 traveling about Oklahoma and western Arkansas interviewing all the Confederate veterans still living and recording their stories. Much of the detail for *Rifles for Watie* (1957) was drawn from these reminiscences and from journal accounts. Fighting the Civil War in these western states were mixed-blood Cherokees and other Indians more concerned with their own political problems than with the issues of slavery or states' rights. The hero of the book is Jefferson Davis Bussey, a farm boy who joined the Union forces, became a scout, and was temporarily enrolled with Stand Watie's Cherokee rebels. The book, which won the Newbery Medal, threw interesting new light on the Civil War, told a fast-moving story, and presented a likable young protagonist with whom boys could identify.

As the centenary of the Civil War drew near, floods of books about it began to appear. Among the many factual books a few good stories stood out. *Jed: the Story of a Yankee Soldier and a Southern Boy* (1960) by Peter Burchard told of sixteen-year-old Jed, already a veteran fighter for the Union, who rescued and restored to his home a small boy, passionate in his Confederate convictions. The people of the book act and respond like ordinary people. It is a deeply felt fragment of life, much more telling than the most realistic accounts of battle.

Across Five Aprils (1964) by Irene Hunt was the most important Civil War story for young people to appear during the centennial period. The plot is the Civil War itself, with all its subplots of conflicts within families and communities, of misery, suffering, cowardice, courage, love, and mercy. In the foreground is a closely knit farm family of southern Illinois enduring through the bitter years from April 1861, to Lincoln's death in April 1865. The story is confined within the small frame of the farm, its immediate surroundings, and the nearest village, and, although not told in the first person, events and impressions are related through the mind and emotions of the boy Jethro.

An unusually fresh love story was Bianca Bradbury's *Flight into Spring* (1965), which told the story of Sally Day, a Maryland girl, married to Charles Horne, who had been an officer in the Union Army. Going to Connecticut to live with his parents, she was completely unprepared for the bitterness and antagonism that met her. There are few tragic overtones, for the reader experiences the postwar period through the emotions of a gay young girl who had been fairly well protected from the harsh realities of the time. But the book has depth in the character of unquenchable Sally, who, in spite of failures, so loved her Charles that she persisted in trying to adjust to his dour, unresponsive parents.

Other Period Stories

In 1927 Caroline Dale Snedeker turned from ancient scenes to tell the story of *Downright Dencey*, an unforgettable child in Nantucket a hundred years ago. The first time she set foot on the island of Nantucket, Mrs. Snedeker had felt that "something" was there; a shadowy form of a Quaker who had lived in one of these charming old houses, a book character, which, as it grew clearer, became Dencey herself. It is hard to believe that *Downright Dencey*, with all its vitality, was written in great sorrow. Mrs. Snedeker's husband, who had been the inspiration for her writing, the critic who had insisted only on her best, had died, but his faith in her was justified. She created in Dencey the most zestful of all her vivid characters and told a story full of atmosphere and humanity that has been a source of continuing pleasure through the years.

From the publication of Forrestine Hooker's *Cricket, A Little Girl of the Old West* in 1925 on to the present, family records and childhood memories have been the sources of many stories. Beginning with *Melissa Ann* (1931) Ethel Parton (1862–1944) wrote six books laid in Newburyport, Massachusetts, between 1800 and 1870, gathering some of her material from printed chronicles but much more from memories of her own childhood in Newburyport, from stories passed down through generations of old, deeply rooted families, and from incidents in the background of her own family told by her grandmother and aunt. The other titles were *Tabitha Mary* (1933), *Penelope Ellen* (1936), *Vinny Applegay* (1937), *The Lost Locket* (1940), and *The House Between* (1943). *The Year Without a Summer* (1945) was outside the Newburyport chronicles but it too was drawn from family accounts of the icy summer of 1816.

In 1935 appeared *Caddie Woodlawn* by Carol Ryrie Brink, which won immediate and well-deserved popularity and the following year was awarded the Newbery Medal. Stories told by her grandmother of her childhood in Wisconsin in frontier days had enlivened Mrs. Brink's own growing years and had made her feel the reality of the child Caddie Woodlawn long before putting her into a book.

Robert Lawson's last book, *The Great Wheel* (1957), was different in mood and subject from any of his others but just as full of fun and just as appealing to boys and girls, and authentic historical fiction. When

Conn was a small boy in his Irish village an old wise woman, studying the tea leaves, told him that his fortune lay to the west, "and one day you'll ride the greatest wheel in all the world." She was right for Conn not only rode on the first great Ferris Wheel built for the World's Columbian Exposition in Chicago in 1893, but he was one of those who helped to build it.

Samuel Hopkins Adams (1871–1958), the American novelist, near the end of his long life wrote a period story for children laid in 1816— "Eighteen-Hundred-and-Froze-to-Death"—telling with verve the story of *Chingo Smith of the Erie Canal* (1958), a resilient, Huck-Finn kind of boy, who could cope with any adventure that thrust itself his way, taking him on to many places besides the Erie Canal. Historically authentic, told with amusing dialogue, the story is often funny, and the scenes of the building of the canal and readying of the boats to ply the canal reel and moil with life and excitement.

Laura Ingalls Wilder and the "Little House" Books

To the great collection of books based on memories and family records, Laura Ingalls Wilder (1867–1957) made the most unusual contribution. Beginning in 1932 with *Little House in the Big Woods* she told in seven volumes the story of a pioneer childhood. Everything is true; not even the names are changed. The Ingalls family included Pa and Ma and the four little girls: Mary, Laura, Carrie, and Grace. Everything that happens in the books happened to them. In another book, *Farmer Boy* (1933), Mrs. Wilder told about the Wilder family of boys and especially of Almanzo Wilder's childhood on a prosperous farm in northern New York state a hundred years ago. In *Little House in the Big Woods* Laura Ingalls was five years old. The time was in the 1870's when pleasures were simple: a slaughtered pig meant a white bladder balloon for two little girls to play with; a pair of mittens and a stick of candy in a Christmas stocking could make eyes shine with happiness; a trip to town was a great adventure. At night, from her bed, Laura could hear Pa's fiddle softly playing, see the firelight gleaming on his brown hair and beard and glistening on the honey brown fiddle, and watch Ma gently rocking and knitting. In Mrs. Wilder's books the children of a very different world can still grasp a bit of the security of a time that is gone.

In *Little House on the Prairie* (1935) the Ingalls family moved west in a covered wagon to make their home in a cabin on the Kansas prairie. In *On the Banks of Plum Creek* (1937) they moved again by covered wagon to Minnesota to live in a dugout.

All around that door green vines were growing out of the grassy bank, and they were full of flowers. Red and blue and purple and rosy-pink and white and striped flowers all had their throats wide open as if they were singing glory to the morning. They were morning-glory flowers.

Laura went under those singing flowers into the dugout. It was one room, all white. The earth walls had been smoothed and whitewashed. The earth floor was smooth and hard.[1]

Pa could never be happy when houses began to fill up the open spaces, and in *By the Shores of Silver Lake* (1939) they moved again, this time to De Smet, South Dakota. Then Ma persuaded her husband that the girls' education was more important than pioneering so here they stayed through *The Long Winter* (1940), *Little Town on the Prairie* (1941), and *These Happy Golden Years* (1943). The last book tells of Laura's year of teaching school to help with Mary's education and of her marriage to Almanzo. The reader enjoys the books with all his senses. He feels the winter cold in the little cabin or the softness of summer dust on bare feet, and he smells and tastes. Ma could do wonders with the simplest ingredients; and, though sometimes the Ingalls were close to starvation, as they were while a blizzard raged that long winter, they had times of feasting. Readers, who are reluctant eaters at their own tables, may eat their way with relish through the Wilder books.

Through the years boys and girls alike have loved these stories. There is much about the unadorned, courageous life of the Ingalls family to delight them. The details of soap and candle making, of building a log shelter, of making a button lamp to save oil, are natural and fascinating parts of the story. Laura and her sisters are far from perfect. They quarrel, show jealousy, are disobedient. And they are punished, but always justly and with logic. No matter how rough was the living, no matter under what circumstances the family had to get along, beauty was always important. Outside was the beauty of the wide plains or of a flower that bloomed in front of the little sod house; inside was the china shepherdess standing on its own little shelf that Pa had made for Ma with great care.

Helen Sewell illustrated with pleasant stylized drawings the first three of the Wilder books. On later ones Mildred Boyle collaborated with her. In 1953 a new edition of the Laura Ingalls Wilder books was published with illustrations by Garth Williams. Before making the pictures Mr. Williams visited Mrs. Wilder in Mansfield, Missouri, where she and Almanzo Wilder then lived, retraced much of the route of the covered-wagon journeys, and visited the settings of the different homes and the scenes of important events in the stories.

No other writer for children has given such a complete picture of a

[1] Laura Ingalls Wilder, *On the Banks of Plum Creek* (New York, Harper, 1953), pp. 9–10.

period in America's past, of a time when the individual drew his security from the strength of his closely knit family life, when outside influences emphasized family unity instead of destroying it. At the same time Mrs. Wilder told stories that children enjoy; her realism is charged with tenderness and humor.

Adventure in New Spain

Nina Brown Baker's *Juan Ponce de León* (1957) brought sympathetic insight to her story about the man who had trained during his youth in Spain to be a knight, came to New Spain on Columbus's second voyage, and eventually earned the title of "Father of Puerto Rico." The line between biographical fiction and fictionalized biography is slender and, in the case of an honest, alive, and fundamentally accurate book, unimportant. Mrs. Baker could feel the man behind the records and gave her account the animation of an adventure story.

Odyssey of Courage (1965), the story of Alvar Núñez Cabeza de Vaca, by Maia Wojciechowska is another biographical adventure that belongs here. During the trek westward from Florida, full of suffering and grueling adventures by sea and on the long overland journey, Cabeza de Vaca, although enslaved by the Indians, came to love them. He died a martyr to his sense of justice and to his ideals of peace and brotherhood.

Betty Baker's dedicated interest in the American Indian, especially of the southwest, has been the inspiration for several books, including two historical novels. *Walk the World's Rim* (1965) tells a story of the four survivers of Cabeza de Vaca's disastrous journey who found refuge among the friendly Avavare Indians of what is now Texas. The book is chiefly about Esteban, the Negro slave of Andrés Dorantes, and is told from the point of view of an Indian boy to whom Esteban was a hero. It is a deeply felt story; Esteban will be a hero to readers too. Betty Baker's *Killer of Death* (1963), the story of the son of an Apache chief, moves the reader to strong empathy with the Indians of the southwest during the nineteenth century.

The King's Fifth (1966) by Scott O'Dell is told by a young cartographer who left the summer camp of Coronado's army with six others and struck out into unknown land in search of the gold of Cibola. The adventure is over when the story begins. Young Esteban de Sandoval is a prisoner in the Fortress of San Juan de Ulua in Vera Cruz in New Spain, awaiting trial for withholding the King's Fifth of the treasure. In telling the long story of the search for gold, Esteban interrupts from time to time to report on the trial that begins on his seventeenth birthday. He had started out, little more than a child, interested only in the opportunities for map making that the journey would give him, but found that even he was not immune to the awful lust for gold. The writing is subtle, beautiful, and the complex structure of the story, instead of hampering the flow of events, is a significant device, giving perspective on the journey, the adventures, the fates of the others on the expedition, and on the development of Esteban's character. The book is an important literary accomplishment and a splendid story.

Mexico

Hervey White's *Snake Gold* (1926), the story of a thrilling search for Aztec treasure, was acclaimed by Henry Beston as one of the finest boys' books yet written by an American. He said, "It is the work of an artist, it has beauty and distinction of style; the story it tells is romantic and moving, and its protagonists are living flesh and blood."[1]

Since that book appeared, many picture books and tales for young children with Mexican settings have been published, but few writers have used the colorful, varied background of Mexico for adventure stories. *Jeremy Craven* (1958), by an English writer, Joyce Collin-Smith, is therefore unique, and as well an extraordinary artistic achievement and a thrilling story.

Jeremy, a shy, sensitive boy, was suddenly whisked away by his Uncle Titus from the cold sparseness of a London orphanage to the animation, turbulence, and heat of revolutionary Mexico in 1911. Uncle Titus was an opportunist, volatile and unpredictable, whom Jeremy was prepared to adore but not to understand. The complex characterizations are wholly convincing, the exciting historical background is accurate, the viability of Jeremy's personality and of his friendship with the Indian boy Julio, give the book heart. The descriptions are brief but so telling that they fill the mind with the sights, sounds, and smells of Mexico.

Children gain little from books that belabor morals or obviously espouse causes, and they seldom have the patience to read them. They do learn from experience, actual or vicarious, if the experience touches their emotions. Historical fiction for young people today is far more than the recounting of battles, escapes, and rescues. In the past quarter of a century it has increased in the honesty of portrayals of events and periods and the reality of the presentation of people of all kinds. It can help children understand history and the part every seemingly unimportant person plays in the human story. Along with great fantasy and other adventure tales it can contribute to the creation of the climate that fosters understanding minds and compassionate hearts.

[1] Anne Carroll Moore, *The Three Owls, Second Book* (New York, Coward-McCann, 1928), pp. 44–45.

Bibliography

Forbes, Esther. *Johnny Tremain*. Boston, Houghton Mifflin, 1943.

Fuller, Muriel. *More Junior Authors*. New York, H. W. Wilson, 1963.

The Horn Book. Reprint from the "Laura Ingalls Wilder Issue" (Dec., 1953).

Kunitz, Stanley J. and Howard Haycraft, eds. *The Junior Book of Authors*. 2d ed., rev. New York, H. W. Wilson, 1951.

Miller, Bertha Mahony and Elinor Whitney Field, eds. *Newbery Medal Books: 1922–1955*. Boston, The Horn Book, 1957.

Moore, Anne Carroll. *The Three Owls, Second Book*. New York, Coward-McCann, 1928.

Skinner, Constance Lindsay. *Beaver, Kings and Cabins*. New York, Macmillan, 1933.

Wibberley, Leonard. "The Treegate Series." *The Horn Book*, Vol. 38 (April, 1962).

Wilder, Laura Ingalls. *On the Banks of Plum Creek*. New York, Harper, 1953.

6

Backgrounds of Understanding

After the First World War attention turned from the politicians and military leaders, who had failed to keep man out of the dreadful cataclysm, to the educators and humanists who advocated knowledge and understanding of other peoples—"Understanding brings tolerance, tolerance friendliness, friendliness peace." It was a philosophy Americans were glad to accept, for many of them, even if they could not remember life in the "old country," still had relatives there or could trace their immediate ancestors to Ireland or Germany, Italy or Russia. America had so recently been called the "melting pot" it was not difficult to turn the eyes of Americans back on their origins. Interest revived in the folk arts that had been brought by new Americans from the Old World. Travel became again the favorite recreation of, not only the well-to-do, but students, teachers, and anyone who had leisure, and money that could be exchanged advantageously into the currency of other countries. Behind it all was the justification of "knowing our neighbor countries" for, with all the scientific progress, the world had suddenly become "small"; there could be no isolation in a world that could be encircled by two young men in an airplane in eight and one-half days.

A New Slant on History

The student began to review history, questioning the reason or the need for wars. Why could not even a new country, built firmly on the platform of equal rights for all men, keep out of war? It is not surprising that, beginning with Van Loon's *The Story of Mankind* (1921), there should be a growing list of important books of history for young people.

Born in Holland, Hendrik Willem van Loon (1882–1944) came to the United States as a young man. His wish to learn English well had been inspired by his reading of *Henry Esmond* and he brought with him a reverence for the English language equaled in intensity by what he considered the object of his life: the humanization and popularization of history. Stimulated rather than discouraged by the opposition of conservative historians, he succeeded in his aim to bring to life, for great numbers of people, the personalities who played their parts in history and in the cultural and scientific development of mankind.

It is significant that the first book to receive the Newbery Medal had a vital influence on the whole field of children's books. *The Story of Mankind* was a revolutionary approach to history. Here was a book of history that did more than present facts. It brought to life man and his world from the very beginning of life on earth. If history could be presented with such originality, what need for any writer to hold to a prescribed pattern? Had Hendrik van Loon done nothing more than open the gates of the twenties to each writer's and artist's original approach, to release the creative impulses in writing for children, he would have made an important contribution to literature for children.

There have, no doubt, been two points of view on the writing of history since the earliest storytellers recounted the feats of the tribal heroes: should history be an objective chronicle or should it search out the reasons behind events? The great historians of the nineteenth century, Macaulay and Carlyle, Motley and Parkman, bore out Francis Parkman's creed that faithfulness to history involved far more than scrupulous and patient research into special facts. But their influence did not affect the attitude toward history books for the child. Hendrik van Loon was the first writer who, believing that history could be exciting reading for the child as well as the adult, succeeded in making it so.

He saw history as the "mighty Tower of Experience, which Time has built amidst the endless fields of bygone ages." His point of view was that of one "born and educated in an atmosphere of the old fashioned liberalism which had followed Darwin and the other pioneers of the nineteenth century"; it was influenced by Montaigne, Erasmus, and Anatole France. His perspective was that of a teacher and philosopher who never loses faith in mankind and who can find in his hopes consolation "for the errors, for the crimes and the injustices which still pollute and afflict this earth." His rule in selection from the vast amount of material was this: "Did the country or person in question produce a new idea or perform an original act without which the entire human race would have been different?" His manner was that of a storyteller to whom there is no more thrilling tale than the account of mankind itself.

The best children's books free the child's imagination and intellect from the bonds of the commonplace but some few have done this service not only to the children, but to writers as well. *The Story of Mankind* is one of these.

Virgil Mores Hillyer, headmaster of the Calvert School, Baltimore, had rebelled at the limited viewpoint of the history books of his childhood, and those that later as a teacher he found available. Convinced that man's wonderful story could not be bound within the limits of countries, he tried out a new approach with his classes of nine- and ten-year-old children, giving a panoramic view of history epoch by epoch, adding interesting explanations and amusing comments, writing and rewriting to achieve the reaction from the children that history deserved, until the result was *A Child's History of the World*, published in 1924. Later, in *A Child's Geography of the World* (1929), he brought to geography the same originality and humor.

Beginning with the first volume of their *A History of Everyday Things in England* (1918), Marjorie Quennell and Charles Henry Quennell introduced into this period the history book that re-creates background, bringing historic figures to life against the detailed picture of everyday customs and standards of courtesy, of the social, religious, and economic life of their times. The fourth volume, published in 1935, carries man through the changes brought on by mechanical inventions and improvements into the industrial age. Between the first and last volumes of English history the Quennells wrote other histories, picturing life in the stone, bronze, and early iron ages, in Roman Britain, in Anglo-Saxon and Norman times, and in ancient Greece. The whole series of books made up a treasure house of information on the life of man through the ages, written with vitality and enthusiasm.

Some years later Alfred Duggan brought a similar sense of immediacy to his history books. In *Growing up in 13th Century England* (1962) he pictured typical families of five different social strata—earl, knight, peasant, merchant, craftsman—giving an abundance of specific details relating to ways of living—lessons, dress, meals, different types of education, the guild system, apprenticeships, and marriage customs. He used the same presentation in *Growing up with the Norman Conquest* (1966).

By 1930 the trend in historical writing was definitely toward a social and economic approach, the kind of history that teaches, in the words of Gertrude Hartman, that each generation has its work to do in making the world a better place to live, each one creating something upon which the next generation builds. Remembering with dissatisfaction the teaching of history in her childhood, Gertrude Hartman was interested in the developing theories and educational methods of the twenties and, in 1923, became the first editor of *Progressive Education*. She gave up the post seven years later to devote her time to writing. Her first history was *The World We Live In and How It Came To Be* (1931). In a lucid style and with a fine selection of pictures, she told the story of man's progress from earliest times, examining the original impetus for great social movements.

Genevieve Foster confessed to being confused by history as taught in her childhood. "And the more I learned in high school and college, the more confused I became." She had been illustrating children's stories for some time when she decided to try to find out what she had always wanted to know about history and write a book about it "that children, and perhaps their fathers and mothers too, might like to read." The result was several unusual histories, each having one significant figure as a focal point, and each covering the events throughout the world during the life span of that one great leader: *George Washington's World* (1941), *Abraham Lincoln's World* (1944), *Augustus Caesar's World* (1947), *The World of Captain John Smith* (1959), and *The World of Columbus and Sons* (1965). Written well and illustrated with her numerous lively drawings, the books were markedly successful in correlating world events, political, economic and cultural, during each given period in history.

In 1945 Katherine B. Shippen entered the field of historical writing for young people with *New Found World*, a book about the Latin American countries. She had majored in history at Bryn Mawr College and traveled widely. She taught in various schools, and for several years held the post of Curator of Social Studies at the Brooklyn Children's Museum. Through all of her studying and teaching it was people who were important to her—the people who have made history, and the children to whom she interpreted the past. Thus she is typical of the historians of this era, presenting history through the people who lived it. Each of her books is a living story, whether she is telling of the discovery and development of the treasures of the American earth in *The Great Heritage* (1947), or tracing the pattern of the discovery, the harnessing and the development of electrical energy, in *Bright Design* (1947), or giving the background of immigrations and showing how they are woven into the fabric of America in *Passage to America* (1950).

Beginning in the forties books appeared that illuminated man's story through the history of one aspect of a period, one activity, or one movement. Outstanding among these was Elizabeth Chesley Baity's *Man Is a Weaver* (1942), which, in telling the story of textiles through the ages, showed it as integral to the long colorful story of mankind. In *Armor* (1963) Sean Morrison threw light on people through the ages in a discussion of warfare and the development of battle dress, illustrating the text with his own excellent drawings. Much can be learned about man in the study of one historic movement as Franklin Hamilton showed in *The Crusades* (1965). Set in motion by idealistic motives the crusades deteriorated to selfish scheming, struggles for power, and treacherous making and unmaking of alliances. "That the crusades went so far astray from their pious purpose tells us much not only about medieval man but also about all the follies of humanity."

Informational Series

Series books have been familiar since the beginning of children's book-publishing programs. Early series, both fictional and informational, were usually, like the nineteenth century *Peter Parley* books or the *Rollo* books, written under one authorship. Later informational series have been, for the most part, motivated by publishers. Publishing books in uniform length and format can be economical in manufacturing, promotion, and marketing. It can foster good organization of material' and bring out new subjects and points of view. It does, however, emphasize writing by assignment and it discourages individuality.

The headlong impetus in the late fifties to improve educational methods and school texts was bound to touch children's pleasure reading. More informational books in all areas were published and more and more informational series were initiated. Many companies that had never before published children's books suddenly opened juvenile departments. Deciding to have a children's book department was easy; finding good books to publish was not. Most publishers, however, were acquainted with specialists in different areas. The quickest possible way to find manuscripts was to invite specialists to write for a new series. Most of the many informational books published in the fifties and sixties were inviting to look at, profusely—and usually colorfully—illustrated. Few were written in a style to keep a child reading for pleasure.

The quality of publishing, like everything else, depends on the knowledge, imagination, and sensitivity of those determining policies and making judgments. Certain series have made rather special contributions; individual books in series have sometimes been outstanding. Whenever these are considered in this chapter they are discussed as books, not as items in a series.

American History

In 1932 Leo Huberman's *"We, the People"* was published, a social and economic history of the United States, studded with apt quotations and showing the courage and cruelty, the necessity and greed—all the human forces, good and bad, that went into settling and building the country. In *These United States and How They Came to Be* (1932) Gertude Hartman emphasized economic and cultural aspects of American life, particularly as affected by discovery and invention.

In 1959 appeared Gerald W. Johnson's *America is Born, A History for Peter*, the first of a projected three volume work intended to cover the history not of the American republic, but of "the growth of the American spirit." Mr. Johnson was inspired to write a book that would help to give his grandson an understanding of "what being an American means." He showed that it is a "continued story" that goes far back with good and bad included because "they all belong to it, and if you leave out the bad parts you will never understand it all." Humor and perspective on people are here as well as events, the story flowing as easily as if Mr. Johnson were indeed telling it to Peter, and with steady interest that holds the reader as it would the listener. *America Grows Up* (1960) and *America Moves Forward* (1960) followed, bringing the story up to the mid-fifties. To explain the three branches of the government Mr. Johnson wrote *The Presidency* (1962), *The Supreme Court* (1962), and *The Congress* (1963). In *The Cabinet* (1966) is shown the imprint made by each president on his cabinet, the important ones analyzed with unusual insight. Mr. Johnson's books for boys and girls are significant for their clarity, good writing, and enthusiasm that stimulate and interest the reader whatever his age.

Margaret Coit, a professor at Fairleigh Dickinson University and a Pulitzer Prize winner (for *John C. Calhoun: American Portrait*), covered in *The Fight for Union* (1961), the years between 1819, when Thomas Jefferson saw the approaching end of his life and of his dreams for a united country, and 1859, when John Brown was hanged. In many history books the forty years of debate and controversy, political maneuvering, and efforts at compromise come through as little more than a dull prelude to the Civil War. Miss Coit's strong sense of drama, her brilliant imagination, appreciation of humanity, and the lucidity and pace of her style make the reader feel the tension, movement, and the life of the period. Her *Andrew Jackson* (1965) is a vivid and perceptive biography.

Jacqueline Overton's *Long Island's Story* (1929) set a high standard for regional histories. Because of her own and her family's childhood memories of Long Island, she brought personal affection as well as careful research to this history.

The West was represented in the thirties by Julia Davis's dramatic narrative of the Lewis and Clark expedition, *No Other White Men* (1937), and Howard Driggs' *The Pony Express Goes Through, An American Saga Told by Its Heroes* (1935), made up of stories told to the author by riders and station agents for the Pony Express. Fifteen years later appeared Samuel Hopkins Adams's *The Pony Express* (1950), a lively account of the intrepid young riders who carried mail in relays from California to St. Joseph, Missouri, through snow and heat, across mountains and desert, and often faced encounters with outlaws and hostile Indians.

In the forties the trend toward regional histories is marked. Lena Barksdale's *That Country Called Virginia* (1945) and Robert Glass Cleland's *California Pageant* (1946) were both written with accuracy and perspective and make moving drama of historical events.

Henry Billings in *All Down the Valley* (1952) sustained the human interest throughout the story of the Tennessee Valley from the pioneer settlement of 1779 to the creation of the Tennessee Valley Authority in 1933 and its development up to 1950. This is an engineer's study but the inclusion of several generations of the Medford family from

1865 to 1950 gives focus to the concern with people and makes it a social history as well as the story of a massive engineering feat. It shows "how people and water can work together to each other's mutual benefit; how natural resources can be brought into balance with human resources." Mr. Billings' own drawings illuminate the text, showing designs of dams and locks, floodgates and spillways.

Samuel Eliot Morison, a well-known historian, brought both humor and scholarship to *The Story of the "Old Colony" of New Plymouth 1620–1692* (1956), clearing away stereotyped notions of grim fanatics, presenting the Pilgrims as interesting individuals, and giving a clear picture of the voyage of the *Mayflower*, the establishment of Plymouth Colony, and the life of its people up to the annexation by the Massachusetts Bay Colony.

By the sixties writers were beginning to realize that individual social movements often had the drama to make absorbing books for young people. In *Women's Rights* (1966) Olivia Coolidge gave life to the suffrage movement by spirited vignettes of the women who carried it on for more than seventy years, through nineteen congresses. She also related it to other forces that were shaping the nation—the Civil War, immigration, industrialization.

The American Indian

Two writers who during the fifties and sixties devoted themselves most consistently to studying and writing about the Indians of America were both foreign born: Sonia Bleeker in Russia, Robert Hofsinde in Denmark. Both came to the United States as young people and continued to live here. Sonia Bleeker, whose husband is the writer Herbert S. Zim, after looking for books that would tell her two young sons how the Indians lived, found none and decided to write one herself. As their home was in New York, the most available place to study Indians was the Onondaga Reservation near Syracuse. She, therefore, wrote her first book about the Iroquois: *Indians of the Longhouse* (1950). Within the decade she wrote a series of books about the ways of life of different North American Indian peoples.

Robert Hofsinde's first encounter with American Indians was as a young man in the north woods of Minnesota after he had completed some scientific drawings for the Museum of Science in Minneapolis. He rescued an Indian boy who had fallen into a pit trap, became his friend, and was later initiated as an Ojibwa and given the name Gray-Wolf. His growing interest in the Indians prompted him to learn about other tribes. A visit among the Blackfeet of Montana led to further acquaintance with northern tribes; a stay among the Navajos of Arizona was only the beginning of his first-hand acquaintanceship with the southwestern tribes. His early books were chiefly concerned with Indian crafts and costumes. Later ones included *Indian Picture Writing* (1959), *Indian Fishing and Camping* (1963), *Indian Warriors and Their Weapons* (1965), and *The Indian Medicine Man* (1966). His books are illustrated with his own detailed drawings.

In *The Story of the Totem Pole* (1951) Ruth Brindze gave the origins and uses of the poles of the Indians of the Northwest, information on how to read the carvings, and stories about specific poles. The illustrations, very important in clarifying the text, are by Yeffe Kimball, of Indian origin and an authority on Indian art.

Theodora Kroeber's *Ishi, Last of His Tribe* (1964) is a tragic story of the proud Yahi tribe of American Indians, whose ancestors had lived for thousands of years in the western foothills of Mount Lassen in northern California. The white men brought to California by the gold rush had killed or driven from their homes the true native sons. The story here is fiction only as it attempts to relate the grievous history through the mind and heart of the Yahi people, and of Ishi, particularly, found by an anthropologist and taken to the Museum of Anthropology in San Francisco where his language and story were learned.

Negro History

In spite of all the interest of the thirties and forties in regional history and in minority groups, it was not until 1948 that the first important history of the Negro was published—Arna Bontemps' *Story of the Negro*.

Arna Bontemps was a very small boy when his father left Louisiana in search of the kind of place he had dreamed of in which to bring up his children. He settled upon Los Angeles, and there his son had a happy childhood, with only occasional reminders that, as a Negro, he must prove his abilities. During Arna Bontemps' college years he began to write poetry, for which he early received recognition. It was not, however, until he had gone to New York to teach, married, and had two children that he began writing children's stories. Later his anthology of Negro poetry and his biographies were published, all his work adding to his stature as a writer and as a man with unusual perspective and understanding of human beings. In *Story of the Negro*, brought up to date in 1955, Mr. Bontemps traced the history of the Negro people from earliest times, described a few of the many kinds of African Negroes and the variety of cultures, and portrayed some of the great men who played important roles in the shameful story of slavery. He gave a well-rounded picture and an excellent background for understanding the American Negro and the progress made despite centuries of segregation and unequal opportunities.

The Russian launching of Sputnik was only one of the factors that stimulated Americans to reevaluate their schools. The other was the

United States Supreme Court decision of 1954, the first step in bringing about the desegregation of public schools "with all deliberate speed." Taken for granted by many, shocking to many others, was the discovery of the paltriness of the education of most Negroes and of the appalling inferiority of most public schools in Negro neighborhoods. Few of the Negro children had any educational preparation for transference to other schools that might be better, but were often far from excellent.

One more tinder was added to the others, touching off the publication explosion. School readers and other textbooks were found inappropriate or meaningless to Negro children in both rural and urban areas. New types of schoolbooks began to be published. Books of literary quality were naturally slower to appear but gradually books of distinction and originality about Negro children and by Negro authors evolved to broaden and enrich children's literature.

Forever Free. The Story of the Emancipation Proclamation (1963) by Dorothy Sterling is a chronicle of the continuous struggle for freedom in which many unknown heroes took part. The author's research was extensive, her writing sparked by enthusiasm and passion. Margaret Warren Brown in *The Horn Book*, June 1963, paid tribute to Dorothy Sterling "for *Forever Free, Captain of the Planter, Mary Jane,* and *Freedom Train,* all noble books—not tracts—which do much to correct the lopsidedness of the traditional view of the Negro's role in history and to give long-neglected patriots their rightful place in the American heritage."

Betty Schechter's *The Peaceable Revolution* (1963) told the story of nonviolent resistance to oppression as exemplified by Thoreau, Gandhi, and Martin Luther King. Johanna Johnston in *Together in America: The Story of Two Races and One Nation* (1965) gave an account of the joint achievement of people of European and African descents in America.

In three provocative volumes Milton Meltzer gathered selections from letters, journals, newspapers, and diaries, and allowed the Negro to speak for himself through three hundred years of oppression. In the first book, *In Their Own Words. A History of the American Negro 1619–1865* (1964), the Negro's struggle for recognition and for rights as a human being begins. His voice is often sad, but notably lacking in bitterness. In the second, *In Their Own Words. A History of the American Negro 1865–1916* (1965), the voice is more articulate, more bitter —half a century has passed since his liberation yet little progress has been made in the recognition of his stature as a citizen. In the final book, *In Their Own Words. A History of the American Negro, 1916–1966* (1967), the voice speaks with the fervor of renaissance and the urgency of revolution.

The Far East

Elizabeth Seeger's *The Pageant of Chinese History* (1934) was the first good history of China for children, and the first important book for children that dealt with Chinese culture. In 1923 Elizabeth Seeger was asked to teach history in a progressive school in New York City. In an effort to make the curriculum truly comprehensive she looked for books on the Orient that would be useful to twelve-year-old children, finding a little about Japan but nothing about India or China. She set about writing a sketch of Chinese history for the children, while her friend Dhan Gopal Mukerji wrote a similar one of the history of India. *The Pageant of Chinese History* was an amplification and completion of the sketch made for her school children. Out of the vast amount of material she made excellent selection, telling a fascinating story, and never, in the chronicle of events, losing sight of the people themselves.

Sixteen years later Elizabeth Seeger's *The Pageant of Russian History* (1950) was published, showing the same careful study and integration of material, and presented with color and imagination.

Robert Newman's *The Japanese: People of the Three Treasures* (1964) is a creatively organized and interestingly told history of the Japanese. Beginning with the legendary origin of the Three Treasures —the Mirror, the Sword, and the Jewel—recognized as the symbols of the right of the imperial family to rule, it carries the account through the middle of the seventeenth century, when Japan cut herself off from the rest of the world, and treats aspects of Japanese life represented by the Treasures. The final chapters discuss the samurai, strong during Japan's feudal period—their traditions and code still alive during the Second World War—their period ending when the Japanese ceased to be "the People of the Sword . . . alone. They became once more what they had been originally, the People of the Three Treasures."

The Ancient World

Although the tomb of Tutankhamon in the Valley of the Kings was unearthed in 1922, causing a wave of popular interest in ancient Egypt, it was not until fifteen years later that the first readable history of Egypt for children was published. In that same year appeared Lucile Morrison's novel of ancient Egypt. This delay between cause and effect, between inspiration and accomplishment, is frequently to be noticed in children's literature, so often is a children's book written as a result of some event, stimulation, or influence in the writer's childhood.

Like other writers with a strong interest in people, Enid La Monte Meadowcroft made *The Gift of the River* a story primarily of the people of ancient Egypt. Although it is a history of a far-away time, incorporating quotations from ancient sources, the organization of material is so good and the style so clear that the younger children can read it with pleasure.

The contemporary quality of ancient Egyptian art was caught in *Never to Die, The Egyptians in Their Own Words* (1938), selected and arranged with commentary by Josephine Mayer and Tom Prideaux. Through the literature and art of Egypt, presented chronologically, the Egyptians themselves are revealed.

One of the earliest writers to make of archaeology a fascinating journey of discovery for children was Jennie Hall. Her *Buried Cities*, published in 1922, describes the excavations of Pompeii, Olympia, and Mycenae, and shows how, through the findings, can be built up a picture of the early life of the peoples of these civilizations.

In 1924 the Carnegie Foundation sent out an archaeological expedition to Yucatan. One of the members of the party was Anne Axtell Morris, who put her experiences in a book, *Digging in Yucatan* (1931), telling not only her adventures, details of reconstruction, and amusing anecdotes relating to the expedition itself, but weaving through it Mayan legends and bits of historic adventure. In her introduction to her later book *Digging in the Southwest* (1933) her definition of archaeology shows her imaginative approach to an exciting career: "Archaeology might be defined as a rescue expedition sent into the far places of the earth to recover the scattered pages of man's autobiography."

Anne Terry White's *Lost Worlds* (1941) was an excellent introduction to the science of archaeology, telling the story of the successful search for the records of the lost civilizations of Crete, Egypt, Babylonia-Assyria, and the Mayan civilizations of Central America.

In *Land of the Pharaohs* (1960) Leonard Cottrell made a parenthetical observation: "It is a curious fact that many great Egyptologists began very young, often as early as twelve years of age"; and then proceeded to give such a fresh account of ancient Egyptian civilization and history and of the archaeologists responsible for making this knowledge available that it would be surprising if he did not arouse the enthusiasm of many other prospective Egyptologists. Mr. Cottrell in *The Secrets of Tutankhamen's Tomb* (1964) supplemented dramatically his earlier book. His *Digs and Diggers: A Book of World Archaeology* (1964) is an important comprehensive discussion of archaeology: Middle Eastern, Asian, European, and American.

Good Digging: The Story of Archaeology (1960) by Dorothy and Joseph Samachson includes the history and development of the science of archaeology. *Portals to the Past* (1963) by Katherine B. Shippen, written with style and life, emphasizes the scientific approach to archaeology, calling attention to new discoveries in both old and new locations and to the fact that in all areas of archaeology new frontiers for discovery are waiting for new generations.

Elizabeth Chesley Baity, growing up in Texas, had always been interested in Indians, who had left behind them their flint arrowpoints; and in dinosaurs, "who had obligingly left their footprints in some of the rocks at our place." Even before them, sea animals had left their bones to become fossilized in rock, "or to end up ignominiously as doorstops." Because of her work as a member of the world Literacy and Christian Literature Team and her husband's as a director in the World Health Organization, she has lived and worked in many parts of the world, including Pakistan, South Sudan, and Tanganyika. Her *Americans Before Columbus* (1951), illustrated with many photographs and with drawings and maps by C. B. Falls, is an outstanding book. In it are discussed the ice-age fossils and the archaeological remains of all the Americas as a background for her interpretation of the people who lived in the Americas before the fifteenth century. In *America Before Man* (1953) she presented with scientific accuracy and creative excitement the story of the American continent from its formation through its geological changes.

Anne Terry White's *Prehistoric America* (1951) is much shorter and simpler in treatment than Mrs. Baity's book on the same subject, but it too makes the past live. Victor W. von Hagen wrote on the three major cultures of the Western Hemisphere. *The Sun Kingdom of the Aztecs* (1958), *Maya, Land of the Turkey and the Deer* (1960), and *The Incas, People of the Sun* (1961), recount the history and vividly re-create the daily life, customs, beliefs, and festivals of each.

Hans Baumann, a former Bavarian school teacher, made the most of the extraordinary fact that many of the caves containing prehistoric paintings were discovered by children. His *The Caves of the Great Hunters* (1954), translated from the German by Isabel and Florence McHugh, tells the story of the discovery made in September 1940 by four boys of Montignac when they climbed Lascaux hill, their favorite haunt, following their dog through a hole in the earth into a series of caves that they had not known existed. Into the account is woven the story of the discovery of other cave paintings, particularly of those in Altamira, Spain, found by a five-year-old girl. Mr. Baumann had not only explored all the caves himself but he had as his guides some of the very boys who made the first discoveries. His book reads like the adventure story it is, charged with the excitement and mystery of archaeological discoveries. Mr. Baumann also wrote *The World of the Pharaohs* (1960), a detailed account of Egyptian archaeology with a thread of story woven through it, and *Gold and Gods of Peru* (1963).

Walter A. Fairservis, Jr., a distinguished archaeologist and anthropologist, based much of his *Egypt, Gift of the Nile* (1963) on recent discoveries. In that and in *Mesopotamia: The Civilization That Rose Out of Clay* (1964) he gave life to ancient civilizations.

The *Quest of the Dead Sea Scrolls* (1965) by Geoffrey Palmer gives an account of the 1947 discovery of the ancient manuscripts by a young Bedouin goatherd, and of their archaeological significance, and discusses the contents of the most important. Thomas Caldecot Chubb's *The Byzantines* (1959) is a well-documented account of Byzantine culture in all its richness and variety.

Shirley Glubok, a lecturer at the Metropolitan Museum of Art, compiled pictures and wrote interpretive text for *The Art of Ancient Egypt* (1962), a book of reproductions of Egyptian wall paintings, mummy cases, statues, hieroglyphs, and everyday art objects. She was responsible also for *The Art of Lands in the Bible* (1963) and similar volumes on the Eskimo, Africa, and other lands and cultures.

May Edel's background for writing *The Story of People* (1953) included not only extensive scientific knowledge and scholarly research but a year of living with a primitive African tribe. She began her book with the discoveries made by Franz Boas when he lived among the Eskimos, continuing with the study of other groups, and concluding with proof that "our civilization has grown from contributions made by many different people," and that indeed all men are brothers. Her *The Story of Our Ancestors* (1955) is a clear, lively discussion of the evolution of man.

Voyages, Explorations and Discoveries

In 1933 Ingri and Edgar Parin d'Aulaire told the story of *The Conquest of the Atlantic* through the ages, from the Vikings to Balbo's flight in 1930, their splendid lithographs adding eloquence to a dramatic presentation. Two years later appeared Leonard Outhwaite's unusual book *Unrolling the Map, The Story of Exploration* (1935), which describes "All the Great Adventures by Land and Sea from Hannu, 2750 B.C., to Picard, 1935," with Gordon Grant's drawings of ships and many specially devised maps to add to its attractiveness and value.

In Mary Seymour Lucas' story of exploration, *Vast Horizons* (1943), not only are the leaders from Genghis Khan onward portrayed and the historic results of great expeditions, from the thirteenth century to 1940, described, but the reader is made aware of the sweep and excitement of exploration and of all the great company of little people—the unknown participants in the Crusades, the sailors, the small merchants, the ordinary young men who were caught by the thrill of exploration. Throughout the story are woven the words and music of fourteen songs, sung by travelers and explorers—songs of the Crusaders, Portuguese and Mongol folk songs, and melodies from the Gold Coast.

Many books about twentieth century exploration have been published for boys and girls. Some of the explorers themselves have written firsthand accounts of their expeditions for children, or selections of particular interest to young people have been made from their writings. In the twenties and thirties the names of William Beebe and J. E. Williamson under the sea, Admiral Richard Evelyn Byrd and Lincoln Ellsworth in the air and at the poles, were nearly as familiar to young people as the historic explorers of continents. Of the records made by the explorers themselves, Stefansson's *Hunters of the Great North* (1922) was the first. Vilhjalmur Stefansson (1879–1962), born of pioneer stock, growing up on a ranch, was nevertheless influenced in his early years by people who "came from countries in Europe where literary ambitions take the place of money making dreams." He went to college intending to be a poet. Halfway through college he turned to anthropology, which became his great interest. *Hunters of the Great North* was written after a background of ten northern winters and thirteen summers. It tells the events leading up to his becoming an explorer and the vivid impressions of his first year among the Eskimos. To Stefansson, an explorer "needs a mind to see visions no less than he needs the strength to face a blizzard." This exciting book is evidence of the power of the imagination that directs the lives of all who willingly face the unknown.

Africa

For many years explorers and adventurers in the jungles of Africa have given accounts of their experiences that children have enjoyed. Rafaello Busoni turned back to an earlier day in his *Stanley's Africa* (1944), an absorbing account of Sir Henry Morgan Stanley's explorations, which gave at the same time an excellent overall picture of Africa, her great variety in land and people, her many problems. Henry Stanley is revealed as a courageous, determined man, whose miserable childhood was no doubt behind his tremendous drive toward success. Mr. Busoni's father was Italian, his mother Swedish, his birthplace Germany, and even as a small boy he traveled frequently. International influences were at work all during his growing years. As an artist he was self taught and had his first exhibition in Switzerland when he was only seventeen. He had already done some illustrating before he fled to the United States from Nazi Germany. It was through illustration that he entered the children's book field here. His special interest in geography and his knowledge of many lands are reflected in his books, and his vivid, disciplined writing gives reality to Stanley's extraordinary career and to the great continent of Africa.

During the forties a number of explorers, including Attilio Gatti and Theodore Waldeck, wrote about their experiences exploring in Africa. By the fifties children's books about the African jungles were superseded by those concerned with the political awakening of the different peoples of Africa and the transition to independence of colony after colony. Attention was focused on emerging social, economic, and political problems. Among the books of current history, soon displaced by others evaluating new problems in the ever changing story, was one of more lasting value, *The Land and People of South Africa* (1955) by Alan Paton, author of *Cry, the Beloved Country*, a novel written with wisdom, love of country, and desire to make better understood the many-faceted race problems.

In the next decade Colin Turnbull's *The Peoples of Africa* (1962) attempted to describe the basic tribal cultures and to assess the impact of Western civilization on Africans. Although taking exception to a few points, Cyrus A. Kamundia of Kenya called Mr. Turnbull's book "factual, scholarly, and sympathetic without being pedantic or patronizing." Mr. Kamundia commended Sidney Lens for the accurate simplicity of his book *Africa—Awakening Giant* (1962), which takes the reader through the currents that changed the relation of Africa with the rest of the world to the present nationalist revolution.

A book that is a landmark, and that points the way to make the people of the varied countries of Negro Africa better understood is *Africa Is People* (1967) by Barbara Nolen. It is an anthology of selections by African authors and others, chiefly anthropologists and artists, who have made Africa their home, and an introduction to the wealth of material from contemporary Africa. Because of the abundance, selections were limited to nonfiction "with priority given to autobiographical accounts by Africans themselves of the last fifty years."

People of Other Lands As Seen Through Their Art and Culture

As early as 1929 Susan Smith in *Made in America* had brought history to life by means of her studies of the arts and crafts of Americans during the Revolutionary period. In *Made in Mexico* (1930), she gave reality to the Mexican people today in her appreciation of art in their daily lives. Other writers also realized that the influence of ideas on the rest of the world, carried by means of crafts and culture, was a more fundamental and natural tie between peoples than the mechanical inventions. Among those writers were Cornelia Spencer, who had lived much of her life in China and was particularly well equipped to show the cultural influence of the Chinese people in *Made in China* (1943); and Margaret Ayer, whose childhood home was Thailand and who showed clearly the daily life of the people in *Made in Thailand* (1964).

In books for young people many lands have been seen through writers' childhood memories. Chiyo Kiyooka, the daughter of Madame Etsu Sugimoto, author of *A Daughter of the Samurai* (1925), wrote, in her turn, of her experiences in returning to Japan after ten years of life in the United States. *Chiyo's Return* (1935) is full of the fascinating contrasts of life, customs, and traditions of the two countries, her mother's experiences in reverse. Shidzué Ishimoto, born to an ancient family in Japan, told in *East Way, West Way* (1936) the story of her childhood at home and in the Peeresses School, giving a picture of the manners, traditions and old ceremonies of the aristocracy at a time when Western ideas were changing ways of thought. In *The Happy Grove* (1933), taken from his book *Grass Roof*, Younghill Kang told the story of his boyhood in a Korean village.

In *Myself When Young, A Boy in Persia* (1929), Youel Benjamin Mirza told of his childhood in Persia, describing his village and the people, and the great change in his life when he came, at the age of fifteen, to New York. The account of Turkey and her people in *Turkey, Old and New* (1947) by Selma Ekrem is based on the author's knowledge of her country, where her growing years were colored by the changes that were revolutionizing age-old attitudes and ways of life.

Out of memories of his childhood in South Africa Jan Juta wrote *Look Out for the Ostriches* (1949), thrilling stories of nature seen through the eyes of a boy whose life counted to himself only when it was lived out of doors.

Gudrun Thorne-Thomsen, one of the great oral storytellers of this century, interpreted the country of her inheritance with imagination and authority, giving *In Norway* (1948) unusual perspective and wholeness. This book, with Helene Ebeltoft Davis's *The Year Is a Round Thing* (1938), which tells of a year of family life above the Arctic Circle, and Sigrid Undset's *Happy Times in Norway* (1942), a sensitive and beautiful glimpse of her own family through whose lives the changing seasons and the festivals weave a glowing pattern, give a living picture of Norway.

In *At Home in India* (1956) Cynthia Bowles told of living in India between 1951 and 1953 while her father was United States ambassador. She went to school with Indian girls, visited in her friends' homes, lived in villages, and observed the work of public health nurses and other village services, and did volunteer work in a New Delhi hospital. Her book was an inspiration to others who also might be just such ideal ambassadors to the young people of other countries.

The West Indies: Islands in the Sun (1967) by Wilfred Cartey is a social and political history that is humanized by the author's love for the islands and the quotations from literature, especially poetry and song, woven through it.

The Artist as Geographer and Historian

In accepting children's books as an important medium of expression the artist has not been limited. He has entered into all aspects of children's bookmaking and all subjects of children's literature. In few places has he made a more practical contribution than in geography. No one but an artist could turn a map into a field of discovery and adventure for a small child. With the publication of Vernon Quinn's *Picture Map Geography of the United States* (1931), illustrated with picture maps by S. Johst, the making of picture geographies and picture histories began. There were more by Mr. Quinn, and others, profusely illustrated in color by Mable Pyne, Arensa Sondegaard, and many other writers and illustrators. Between 1940 and 1950 was published a group of picture-story books of America called *The Regions of America Series* which, chiefly through the dramatic and colorful lithography of their artist, Cornelius H. DeWitt, make history and geography exciting for young children.

Holling C. Holling made an unusual contribution to geography in his beautiful *Paddle-to-the-Sea* (1941). With simple, dramatic text and striking illustrations in color he showed the journey made by a little wooden figure in a tiny canoe, launched on Lake Nipigon by the Indian boy who had made it, which floated through the Great Lakes, the St. Lawrence River, and into the sea. Mr. Holling wrote and illustrated other books, also, with great imagination, among them *Tree in the Trail* (1942) and *Seabird* (1948). They are like windows on other times and places.

In *Oars, Sails and Steam* (1952) Edwin Tunis traced the development of ships with clear text and many detailed drawings from the first boat ("it's a good guess that the first boat of all was just a log") to the great transatlantic liners. The book was only a beginning. *Weapons* (1954) and *Wheels* (1955) followed, the historical facts authentic, the many drawings meticulously accurate in every detail, the books beautifully designed, and the pages uncrowded. Particularly important to those interested in American history are *Indians* (1959), *Frontier Living* (1961), *Colonial Living* (1957), and *Colonial Craftsmen and the Beginnings of American Industry* (1965). In illuminating the ways of living in the early years of the country, no historian has been more successful than Mr. Tunis in his handsome books.

John O'Hara Cosgrave II (1908–1968) told the chronological history of American ships from Indian canoes to Polaris submarines in *America Sails the Seas* (1962) with over two hundred beautiful pictures in color. The ships of each period are minutely described in good text and detailed diagrams of interiors and riggings. The books by Mr. Cosgrave and Mr. Tunis are characteristic of some of the most distinguished books of every era; they were created with attention to the special needs and interests of young people but belong to the mainstream that gives refreshment and pleasure to people of all ages and backgrounds.

Among the numerous informational series published in the fifties and sixties were many on life in other countries. The text was often little more than an encyclopedia entry slightly expanded. Illustrations, mostly photographs, were numerous, usually good but not good enough to redeem the undistinguished text. Many were slight books, intended to give the young child merely a glimpse of life in other lands. Some of the best were done by Sonia and Tim Gidal. The distinguished Swedish photographer Anna Riwkin-Brick created several, telling her story almost entirely with photographs, sometimes taking a Swedish child to visit another country as in *Eva Visits Noriko-San* (1957). One of her most charming, *My Swedish Cousins* (1960), has stunning photographs of five different regions in Sweden, tied together with Astrid Lindgren's pleasant story of the midsummer visit of seven young cousins to their grandmother.

New Approaches to History

By the late fifties and all through the sixties new historians, journalists, and news commentators were writing for young people. Robert Goldston stands out among them for his perception, objectivity, and the energy and clarity of his writing style. His interest in Spain resulted in an excellent book, called simply *Spain* (1967), about the country and people, and a lucid, reasoned treatment of one of the great tragedies of the century, *The Civil War in Spain* (1966). He succeeded remarkably well in helping readers to grasp the intricacies, contradictions, and portents of the Spanish Civil War.

From time to time abridgments of important books have been published in attractive form to invite young people who might be put off by a complete work. Often these have seemed unnecessary, or to underestimate the ability and interest of boys and girls.

An abridgment for which there seemed good reason was one of *The Voyage of the Beagle* by Charles Darwin. The original is a work of more than five hundred pages, much of it unnecessary to the general reader, but it records the painstaking groundwork for a theory that had major effects on scientific thought, presents one of the great adventures of all time, and reveals a unique personality. Millicent E. Selsam's arrangement of *The Voyage of the Beagle* (1959) was a superb example of abridgment and editing. She carefully indicated all omissions, did not change Darwin's words, and added to the book newly available material from Darwin's letters.

Young people of the fifties, even before the accelerated courses in schools gave them better understanding of current history and scientific advancements, were exposed through television to a wider world than children had ever known before. Although the benefits of mass media may have been negligible to many children, to others they have been valuable. One of the noticeable trends of the sixties was the readiness of many children for advanced material and the efforts of writers and publishers to fill the need. A significant development was the publication for young people of selections from original sources. For *America;*

Adventures in Eyewitness History (1962) Rhoda Hoff chose brief, dramatic selections from letters, diaries and documents to tell the story of the United States. The collection is bounded by Governor William Bradford's account of the first landing at Plymouth in 1620 and a little Jewish girl's story of the day in 1893 when her father took his three children to school in the new land where education was free to all and, "by the simple act of delivering our school certificates to the teacher he took possession of America." Miss Hoff brought the same raw material of history, "a message from the heat of battle," to illuminate the stories of other countries, including *Africa: Adventures in Eyewitness History* (1963), which begins with an account by Herodotus and ends with one by Robert Moffatt, missionary father-in-law of David Livingstone; and *China: Adventures in Eyewitness History* (1965), from 651 B.C., when a treaty was signed, to 1936 when Mao Tse-tung wrote about his early life.

Robert Meredith and E. Brooks Smith carefully edited and abridged selections from Governor Bradford's *Of Plimoth Plantation* and Edward Arber's *The Story of the Pilgrim Fathers* for their *Pilgrim Courage* (1962), which tells the story of the Pilgrims in the Old World and in the New up to the First Thanksgiving. The same historians collaborated on the selection and editing of original sources for other books: Pedro de Casteñada's account of the exploration of the Southwest, *Relación de la jornada de Cibola,* calling it *Riding with Coronado* (1964), and *The History of the Life and Actions of Admiral Christopher Colon* by Columbus's younger son, Ferdinand, calling it *The Quest of Columbus: A Detailed and Exact Account of the Discovery of America with the Many Difficulties, Dangers, and Triumphant Return* (1966). Shirley Glubok edited and abridged the A. P. Maudslay translation of Bernal Díaz del Castillo's *The Discovery and Conquest of Mexico, 1517–1521* in *The Fall of the Aztecs* (1965).

These and other books demonstrated the growing respect for the intelligence of young people and their readiness for all types of books that might enable them to view the world from "the Mighty Tower of Experience."

Bibliography

Fuller, Muriel. *More Junior Authors.* New York, H. W. Wilson, 1963.
Hofsinde, Robert. "Brother of the Indian." *The Horn Book,* Vol. 36 (Feb., 1960).
Kamundia, Cyrus A. "Books About Africa." *The Horn Book,* Vol. 39 (Feb., 1963).
Kunitz, Stanley J. and Howard Haycraft, eds. *The Junior Book of Authors.* 2d ed., rev. New York, H. W. Wilson, 1951.
Lindquist, Jennie. "Series." *The Horn Book,* Vol. 29 (April, 1953).

7

One World in Children's Books

The children's books with backgrounds in foreign lands that appeared in great numbers in the twenty years following the First World War were an emphatic indication that children's books would express the times as never before. The years between the wars became an era of exploration, not of new frontiers, but of the world of humanity. Among the shiploads of tourists pouring into Europe were many primarily interested in knowing the people of countries that had suddenly become neighbors.

Then in the twenties, this widening interest began to find expression in books for children. Living vicariously in other lands where children like themselves lived, played, and went to school in enchantingly unfamiliar surroundings was an easy and delightful experience, when the stories were true to life and untouched by pedagogy.

Forerunners of the Realistic Foreign Background Story

Paving the way for the traveler-writers were a few storytellers who had grown up or lived long in foreign lands and who had already discovered the satisfaction of writing for boys and girls. Among these was Katharine Adams, who, beginning with *Mehitable* (1925), drew on her life in France, Sweden, Ireland, and England to write a number of books popular with girls, chiefly for the romantic atmosphere that she could create in any setting.

Of greater literary importance was Evelyn and C. Kay Scott's *In the Endless Sands* (1925), a story of two children lost on the Sahara Desert. A quality of remoteness kept the book from wide popularity, but it was significant that distinguished writers should recognize the child's right to strange, new experiences in his books.

Sonia Lustig drew from her own background in *Roses of the Winds* (1926) to give a colorful picture of the life of a noble Russian family exiled to the Caucasus.

John Eyton's *Kullu of the Carts* (1929) has a fascinating background of India. It was rare in the period to find a children's book that faced so realistically the facts behind a child's rebellion. Drew, the half-English, half-Indian boy, could defy the conservative pattern of his life laid down by a cold father and unsympathetic sisters to run away from his British inheritance to the warmth and adventure of native life. He remained a nonconformist to the end of the book. Mr. Eyton's prose is a pleasure. Adult readers may see social retribution ahead for Drew, but children see him forever driving on with Kullu behind the slow bullock carts down the dusty roads of India.

Out of Erick Berry's experiences living in West Africa, and later traveling with her husband, Herbert Best, through the villages and towns along the desert and up the tributaries of the Niger, evolved the six stories in *Girls in Africa* (1928). Each story gives a glimpse of a different aspect of West African civilization.

Elizabeth Cleveland Miller's knowledge of the people and ways of life of Albania grew from experiences at the end of the First World War, when she worked with the Red Cross to find and rehabilitate the war's lost children. *Children of the Mountain Eagle* (1927) is laid in the Albanian mountains. *Pran of Albania* (1929) is the story of a girl who has the courage to speak out in the council of chiefs against the ancient custom of the blood feud. *Young Trajan* (1931), a gentle love story, is an early example of the drama of social issues in a book for young people.

Alexander Finta's *Herdboy of Hungary* (1932) is an autobiographical story of a young boy's life on a Hungarian cattle ranch. The vastness of the Hungarian plains is in this book, the extravagant jokes of the cowherds and their big-hearted laughter; in all this bigness Sandor seemed disproportionately small, but he had amazing resilience, a quick brain and a wide imagination, and his heart held boundless love for the ancient horse, Mocskos. The author's remarkable illustrations underline the exaggeration of the story and have the same touch of wildness and excitement.

These foreign background stories of the twenties and early thirties, and others by Dorothy Rowe, Kurt Wiese, Herbert Best, and Helen Damrosch Tee-Van were setting the pace for the many to come in the next decade, showing that people who had grown up in other lands, who had lived or worked abroad, had something rich and delightful to share with children in story books.

Stories of Family Life and Everyday Adventures

At the beginning of the thirties, Eleanor Frances Lattimore, who had clear recollections of a childhood spent in China, wrote *Little Pear* (1931), the story of a mischievous Chinese boy. This was the first in a long series of stories of everyday children that the youngest readers could read for themselves. The simple directness of the writing and the sincerity and naturalness of the stories, with their engaging children and accurate settings, gave them a rather special place in children's literature.

Arna Bontemps and Langston Hughes, both poets, brought to their *Popo and Fifina* (1932), the story of two little Negro children of Haiti, an appreciation of that country and knowledge of childhood everywhere. There are both reality and the charm of strange settings in stories by Caroline Singer and Cyrus LeRoy Baldridge, Kathleen Morrow Elliot, Elizabeth Steen, and many others.

The growing interest at this time in foreign backgrounds was pointed up by the awarding of the Newbery Medal in 1933 to a realistic story of China, *Young Fu of the Upper Yangtze* (1932) by Elizabeth Foreman Lewis. Several years of teaching in various parts of China under a mission board had given her a thorough knowledge of China. Her love and admiration for the country and people had impelled her to write. For six years she wrote short stories of China for children's magazines, and out of a number of these grew her first book, *Young Fu*, the story of a coppersmith's apprentice newly come from the country to Chungking. *Ho-Ming, Girl of New China* (1934) is an even more sympathetic character portrayal.

Monica Shannon was born in Canada and spent her childhood on a great stock farm in the Bitterroot Valley of northwestern United States. She remembered the Bulgarian immigrants who worked on the ranch and who kept many of their native customs. Her love of the land and appreciation of the beauty of the wide sweep of grain, the thousands of red cattle, the snowy peaks of mountains all around, are reflected in *Dobry* (1934) for which Miss Shannon received the Newbery Medal. It is the story of a Bulgarian peasant boy, of his longing to be a sculptor, of his mother's incomprehension of his wish to leave the fields that she fairly worshiped, and of his eventual uprooting from the village. Woven through are the stories told by Dobry's old grandfather.

Such truth and humor as one finds in Marie Hamsun's *A Norwegian Farm* (1933), translated from the Norwegian, could create added interest in family adventures in other parts of the world. It is chiefly the story of the four Langerud children and their parents through the seasons of one busy year. The author, the wife of the novelist Knut Hamsun, wrote about her own children in this story and its sequel, showing remarkable objectivity as well as understanding in her characterizations.

Joy in the freedom and goodness of daily life pervades Kate Seredy's story of life on a farm in the Hungarian plains. *The Good Master* (1935) tells about the wild little tomboy Kate, newly come from Budapest to share the warmth and kindness of her uncle's home and to enjoy the companionship of her cousin Jancsi. The customs of the people of the Hungarian plains, their festivals and legends, are all part of the happy development of two appealing children, whose lives are made secure by the loving understanding of Jancsi's father, the Good Master. Twenty years later Kate Seredy used Prague as the background for her gracefully sentimental *Philomena* (1955). Miss Seredy's pictures illustrate both books.

Hilda van Stockum's inheritance is both Dutch and Irish; she lived in Holland, Ireland, and in other parts of the world before she grew up. Many of her characters are drawn from loving memory of members of her family. Her first book, *A Day on Skates* (1934), was one of the most delightful of the early picture-story books for the younger children. Miss van Stockum's own lively drawings in black and white sprinkle the pages, and her eight full-page pictures in color show entrancing scenes of children joyously skating on the canals or playing in the snow. Holland was also the setting for her *Kersti and Saint Nicholas* (1940), another enchanting picture-story book about a naughty child who got the better of St. Nicholas. Between the two picture-story books came *The Cottage at Bantry Bay* (1938), her first full-length book and the first of three stories about the loveable O'Sullivan family living in a little cottage in Ireland under the shadow of the Kerry Mountains. Full of vitality, and true to childhood and to Irish family life *The Cottage at Bantry Bay* was immediately popular. In addition to the Irish stories two books about Holland followed, also with her own illustrations. After her husband, E. R. Marlin, was transferred to Washington and later to Montreal, she wrote stories about the Mitchell family with settings in both cities. No doubt her own six children were models for some of the characters in these later books.

Ludwig Bemelmans (1898–1962) was born in the Austrian Tyrol and came to America when he was sixteen. His first book, *Hansi* (1934), was the result of a suggestion from May Massee, the children's book editor at the Viking Press, when she saw some of the landscapes he had painted on the window shades of his apartment to remind him of his birthplace. *Hansi*, the story of a small boy who spends his winter vacation high in the Tyrolean mountains, is an echo of his own childhood. The illustrations in color by Mr. Bemelmans made it another one of the early, very distinguished picture-story books. *The High World* (1954), with appeal to older boys and girls, is also laid in the Tyrol.

France

René Bazin's *Juniper Farm* (1928), translated from the French by Margery Bianco, related simple, homely events on a French farm where four children passed their childhood. It was a pleasant, wholesome book but lacking in any strong story interest. In the thirties an entertaining book gave glimpses of France, but the main characters were American children. The boy and girl of Marjorie Fischer's *Street Fair* (1935) escaped from conventional sightseeing in Paris to explore southern France in their own way. Cyrus Fisher's *The Avion My Uncle Flew* (1946) has an American protagonist but gives the reader a happy experience in a village in central France. Told in the words of thirteen-year-old Johnny Littlehorn, it is a story of mystery and suspense, and also of Johnny's change from a spoiled, sulky invalid to an enthusiastic, healthy boy through his friendly association with the villagers and his ingenious Uncle Paul. The book has originality, and the French words and phrases sprinkled throughout add amusement and flavor.

In the fifties a number of stories with French background appeared. Some were translations from the French, others by authors native to France but living in the United States, like Claire Huchet Bishop. Some years before she came to America Claire Huchet had opened in Paris, on behalf of an American committee, L'Heure Joyeuse, the first French children's library. There she started telling stories. One of her stories was "The Five Chinese Brothers." Years later, married to an American, she told that same story in the New York Public Library. She wrote it down, and her writing career in the United States began. *Pancakes-Paris* (1947) grew out of her wish to help Americans understand the suffering of French children during seven years of war. Other stories with French settings followed, including *All Alone* (1953), the story of a ten-year-old village boy who, quite by himself, took the family's three heifers—"the family's fortune"—up Little Giant, six thousand feet above the valley, to summer pasture. His father's parting words reminded him to keep to himself, to pay no attention to anything except his own animals. Marcel's feeling of aloneness, his joyous exhilaration when he first breathes the high clear air, and his terror of the storm are intense experiences for the reader. Illustrated by Feodor Rojankovsky with pictures that add a great deal to the drama and the mountain atmosphere, it is a beautiful, simple, nearly perfect book.

After a book of French Canadian folk tales and *Wings Against the Wind* (1955), a story about a Breton fisherman and his pet gull, Natalie Savage Carlson wrote the first of a group of books with genuine Gallic flavor that delight little girls, *The Happy Orpheline* (1957). The French orphan of the title is Brigitte, one of twenty orphans under the care of Madame Flattot, who said, "I wanted twenty children when I was first married, but since I never had any children of my own, working here is my second choice." None of the orphans wanted to be adopted; they were much too happy as one big family. In the second story about the orphelines a baby boy is found in a basket at the gate of the crumbling old orphanage, and the orphelines manage to postpone the day that they must give him up. In the third book the children are to have a pet and they quarrel—rare for the orphelines—because they cannot agree upon the kind. In the fourth book, *The Orphelines in the Enchanted Castle* (1964), the children are moved to a spacious old castle in Fontainebleau, where they are joined by thirty boy orphans who tease the girls unmercifully and are anything but the "noble knights" that the orphelines had expected. The stories are written with so much zest and wit, and the many illustrations, by Garth Williams for the first two, Fermin Rocker for *A Pet for the Orphelines* (1962), and Adriana Saviozzi for the fourth, are so lively and appealing that the books can be enjoyed by fairly new readers. There is no writing down and no obvious simplification of style but each book catches the reader's interest so quickly and holds it so steadily that the child forgets she is reading and knows only that she is enjoying a good book. Among several books with French settings by Mrs. Carlson are *Luigi of the Streets* (1967), which shows Marseilles with its variety of peoples and tongues and temperaments, and *The Family under the Bridge* (1958), which tells about three homeless children and their distraught mother, befriended by Armand, an old hobo who lets them share his corner under one of the bridges of Paris. Natalie Savage Carlson has written many books with a variety of settings. There is humor in all.

The Horse without a Head (1958), translated by John Buchanan-Brown, introduced Paul Berna, a French writer who is skillful in portraying sturdy, independent children. The gang in this story are boys and girls all under thirteen, and a great many dogs, who manage to outwit thieves who have stolen their prize plaything—a wooden horse mounted on tricycle wheels. A town on the Riviera is the setting for *The Knights of King Midas* (1961), and a boarding school in the Loire valley for *Flood Warning* (1963). Good local color, lively characters, and well-developed plots characterize his books.

The simple eloquence and the distinct setting and atmosphere of a French village in Suzanne Butler's *Starlight in Tourrone* (1965), with Rita Fava Fegiz's lively pictures, make this variant of a familiar Christmas theme seem quite new. Despite the apathy of the grownups the children prepare to reenact the March to the Star, the traditional Christmas Eve ceremony no longer performed in Tourrone. Their exuberant faith sweeps aside the indifference of their elders.

Switzerland

Clear memory of the exhilaration and quiet joy that experience in the mountains can give to children informs two appealing stories: Erna M. Karolyi's *A Summer to Remember* (1949), the story of a little Hungarian girl's summer in Switzerland at the close of the First World War; and *The Shooting Star* (1954) by Margot Benary-Isbert, translated from the German by Richard and Clara Winston, the story of a nine-year-old German girl's winter in the high Alps.

Scandinavia and the Far North

The northernmost tip of Norway is the setting for Rafaello Busoni's story of a Lapp tribe, and of single-minded Somi, who was determined his people should have a wooden church in a place where no trees grew, where no roads existed, and where there was no port. In *Somi Builds a Church* (1943) the reader becomes deeply involved in the labor and sacrifice to accomplish what had seemed, to all but Somi, an impossibility. The tundras are also the setting for Faith Yingling Knoop's *Lars and the Luck Stone* (1950), a story strong in human interest about a Lapp boy's adventures when he tries to find a herd of reindeer stolen from his father.

Steingrimur Arason drew on memories of his boyhood to give a clear idea of Icelandic life in *Smoky Bay* (1942). *Eskimo Boy* (1951) by Pipaluk Freuchen is an epic tale, translated from the Danish, that progresses from great suffering to triumph, telling of Ivik, who sees his father killed in a walrus hunt and knows that he, a small boy, must now provide food for his family.

Danish background and people are seen with warm affection in *Lotte's Locket* (1964) by Virginia Sorenson, the story of a child's last year to live in the old farmhouse that had been the home of seven Lottes before her. Adjustment to her mother's marriage to an American and to leaving Denmark makes Lotte more observant than ever of her country and her home. Mrs. Sorenson's people are always real, and Lotte and the grownups, who must help her see beyond her selfish preoccupations, are very perceptively characterized.

Translations from the Swedish have given varied glimpses of Sweden. Edith Unnerstad's Larsson family of *The Saucepan Journey* (1951) travel from Stockholm to Norrköping to sell the father's whistling saucepan. *The Spettecake Holiday* (1958) is spent by two appealing children on a farm in southern Sweden, and *The Journey with Grandmother* (1960) tells about the Dalecarlians who traveled to Finland and Russia at the beginning of the century to sell their haircraft.

Astrid Lindgren, in her Noisy Village stories, made charming and understandable for the younger children a Swedish village and its people. *Rasmus and the Vagabond* (1960), a carefree story of adventures on the open road, gives the nine- and ten-year-olds humor, suspense, and engaging characters. The many books by Astrid Lindgren and Edith Unnerstad make readers everywhere feel happily at home in Sweden.

Karin Anckarsvärd's *Doctor's Boy* (1965) is a warm story of the son of a horse-and-buggy doctor at the beginning of the twentieth century and of the boy's natural, happy relationship with his father. The characterizations of the children in Gunnel Linde's *The White Stone* (1966) are extraordinarily strong.

Italy

Valenti Angelo's *Nino* (1938) is a rare and lovely story of the artist-author's childhood in Tuscany. His *The Marble Fountain* (1951) is laid in the same little village after the Second World War. Two orphan brothers come to live with relatives in the once beautiful village, now almost ruined by the war, and play a part in its restoration. Piccolo, the seven-year-old, imaginative and full of the wonder of living, is particularly memorable.

Ann Weil's *Red Sails to Capri* (1952) tells with humor and excitement of the discovery of the Blue Grotto and has as its setting a beautiful mountainside village in Italy.

Against a vivid re-creation of Venice, David Fletcher told, in *The King's Goblet* (1962), an exciting story of a summer that brought to a fifteen-year-old Venetian boy new friends, a mystery to solve, and a way out of his despondency over the future. The combination of an absorbing plot and a sense of actually living in the magical city makes the book extraordinary.

An earlier book by Mr. Fletcher, with appeal to younger children, *Confetti for Cortorelli* (1957), tells of the efforts of the ingratiating orphan Angelo to assemble a costume for the carnival. So great is the author's affection for Sicily that he brings the reader right into the charming little town; and so perfectly does the story belong to the setting that the character of the people emerges with liveliness and humor through Angelo's activities. The atmosphere of another Sicilian town is clearly evoked in Edward Fenton's *A Matter of Miracles* (1967).

Holland

Meindert DeJong came with his parents to the United States from the Netherlands when he was eight years old. His "childhood village of Wierum, tight against the dike of the North Sea," has been one of the important "wells" out of which his books have come. "I have been extraordinarily lucky," he said, "in having had the childhood in the Netherlands that I left behind stay fixed in me forever, as if set in amber." *The Wheel on the School* (1954), for which he received the Newbery Medal, is a melding of childlike concepts and subtle perceptions. The story is very simple: the six school children in the village of Shora hope that, although storks have not nested in Shora for many years, they will come again if a wheel can be mounted on the schoolhouse roof as a nesting place. The children set out individually to find a wagon wheel, each one encountering different complications, making different acquaintances, overcoming different obstacles, but finally all succeeding as a group. Finding a wheel, getting it firmly mounted on the roof of the school, and then waiting for the storks become the most important things in the world to the reader.

Also drawn from Mr. DeJong's childhood source was *Far Out the Long Canal* (1964), less diverse in its characters and events but also perfect in its expression of place and time and a child's personality. Moonta had been ill with pneumonia four years before, during the last big freeze, and until now there had been no ice for skating. So here he was, a great boy of nine, pushing a little red chair along the frozen canal while all his contemporaries were flying ahead. Despite adventures and misadventures, by the end of the day Moonta had not only learned how to skate but he had learned a great deal about people. The scene is wonderfully appealing: winter in a little North Sea coast village, the canals alive with flying skaters. The naturalness of the characters and the tender, humorous understanding of the intensity of a little boy's yearnings give the book depth and reality.

Few writers can see to the core of a child's emotions as Mr. DeJong does and interpret them without slipping into hypersensitivity or sentimentality. Sometimes the poetic iteration of his style verges on monotony. But not in these two books. Had he written nothing more than these, *The House of Sixty Fathers*, and *The Tower by the Sea*, Meindert DeJong's place in children's literature would be secure. He has done more, however—unusual animal tales that are considered elsewhere.

Spain

When El Bigote harnessed Fedro, his mule, to the water wheel, he bound an old sack over his eyes, gave him a light blow and told him, "Now you are going to Granada. He who sees Granada sees paradise. Giddap, Fedro! It's a long way to Granada." And poor Fedro walked around and around. One day the bandage slipped and, in a rage over the way he had been treated, Fedro ran away—to Granada. To *The Song of the Lop-Eared Mule* (1961) Natalie Savage Carlson transfers the color and gaiety of southern Spain and the lively wit of the people.

In *Don Tiburcio's Secret* (1960) by Jeanne Loisy, translated from the French by James Kirkup, the setting of central Spain is so vivid that the story, filtered through its brilliant sunshine and biting winds, its ruined castles, and lively market places, gives the reader a sense of having lived there. The characters, too, are important and real, the sharp-tongued old grandmother, the father, who is honest only when he has to be, and Pepito, the half Gypsy boy who lives by his wits, who is poor and often hungry but is never to be pitied.

Maia Wojciechowska's *Shadow of a Bull* (1964), a Newbery Award book, has as its setting another perfectly realized village in Spain, its people patiently waiting for Manolo to grow up and bring fame to Arcangel as his father, the greatest bullfighter in Spain, had done. Dreading his twelfth birthday when he must face his first bull, just as his father, whom Manolo had never known, had done, Manolo doggedly prepared to follow in his father's footsteps. No manifesto for or against bullfighting, this is a perceptive story of a boy torn between loyalty and the need to be himself. The book has many facets: an understanding of bullfighting background and the symbolic role of the torero (the "killer of death"), the agonies of an adolescent boy's longing to be understood and recognized for himself, and the phenomenon of the oneness of viewpoint of all the people of a village.

The lovely island of Formentera in the Balearics is the setting for *The Island of Fish in the Trees* (1962) by Eva-Lis Wuorio. Two little girls set off early in the morning to find the doctor to mend their broken doll. Through the village, to the port across the bay, to the windmills, and eventually to the lighthouse they go, making new friends and gathering gifts all along their way. Doublespreads and frontispiece in full color by Edward Ardizzone reflect the warmth of the story and the sun-drenched island where silvery fish hang drying from branches of trees.

Lebanon

Crystal Mountain (1955) by Belle Dorman Rugh, set in Lebanon, is the story of a family of American boys who share the freedom they enjoy in the strange land with a lively English tomboy. Mrs. Rugh had lived in Lebanon as a child, but she made no contrived effort to picture the country. Nevertheless, the story she told is so full of zest and set so naturally in the country she loves that Lebanon becomes familiar and beautiful to the reader. The characters, including a most unconventional English governess, are wonderfully alive and interesting.

Greece

Edward Fenton has written many books with a variety of backgrounds. His love for Greece, where a few of his stories are laid, gives them special warmth. Particularly strong is the sense of place in his *Aleko's Island* (1948). The place is a Greek island surrounded by blue sea and arched by blue sky, and rich with its past, across which Aleko travels with a philosophical itinerant painter.

Throughout Joice M. NanKivell's *Tales of Christophilos* (1954), stories about a goatherd living at the foot of Mt. Athos in Greece, are woven the superstitions and customs of the people. The stories are told in beautiful prose rich in humor and in the details of the environment.

Islands of Ireland and Scotland

Eilís Dillon in a number of books published over a few years made remote islands off the coast of Ireland familiar to boys and girls. *The Sea Wall* (1965) tells how old Sally MacDonagh, who could not persuade the people of Inisharcain to mend the sea wall, took into her confidence her grandson and his friend, and by secret and ingenious planning they succeeded in doing together what Sally alone had not been able to accomplish in twenty-nine years. The unusual overtones, convincing atmosphere, and superb storytelling make The CORIANDER (1964) the most exciting of all Miss Dillon's books. The wreck of the ship was a rich prize for the people of Inishgillan, for from it they acquired cargo and other treasures but, most important, they captured the ship's doctor and hid him from the authorities. The attitudes and viewpoints of the islanders, often at variance with the law, and the subtle distinctions between right and wrong, add fascinating complexities to the plot and show the author's remarkable understanding of people.

The re-creation of the atmosphere of the Isle of Skye is very clear in Allan Campbell McLean's *Storm over Skye* (1957) about two brothers who solve the mystery of sheep stealing that had been turning neighbors against each other. Also laid in Skye is Margaret MacPherson's *The Shinty Boys* (1964), which tells a great deal about school boys and shinty, an ancient form of hockey, of vital concern to the boys of this island. Most important are the skillful characterizations, the beauty of Skye, the little crofts with their sturdy, hard-working people, and the daily rhythm of the island life.

Russia

The feeling of the countryside, woods, swamp, birds and animals is vivid in Mikhail Mikhailovich Prishvin's *The Treasure Trove of the Sun* (1952), translated by Tatiana Balkoff-Drowne. It is a story of peasants of Northern Russia and two gallant, happy children, who succeed in making a home by themselves after their parents' death. The illustrations by Feodor Rojankovsky perfectly suit the story.

Nicholas Kalashnikoff told of his childhood in the Siberian village of Nikolsk in *My Friend Yakub* (1953). Most important to young Nicholas were his love for the animals and his friendship with Yakub the Tartar, who cared for them. The writing is strong and beautiful. The personality of Yakub is vivid and memorable as is the character of Turgen of *The Defender* (1951), also by Kalashnikoff. Turgen was a mountain shepherd of northern Siberia, defending the last of the wild rams in that section of the mountains. Pervading the story are his gentleness and kindness to animals and to two young children and their mother.

Against the background of a Ukrainian village that the author Marie Halum Bloch had known as a child are shown in *Aunt America* (1963) individual reactions to the forces at work in a dictator regime. Not until Aunt Lydia came from the United States to visit did eleven-year-old Lesya love her father for his courage in not submitting to the authorities, and appreciate the difference between docilely accepting subjection to live in comfort, and facing the danger of prison to be free. The plot is contemporary, the theme and the sharply portrayed emotions are timeless.

In *Katia* (1967) by Catherine Almedingen, adapted and translated by E. M. Almedingen, is told the story of a vanished era. Based on a memoir of eight years in the childhood of a girl who grew up to be a writer and translator of children's books and the editor of a famous Russian children's magazine, the story tells of Katia's life from her mother's death when she was five until she entered the "gloomy vaulted hall of the Catherine Nobility Institute in Moscow," and she knew her childhood was ended. The details of luxurious living in a well-to-do family in Czarist Russia give the book the romantic atmosphere of an almost fairy-tale world, but the children are completely real.

Australia

In *Red Heifer* (1934) Frank Dalby Davison gave a tragic picture of the Australian bush and the passing of the wildlife before the encroachment of civilization. In the fifties Mary Elwyn Patchett began writing stories based on her childhood on a great cattle station in the New South Wales-Queensland district. In the sixties the books of several Australian writers were published in the United States. *The Boundary Riders* (1963) introduced Joan Phipson with a story of three children who set off to check the boundary fence. They had prepared to be gone for three days but, caught in a storm and hopelessly lost, they had several days of discomfort and harrowing adventures before the search for them even began. So vivid are Australia's vastness and rugged beauty, so logical the disasters, and so natural the people that the reader feels he is sharing an actual experience. Other books by Mrs. Phipson followed, including two about the enterprising children of the Barker family and one, *Birkin* (1966), set in a little Australian town where a black bull calf served as a catalyst in changing the lives of several children. Reginald Ottley's *Boy Alone* (1966), the story of a wood-and-water choreboy, shows more clearly than any other the atmosphere of life on an isolated cattle station "outback."

For the older boys and girls Jon Cleary's *The Sundowners* (1965), originally published as an adult book in 1952, tells of the adventures of an Australian drover's family, from the point of view of the fourteen-year-old son. It is an absorbing story with sharp reality of setting and depth and honesty in characterizations.

China

Margery Evernden told two tales of adventure against a background of old China: *The Secret of the Porcelain Fish* (1947) and *The Runaway Apprentice* (1949). In the first is highlighted the ancient craft of porcelain making, and in the second the traditions and skills of the shadow players. In both books is the successful fusion of colorful setting, interesting plots, and well-drawn characters.

Carolyn Treffinger's *Li Lun, Lad of Courage* (1947) tells of a fisherman, who, shamed by his son's fear of the sea, imposed upon him a strange and bitter punishment: he gave Li Lun seven grains of rice and commanded him to plant it at the top of Lao Shan and not to return until he had grown seven times as many grains as he had planted. The story has the simplicity, strength, and timeless quality of legend.

Su-Mei's Golden Year (1950), a humorous, understanding story by Margueritte Harmon Bro, was one of the last books about Chinese family and village life, set in a time before mainland China became the People's Republic of China. Stories of family life and everyday adventures of the fifties and sixties have yet to come out of the two Chinas.

Japan

Elizabeth Janet Gray told a gentle, perceptive story of Japan shortly after World War II in *The Cheerful Heart* (1959). The daily lives of Tomi, her six-year-old brother, her parents, and grandfather are surprisingly like those of a family in America, but woven through are poignant memories of the war years and the little important differences that belong to a story of Japan.

Yoshiko Uchida, whose dual background makes her especially fitted to show Japan to American readers, told a story of a ten-year-old Japanese girl's visit to relatives in California in *The Promised Year* (1959). Her *In-Between Miya* (1967) gives contrasting glimpses of Japanese village and city life, telling the story of the daughter of a village priest.

Momoko Ishii, Japanese author, editor, and translator of numerous English and American children's books into Japanese (including *Winnie-the-Pooh*), wrote an appealing story of contemporary Japan, published in Tokyo in 1963, called *The Dolls' Day for Yoshiko* (1966), translated by Yone Mizuta.

Korea

The Happy Days (1960) by Kim Yong Ik is a story of rural Korea and of a group of village children bound together by their affection for the village barber who became their teacher when he opened a little night school in his shop. Intricate details of people's lives are related in poetic prose and the book is full of unusual but convincing characters.

India

Long before they had been given any glimpse of Indian village and country life, English-speaking children had seen the Indian jungle through the eyes of Kipling and Mukerji. A few stories of Indian child life had been published in the thirties but, as a setting for family stories, India did not have wide appeal for American children until Jean Bothwell began writing. Later books had more colorful and complicated plots but, for true interpretation of children and beauty of setting, her *Little Boat Boy* (1945), *River Boy of Kashmir* (1946), and *Little Flute Player* (1949) are outstanding. Miss Bothwell succeeded unusually well in making India credible and interesting even to quite young readers, and in portraying children who slip easily into the reader's affections.

Later stories of family life in India included Caroline Davis's *Jungle Child* (1950), based on childhood memories of the country in the early twentieth century, about a small British tomboy whose life was divided between identifying with the Indians of village and jungle whom she knew in her unrestricted freedom, and struggling for attention from her father who had paid her little notice after her mother's death; and *Sun in the Morning* (1950) by Elizabeth Cadell that shows the country through the eyes of European girls to whom India was home.

Africa

The more unfamiliar a land, the more didactic are the children's books about it likely to be. For many years there have been books with African settings, but most of them have been so contrived to show the culture and customs of the people that they are lacking in conviction and vitality. A few exceptions, like Herbert Best's *Garram the Hunter* (1930), about a boy of the Hill tribes and his wonderful dog, are more adventure than stories of everyday life.

Far better than others was Reba Paeff Mirsky's *Thirty-one Brothers and Sisters* (1952), based on information furnished by Zulu students in the United States, with details carefully checked by authorities in Africa. The unusual setting, the kraal of a Zulu chief with a family of six wives and thirty-one children, has interest, and the characterization of the brave, appealing ten-year-old girl Nomusa gives the story life.

Latin America

Artists had been enjoying the color and atmosphere of Latin America for years. René d'Harnoncourt had done striking illustrations for Elizabeth Morrow's *The Painted Pig* (1930), the story of what happened to a little Mexican boy when he wanted a painted pig with a rosebud on its tail, making of the simple story a distinctive picture book. Constance Lindsay Skinner, Hervey White, and others had found adventure there in the twenties, but not until the Second World War cut them off from European scenes, did many writers discover that neighbor republics held stories galore, friendly stories of everyday children, as well as tales of adventure. Only a few of the most convincing can be mentioned here. Elizabeth Kent Tarshis created a real Mexican village and gave its people life and humor in *The Village That Learned to Read* (1941), the story of a new school in the village and of Pedro, who alone did not want to learn to read. Ruth Sawyer's understanding of children everywhere gives truth to her story of a little Mexican boy and his burro in *The Least One* (1941). Of Alice Dalgliesh's several stories of everyday children, her *The Little Angel* (1943) is the gayest. A colorful story of Rio de Janeiro in the days of Dom Pedro I, it tells of a very engaging family, especially of Maria Luiza and the little sister who was an angel in the Ash Wednesday procession to Santo Antonio.

Ann Nolan Clark, as materials specialist for the Institute of Inter-American Affairs, worked so closely with the people of different Latin American countries in the preparation of textbooks for their schools that each of her story books seems to have grown naturally out of the country of its setting, to be *of* the people rather than merely about them. *Magic Money* (1950) is just such a living portrayal of the life of a Costa Rican family, with a small boy's love for his grandfather filling the story with warmth. Her *Secret of the Andes* (1952) is the story of a Peruvian boy, Cusi, and of the old Indian Chuto, who in the Hidden Valley of the high Andes taught Cusi the history of the Incas, their tribal secrets, and their ways of shepherding the llamas. For the poetic story Ann Nolan Clark received the Newbery Medal. With Jean Charlot's strong pictures it is beautiful to look at as well as to read. Among Mrs. Clark's other books are *Looking-for-Something* (1952), a story of Ecuador for young children; and *Santiago* (1955) about an Indian boy of Guatemala.

Dorothy Rhoads's *The Corn Grows Ripe* (1956) is an absorbing story, rich in Mayan tradition, of a high-spirited twelve-year-old boy who had avoided responsibilities until his father was injured. Jean Charlot's illustrations are as perfectly suited to this story set in Yucatan as they are to Mrs. Clark's *Secret of the Andes*.

Helen Rand Parish's *At the Palace Gates* (1949) has unusual zest. It tells of a nine-year-old Indian boy who finds familiar vicuñas in the palace gardens of the bewildering city of Lima, and through them realizes unbelievable good fortune.

In *The Two Uncles of Pablo* (1959), Harry Behn's first prose narrative, are two delightful pictures of Mexico: the little sunparched farm in the mountains where Pablo left his family to go with Uncle Silván and the beautiful donkey Angelito; and the town of San Miguel, their destination, where Pablo hoped to go to school to learn how to read the letter that Uncle Silván carried. Mr. Behn's knowledge of children is wonderfully clear in the portrait of Pablo with his simple dignity, his childlike tolerance of the strange ways of adults, and his understanding of animals and people.

Ella Thorpe Ellis's *Roam the Wild Country* (1967) is a thrilling tale of three boys and an old gaucho who took a herd of two hundred and fifty Arabian horses out of drought-stricken northern Argentina across the high Andes to greener pastures.

Animal Tales and Stories of Jungle Life

Dhan Gopal Mukerji (1890–1936) brought very special attributes to his interpretation of the Indian jungle. First of all he himself was a child of the jungle. His home was on its edge, and the holy men, while he was still a little boy, took him into the jungle at night to watch till dawn, and taught him that the animals were his brothers. As a young man he came to America, where he received a Western education, became a lecturer, married, and after twelve years' absence, returned to India. Then the urgency of his childhood memories demanded expression in books that would make India better understood by American boys and girls. His first book, *Kari the Elephant* (1922), is the story of an elephant in captivity and the young boy who cared for him; his second, *Hari the Jungle Lad* (1924), tells of a boy's life in the jungle and of his learning the laws and ways of the jungle to fortify him against the "risks of book learning." Other books followed—*Jungle, Beasts and Men* (1929), *Ghond the Hunter* (1928), *The Chief of the Herd* (1929), all of which were drawn from his childhood love and knowledge of the jungle and point up reverence for all nature.

In *Gay-Neck*(1927), for which he received the Newbery Medal, he used a wider canvas than in any of his other books. The story of a carrier pigeon, it has sweep and excitement, beginning in Calcutta, thence across the Himalayan Mountains, and to France during the war. There is beauty in his language and his unique style, and certain ornate passages create a harmonious setting for the moral precepts and the prayers for serenity and wisdom woven through the stories.

It was nearly twenty years after Mukerji began to write before other significant stories of the Indian jungle appeared. *Gift of the Forest* (1942) by Reginald Lal Singh and Eloise Lownsbery, with sensitive understanding of the Indian people and village life, tells the story of a boy who reared and loved a tiger cub and, when he was grown, gave him back to the forest.

Post Wheeler's *Hathoo of the Elephants* (1943) has authentic background in the Indian traditions regarding elephants. The story of an English baby, reared in the jungle by a leopard and an elephant, has kinship with the legends that inspired Kipling, but this story has its own flavor and fascination. Post Wheeler's years in India gave him opportunity for the study of individual elephants, and the interpolations of the talking elephants in the story, which might seem flights of imagination, are based on Mr. Wheeler's firm belief in their ability to communicate intelligently with each other.

Other writers have made vivid in their stories the life of the jungle: Jo Besse McElveen Waldeck, the jungle of British Guiana; Attilio Gatti, the African jungle; and Florence Stuart, the forests of the Philippines.

Willis Lindquist's *Burma Boy* (1953), an absorbing story with authentic setting, tells of courageous, thirteen-year-old Haji, who dared to go into the jungle to find and save the life of the great leader of the elephant herd, who had gone wild.

During the fifties René Guillot wrote many stories of jungle life and wild animals, among them *The Elephants of Sargabal* (1957) inspired by legend. A. T. W. Simeons, a physician who had spent many years in India, gave the unusual background of cheetah training in *Ramlal* (1965), an exciting story of an orphan boy befriended by the Maharajah.

Throughout this study translations have been considered as a natural part of the body of American children's books. Without them, just as without British publications, the study would be incomplete. The point of view in this volume is on books available to American boys and girls, especially those books that have had influence on the flow and development of children's literature, and those that seem to have the potentiality for influence. Once a book has been translated into the language of a country, and accepted by the children who read that language, it has joined the pageant of experiences, delights, emotional and mental stimuli and excursions into new worlds to which good books belong.

Bibliography

Fuller, Muriel. *More Junior Authors*. New York, H. W. Wilson, 1963.

Hürlimann, Bettina. *Three Centuries of Children's Books in Europe*. Translated and edited by Brian W. Alderson. London, Oxford University Press, 1967.

Kunitz, Stanley J. and Howard Haycraft, eds. *The Junior Book of Authors*. 2d ed., rev. New York, H. W. Wilson, 1951.

Moore, Anne Carroll. *My Roads to Childhood*. Boston, The Horn Book, 1961.

Unnerstad, Edith. "Journey to Dalecarlia." *The Horn Book*, Vol. 39 (Dec., 1963), pp. 580–587.

· 8 ·

Experiences to Share

It is the endless variety of children—a variety often concealed beneath the surface of the similar—that is most striking even when we compare them with their seniors. . . .

Men in their late thirties, forties and early fifties are practically contemporaries. They may share much the same tastes, pursuits, outlook and incentives; common sense and worldly wisdom being effective solvents. They mix easily. A little picnic party on the other hand consisting of an infant of two, a girl of about four, a boy of six, a girl of ten and a "young person" aged fourteen and a quarter, is another matter, even though a French governess of forty, seated on a neighboring tree-stump and reading a yellow-back, is present to keep the peace. The generations, so to speak, of children are minute.

—WALTER DE LA MARE[1]

The very essence of childhood is change. The age of complete egotism progresses to the age of wonder, then to the age of action, and thence to the age of self-analysis and insecurity. The child's reaction to the world and to other people has all the variety of these changing emphases and generations. There is drama in each change and even greater drama in the child's adjustments. Then there are all the subtle shadings and overlappings of these phases, and the endless variations of individualities, for "no child is in all respects either average or even normal." It is no wonder that there is substance for the creative writer in childhood itself, without groping for a plot, a mystery, or an adventure. Many writers would like to depend wholly on this, calling on their memories of childhood, writing out of nostalgia. Unfortunately those memories, often incomplete and imperfect, result in an idealization of childhood, tender and sometimes lovely, but without essential truth and without the objectivity and form to make a good story. A few writers can deal with the everyday events of childhood and give them drama.

[1] Walter de la Mare, *Early One Morning in the Spring* (New York, Macmillan, 1935), pp. 63–64.

Stories of Family Life and Everyday Adventures

Eleanor Estes has memories of a happy childhood in West Haven, Connecticut, "a perfect town to grow up in." As a children's librarian she came to know other children besides the one she had been and to understand what gave them pleasure. Her mother, who had loved books, could quote at length from the great poets, and was a born storyteller, helped develop her literary taste and judgment. When she began to write, her native genius, radiant humor, and very special understanding of children were evident. It is difficult to remember when we have not known the Moffats—Jane, Rufus, Sylvie, Joey and their mother—their friends and neighbors on New Dollar Street, and the important inhabitants of the town of Cranbury. The events of the stories themselves are often commonplace, but the turn they take is never ordinary. The children are ingenious and enterprising, but never unrealistically so, the one-track pattern of their minds is the perfect vehicle for the pursuit of a plan to an often surprising conclusion. Mrs. Estes' writing is as inevitably full of surprise as it is of fun, and the characters are completely realized. Throughout the three books, *The Moffats* (1941), *The Middle Moffat* (1942), and *Rufus M.* (1943), each character remains himself, changing with time, of course, but growing in his own pattern. It is good to know that these books have been translated into several European languages and into Japanese, and that American children are represented in other lands by *The Moffats*.

A new family, also of Cranbury, Connecticut, was introduced in *Ginger Pye*: Rachel and Jerry Pye, their dog Ginger, their father, quite a famous "bird man," and their mother, the youngest mother in Cranbury. Rachel and Jerry were famous for their Uncle Bennie, who, in turn, was famous for being an uncle at the age of three. *Pinkey Pye* (1958) was a deserted kitten who joined the family while they were summering at Fire Island and proved herself a most intelligent cat, even learning to type. The wellspring of Mrs. Estes's childhood seems inexhaustible. Later books with settings, characters, and problems, quite different from those of the families of Cranbury, still seem to receive their life from that rich and original source.

When *Ginger Pye* (1951) won the Newbery Medal, Frances Clarke Sayers wrote about Eleanor Estes:

> To this observer it seems that the vitality of Eleanor Estes derives from the fact that she sees childhood whole—its zest, its dilemmas, its cruelties and compassion. She never moves outside that understanding, because she never needs to lean upon the crutch of adult concepts or explanations. Her stories move and have their being in their own complete world, peopled by children. There are wonder-

ful adults in them, to be sure, but they are adults as children see them, smiling or cross, largely divided as children instinctively divide their world into those who are for and those who are against children.[1]

The family-career stories by the English writer Noel Streatfeild were popular in the thirties and forties. Beginning with *Ballet Shoes* (1937) they told stories of families of children aiming toward specific careers, in the ballet, the theater, films, tennis, and, the best of them all, in the circus—*Circus Shoes* (1939), called in England, *The Circus is Coming*. In all of the stories events move rapidly and each child is a definite individual. Miss Streatfeild's spirited, amusing autobiographical novel *A Vicarage Family* (1963) shows very clearly the abundant resources of a lively childhood.

Margery Bianco drew on the memories of her own childhood and that of an older sister in *Bright Morning* (1942) and brought to life two appealing little girls against a background of Victorian London. The charm of the familiar is here and the wonder of the unfamiliar. Chris is eight, Emmie about five, and little girls reading about them can recognize kindred spirits. To them it is very satisfying that Emmie does *not* resist the temptation to lick the roses on the wallpaper when she is faced up to the wall in punishment. And it is exciting and funny to go into the ocean with them from a bathing machine.

In contrast, Mrs. Bianco's *A Street of Little Shops* (1932) is a child's view of an American village. Almost every woman remembers a "baker's daughter" in her childhood, and her counterpart will inhabit the memories of the mid-century girls in the 2000's. The little milliner who made "hats for horses," Mr. A. and Mr. P. and the others touched realism with nonsense—reminders that real life should not be taken too seriously. *Forward Commandos!* (1944) is a story of five New Jersey boys during a summer full of realistic play and some exciting experiences in actuality. Perception, imagination, the storyteller's skill, and the poet's ear for rhythm and style were united in each of her very different books.

Windy Foot at the County Fair (1947) and its sequel, by the poet Frances Frost, may be primarily a story of a small boy and his pony amidst the excitement of the fair, but the quality that one remembers is the closeness of family relationships. Reading Frances Clarke Sayers' *Tag-Along Tooloo* (1941), one is amused by a small girl's struggles to keep up with the activities of a big sister, but, in recalling the story, it is the depth of loyalty between sisters that first comes to mind. The events in Gertrude Robinson's *Father and the Mountains* (1950) may

[1] Frances Clarke Sayers, *Summoned by Books* (New York, Viking, 1965), p. 118.

become confused in memory, but one does not soon forget the family pride and devotion.

Family relationships are interesting in all of Lee Kingman's books. In *The Best Christmas* (1949) the feeling of family loyalty and unity is especially moving. In *Windfall Fiddle* (1950) Carl Carmer's re-creation of childhood early in the twentieth century in upstate New York has regional flavor but is more important for the sense of the child's secure place in his family. Lavinia Davis's books, whether summer-vacation stories or horse-and-children stories, are as interesting for the families in them as for their ingenious mysteries. And individuals are important too—Jamie of *The Secret of Donkey Island* (1952), next to the youngest of the doctor's five children, sometimes felt "kind of squeezed." Jennie Lindquist's *The Golden Name Day* (1955) grew naturally out of the everyday life of a happy Swedish-American family and of the author's sympathetic understanding of children.

A book that very quickly found its place in children's lives was Sydney Taylor's *All-of-a-Kind Family* (1951). The stories that make up the book are from Mrs. Taylor's very happy childhood in a family of five little girls living on New York's lower East Side. Jewish customs have their natural place in the family life that is full of variety, interest, and the special joy that the immigrant parents could make their children feel—joy in being alive in a free country with a few pennies to spend. The incidents that showed how large a part the library played in the children's lives brought this comment from Anne Carroll Moore:

> I, who drew from the lower East Side of New York inspiration needed to serve a city of many races with books and understanding librarians, feel that *All-of-a-Kind Family* has given reality to a dream of years—of hearing from the children themselves what the library meant to them in childhood.[1]

Elizabeth Enright (1909–1968), who had begun her career in children's books as an illustrator, turned to writing her own stories. When in 1939 her second book, *Thimble Summer* (1938), a story of a little Wisconsin farm girl, received the Newbery Medal her career as a writer of realistic stories for children was well launched. In *The Sea Is All Around* (1940) she took the heroine, an Iowa child, to live on a New England island, where the strange wintry beauty of her new home gave a special quality to what would otherwise have been ordinary experiences. With *The Saturdays* (1941), she began a series of stories about the four children of the Melendy family, modern, self-sufficient, imaginative young people, who could find adventures and excitement in the country as well as on occasional trips to New York. After a number

[1] Anne Carroll Moore, "The Three Owls' Notebook," *The Horn Book*, Vol. 28 (Feb., 1952), p. 23.

of years during which Miss Enright wrote short stories and novels for adults and enjoyed—with very observant ears and eyes—her growing sons, she wrote *Gone-Away Lake* (1957). One of the freshest of books to appear in many years, it is a mingling of summer fun, a feeling for nature and humorous situations with strongly individualized characters of widely separated generations, and an original setting and plot. Two cousins, Portia and Julian, while exploring unfamiliar woods and swampland, discover what had once been Lake Tarrigo surrounded by ornate little Victorian summer cottages, but which was now only a swamp, circled by deserted and crumbling ruins. All, that is, except two were deserted. In those derelict cottages two old people, Miss Minnie Cheever and her brother, had each made a home, living in turn-of-the-century style. The children keep their discovery of the vanished lake and their friendship with the old people a secret from their families until a younger brother follows them, precipitates a crisis, and brings the story to a satisfying conclusion. Genuine humor, originality, and life are enduring qualities. *Return to Gone-Away* (1961) lacks the surprise of the first book but is expertly written, humorous, and alive.

William Mayne, claimed by one English critic to be "probably the most original of children's authors writing today," began his work early in the fifties. His third book, *A Swarm in May* (1957), published in England in 1955, was the first to be published in the United States and is still considered by some to be his best. The setting is a Cathedral Choir School and the plot is closely related to a tradition dating back to the Middle Ages. The youngest Singing Boy is always the Beekeeper; he must "come before the Bishop one Sunday in May, to sing a short solo and recite the ritual assuring the Bishop that the organist will supply good beeswax candles for the Cathedral throughout the coming year." John Owen's reluctance to be Beekeeper, his eventual appreciation of the importance of the duty, and the discovery of a forgotten passage high in one of the cathedral towers and of an old, old secret are different facets of a uniquely delightful story. Mr. Mayne's settings are most often Yorkshire villages, his characters ordinary middle-class people—except that they are never really ordinary. To browse through a number of his books at the same time is to realize how many people he has brought to life in print and how complete an individual each one is. The children disagree, sometimes quarrel and weep, but the atmosphere that one remembers in his many stories is good humor. The relationships are affectionate and amusing, the dialogue full of quips and jokes and amiable insults. *Sand* (1965) is an especially good example of the individuality of characters, *The Battlefield* (1967) of the quick wit and the lively give and take in the conversations. The Yorkshire dialect sprinkled through the stories is less confusing to American children, I believe, than Mr. Mayne's tendency to make three words do the work of twenty.

He has been called a "verbal magician" and his genius in finding the right word and his ability to tell a story almost entirely through dialogue are continually astonishing. The abundance of details packed into a few lines demands the most careful attention or the thread of meaning is lost. There is no racing through Mr. Mayne's books, and herein may lie the reason for the reluctance of some children to read them.

The plots of Mr. Mayne's stories are often closely related to natural phenomena, to old traditions, and historic events. A strain of fantasy can slip easily in and out of a story as it does in *A Grass Rope* (1962) when the children try to find out the truth about an old legend concerning a unicorn, a pack of hunting hounds, and a treasure inside the hill. Nan did not believe in the story at all. Adam thought it was true without magic, but Mary, the youngest, believed in magic and wove a grass rope to catch the unicorn.

Storm from the West (1964) is one of Barbara Willard's most vigorous and interesting stories. When English Mrs. Lattimer, with two children, married American Mr. Graham with four, the combined families vacationed together at the Lattimers' beloved Kilmorah, their old cottage in the west of Scotland. Here were six positive, intelligent, highly individual personalities—none of them short on determination—forced to share the people they loved most. The inevitable clashes are dramatic and often amusing. The Scottish setting with its beauty and its special demands finally brought the families together in a "clan."

Memorable Personalities

A few book children emerge as unforgettable individuals, sometimes because of the unusual activities in which they take part, but more often because of their authors' complete realization of them. Families play their parts and everyday incidents abound, but the characters stand out above their surroundings and touch events with the magic of their special personalities. Lucinda of *Roller Skates* (1936) is one of these.

Ruth Sawyer need not experience events to bring them to reality. Her lively imagination can do that. She need not *be* every one of her characters to make them live, for the warmth of her personality enfolds people and makes her know them. But Lucinda is a reflection of the child she really was. She was ten the year that she skated around New York, knew Tony at the fruit stand, Mr. Gilligan and his hansom cab, Patrolman M'Gonegal, sympathetic Uncle Earle, and precious Trinket. Her father was an importer and her mother had gone abroad with him, and New York lay waiting for her to discover. Most children love an opportunity for adventure, but few people can so forget themselves that their personalities extend in an outflowing stream, growing richer with every new friend. But the ten-year-old, whom we know as Lucinda, could and did, and we have the story of her year of joyous adventure to prove it. Ruth Sawyer received the Newbery Medal for

Roller Skates. *The Year of Jubilo* (1940) tells of another year in Lucinda's life—her fourteenth. The setting is Maine, where her family lived in much reduced circumstances. Lucinda had to adjust to many changes and to meet them on equal terms with her brothers. Growing in strength and courage, Lucinda kept her buoyancy and zest for living, her gift for friendship, and her appreciation of nature—even the cold beauty of the state of Maine that she had known before only as a summer playground. The book makes possible a deeper acquaintance with Lucinda and is far more than a sequel to *Roller Skates*.

The hero of *Tumbledown Dick: All People and No Plot* (1940) by the English novelist Howard Spring has a certain kinship with Lucinda in his wide-eyed delight in the discovery of Manchester as a city of surprises. Dick was blessed with the good fortune to have uncles with most interesting pursuits. Oswald Tubbs was a conjurer, Uncle Henry had a pet shop—"Birds, Beasts, Reptiles, Fishes" said the sign—but his special love for goldfish kept him in a state of melancholy, for each time he sold one he saw it doomed, because when it came to goldfish, according to Uncle Henry, "People have got no sense." There is plenty of plot despite the title, and delightful characterizations that make this a rare book.

A whole family of memorable personalities was introduced to children in four books by E. C. Spykman (1896–1965) that stem from her own childhood. The four young Cares led adventurous lives in the early 1900's when adults seemed to be very certain of the rightness of their pronouncements and their actions, giving children the security to escape into their own dangerous worlds. Events in the first two books, *A Lemon and a Star* (1955) and *The Wild Angel* (1957), are chiefly from the point of view of Jane who was ten when their father brought home a beautiful stepmother whom the children eventually called Madam. She was tolerant, and understanding but soon preoccupied with her own young children, so Theodore, Jane, Hubert, and Edie continued to be left largely to their own devices. Irrepressible, intelligent, extremely inventive, frequently rivals, but quick to collaborate on mischief, they were, like all children, intense believers in justice, and they often exploded with righteous indignation over the illogical world of adults. The last two books, *Terrible, Horrible Edie* (1960) and *Edie on the Warpath* (1966), are told from the point of view of the youngest child, ten-year-old Edie, whose older sister and brothers, all in their teens, often made life unbearable for her. Elizabeth Enright wrote of the children in Mrs. Spykman's books:

> Each of these children lived with an almost electrical reality. I should say *live*; they do. Not many writers of children's books dare to make children as real as they are; not many know how. Here was a writer who did. The Cares children fight, feud, laugh, cry,

hate, enjoy, adventure, are bad as can be, magnanimous on occasion, loyal to each other in their own way, interesting always. And *funny*. I laughed out loud many times as I read. When I came to the end, I was sorry and felt deprived that there was no more.[1]

Librarians sometimes have a difficult time supplying "funny books" to children, yet there are many more funny books than there are truly humorous ones, in the sense that "humor illustrates some fundamental absurdity in human nature or conduct." Most of the books just discussed are truly humorous: those by Eleanor Estes, Elizabeth Enright, Ruth Sawyer, Howard Spring, and E. C. Spykman. Books that are genuinely humorous may be rare but they are also very likely to survive from one generation to the next, with the result that gradually a fine stock is building up to make each new generation of children richer in humorous books than the one before. Because often truly humorous books have much that also qualifies in the child's mind as *funny* they are the most appropriate books to share in a family group in which different generations and different ages of children are represented.

Another of these rare books is *Homer Price* (1943). Robert McCloskey's claim that he merely thinks up words to tie his pictures together is scarcely born out in *Homer Price*. It may be one of those books that authors claim write themselves. Whatever the circumstances, Homer is revealed in story as well as pictures with complete spontaneity. Robert McCloskey was, no doubt, just such an ingenious boy as Homer, and the pictures of Homer surrounded by coils of wire, bits of electric motors, and parts of broken-down radios could only have been inspired by childhood memories. Homer is a typical American boy and, as extravagantly funny as his exploits often are, there is far more truth in this glimpse of America than in many seriously purposeful books. James Daugherty wrote this about *Homer Price*:

> It is America laughing at itself with a broad and genial humanity, without bitterness or sourness or sophistication. The whole thing culminates magnificently in the final story when "the wheels of progress" come to Centerburg, and here McCloskey puts on a full philharmonic of fun and satire. One closes the book with the comforting feeling, however, that although Centerburg can and does take the machine age in its stride, the salt and character, the humanities and individualism of Our Town remain triumphant and that democracy will keep her rendezvous with destiny, musical mousetraps, and all.[2]

[1] *Book Week*, September 12, 1966.
[2] James Daugherty, "Comment on *Homer Price*," *The Horn Book*, Vol. 19 (Nov.–Dec., 1943), p. 426.

From the Mixed-up Files of Mrs. Basil E. Frankweiler (1967) by
E. L. Konigsburg was one of the most original of books to appear for
many years and a completely contemporary story. The main characters
are a sister and brother from an upper-middle-class suburb of New
York. They remain natural children—though independent and somewhat precocious—without the sophistication that tinges the numerous
self-conscious attempts made to portray children of the sixties. Claudia
decided to run away from home, not because she was angry or unhappy,
but because she believed that her family took her for granted as the
oldest child and the only daughter. She took with her her middle brother
because he could be depended upon to have money. They ran away to
the Metropolitan Museum of Art because Claudia liked to be comfortable and she wanted a place to run to that could be indoors and pleasant
and beautiful. Adapting to life in the museum for a week without being
discovered required considerable ingenuity but they managed it. The
account of their adventure is set down by an elderly woman in a letter
to her lawyer, which in itself is a departure, and a happily successful
device. For *The Mixed-up Files*, Mrs. Konigsburg received the Newbery
Medal.

An earlier story, *Jennifer, Hecate, Macbeth, William McKinley,
and Me, Elizabeth* (1967), although less unconventional in characters,
events, and framework, is also a refreshing book. Elizabeth, the willing
follower, tells the story. Jennifer, a Negro girl, awes Elizabeth by her
aloof air and her wide reading background. She is the leader in an
elaborate game of witch and apprentice until a crisis sweeps all pretense
aside and the girls become just good friends.

Mrs. Konigsburg is far more than a skillful technician challenged by
the complex structure of one story and the subtle character developments
in the other. The situations in both stories are in tune with the personalities and imaginations of the children involved. The style in *Jennifer. . .*
maintains the flavor of an articulate fifth-grader; in *From the Mixed-up
Files. . .* it has the dignity and wry humor of a well educated, literate
woman, enlivened by her enjoyment of the discoveries she has made
about the children's characters and personalities. The books are very
much alive.

Everyday Children at Home and at School

Many children arrive at a point in their reading when only stories
about children like themselves will satisfy them. Identification with
everyday children whose lives may be very much like the reader's own
is easy. It can be comforting when one needs a friend and reassuring
when changes must be faced. Even the simplest experiences in a book
that a young child can read for himself take on glamor merely from
being enclosed in print—to which the child has the key. Stories of

commonplace people and events, however, seldom last more than one reading, and even the better ones seldom live more than a generation. Things of the imagination do not change, but manners and customs become outmoded, and the stories that picture ordinary activities of everyday children may be received with a happy sense of recognition when they first appear and, within a decade, seem old-fashioned—a term of opprobrium when applied by children to books that are not *au courant*.

"*B*" *Is for Betsy* (1939), written and illustrated by Carolyn Haywood, was followed by other books about Betsy and later by books about Eddie, and by a new wave of interest among other writers in telling simple, realistic stories of the school and homelife of present-day children under ten. Eleanor Frances Lattimore, whose earlier books had been about Chinese children, began writing and illustrating easy-reading stories about present-day American children. The child characters of both of these writers had more reality than many of their followers, and sometimes the plots had substance. Miss Lattimore's *The Bus Trip* (1965), for instance, has real suspense in the account of how a responsible nine-year-old coped with unforeseen complications and emergencies and got herself and her small brother from Florida to their grandparents in Philadelphia. And Carolyn Haywood's *Eddie's Green Thumb* (1964), the story of how Eddie's efforts for the school gardening project grew to complicated dimensions, has in common with others the spontaneity and liveliness of the author's books of twenty-five years before.

Wilson Gage in *Dan and the Miranda* (1962) captured the child's speech and attitudes and made nature something not merely to be studied but to be enjoyed. While he was looking for a subject sufficiently "scientific" for next year's science-fair project, Dan became so interested in spiders that he was reluctant to mount them in plastic, and decided regretfully that he was just "unscientific." As in her *A Wild Goose Tale* (1961), the author's accurate observations of nature are unobtrusive and her enthusiasm is contagious.

Rebecca Caudill showed in three books that she is as skillful in writing stories for the youngest readers as she is in writing novels. Her *A Pocket Full of Cricket* (1964) with beautiful illustrations by Evaline Ness and *Did You Carry the Flag Today, Charlie?* (1966), illustrated by Nancy Grossman, are contemporary school stories with completely real characters. *A Certain Small Shepherd* (1965), illustrated by William Pène du Bois, is a very beautiful Christmas story with a setting in the Kentucky mountains.

Ursula Nordstrom's *The Secret Language* (1960) has the distinction of being a boarding-school story for younger readers. It is important, however, for the understanding of the child's world that comes through the simple, direct storytelling and heightens the reality. Victoria was eight when she first arrived at boarding school and she suffered agonies of homesickness until she made friends with Martha, who had a "secret language." In the security of their friendship they dared to be non-conformists, united in their hatred of the housemother and in their determination not to show any liking for the pleasant woman who replaced her. Little girls can as readily identify with Victoria and Martha as they used to do with the heroines of Eliza Orne White's stories.

With the third-grader *Henry Huggins* (1950) Beverly Cleary began a long succession of books that have been much enjoyed by children between seven and ten. *Ellen Tebbits* (1951) is about a third-grade girl. Henry, his sister, and his dog appear in a number of stories, and the story about *Mitch and Amy* (1967), twin fourth-graders was no doubt inspired by Mrs. Cleary's own twin son and daughter. Rarely in easily read books are family relationships so well handled as they are in Mrs. Cleary's stories. She has an acute ear for children's dialogue, a strong sense of humor, and skill in translating children's actions and predicaments to the printed page that make all her books amusing, some of them very funny.

Keith Robertson's *Henry Reed, Inc.* (1958) was told as a journal, Henry's very Private Journal, not a diary because "diaries are kept by girls." Henry's record of his adventures in research—he was influenced by nearby Princeton University—are very funny. The book stimulated some labored attempts by other writers at telling a story through a journal or diary, a return to an old device often used by writers to make the first person account seem natural.

The Lone Child

The plight of the orphan has long been a favorite theme in children's stories, but from the forties on story-book orphans bear little resemblance to their patient predecessors, and many of their stories are told with humor and without sentimentality. Their state of orphanhood often presents opportunity for unusual adventure. It would be difficult to find more self-reliant children than the young Bounces in Evelyn Sibley Lampman's *The Bounces of Cynthiann'* (1950). Doris Gates's *Sensible Kate* (1943) is a child with character. Even though she is "not cute nor pretty, merely sensible" she quickly wins the reader's heart. Helen Fern Daringer's *Adopted Jane* (1947) is another appealing child with ability to assume responsibility beyond her years.

In *The Lavender Cat* (1944) Janette Sebring Lowrey told with beautiful restraint the story of a homeless boy. The setting is a bit of Texas "years ago when the woods were free and the towns were few and far between," yet it has overtones of the Irish fairy tales that Shawn told to the boy, Jemmy, and the feeling of the woods and the river around him. It is the story of Jemmy, living unwanted with the charcoal burners, and of the little cat he found who led him unerringly to the right fireside for him.

Ellen of Nancy Barnes's *The Wonderful Year* (1946) is an only child for whom the much dreaded change from her home in Kansas to the ranch in Colorado turned out to be a wonderful experience, quite, she believed, the most perfect of her life. Her parents are definite people, as important as Ellen to the story because their attitude toward Ellen, their respect for her individuality, and their wisdom in helping her to grow are largely what make Ellen an appealing person.

A nameless, orphan crop picker, starving, exhausted, and still suffering from the shock of an accident that had taken the one person who had been kind to him, wandered into Montana sheep-grazing country and was befriended by a woman sheepherder. *The Loner* (1963) by Ester Wier is the story of his mistakes and struggles to succeed in Boss's eyes and to earn the name that she helped him find for himself in the Bible—David. The vast, rugged country and the harsh life of the sheep-herders are clearly seen. The storytelling is poignant and restrained.

Eleanor Cameron's *A Spell is Cast* (1964) is laid in a castle-like house on the California coast, where young Cory had come to spend a summer with the parents of her foster mother, a famous monologist. Cory hopes in her heart that it will be more than a visit. From its opening the story is absorbing and real. It is creative storytelling at its best—style, plot, characterizations, atmosphere, and flavor give importance and intensity to what might have been, in less skillful hands, just another story of an appealing child longing for a home.

Several especially interesting books from Britain, stories of lonely girls, have great vitality in the portrayal of people and relationships. Stella Weaver's talent for creating atmosphere of place is vivid in *A Poppy in the Corn* (1960), laid on the Cornish coast and telling the story of Teresa, a war orphan who came to live in a home with two sons and a daughter, Anna. Having, within her memory, known only a concentration camp or an orphanage, Teresa felt like an outsider. The personalities of the children and their development as tensions grow are sensitively drawn, and the story is absorbing. The setting of southern Ireland, where two English children spend the summer, is clear and beautiful in the same author's *The Stranger* (1956).

Cordelia Jones's *Nobody's Garden* (1966) is also a story of a child's adjustment to the aftermath of war in which her parents had been killed. Outgoing, blunt, tactless, but amiable, Hilary took Bridget under her wing and tried to bring her out of her abnormal shyness. The first step in companionship was the discovery of a common love for *The Secret Garden*. Then the girls found and began to work in an overgrown garden of a bombed-out house and Bridget was on the way to becoming a normal, happy child.

The interaction of personalities is understandable and realistically portrayed in Margaret Storey's *Pauline* (1967), about a proud, intelligent child who comes to live in the home of relatives with whom she has little in common, and of her adjustment, particularly, to a very patronizing but well-meaning uncle.

Holiday Adventures

In the tradition of E. Nesbit and in interesting contrast to the books about solitary children are stories presenting groups of children, often of varying ages, who share in activities and adventures, each child holding a special place in the group, with interest centering on no one child for any length of time.

The first writer to reach near-perfection in this type of story and to have a marked influence on realistic stories both in England and America was Arthur Ransome (1884–1967). Mr. Ransome had been writing for many years, had collected fairy tales in Russia, and had been a newspaper correspondent during the First World War and the Russian Revolution. Sailing his own little ship about the Baltic, he had traveled to China and Egypt and other far countries and written about them in the *Manchester Guardian*. Then he had gone back to the English Lake Country, which held memories of sailing, fishing, and camping on an island, and wrote *Swallows and Amazons* (1931) for the grandchildren of the friend who had shared those adventures. He made the Lake Country real for children in America as well as England. Unhampered by grownups the children lose themselves completely in their play, demonstrating the self-reliance, common sense, and free imaginations that are natural to the average child. Sometimes the children are up against a real challenge, as they are in *We Didn't Mean to Go to Sea* (1938), when the yacht on which they are sailing around Harwich Harbor drifts out to sea, but their play life amply prepared them for such an emergency. The only adults allowed to have any large share in their lives are those who make possible more highly colored or romantic experiences than they could have by themselves: Captain Flint, who took them with him on a trip around the world in *Missee Lee* (1942), or the old seaman *Peter Duck* (1933), who shared their adventures with buried treasure and pirates.

So reasonable are all the children's adventures, so spontaneous the fun, that readers are inspired to create for themselves similar adventures. Probably no writer since E. Nesbit had so much influence on children's play as did Arthur Ransome, and few writers of this century have had as many imitators in England and America.

The people of Elisabeth Kyle's *Holly Hotel* (1947) are so real that the reader is certain that if he visited the village of Whistleblow in Scotland, he would find Mrs. Maitland and Molly, the minister and his boy

Sandy, Sally with her kitten, Peter Murchison at his inventing and Rowena at the post office, with the young Roches coming for their holidays, and Mungo Kerrigan and Mr. Brown dropping in for a return visit to the scene of their rivalry. Nora Unwin's pictures emerge onto the pages as if they came from within the story.

Books like *Holly Hotel*, with a plot enhanced by a mystery, atmosphere, and good characterization, and that remain true to natural childhood are rare. During the forties and fifties a trend could be noticed toward a type of mystery story in which groups of children track down criminals, with far from childlike purpose and technique, finally outwitting not only the criminal but the police. This was an unfortunate deterioration of the plot and treatment in Erich Kästner's *Emil and the Detectives*, which came to us from Germany in 1930. Emil's single purpose—very true to boy nature—was not primarily to capture a thief but to get back his stolen money, and the boys of Berlin entered the chase to right a wrong done to one of their kind. Leadership, teamwork, determination, not violence, got Emil's money back and caught a thief. The emphasis in later stories of this kind was less childlike.

Richard Church in *Five Boys in a Cave* (1951) told a gripping story that begins as a normal holiday adventure but that soon involves the boys in grave danger. The character development is convincing, as the individual boys respond differently to the demands of courage and initiative.

Mrs. Wappinger's Secret (1956) was the first of several humorous stories by Florence Hightower that invariably have a great variety of well realized, unconventional characters. Especially interesting is the friendship between Charlie and elderly, eccentric Mrs. Wappinger, who became his accomplice in a search for treasure.

In Philippa Pearce's *The Minnow Leads to Treasure* (1958), published in England as *Minnow on the Say*, two boys become acquainted after one has found the other's drifting canoe, and they spend their holidays searching for hidden treasure. The characters are very perceptively drawn, but, most important of all, the book has the power to transport the reader into another setting. Unforgettable are the pleasure of sharing an interesting pursuit with a congenial companion, the charm of boating on a beautiful English stream, and the peace and relaxation of summer holidays.

Equally delightful but more lively is the vacation spent by four children in *The Paleface Redskins* (1958) by Jacqueline Jackson. As soon as school was out the family set off for the lake, where the younger three were joined by an old friend and they became once more a united tribe of Potawatomis—Chief Thunder Cloud, Owl Eyes, White Feather, and Papoose, later advanced to the status of brave and named Crafty Fox—ready for a summer of adventure. The book is contemporary in its feeling but very true to the inventive summer play of any generation of American children lucky enough to have the space to give free rein to their imaginations and who are not repressed by too much adult supervision. Mrs. Jackson's ear for children's dialogue and her perception of their feelings and attitudes are acute. The book is funny, and the flashes of insight into children's emotions give it an extra dimension.

Hurdles to Clear

It takes a long time to grow up, think children coping with the complexities that they are heir to. Without basis for comparison, the child sees a mountain where an adult sees only a curve on the horizon. But sometimes also a very small thing assumes such importance to the child that it helps him to turn the corner from despair to joy. In Catherine Storr's *The Freedom of the Seas* (1962), for instance, Robin, youngest of the family, is often made to feel inferior by the competence of the other children and longs for something that will help him to be better than anyone—at something. He found a shell, named it the Freedom of the Seas, and, following its magic, not only learned to swim but discovered his own uniqueness.

Children keep many talismans that grownups never hear about. Adults can more easily understand, and remember, the child's need for something alive to love and to talk to—privately. It has become the theme of many a story. Ben, the lonely middle child in a large London family, longed for a dog. The unperceptive attempts of adults to help him only made his longing so intense that at last he had to imagine a dog for himself, "a dog so small that you could only see it with your eyes shut." In *A Dog So Small* (1962) Philippa Pearce told a story that comes close to tragedy but that ends, not in exactly what Ben wanted, but in a wholehearted acceptance of reality. The book is an extraordinary accomplishment.

Built around the same longing, but satisfied in a very different way is *A Dog on Barkham Street* (1960) by Mary Stolz. Into Edward's life came his Uncle Josh, a wanderer and a self-acknowledged hobo. With him came a companion, a beautiful collie, Argess. Friendship with Uncle Josh even more than with Argess helped Edward to solve his problems, but Argess was the talisman.

Rumer Godden's intuitive understanding of children that gives such special life to her books about children was never more evident than it is in *The Kitchen Madonna* (1967). In a number of her stories about dolls and children she showed that creating something with one's hands and ingenuity can help solve many problems. The same idea is implicit here. Sensing the unhappiness of Marta, the new maid in a fine London house, aloof, uncommunicative Gregory set about making a holy picture for her, hoping that it would give to the sterile, modern kitchen a touch of her Ukrainian home. His and his sister's embarrassment at the museum and at an expensive jeweler's where they went to learn what an icon looked like, and the difficulties in finding the materials to make it are recounted with insight and humor. In a beautiful climax the reader sees with complete clarity the joyful triumph when the picture is done, and Gregory is ready to make another—a hat-shop Madonna for the milliner who was kind to him.

The repeated pronouncements from cities during the fifties and sixties that children need books about their actual world, books to prepare them for the harsh realities of life, have sounded like the grownups Paul Hazard deplored, who "want to suppress that happy interval of years in which we live without dragging the weight of life about with us." Children resist, often successfully, the weight their elders thrust upon them, and, as Paul Hazard also said, they "reject the books that do not treat them as equals." To himself the child will explain the world about him in his own terms—more often symbolic than linguistic—but he is not willingly shut away from it.

Unfortunately, only a few writers in any era have the genius to present the severest realism with balance and appealing characters in stories that place the child in our turbulent world, and that also touch his core of wonder and leave him undefeated. Limited human experience can only be extended through imagination. Books that are revelations of life, *that demand involvement*—and those are chiefly fiction—can prepare the child as knowledge alone can never do.

Erik Haugaard, who is never didactic, through whose books the reader grows and begins to see a place for himself in an ungentle world, wrote:

> All my books have had a purpose; they have a rudder and sails that could be set to steer a certain course. In each of them I wished to express something specific—a significant comment on humanity. . . .
>
> In *The Little Fishes* I wanted to tell not only what happened to the victims of war but also how a person could survive, how in degradation he could refuse to be degraded. Our history books tell about the victories and defeats of armies; I wanted to tell about the defeat and victory of human beings.[1]

Robert Burch has the humor and humanity to give in his seemingly simple stories of underprivileged American children honest comments on life that strengthen hope. For his children's books Robert Burch has drawn on rural Georgia, where he was born and grew up with seven brothers and sisters. *Skinny* (1964) is the story of the illiterate or-

[1] Haugaard, Erik Christian. "A Thank You Note and a Credo," *The Horn Book*, Vol. 44 (Feb., 1968), p. 14.

phaned son of a share-cropper, who, while waiting to get into an orphanage, spent the summer helping Miss Bessie run her hotel. Uncomplicated, friendly, with the philosophy to meet whatever life hands to him, Skinny is one of the most engaging of book children. In Mr. Burch's *Queenie Peavy* (1966), his heroine's vulnerability to teasing because she had a father in prison was covered by a braggadocio that prompted her to excel at a number of things, "most of them unworthy of her attention." The account is as dispassionate as a case study, but considerably more convincing, and Queenie is so real, and so amiable in her defiance, that the reader becomes deeply involved in everything that concerns her. As in many such actual situations, Queenie cannot be rid of the obstacle that makes life difficult and often disheartening for her but she learns how to accept her particular problem. Mr. Burch writes with a wonderfully clear understanding of children.

My Brother Stevie (1967) by Eleanor Clymer is another wholly "realistic" story of a girl burdened with a feeling of responsibility for her eight-year-old brother. She tells of her discouragement and fear as she sees Stevie moving rapidly toward delinquency with a gang of older boys.

John Rowe Townsend's *Good-bye to the Jungle* (1967) begins with the Thompson family's leaving the Jungle—a dilapidated soon-to-be-demolished section of an English town. Kevin and Sandra, fifteen and fourteen years old, hope life will be more respectable, especially for their young cousins Harold and Jean, Uncle Walter's own children. They are not surprised that Walter does not reform in the new surroundings, and they expected little of Doris, the woman who had lived with Walter since his wife left him. Slowly, however, Doris seemed to breathe with a little more self-respect. The characterizations are excellent. Walter and Doris are among the most degraded "parents" to be found in children's literature, but they are entirely believable. The children are as different from each other as children inevitably are, and their loyalty to each other gives them the strength to face a world that has often been unkind. There is not a trace of false sentiment, nor is the story overly grim. It is often exciting, sometimes funny, and always absorbing. Kevin and Sandra with their pride and pluck and dogged resolution are real and memorable. The book is a refutation of the criticism that books for children fail to present life realistically. This book presents the seamy side of reality with honesty and humor.

New knowledge and new techniques in the treatment and rehabilitation of children with physical handicaps has been accompanied by a growing number of contemporary stories about such children. Most people see children as far more vulnerable than grownups to the inevitable pains and problems of living; a child with a major handicap has, therefore, such special poignance that he makes a tempting subject for a story. Since 1950 books about handicapped children have been far more competently written than they were before, and in them the handicaps have been handled in line with approved medical and psychological practice. Few books, however, written within the convention of a period survive from one generation to the next. A story that rises from a great mind, from deep spiritual reserves, created out of human understanding and universal truth gives the child strength for growing; but only if it first commands his interest. When a story is concerned with convincing characters and has a wider focus than a handicapped child's immediate environment it may give a child both entertainment and emotional release. In *Mine for Keeps* (1962) Jean Little deals specifically with a handicapped child; in all her books very personal human problems must be solved. Her major concern, however, is with individual people of many sorts, their strengths and weaknesses, and the changes in their relationships to each other.

Regional Stories

The critical Depression years, which touched nearly every phase of American life, naturally made their mark on children's literature. The shifting of population that accompanied the economic disasters brought new awareness of different areas of the country. Writers began to deplore the "absence of stories related to the modern world."

Lois Lenski, who had been creating picture books and writing period stories for a number of years, began with *Bayou Suzette* (1943) to give children a series of social and economic pictures of different regions and ways of life in America.

Her avowed purpose was to help children "see beyond the rim of their own world." Her intense interest in people, particularly children, prompted the writing of the series, and took her to live in each region before setting her story there. For the most part she succeeded in her desire to show "through an artist's interpretation, a deeper meaning in the commonplace," to make us "see others as ourselves." *Bayou Suzette* is set in the Louisiana Bayou country, *Strawberry Girl* (1945), which won the Newbery Medal, among the Florida Crackers, *Boom Town Boy* (1948) in the Oklahoma oil fields, *Cotton in My Sack* (1949) among the Arkansas cotton pickers. The most convincing of all is *Judy's Journey* (1947), a story of a family of Alabama sharecroppers who leave their little shack to follow the harvests from Florida to New Jersey. This is written with vigor and force, out of sincere indignation over the lot of the children of migratory workers.

Doris Gates's *Blue Willow* (1940) came out of her experiences as a children's librarian in the San Joaquin Valley, where she saw hundreds of children of migratory workers. Telling stories in the migrant camps she came to know the children and their dreams as a storyteller can know them and to realize that the thing they invariably wanted most in the world was a permanent home. Gradually the story of Janey Larkin grew. The most precious thing Janey owned was a willow plate, her one tie with the only real home she had ever had. Her greatest longing was to have a home again where the willow plate would have a proper place. With this theme Miss Gates constructed a story that has suspense, a vivid sense of place, and very human characters.

Also about migrant farm workers, a story perfectly constructed and strong in its simplicity, is *Roosevelt Grady* (1963) by Louisa R. Shotwell. The mother and nine-year-old Roosevelt, hungry for schooling, were the ones who most longed for a "stay-put" place. Peter Burchard's illustrations show the Negro family with great sympathy and warmth. Miss Shotwell's later book *Adam Bookout* (1967) presents an appealing orphan in a contemporary setting in Brooklyn.

The characterizations of Robin and her family in Zilpha Keatley Snyder's *The Velvet Room* (1965) are exceptionally real. For three years the Williams family had been migrants following the California harvests, when the old Model T broke down near the McCurdy ranch and Dad found a permanent job there. It was like a miracle to Robin, who saw the world through a magical aura.

The special interest in regional stories encouraged writers to find stories in parts of the country they knew best, thus backgrounds were drawn with authenticity and often lovingly. Such books are rich in atmosphere, with characters and situations indigenous to their surroundings. There is perfect integration of people and setting in Katherine Wigmore Eyre's enchanting story of New Orleans, *Lottie's Valentine* (1941), Frances Clarke Sayers' stories of Texas, Marguerite de Angeli's picture-story books of Pennsylvania, Lee Kingman's stories of Finnish-American people on Cape Ann, and numerous others. Important forerunners included Marian Hurd McNeely's story of the Dakota prairies, *Jumping Off Place* (1929), Alice Dalgliesh's stories for young children laid in Canada near the Bay of Fundy, and Florence Crannell Means's books with Colorado settings, *Penny for Luck* (1935) and several others.

Valenti Angelo, having told of small Nino's life in Tuscany, brought him to America in *Golden Gate* (1939) and began a series of books in which he pictured with understanding and kindness the lives of newcomers to America. Whether his story is laid on Telegraph Hill, in the San Joaquin Valley, in Greenwich Village, or in a little town on the Nevada desert, it has a vivid setting and a sense of deep religious faith.

Stephen Meader, at his best in stories that grew out of his childhood in New Hampshire, and experiences with animals and the woods, told of outlaws and bootleggers in *King of the Hills* (1933), but the real fascination of that story lies in the New Hampshire mountains and the great buck with twelve-pointed antlers. *Lumberjack* (1934), with its details of lumbering in New England, was based on experiences in camp when his father was operating his portable sawmill in New Hampshire and southern Maine. One of his most important books is *Red Horse Hill* (1930), with its farm background and its appealing boy hero. But Cedar, the horse born in the snow, whose whole career is bound up in New Hampshire winters, is the center of interest.

Uncle Andy's Island (1950) by Anne Molloy is unmistakably the Maine coast; *This Boy Cody* (1950) by Leon Wilson, who served on the staff of the Cumberland Mountain Folk School in Tennessee, was well acquainted with people and events like those of his story; Ralph Moody's *Little Britches* (1950) tells the story of an eastern family's experiences with a Colorado ranch in the first decade of the twentieth century. Frances Clarke Sayers' *Ginny and Custard* (1951) tells of a little girl's happy year exploring Los Angeles with an understanding mother and father.

Three books by Virginia Sorensen have well-realized regional settings: *Curious Missie* (1953) is set in the Alabama cotton country; *Plain Girl* (1955), laid among the Amish of Pennsylvania, shows with sympathy the struggle between the generations. *Miracles on Maple Hill* (1956) for which Mrs. Sorensen received the Newbery Medal is laid in rural Pennsylvania and tells about two city-bred children who learn the joys of country living, discovering that each season brings its own miracles.

Jesse Stuart's *The Beatinest Boy* (1953) is laid in the author's own Kentucky mountain region. Gurdon S. Worcester's *The Singing Flute* (1963), its setting on Cape Ann, Massachusetts, is a story of a girl of Finnish descent, caught in the midst of a many-years-long quarrel between her father and her uncle. It has great strength and rhythm in style, and the plot, built from conflicts in the real world, has the drama and irrevocability of legend.

Social Problems and Interest in Minority Groups

Prejudice and bigotry have no place in the world of normal childhood, but children soon reflect the attitudes around them. In their zeal to make children look with kind and tolerant eyes on the dark-skinned child in their classroom, many writers forget that some happy children have never looked at them in any other way. The obviously written story may point out differences of which an unspoiled child is unaware. The writers who are on true terms with childhood, who see children whatever their race or background, as just children, can tell stories with qualities of universality. These stories may survive as literature after Americans have reached the state of grace when inequalities due to race, nationality, or religion belong to history. Books like E. L. Konigsburg's *Jennifer, Hecate, Macbeth, William McKinley, and Me, Elizabeth*, Mrs. Snyder's *The Egypt Game*, Louisa Shotwell's *Roosevelt Grady*, or Sydney Taylor's *All-of-a-Kind Family* can benefit the child who needs to shake off prejudice and do no harm to those who have never lost their natural delight in all people who are kind and just and pleasant company.

Grace Moon, whose *Chi-Weé* was published in 1925, was on such terms with childhood. She and her husband, the artist Carl Moon, had lived, worked, and traveled in the Indian country for many years and had known that the Indians were their friends. The book tells of the life of a little Pueblo Indian girl. Many years later Ann Nolan Clark in *Little Navajo Bluebird* (1943) gave another sensitive interpretation of Indian childhood.

In 1931 Laura Adams Armer's *Waterless Mountain*, a Newbery Medal book, was a sincere attempt to interpret Navajo Indian life through the eyes of an Indian boy who had a vocation to become a medicine man. The introspection and mysticism of the book made it difficult reading, but Mrs. Armer's understanding of the Indians, gained through years of studying their art, particularly their sacred sand paintings, gave the book significance. It was an important forerunner of a number of stories written to make better understood the Indians' problem of reconciling two ways of life.

Purpose is thoroughly integrated in the plot of Jonreed Lauritzen's *The Ordeal of the Young Hunter* (1954), a strong, well-told story of contemporary Navajo Indian life. Alice Marriott, Evelyn Sibley Lampman, and numerous others have shown understanding of the Indians in good, suspenseful stories.

Among the few fine stories of a child who is "different," one stands out for subtlety, good writing and perfect understanding of childhood: *The Hundred Dresses* (1944) by Eleanor Estes. The children who tease and ridicule Wanda only because the others do it always have a sense of uneasiness, an unrecognized feeling that in separating Wanda from them they are doing some indefinable harm not only to her, but to themselves. The young child, untouched by prejudice, may see a child with a darker or lighter skin than his, or with clothes that are strange, as someone especially interesting, especially lovable. But the older child who feels the pressure to conform to patterns of society or of his peers may see the unfamiliar in another human being as something to be scorned. The lesson that the two little girls learn in *The Hundred Dresses* is never spoken, and realistically they themselves never have an opportunity to make up to Wanda for what they have done.

Any successful story must enlist sympathy for its characters. The lot

of the disadvantaged child is natural substance for interesting fiction—
that is why orphans have appeared in children's books for centuries.
The Hundred Dresses makes a strong, unforgettable impact and leaves
the reader thinking beyond the last page.

By the late fifties concern with immigration from Puerto Rico to
American cities reached the pages of children's books. The problems
involved adapting to the ways of a strange land and often to existence
in a great, cold city after country living. Many stories were built around
such adjustments. Less specifically immediate and more natural is the
weaving of events in the life of Simone Orgella and of her cousin from
San Juan, through Franny Davis's story, *The Noonday Friends* (1965)
by Mary Stolz.

It is largely to the older boys and girls that writers of the thirties
and forties addressed purposeful stories presenting special social problems or emphasizing the incompatibility of democracy with racial and
religious intolerance. Often the stories were little better than propaganda.
But the very complexities of social life create story plots and these have
naturally found their way into books for modern young people. Phyllis
Whitney's *Willow Hill* (1947) was one of the more convincing of these
stories. John Tunis in *All-American* (1942) and his other stories of
college athletics or professional baseball was unusually successful in
integrating his theme with his plot and characterizations.

Among writers dealing with the special problems of minority groups,
Florence Crannell Means is one whose work often attains real stature.
Any need that she may feel for the interpretation of people with special
problems is merged, in the best of her books, in the humanity of her
characterizations. She does not preach, she merely presents to her
readers people who become their friends.

Florence Crannell Means's father was a Baptist clergyman, a scholar,
poet, and wit. Her memories are full of the books enjoyed in the family
and the people of many races who visited her home. The family moved
to a village in the mountains near Denver when Florence was a young
girl. *At the End of Nowhere* (1940) is a happy reliving of some of
her experiences then. Integral to her writing has been her wish to give
to children the association with other peoples that was so happy a part
of her childhood.

Out of first hand experiences among the Indians of the Southwest
came two stories of Indian life showing the conflicts between the Indian's traditional beliefs and customs and the white man's ways: *Tangled
Waters* (1936), a story of the Arizona Navajos, and *Whispering Girl*
(1941), of the Hopi Indians.

Shuttered Windows (1938) grew out of a visit to Mather College
in South Carolina, where Mrs. Means came to know the girls so well
that they asked her to write a book about them and, later, gave her

suggestions for revisions and changes. It is the story of a Northern Negro girl whose sense of duty to her people took her to live with her great-grandmother on a little island off the coast of South Carolina, of her difficult adjustment to vastly different attitudes and customs, and her growing understanding and appreciation of the island people.

In *Great Day in the Morning* (1946) is another perfectly realized character. Lilybelle, a Negro girl with determination and strength of purpose, has much in common with Penny of *Penny for Luck*. Lilybelle's story is dramatic and tender, interpreting with insight the lessons that only life itself can teach.

The Moved-Outers (1945) was written out of strong feeling but with so much restraint that it has extraordinary force. It tells about the Japanese and American-Japanese who were evacuated from the Pacific Coast during the tense months following Pearl Harbor. It is less a story of the uprooting of a race of people from their homes than it is of the reactions of individuals of many backgrounds, many different temperaments, whose lives were changed by one of the most tragic experiments the United States has ever made. Moved to write this story by the intensity of her sympathy and the courage of her convictions, Mrs. Means did it with remarkable objectivity and fairness. She did not need to editorialize; the implications as well as the drama are in the natural and honest presentation.

Stories About Negro Children

Civil Rights legislation, school integration, and nonviolent demonstrations to hasten the reality of Negro freedom and equal rights found expression in many stories for children during the fifties and early sixties. Stories were built on the problems of Negro life in the South, on the adjustments of Southern Negro families to life in Northern industrial cities, and on many specific dramatic events in the long delayed movement toward making equal rights actual. Dorothy Sterling's *Mary Jane* (1959) was one of the early stories about a Negro child in a newly integrated school. *The Empty Schoolhouse* (1965) by Natalie Savage Carlson brought out the part played by outside agitators in holding back school integration. So rapidly, however, did attitudes shift as the Negro revolution gained in momentum that even such well-written stories soon seemed dated.

Frank Bonham's *Durango Street* (1965), a powerful story of a Los Angeles Negro ghetto, made understandable the protagonist's statement that the "only way to stay alive in a big-city jungle was to join a fighting gang—before some other gang decided to use you for bayonet practice." Nat Hentoff's *Jazz Country* (1965) reversed the familiar pattern by telling of a white boy who struggled for acceptance in the predominently Negro world of jazz. The recognition that textbooks should be more closely related to children's lives prompted the rapid production also of books for children's pleasure reading with urban settings and Negro characters. Few had vitality. Almost all were obviously contrived. The dramatic situation of Paula Fox's *How Many Miles to Babylon* (1967) was one that made ghetto living tragically real to more fortunate children.

Sometimes, through the purposeful earnestness engaging characters emerged, like Evan of Elizabeth Starr Hill's *Evan's Corner* (1967). Few books reflecting contemporary problems, however, had the naturalness and poignance of the understatement in *Roosevelt Grady*, or *A Certain Small Shepherd*.

Stories about Negroes were scarcely an invention of the sixties, although many educators and critics seemed unaware of those that had gone before. The poet Arna Bontemps began writing for children in the thirties. In addition to biography and history, he wrote two stories. His *Sad-Faced Boy* (1937) told of three Alabama Negro boys who beat their way to New York City and had some amusing and surprising adventures there. *Lonesome Boy* (1955) is a poetically written short story with a haunting folk-tale quality.

Hope Newell's *Steppin and Family* (1942) and Ellen Tarry's *My Dog Rinty* (1946), both about Negro children, emphasized natural children in natural situations.

Growing Up

The recognition in the thirties of a growing audience of older boys and girls stimulated special service to them in libraries and specific concern for them in the children's book departments of publishing houses. To writers it presented very inviting aspects. It was an uncrowded field, for few stories about adolescents had survived from the past. Growing boys enjoyed seeing themselves in *Huckleberry Finn*, and girls had been able to identify themselves with one of the March sisters of *Little Women*, but except for those stories boys not ready for adult books found their chief reading pleasure in adventure tales; and the girls, who yearned for romance in their books, turned to the sentimental, extremely unrealistic adult novels that prevailed in the years before the First World War.

In many ways, writing realistically of young people who were almost adults was easier than writing about an almost forgotten childhood. The pangs of adolescence for many people were well remembered. All the conflicts that must inevitably arise in the adjustments to family, to the future, to society in general, gave material for drama and resulted in novels of contemporary young people that gradually developed into a new branch of children's literature.

In 1931 Marian Hurd McNeely's *Winning Out* gave reality to the personalities of two sisters and their different ways of facing the future. In 1934 Margaret Thomsen Raymond's *A Bend in the Road* was unprecedented in having a heroine who could rebel against parental authority to the extent of running away from home to make her own living.

Shortly after this came Margery Bianco's *Winterbound* (1936) and *Other People's Houses* (1939). Mrs. Bianco spoke of writing these books as experiments, "because I have always been interested in everyday stories as long as they were real." The stories do have reality; the things that happen to Dale, who had to make her own living and took any job available, have happened to many girls, and the four young people who face their first winter in the country with new responsibilities for the comfort and happiness of their home have many kin in real life.

The United States at the beginning of the Second World War is the setting for *The Welcome* (1942). Seldom does one find a writer who can so successfully step inside a boy, and from that vantage point coordinate the contradictions of his emotions and actions, as did Babette Deutsch in this story. Thursty is alive. Even understandable are the emotions that prompt his unkind hazing of Ernst, the refugee boy in his class, and his rare flashes of perception. The Welcome is a haven for refugee children, run by a personable young woman who is herself a refugee. It is fortunate for their future outlook that Thursty and his friends, through a strange combination of circumstances, become involved in The Welcome. There is no quick conversion to humanitarianism; the boys remain true to character, but their interest is challenged by the almost unbelievable courage of the people they meet in this strange world of refugees. Among the familiar incidents of the war, almost too poignant to bear at the time, were the broadcasts between the young evacuees and their parents. The book is a convincing portrayal of one of the many dramas, by-products of the war, that so vitally affected children everywhere.

Rebecca Caudill's *Barrie & Daughter* (1943), laid in the Kentucky mountains fifty or so years ago, has not only realistic characters but the excitement of mountain feuds, dishonest politics, and a girl's determination to help her father in a fight for justice. Janet, of Alice Dalgliesh's *The Silver Pencil* (1944), is a complete personality, wholly credible and human. So well portrayed is her childhood in Trinidad, school years in England, and her experiences as a young woman in America training to be a teacher that the book becomes an engrossing personal experience for the reader. Marjorie Hill Allee and Elizabeth Janet Gray both told stories of college girls and their problems. Two others that stand out for their unusual perception are Janette Sebring Lowrey's *Margaret* (1950) and Madeleine L'Engle's story of an American girl in an international boarding school in Switzerland, *And Both Were Young* (1949).

Elsie Singmaster's *The Isle of Que* (1948), laid on a peninsula in the Susquehanna River, is concerned chiefly with Tim, the youngest of the Yoder children, his maturing, and his learning courage. The story reaches a climax in the wonderful description of the Susquehanna in flood. There is fine economy of words, and complete characterizations.

Very soon after teen-agers were noticed as a special audience for books about their own special difficulties, writers began to make the most of the problems of choosing a career. The trend to write career stories, with the *Sue Barton* (1936) books by Helen Dore Boylston, among the first, grew to become an appalling vogue in the late thirties and early forties. The books may have thrown a certain light on different jobs and professions, but they were written to pattern, were completely unrealistic and lacking in any literary distinction. To the child who wanted facts they gave superficial glamor. To the romantic girl they were stories of modern Cinderellas who might be themselves: under the guise of stories about real situations they built false impressions and hopes.

The boys did not fare so badly. There were few career books, as such, about young men, but from time to time appeared such a story as Hubert Skidmore's *River Rising!* (1939), full of action and suspense, about a courageous young man teaching school in a lumber camp in the Blue Ridge Mountains to earn money for a medical education. There were realistic stories of farming with all its hard work and discipline, disappointments and satisfactions. Douglas Gorsline's *Farm Boy* (1950) was a particularly good one of these. A refreshing book was *Green Treasure* (1948) by M. I. Ross, which tells in lively fashion of a boy's adventures in the pursuit of his consuming interest—plant exploration.

Concern with girls' career stories began to taper off in the forties giving place to an increasing number of well-written love stories. A hint of romance was to be found in most stories for the older girls, but in the new books love was not confined to a tender moment on the last page.

In *High Trail* (1948) Vivian Breck wove a natural, appealing love story through an account of hardship and near-tragedy on a mountain-climbing expedition in the Sierra Nevadas. Her *Maggie* (1954) is an exciting and emotionally true story of a defiant marriage, told against a background of Mexican west-coast mining country, an unconventional setting for a young woman of 1900 who had been reared in the affluence of one of San Francisco's socially prominent families. Alive, absorbing, and very well written, the book was exceptional in this period for the honesty of its discussion of love and marriage.

Mary Stolz, in *To Tell Your Love* (1950), tells of seventeen-year-old

Anne's unhappy summer spent in loving too much a young man who no longer loved her, and weaves through Anne's story the sadness of another love affair that culminated in too early marriage, and the joy and understanding that belonged to the mature love story of her older sister. The love story, even for young girls, was no longer in the lavender-and-old-lace tradition; the best ones were sincere interpretations of life.

All through the fifties and early sixties Mrs. Stolz wrote realistic, honest books about young people. Almost every obvious problem characteristic of the experiences of teen-age girls has been met in one of her novels. Here is a sampling. *The Organdy Cupcakes* (1951) is about three student nurses who, despite differences in temperament, become close friends. It has less glamor and far more reality than any nursing story before it. In *The Sea Gulls Woke Me* (1951) sixteen-year-old Jean has a summer away from a dominating mother. Overweight is Bessie Muller's problem in *In a Mirror* (1953). In *Ready or Not* (1953) sixteen-year-old Morgan Connor has to keep house in a low-cost housing development in New York for her young brother and sister and an impractical father. There is no strong understanding between the father and his children, but an underlying current of affection sustains them.

Because of Madeleine (1957) is a study of the catalytic effect on several lives of one young nonconformist. In *Wait for Me, Michael* (1961) fifteen-year-old Anny falls in love with a friend of her mother's. Mrs. Stolz's great talent is the creation of living characters, every one of whom is different from the others. Some of her early books written in the first person are extremely introspective. Later ones have more objectivity. The characters grow and often the reader does also. Mrs. Stolz's stories can be reassuring for girls and good reading for almost any age. After *Who Wants Music on Monday?* (1936) Mrs. Stolz began to write about younger children. She had already told some humorous animal fables, and her *The Dog on Barkham Street* (1960) showed that her understanding of people is not limited by age or sex.

In telling the story of a family's adjustment to a spoiled young orphan cousin who has come to live with them—and hers to the family—Madeleine L'Engle in *Meet the Austins* (1960) showed even deeper knowledge of young people than she did in *And Both Were Young*, one of the most perceptive books of its period. The Austin family is normal in its noise and minor quarrels, small disasters and confusion, but far from ordinary in its enjoyment of books and music, and its emphasis on fundamental values. Full of warmth and love and idealism, the book is also completely real. *The Moon by Night* (1963) in which the Austins take a camping trip from New England to the Southwest, North, and back across Canada is thought-provoking and exciting. The book is contemporary in feeling, incident, and characterizations, and the journey full of convincing adventures and unusually interesting encounters with people.

So clearly does Irene Hunt see the people who make up Julie Trelling's world in *Up a Road Slowly* (1966) and so vividly does she bring them to life that the reader is quickly and intensely interested in them. Julie was seven when her mother died and she went to live with her mother's sister and brother in their old country home. Aunt Cordelia, who taught the country school, was strict, precise, and seemingly inflexible, but Julie grew to appreciate her extraordinary depths of kindness and understanding. Handsome Uncle Haskell was an alcoholic and a pathological liar with a cynical poise that Julie saw shaken only once, but he too played an important part in her life for she saw him more clearly than many others did and she loved him. This beautifully written story of a young girl's growing to maturity received the Newbery Medal.

Many novels have been published for young people, and the level of writing in them since 1950 has been unusually high. Only a few of them can be briefly noted.

Elisabeth Friermood invariably found unusual situations about which to create her many books. In *Ballad of Calamity Creek* (1962) a young girl teaching in a mission school in the Kentucky mountains found that she was gaining more from the mountain people than they were learning from her. Of special interest is the concern with folk music about which Ann learned when she helped a young man, who for his doctoral dissertation was tracing the origins of the mountain people through their folk songs and ballads. Mildred Lee's *The Rock and the Willow* (1963) tells with great insight of the oldest daughter of an Alabama farm family whose dream of going to college seemed quite impossible. In Janette Sebring Lowrey's *Love, Bid Me Welcome* (1964) the vivid portrayal of a small Texas town and its people at the beginning of the century make the background of Margaret's love story as interesting as the story itself. Among Betty Cavanna's many books was one with an unusual situation perceptively handled, *Jenny Kimura* (1964). Tokyo had always been the home of Jenny Kimura Smith, living with her parents in a house that expressed, as did their life, "the best of two worlds." She was sixteen before her American grandmother invited her to spend a summer in the United States, a summer that demanded of Jenny all the courage and grace that she had inherited from her two worlds. Robinson Barnwell's *Shadow on the Water* (1967), with its setting on a South Carolina farm in the thirties, has characters with which the reader becomes deeply involved.

Joseph Krumgold's three books, different in settings, characters, mood, and style are, nevertheless, related. They make up, in a sense, a trilogy having for its basic theme the problems of adolescence: of understanding the loved and imperfect people around one and being respected by them as a mature person, of accepting the world of people with widely divergent views and attitudes, and of recognizing the values fundamental to the wholeness of one's personality and life.

. . . *And Now Miguel* (1953) is laid among the sheepherders of New Mexico. Miguel tells of his longing to go with the men of his family to take the sheep into the Sangre de Cristo mountains to summer pasture. But with each spring, his father tells him that he is not yet ready.

Onion John (1959) is laid in a small New Jersey town and introduces problems slightly more complex. Andy understands and admires Onion John, an immigrant hobo living on a little garden patch at the edge of town. When the town tries to improve Onion John and turn him into a "proper citizen" Andy understands the man's resistance and resents his father's interference in Onion John's life. The first wedge of discord is driven between father and son.

Henry 3 (1967) is the son of a man who has at last reached the top. As a vice president of his company he has been able to move his family to "the finest, executive-type development in the New York City area." Henry, who had lived all over the country and had had few close friends, was soon accepted by the sons of the most important families. Then a misunderstanding brought disfavor to his father and disillusionment to him until a disaster that swept away hypocrisy and misunderstandings gave Henry his first confrontation with the essential strengths and weaknesses in people of all kinds.

Mr. Krumgold received the Newbery Medal for each of his first two books. *Henry 3* is even stronger in the development of the theme and characterizations, and more absorbing and exciting in plot.

Emily Neville's *It's Like This, Cat* (1963), for which she received the Newbery Medal, gives a wonderful sense of the sights, sounds, and smells of New York City. Dave Mitchell, fourteen and rebellious—"My father is always talking about how a dog can be very educational for a boy. This is one reason I got a cat"—tells his own story of a year of growing up, especially of going through the tunnel of impatience and irritation with his father and coming at last into the light. Mrs. Neville's second book, *Berries Goodman* (1965), has even more interesting characters and situations. It is the story of a city boy, newly arrived in the suburbs, who has his first brush with antisemitism. Berries Goodman and Sidney Fine, who have found much in common, do their best to keep adult prejudices from interfering with their friendship, but they cannot long maintain their easy, happy relationship in the face of parental pressures. Humor and perspective make it an absorbing story, not a social tract. The emotion underlying the straightforward story-telling makes the reader care greatly about the boys and their friendship.

Margaret MacPherson's *The Rough Road* (1965), laid on the Isle of Skye, is the story of a sullen, unhappy boy. Jim's one interest was in raising cattle and when he had a chance to learn about them from casual, outgoing Alasdair MacAskill, he spent every spare minute with Alasdair, even to playing truant from school to help him with the cattle. The climax that changed the course of his life came when he found himself alone with full responsibility for getting the herd of prize animals to Kyle, across to the mainland, and then to the market— Jim who did not have a cent in his pocket, and who had never been off the island before. The characterizations, suspense, and the humor and poignance of Jim's situation make an exceptional story.

Another outstanding book from England about a troubled boy is K. M. Peyton's *The Plan for Birdmarsh* (1966), a story about a boy's deep disappointment when his father sold his property for a marina. Paul had always counted on carrying on the family farm that lay between the village of Birdmarsh and the sea. The well-developed plot includes a mystery involving the life-saving suit Paul's older brother Chris had invented, and comes to an exciting climax. Even more unforgettable, however, and the turning point in Paul's maturing, is the situation when, quite by accident he—not Chris—tests the suit for thirty-three hours in a fog-bound sea. Many stories have been concerned with the changes to the landscape of England by housing and industrial developments, and by the influx of city people to English coastal farming country. Few have the interesting characterizations and the excitement of this one.

Animal Heroes in Realistic Fiction

The first book that was both a great horse story and a great cowboy story was a Newbery Award winner, *Smoky* (1926) by Will James. It introduced into children's literature the West of the cattle ranges, the excitement of the roundup and the rodeo.

Will James's life story reads more like fiction than most novels. He was born in a covered wagon on the Montana prairies, his parents died when he was a very small child. The only thing he remembered about his father was the gift of a saddle and a horse all his own when he was about four years old. He was adopted by a French-Canadian trapper and prospector who taught him the rudiments of reading and writing. Further education Will James carried on by himself, chiefly with the aid of old magazines he had found at cow camps. He was only thirteen when his guardian was drowned, and he tried to heal the hurt of his loss by working to become a cowboy as his father had been. From then on "Horses and cattle and range country was all I knew or cared to know. And I'm still the same, even if I've broke into writing and drawing, for in that work I'm only living my life over again as I put it down on paper." He had always loved to draw and had done it at every opportunity, but it was while he was recuperating from an accident that he began to take his talent seriously and to sell his drawings. It was a natural step from drawing horses to trying to write about them, first magazine sketches in cowboy vernacular, then books, including his life's story, *Lone Cowboy* (1930), and *Smoky*.

A horse at the mercy of good and evil men is a theme that has inevitable appeal, but in the hands of a great storytelling cowboy it resulted in something very different from all the horse stories before it. The effortless way Smoky's story is told, the certainty of the characterization of Smoky, without humanizing or sentimentalizing, and the vivid setting lift this horse story into the realm of literature.

Glen Rounds grew up on Montana and North Dakota ranches and started writing and illustrating after he had roamed the country earning his living at any occupation available at the time. Humor and exaggeration fill his stories, but in *The Blind Colt* (1941) he achieved the perfect balance of perception and humor. It is the unforgettable story of a wild colt born blind, and of the small boy who tamed and trained him.

Marguerite Henry is best known for her horse stories, several of which are based on the history of famous lines of horses: *King of the Wind* (1948), winner of the Newbery Medal, is the story of the Godolphin Arabian, the ancestor of Man O'War and one of the founders of the entire thoroughbred strain; the wild pony of *Misty of Chincoteague* (1947) is descended from the ponies who escaped long ago from the wreck of the Spanish galleon to the lovely island of Assateague off the coast of Virginia; *Justin Morgan Had a Horse* (1954) tells the story of the first in a long line of American horses; harness-racing history was made by the characters—both human and horse—in *Born to Trot* (1950).

One of the best loved of many children's books about dogs is *Lassie Come Home* (1940) by Eric Knight, the story of the faithful collie who, sold to a duke who took her to northern Scotland, escaped and made the four hundred mile trek back to her young master in Yorkshire. Jim Kjelgaard, whose knowledge and love of the wilderness was very evident in his books, drew some notable dog portraits, among them *Big Red* (1945) and *Snow Dog* (1948). Based on childhood recollections was Zachary Ball's *Bristle Face* (1962), a boy-and-dog story laid in rural Tennessee. Among the books of the twentieth century published for adults that children have claimed for their own are a number of animal stories: *Lad: A Dog* by Albert Payson Terhune (1919),

My Friend Flicka by Mary O'Hara (1941), and the poignant story of a boy and his pet deer, *The Yearling* (1938) by Marjorie Kinnan Rawlings; *Old Yeller* (1956) by Fred Gipson, a tale of Texas cattle country in the nineteenth century, and of the ugly stray dog who won a boy's reluctant and, finally, devoted friendship; *The Incredible Journey* (1961) by Sheila Burnford, the story of the long journey of three animal friends—two dogs and a Siamese cat—through the Canadian wilderness to find their home and master; and *Rascal* (1963) by Sterling North, the story of a raccoon.

Cats have more often inspired fantasy than realistic writing, but some engaging cats are represented in realistic stories. Marguerite Henry's *Benjamin West and His Cat Grimalkin* (1947) is less the story of the artist than it is of his cat whose tail furnished Benjamin with the hairs for his first paint brush. Ann Petry gave complete personality to *The Drugstore Cat* (1949), as also did Eleanor Hoffmann to the Siamese cat Thom in her *A Cat of Paris* (1940), which, in addition, has a good realistic background of Paris between the wars. Carolyn Sherwin Bailey's understanding of cats is very evident (as is the illustrator's, Kate Seredy) in *Finnegan II. His Nine Lives* (1953). Finnie was a cat who began life in a New York alley, was adopted by a small boy, and came to live on the "Old Place" (famous because of Miss Hickory) in New Hampshire.

Strange animals frequently take the stage in realistic story books. One of the most surprising, at least to the people of a certain little Minnesota village in the dead of winter, was a moose who found plenty of appetizing fodder in Ivar's father's livery stable. *Honk: the Moose* (1935) reads as though the author, Phil Stong, and illustrator, Kurt Wiese, must have thoroughly enjoyed creating the book.

The same refreshing sense of writing for pleasure characterizes Rutherford Montgomery's *Kildee House* (1949), the story of the recluse who built his home in the Redwood forest expecting to live completely alone, only to find that his house was also the haven for innumerable friends, among them a family of spotted skunks, a family of pack rats, the raccoon "Old Grouch," and the ingratiating "Mrs. Grouch." Taro Yashima translated, adapted, and illustrated *The Golden Footprints* (1960) by Jun Iwamatsu and Hatoju Muku. It is the story of a baby fox captured by a farmer, of the boy Shotaro, who longed to set the fox free, and of the efforts of the parent foxes to rescue it. It creates with skillful understatement a bit of Japan and a way of life. Michel-Aimé Baudouy's *Old One-Toe* (1959), translated from the French by Marie Ponsot, is also the story of the defence of a fox by animal-loving children.

Two unusual stories of birds came in the sixties; *Gull Number 737* (1964) by Jean George, which is also the story of sixteen-year-old

Luke's relationship with his father, an ornithologist; and Farley Mowat's *Owls in the Family* (1961), a very funny story—and delightful to read aloud—about two horned owls, Weeps and Wol, that belong to a boy in Saskatoon.

A paragraph in a biographical sketch of Meindert DeJong by his brother throws a little light on the wellspring of memory and experience of his animal stories:

> The Depression years were upon us and he retreated to a farm, and seemed to find solace in chickens and cows and poorly producing harvests. It brought him close, face to face and soul to soul with all the animals he always loved. Why, he could even make a chicken act human! It laid the groundwork for a kind of writing I had never considered when I kept prodding him to write novels, shorter fiction, poetry.[1]

His love for animals was as much a part of his childhood as was the little village of Wierum on the North Sea. On that strong basis his understanding of them grew. His first book was *The Big Goose and the Little White Duck* (1938), and through the forties his stories were mostly about animals. Without humanizing, he shows animals with the kind of empathy that children feel, and a deep, protective love. In *Good Luck Duck* (1950), a picture-story book, Mr. DeJong was well started on the path that communicates directly with children. In *Hurry Home, Candy* (1953) the dog Candy is always the center of interest. People come and go in the little creature's life; two children love him and are in despair when they lose him, but eventually other interests have displaced their devotion to Candy. To the reader it is Candy's story that must end happily. Two stories of unusual friendships, *The Little Cow and the Turtle* (1955) and *Along Came a Dog* (1958), in which a humble dog and a proud hen become devoted friends, show recognition of the strong variations in animal personalities that is seldom achieved in a story without anthropomorphism or sentimentality.

Few writers have been able to express so movingly a child's intense love for a pet as Mr. DeJong does in a number of his animal stories, especially in *Shadrach* (1953). The story is told through Davie's thoughts, centered on the little black rabbit even before he owned him, and then on his all-absorbing love for his pet. Because he drew from his inner childhood, Mr. DeJong could give a story like *Shadrach* action and suspense to hold readers of any age.

---

[1] David Cornel DeJong, "My Brother Meindert." In Bertha Mahony Miller and Elinor Whitney Field, eds., *Newbery Medal Books: 1922–1955* (Boston, The Horn Book, 1955), p. 430.

Bibliography

Daugherty, James. "Comment on *Homer Price*." *The Horn Book*, Vol. 19 (Nov.–Dec., 1943).

DeJong, David Cornel. "My Brother Meindert." In Bertha Mahony Miller and Elinor Whitney Field, eds., *Newbery Medal Books: 1922–1955*. Boston, The Horn Book, 1955.

de la Mare, Walter. *Early One Morning in the Spring*. New York, Macmillan, 1935.

Haugaard, Erik Christian. "A Thank You Note and a Credo." *The Horn Book*, Vol. 44 (Feb., 1968).

Haviland, Virginia. *Ruth Sawyer*, a Walck Monograph. New York, Henry Z. Walck, 1965.

Moore, Anne Carroll. "The Three Owls' Notebook." *The Horn Book*, Vol. 28 (Feb., 1952).

Sayers, Frances Clarke. *Summoned by Books*. New York, Viking Press, 1965.

9

Companions on the Road

There are many ways of enjoying ourselves, and one of the pleasantest is to meet interesting people.—MARCHETTE CHUTE[1]

The child who has discovered the pleasure of books has discovered that good books are full of interesting people. A biography that catches his interest has an added attraction in being about someone who really did live and knew the delights and frustrations of being human.

Many collective biographies were published in the twenties, intended primarily for school use. Biographies of individual people for children were few, but among them were some that were significant. Stewart Edward White's *Daniel Boone: Wilderness Scout* (1922) was the first important biography of Boone. Its republication in 1926 with James Daugherty's illustrations, that gave it added distinction, launched James Daugherty on the career of illustration for children, and sowed the seed for his own interpretation of Boone in the next decade.

The boyhood chapters of Carl Sandburg's *Abraham Lincoln: The Prairie Years* were published in separate form for young people in 1928 under the title *Abe Lincoln Grows Up*, also illustrated by James Daugherty. This was an exciting recognition that there was place in children's literature for the best of writing and for mature interpretations of the drama of America. Boone and Lincoln—the names for two great forces at the heart of America—were to become closely associated with the name of James Daugherty, one of the great portrayers of America.

At the end of the decade Jeanette Eaton wrote the first of many biographies. She introduced no fictitious incident or dialogue into *A Daughter of the Seine* (1929), the story of Mme. Roland and her part in the French Revolution, crediting young people with the ability to follow the intricacies of the politics of the time. She brought Mme. Roland to life as a human being, imperfect, but lovable and heroic.

[1] Marchette Chute, "Biographies Bring New Companions." In Alfred Stefferud, ed., *The Wonderful World of Books* (New York, New American Library, 1953), p. 50.

Such books set a high standard of quality for biographies for young people; other influences were at work to promote the publication of biographies in quantity: the growing interest in the production of books for older boys and girls and the willingness of publishers to listen to "needs" that teachers and librarians might express. The decade between 1930 and 1940 received the full impact of this trend. A number of important books arose, however, above the mass of commissioned biographies.

The author of *Little Women* was a natural subject for biography. Louisa May Alcott's life was woven so inextricably with the events and people of her books that her biography gave pleasure as a continuation, in a way, of her well-loved stories. *Invincible Louisa* (1933) by Cornelia Meigs reveals the valiant, spirited woman whose life had even more courage, struggle, failure, and success than her stories. A vital, moving interpretation of Louisa Alcott, it was an appropriate choice for the Newbery Medal, which Miss Meigs accepted "on behalf of Louisa."

Constance Rourke (1885–1941) made a notable contribution with *Davy Crockett* (1934), told in a simple vigorous style, picturing vividly frontier life and Crockett's many-sided personality, weaving through the story the legends built up around him. So full of atmosphere is her book that the words she used to describe the originators of the Crockett legends could almost have been applied to her: "Whoever first told them had seen wildcats flash through the branches of a white oak and knew the hunter's life well." This concern with the understanding of the American frontiers led naturally to Audubon's writings and the attempt to portray the man himself. Miss Rourke followed his trails not only in her reading but actually traveling along the Ohio River, through the Mississippi country, through Kentucky, Louisiana, and Florida. Her *Audubon* (1936) clearly shows his personality, the impracticality and genius, charm and generosity, and "almost flawless integrity" of one of the warmest and most colorful characters in American history.

Elizabeth Janet Gray's two biographies were highlights of this period and excellent examples of two kinds of biographical writing. *Young Walter Scott* (1935) begins with lame Wattie's arrival at his home after many years of living as the only child of a loving, gentle aunt. The roughness of his lively brothers bewildered him and the pity of his little sister humiliated him. The book ends with Wattie's pride in at last being able to keep up with the other boys in all their activities, to the puzzlement of his friends, who, admiring Wattie for his many greater gifts, saw him preening himself on his physical prowess.

For nine years Elizabeth Janet Gray had wanted to write the story of Scott's boyhood. She had drawn upon her Scottish background, read widely about Scott and eighteenth century Edinburgh, had herself walked the roads and explored the places Scott had known. The effortless beauty of the writing is indication of the long, sure growth of the story. This is true re-creation of a life and a period and biographical fiction at its best.

Just as truly did she re-create William Penn, the England of his time, and the colony of Pennsylvania in *Penn* (1938), which is pure biography. Mrs. Gray made no attempt to turn his life into a story but the appeal of a story is there, so pertinent is her selection of incident. Penn, renouncing wealth and position to become a Quaker, facing his father's anger, standing firm before the courts of the law, coming to the New World and showing his greatness and wisdom as the governor of Pennsylvania—these high points are woven together with a wealth of authentic detail, to make of an historic figure a living man.

Stories of the pioneers and the builders of America had been woven through James Daugherty's childhood. The tall tales of Daniel Boone told by his grandfather and a boyhood spent on an Indiana farm and in the city of Washington, had laid the foundation for a good understanding of the country's past. He was, however, in England when he first discovered Walt Whitman's poetry and caught the vision of America to which he gave his own interpretation. *Daniel Boone* (1939), for which he received the Newbery Medal; *Poor Richard* (1941); *Abraham Lincoln* (1943); *Of Courage Undaunted* (1951), the account of the Lewis and Clark expedition across the Rocky Mountains to find the passage to the Pacific; and *Marcus and Narcissa Whitman, Pioneers of Oregon* (1953) have in the writing the strength and simplicity characteristic of Mr. Daugherty's pictures. For these books and for his illustrations for numerous other books he has come to stand, as Lynd Ward expressed it,

> . . . in a kind of symbolic relation to our culture, his talent firmly rooted in American experience, his creative motivation well attuned to the techniques of our age, his voice well able to speak out for the values of democratic life.[1]

After writing *A Daughter of the Seine*, which had involved Jeanette Eaton's enthusiastic exploration to find the Paris of Revolutionary times behind the present-day city, it was a natural step backward in time for her to recapture the period of *Young Lafayette* (1932). From Lafayette's career it was a logical progression to her interpretation of Washington, *Leader by Destiny* (1938). The imaginative re-creation of incident and conversation woven into these and later books was based on authentic sources and integrated naturally into the biographical material.

Laura Benét caught the bright, irrepressible spirit of Shelley between

[1] Lynd Ward, "A Note on James Daugherty," *The Horn Book*, Vol. 16 (July, 1940), p. 246.

the ages of nine and eighteen in *The Boy Shelley* (1937). In *Enchanting Jenny Lind* (1939) she re-created the period between 1820 and 1850 and from a vast amount of material—diaries, letters, books and newspapers—she brought to life the Swedish singer who had the world at her feet.

Eleanor Doorly's love for France and her enjoyment of the gentle personality of Jean Henri Fabre glow through her unusual biography, *The Insect Man* (1937). The subtitle describes her approach: "A tale of how the Yew Tree children went to France to hear the story of Jean Henri Fabre in the places where he lived and to see the homes and some of the insects whose life story he has written." Biographers of scientists have found a rich and fruitful field. Each day's work of a research scientist is a suspenseful story, each small success a triumph. Unlike her book about Fabre there is no story within a story in Miss Doorly's *The Microbe Man* (1939). It is a direct, sympathetic portrayal of Louis Pasteur's life and work, based on the René Vallery-Radot *La Vie de Pasteur*.

Laura N. Wood's absorbing account of Raymond L. Ditmars' life, though its mood and setting are so different, sends one's mind back from time to time to *The Insect Man*. Mr. Ditmars' mother, though she would have expressed it differently, had much in common with Fabre's, who said, "Bring up my children to see them going wrong! You'll break my heart. Grass you might have collected, that does for the rabbits. But stones to tear your pockets! Insects that might poison your hands! What do you want with them, silly? Some one has bewitched you."

In her introduction to *Runner of the Mountain Tops* (1939), Mabel L. Robinson described some of the qualities in Agassiz that had caught her interest: "Other men to whom these qualities might apply would, perhaps, make a biographer, who faces all the great men of the ages, hesitate where to choose. There was no choice in my case. Louis Agassiz was the only person whose biography I ever intended to write. I seem always to have known him." She caught and translated into this story something of the imperishable spirit of the man. We see the headlong boy, whose mother bemoaned his tendency "to leap from one splendid unfinished project to the next one which seemed more exciting," the student at Heidelberg and Munich, the teacher back in his native Switzerland drawing people to him because of his outgoing personality and his quicksilver mind, the distinguished immigrant to the United States, the founder of the Agassiz Museum at Harvard University, and one of America's great men. Other biographies of Agassiz were published in the fifties but *Runner of the Mountain Tops* stands out for the conviction and depth of the characterization.

As a publisher of children's illustrated books in Paris, Esther Averill wrote, among a number of books, *Daniel Boone* (1931), handsomely illustrated by Feodor Rojankovsky, and published it in both French and English editions. When the Second World War put an end to her publishing career, she returned to the United States, where *The Voyages of Jacques Cartier* (1937) was published, also illustrated by Mr. Rojankovsky. A new edition of this book was issued under the title of *Cartier Sails the St. Lawrence* (1956).

C. Walter Hodges, already known for his vigorous, imaginative drawings, brought the same qualities to the writing and illustrating of *Columbus Sails* (1939). The story of Columbus's life is told by three men close to him, a monk at La Rabida, a sailor on the voyage, and an Indian whom Columbus had brought back with him to Spain. This is a fresh and exciting interpretation.

Much so-called biography of the thirties was, in reality, very contrived biographical fiction. On the bare facts of a life was built a lively story—a lure for the reluctant reader, and a shield behind which the writer could hide a superficial knowledge of his subject. The books that stand out from the mass of commissioned biographies are evidence that it takes long living with the subject to bring him to life in the printed word, and that some affinity usually exists between subject and biographer.

By 1940 the pot that had been boiling up biographies for young people began to simmer down. Those written out of enthusiasm and natural sympathy began to be numerous enough to be noticeable among the obviously contrived. Although few biographies were written without occasional fictionized passages, the outstanding biographers saw that they had special responsibility in writing for young people to present their subjects with accuracy and honesty. Biographical fiction was recognized as entailing no less background and research than pure biography and, like historical fiction, it required special genius.

Jeanette Eaton's *Narcissa Whitman* (1941), the story of the beautiful pioneer missionary, was moving and credible. In *Lone Journey* (1944) Miss Eaton gave Roger Williams his rightful place as the first great American liberal. Nina Brown Baker with her strong sense of the dramatic brought colorful personalities into children's lives through story biographies of widely different people, among them *Garibaldi* (1944) and *Peter the Great* (1943). Madeleine Goss, in her *Beethoven* (1931) and *Unfinished Symphony* (1941), the story of Schubert, showed appreciation of the creative genius of musicians and imparted enthusiasm for their music as well as interest in their lives. Covelle Newcomb wrote several exciting story biographies, among them *Black Fire* (1940), the dramatic story of Henri Christophe. Phyllis Wynn Jackson brought to life some extraordinary women and their periods in her life of Harriet Beecher Stowe, *Victorian Cinderella* (1947), and in her story of the career of America's first great comedienne, Lotta Crabtree, *Golden Footlights* (1949).

Following Fanny Burney's early diaries Anna Bird Stewart in *Young*

Miss Burney (1947) covered the most important and entertaining years of Fanny's life, picturing the Burneys' illustrious circle of acquaintances, in the midst of which modest, witty Fanny enjoyed her surprising fame. In *Enter David Garrick* (1951) Anna Bird Stewart presented with equal enthusiasm the brilliant, charming man against the fascinating period in London when modern drama was at its beginning.

May Lamberton Becker's (1873–1958) *Introducing Charles Dickens* (1940) would stand out as an important book in any era. Steeped in the work of Dickens, knowing well the people who troop through his stories, Mrs. Becker obviously enjoyed the steps she took to know the man himself. She drew upon letters more than upon any other source, and then "upon people who saw him, listened to him, laughed with him, and wrote down how he looked and acted and spoke. For no one seems to have met Dickens, much less known him well, without feeling that while they were with him something important was happening, worth writing down if they could write, but at all events something not to be forgotten." The people in Dickens's stories were drawn from life and so are inextricably bound up with his life. Mrs. Becker had written widely on the subject of books and reading for children and young people, was for years a discerning critic of children's books; with her daughter, Beatrice Warde, whose home is in England, she kept in active touch with children and books on both sides of the Atlantic through the war years. This biography is a salient testimonial to her high standards and to the lifelong pleasure that Dickens gave her. *Nicholas Nickleby* was the first volume of Dickens that she owned and long before she began this biography, it had "returned to dust," but its work had been done, "It had taken my hand and laid it in that of a friend I was never to lose. 'Child,' it had said, 'this is Charles Dickens.' "

Mrs. Becker's enthusiasm brought Jane Austen completely to life without any fictionizing in *Presenting Miss Jane Austen* (1952). Anne Carroll Moore wrote:

> The distinction of her book, that which sets it apart from biographies written for young people, lies in the simple fact that the author never forgets that she is presenting Jane Austen herself, her family, their life, the places they lived in, Jane's novels, their characters, and as much as is known of how they were written. She relies upon recorded evidence. All is clear and in order in the mind of the author, and she brings her rare associative memory and discriminating taste to a revealing picture of an elusive and delightful personality.[1]

Mrs. Becker's two biographies are nearly irresistible invitations to the books by Charles Dickens and Jane Austen.

[1] Anne Carroll Moore, "The Three Owls' Notebook," *The Horn Book*, Vol. 28 (Aug., 1952), p. 235.

Anna Gertrude Hall succeeded admirably in portraying a many-sided genius in her *Nansen* (1940) and in showing the fearless idealism that led him on many quests. His first, while he was still studying at the University of Christiana, took him on a sealing vessel to the Arctic Ocean to make notes on winds, ocean currents, ice drifts, and animal life. His last, after he had made great scientific contributions and had served his country in many capacities, led him to take active part in the League of Nations in his search for the way to peace. Although the great quiet of the North and the vast ice fields were to become familiar to Fridtjof Nansen, his was a nature that rejoiced in his home and family and close contact with people. "He was a great man; he will seem greater when men who made more noise in his day have been forgotten, and the world has had time to look back and see how he towers above his times."

The poet Babette Deutsch revealed in *Walt Whitman, Builder for America* (1941) the personality of the one who continuously expressed in his poetry the ideals of America and democracy. A selection of his poetry is included at the end and bits of it are introduced frequently through the whole inspired story.

Even as Whitman was America's poetic exponent, Sibelius expressed Finland in music. Elliott Arnold showed in *Finlandia* (1941) how completely were Sibelius's life and love of his country blended in his music. Many biographies of musicians appeared in the next twenty-five years. Especially vivid portrayals of subjects and periods are Hilda White's *Song Without End* (1959), the story of Clara and Robert Schumann, and Elisabeth Kyle's *The Swedish Nightingale: Jenny Lind* (1965).

Published on the five hundredth anniversary of the invention of movable type, and written by Douglas McMurtrie, a distinguished printer, in collaboration with Don Farran, *Wings for Words* (1940) tells the story of Johann Gutenberg from his boyhood and early interest in the cutting of wood blocks to the end of his richly fulfilled life. The part Gutenberg played in the history of printing is the main thread of the story told against the background of Germany in the days of the guilds.

The subjects of biographies have not been limited to the great. Often a relatively unimportant person can throw light upon a period. There is very natural appeal for children in *"Have You Seen Tom Thumb?"* (1942), Mabel Leigh Hunt's telling of the fairy-tale-like story of Charles Stratton, the midget who brought so much fame and fortune to Phineas T. Barnum, who enchanted the Princess Victoria of England and who, with his tiny wife, brought a bit of relief to the war-weary President Lincoln. It is also an entertaining picture of a period when the genial figure of such a man as Barnum could create so much furor. Alice Curtis Desmond's *Barnum Presents: General Tom Thumb* (1954) is a more detailed biography and of interest to older boys and girls. Mrs. Desmond spent her girlhood in Bridgeport, Connecticut, where Tom Thumb lived, heard for years about the famous midget, and was surrounded with reminders of him. She talked with people who knew him and had access to records and a manuscript autobiography written by his wife.

Among biographies of South American leaders appeared, in the early forties, not less than three about Simón Bolivar, leader in the struggle of five South American countries for independence: *He Wouldn't Be King: The Story of Simón Bolivar* (1941) by Nina Brown Baker, *Simón Bolivar: A Story of Courage* (1941) by Elizabeth Waugh, and *The Life and Times of Simón Bolivar* (1943) by Hendrik Willem van Loon. In *American Emperor* (1945) Rose Brown clearly revealed the personality of Dom Pedro II against the background of three generations of Brazilian life and politics.

Southwestern and Latin American explorers received less prejudiced treatment in the fifties than they had earlier. Until 1940 source material had not been easily available, or had never been translated into English. By then, when New Mexico celebrated the four hundredth anniversary of the discovery of Coronado's expedition, little-known or lost documents had come to light, were translated and published. Making the most of the newly available source material, Camilla Campbell in *Coronado and His Captains* (1958) showed in perspective the men who took part in the search for the kingdom of Cibola. Good or bad, loyal or treacherous, they had the nobility and the limitations of human beings of any time. Coronado himself was a wise leader whose courage stemmed not from ambition or greed for gold, but from his strong sense of duty to his country and his pride in living up to the trust placed in him. Evan Jones in *Protector of the Indians* (1958) told the story of Bartolomé de Las Casas, who devoted the last sixty years of his life to securing justice for the Indians. Maud Hart Lovelace in *What Cabrillo Found* (1958) told the exciting story of Juan Rodríguez Cabrillo, who claimed what is now California for Spain. Ronald Syme in *The Man Who Discovered the Amazon* (1958) recounted the extraordinary adventures of Francisco Orellana in Brazil.

As the first European to set foot on mainland North America, Leif Eriksson was a natural subject for biography. In 1951 at least four children's books about him were published. Katherine B. Shippen's *Leif Eriksson, First Voyager to America* (1951) is especially important for its color and detail and the direct, uncomplicated writing that suggests the flavor of the Norse sagas.

Early in the twentieth century the view of the American Indian in history began to undergo a change, but not until the thirties was this new, more rational attitude strongly evident in children's books. From then on Indians who appeared in fiction and in historical accounts were seen with more understanding and presented with greater justice and dignity than before. In the forties and fifties a number of exceptionally good books about Indians appeared. Catherine Cate Coblentz told the brave, but little-known story of *Sequoya* (1946), the lame half-white Cherokee who developed a written language for his people. Esther Averill's *King Philip, the Indian Chief* (1950) is a straightforward, dramatic account of a great, often misjudged Indian leader. Edgar Wyatt's *Geronimo, the Last Apache War Chief* (1952) is a fine biography of one of the best known of the Indian chiefs. In the next year appeared three biographies of Cochise. His love for peace and his desire for friendship with the white men are especially clear in *Cochise of Arizona* (1953) by Oliver La Farge.

Many biographies of other Americans were published through the fifties and sixties. Important among several about John Chapman, who in the early nineteenth century spent his life planting apple seeds throughout the country, is *Better Known as Johnny Appleseed* (1950) by Mabel Leigh Hunt, whose interpretation of the legendary figure is dignified and unsentimental. Authentic historical details give substance to *The Sword and Compass* (1951), Margaret Leighton's exciting fictionized biography of Captain John Smith, whose adventures through seventeenth century England, France, and Turkey are less known than those in the British-American colonies. *Lee of Virginia* (1958) was drawn from Douglas Southall Freeman's four-volume Pulitzer prize biography of *Robert E. Lee*. Leo Gurko's *Tom Paine, Freedom's Apostle* (1957), written in a simple, clear style with the few imagined scenes integrated naturally in the authentic record, is an excellent portrayal of the dedicated, complex man, adored as a champion of the American Revolution, but scorned in his old age, who, far ahead of his time, wrote:

> It is wrong to say God made *rich* and *poor*; He made only *male* and *female*; and He gave them the earth for their inheritance . . . Practical religion consists in doing good: and the only way of serving God is that of endeavoring to make His Creation happy. All preaching that has not this for its object is nonsense and hypocrisy.[1]

Catherine Owens Peare's *The Woodrow Wilson Story* (1963) is a well-balanced account of Wilson's life that emphasizes his integrity and his refusal to compromise principles, and shows also his warm relationships to family and friends. Miriam Gurko in *Clarence Darrow* (1965) brought to life the colorful personality of the great trial lawyer, describing his most famous cases, and making clear the principles behind each. Life courses through Leonard Wibberley's fictionized four-volume biography of Thomas Jefferson: *Young Man from the Piedmont: The Youth of Thomas Jefferson* (1963), *A Dawn in the Trees: . . . the Years 1776 to 1789* (1964), *The Gales of Spring: . . . the Years 1789 to 1801*

---

[1] Leo Gurko, *Tom Paine, Freedom's Apostle* (New York, T. Y. Crowell, 1957), p. 174.

(1965), and *Time of the Harvest: . . . the Years 1801 to 1826* (1966). Books like these about Paine, Wilson, Darrow, and Jefferson showed that stories of lives in which ideas were more important than action could be presented with excitement and vitality by the right biographers. Even the life of a deeply religious, introverted man became intensely interesting as Emmeline Garnett presented it in *Tormented Angel: A Life of John Henry Newman* (*1966*).

Hildegarde Hoyt Swift was the first to write for young people a story of Harriet Tubman, the great Negro woman who played so dramatic a role in the Underground Railroad. *The Railroad to Freedom* (1932) was fiction but based on a solid foundation of fact. Its publication was prophetic but nearly twenty years of apathy had to pass before the appearance of numerous books on Negroes, on social changes of many kinds, particularly those relating to minority groups and civil-rights legislation. Elizabeth Yates's *Amos Fortune Free Man* (1950) was an introduction to a little-known man, born in Africa, brought to the United States as a slave, who lived to become one of the most respected men in his community. The moving story was chosen for the Newbery Medal. Then came Arna Bontemps's story of the Jubilee Singers, *Chariot in the Sky* (1951), in which is felt strongly the impact of slavery and racial discrimination; and Catherine Owens Peare's book about *Mary McLeod Bethune* (1951) with emphasis on her efforts to improve Negro education in the South and the establishment of Bethune-Cookman College. Emma Gelders Sterne wrote another *Mary McLeod Bethune* (1957), an absorbing biography. Two more accounts of Harriet Tubman were published: Dorothy Sterling's *Freedom Train* (1954) which, in a fast-paced story, provides background for the fervor and ingenuity with which Harriet Tubman succeeded in moving people along the devious ways toward freedom; and Ann Petry's *Harriet Tubman, Conductor of the Underground Railroad* (1955), poignant and beautifully written, in which Miss Petry's intuitive understanding of Harriet Tubman's feelings and dreams gives the story depth. Elizabeth Yates's *Prudence Crandall, Woman of Courage* (1955) tells of the Quaker schoolmistress who opened a school for Negro girls in 1833, risking safety and livelihood in her single-hearted devotion to her beliefs. Jean Gould's *That Dunbar Boy, the Story of America's Famous Negro Poet* (1958) is not a deep study of Paul Laurence Dunbar's personality or of the problems and tragedies he faced, but it is an interesting account of a fine and gentle person, who, as a poet, made a unique contribution to American letters. *Frederick Douglass: Slave-Fighter-Freeman* (1959) by Arna Bontemps is an important biography of the great Negro abolitionist. Centered chiefly on his boyhood and youth, it shows the drama of the awakening of a human spirit trapped by an inhumane system and tells of the escape from slavery and the beginning of a career that was to have far-reaching influence.

The first good biography of Gandhi for young people was by Jeanette Eaton, *Gandhi, Fighter Without Sword* (1950). Then came *Mahatma Gandhi* (1950) by Catharine Owens Peare, less dramatic than the Eaton biography, but more detailed. These books introduced to American young people the idea of passive-resistance strikes, and the philosophy behind them. Betty Schechter in *The Peaceable Revolution* (1963) presented the concept of nonviolent resistance as interpreted by Thoreau and Gandhi and related it to the Negro movement against segregation in the 1960's.

Two courageous women were subjects for later biographies: *Lucretia Mott, Gentle Warrior* (1964) by Dorothy Sterling, the story of an often misunderstood gentle crusader who struggled for the rights of Negroes, women, and all minority groups in general; and *Tongue of Flame: The Life of Lydia Maria Child* (1965) by Milton Meltzer, an unfictionized account of the author of the first antislavery volume published in the United States. Mrs. Child could have been a very successful editor and publisher of uncontroversial books and magazines; instead she spent her long and active career in the cause of antislavery and wartime and postwar problems. As the abolitionist Wendell Phillips characterized her, "She was ready to die for a principle and starve for an idea." Dorothy Sterling and Benjamin Quarles collaborated on a collection of biographical sketches of four great Negro leaders: *Lift Every Voice: the Lives of Booker T. Washington, W. E. B. DuBois, Mary Church Terrell, and James Weldon Johnson* (1965).

In a science-centered era there were inevitably many books about scientists and scientific exploration, competently written, timely, and useful. A complete study is not possible here but mention of a few well-written books that emphasize the personalities and the human drama inherent in the accomplishment of scientific contributions will give an indication of the wide variety of subjects covered in biography for young people. In telling the story of people who wanted to fly—from Daedalus and Icarus to Igor Sikorsky and the helicopter—Katherine B. Shippen in *A Bridle for Pegasus* (1943) presented the history of flying as one great panorama. Eric Swenson's *The South Sea Shilling: Voyages of Captain Cook* (1952) is an adventure story of three long voyages taken between 1769 and 1779 that opened a new age in scientific exploration. In Rose Brown's *Bicycle in the Sky: The Story of Alberto Santos-Dumont* (1953), a semi-fictionized biography of the great Brazilian pioneer in aviation, emphasis is on the man and his period rather than on scientific details. Sidney Rosen's *Galileo and the Magic Numbers* (1958) presents the state of scientific thought just before and after 1600, showing clearly the courage and drama of Galileo's rebellion. Mr. Rosen's *Doctor Paracelsus* (1959) is another lively, authentically based biography of a scientist ahead of his time—the alchemist-physician Phillip Theophrastus Bombast von Hohenheim, who spent his life wandering, studying, talking, learning, and finding new ways of treating the sick and wounded.

Marjorie Braymer's *The Walls of Windy Troy: a Biography of Heinrich Schliemann* (1960) is an account of the man who in middle age, but still fired by the stories of Troy that he had read in childhood, began excavations where he believed ancient Troy was buried, and found the foundations of Troy among the ruins of a total of nine cities built one above the other. Margaret Bell wrote an intensely alive account of the German botanist, the first scientist to set foot on Alaskan soil, in *Touched with Fire: Alaska's George William Steller* (1960). Hildegard Hoyt Swift's *From the Eagle's Wing* (1962) is a biography of John Muir "dramatized, not fictionized" through which shines the author's conviction of Muir's greatness and her understanding of this man with "a passionate zest for life, the love of beauty," and "the dedication to his own sense of mission."

Of the many great literary figures, one whose personal life was itself colorful, adventuresome drama is Cervantes, *The Man Who Was Don Quixote* (1958). Reading Rafaello Busoni's biography of Miguel de Cervantes y Saavedra means living for a while in sixteenth century Spain and knowing a man of such extraordinary personal attributes that one is reluctant to relegate him and his world to the past when the book is finished. Cervantes' childhood was chiefly spent in a caravan traveling with his family throughout Spain. He was briefly a student, a secretary in the Vatican, a soldier, a captive of Barbary pirates, a slave in the palace of the Bey of Algiers, an actor and playwright wandering across Spain with a traveling theatrical troupe, and several times a prisoner. It is good to realize that the end of the biography is not the end of his story, that in *Don Quixote* much of the man can be recaptured: his imagination, philosophy, wisdom, humor, and his joyous appreciation of mankind. The profuse black and white drawings by Mr. Busoni, on almost every page, full of life and atmosphere, are like spontaneous impressions dashed off at the scene, evidence of how completely assimilated were the years of research and devotion that went into this account. Few biographies of a writer extend so strong an invitation to read his books.

Charles Norman handled with unusual insight the biography of a man difficult to interpret for children. His *To a Different Drum* (1954) is an excellent brief introduction to Thoreau through well-chosen incidents from his life, comments from friends—Emerson, Alcott, and Hawthorne—and quotations from letters, speeches, and other writings.

Of the many biographies of Andersen one of the most perceptive is also brief, Rumer Godden's *Hans Christian Andersen* (1954). Ruth Franchere's *Willa: the Story of Willa Cather's Growing Up* (1958) is a most appealing story-biography of a lively tomboy, racing across the Nebraska prairie on her pony, interested in everything and everybody, especially the pioneer farmers, immigrants from Central Europe beginning their new lives in soddy huts. Elisabeth Kyle's *Girl with a Pen* (1964) is an absorbing biographical novel about Charlotte Brontë that focuses on the period between her seventeenth and thirty-first years. Two biographies of Emily Dickinson appeared almost simultaneously, written from very different points of view. Polly Longsworth's *Emily Dickinson: Her Letter to the World* (1965) is a distinguished biography, objective and restrained, that makes very clear Emily's independence of spirit, her wit, her pleasure in family and friends, and her mysticism. *We Dickinsons: the Life of Emily Dickinson as seen through the eyes of her brother Austin* (1965) by Aileen Fisher and Olive Rabe was drawn from material in her many letters and told as a personal memoir, revealing her as a beloved member of a close-knit family. Seon Manley's *Rudyard Kipling: Creative Adventurer* (1965) is partially fictional but an accurate and very interesting record. Rosemary Sprague's *Forever in Joy: The Life of Robert Browning* (1965) gives frequent glimpses of Browning's poetry, but the man is always present too—the man to whom life was opportunity for joy. His love for Elizabeth Barrett and their happy marriage is the core of Browning's personal story but only the beginning of the story of the poet. Miss Sprague, a Browning scholar, in honoring man and poet, told an absorbing story.

James Playsted Wood wrote a number of biographies of writers, including *Trust Thyself: A Life of Ralph Waldo Emerson* (1964) and *The Lantern Bearer: A Life of Robert Louis Stevenson* (1965). His *A Hound, a Bay Horse, and a Turtle Dove* (1963) is a critical appreciation of Thoreau that has more detailed background of early nineteenth century New England and Thoreau's contemporaries than the book by Charles Norman. In *The Man Who Hated Sherlock Holmes: A Life of Sir Arthur Conan Doyle* (1965) Mr. Wood showed the warmth he feels toward his marvelously versatile, colorful subject and traced the threads of Conan Doyle's life in his writings. *The Snark Was a Boojum: A Life of Lewis Carroll* (1966) is crisp and witty in its weaving through the book quotations from Lewis Carroll's prose and rhymes, but underlying the whole account is Mr. Wood's understanding of a complex personality.

The basic impulse for these books came out of emotions so deep within him that he was never able to explain the where or whence or how of the writing. . .

Once when a small girl praised him for writing *Alice in Wonder-*

land, he chided her. "Never praise me. I feel myself a trustee, that is all."[1]

Mr. Wood is extraordinary in his ability to lose himself in the life, philosophy, and ambience of each of his varied subjects. He brings them to life without the introduction of fictitious scenes or dialogue.

Nardi Reeder Campion with Rosamond Wilfley Stanton told the story of a contemporary heroine, the first woman in the United States to be made a professor of clinical medicine, in *Look to This Day! The Lively Education of a Great Woman Doctor: Connie Guion, MD* (1965). At the time of the publication of the book Dr. Guion was in her forty-fourth year of teaching at Cornell Medical College. Her childhood in a family of twelve children on a rather impoverished Southern plantation, her efforts to get an education and then to insure the education of the three children younger than herself, and the progress of her career make a gallant, happy story.

Good biographies with strong appeal for young children have been few, and in these the illustrations are important. Ingri and Edgar Parin d'Aulaire wrote and illustrated a number of picture-book biographies: *George Washington* (1936), *Abraham Lincoln* (1939), (for which they received the Caldecott Medal), *Pocahontas* (1946), *Benjamin Franklin* (1950), *Leif the Lucky* (1951), and *Columbus* (1955). Leo Politi's *The Mission Bell* (1953) tells with brief text and full-page pictures in color of the coming of Father Junipero Serra to California. The first of a group of brief biographies with simple, dignified text, illustrated with dramatic pictures by Lynd Ward, was Esther Forbes's *America's Paul Revere* (1946). Others were Stewart Holbrook's *America's Ethan Allen* (1949), and Henry Steele Commager's *America's Robert E. Lee* (1951). May McNeer, the wife of Lynd Ward, wrote biographies of two religious leaders that Mr. Ward illustrated: *John Wesley* (1951) and *Martin Luther* (1953). Genevieve Foster wrote and illustrated two "Initial Biographies," *George Washington* (1949) and *Abraham Lincoln* (1950), using particular care in the selection of incident to make the men and their periods clear to young children. Clyde Fisher, a distinguished naturalist, wrote with enthusiasm *The Life of Audubon* (1949), illustrating the book with Audubon's own paintings and drawings.

The purposeful note in the writing of biography has been apparent throughout forty years. At first stimulated by educational needs for material on outstanding personalities, it extended to include subjects that would help children to understand political and social movements through books about the leaders of the movements. Like this type of

---

[1] James Playsted Wood, *The Snark Was a Boojum* (New York, Pantheon, 1966), p. 174.

writing in realistic fiction, it is topical and often necessary, but seldom literature. The books discussed in this chapter are evidence, however, that biography need not be didactic, can be as interesting as fiction, and often provides inspiration as well as vicarious experiences for boys and girls.

Bibliography

Becker, May Lamberton. *Introducing Charles Dickens*. New York, Dodd, Mead, 1940.

Campbell, Camilla. "A New Look at Heroes of the Southwest." *The Horn Book*, Vol. 35 (Feb., 1959).

Chute, Marchette. "Biographies Bring New Companions." In *The Wonderful World of Books*, edited by Alfred Stefferud. New York, New American Library, 1953.

Gurko, Leo. *Tom Paine, Freedom's Apostle*. New York, T. Y. Crowell, 1957.

Moore, Anne Carroll. "The Three Owls' Notebook." *The Horn Book*, Vol. 28 (Aug., 1952).

Ward, Lynd. "A Note on James Daugherty." *The Horn Book*, Vol. 16 (July, 1940).

Wood, James Playsted. *The Snark Was a Boojum*. New York, Pantheon, 1966.

10

The World Around Us

*One great advantage that a rank amateur has . . . is that every-
thing is amazing.* The most well-known facts made me stand *open-
eyed and I went through our unpeopled days with surprise accompanying me.*—FLORENCE PAGE JAQUES[1]

Even as artists of the twenties made the discovery of children as a
responsive new audience, so scientists began to realize that a new audience was also waiting for them, that through the medium of children's
books—not school texts, but books for pleasure reading—they could
recapture the thrill of their first discoveries and transmit that enthusiasm
to children. Scientific careers, many times, have been the outgrowth of
childhood interests, and the scientist who writes for children joins the
ranks of the other writers in remembering his own childhood and in
giving respect to the interest and curiosity of today's child.

W. Maxwell Reed had been professor of astronomy at Harvard and
Princeton when the curiosity of his young nephew started him writing
a series of letters to answer the boy's questions about the earth. These
letters resulted in *The Earth for Sam* (1930). Illustrated with good
photographs and amusing sketches, the book describes the earth's
changes through various geological periods, gives much information
on prehistoric animals and plants, and opens up to the child the adventure that awaits in the realm of science. *The Stars for Sam* (1931) is
an equally readable presentation of the stars that introduces also the
wonders of explorations into the universe, the possibility for changing
concepts brought about by new discoveries, and the realization that the
frontiers of exploration of the universe are endless.

Mr. Reed collaborated with Wilfrid Bronson in *The Sea for Sam*
(1935), which introduced children to many aspects of oceanography.
And with Jannette Lucas he wrote *Animals on the March* (1937), which
traced the history of many familiar animals from earliest forms to the

---

[1] Florence Page Jaques, "Canoe Country," in *A Sense of Wonder*, compiled by
Dorothy Shuttlesworth (New York, Doubleday, 1963), p. 153.

present. Her twenty years in charge of the Osborn Library of Vertebrate Paleontology in the American Museum of Natural History gave Jannette Lucas excellent preparation for her books. She met Helene Carter, who illustrated one of Dr. Ditmars' books, and out of this acquaintance began a collaboration which resulted in *The Earth Changes* (1937), a vivid account of prehistoric geology. Miss Lucas' history of prehistoric man, *Man's First Million Years* (1941), written after many years of experience at the museum, answered some of the questions for which she had had difficulty in finding answers in the early years of her work.

Out of talks on geology given to young visitors to the museums of the universities of Chicago and Cincinnati grew Carroll Lane Fenton's *Along the Hill* (1935) and *Earth's Adventures* (1942).

Vera Edelstadt's story of water, *Oceans in the Sky* (1946), and Ruth Brindze's *The Gulf Stream* (1945) were only two more of the increasing number and variety of books that stimulate the child's wondering mind.

Alex Novikoff explained evolution in *Climbing Our Family Tree* (1945), profusely illustrated by John English with lively pictures and diagrams. In *Man's Way from Cave to Skyscraper* (1947) Ralph and Adelin Linton gave an authoritative analysis of race, tracing man's culture in all parts of the world from prehistoric times to the present. In *Four Ways of Being Human* (1956) Gene Lisitzky presented an introduction to anthropology through four primitive cultures, showing how man conquered different environments: the Semang of the Malayan jungle, the Eskimos of the Arctic, the Maori of New Zealand, and the Hopi of southwestern United States.

Scientific Developments

In 1930 Amabel Williams-Ellis in *Men Who Found Out* told the stories of the great scientific discoverers: Galileo, William Harvey, Van Leeuwenhoek, Faraday, Darwin, Pasteur, Curie, and others. The development of communications through the ages is the theme of *Heels, Wheels and Wire* (1935) by Frances Rogers and Alice Beard. Gertrude Hartman told true stories of the inventions that have contributed to modern civilization in *Machines and the Men Who Made the World of Industry* (1939). Katherine Shippen in *The Bright Design* (1949) told the stories of the men behind the discovery and the harnessing of electrical energy. Miss Shippen shared her enthusiasm for the work of great biologists in *Men, Microscopes, and Living Things* (1955) and told the story of the development of medicine in *Men of Medicine* (1957), both exceptionally well illustrated by Anthony Ravielli. Lonzo Anderson in *Bag of Smoke* (1942) told the lively story of the Montgolfiers and their experiments with balloons, picturing vividly France in the days of

Louis XVI and the excitement caused by these early experiments in aeronautics.

William H. Crouse deftly removed the veil of mystery from radar and atomic energy, and such everyday wonders as the telephone, motion pictures, and television in *Understanding Science* (1948). M. Ilin made amusing an account of man's efforts and devices for the measurement of time in *What Time Is It? The Story of Clocks* (1932) and his story covering the earliest forms of writing and record-keeping to the present in *Black on White, The Story of Books* (1932). Thomas Hibben told the history of tools in *The Carpenter's Tool Chest* (1933), showing also, with profuse and fascinating illustrations, their development and uses.

From the beginning of the fifties to the mid-sixties children's books on almost every aspect of science accumulated with such rapidity that the problem of evaluating and reviewing them became almost insurmountable. Science books for children and young people were reviewed occasionally in science magazines, from time to time professional groups compiled lists of recommended titles, and librarians throughout the country met the challenge in various ways. Scientific changes and new developments occur so rapidly that science books need constant revision and updating. Many become obsolete after a few years and, although especially important in the lives of children of the technological age, they can rarely be considered literature and seldom influence literary trends.

Scientists often, however, are writers and, now and then, excerpts of their writings have been presented so skillfully that they are significant additions to children's literature. In *Stars, Mosquitoes and Crocodiles* (1962) Millicent E. Selsam selected excerpts from Alexander von Humboldt's thirty-some volumes that cover five years and more than forty thousand miles of travel in the Orinoco, Amazon, and Andes of South America, joining the passages with biographical and interpretive connecting links. This direct presentation of Von Humbolt's observations is far more interesting and provocative than accounts about him. Dorothy Shuttlesworth's *A Sense of Wonder* (1963) is made up of selections from the work of twenty writers on nature, among them Roy Chapman Andrews, Rachel Carson, Raymond Ditmars, Jean Henri Fabre, Albert Einstein, and John Muir.

For the general reader Russell Freedman's *2000 Years of Space Travel* (1963) is of great interest. It is primarily a history of the *idea* of space travel that has fascinated man, probably, from his beginning. Ancient theories about the universe, scientific discoveries, classic tales of science fiction from Lucian's *True History* and Francis Godwin's *The Man in the Moon*, to the stories by Poe, Jules Verne, and H. G. Wells are included, and the relationships between the dreams and stories and the discoveries are shown.

Although, by official reckoning, the space age began on October 4, 1957 with the Russian launching into orbit of Sputnik I, the earth's first artificial satellite, factual books for young people about space ships and space travel had been appearing from the beginning of the fifties. By 1954 publication could scarcely keep pace with scientific development, and by 1957, with the launching of Sputnik, the quantity of books on space, space travel, planets, and related subjects was overwhelming. Only a few authors and books can be mentioned in an attempt to indicate the areas of special emphasis in science publications for children.

On July 1, 1957, began the greatest coordinated scientific effort in history, the International Geophysical Year in which approximately thirty thousand scientists from sixty-six countries participated. When the I.G.Y. ended on December 31, 1958, scientific investigations had been carried out in fourteen different areas, including space, oceanography, glaciology, and meteorology; and a new organization had been founded, the International Geophysical Cooperation. Children's books soon reflected the widening interest in all areas of science. Margaret O. Hyde's *Exploring Earth and Space* (1957) gave background on the aims and projects of the I.G.Y. and looked ahead to important developments that would probably result from the massive scientific effort.

Isaac Asimov, associate professor of biochemistry at Boston University, author of science fiction, and a most versatile writer also in the fields of nonfiction science, history, and etymology, was writing for young people as well as for adults all through the fifties and sixties. Among his many books are *Inside the Atom* (1956), *Words of Science* (1959), *Satellites in Outer Space* (1960), and *The Kingdom of the Sun* (1960), the history of man's comprehension of the solar system. His *The Clock We Live On* (1959), a comprehensive discussion of time, brings in astronomy, geography, history, and even psychology to help in the understanding of clocks and calendars. The zest, clarity, and persuasion of Mr. Asimov's writing give interest to any subject. His *The Kite That Won the Revolution* (1963) is a most original and imaginative mingling of science and history. Tracing the history of electricity up to Benjamin Franklin's time, he showed how Franklin's scientific achievements won the interest and opened the doors of the French aristocrats, who provided money and men to make possible the victory of the American Revolution.

Franklyn M. Branley, Associate Astronomer of the American Museum-Hayden Planetarium, New York City, began his career as a teacher, his own driving interest in science stemming from his response to the enthusiasm of his pupils. Among his many books are *Exploring by Satellite* (1957) with unusually good illustrations by Helmut Wimmer, *Solar Energy* (1957), and *The Nine Planets* (1958). Mr. Branley also wrote the text for a number of science-picture books for young elementary school children, including *Snow Is Falling*, illustrated by Helen Stone (1963); and *Flash, Crash, Rumble and Roll*, (1964) illustrated by Ed Emberley, an explanation of thunderstorms.

Lynn Poole's successful television programs were the basis for some of his many books, among them *Diving for Science* (1955), *Ballooning in the Space Age* (1958), *Deep in Caves and Caverns* (1962), and *Insect-Eating Plants* (1963). J. Bronowski and Millicent E. Selsam in *Biography of an Atom* (1965) traced the life of a single carbon atom from its production inside a star, through its broadcasting into space by the star's explosion, to its subsequent coming to earth. Frank X. Ross wrote *Weather; the Science of Meteorology from Ancient Times to the Space Age* (1965). Ruth Brindze discussed tides in *The Rise and Fall of the Seas* (1964). Arthur Clarke in *The Challenge of the Sea* (1960) considered the importance of the underwater frontier to the future of man. Irving Adler's *Time in Your Life* (1955), with illustrations by Ruth Adler, develops the subject more fully than does M. Ilin's *What Time Is It?* Among a number of other books by the Adlers, of great interest to children of elementary school age are *Tools in Your Life* (1956), *Magic House of Numbers* (1957), and *Color in Your Life* (1962).

Herman and Nina Schneider's collaboration resulted in very good reading on a variety of subjects: *You Among the Stars* (1951), *Rocks, Rivers and the Changing Earth* (1952), *More Power to You: A Short History of Power from the Windmill to the Atom* (1953), and many others.

Willy Ley's *Engineer's Dreams* (1954) discusses certain projects that are possible from the point of view of engineering, but quite impossible for reasons unrelated to engineering, some of which, nevertheless, might in time come to pass.

Anthony Ravielli's *Wonders of the Human Body* (1954) is an introduction to anatomy, the brief text accurately technical in the use of scientific terms, imaginative in the analogies to machines and familiar objects, and made especially clear by the author's handsome drawings and diagrams. His *An Adventure in Geometry* (1957) is a beautifully lucid introduction to geometry, illustrated with his own drawings. *String, Straightedge, and Shadow* (1965) by Julia E. Diggins is a lively account of the beginnings of geometry from prehistoric man to Euclid.

The Romance of Writing (1956), written and illustrated by Keith Gordon Irwin, is a clear, comprehensive, and readable account of the evolution of writing from Egyptian hieroglyphics to modern letters, numbers, and signs. In *Map Making: The Art That Became a Science* (1960) Lloyd A. Brown, a noted American cartographer, traced the history of map making from ancient times to the present, showing how what began as a crude form of art developed into an exact science. John Laffin told the intriguing history of cryptography in *Codes and Ciphers: Secret Writing Through the Ages* (1964).

Beryl and Samuel Epstein told the story of antibiotics in *Medicine from Microbes* (1965); and Keith Gordon Irwin told the story of chemistry from ancient alchemy to nuclear fission in *The Romance of Chemistry* (1959), and of physics from Archimedes to Fermi in *The Romance of Physics* (1966).

The coating of scientific fact with fantasy, characteristic of many informational books of the nineteenth century and noticed as late as the nineteen sixties in occasional European children's books, was not generally acceptable in the United States after the thirties. Imaginative approaches, nevertheless, were evident in such books as Marion B. Cothren's *This Is the Moon* (1946) in which, along with a scientific account of the moon, its relation to the earth, and its place in the solar system, were included moon myths from many lands, interesting facts, superstitions, legends, poems, and rhymes about the moon.

The most striking difference between factual books before and after the thirties was in the abundance of illustrations and the obvious collaboration of writer and artist. Author-artists Maud and Miska Petersham pioneered in the field of informational picture books, beginning with *The Story Book of Things We Use* (1933), *The Story Book of Wheels, Ships, Trains, Aircraft* (1935), *The Story Book of Foods from the Field* (1936), and *The Story Book of Things We Wear* (1939). The simple text was kept to a minimum and on every page were illustrations in full color. Few informational picture books were as well loved by young children unless, perhaps, those of Lois Lenski. Beginning with *The Little Auto* (1934) her little picture books in black and white give accurate information, call the parts of trains, automobiles, and everything she describes by their correct names, and show the logical exploits of Pilot Small, Engineer Small, Farmer Small, or whatever name the particular book has called Mr. Small to adopt.

Other informational picture books cover such widely different subjects as Kurt Wiese's *You Can Write Chinese* (1945), Henry Billings' *Diesel Electric 4030* (1950), Madeleine Gekiere's *Who Gave Us . . . Peacocks? Planes? & Ferris Wheels?* (1953), and Al Hine's imaginative approach to geography, *Where in the World Do You Live?* (1962). The science-picture books for which Herbert S. Zim wrote the text, with several different artists collaborating, are on subjects varying from *Parachutes* (1942) to *The Universe* (1961). In *The World is Round* (1963) Anthony Ravielli sketched the history of the changing concepts of the earth's shape in clear text and beautiful pictures in color.

The Wonders of Nature

In 1948 appeared a translation from the Russian, *White Birds Island* by Georgi Skrebitsky, the story of two boys stranded for a day and a night on an island inhabited by countless birds. Despite mannerisms in the writing that detract from the story, the book is significant for beautiful descriptions and an exuberant joy in nature.

This same utter pleasure in nature is found in Addison Webb's *Song of the Seasons* (1950). Here a distinguished naturalist described with humor and beauty the changing seasons and how they affect the lives of many wild creatures.

Wilfrid Bronson had always liked to draw—wild animals, especially. Every possible summer, while he was growing up, he spent on a farm, in a camp, or a mountain hotel, anywhere he could both earn a living and be close to wild things. After art school and then service in the First World War, he was staff artist for five years on a project to create a museum of oceanic animals, making three long voyages into tropical seas. Out of this experience came his first book, *Fingerfins* (1930), the tale of a Sargasso Fish. After an expedition to the Galapagos Islands, he wrote about penguins in *Paddlewings* (1931). *Pollwiggle's Progress* (1932), the story of a bullfrog, was written after exploring around his own home in the Catskills. Of his many books about animal life, one of the most unusual was *Children of the Sea* (1940), the story of the friendship between a small boy and a dolphin, full of accurate and fascinating information on sea life and on dolphins in particular. Whatever the subject, Mr. Bronson's writing is enlivened with imagination and humor.

In *Hexapod Stories* (1920) Edith Patch told the life story of several insects through the year's cycle of changing seasons, showing the pleasure even quite young children could receive from true stories from nature. Her many books stimulated first-hand observation of animal life. Clarence J. Hylander in his series beginning with *Out of Doors in Spring* (1942), and Harriet Huntington in *Let's Go Outdoors* (1939), *Let's Go to the Seashore* (1941), and the others, brought fresh appeal to nature books.

Francesca R. La Monte and Micaela H. Welch, both of the American Museum of Natural History, made an important contribution in *Vanishing Wilderness* (1934), which describes the lives and habits of nineteen animals in danger of becoming extinct.

For four years Clifford H. Pope led one branch of the Central Asiatic Expeditions of the American Museum of Natural History, exploring the eastern half of China to collect vertebrates. *China's Animal Frontier* (1940), his account of the people with whom he worked, his many experiences with the language, transportation, food, and all phases of the expedition as well as the animals that were its object, is entertainingly written and full of humor. This book had been pre-ceded by *Snakes Alive* (1937), an account of adventures hunting snakes in both America and China.

Raymond Ditmars, whose childhood interest in snakes first met with dismay at home and later was accepted reluctantly, led him eventually to a chance to turn his hobby into a profession as a member of the staff of the New York Zoological Park, and won for him many honors from scientific societies. His pleasure and enthusiasm in sharing with his two daughters the fun of collecting and exploring come through the pages of the books he has written for boys and girls. The first, *The Book of Zoography* (1934), which describes the behavior and habitat of various animals, some to be found in the zoo, and other more rare creatures, was followed by several other books, all further interpreted by Helene Carter with beautiful illustrations and pictorial maps.

The Science of Life (1961) by the author-illustrators Lois and Louis Darling is a beautiful book in form and content. The excellent illustra-tions are well integrated with the meaning of the text and arranged to contribute handsomely to the format. Although few books could equal it in the quality of writing and illustrations, it was characteristic of the efforts of scientific writers of the sixties to meet the interest of children, whose learning in many areas of science was accelerating faster than ever before. The book goes into greater depth than the usual review of biology. Both art and the biological sciences have been life-long inter-ests of Louis Darling, who with his artist wife has collaborated on a number of fine books for young people.

Throughout the fifties and sixties Millicent Selsam wrote animated accounts of many aspects of animal life and nature. *The Language of Animals* (1962) is an exploration of animal communication based on the findings of scientific experimentation with fish, reptiles, birds, mam-mals, and insects. *How Animals Live Together* (1963) gives a variety of examples of group behavior. Kathleen Elgin illustrated both books.

Dorothy Sterling's *The Outer Lands: A Natural History Guide to Cape Cod, Martha's Vineyard, Nantucket, Block Island, and Long Island* (1967), illustrated by Winifred Lubell, is a beautiful basic introduction to salt-water ecology.

Glen Rounds's relaxed writing, eloquent with his love of nature, can sharpen observation and inspire pleasure in animals, the outdoors, and the amazing activities and changes that transpire every moment in even the smallest "wildlife preserve." Human beings do not intrude in such life-cycle stories as *Lone Muskrat* (1953) and *Beaver Business* (1960), nor in the delightful sketches of the behavior of birds, small animals, and insects in *Rain in the Woods and Other Small Matters* (1964) and other collections of nature essays. Mr. Rounds's line draw-ings sprinkled through the text enliven his books.

Valley of the Smallest (1966) contains many beautiful descriptions of plant life and animal activities in a valley of the Colorado Rockies. The author, Aileen Fisher, a poet-naturalist, recorded her observations near her mountain home, centering interest on the smallest animal there, the shrew.

In *Animals Nobody Knows* (1940) Ivan Sanderson's concise, delightful text and fine drawings describe twenty-one animals. The importance of illustrations in this and many other books is equal to the text in making animals interesting and clearly understood. Beautiful black crayon drawings by Carl Burger illustrate Will Barker's book on animal hibernation, *Winter-Sleeping Wildlife* (1958). Adrien Stoutenburg's *Wild Animals of the Far West* (1958) is illustrated with excellent drawings by Ruth Robbins.

Jocelyn Arundel's *The Wildlife of Africa* (1965) discusses the relentless destruction of animals and the means by which certain species are being saved from extinction. The author's enthusiasm for animals comes through in her writing, which has basis in first-hand experiences on safaris in Africa and in work for the International Union for Conservation of Natural and National Resources.

Animal Stories Based on Scientific Fact

In 1928 appeared a translation from the German that was hailed as a masterpiece. It was the life story of a forest deer, told by a poet with a deep feeling for nature. The animals spoke and reacted with human emotions to beauty and love and crisis. This was *Bambi* by Felix Salten, published as an adult book but claimed by children who love speaking animals in fantasy and have patience with speaking animals even in books that are supposedly true to life. There are beautiful passages in *Bambi*, and the sympathetic reader may feel that these offset the sentimentality and the humanizing of creatures that are essentially appealing without human attributes.

A number of writers have related the life cycles of wild animals accurately and, recognizing drama inherent in the stories, have written scientifically sound, absorbing books. Ernest Harold Baynes's *Polaris* (1922), the story of an Eskimo dog, was among the first. Alice Gall and Fleming Crew, brother and sister, relived their childhood pleasure in nature in the books they wrote together: *Ringtail* (1933), the story of a raccoon, *Bushy Tail* (1941), the story of a chipmunk, and others. Books by John and Jean George, *Vulpes the Red Fox* (1948), *Vison the Mink* (1949), and the story of a raccoon, *Masked Prowler* (1950), are excellent examples of unfictionized life-cycle stories. Frank Conibear and J. L. Blundell, without any humanizing, revealed the social instinct that controls the life pattern of the beaver in *The Wise One* (1949); and Theodore J. Waldeck's thorough knowledge of the jungle and of the wild animals makes possible the drama of such books as *The White Panther* (1941).

Harold McCracken was little more than a boy when he was working for the Canadian National Railroad, far up in the Canadian Rockies of British Columbia, and hunting bear and deer with the Cree Indians. Later he organized an expedition to collect big-game specimens for the Ohio State Museum and had some extremely hazardous experiences before he succeeded in bringing out five of the giant Alaskan grizzlies. Love of adventure, knowledge of the animals and the country about which he wrote, and the scientist's respect for all creatures gave *The Biggest Bear on Earth* (1943), *The Last of the Sea Otters* (1942), and the rest of his books dignity and excitement.

In addition to his vigorous, well-written stories about dogs—*Big Red* (1945) was the first about champion Irish Setters—Jim Kjelgaard wrote several books about wild animals. His stories, laid almost invariably in mountain, desert, or wilderness, have suspense and atmosphere. People appear but are subordinate to the animals in the books by Joseph Wharton Lippincott, which have scientific accuracy and authentic wilderness settings. *Wilderness Champion* (1944) is the story of a red setter pup lost in the Canadian mountains and raised by a great wolf. *Wahoo Bobcat* (1950), laid in the Florida swampland, is about the friendship between a boy and a hugh bobcat. *Old Bill, the Whooping Crane* (1958) brings home to the reader the importance of conservation programs, but its absorbing interest lies in the reality of the settings and the sense it gives the reader of being an eye witness to the fabulous bird migrations.

Natural Science Picture Books

Dorothy Lathrop's animal pictures, drawn from life, are as beautiful as they are scientifically accurate. *Who Goes There?* (1935) is a story of the animals' Christmas in the winter woods; *Presents for Lupe* (1940) of a South American red squirrel; *Puppies for Keeps* (1943) of four Pekingese puppies. Her love and sympathy for every living creature that glow through all of her books about animals were perfectly expressed in *Let Them Live* (1951). Twenty different varieties of birds and animals are presented, from the snowy egret to the woodchuck, in exquisite pictures and good text, giving a far greater realization of the need to protect wildlife than almost any book on conservation.

Berta and Elmer Hader's knowledge and love of animals is evident in their many books. Outstanding is *The Big Snow* (1948), winner of the Caldecott Medal, an account of the animals during an especially difficult winter, but one that is very beautiful in a picture book.

Mary and Conrad Buff told the story of the first year in the life of two fauns in *Dash and Dart* (1942) with simple rhythmic prose and exquisite pictures. *Big Tree* (1946) is the story of five thousand years in the life of a Sequoia tree; the pictures capture the mood and pattern of the redwood forests.

Photography is obviously of great value in illustrating informational publications especially natural-science books, only a few of which can be mentioned here. In *A Fruit Is Born* (1960) by Jean Michel Guilcher and Robert Henri Noailles the remarkable close-up photographs inspire a sense of awe at the beauty and variety of nature, although the textual presentation of the development of the fruits of different groups of plants is quite matter-of-fact. Excellent photographs by the author illustrate a new approach to the study of seeds in *The Amazing Seeds* (1965) by Ross Hutchins. For *Easter in November* (1964) Lilo Hess focused on Araucana chickens and their laying of eggs in varied pastel colors. Graphic shots show the different stages of the chick's breaking through the shell. *The Gull's Way* (1965) by Louis Darling shows in clear text, numerous drawings, and many beautiful photographs a few weeks in the life of a family of herring gulls on an uninhabited island off the coast of Maine.

In *Life Story* (1962) Virginia Lee Burton presented the story of life on earth as a marvelous drama, each right-hand page a stage setting in full color showing the changes from one geological period to another, with clear, explanatory text opposite each picture. It was an ambitious project, certainly, to present the continuity of life in a picture book, and many years of research went into it. Miss Burton succeeded in making a beautiful book and in giving the reader a sense of his own place in the flow of time and creation.

Millicent E. Selsam wrote the text for a great many science-picture books for young children, including *See Through the Forest* (1956) and *Birth of an Island* (1959) with illustrations by Winifred Lubell, and *See Along the Shore* (1961) with illustrations by Leonard Weisgard. Marie Neurath wrote and illustrated *The Wonder World of Birds* (1953) and several other natural science picture books. Alice Goudey wrote the text and Adrienne Adams made the illustrations for a beautiful book about shells, *Houses from the Sea* (1959), and one about butterflies, *Butterfly Time* (1964). Marie Nonnast illustrated Alice E. Goudey's life-cycle story of the herring gulls in *Graywings* (1964).

I Like Butterflies (1960) by Gladys Conklin, with illustrations by Barbara Latham, and other books about bugs, birds, and lizards are attractive and scientifically accurate, presented from the point of view of young children just beginning to be excited about nature.

The Storm Book (1952) by Charlotte Zolotow, illustrated by Margaret Bloy Graham, with poetic text and beautiful doublespreads in color, makes a thunder storm descending on a little boy's quiet country home a thrilling and wonderful experience.

Art and Architecture

Katharine Gibson's *The Goldsmith of Florence* (1929), illustrated with splendid reproductions, grew out of the author's experiences as a storyteller in the Cleveland Museum of Art. Against vivid historical background is information about unknown craftsmen—the illuminators of manuscripts, the tapestry weavers, medieval woodcarvers and armorers—as well as stories of the great, Cellini, Donatello, Della Robbia, and others.

Writing in the lively style of *A Child's History of the World*, V. M. Hillyer and E. G. Huey told the stories of painting, sculpture, and architecture in *A Child's History of Art* (1933). In *Art in the New Land* (1945) Charlie May Simon told stories of some American artists and their work, from the unknown traveling portrait painters of colonial days to the artists of the twentieth century.

Treasure to See, A Museum Picture-Book (1956) by Leonard Weisgard is a beautiful picture book that imaginatively prepares children for their first visit to a fine arts museum.

In Douglas and Elizabeth MacAgy's *Going for a Walk with a Line: A Step into the World of Modern Art* (1959) examples of contemporary masterpieces are reproduced in full color and in black and white, linked together by brief poetic text to make a stimulating introduction to modern art. In *The Pantheon Story of Art* (1964) Ariane Ruskin told the story of painting and sculpture from cave painting to the present. The writing is lucid and enthusiastic and the book is illustrated generously with excellent reproductions in color and in black and white. In *Famous Artists of the Past* (1964) Alice Elizabeth Chase, on the staff of the Yale University Art Gallery, dramatized the important elements in the lives and work of twenty-seven great painters and sculptors. Her *Famous Paintings* (1951) is an excellent introduction to art. With brief text and beautiful photographic reproductions Marion Downer in *The Story of Design* (1963) showed the development of design in different countries from prehistoric times to the present.

Photographs by Alfred H. Tamarin of frescoes, statues, vases, and other works of art found at Tarquinia are combined with good brief text to give glimpses of an ancient and highly developed civilization in *The Art of the Etruscans* (1967), one of several books about the art of different cultures by Shirley Glubok. Christine Price's *Made in the Middle Ages* (1961), *Made in the Renaissance* (1963), *The Story of Moslem Art* (1964), and *Made in Ancient Greece* (1967) are beautifully designed books. The clear, evocative text and the many reproductions of art objects, and those suggesting everyday occupations, illuminate history.

In a very original book *What's in a Line?* (1951) Leonard Kessler told in rhymed text and in pictures some of the many things a line can do: it can be a name, or tell a story, it can turn into a picture of a house, a wheel, an animal, ". . . because a line is only an idea caught and set down in little marks."

Do You See What I See? (1959) by Helen Borten interprets in brief text and many pictures the world in terms of composition in art. In *A Picture Has a Special Look* (1961) Mrs. Borten showed why different materials make pictures that are different in appearance and in feeling. The special quality of each medium is clearly explained in the text and shown in the pictures: the grainy lines and silveriness of pencil, the roughness or the hard, shiny colors of crayons, the lines fine as hair of the pen, the bold lines and flowing shapes of brush and ink, the transparency of water colors, and so on. The original idea was executed most successfully to make a picture book that is inviting and stimulating.

In *The Blue Cat of Castle Town* (1949) Catherine Cate Coblentz wove an imaginative story around the work of the early craftsmen of Castleton, Vermont. The thread of story tells how a cat happened to be pictured on a carpet that now hangs in the Metropolitan Museum of Art.

In *The Bayeaux Tapestry: The Story of the Norman Conquest: 1066* (1966) by Norman Denny and Josephine Filmer-Sankey the complete tapestry is reproduced as a unified historical narrative to make a very beautiful picture book. On every page text in large type narrates events shown in the illustration; a paragraph in smaller type comments on the background and clarifies details.

Louise Lamprey's *All the Ways of Building* (1933) is a comprehensive and extremely interesting account of architecture in all parts of the world, showing how history, climate, topography, and ways of life have influenced it. Miss Lamprey is one of the writers who link this period of children's books with the early years of the century. Her history of architecture is notable evidence of her understanding of children's wide interests and her belief that books for them should be accurate, interesting, and well written. Among many later books about architecture, Carl E. Hiller's *From Tepees to Towers: A Photographic History of American Architecture* (1967) is an outstanding introduction to the subject.

Music

How Music Grew from Prehistoric Times to the Present Day (1925) by Marion Bauer and Ethel Rose Peyser, an important and comprehensive history of music for young people, was revised in 1939 and brought up to date to include chapters on American and twentieth century music.

Fannie R. Buchanan in *The Story of How Man Made Music*

(1936) traced the history of the different types of musical instruments, the making of a song, of oratorios and operas, the beginning of bands, the stories behind folk music and the great musicians through whose genius certain musical forms have achieved immortality.

The Heritage of Music (1963) by Katherine B. Shippen and Anca Seidlova is a survey of the history and development of Western music from the earliest primitive forms, to experimentation with atonality and electronic music of the twentieth century. Integral to the whole story of man, music is related here to history and ways of life, with perceptive sketches of great composers accenting periods and changes.

Ernest La Prade's *Alice in Orchestralia*, published in 1925, with its information about the instruments of the orchestra set within a fantasy, was full of whimsical plays on words (Alice has an underground ride on a "tuba" and visits the city of Fiddladelphia), but at the end of the book there was a straightforward description of instruments for the child who really wanted to know and perhaps lacked the patience to follow Alice's adventures. In interesting contrast was Harriet Huntington's *Tune Up; The Instruments of the Orchestra and Their Players* (1942) with its simple, concise text and good photographs of instruments in the hands of young players. Mr. La Prade wrote a foreword to this new book about the orchestra, commending Miss Huntington for succeeding in "conveying a suggestion of the esthetic enjoyment which these beguiling contrivances hold for the ear."

Opera Story Books

The narrative adaptation by Frances Frost of Gian-Carlo Menotti's opera *Amahl and the Night Visitors* (1952) preserves the exact dialogue of the opera. Illustrated in black and white and in strong Christmas colors by Roger Duvoisin, the book takes its place as a story that young children can enjoy even without knowledge of the music. It gives pleasure to all ages familiar with the opera.

Warren Chappell's first "musical picture book" was *Peter and the Wolf* (1940). A Russian folk tale, the basis for Serge Prokofieff's opera, presented as an orchestral narrative by Serge Koussevitzky and the Boston Symphony Orchestra, was made into a distinctive book, designed and illustrated in color by Warren Chappell, with the actual music of the important themes included. Other books in the same format followed, the stories of some of them adapted by Mr. Chappell, all of them designed and illustrated by him. Among them are *The Nutcracker* (1958), based on the Alexander Dumas *père* version of the story by E. T. A. Hoffmann with themes from Tchaikovsky's ballet music; *The Sleeping Beauty* (1961) with musical themes also by Tchaikovsky; *The Magic Flute* (1962), Mozart's opera story, adapted by John Updike with Mozart's musical themes included; and *The Ring* (1964) for which John Updike retold *Siegfried*, the third of the four operas comprising Wagner's "Ring" cycle, with the musical themes included.

Songs

Many delightful books of songs appeared through the fifties and sixties, made especially inviting by the illustrations. *A Cat Came Fiddling* (1956) by Paul Kapp was illustrated by Irene Haas. *Frog Went a-Courtin'* (1955), retold by John Langstaff, was illustrated by Feodor Rojankovsky, who received the Caldecott Medal for the illustrations. Mr. Langstaff gathered four very old Christmas carols for *On Christmas Day in the Morning!* (1959) with piano settings by Marshall Woodbridge and detailed illustrations in luminous color by Antony Groves-Raines. The Provençal carol attributed to Nicholas Saboly in the seventeenth century, *Bring A Torch, Jeanette, Isabella* (1963), was made into a picture book by Adrienne Adams, whose glowing illustrations are warm with the beauty and humanity of the traditional festival.

Lullabies and Night Songs (1965), edited by William Engvick with music by Alec Wilder and illustrations by Maurice Sendak, is a large, handsome book; the illustrations in soft colors vary in mood—lively, dreamy, nonsensical. A few of the pictures are reminiscent of Randolph Caldecott, whom Mr. Sendak has recognized as a preceptor and an inspiration. Some of the songs were set to music here for the first time, "as they seem to ask to be sung as well as read. Some of the rollicking ones are not strictly lullabies, but aim to end the day with laughter and delight. These we call night songs. The collection does not pretend to be definitive; it simply celebrates the magic world of a happy, sleepy child."

The Theater

Shakespeare and the Players (1949) by C. Walter Hodges traces the growth of the theater of Elizabethan times. Shakespeare's position is shown and included are brief sketches of other well-known playwrights of the times, information about the Globe Theatre itself, and many details, which Mr. Hodges' interesting sketches make even more clear. In *Shakespeare's Theatre* (1964) Mr. Hodges recounted in concise text and beautiful, detailed illustrations the development of the Elizabethan theater from the early medieval religious dramas to a sixteenth century Globe Theatre performance of Shakespeare's *Julius Caesar*.

Seven Stages (1965) by Geoffrey Trease traces the rise to fame of seven people against the brilliant settings of their theater worlds, "each memorable for the strength of personal achievement in the theater arts": Christopher Marlowe, Sarah Siddons, Henry Irving, Molière, Verdi, Jenny Lind, and Anna Pavlova.

In *Pantomime, the Silent Theater* (1964) Douglas and Kari Hunt surveyed the art of pantomime from its primitive beginnings through its development in various countries, to its use in motion pictures, television, and the theater.

In *Punch and Judy; a Play for Puppets* (1965) Ed Emberley contributed a brief history of the puppet Punch and an illustrated cast of characters as an introduction to the script for the famous old Punch and Judy show, and made gaily colored picture sequences to accompany the text.

Agnes de Mille's enthusiasm for the dance and her dedication to it as an art form make *To A Young Dancer; a Handbook* (1962) an inspiration for the dancer and an illuminating experience for appreciative spectators.

Religions of the World

In 1944 Florence Mary Fitch met a need that had long been felt in *One God: The Ways We Worship Him*. With beautiful photographs and clear text it describes the ways of worship, religious festivals, and observances of Jews, Catholics, and Protestants. In *Their Search for God, Ways of Worship in the Orient* (1947), Miss Fitch showed not only the important ceremonies and festivals relating to the religions of the Orient but religion as an expression of a way of life. Her third book, *Allah, the God of Islam* (1950), is a companion volume to the others, giving in photographs and excellent text the story of Mohammedanism, its history, customs, laws, and the art, music, and ways of the Moslems. Miss Fitch wrote out of a lifetime of study, bringing to boys and girls an understanding of peoples as well as religions.

The Good Ways (1950) by Delight Ansley grew out of a series of discussions and assembly programs on various forms of religion and their place in the world with which the author, a librarian in a preparatory school in Pennsylvania, assisted. She recounted the origins and history of the most important religions of the world and drew interesting comparisons, pointing out the differences between religions and the many points of agreement—"all forms of religion are the attempt of mankind to reach harmony with God."

In *The Story of the World's Religions* (1967) Katharine Savage states as her purpose "to tell the story of the birth and growth of world religions, to fit them into their historical settings, and to outline their basic beliefs." With a straightforward, unbiased approach she showed how ancient forms of worship contributed to the evolvement of the major religions of the present, and illuminated the foundations of faith.

The books mentioned in this chapter suggest the variety and general excellence of a substantial body of informational books that can be sifted from the proliferation of publications appearing between 1920 and 1967. No attempt has been made to list even representative samplings of the hundreds of books covering many subjects that have proved their value through many years and frequent revisions but that are read for pleasure only by ardent young specialists. The purpose here has been to present reminders of books of an informational nature written and illustrated with a verve that extends their appeal beyond the circle of special enthusiasts to the multitude of boys and girls with lively curiosities and open minds waiting to glimpse every bit of wonder and beauty the world can offer them.

Bibliography

Fuller, Muriel. *More Junior Authors*. New York, H. W. Wilson, 1963.

Jaques, Florence Page. "Canoe Country." In Dorothy Shuttlesworth, comp., *A Sense of Wonder: Selections from Great Writers on Nature*. New York, Doubleday, 1963.

Kunitz, Stanley J. and Howard Haycraft, eds. *The Junior Book of Authors*. 2d ed., rev. New York, H. W. Wilson, 1951.

Moulton, Priscilla Landis. "An Experiment in Cooperative Reviewing by Scientists and Librarians." *The Horn Book*, Vol. 42 (June, 1966), pp. 345–349.

· 11 ·

The Artist as Storyteller

Taste, the ability to discriminate, to cast off the false, the unworthy, and to retain the genuine; the capacity to see what is before us, to be alert; the pleasure in what is harmonious and at the same time various; the poise that is born of inner rhythm and balance—all these are best formed in early childhood.

—MARCIA BROWN[1]

The practice of illustration, as I see it, is in one respect quite different from easel or mural painting, for it necessarily refers to something outside itself. The subject matter, the literary content, assumes a new significance, and the illustration must reflect this. From my point of view, the illustrator should not enter upon his task with too fixed a conception; he should not have in mind too pronounced a pattern. The illustration is not pre-composed, but it must be allowed to grow, so to speak, from the seed of the impulse. Upon reading a poem or a work of fiction or history, I *see* a picture, and I go to work . . . and I try to bring the picture to life, to develop and make actual that subjective impression. This subjective impression is, by definition, my own, not the author's although he provides the stimulus.

—BOARDMAN ROBINSON[2]

Looking back through the profusion of picture books in color, in black and white, large and small and many shapes, which have hailed down from publishers' desks and printers' presses for more than forty years, it is difficult to realize that, with the exception of C. B. Falls's *A B C Book*, published in 1923, no significant picture books were published in America in the first seven years of the twenties. Leslie

[1] Marcia Brown, "Distinction in Picture Books," in *Illustrators of Children's Books: 1946–1956*, compiled by Bertha Mahony Miller, Ruth Hill Viguers, and Marcia Dalphin (Boston, The Horn Book, 1958), p. 2.
[2] Quoted in "Bench Marks for Illustrators of Children's Books" by Warren Chappell. *The Horn Book*, Vol. 33 (Oct., 1957), p. 420.

Brooke had kept alive the tradition of the great English picture-book artists of the nineteenth century, entering this decade with the publication of *Ring o' Roses* in 1922, and important books had come from other countries, but not until 1927 did a true picture book make its first appearance in America. If, by a true picture book one means a book in which pictures tell a story with little need of text, there can be no doubt that William Nicholson had accomplished this in *Clever Bill* (1927). The brief text serves the purpose of naming the characters, but the pictures tell the story, and a story full of action and swift movement it is. This was the beginning—a story told in pictures by an English artist but first published in the United States. The next year appeared another landmark in the field of American picture books, *Millions of Cats*.

Writing of Wanda Gág, Lynd Ward said:

> Her *Millions of Cats* was an extension into the field of children's books of those same qualities of freshness and simplicity that distinguished her work in the field of prints. At that time it was still a little heretical for an artist whose reputation was grounded in what the critics call one of the "fine arts" to work seriously and without pretentious apology in the field of illustration for children. The children of America, of course, are immeasurably richer because of what Wanda Gág brought them within the covers of her books.[1]

In reviewing the life of the author-artist of this first true "picture book" by an American artist it seems the most natural thing in the world that *Millions of Cats* should have come into being from the genius of Wanda Gág. It has the sureness of the tale told for generations. It could only be the conception of an artist steeped in traditional lore. At a time when originality of artistic expression was only beginning to be encouraged, Wanda Gág dared to be herself, and the immediate success of her first book proved that children were ready for her fresh expression, which was at the same time perfectly in tune with the storytelling tradition. The pictures of *Millions of Cats* tell the story with vitality and atmosphere; yet the story can stand alone.

Wanda Gág was born in New Ulm, Minnesota, a little European town in the midst of the New World. Her father, Anton Gág, had come with his parents from Bohemia when he was a young boy. Her father was an artist, though he had to turn his talent into very practical channels to earn a livelihood. Her mother, also of Bohemian heritage, had a great deal of artistic ability. Wanda and her five younger sisters and one brother grew up taking drawing as a matter of course. She realized with some surprise when she entered school that to everyone

[1] Lynd Ward, "Wanda Gág, Fellow Artist," *The Horn Book*, Vol. 23 (May-June, 1947), p. 195.

drawing was not as natural as eating and sleeping. Wanda was young when her parents died, but sheer determination and working together saw all the children through high school and Wanda carrying out her artistic ambitions. When she had finally reached the point where she could earn a good living with commercial work she gave it up so that she could devote herself to her own artistic expression. Among the things she had done during the lean years were some children's stories, which had not met with any enthusiasm so she had filed them away among her rejections. Her efforts to draw in her own way had gratifying results. She found her work selling; a New York gallery gave her a one-man show, and she came to the attention of Ernestine Evans on the staff of a new publishing company. The nucleus of *Millions of Cats* came out of the "Rejection Box" and in 1928 Wanda Gág was launched on a career in which she could share her rich talent and her warm joyful spirit in pictures and stories. In the words of Anne Carroll Moore she "became quite unconsciously a regenerative force in the field of children's books, published in the United States from the year 1928."[1]

By 1930 new developments in photo-offset lithography were available in America, making possible large editions of illustrated books at low cost. Artists who had been experimenting through the twenties were now to see children's books as a great potential outlet for their genius; were to find themselves as well known and well loved by the children as the storytellers. From this time on, the importance of illustration in children's books was granted, and the true picture book, the book in which the pictures tell the story without the need of text, or in which the story can be told only by the complete integration of pictures and text, came into its own in America.

By the first half of the thirties the snowball was rolling. Wanda Gág had published three more picture books—*The Funny Thing* (1929) and *Snippy and Snappy* (1931) and her *A B C Bunny* (1933), illustrated with beautiful lithographs, full of action and rhythm, one of the loveliest of picture books for young children. Emma Brock's first picture book, *Runaway Sardine* (1929), had appeared. Kurt Wiese had started writing and illustrating his own picture books and had made the gay pictures for Marjorie Flack's *The Story About Ping* (1933), the small duck on the Yangtze River, destined to be a favorite with small children for years to come. Helen Sewell turned from illustrating other people's stories to making her own first picture book, *A Head for Happy* (1931), and Elizabeth MacKinstry made of the story of *Aladdin and the Wonderful Lamp* (1935) a brilliant, rich picture book. L. Leslie Brooke formed a link with an earlier period with *Johnny Crow's New Garden* (1935) and his irresistible illustrations for Robert Charles's

---

[1] Anne Carroll Moore, "Art for Art's Sake," *The Horn Book*, Vol. 23 (May-June, 1947), p. 157.

nonsense rhyme, *Roundabout Turn* (1930). Ellis Credle published a picture book with a distinctly regional atmosphere and childlike humor, *Down, Down the Mountain* (1934), a story of two children who lived high in the Blue Ridge Mountains. Applying the centuries-old art of batik to paper, Marie Hall Ets very effectively illustrated her own story, *Mr. Penny* (1935), engaging nonsense about the animals on kind old Mr. Penny's farm.

All during the first thirty years of the century, European as well as English picture books were imported and occasionally published in English translation. Siri Andrews translated from the Swedish *Aunt Green, Aunt Brown, and Aunt Lavender* (1928) and others of Elsa Beskow's picture books that had been delighting children in Sweden since 1892. *L'Histoire de Babar, le Petit Éléphant* by Jean de Brunhoff (1899–1937) made a great stir in Paris in 1931 and two years later *The Story of Babar* (1933) was published in the United States. This was the beginning of a long series of books about the elephant Babar, which was continued after the artist's death by his son Laurent.

In 1930 Bertha Mahony and Elinor Whitney compiled *Contemporary Illustrators of Children's Books* under the imprint of The Bookshop for Boys and Girls, Women's Educational and Industrial Union in Boston. This book was the first to give serious consideration to children's book illustration. A more ambitious project was *Illustrators of Children's Books: 1744–1945*, compiled by Bertha E. Mahony, Louise Payson Latimer, and Beulah Folmsbee, including historical and critical essays on children's book illustration in England and America, a chapter by Maria Cimino on Foreign Picture Books in a Children's Library, other chapters showing the vitality and various aspects of the contributions of artists to books for children, and biographical sketches and bibliographies of more than three hundred and fifty illustrators living at the time of the compilation of the book. In 1958 a supplement was published, including five hundred artists and bringing up to 1956 the consideration of illustrators of children's books.[1] Since the publication of those three volumes the interest in children's book illustration has grown tremendously and numerous books on the subject are now available.

The importance of the illustrator has been pointed up frequently in this volume, for he has come to be a partner in the creation of many books for the youngest children. Picture books and profusely illustrated books have been mentioned in other chapters when they could be naturally or appropriately included in the discussion of specific subjects or writers. The term "children's literature" now includes the best that

---

[1] A second supplement, *Illustrators of Children's Books: 1956–1966*, compiled by Lee Kingman, Joanna Foster, and Ruth Giles Lontoft, was published by The Horn Book, in 1968.

both writers and artists have contributed to boys and girls. Neither a detailed discussion of the contributions of the great children's book illustrators, nor their philosophies and techniques can be covered here. In this chapter it is possible to include only a few of the true picture books and other illustrated books for young children—often referred to as picture-story books—that represent those artists who have already influenced children's books and those whose work has so universal an appeal that it may survive to stand forth in later histories of the children's books of our period.

Throughout the study of American children's books one is impressed by the number of authors and artists who came from many parts of the world to make their home in America and who have enriched American children's literature by their unique contributions. Fritz Eichenberg, Ludwig Bemelmans, Roger Duvoisin, Feodor Rojankovsky, Jean Charlot, Rafaello Busoni, René D'Harnoncourt, Fritz Kredel, Miska Petersham, the d'Aulaires, Beni Montresor, Leo Lionni, and Tomi Ungerer are only a few of them.

Shortly after Ingri and Edgar Parin d'Aulaire had come to live in the United States, Anne Carroll Moore suggested that they might do a picture book together. At first they had resisted the idea, being fearful that such collaboration would interfere with their work as individual artists. Experimenting, they found that working together on picture books they could make a third distinctive contribution, which also gave them pleasure and satisfaction. Their first book, *The Magic Rug* (1931), was a colorful picture-story book illustrated with lithographs done directly on stone, a technique which they have continued to use in many other books. *Ola* (1932) was a picture book of a boy's wintertime adventures in Norway, authentic both in detail and spirit, with large lithographs in full color and in black and white. Other books drawn from the background of Ingri's happy childhood in Norway appeared, but their new homeland interested them to such an extent that many of their books have been interpretations of the history and spirit of America.

In the latter half of the thirties new artists entered the field with distinguished books in great variety. *Little Tim and the Brave Sea Captain* (1936) by the English artist Edward Ardizzone brought real sea adventure to the young child with dramatic pictures of life on shipboard and a storm at sea. The Caldecott Award was established in 1938 and the first artist to receive the medal was Dorothy P. Lathrop for *Animals of the Bible* (1937). In *Mei Li* (1938), the second book to win the Caldecott Medal, Thomas Handforth told an appealing story of a small Chinese girl's adventures at the New Year fair and caught the magic of North China in beautiful pictures as no other picture book artist has yet done; Ludwig Bemelmans' enchanting *Madeline*

(1939) with its gay colored pictures was straight out of Paris; *Andy and the Lion* (1938) proved that the medium of the picture book was not too limited for even the vigor and scope of James Daugherty's drawings, and introduced a real American boy into picture books. Munro Leaf and Robert Lawson collaborated to create a wonderful bit of satire, *The Story of Ferdinand* (1936), and later a gay glimpse of Scotland, *Wee Gillis* (1938); and Robert Lawson won the Caldecott Medal for *They Were Strong and Good* (1940). Dr. Seuss's first book, *And to Think that I Saw It on Mulberry Street* (1937), introduced a new master of nonsense.

Originality and variety marked this rich era of picture books. There was a welcome for the most fantastic nonsense, for the delicately illustrated tiny books of Tasha Tudor, and for the dignified beauty of *I Am a Pueblo Indian Girl* (1939) by a young American Indian, Louise Abeita, with pictures by artists from Navajo, Apache, and Pueblo tribes.

Notable among picture-book artists who, in the thirties, were moving away from traditional styles and techniques were Roger Duvoisin and Leonard Weisgard. Working through more than thirty years, they continued to show fresh viewpoints, never losing their ability to speak directly to children. Both of them have written the stories for some of their books; both also have given sensitive, creative interpretation to the writing of others. Alvin Tresselt wrote the text for several of Mr. Duvoisin's books.

Leonard Weisgard and Margaret Wise Brown (1910–1952) began collaborating on picture books in the thirties. Mr. Weisgard illustrated nearly one fourth—more than any other artist—of Margaret Wise Brown's approximately one hundred books. One of her publishers, William R. Scott, spoke of her stories having "an elusive quality that was Margaret Wise Brown" and "simplicity, directness, humor, unexpectedness, respect for the reader and a sense of the importance of living."[1] She herself spoke of children wanting "words better arranged than their own, and a few gorgeous big grownup words to bite on."[2]

At the beginning of the forties H. A. Rey introduced *Curious George* (1941), the first of a series of funny stories about an adventurous little monkey. Louis Slobodkin was inspired by his small sons to make his first picture books, *Magic Michael* (1944) and *Friendly Animals* (1944). Marie Hall Ets wrote an enchantingly childlike book, *In the Forest* (1944), illustrating it in black and white, using her familiar paper batik method.

[1] Louise Seaman Bechtel, "Margaret Wise Brown, 'Laureate of the Nursery,'" *The Horn Book*, Vol. 34 (June, 1958), p. 184.
[2] *Ibid.*, p. 180.

In the thirties, when her sons were at "the picture book age," Virginia Lee Burton (1909–1968) had begun making picture books, among them *Mike Mulligan and His Steam Shovel* (1939). *The Little House* (1942) for which Miss Burton received the Caldecott Medal is a particularly beautiful example of color and design in picture books, but it has drama, too, in the changing seasons, and in the gigantic city growing close and black about the little house. Another story about machines, so loved by small boys, followed—*Katy and the Big Snow* (1943), Katy being a snow shovel and "the pride and joy of the Gloucester Highway Department." Virginia Lee Burton and her husband, George Demetrios, a sculptor and teacher, founded the Folly Cove Designers in Gloucester, Massachusetts.

Robert McCloskey's *Lentil* (1940) marked the second entrance of an American boy into a picture book and showed a typical, small American town at the beginning of the century. His first Caldecott Medal winner, *Make Way for Ducklings* (1941), is clearly set in Boston but it tells a story that delights children everywhere and within a few years became recognized as a classic. His *Blueberries for Sal* (1948) is fragrant with the pines and sundrenched bushes of Mr. McCloskey's Maine Island home and warm with family closeness and the fun of summer adventures.

Lynd Ward illustrated a number of books, but his entrance into picture books was made with his illustrations for Hildegarde Hoyt Swift's *Little Red Lighthouse* (1942).

The variety in subject matter as well as in artistic treatment in several early winners of the Caldecott Medal is interesting. Louis Slobodkin's casually humorous, slightly impressionistic drawings illustrate James Thurber's fairy tale, *Many Moons* (1943). Elizabeth Orton Jones's idealized children illustrate Rachel Field's *Prayer for a Child* (1944). Maud and Miska Petersham's illustrations for *The Rooster Crows* (1945), a book of American rhymes and jingles, have crispness and action. In the next two years the medal went to two very different examples of mood-creating, rather than storytelling, picture books: *Little Island* (1946) by Golden MacDonald, a penname for Margaret Wise Brown, illustrated by Leonard Weisgard, and *White Snow, Bright Snow* (1947) by Alvin Tresselt, illustrated by Roger Duvoisin.

Alice Dalgliesh, children's book editor for Charles Scribner's Sons, gave Leo Politi the incentive to write and illustrate *Pedro, the Angel of Olvera Street* (1946). *Pedro, Juanita* (1948), and his Caldecott Medal winner, *Song of the Swallows* (1949), show his enjoyment of the warmth and color of the Mexican heritage of southern California. *Timothy Turtle* (1946) by Al Graham, with pictures by Tony Palazzo, demonstrates fine collaboration of artist and author. Bettina told with lovely colors and childlike imagination and humor the story of the little donkey *Cocolo* (1948) on a Mediterranean island where she had spent childhood summers. Dahlov Ipcar wrote and illustrated *Animal Hide and Seek* (1947). Mark Simont and Ruth Krauss in *The Happy Day* (1949) showed that color was not always needed to create atmosphere, that text could be brief and still consequential, and that artist and author working together could achieve perfect unity in a book. Marcia Brown in *Little Carousel* (1946) and *Henry Fisherman* (1949) showed her understanding of children everywhere, her appreciation of the potentialities of the modern picture book, and suggested the versatility with which she would be able to meet the demands of other books.

Then came the nineteen-fifties, and the deluge. Despite the overwhelming mass of cheaply produced, garishly illustrated publications, the discerning adult could find well-written, well-illustrated books. Artists already known from the forties were adding new titles to the parade of picture books: Fritz Eichenberg, Bettina, Edward Ardizzone, Leonard Weisgard, Feodor Rojankovsky, Roger Duvoisin, Leo Politi, Berta and Elmer Hader, Maud and Miska Petersham, Garth Williams. Ludwig Bemelmans wrote and illustrated two more Madeline books, one of which, *Madeline's Rescue* (1953), won the Caldecott Award. Lynd Ward's *The Biggest Bear* (1952), also a Caldecott Medal winner, a vigorous story of the northern woods, is strong in humor despite the somber darkness of the watercolor drawings. Will Lipkind and Nicholas Mordvinoff began collaborating on picture books, beginning with *The Two Reds* (1950), with the artist Mr. Mordvinoff, winning the Caldecott Medal for *Finders Keepers* (1951), and continuing beyond the decade. Dahlov Ipcar wrote and illustrated in strong flat colors *One Horse Farm* (1950) and other animal books. Françoise Seignobosc, a French artist, with the pseudonym Françoise, who worked closely with her American publisher, had earlier illustrated a Mother Goose and an ABC, but her lovely childlike storytelling picture books began with *Jeanne-Marie Counts Her Sheep* (1951), illustrated in spring-garden colors. English artist Rowland Emett made a picture book about the famous engine in *Punch*, *New World for Nellie* (1952), a nonsense extravaganza in delicate line-and-wash drawings.

Marc Simont's illustrations for Janice May Udry's *A Tree Is Nice* (1956) received the Caldecott Medal. Marie Hall Ets, in addition to other books in the style of *In the Forest* wrote and illustrated *Play With Me* (1955), a gentle story, with pictures in soft colors, for the youngest children. Her illustrations for *Nine Days to Christmas* (1959), a Mexican story on which she had collaborated with Aurora Labastida, received the Caldecott Award. Marcia Brown made several picture books, each one different from the others in subject, style, and technique, including *Dick Whittington and His Cat* (1950) and her lovely interpretation of an Andersen tale, *The Steadfast Tin Soldier* (1953). Barbara Cooney, already known for her illustrations for stories for older children, retold one of Chaucer's *Canterbury Tales* and illustrated it in a stunning picture book, *Chanticleer and the Fox* (1958), which received the Caldecott Medal. Taro Yashima, inspired by his little daughter, drew on his childhood in Japan to create a beautiful book, *The Village Tree* (1953), and several others—one of the strongest and most unusual being *Crow Boy* (1955). William Pène du Bois created his most beautiful picture book, *Lion* (1956). Robert McCloskey collaborated with Ruth Sawyer to make a lively picture book with genuine folk-tale quality, *Journey Cake, Ho!* (1953). Two of his new books were more important for mood and atmosphere than plot: *One Morning in Maine* (1952), and his first picture book in color, *Time of Wonder* (1957), for which Mr. McCloskey received the Caldecott Medal a second time. André François illustrated John Symonds' lively story, *Magic Currant Bun* (1952). In *See and Say* (1955) Antonio Frasconi with three- and four-color woodcuts created a very contemporary picture book of objects, each one identified in four languages. Juliet Kepes's *Beasts from a Brush* (1955) is a most unusual picture book with line drawings of beasts straight from the imagination of an artist who saw them ". . . on walls, in puddles, in spludges/ In ink drops and scratches and all sorts of smudges/ In clouds in the sky and cracks in a storm . . ." and drew them to entertain her own children. A number of picture books with lively stories, the kind young children return to again and again, appeared in the fifties: the first of a popular series, *The Happy Lion* (1954) by Louise Fatio illustrated by Roger Duvoisin; the first of Eve Titus's stories about a resourceful mouse, *Anatole* (1956), illustrated by Paul Galdone; Tomi Ungerer's *Crictor*, (1958) about a friendly boa constrictor; Phyllis Krasilovsky's *The Cow Who Fell into the Canal* (1957) illustrated by Peter Spier; Gene Zion's stories about the dog Harry, illustrated by Margaret Bloy Graham, beginning with *Harry the Dirty Dog* (1956); Don Freeman's *Pet of the Met* (1953) about another enterprising mouse; and James Flora's *The Fabulous Firework Family* (1955).

Many of the artists of the fifties continued making picture books through the sixties: Taro Yashima, Lynd Ward, Marcia Brown, Don Freeman, Margaret Bloy Graham. Peter Spier, who had drawn on memories of childhood in Holland for *The Cow Who Fell in the Canal*, illustrated with lovely autumn colors and fascinating detail an old song, *The Fox Went Out on a Chilly Night* (1961). Roger Duvoisin made an especially beautiful book with text by Alvin Tresselt, *Hide and Seek Fog* (1965). Tomi Ungerer wrote and illustrated *The Three Robbers* (1962), which has more plot and suspense than his others and as much amusement. Among several beautiful books by Leo Lionni, *Inch by Inch* (1960) with its spacious pages is especially satisfying to the youngest children. Garth Williams illustrated the first of a series of engaging moral tales by Russell Hoban, *Bedtime for Frances* (1960). Barbara Cooney moved from the scratchboard to other media and techniques for a fresh, amusing book made from Francis Steegmuller's French translation of "The Owl and the Pussy-Cat," *Le Hibou et la Poussiquette* (1961), and for a harmoniously illustrated edition of the old rhyme, *The Courtship, Merry Marriage, and Feast of Cock Robin and Jenny Wren, to which is added the Doleful Death of Cock Robin* (1965). Kurt Wiese illustrated Claire Huchet Bishop's accumulative counting story, *Twenty- two Bears* (1964). Evaline Ness, who through the fifties had illustrated many books for older children, began illustrating picture books, *Lonely Maria* (1960) by Elizabeth Coatsworth, several folk tales, and *Sam, Bangs, and Moonshine* (1966) for which she received the Caldecott Award. Beni Montresor, after illustrating several fanciful stories of his own, made the pictures for *May I Bring a Friend* (1964) by Beatrice Schenk de Regniers, a beautifully designed book, childlike in conception, for which he received the Caldecott Medal. Mr. Montresor, a stage designer, found picture books a natural extension of his art. *The Magic Flute* (1966) with text by Stephen Spender was based on his sets for a new production by the New York City Opera Company of the Mozart opera.

Ezra Jack Keats was illustrating during the fifties, but he became known as a picture-book artist during the sixties, received the Caldecott Medal for *The Snowy Day* (1962), and showed in the full-color pictures for *Jennie's Hat* (1966) unusually imaginative use of college. Many of Margot Zemach's illustrations have been for folk-tale picture books. Her *Mommy, Buy Me a China Doll* (1966) is an adaptation by Harve Zemach of an Ozark folk song, illustrated harmoniously with earthy reds and browns. Ed Emberley's strong sense of design is evident in *One Wide River to Cross* (1966), an adaptation by Barbara Emberley of a Negro spiritual, and in his Caldecott Medal winner, *Drummer Hoff* (1967). Clement Hurd with linoleum-block prints on the grain of weathered wood created pictures that are soft, flowing, and wet looking, most fitting for the story by Evans G. Valens, Jr., of two flying fish, *Wingfin and Topple* (1962). Uri Shulevitz showed his closeness to the child's world of fantasy— a city child—in *One Monday Morning* (1967). Ati Forberg's illustrations for Dorothy Levenson's *The Magic Carousel* (1967) have swift flowing movement and strong imaginative quality. John Larrecq made an enchanting picture book of Theodora Kroeber's *A Green Christmas* (1967), the story of two Colorado children's first California Christmas.

Contemporary Japan was presented in picture books by Masako Matsuno, illustrated by Kazue Mizumura; Thailand by Jacqueline Ayer. Both Japan and Thailand inspired books written and illustrated by Arnold Dobrin.

A number of amusing, adroit little books were published during the fifties and sixties like Ruth Krauss's book of "definitions," *A Hole Is to Dig* (1952), illustrated by Maurice Sendak, or Sesyle Joslin's *There Is a Dragon in My Bed* (1961), illustrated by Irene Haas. These meant more to adults than to children, and may have helped to capture the sophisticated interest in children's books. With every generation, adults must be won to the idea that good children's books have interest and vitality as do any books that qualify as literature. The occasional engaging tour de force is sometimes a lure.

Maurice Sendak's *Where the Wild Things Are* (1963) was welcomed immediately by children, more tentatively by adults, and received the Caldecott Medal. The first children's book Mr. Sendak had illustrated was Marcel Aymé's *The Wonderful Farm* (1951). Then came *A Hole Is to Dig* (1952). All through the fifties his illustrations extended the text or gave an extra dimension to the stories of others. The first book he both wrote and illustrated was *Kenny's Window* (1956). In his paper accepting the Caldecott Medal for *Where the Wild Things Are* (1963) he paid tribute to Randolph Caldecott as "one of my favorite teachers":

> One can forever delight in the liveliness and physical ease of Caldecott's picture books, in his ingenious and playful elaborations on a given text. But so far as I am concerned, these enviable qualities only begin to explain Caldecott's supremacy. For me, his greatness lies in the truthfulness of his personal vision of life.[1]

Mr. Sendak expressed his own dedication behind his work thus:

> It is my involvement with this inescapable fact of childhood— the awful vulnerability of children and their struggle to make themselves King of all Wild Things—that gives my work whatever truth and passion it may have.[2]

Most of the great illustrators and writers for children have felt a similar dedication. Most of them, too, have not lost contact with the inner child and so have been able to speak naturally to children. Mr. Sendak not only understands the uniqueness of those who can communicate directly with childhood, he is articulate. He has a capacity to

[1] Maurice Sendak, "Caldecott Award Acceptance." Lee Kingman, ed., *Newbery and Caldecott Medal Books: 1956–1965* (Boston, The Horn Book, 1965), p. 248.
[2] *Ibid.*, p. 250.

put into words what many only feel, and has done much in a seemingly crass, insensitive era to raise the status of literature for children.

One of the most unusual picture books to be published in the United States was *The Animal Frolic* (1954). That a picture book for twentieth century children could come out of twelfth century Japan is not a likely thought. But Velma Varner had seen the special Exhibit of Japanese Painting and Art at the Metropolitan Museum of Art in 1953 and had realized that the frolicking rabbits, monkeys, and frogs of Toba Sojo's "Scroll of Animals" had

> all the simplicity, vigor, humor, artistry, and story appeal that we dream of finding in books for children. Here was a great work of art that had never before been seen in this country and in another few months would again be tucked away in the Temple of Kozanji in Kyoto, Japan. It needed to be made available to children.[1]

Miss Varner wrote the brief text and many people cooperated in the accomplishment of the project of making a beautiful picture book from the masterpiece of Japanese art.

Throughout the fifties and sixties the importation of picture books from abroad accelerated steadily. *A Bell for Ursli* (1950) by Selina Chönz introduced Alois Carigiet's extraordinary pictures, as brilliant and clear as the atmosphere of the mountain setting. Later books, however, were disappointing because the stories lacked substance and the pictures varied little in composition and technique from those in his first books. Many European picture books were collections of beautiful or unusual paintings tied together with very slight text. These books did not satisfy children who look for a good story. Many other books, however, were immediately enjoyed. The work of Edward Ardizzone, Felix Hoffmann, Hans Fischer, and Raymond Briggs has been mentioned. Among others whose books have brought continuing pleasure are Celestino Piatti, Harald Wiberg, Egon Mathiesen, Paul Nussbaumer, Rainey Bennett, Hans P. Schaad, and Fuku Akino.

From England came books by Victor Ambrus and William Stobbs, both of whom had illustrated many books for older children before turning, in the sixties, to picture books. Beginning with *Brian Wildsmith's A B C* (1963), Mr. Wildsmith created a series of brilliant picture books, including individual books made from three fables of La Fontaine. As a color artist Mr. Wildsmith has few peers. The tendency, however, to allow the pictures to overpower the text was noted in his collection of Mother Goose rhymes.

An Italian artist who has given boundless delight to American children ever since several of his "toy books" were published in the

[1] Velma Varner, "The Scroll of Animals," *The Horn Book*, Vol. 30 (April, 1954), p. 70.

United States during the fifties is Bruno Munari. *Bruno Munari's A B C* (1960) and *Bruno Munari's Zoo* (1963) are outstanding among picture books of the sixties published in the United States. Maria Cimino wrote:

> Bruno Munari's greatness lies, I think, in his view of the world, which is personal and poetic. His extraordinary originality and his rightness as a creator of children's books rest in turn on the fact that for all his technical proficiency and plastic skills he has been able to retain the fresh eye of childhood and an untrammelled imagination. It is not their formal beauty alone, it is above all their vitality and spontaneity, that make his picture books unforgettable.[1]

The Artist Versus the Comic Book

The problem of the so-called comic book, the twentieth century embodiment of sensational material that has plagued parents, educators, writers, and artists for generations, was met in various ways. Parents whose children had from infancy, poetry, stories, and well-written, well-illustrated books that truly *entertained* found that the "comics" were but a passing phase. Librarians were challenged to keep their collections lively, their libraries inviting, and to emphasize books that were exciting and truly funny. Artists felt a special challenge, for they, more than others, recognized in the comic book the slipshod techniques, the poor drawing, the insult to children's inherent artistic taste. Helen Sewell, not content merely to regret the hold of the comics on children, set out to analyze it, deciding that their popularity was due to the vigorous subject matter, their availability, and the form itself—a story told in pictures. She was experienced in telling a story in pictures; it remained for her to select subjects to compete with the comics, and this she did in a book called *Three Tall Tales* (1947), stories told in well-drawn pictures that are genuinely comic. Even earlier, Virginia Lee Burton had set out to make a book to compete with the comic books for the interest of her own young sons, the result being *Calico, the Wonder Horse* (1941), a story of cowboys and highway robbers, well drawn, and full of suspense and humor. As early as 1938 Nikolay Radlov in *The Cautious Carp* had used the comic book form to tell some funny stories with very good pictures. The one thing none of these artists could compete with was the availability of the "comics," for the production costs of a well-drawn and well-reproduced picture book could not approach the cheapness of the comic book.

---

[1] Maria Cimino, "The Picture Books of Bruno Munari." In Frances Lander Spain, ed., *Reading Without Boundaries* (The New York Public Library, 1956), p. 54.

Through the years many things have conspired to compete with good books to take the children's time. But though the radio came, children continued to read. Motion pictures, if anything, stimulated the reading of certain books. Comics attracted chiefly the children who had never discovered good books. Television caused consternation for a time. Whatever the future brings, children *who have once known it* will come back to the joy of creation that is waiting for them in books.

Illustrators of Mother Goose

For hundreds of years artists have been illustrating traditional rhymes and stories. Even though thousands of original stories and verses for young children have been published in this century, few rhymes are as spontaneous as Mother Goose, and few stories have the suspense and satisfying plots of traditional folk and fairy tales. Artists, realizing this and remembering their childhood favorites, have turned with obvious delight to the making of picture books from old rhymes and stories.

Maurice Sendak wrote about the difficulty of illustrating Mother Goose, first, because of the elusive quality and then because:

> . . . they have about them a certain baldness that betrays the unwary artist into banalities; the deceptively simple verse seems to slip just out of reach. . . . Characteristic of the best imaginative writing, they evoke their own images, thus placing the artist in the embarrassing position of having to contend with Mother Goose the illustrator as well as the poet.[1]

Each decade has, nevertheless, produced new editions of Mother Goose rhymes. An outline of changing social and educational attitudes and of differing tastes in art might be traced in a study of the many editions of Mother Goose. Only a few published since 1920, distinctive for their illustrations, can be mentioned here: Leslie Brooke's *Ring o' Roses* (1922), in the tradition of Randolph Caldecott, but no mere imitation, has full-page pictures in color and many drawings in black and white and is one of the most satisfying of first books for the youngest children; Joseph Low's *Mother Goose Riddle Rhymes* (1953) is a rebus Mother Goose with brilliantly colored pictures reminiscent of old woodcuts; Marguerite de Angeli's *Book of Nursery and Mother Goose Rhymes* (1954) is comprehensive and illustrated prolifically with lively, happy pictures; Harold Jones's illustrations in lovely color for Kathleen Lines's collection *Lavender's Blue* (1954) have an engaging old-fashioned quality; Philip Reed's *Mother Goose and Nursery*

[1] Maurice Sendak, "Mother Goose's Garnishings," *Book Week*, Oct. 31, 1965, p. 5.

Rhymes (1963) is a beautifully designed book with handsome wood engravings in six colors inspired by the wood cuts in John Newbery's eighteenth century *Mother Goose's Melody.* Barbara Cooney illustrated Hugh Latham's translation *Mother Goose in French* (1964) with gay, suitably Gallic pictures. Raymond Briggs's *The Mother Goose Treasury* (1966), includes over four hundred rhymes and twice as many illustrations. Except for a very few, the rhymes are from the Iona and Peter Opie collection. The book is unified, despite the variety of moods and approaches in the illustrations which catch the many nuances and variations of humor—satiric, earthy, gentle, or funny—in breath-taking exuberance.

Among numerous individual picture books created from Mother Goose are two published in 1967 by Peter Spier and Ed Emberley, both called *London Bridge Is Falling Down.* Mr. Spier's book is done in line and color drawings full of intricate detail; Mr. Emberley's, delicately colored and more contemporary in style, includes the song and the game.

Folk and Fairy Tale Picture Books

Walter Crane in the nineteenth century set a high standard for the illustration of fairy tales with his handsome full-page drawings for "Cinderella," "The Sleeping Beauty," and others. Leslie Brooke at the beginning of the twentieth century again set high standards for the illustration of fairy tales. One of the earliest of American picture-book folk tales was Pura Belpre's translation of a well-loved tale out of her childhood in Puerto Rico, *Perez and Martina* (1932), with Carlos Sanchez's illustrations in bright colors. Boris Artzybasheff reinterpreted a Russian folk tale, *The Seven Simeons* (1937), with brilliant line drawings accompanying his subtle, humorous text. Then came Claire Huchet Bishop's *The Five Chinese Brothers* (1938), a retelling of an old Chinese folk tale perfectly interpreted by Kurt Wiese with irresistibly funny drawings. Josephine Bernhard adapted the Polish tale *Lullaby: Why the Pussycat Washes Himself So Often* (1944) and illustrator Irena Lorentowicz made it into an unusual picture book. A twelve-year-old Chinese boy, Plato Chan, made remarkable drawings for his favorite version of an old tale, which his mother Chan Chih-yi adapted, *The Good Luck Horse* (1943). Marcia Brown, whose ability as an artist and a storyteller had been thoroughly tested in working with children in libraries, retold the old story *Stone Soup* (1947) and illustrated it with pictures that have great humor and folk feeling. Miss Brown made several picture books from old tales, including *Cinderella* (1954) and her Indian fable *Once a Mouse* (1961), illustrated with strong woodcuts in color, both of which won the Caldecott Medal.

The Swiss artist Felix Hoffmann turned *The Sleeping Beauty*

(1960) into an exquisite picture book, *The Seven Ravens*, with the characters in modern dress, into an unusual one, and *The Wolf and the Seven Little Kids* (1959) and *The Four Clever Brothers* (1967) into very amusing ones. Among a number of picture books by Hans Fischer (1909–1958), also Swiss, are adaptations of old tales, including *The Traveling Musicians* (1955), *The Good-for-Nothings* (1957), and *Puss in Boots* (1959). His drawings are witty and alive and were executed in a wonderfully fluid line. Bettina Hürlimann commented, "What animals he draws! Hens, cats, goats, fish, rabbits, ducks—he does not simply draw them but writes them on the paper like letters."[1] Ruth Robbins's retelling of the Russian tale *Baboushka and the Three Kings* (1960) was illustrated by Nicolas Sidjakov, who received the Caldecott Medal for his work. The book is beautifully designed, the stiffness and angularity of the figures, the clean colors—blue, red, and yellow—make the book at once contemporary and strongly traditional.

The illustrations in warm, glowing colors of Adrienne Adams's fairy-tale picture books are full of atmosphere and changing moods. Among them are *The Shoemaker and the Elves* (1960), *Snow White and Rose Red* (1964), and *The Twelve Dancing Princesses* (1966), based on the Lang version. In the same year Uri Shulevitz illustrated the Grimm variant of *The Twelve Dancing Princesses* in flat, poster-like colors, as appropriate for the short, matter-of-fact version as Miss Adams's rich, atmospheric drawings are for the more romantic variant. Evaline Ness made picture books from two of Joseph Jacobs' English tales: *Tom Tit Tot* (1965) and *Mr. Miacca* (1967), the latter set most surprisingly and delightfully in Victorian England. Nonny Hogrogian made a picture book from *Always Room for One More* (1965), Sorche Nic Leodhas's version of an old Scottish song, for which Miss Hogrogian received the Caldecott Medal. She also made an exquisite picture book from Yulya's Russian Lullaby, *Bears Are Sleeping* (1967), and a humorous book from an old Russian story, *A Tale of Stolen Time* (1966), showing her ability to work in different media and techniques.

Paul Galdone made some lively, attractive folk-tale picture books, among them *The Hare and the Tortoise* (1962). Ronni Solbert, Margot Zemach, Janina Domanska, Christine Price, Madeleine Gekiere, and others have created picture books from old tales, each artist bringing his unique vision to the interpretation.

The picture-book folk and fairy tales are a manifestation of the visual–mindedness of the fifties and sixties. For hundreds of years folk and fairy tales were the resource, the stock in trade, of the

---

[1] Bettina Hürlimann, *Three Centuries of Children's Books in Europe* (London, Oxford University Press, 1967), p. 240.

oral storytellers. They were meant to be told and meant to be heard. They had been told and retold and polished in the retelling for so many generations that they sounded right. Suddenly storytellers and listeners vanished. There were only viewers.

The child to whom good picture books are not available misses a great deal of pleasure and a chance to grow in his appreciation of art. The child who has never heard a well-told story, who has never learned to listen, is also deprived. One cannot take the place of the other without loss to the child.

Picture-Story Books

There was no precedent for the picture-story books that came into their own in the 1930's, the first decade of lower reproduction costs, those books in which profuse illustrations further interpret the story but do not supplant the text in importance. Only a few of the great story books of the past made their entrance into the world already adorned with pictures to point up the humor and add an artist's explication of characters and background. Yet in a very few years, especially in books for younger children, the artist attained a place of equal importance with the writer. In many cases this necessary partnership of artist and author has stimulated an artist to experiment in writing his own stories.

Dorothy Lathrop, who was already known for her distinguished illustrations for the books of other authors, was one of the first artists in this decade to turn to the making of her own books. In 1931 appeared her first book, *The Fairy Circus*, and between then and 1962, when *The Dog in the Tapestry Garden* was published, she wrote and illustrated many beautiful picture-story books of small animals. Through the twenties Boris Artzybasheff (1899–1965) had been illustrating the work of others. In *Poor Shaydullah* (1931) he wrote his own story for his drawings. A few, like Ludwig Bemelmans and William Pène du Bois, told stories with words and pictures that seemed to have evolved at the same time. Maud and Miska Petersham's story books of this decade grew out of family relationships—a well-loved aunt and their little son and his friends and toys—and Miska's Hungarian background. *Miki* (1929) was written for their little boy and was full of Miska's memories of his childhood in Hungary.

Berta and Elmer Hader's many picture-story books, full of the warmth of their pleasure in people and of their love for animals, began to appear in this decade, with *Spunky* (1933) taking a secure place among pony stories.

The picture-story book filled a need that had never been met before, had perhaps not even been recognized—that of maintaining the child's interest in books through the difficult and sometimes long period of mastering the mechanics of reading, until his eighth or ninth year. Perhaps experimentation with new techniques in the teaching of reading prolonged this period of learning and made of particular value those books that were more than picture books, but that had pictures in abundance to hold the child's interest. Perhaps the ever increasing number of children to be educated had emphasized the arduousness of the process of learning to read. Whatever its cause, the need was there, and in helping to fill it the picture-story book often became the average adult's idea of "a modern children's book."

This catering to the taste of the adults who buy the books has often led to the emphasizing of form and illustration rather than content, with the result that a beautiful looking book sometimes has only its outward appearance to recommend it, possessing as a book no real substance or quality of permanence. It has led also to the mass production of picture-story books. Among the most expensive types of books to publish, they could only be sold cheaply when produced in large quantities. To do this the publisher has turned printer, or more often printer has become publisher, and writers and illustrators have been commissioned to work as craftsmen rather than as artists. It is not surprising that the bulk of publications for children are merchandise, not literature. Now and then a good book has appeared among the many poor ones, but only occasionally. The vast majority are ephemeral. Like cheap toys they are used, thrown away, and forgotten. The harm they do is in obscuring by their very brightness and availability the real books of which too many grownups are unaware.

Progressive education and the growth of the nursery school movement had their influence in the twenties on realistic writing for young children. Lucy Sprague Mitchell was one of the first advocates of the need of the small child for stories within his own experience, concerned with his modern world. Her *Here and Now Story Book* (1921) told simple little tales of the small child's everyday activities. There was emphasis on the way things feel and sound and look to the young child, with little or no plot. Other writers followed in her lead but few of these stories outlived the twenties. They did serve, however, to bring to the attention of publishers the special needs of the pre-school child. This recognition, coinciding with the popularization of printing processes, gave added impetus to the publication of picture books and picture-story books.

A few realistic stories for children that lived beyond the period were those with definite plot in which the familiar was presented with imagination and humor. *The Poppy Seed Cakes* (1924) by Margery Clark, the pseudonym for Mary E. Clark and Margery C. Quigley, was one of these. *Pelle's New Suit* (1929), Elsa Beskow's one realistic picture book to be published in America, was acceptable to the advocates of the here-and-now school. It has been loved through the years, however, for the very unfamiliarity of its charm in telling how Pelle's new suit grew from his pet sheep's wool to its first wearing by Pelle on a bright Sunday morning. By the forties there were such realistic picture-story books as Lavinia Davis's *Roger and the Fox* (1947), with pictures by Hildegard Woodward, full of a little boy's pleasure in the winter countryside.

For generations the youngest readers have longed for books that they can read for themselves, and for generations all but a few of those books have been the dullest of primers and blatantly vocabularized readers. The focus in the fifties on the need to improve textbooks suddenly threw light on a new field of exploration for writers and artists. *The Cat in the Hat* by Dr. Seuss and *Little Bear* by Else Holmelund Minarik, illustrated by Maurice Sendak, both published in 1957, were received with so much delight that the floodgates opened. Series after series of easy reading picture-story books appeared, far more titles than a child could read during the short period between beginning to read and being ready for more substantial fare. The poorest are only slightly better than the comics. The best of the stories are original and funny, the texts, though simple, are not condescending, nor are the vocabularies obviously limited. Else Minarik and Maurice Sendak collaborated on several about Little Bear, and on *No Fighting, No Biting!* (1958). Betty Baker wrote an engaging Indian story *Little Runner of the Longhouse* (1962) that Arnold Lobel illustrated. Crosby Bonsall wrote and illustrated *What Spot?* (1963) and *The Case of the Hungry Stranger* (1963). Margaret Bloy Graham illustrated *Harry and the Lady Next Door* (1960) by Gene Zion and wrote and illustrated *Be Nice to Spiders* (1967). These and other books proved that simple stories could be told with wit and style.

There is as much variety of subject in picture books and picture-story books as in all of children's literature: foreign background stories like Helen Garrett's gay Mexican tale, *Angelo, the Naughty One* (1944) with pictures by Leo Politi; period stories like Marguerite De Angeli's *Skippack School* (1939), Barbara Cooney's *The Little Juggler* (1961), and Ruth Robbins's *The Emperor and the Drummer Boy* (1962), illustrated by Nicolas Sidjakov; regional stories like Katherine Milhous's books about the Amish people, *Lovina* (1940), and her Caldecott Medal book, *The Egg Tree* (1950); imaginative tales like Elizabeth Orton Jones's *Twig* (1942), William Pène du Bois's *The Three Policemen* (1938) and *The Great Geppy* (1940), Louis Slobodkin's *The Late Cuckoo* (1962) and Hardie Gramatky's *Little Toot on the Thames* (1964); talking animal tales—Esther Averill's series, beginning with *The Cat Club* (1944), Rumer Godden's *Mouse House*

(1957) illustrated by Adrienne Adams, Jan Wahl's *Pleasant Field-mouse* (1964) illustrated by Maurice Sendak, and many of Robert Lawson's books; doll stories like Elizabeth Orton Jones's *Big Susan* (1947), and Pamela Bianco's *The Doll in the Window* (1953) and *Toy Rose* (1957); newly illustrated classic stories—Marcia Brown's interpretation of Andersen's *The Wild Swans* (1963), and Blair Lent's of *The Wave* (1964), adapted by Margaret Hodges from a story by Lafcadio Hearn; stories of the world between wonder and reality, so gracefully entered by way of Madeleine Ley's *Enchanted Eve* (1947) with Edy Le Grand's illustrations, Dorothy Lathrop's *The Dog in the Tapestry Garden* (1962), and Jean Merrill's story inspired by an old Chinese tale, *The Superlative Horse* (1961), with drawings by Ronni Solbert. In these and many others the beauty, humor, and appropriateness of the pictures extend the delight of the well-told stories.

Throughout three decades of picture-book publishing in the United States a strong philosophy has been growing: the child is entitled to the best that writers and artists can give; the picture book is for the child and demands more of the artist than a display of virtuosity.

If it were possible to see an exhibition of only the books mentioned in this chapter one would find represented a tremendous variety of techniques, media, attitudes, subjects, and approaches. Children have the right to all kinds of artistic expression. They should have the best of the past, and the best of their own time, in all its variety—representational, abstract, impressionistic, or unclassifiable.

> Illustrators should be interested in the past, and should learn from it. . . . Shakespeare and Molière drew on their forerunners, Rubens spent much of his time in Spain copying paintings in the Prado, and Rembrandt made dozens of copies of Persian miniatures. In each case the result was something new. It cannot be said too often that art thrives on continuity, and that the work of any individual becomes a part of the general heritage.[1]

Those who merely imitate never reach their goal. Those who learn from their great predecessors may achieve something beyond even their dreams of greatness.

[1] Warren Chappell, "Illustration Today in Children's Books," *The Horn Book*, Vol. 17 (Nov.-Dec., 1941), p. 450.

Bibliography

Bechtel, Louise Seaman. "Margaret Wise Brown, 'Laureate of the Nursery.' " *The Horn Book*, Vol. 34 (June, 1958).
Chappell, Warren. "Bench Marks for Illustrators of Children's Books." *The Horn Book*, Vol. 33 (Oct., 1957).

Chappell, Warren. "Illustration Today in Children's Books." *The Horn Book*, Vol. 17 (Nov.-Dec., 1941).

Gág, Wanda. *Growing Pains*. New York, Coward-McCann, 1940.

Hürlimann, Bettina. *Three Centuries of Children's Books in Europe*. London, Oxford University Press, 1967.

Kingman, Lee, ed. *Newbery and Caldecott Medal Books: 1956–1965*. Boston, The Horn Book, 1965.

Mahony, Bertha E., Louise Payson Latimer, and Beulah Folmsbee, comps. *Illustrators of Children's Books: 1744–1945*. Boston, The Horn Book, 1947.

Miller, Bertha Mahony and Elinor Whitney Field, eds. *Caldecott Medal Books: 1938–1957*. Boston, The Horn Book, 1957.

Miller, Bertha Mahony, Ruth Hill Viguers, and Marcia Dalphin, comps. *Illustrators of Children's Books: 1946–1956*. Boston, The Horn Book, 1958.

Moore, Anne Carroll. "Art for Art's Sake." *The Horn Book*, Vol. 33 (May-June, 1947).

Opie, Iona and Peter, eds. *The Oxford Dictionary of Nursery Rhymes*. London, Oxford University Press, 1951.

Scott, Alma. *Wanda Gág, The Story of an Artist*. Minneapolis, University of Minnesota Press, 1940.

Spain, Frances Lander, ed. *Reading Without Boundaries*. New York, The New York Public Library, 1956.

Varner, Velma. "The Scroll of Animals." *The Horn Book*, Vol. 30 (April, 1954).

Ward, Lynd. "Wanda Gág, Fellow Artist." *The Horn Book*, Vol. 23 (May-June, 1947).

· 12 ·

Poetry

Children see a world in every least thing. It is too bad we have to teach them to forget how to see.—HARRY BEHN[1]

Anyone who has heard, who has really listened, to children playing is surprised and sometimes enchanted by the rhyme and rhythm of their verbal accompaniment to games. Verse, like song, is natural to human life; poetry should never *have* to be introduced to children. It needs only to be kept alive in their minds and hearts by continuous aural availability, and allowed to grow by steady and natural feeding. Nursery rhymes are important but not enough. The child should always have poetry. The great inheritance of poetry is varied enough for every temperament and mood.

Ever since the mid-fifties, poetry has been accepted, even emphasized, as a legitimate part of the school curricula, important to encourage in children's libraries, and necessary, of course, for conscientious parents to give to their offspring. This has been wonderfully encouraging. The hope is that poetry will be as natural a part of children's lives as nursery songs and counting-out rhymes. The danger in *presenting* poetry is that it is so often done self-consciously. The one who presents expects a response. Because the child is skillful at hiding it, we are often unaware of his inner upwelling of emotion. Sometimes when a response is required, the quick spring of wonder vanishes.

Elizabeth Nesbitt, whose portion of this volume includes the years 1890 to 1920, speaks of the period culminating in the work of a "truly great literary artist, whose poetry for children takes its place among the great poetry of the English speaking world." The work of this great literary figure—Walter de la Mare (1873–1956)—links the periods. *Peacock Pie* (1920) was published in the United States seven years and one world war after its publication in England. *Down-Adown Derry* (1922) is poetry about good and bad fairies, lost children, witches, and other magical creatures. *This Year: Next Year*

---

[1] Harry Behn. *Chrysalis* (New York, Harcourt, 1968), p. 43.

(1937) was a collaboration of the poet with Harold Jones, the illustrator. Mr. de la Mare wrote verses to the artist's pictures, the result—a lovely expression of the physical world of the young child. *Poems for Children* (1930) includes a selection from earlier books with twenty new poems. *Bells and Grass* (1942), compiled when the poet was nearly seventy, includes mostly poems about children, animals, birds, and grownups, among them some of his earliest poems never published before. Most of Walter de la Mare's poems for children and about children were included by him in *Rhymes and Verses* (1947).

> Walter de la Mare was a poet who believed in the beauty and everlastingness of the human spirit. And he saw these flashes of eternity . . . at their loveliest and strongest in childhood. His poetry has, in the first place, quality of a very high and individual order, and in the second, it concerns itself with that cosmos which is essentially the cosmos of childhood. Lear and Carroll were witty poets, Wordsworth was in deadly earnest, Blake saw children as a mystic enjoys heaven, Stevenson's children were wistful or gay, Allingham's fanciful, Christina Rossetti held hers in her arms. But Walter de la Mare wrote as if he were a child himself, as if he were revealing his own childhood, though with the mature gifts of the authentic poet. His children are true to childhood.[1]

In his poems of a child's simple everyday life, in his fairy poetry, in those poems in which fancy and reality mingle, in the mystical poems that are felt rather than understood, in his nonsense verse—in all his wonderful variety he recovered "the intense delight, the untellable joy and happiness and fear and grief and pain . . . of an all but forgotten childhood."[2]

Unsurpassed for its joy in poetry and for the quality that invites the reader to explore further is Walter de la Mare's *Come Hither* (1923), a collection of lyrical and imaginative poems from many sources. Its introduction and the notes and appreciation at the end, "written about and around the poems," give the book, though it represents the work of a great variety of poets, beautiful accord and unity.

Tom Tiddler's Ground, published in England in 1931, is Mr. de la Mare's anthology for younger children. As in *Come Hither*, there are notes in the back of the book that add insight and a great deal of pleasure to the reading of the poems. Games and nursery rhymes, lyrics, storytelling poems—many kinds by many different poets are included. Only a few are so-called children's poems, but the selection was made with children in mind. In his introduction Mr. de la Mare said, "Some of the poems are serious some are tragic; many are easy to

[1] Leonard Clark, *Walter de la Mare*, a Walck Monograph (New York, Henry Z. Walck, 1961), pp. 43-44.
[2] Walter de la Mare, *Bells and Grass* (New York, Viking, 1942), p. 9.

understand, a few will be difficult. But I do not know of any true poem, however sorrowful it may be, that is not a comfort to read and to remember and a good deal else beside."

Eleanor Farjeon's (1881–1965) poetry is full of games. Her children are always dancing, playing, finding things, rushing off to school— just being children. Yet she never seems to be observing them, only saying what she always knew. Her understanding of children was as natural as breathing.

Eleanor Farjeon's childhood was full of variety and color. She never had any formal schooling but grew up in an atmosphere "rich with imaginative suggestion." She read omnivorously from her father's large library and was writing her own things by the time she was seven. All four children were very creative, their nursery life was filled with imaginative activity, their father made Christmas the most glorious of festivals. It is no wonder that *Come Christmas* (1927), one of her earliest collections of poetry, should contain some of the gayest and some of the loveliest Christmas poetry in children's literature. Numerous collections of her poetry have been published. *Joan's Door* (1926), *Over the Garden Wall* (1933), and *Sing for Your Supper* (1938), with poems from *Come Christmas*, were included in *Poems for Children* (1931), a various collection: fairy poems, verses of the country and the city, songs about children of other countries, poem portraits of very different children, dog verses, school-time verses, songs of the seasons and of Christmas. There is in all her poetry a great variety of verse patterns, delightful use of words, love of nature as a child loves it, gaiety, spontaneity, rhythm, and music. "I can hardly remember the time when it did not seem *easier* to me to write in running rhyme than in plodding prose," she said. *Then There Were Three* (1965) included the poetry from three collections: *Cherrystones*, *The Mulberry Bush*, and *The Starry Floor*. Along with her rollicking jingles and nonsensical fantasies, one often finds such an inspired poem as "The Earth," seen as a child from another planet might see it.

A later edition of *Poems for Children* (1951) contained the same poems included in the earlier one and twenty others, hitherto published only in England. *The Children's Bells* (1960) is a rich and varied selection made by Eleanor Farjeon herself from several collections of her verse and from her story books. Included are poems loved but almost lost to Americans combined with many never known in the United States.

Joseph Auslander and Frank Ernest Hill's *The Winged Horse* (1927) tells the story of poetry. It traces the primitive beginnings to the first poets, through the poetry of the great Greeks and Romans, then to Petrarch and his influence on the poetry of England. From there on the story touches the mountain peaks of poetry in the English language.

Anthologists have kept in mind the great poetic heritage of the English language including, among the rhymes and poems out of childhood, many of the world's loveliest lyrics and the great storytelling poems. It is, however, the poets' choice, those anthologies made by the poets themselves that stand out as beacons above the many useful, often delightful collections of the period. Sara Teasdale's *Rainbow Gold* (1922) emphasized the poetry of Shakespeare, Shelley, Blake, Tennyson, Rossetti, and others from the past and included certain contemporary poets but few poems written primarily for children. Louis Untermeyer made some fine collections of poetry, drawing from a wide variety of sources, old end new. The poems included in his *This Singing World* (1923), selected largely from the work of living poets, have an appeal to widely different tastes.

Selections were made from the work of contemporary poets with children in mind: Edna St. Vincent Millay's *Poems Selected for Young People* (1929); a collection by Vachel Lindsay, *Johnny Appleseed and Other Poems* (1928); Alfred Noyes's *Forty Singing Seamen* (1930); Carl Sandburg's *Early Moon* (1930); Sara Teasdale's *Stars Tonight* (1930); Emily Dickinson's *Poems for Youth* (1934); Robert Frost's *Come In and Other Poems* (1943); Countee Cullen's *The Lost Zoo* (1940). Later selections made with young people in mind were *You Come Too* (1959) by Robert Frost and *Wind Song* (1960) by Carl Sandburg. *Walt Whitman's America* (1964) includes selections by James Daugherty from *Leaves of Grass*, *Specimen Days*, and *Portraits of Lincoln*, with Mr. Daugherty's rugged, appropriate drawings.

Through the twenties and thirties the poets of childhood were many. The work of some was amusing for a while, and then it faded. The verse of others, Rose Fyleman's for instance, was popular for several decades and then suddenly became dated. Some of the poets of those years continue to speak to boys and girls.

Under the Tree (1922) by Elizabeth Madox Roberts revealed a lyrical poet of strong individuality who could see through a child's eyes, with a child's wonder and imagination, and whose expression was both poetic and childlike. Much is familiar to the child hearing these poems, and for the adult they evoke clear memories.

Rachel Field's (1894–1942) first book of verse was *The Pointed People* (1924). Although her small volume did not excite as much comment as A. A. Milne's first book, published in the same year, it introduced a poet of childhood who understood the child's point of view and who would capture in her poetry some of the elusive moods of childhood. In *Taxis and Toadstools* (1926) she interpreted in rhyme city and country as a child sees them. *Poems* by Rachel Field (1957) included six poems not published before and selections from her earlier books: *Pointed People, Branches Green, Christmas Time, Eliza and the Elves,* and *Fear Is the Thorn.*

A. A. Milne's (1882–1956) *When We Were Very Young* (1924) and *Now We Are Six* (1927) enjoyed immediate and phenomenal success. The fun and surprise in them and the gaiety evoked by their exact meter, amusing rhymes, and pictorial quality have made them almost universally known among English-speaking children. Mr. Milne had the inspired collaboration of the artist Ernest H. Shepard, who came to be considered the only possible illustrator for A. A. Milne's work.

The inspiration of a small son and close observations of a young child's attitudes and activities were at the heart of Mr. Milne's perception, but memory of his own childhood was keen and the child who emerges from these verses is a composite picture of childhood. In his poems children can see themselves, while adults catch nostalgic glimpses of the children they once were, the children they once knew, or see revealed the very children to whom they are reading the rhymes.

The variety of rhythm and rhyme, the fun with words and the nonsensical play upon them, and the storytelling qualities give the verses wide appeal. Children recognize themselves in such poems as "Binker" and "Lines and Squares." Some of the verses speak two languages. The children's elders may be the ones to enjoy the whimsy of "The Dormouse and the Doctor" but children relish such metrical words as "Delphiniums (blue) and geraniums (red)." "Sneezles" and "Rice Pudding" bring amused recognition to parents. To children the first is a delight because of its funny words, the other for giving them a momentary feeling of superiority because of the familiar naughtiness of another child.

While it is for enjoyment of the child's world rather than the world of nature that one turns to Milne, there is, now and then, as in "The Charcoal-Burner," brief forgetfulness of self in an awareness of beauty:

> And the moon swings clear of the tall black trees,
> The owls fly over and wish him goodnight,
> Quietly over to wish him goodnight . . .

But Mr. Milne did not forget. It was a young child's thoughts he was recording and the child must relate the experience to himself. The poem concludes:

> Oh the charcoal-burner has tales to tell!
> And he lives in the Forest and knows us well.

The ego of the young child feeds on the foolishness of grownups—the humility of kings—and such storytelling poems as "The Old Sailor,"

"The King's Breakfast," and "Disobedience" are exceedingly droll to children and to their elders. Mr. Milne quickly became the acknowledged master at capturing both the supreme egotism and the artless beauty of little children.

Skipping Along Alone (1931), a book of children's poems by a New England poet, Winifred Welles, was also inspired by the poet's little boy. Her mature verse had received praise and showed potentialities that her early death kept from complete realization. The imaginative quality of the poems, the sensitive mingling of realism and fantasy, make her one book of children's poetry singularly beautiful.

Dorothy Aldis, beginning with her first book of verse, *Everything and Anything* (1927), gave much delight to small children. Her knowledge of what is funny, her accurate pictures of the things small children do, and her understanding of why they do those things made her verses favorites. Her verse forms have little variety but children enjoy her accurate interpretation of their ways of seeing and doing.

The publication of Hilda Conkling's *Poems by a Little Girl* in 1920 caused a stir because the poems had been written by a child of nine. The mother, Grace Hazard Conkling, also a poet, had recorded, unknown to Hilda, the poetic expression that seemed so natural to the child and the songs and verses that she "told" her mother. Attention to the verses themselves revealed a response to nature and poetic phrasing found often, but fleetingly, in young children when they first begin to interpret with language the wonders around them. Few children, however, have mothers who recognize this rare quality and fewer are the mothers who can encourage such expression without destroying its spontaneity. *Shoes of the Wind* (1922) followed, and a selection of poems from the two books a little later, but no other poetry of Hilda's childhood was published.

Frances Frost's first collection of poetry, *Pool in the Meadow* (1933), introduced a new poet of nature. Her poems call up quick sensory responses. There are vivid pictures, and the touch of the wind, the warmth of the sun, the smell of the rain and the taste of apples.

> In the firelit, winter
> Nights, they'll be
> The clear sweet taste
> Of a summer tree!

Elizabeth Coatsworth began to write when the imagist poets were flourishing in the United States and "singing filled the air." She responded to the freedom to let a poem take its own form, not to be bound by one "school" of poetry or another, and she has:

. . . gone on writing, still feeling something of that first excitement. I have written in blank verse and written in rhyme. The form has never seemed important. Even when the poems may be shadowed in content, they were written in a mood of exhilaration, always rapidly, with the immediacy of sketches.[1]

It is not surprising that since, as a poet, she turned to the writing of children's stories, poetry is often to be found in the pages of her story books, setting the mood for a chapter or a tale. The images are clear and sharp; there is music too, and great variety in her meter and verse forms. She has given to children a whole gallery of pictures: "The two little girls in their gay fresh dresses . . . are riding painted horses on an old merry-go-round"; the teakettle "on the black kind knees of the woodstove"; and mermaids—"They comb their hair in shadowy caverns, they string their pearls in the valleys of sleep"; and many others. Among the collections of her poetry are *Summer Green* (1948), *Poems* (1957), and *The Sparrow Bush* (1966). The last she calls "rhymes." "One doesn't look for beauty in rhymes, though sometimes one may find a little. One may even find a sudden shaft of strangeness."[2] Whether in rhymes or poetry, she creates mood and gives surprise. Nature, people, history, places far and near have inspired her poetry— her record of "delight in the world and in living."

When Eleanor and Herbert Farjeon put their imaginations and humor into rhythm and rhyme they could make even English history gay. Though *Kings and Queens* (1932) and *Heroes and Heroines* (1933) are probably not read for their history, there is no doubt that with the reading of them bits of history may suddenly have meaning and cling to the memory. Best of all, they are fun.

There have also been poetic interpretations of American history. Hildegarde Hoyt Swift, with rhythmic, moving poetry, and Lynd Ward, with strong pictures, together made in *North Star Shining* (1947) a dramatic presentation of the American Negro. In *A Book of Americans* (1933) we see history through the eyes of a distinguished poet richly endowed with humor. Stephen Vincent Benét and his wife, Rosemary, must have had a jolly time writing the verses for *A Book of Americans*, and no doubt their three children had a part in the fun. Many of the poems seem to have grown out of family sharing. Wisdom is here as well as humor, and from time to time a verse has the power of great poetry.

Probably never were so many people speaking "out of the child's world" as during the fifties and sixties. Playful rhymes of the child's day, childlike nonsense and imaginative speculations, verses about clocks, old houses, telephones, about sounds and colors, about bugs and

[1] Elizabeth Coatsworth, *Down Half the World* (New York, Macmillan, 1968), p. viii.
[2] Elizabeth Coatsworth, *The Sparrow Bush* (New York, Norton, 1966), p. 8.

worms and animals of all kinds—they are gay, whimsical, inventive, and can add zest and liveliness to the young child's day. William Jay Smith, Beatrice Schenk de Regniers, Karla Kuskin, Myra Cohn Livingston, Mary O'Neill, Kaye Starbird, Gwendolyn Brooks, Eve Merriam, and Patricia Hubbell are among the many who have written engaging verses that often catch the child's way of seeing and hearing. Occasionally one does find beauty and an unexpected "sudden shaft of strangeness."

Poetry-Picture Books

Aileen Fisher has written prolifically of nature, and the child's response to it and to small creatures of all kinds. *Cricket in a Thicket* (1963), illustrated by Feodor Rojankovsky, and *In the Woods, In the Meadow, In the Sky* (1965), illustrated by Margot Tomes, have delightful pictures accompanying the short poems. The verses are spontaneous, the meter and rhythm precise, and Miss Fisher's point of view is the child's. A number of her long poems are the texts for picture books that have a great deal of atmosphere; among them *Going Barefoot* (1960) and *In the Middle of the Night* (1965), both illustrated by Adrienne Adams, *Like Nothing at All* (1962), illustrated by Leonard Weisgard, and *Listen, Rabbit* (1964) by Symeon Shimin.

Poetry, especially that which children enjoy most, is so rich in imagery one wonders if the child of the picture-viewing era is ever challenged to make his own mental images. Undoubtedly, children are drawn to poetry-picture books by the illustrations; and, so beautiful are many of them, there is little doubt that the artists accomplished their assignments with pleasure. Whatever our questions, poetry-picture books give a great deal of delight. In a variety of unusual ones an interesting progression of the poetry-picture book may be seen: Eleanor Farjeon's *A Prayer for Little Things* (1945), illustrated by Elizabeth Orton Jones; Elizabeth Coatsworth's *The Peaceable Kingdom and Other Poems* (1958), illustrated by Fritz Eichenberg; *Beyond the High Hills* (1961), Eskimo poems collected by Knud Rasmussen and illustrated with color photographs by Guy Mary-Rousselière; Richard Lewis's compilation of translations of haiku of such Japanese poets as Issa and Buson, *In a Spring Garden* (1965), illustrated by Ezra Jack Keats, who in choosing to use "imagery and style familiar to my own world" gives the impression of the universality and timelessness of all great poetry and art; *Hand in Hand We'll Go* (1965), ten poems by Robert Burns, illustrated with glowing woodcuts by Nonny Hogrogian; and Kazue Mizumura's own translation into visual images of seventeen poems "in the spirit of the Japanese haiku," *I See the Winds* (1966).

The word play of satirist Michael Flanders needs no pictures to sharpen the wit, but the strange animals that the artist Marcello Minale was inspired to draw for *Creatures Great and Small* (1965) make an unusual and funny picture book. Surprising pictures of animals by Milton Glaser accompany Conrad Aiken's nonsense poems in *Cats and Bats and Things with Wings* (1965).

Noah inspired two poets in the mid-sixties. British George Macbeth made his own version of the animals and the Ark, *Noah's Journey* (1966). His poems have ruggedness and fiber, and the illustrations by Margaret Gordon in contemporary style and brilliant full color seem very appropriate. The American poet Norma Farber was not so fortunate. With her quick imagination and her confidence in handling words she gave vitality to a most original story of the Ark, *Did You Know It Was the Narwhale?* (1967). The heaviness of some of the pages and the archness of the drawings detract from a poem that has subtlety and imagery and that needed more chimerical illustrations or none. Not all poetry needs to be turned into a picture book.

From 1950 on there was almost as much verse as prose in picture books, often verse with feeble rhyme and inaccurate rhythm. In contrast Edgar Parker's *Stuff and Nonsense* (1961) was a great relief. Precise meter and rhyme carry his nonsensical narrative poems. They read aloud wonderfully well, are very funny, and have good sense in the nonsense. His drawings are as meticulous as his rhyming and appropriate accompaniments to the poems.

Poets of the Fifties and Sixties

Within a short time after the mid-point of the twentieth century had been reached, it was very evident that two American poets had emerged whose poetry should be long known and loved.

As a child, Harry Behn lived in an Arizona mining community and spent a good part of his childhood playing with Indian boys and pretending he himself was one.

> . . . nothing has ever meant more to me than the lore I learned as a child from Indians. . . . They were our instructors in good manners, in careful observation of natural signs, in being responsive to the spirit in everything that lived and grew on the earth. . . . For many years I tried to be civilized, but gradually my early training in the ceremonies of innocence became dominant. Today I am dedicated to the primitive business of composing poetry and telling stories, not for grownups but for children. Like all aborigines, children are accustomed to thinking about the beginnings of things, the creation of beauty, the understanding of plants and animals, of how alive stones and stars and wild flowers are, and how wonderfully different each is from the other.[1]

[1] Behn, *op. cit.*, p. 12.

Mr. Behn's memory of childhood illuminates his work. He has, like Walter de la Mare, a respect for childhood and deep appreciation of it that are reflected in his poetry. Of all the champions of children, his voice is the clearest. In *Chrysalis* (1968) he speaks with assurance and immediacy.

The first of his books of poems was *The Little Hill* (1949), followed by *All Kinds of Time* (1950), *Windy Morning* (1953), *The Wizard in the Well* (1956), and a story in verse,*The House Beyond the Meadow* (1955), that creates a true sense of enchantment. Mr. Behn's own drawings, simple, decorative, and often humorous, illustrate his books most fittingly.

Harry Behn is a master of the haiku in English. Following the exacting rules for the form in his translations, he tries to do "what the author might have done if English had been his language." *Cricket Songs* (1964) is a collection of his translations of Japanese haiku, each one "the imprint of an experience of illumination." The poetry in *The Golden Hive* (1966) appeals more to older children than that in the first four books. Most of Mr. Behn's poetry is inspired by nature in all its variousness as seen through the fresh imaginations of children. Even the simplest verses fulfill an important requirement: "Any thing or experience, to become a poem, must be presented with a careful incompleteness of information."

David McCord was called by the poet Samuel Morse one of the "most accomplished poets who have chosen children as their special audience."[1] When his *Far and Few, Rhymes of the Never Was and Always Is* (1952) appeared, illustrated by Henry B. Kane, Anne Carroll Moore wrote:

> Here are "loving words" freshly minted and invigorated by their application to what children see and touch, feel and know, instinctively. Love of poetry is born and bred and nourished by such a book as this and the drawings . . . are in the mood of rhymes which range from pure nonsense to pure beauty.[2]

Other books by Mr. McCord, *Take Sky* (1962) and *All Day Long* (1966), also illustrated with humor and perception by Henry B. Kane, merited the same enthusiasm. His play with words is so spontaneous, so deceptively easy; his memory and his understanding of childhood are so keen, his humor both contemporary and ageless, that his poetry seems to have always been part of the literary heritage of the English-speaking child.

[1] Samuel French Morse, "Speaking to the Imagination," *The Horn Book*, Vol. 41 (June, 1965), p. 256.

[2] Anne Carroll Moore, "The Three Owls' Notebook," *The Horn Book*, Vol. 28 (Oct., 1952), pp. 310–311.

Among poets who turned from the grownup world to writing for children was John Updike, who wrote fresh poems of the seasons, faultless in rhythm and rhyme, for a lovely picture book *A Child's Calendar* (1965), illustrated by Nancy E. Burkert. John Ciardi wrote facile, often highly amusing, contemporaneous poems, capitalizing on manners and relationships between generations. *John J. Plenty and Fiddler Dan* (1963), a new, poetic version of an old fable, was a pleasant change from Mr. Ciardi's many frustrated adults and subversive children.

Among British poets especially enjoyed in the United States is James Reeves. His *The Blackbird in the Lilac* (1959) has variety seldom found in a volume by a single poet. His poetry sings and plays; is full of people—charming, eccentric or both; it has mystery and gentle ghosts, flowers and weather, birds and beasts. *Prefabulous Animiles* (1960) contains wildly strange creatures in racing rhymes. Robert Graves's poetry in *The Penny Fiddle* (1960) gives the child something to ponder. That book and his *Ann at Highwood Hall* (1966) have a great deal of imagery and inner meaning. They are as stimulating to the imagination as fairy tales—some of them seem to be fragments of fairy tales. The books of both of these poets were illustrated harmoniously and delightfully by Edward Ardizzone.

The only book of poems by E. V. Rieu, a distinguished English classicist, to be published in the United States is *The Flattered Flying Fish and Other Poems* (1962), full of humor and nonsense that grow funnier with each reading. In the words of Eleanor Graham, he "finds relaxation and refreshment in experiment with rhythms and weaving into them unexpected effects of levity."

Ian Serraillier gave children a vigorous, narrative poem in *The Challenge of the Green Knight* (1967), his retelling of *Sir Gawain and the Green Knight*. It reads smoothly and quickly yet retains the subtlety and heroic proportions of the original. In poetry, as in other areas of children's books, the work of British writers is deeply rooted in traditional literature, contributing an important dimension to contemporary children's literature.

In 1957 appeared two new editions of translations of *Platero y Yo* by Juan Ramón Jiménez. The more nearly literal translation by William and Mary Roberts had a few cuts. *Platero and I*, translated by Eloïse Roach, is uncut and was originally published in 1947. The new edition, illustrated by Jo Alys Downs, is true to the spirit of the Spanish poetic classic.

Rumer Godden's exquisite translation from the French of the poems by Carmen Bernos de Gasztold, *Prayers from the Ark* (1962) and *The Creatures' Choir* (1965), have great meaning for children. In her foreword to the second book, Miss Godden wrote, "Carmen de

Gasztold has been able to find for each beast its authentic voice, and this in a refreshing, matter-of-fact way; yet each large or infinitesimal, favoured or ill-favoured, bold or timid creature wafts up, as in the Prayers, an unexpected grain of incense that consecrates its wild or tame work-a-day self."

A Crocodile Has Me by the Leg (1967) is made up of poems found in Africa by travelers and scholars, selected, translated into English, when necessary, and edited by Leonard W. Doob, Chairman of the Council of African Studies at Yale University. The poems are simple, lively, and musical, and the well-designed book, illustrated with stunning woodcuts in black and red by Solomon Irein Wangboje, is a happy introduction to African thought and life.

Beautiful and most poignant of all the books from abroad is . . . *I Never Saw Another Butterfly* (1964), a collection of children's poems and drawings from the Theresienstadt Concentration Camp, 1942–1944, selected from many in the archives of the State Jewish Museum in Prague.

Characteristic of the resurgence of interest in poetry in the late fifties and sixties is a series under the editorship of Lillian Morrison. Each book includes a biographical and critical foreword by an authority on the poet and introduces the poet through an inviting and representative selection of his work. Among the many attractive volumes of the series, published in 1964, were selections of the poetry of Robert Browning, William Wordsworth, Walt Whitman, and Emily Dickinson, the poets introduced and the poems selected, respectively, by Rosemary Sprague, Elinor Parker, Lawrence Clark Powell, and Helen Plotz.

An extraordinary number of important and inviting poetry anthologies were published during the fifties and sixties. William Cole was responsible for collections of humorous poetry, seasonal poetry, story poems, and others; Katherine Love compiled two delightful collections; Gerald D. McDonald made a collection of poems of particular interest to boys, *A Way of Knowing* (1959); Elinor Parker an anthology of poems translated from world literature, *The Singing and the Gold* (1962); Louise Bogan and William Jay Smith, *The Golden Journey* (1965); Padraic Colum a collection of poems to be read aloud, *Roofs of Gold* (1964); Sara Hannum and Gwendolyn Reed, a collection of modern poetry, *Lean Out of the Window* (1965). Helen Plotz brought an unusually fresh viewpoint to an anthology with *Imagination's Other Place* (1955), poems of science and mathematics, and later *Untune the Sky* (1957), poems of music and the dance. Lillian Morrison compiled *Sprints and Distances, Sports in Poetry and Poetry in Sports* (1965). Horace Gregory and Marya Zaturenska presented an inspiriting invitation to poetry in *The Crystal Cabinet* (1962).

Poetry is never away, apart, beyond. It is within. All we have to do, then, to find the source of poetry is to track back within ourselves, back to the beginnings of the ancient energies that have come to us in myth recorded in their sibylline books of inherited experience.

Poetry is such experience fractured and reformed into shapes that the mind (the whole mind, mind you) can assimilate. Poetry is a pursuit (in words) of all beautiful mysteries, their capture, death, and transfiguration.[1]

---

[1] Behn, *op. cit.*, pp. 89–90.

Bibliography

Behn, Harry. *Chrysalis. Concerning Children and Poetry.* New York, Harcourt, 1968.

Clark, Leonard. *Walter de la Mare*, a Walck Monograph. New York, Henry Z. Walck, 1961.

Coatsworth, Elizabeth. *The Sparrow Bush.* New York, Norton, 1966.

Colwell, Eileen H. *Eleanor Farjeon*, a Walck Monograph. New York, Henry Z. Walck, 1962.

de la Mare, Walter. *Bells and Grass.* New York, Viking Press, 1942.

―――― *Come Hither.* New York, Knopf, 1957.

―――― *Tom Tiddler's Ground.* New York, Knopf, 1961.

Farjeon, Eleanor. *A Nursery in the Nineties.* London, Oxford University Press, 1960.

Moore, Anne Carroll. "The Three Owls' Notebook." *The Horn Book*, Vol. 28 (Oct., 1952).

Morse, Samuel French. "Speaking to the Imagination." *The Horn Book*, Vol. 41 (June, 1965).

Opie, Iona and Peter. *The Lore and Language of Schoolchildren.* London, Oxford University Press, 1959.

Smith, Lillian H. *The Unreluctant Years.* Chicago, American Library Assoc., 1953.

· 13 ·

Looking Ahead

Because any concern with childhood means looking ahead, a discussion
of the literature of childhood cannot be left with the past. What of the
next fifty years? More books, no doubt. More good books, we hope.
The work of a few poets and storytellers who began in the twenties
spans nearly half a century. In every decade new writers and artists
come to the fore, showing in their books fresh outlooks and new ways
of working. The children's books of every new year prove again that
there is no pattern for good literature. Apart from sincerity and
excellence of writing, the requirements are originality and personal
involvement—each writer working to say what he alone can say.

Not all the good books of this period will live, but their special
qualities, becoming part of the lives of the children who knew them,
will influence writers of the future. Many fine books that deserve to be
read generation after generation may be lost in the confusion of pedantry,
technology, and good intentions that confound the mid-century. Increased costs in bookmaking may direct the attention of publishers to
salability instead of excellence; but, on the other hand, only the buyers—
parents, teachers, and librarians—can influence publishers to keep
available the best of the old and to make available the best of the new.

Eventually, trends and series of our time will be forgotten, but a
few books that were part of those series and trends will stand out and
take their places in the literature of a new era of children's books, forming another link in the chain. Fashions in writing, timeliness of subjects,
are important for a moment, but certain books link the past with the
present, the present with the future. Epic stories, legendary tales and
folklore, *Hakluyt's Voyages*, *Robinson Crusoe*, and *Pilgrim's Progress*,
as they have linked the present, will join the future to the past, influencing new writers and finding always a fresh audience among the
children.

In the early days of the century discriminating critics of children's
books were needed to show the way in an unexplored forest. The trees
have now given place to a jungle of towers and pinnacles. The old

roads are still there—enjoyment of good books, fine pictures, beautiful music—but guides are needed. The discerning critic who can communicate to children his enthusiasm for good books is more important than ever before. The span of childhood is brief, and relatively few are the books each child can know during that enchanted period.

Children's books are always an expression of their times. Critics in the future may look with condescension on the didacticism of the books of our day, the self-consciousness of our social and moral concerns. Of the great mountain of books of which we have been speaking, perhaps those will live that not only reflect our times—troubled, dramatic, and fantastic though they may be—but that are an expression of childhood itself, its joys and anguish, its love, its dreams and wonder.

Index